BANKRUPTCY LAW MANUAL

by

BENJAMIN WEINTRAUB
Counsel to the firm of Levin & Weintraub, New York City
Member of the National Bankruptcy Conference

and

ALAN N. RESNICK
Associate Dean and Professor of Law
Hofstra University Law School

WARREN, GORHAM & LAMONT
Boston
New York

By WARREN, GORHAM & LAMONT, INC.
210 South Street
Boston, Massachusetts 02111

ISBN 0-88262-494-6
Library of Congress Card Catalog No. 80-52860

PRINTED IN THE UNITED STATES OF AMERICA

We dedicate this book to the Weintraub family
Jeanne, Elinor Crames, and Charles
and to the Resnick family
Jill, Brian, and Craig

PREFACE

The Bankruptcy Reform Act of 1978 is the first comprehensive bankruptcy statute since 1898. The Reform Act, which contains the new Bankruptcy Code, affects almost every aspect of procedural and substantive bankruptcy law. The new statute has many significant features, such as the provisions assuring adequate protection for secured creditors' rights, improving exemptions afforded debtors, modernizing the rules on preferences and other trustee's avoiding powers, and creating a more independent bankruptcy court with broad jurisdiction. The merging of Chapters X, XI, and XII of the former Bankruptcy Act into the new chapter 11 dealing with reorganizations and the reforms relating to debt adjustments for individuals with regular income under chapter 13 are some of the most dramatic changes resulting from the 1978 Act. In view of these comprehensive changes in the law, the time is ripe for a new book on the subject.

This book is a one-volume practical guide to bankruptcy and debtor relief written for several audiences. The lawyer already familiar with the intricacies of bankruptcy law under the former Bankruptcy Act will find it useful in learning the practical consequences of the recent statutory reforms. In fact, the footnotes often draw comparisons with the former Act, cite old cases that undoubtedly will be used as precedents for interpreting provisions of the new Code, and point out judicial decisions that have been overruled by the law. We did not assume, however, that every practitioner who will use this book will have had experience in the bankruptcy field. Lawyers unfamiliar with this area who are seeking a clear and concise introduction to bankruptcy and its alternatives should find it in the chapters that follow. Legal educators and students should find an appropriate balance of statutory analysis, judicial interpretation, and practical guidance to make this book useful as a learning device. Moreover, this book can be read and used by bankers, credit executives, accountants, and debtors who seek to acquire a basic understanding of bankruptcy and debtor relief without the discomfort of struggling through unnecessary "lawyers' language." For the convenience of all readers, we included in the appendices the new Bankruptcy Code in its entirety, as well as up-to-date forms.

Any book of this type must, to some extent, reflect the experiences of its authors. We believe that the combination of our different professional backgrounds has contributed significantly in producing an informative book appropriate for the several audiences mentioned above. One of us has actively practiced law in the field of bankruptcy for fifty years and has lectured to lawyers, accountants, bankers, credit executives, and students. The other is a professor of law and consultant who has spent years immersed in the complex web of statutes, legislative history, and case law relating to bankruptcy. As a result of our combined experiences, this book contains practical information as well as insights and interpretations going well beyond the mere paraphrasing of the new Code.

We gratefully express our appreciation to three students at Hofstra University School of Law who assisted us in the preparation of this book: Wendy Finkel '81, Donna Bookin '80, and Judith Croiter '81. We also thank Betty Presti and Gay Glowacki for their valuable secretarial services. The skill and dedication (and occasional good humor) of these students and secretaries made our task easier and much more pleasant than it would have been without their assistance. We also thank the staff of the Hofstra Law Library for providing us with essential resource materials.

We also express our gratitude to the firm of Levin & Weintraub for their valuable thoughts with respect to some of the practical applications of the Bankruptcy Code and for making available materials of their current cases. Our thanks are also due to their secretarial staff for unstinting aid despite a busy law practice.

Finally, we thank our publisher who gave us continuous assistance in the development of the format of this book and who had the vision to sponsor the writing of this book long before the Bankruptcy Reform Act became law.

BENJAMIN WEINTRAUB
ALAN N. RESNICK

July 15, 1980

SUMMARY TABLE OF CONTENTS

DETAILED TABLE OF CONTENTS

Chapter 1

LIQUIDATION AS A DEBTOR'S REMEDY: THE VOLUNTARY CASE

Chapter 2

LIQUIDATION AS A CREDITOR'S REMEDY: THE INVOLUNTARY CASE

Chapter 3

DISCHARGE OF DEBTS IN LIQUIDATION CASES

Chapter 4

PROPERTY OF THE ESTATE AND EXEMPTIONS

Chapter 5

CREDITORS, CLAIMS, AND INTERESTS

Chapter 6

BANKRUPTCY COURTS AND OFFICERS

Chapter 7

THE TRUSTEE'S POWERS

Chapter 8

REORGANIZATION

Chapter 9

DEBT ADJUSTMENTS FOR INDIVIDUALS WITH REGULAR INCOME

Chapter 10

ALTERNATIVE INSOLVENCY PROCEEDINGS

INTRODUCTION: THE SOURCES OF BANKRUPTCY LAW

The reader should become familiar with the various sources of bankruptcy law cited throughout this book. An understanding of the contribution that each source makes to the substantive or procedural aspects of bankruptcy will be useful to the practitioner in locating relevant provisions of the law.

(1) *U.S. Constitution.* The oldest source of American bankruptcy law is the U.S. Constitution. Specifically, Article I, Section 8, Clause 4 gives Congress the power "to establish . . . uniform Laws on the subject of Bankruptcies throughout the United States." Congress exercised this power rather unsuccessfully three times within the first hundred years of the life of this nation.[1] Congress enacted bankruptcy statutes in 1800,[2] 1841,[3] and again in 1867,[4] but each was repealed shortly after enactment. It was not until 1898 that Congress passed a comprehensive bankruptcy statute which still plays an important role in modern bankruptcy law.

(2) *National Bankruptcy Act of 1898.* The National Bankruptcy Act of 1898[5] (referred to in this book as the former Act) governed bankruptcy cases for approximately eight decades. The focus of the former Act for the first forty years was "straight bankruptcy" resulting in liquidation of the debtor's nonexempt assets. In 1938, however, as a result of the Chandler Act[6] amendments, Chapters X (Corporate Re-

---

[1] See Countryman, "A History of American Bankruptcy Law," 81 Com. L.J. 226 (1976).

[2] 2 Stat. 19 (1800), *repealed by* 2 Stat. 248 (1803).

[3] 5 Stat. 440 (1841), *repealed by* 5 Stat. 614 (1843).

[4] 14 Stat. 517 (1867), *repealed by* 20 Stat. 99 (1878).

[5] 30 Stat. 544 (1898).

[6] 52 Stat. 840 (1938).

organizations), XI (Arrangements), XII (Real Property Arrangements), and XIII (Wage Earners' Plans) were added to the Act to provide for debtor rehabilitation as an alternative to liquidation.

The former Act is a significant source of bankruptcy law for several reasons. First, it continues to govern all cases that were commenced prior to September 30, 1979, its provisions still applicable to those complex cases which may continue for several years. Second, many of the provisions and policies of the new Bankruptcy Code are derived from the former Act. Accordingly, the legislative history and the judicial interpretation of the former Act may be relevant in understanding the new Code. More specifically, there is no doubt that case law under the former Act serves as precedent when courts apply the provisions of the Bankruptcy Code.

(3) *Bankruptcy Rules of Procedure and Official Forms.* In 1973, the Supreme Court promulgated rules and forms, as approved by the Judicial Conference of the United States, to govern the procedural aspects of bankruptcy cases.[7] The Bankruptcy Rules were designed for use in cases which were governed by the former Act. Bankruptcy Rules of Procedure and Official Forms applicable to cases under Chapters X, XII, and XIII were added in 1975. The rules promulgated in 1973 and 1975 are referred to as the Bankruptcy Rules and are cited throughout this book as B. Rule.

(4) *Bankruptcy Reform Act of 1978.* The most significant development in bankruptcy law in the past two generations is the Bankruptcy Reform Act of 1978. It repealed and replaced the former Bankruptcy Act[8] and made comprehensive changes in almost every aspect of bankruptcy law.

The Bankruptcy Reform Act is divided into four titles. Title I, which is the most important, contains the new Bankruptcy Code. Titles II and III contain amendments to various federal statutes relating to court structure, jurisdiction, venue, and many other aspects of bankruptcy. Title IV governs the transition from the former Act to the provisions of the Reform Act.

It is interesting to note that the Reform Act provides that the Bank-

---

[7] The Supreme Court's authority for prescribing bankruptcy rules is contained in 28 U.S.C. § 2075.

[8] Pub. L. 95-598, 92 Stat. 2549 (1978). See Resnick & Wypyski, *Bankruptcy Reform Act of 1978: A Legislative History* (1979), for selected legislative documents that trace the development of the Bankruptcy Reform Act.

ruptcy Rules of Procedure and Official Forms in effect on September 30, 1979, will apply to cases commenced under the new Code "to the extent not inconsistent with the amendments made" by the Reform Act, until new rules are prescribed to replace them.[9] As of this writing, new rules have not been promulgated by the U.S. Supreme Court.

(5) *Bankruptcy Code.* As discussed above, Title I of the Bankruptcy Reform Act of 1978 consists of the Bankruptcy Code. The Code, which contains all the substantive bankruptcy law applicable to cases commenced on or after October 1, 1979, has become Title 11 of the U.S. Code and sections of the Code are cited throughout this book as 11 U.S.C. § —. Because the Code is now the primary source of bankruptcy law, a copy of the complete Code is set forth in Appendix A.

The Bankruptcy Code is divided into the following eight chapters:

Chapter 1. General Provisions
Chapter 3. Case Administration
Chapter 5. Creditors, the Debtor and the Estate
Chapter 7. Liquidation
Chapter 9. Adjustment of Debts of a Municipality
Chapter 11. Reorganization
Chapter 13. Adjustment of Debts of an Individual With Regular Income
Chapter 15. United States Trustees

There are four types of cases that may be commenced under the Code:

(1) Liquidation (Chapter 7)
(2) Municipal debt adjustment (Chapter 9)
(3) Reorganization (Chapter 11)
(4) Debt adjustment for an individual with regular income (Chapter 13)

Except for municipal debt adjustments, the different types of bankruptcy cases are examined and discussed at length in the first nine chapters of this book. The final chapter of the book analyzes the various alternatives for debt relief under state and common law.

(6) *Suggested Interim Bankruptcy Rules and Forms.* As discussed

[9] Bankr. Reform Act § 405(d).

above, the Bankruptcy Rules of Procedure and Official Forms which governed cases under the former Act are applicable to cases under the new Code to the extent that they are consistent with the Code.

The Supreme Court appointed an Advisory Committee on Bankruptcy Rules of the Judicial Conference of the United States to undertake a complete revision of the procedural rules and official forms in light of the new Code. This task is a formidable one that probably will take several years to accomplish. However, in 1979 the Committtee drafted Suggested Interim Bankruptcy Rules and Forms for guidance until the new rules are formulated. Although these suggested rules have not been prescribed by the Supreme Court, they may be binding if adopted as local court rules or if made applicable by the bankruptcy judge in the exercise of discretion. These rules are cited throughout the book as Sugg. Int. B. Rule. Many of the Suggested Interim Bankruptcy Forms are contained in Appendix B.

Chapter 1

LIQUIDATION AS A DEBTOR'S REMEDY: THE VOLUNTARY CASE

¶ 1.01 WHAT IS LIQUIDATION?

The most common form of relief sought by debtors under the bankruptcy laws is liquidation, which lawyers often refer to as a "straight bankruptcy." Liquidation, which is governed by chapter 7 of the Bankruptcy Code, is one of the four types of bankruptcy cases available to debtors.[1] The first chapter of this book deals with the voluntary petition for liquidation. Involuntary petitions for liquidation are discussed in Chapter 2, and petitions for the other forms of relief are discussed in Chapters 8 and 9.

¶ 1.02 SHOULD THE DEBTOR FILE A VOLUNTARY PETITION FOR LIQUIDATION?

This chapter and the succeeding chapters are designed to assist the debtor and the debtor's counsel in deciding whether or not to file a voluntary bankruptcy petition for liquidation. In making this decision, the debtor should consider the purposes of liquidation, as well as the alternative means of obtaining relief from indebtedness.

[1] Consideration of Purpose

[a] Discharge of Debts

One of the primary purposes of bankruptcy is discharging debts to give an honest debtor a new opportunity in life without the pressure and discouragement of substantial indebtedness.[2] It is not surprising, therefore, that voluntary bankruptcy petitions often represent the debtor's dream of complete forgiveness of all debts with little or no cost or obligation on the debtor's part. There are many caveats, however, which must be considered carefully before the debtor plunges head first into the bankruptcy court.

[b] Opposition to Discharge

Under the Bankruptcy Code, a discharge in a liquidation case is given to individual debtors only, not to partnerships or corporations.[3]

---

[1] Although liquidation of assets may be accomplished under chapter 11 of the Bankruptcy Code (Reorganization), that chapter is designed primarily for rehabilitation. See 11 U.S.C. § 1123(b)(4), and Chapter 8 *infra.*

[2] The U.S. Supreme Court, commenting on the former Bankruptcy Act, stated: "One of the primary purposes of the Bankruptcy Act is to 'relieve the honest debtor from the weight of oppressive indebtedness and permit him to start afresh free from the obligations and responsibilities consequent upon business misfortunes.' " Local Loan Co. v. Hunt, 292 U.S. 234, 244 (1934) (quoting from Williams v. U.S. Fidelity & Guar. Co., 236 U.S. 549, 554-555 (1915)).

[3] 11 U.S.C. § 727(a)(1). A corporation was entitled to a discharge

Moreover, an individual's right to a discharge is not absolute. The individual debtor must consider whether grounds exist to oppose a discharge. Such situations as having made fraudulent transfers of property within the previous year or having obtained a discharge in a prior bankruptcy case within the previous six years constitute grounds for the denial of a discharge,[4] and they may be a sufficient deterrent to filing a bankruptcy petition. The importance of objections to discharge[5] makes it necessary for the debtor's lawyer to consider whether the debtor acted dishonestly in connection with the debtor's assets or business or whether the debtor committed other acts that would result in the denial of a discharge.

[c] Exceptions to Discharge

Usually, the filing of a voluntary bankruptcy petition for liquidation does result in a discharge of debts for individuals. However, even if a discharge is obtained, certain debts are nondischargeable and will survive bankruptcy.[6] For example, certain income taxes that accrue prior to the filing of a petition and obligations to pay alimony and child support are not discharged in bankruptcy. It is important, therefore, that the amount of nondischargeable debts be appraised against the amount of the dischargeable liabilities. If nondischargeable tax obligations amount to $25,000 and dischargeable debts amount to only $1,000, it would probably not serve any useful purpose for the debtor to expend the money and time to commence a bankruptcy case[7] after which he would be subjected to the status of being a debtor in bankruptcy[8] and would still be required to pay $25,000 to the Internal Revenue Service.

---

under the former Act. See Former B.A. § 14(a); B. Rule 404. Also, a partnership was a "person" entitled to a discharge under the former Act, even though it may be composed of several individuals. Former B.A. §§ 1(23), 14(a).

[4] See 11 U.S.C. §§ 727(a)(2), 727(a)(8).

[5] See Chapter 3 *infra* for a discussion of objections to discharge.

[6] See 11 U.S.C. § 523, and Chapter 3 *infra.*

[7] Prior to 1973, a bankruptcy was often referred to as a "bankruptcy proceeding." The Bankruptcy Rules, however, use the term "bankruptcy case" to embrace all matters of administration and all controversies that arise during the bankrupcty. The narrower term "bankruptcy proceeding" refers to a litigated dispute arising within a "bankruptcy case." See B. Rules 101, 703. The Bankruptcy Code continues to use the same terminology as used in the Rules. See 11 U.S.C. § 301, and Chapter 6 *infra,* on the types of disputes litigated in the bankruptcy court.

[8] Under the former Bankruptcy Act, the debtor was labeled a "bank-

[d] Disposition of Assets

Although debtors like to believe that a discharge of debts is the sole purpose of the bankruptcy laws, there is another purpose that is designed to benefit creditors: the conversion of the bankrupt's assets into cash for equal distribution among creditors.[9] Accordingly, the debtor must realize that bankruptcy is likely to result in the loss of property. Upon filing a petition, the property belonging to the debtor, with the exception of certain property exempted under federal, state, or local laws, will become part of the debtor's estate to be liquidated for distribution to creditors.[10] Therefore, the loss of assets in a particular case must be considered when contemplating the filing of a petition. For corporations and partnerships, which are not discharged in bankruptcy, the liquidation and equal distribution of assets between creditors is the primary purpose for filing a petition. Moreover, in a partnership bankruptcy, the liquidation of the partnership assets could reduce the claims that creditors may assert against the general partners.

[2] Alternatives to Voluntary Liquidation Under the Bankruptcy Code

In addition to filing a petition under chapter 7 for liquidation resulting in a distribution of assets, the debtor may seek other forms of relief under the Bankruptcy Code. Debtors who are engaged in business, including sole proprietors, partnerships, and corporations, may wish to continue their businesses and avoid liquidation. Under chapter 11 of the Code, the debtor may seek an adjustment of debts, either by reducing or by extending time of payment, or may seek an even more comprehensive reorganization.[11] Individual debtors and sole proprietors

---

rupt." Former B.A. § 1(4). The Bankruptcy Code substituted the word "debtor" for "bankrupt" to soften the stigma attached to being the subject of a bankruptcy case.

[9] See Burlingham v. Crouse, 228 U.S. 459, 473 (1913), in which the Supreme Court wrote that it is "the two-fold purpose of the Bankruptcy Act to convert the estate of the bankrupt into cash and distribute it among creditors and then to give the bankrupt a fresh start. . . ." For a discussion on creditors' claims and priorities in distribution, see Chapter 5 *infra*.

[10] See 11 U.S.C. §§ 522 and 541, and Chapter 4 *infra*, on property of the estate and exemptions.

[11] Under the former Bankruptcy Act, corporations seeking a corporate reorganization had to proceed under Chapter X of the Act. Debtors, including individuals, partnerships, and corporations, who wanted to effectuate an arrangement with creditors had to proceed under Chapter XI of the former

of small businesses who have regular income may seek an arrangement with creditors under chapter 13 of the Bankruptcy Code.[12]

Other alternatives for debtors, such as assignments for the benefit of creditors and state court receiverships, are available under state law. Because state liquidation procedures do not result in a discharge of debts, it is not common for individuals to take advantage of them. However, corporations and partnership entities, which do not receive discharges in bankruptcy, often find that these state procedures are less troublesome and less costly. But since these statutes do not usually authorize the vacation of liens obtained through legal proceedings, care should be taken before using this alternative. Extrajudicial arrangements for business debtors may be another road to the adjustment of debts or liquidation. These alternatives for debtor relief will be discussed in more detail in Chapter 10 of this book.

[3] Choice of Voluntary or Involuntary Proceedings: Should the Debtor Wait?

Since a debtor may file a voluntary petition or creditors may file an involuntary petition,[13] the question often arises: Should a debtor file a voluntary petition when experiencing financial difficulty, or should he wait for the inevitable involuntary petition to be filed while continuing the business as long as possible and letting the motor idle? A debtor is often inclined to wait until creditors assume the initiative because the ultimate goals of voluntary or involuntary bankruptcy are the same—namely, a discharge to the debtor and liquidation and distribution of the estate.

In making this decision, the debtor should consider several disadvantages of a wait-it-out policy. First, creditors will continue to try to collect their claims, which is often disturbing to the debtor. The debtor who will welcome the protection of an automatic stay may as well benefit from it early.[14] Employed debtors should be concerned about possible embarrassing wage garnishments. Second, creditors may

---

Act. Owners of real property were permitted to seek arrangement with creditors under Chapter XII of the former Act. The Bankruptcy Code combines the concepts of former Chapters X, XI, and XII into new chapter 11 entitled "Reorganizations." See Chapter 8 *infra*.

[12] See 11 U.S.C. § 109(e) as to who may be a debtor under chapter 13, which not only replaces Chapter XIII of the former Act but is expanded to include individuals other than wage earners. See Chapter 9 *infra*.

[13] Involuntary petitions are discussed in Chapter 2 *infra*.

[14] See ¶ 1.09 on automatic stays.

levy on assets long before an involuntary petition is filed, so that a trustee may be unable to void the transfer.[15] This may result in less property in the estate for the trustee to use to pay nondischargeable claims, such as alimony or taxes.[16] Third, sheriff sales after levy are likely to realize sums far below the prices received at a well-advertised bankruptcy sale, resulting in less money for payment of nondischargeable claims. Fourth, in the case of a voluntary petition, the debtor has time to consult with a lawyer to plan for bankruptcy and to carefully prepare schedules and statement of affairs. In contrast, debtors who are served with involuntary petitions often do not consult with lawyers in time to plan carefully for the bankruptcy. Also, the longer a person remains insolvent and in a desperate financial condition, the more likely it is that the debtor will commit an act that would later bar a discharge in bankruptcy. For example, the hopelessly insolvent debtor may neglect to continue to keep or preserve books and records.[17] Moreover, an involuntary petition may be filed in a district that is not suitable for the debtor, which can cause extreme inconvenience, especially in the case of a debtor engaged in business who desires a reorganization. These disadvantages should be weighed against the possibility that the debtor may be able to improve his financial situation so as to avoid bankruptcy altogether before an involuntary petition is filed.

¶ 1.03 WHO MAY FILE A VOLUNTARY PETITION?

[1] Individuals

A voluntary petition for liquidation may be filed by a natural person, regardless of whether the debtor is insolvent or whether the person is entitled to a discharge of debts.[18] For example, a debtor who received a discharge within the previous six years may not receive another discharge,[19] but, nevertheless, he may file a petition, proceed as a debtor under chapter 7, and effect an orderly liquidation of property. Infants may file petitions when legally obligated to pay debts, such as those

---

[15] See Chapter 7 *infra* on the trustee's avoiding powers.

[16] See Chapter 3 *infra* on dischargeability of claims.

[17] See 11 U.S.C. § 727(a)(3), and ¶ 3.03[3].

[18] See 11 U.S.C. § 109(a). "Person" is defined in the Bankruptcy Code to include individuals. 11 U.S.C. § 101(30).

[19] 11 U.S.C. § 727(a)(8).

arising from the purchase of necessities.[20] Courts have permitted insane persons to file petitions when acting through authorized guardians.[21]

The Bankruptcy Code requires that the petitioning debtor either resides in the United States or has a domicile, place of business, or property in the United States.[22] An alien, therefore, is eligible to become a debtor under the Bankruptcy Code so long as any one of these requirements is met.

A decedent's estate may not file a bankruptcy petition,[23] but the death of the debtor after the filing does not terminate the administration of the bankruptcy estate.[24]

[2] Partnerships

The bankruptcy laws consider a partnership as a separate legal entity distinct from the individual partners.[25] Accordingly, a partnership may file a voluntary petition either with or without one or more of the individual partners. This rule also applies to limited partnerships that have at least one general partner. Although it is possible for a partnership petition to be filed without any partner becoming an individual bankrupt, it is more common for individual partners to file their personal petitions along with the partnership petition.[26] The filing of individual petitions by partners is advisable because the filing of a partnership petition, in and of itself, does not discharge the individual partners from their personal liability to partnership creditors or from liability on personal obligations.

---

[20] See *In re* Walrath, 175 F. 243 (N.D.N.Y. 1910).

[21] See Hilliard v. McCrory, 134 P.2d 1057 (Colo. 1943); *In re* Clinton, 41 F.2d 749 (S.D. Cal. 1930).

[22] 11 U.S.C. § 109(a).

[23] See *In re* Estate of Hiller, 240 F. Supp. 504 (N.D. Cal. 1965).

[24] Bankruptcy Rule 118 provides that in the event of death or insanity of the debtor after the petition is filed, the bankruptcy estate is to be administered and the case concluded in the same manner, as far as possible, as though the death or insanity had not occurred. This Rule continues to apply because the new Bankruptcy Code does not address this problem.

[25] The Bankruptcy Code provides that any "person" may be a debtor under the Act. "Person" is defined so as to include partnerships. See 11 U.S.C. § 101(30).

[26] Because the Bankruptcy Code does not permit the filing of joint petitions unles the petitioners are husband and wife, unmarried partners who wish to file petitions as individuals and on behalf of the partnership entity must file separate petitions. Nonetheless, the court may consolidate or jointly administer the cases when appropriate. See 11 U.S.C. § 302(a); B. Rule 117.

The treatment of partnership petitions has been changed slightly by the new Bankruptcy Code. Under previous law, a voluntary petition could have been filed by any one or more general partners on behalf of the firm. If fewer than all of the general partners joined in the petition, the former Act required that the petition allege that the partnership is insolvent.[27] Although a general partner who did not join in the petition had the right to contest this "quasi-involuntary" petition by challenging the insolvency allegation,[28] the petition was treated as a voluntary petition nonetheless.

The Bankruptcy Code is similar to the former Act in that a partnership petition executed by all general partners commences a voluntary case. However, the Code departs from the former Act by treating a petition signed by fewer than all of the general partners as an involuntary petition for all purposes.[29] Thus, a partner who does not join in the petition has the right to file an answer contesting the petition, in which case the court may order relief under the Code only if grounds for an involuntary petition are found. Involuntary petitions are discussed in Chapter 2 of this book.

Filing a petition as an individual may be sufficient to protect the interests of a general partner without the partnership entity becoming a debtor under the Code. A partner who only files an individual petition may receive a discharge from both the partnership and individual debts. There are situations, however, in which a partner would want to have a petition filed against or on behalf of the firm. Suppose that a general partner has reason to believe that other partners embezzled partnership property, causing the insolvency of the firm. When the innocent but insolvent partner files a petition as an individual, it may also be desirable to file an involuntary petition against the firm so that a partnership trustee can be appointed to investigate and recover fraudulently transferred property. The partnership trustee may succeed in re-

---

[27] Former B.A. § 5(b).

[28] See B. Rule 105(b).

[29] 11 U.S.C. § 303(b)(3)(A). Treating a petition by less than all of the partners as an involuntary petition *against* the partnership instead of a voluntary petition on behalf of the firm is consistent with prevailing state law which prohibits less than all of the partners from assigning assets for the benefit of creditors or otherwise doing any act which would make it impossible to carry on the ordinary business of the partnership without authorization by the other partners. Uniform Partnership Act § 9(3); See Bumb v. Bennett, 333 P.2d 23, 27 (Cal. 1958), where the court upheld an assignment for the benefit of creditors executed by one of the partners because the other partner had assented to the assignment orally.

covering enough assets to pay at least a portion of the innocent partner's nondischargeable claims.

[3] Corporations

Although a corporation will not receive a discharge of debts, it may file a voluntary petition for the purpose of liquidation and the distribution of assets to creditors. Voluntary petitions may be filed on behalf of charitable or other nonprofit corporations as well as business corporations.[30]

Whether a board of directors has the authority to file a petition without approval of the shareholders is determined by state law.[31] Generally, officers of the corporation have no authority to file a petition without approval by the board of directors.[32] Problems arise when the board of directors is deadlocked by a 50–50 vote. In such instances, no officer is authorized by either faction to file a voluntary petition seeking any form of relief under the bankruptcy laws.[33] Moreover, the fact that a prior state court proceeding, such as a receivership or assignment for the benefit of creditors, is pending is not a deterrent to the

---

[30] The Bankruptcy Code defines "person" to include a corporation, and a "person" is eligible to file a liquidation petition. 11 U.S.C. §§ 101(30), 109(a).

[31] Where state law provides that the board of directors shall manage the business of the corporation, the board has authority to file a voluntary petition in bankruptcy. See Boyce v. Chemical Plastics, Inc., 175 F.2d 839 (8th Cir.), *cert. denied* 338 U.S. 828 (1949); *In re* High-Low Tank Car Serv. Stations, Inc., 254 F.2d 363 (7th Cir. 1958). See also *In re* Park Towers Corp., 387 F.2d 948 (2d Cir. 1967), in which the court held that a stockbroker may not file a bankruptcy petition on behalf of the corporation without authority from the board of directors.

[32] See *In re* Community Book Co., 10 F.2d 616 (D. Minn. 1926); *In re* Jefferson Casket Co., 182 F. 689 (N.D.N.Y. 1910), where failure to show authorization for filing the petition deprived the court of jurisdiction to adjudicate the corporation a bankrupt under the former Act. But see Regal Cleaner & Dyers, Inc. v. Merlis, 274 F. 915 (2d Cir. 1921), where equity permitted the president to file an answer denying the allegations of an involuntary petition without the authorization of the board of directors; Whittaker v. Bacon, 17 Tenn. App. 67, 65 S.W.2d 1083 (1933), which held that a voluntary petition filed by the president of a corporation did not have to show authorization by the board of directors.

[33] However, a faction of a deadlocked board of directors may be able to seek a judicial dissolution of the corporation and the appointment of a receiver under state law. See N.Y. Bus. Corp. Law §§ 1104, 1113 (McKinney 1963); O'Connell, "Dissolution as a Remedy for Dissension and Deadlock in the New York Closely-Held Corporation," 19 Buffalo L. Rev. 585 (1970).

filing of a voluntary petition seeking liquidation or reorganization under the bankruptcy laws.[34]

[4] Unincorporated Organizations

The Bankruptcy Code provides that, upon proper authorization, a corporation may file a voluntary petition, but the word "corporation" is defined broadly to include joint stock companies, unincorporated companies and associations, and partnership associations organized under a law that makes only their subscribed capital responsible for their debts, and business trusts.[35] Trusts that are not conducting a business are not included. For example, a private family trust[36] or an employee profit-sharing trust[37] may not file a petition. A labor union is an unincorporated association eligible to file a voluntary petition.[38]

[5] Stockbrokers and Commodity Brokers

A stockbroker or commodity broker may file a voluntary petition for liquidation under chapter 7. The reader involved in such a case, however, should be aware that Subchapters III and IV of chapter 7 contain special provisions dealing solely with stockbroker and commodity broker liquidations. These provisions are necessary because of a sensitivity to the protection of investor customers, and because of the vital role of the Securities and Exchange Commission, Security Investor Protection Corporation, and Commodity Futures Trading Commission in broker liquidations. Anyone involved in a broker liquidation case should be sure to consult these portions of the Code.

[6] Exceptions: Debtors Who May Not File Petitions for Liquidation

Bankruptcy is available only to those persons who reside in the United States or who have a domicile, place of business, or property in

---

[34] See *In re* Denton & Haskins Music Pub. Co., 10 F. Supp. 802 (S.D.N.Y. 1935). In such a situation, the receiver or assignee must turn over property of the estate to the bankruptcy trustee. See 11 U.S.C. § 543.

[35] 11 U.S.C. § 101(8).

[36] See Pope & Cottle Co. v. Fairbanks Realty Trust, 124 F.2d 132 (1st Cir. 1941).

[37] See Associated Cemetery Management, Inc. v. Barnes, 268 F.2d 97 (8th Cir. 1959).

[38] See Highway & City Freight Drivers v. Gordon Transports, Inc., 576 F.2d 1285 (8th Cir. 1978). See also Note, 12 Creighton L. Rev. 847 (1979).

the United States. Debtors, including individuals, partnerships, and corporations, who have none of these connections with the United States are not eligible to file bankruptcy petitions.[39]

Governmental units, including municipalities, agencies, and other government bodies, may not commence a bankruptcy case for liquidation.[40] This exclusion applies even if the municipality is incorporated. Municipalities may, however, seek relief under chapter 9 of the Bankruptcy Code for the adjustment of their debts. Railroads that are common carriers are also ineligible to commence a liquidation case under the Code, but may seek relief from indebtedness under chapter 11.[41]

Voluntary petitions may not be filed on behalf of domestic insurance companies, banking institutions,[42] and credit unions. These entities must be liquidated under separate regulatory laws designed to deal with the special concerns relating to these businesses. This exclusion also applies to foreign insurance companies, banking institutions, and credit unions that are engaged in such business in the United States. However, these types of foreign institutions not engaged in business in the United States but having assets in the United States may petition for voluntary bankruptcy.[43] The rationale for this rule is that foreign insurance companies, banking institutions, and credit unions not conducting business in the United States are not eligible for supervised liquidation under the various regulatory laws of this country, and therefore, bankruptcy is the only means available for liquidating their assets in the United States.

¶ 1.04 WHERE TO FILE THE PETITION: JURISDICTION AND VENUE

One of the first questions that comes to mind after deciding to commence a bankruptcy case is: "Where is the petition to be filed?"

---

[39] 11 U.S.C. § 109(a).

[40] Only "persons" may file voluntary petitions, and the Bankruptcy Code excludes governmental units from the definition of "person." 11 U.S.C. § 101(30).

[41] 11 U.S.C. §§ 109(b)(1), 109(d).

[42] The excluded banking institutions include all banks, savings banks, cooperative banks, savings and loan associations, building and loan associations, and homestead associations. 11 U.S.C. § 109(b)(2).

[43] 11 U.S.C. § 109(b)(3). This section follows Israel-British Bank (London) Ltd. v. FDIC, 536 F.2d 509 (2d Cir.), *cert. denied* 429 U.S. 978 (1976), in which the court held that a British bank that borrowed American dollars and Eurodollars from U.S. banks and maintained deposits in U.S. banks, but did not engage in any banking business in this country and was

Power to deal with bankruptcy matters is exclusively in the federal government under Article I of the Constitution. In the exercise of that power, Congress gave exclusive jurisdiction over bankruptcy cases to federal district courts and created bankruptcy courts as adjuncts to the U.S. district courts. The bankruptcy courts are presided over by bankruptcy judges who have the power to grant relief under the bankruptcy laws. Therefore, only federal courts have jurisdiction to entertain bankruptcy petitions.[44]

The former Bankruptcy Act placed territorial limits on the bankruptcy court's power to adjudge persons bankrupt. Although these territorial limitations were couched in terms of jurisdictional limitations of the bankruptcy court, many courts treated them as relating to venue and not jurisdiction.[45] This distinction is important because the lack of jurisdiction cannot be waived by the parties, whereas lack of venue is a personal defense that may be waived by failure to object promptly. The Bankruptcy Reform Act makes it clear that territorial limitations relate to venue only and not jurisdiction.[46] The debtor should file the petition with the clerk of the U.S. district court in a federal district that has proper venue. After the filing, the clerk will refer the case to a bankruptcy judge.

The debtor has a choice of filing the petition in the judicial district where, for the longest portion of the 180-day period immediately preceding the filing,[47] the debtor either had (1) a residence, (2) a domicile, (3) principal assets, or (4) a principal place of business.

[1] Venue for Individuals

A case that illustrates venue requirements for natural persons is *In re Carnera,*[48] which involved an Italian prizefighter who came to

---

not licensed to do business in any state, was eligible to file a bankruptcy petition under the former Bankruptcy Act.

[44] See Chapter 6 *infra* on bankruptcy courts and officers.

[45] See Bass v. Hutchins, 417 F.2d 692 (5th Cir. 1969); *In re* Eatherton, 271 F.2d 199 (8th Cir. 1959).

[46] See 28 U.S.C. §§ 1472 and 1477(b), *as amended by* B.R.A. § 241(a).

[47] 28 U.S.C. § 1472(1), *as amended by* B.R.A. § 241(a). This section supersedes Bankruptcy Rule 116 (a)(1), which allowed the location of assets as a basis for venue for individuals only if the debtor had no residence, domicile, or place of business in the United States.

[48] 6 F. Supp. 267 (1933). Although this case was decided under the former Bankruptcy Act, its reasoning is applicable to cases under the Bankruptcy Reform Act.

compete in the United States. He filed a bankruptcy petition, and thereafter, a judgment creditor made a motion to dismiss it. The court found that the debtor was only a temporary visitor to our shores and not a resident or domiciliary of this country. The court found, however, that for the greater part of the six-month period prior to filing the petition, Mr. Carnera conducted business at his hotel, where he negotiated contracts and performed other tasks. This activity was sufficient to constitute his principal place of business, and the court denied the motion to dismiss.

The place of the debtor's employment is not a principal place of business. It has been held that a salaried employee does not have his own principal place of business and that venue for an employee must be based on domicile or residence.[49]

[2] Venue for Corporations

The application of the Bankruptcy Rules to corporate debtors raises the problem of determining the residence or domicile of a corporation for venue purposes. For example, suppose a debtor is incorporated under the laws of Delaware and is licensed to do business in Vermont, but conducts all of its business and has all of its assets in New York. Where does the corporation reside for venue purposes? May the corporation file a bankruptcy petition in Vermont? Prior to the Bankruptcy Reform Act, the relevant law expressly provided that venue for corporate petitioners was based on location of the corporation's principal place of business or its principal assets, and therefore, it was not necessary to determine the residence of a corporation.[50] The Bankruptcy Reform Act, however, makes residence a basis of venue for corporations as well as for other debtors.[51] It may be expected that bankruptcy courts will deal with this problem the same way that courts deal with corporate residency for purposes of venue in diversity actions in the district court. The venue statute governing district courts provides that "a corporation may be sued in any judicial district in which it is incorporated or licensed to do business or is doing business, and such judicial district shall be regarded as the residence of such corporation for venue purposes."[52] If this statute applies to corporate petitions in bankruptcy, the corporation in the above example has the choice of commencing

[49] See Higgins v. State Loan Co., 114 F.2d 25 (D.C. Cir. 1940).

[50] See B. Rule 116(a)(2).

[51] See 11 U.S.C. § 1472(1).

[52] 28 U.S.C. § 1391(c).

a bankruptcy case in either Vermont, Delaware, or New York. However, courts are in disagreement as to whether this statute applies to corporate plaintiffs as well as corporate defendants. Several courts have held that corporate plaintiffs are not covered by this statute and that they reside only in the state of incorporation.[53] Other courts have held that the statute does govern corporate plaintiffs.[54] Whether this statute will apply to corporate petitioners in bankruptcy cases under the Reform Act is a question that remains unanswered. In any event, the corporation may file the petition in any district in the state of incorporation or in the district where its principal assets or principal place of business have been located.

If a debtor corporation is the subject of a pending bankruptcy case, parent and subsidiary corporations, as well as certain other entities closely affiliated with a debtor corporation, may file a voluntary petition on their own behalf in the same district as the affiliated debtor without meeting any other venue requirements.[55] For example, if *ABC* Corporation properly files a petition in the Southern District of New York, its wholly-owned subsidiary corporation, *XYZ* Corporation, may file a petition on its own behalf in the same district despite the absence of a place of business, assets, domicile, or residence in New York.

[3] Venue for Unincorporated Associations and Partnerships

In determining the place of residence of unincorporated associations and partnership entities, the U.S. Supreme Court held that an unincorporated association may be sued to enforce a federal right in any federal district court in which it is doing business, which is its residence for venue purposes.[56] This same rule had been applied to labor unions[57] and partnerships.[58] Whether the same rules will

---

[53] This is the prevailing view. See, e.g., American Cyanamid Co. v. Hammond Lead Prods., Inc., 495 F.2d 1183 (3d Cir. 1974); Manchester Modes, Inc. v. Schuman, 426 F.2d 629 (2d Cir. 1970).

[54] See A.P. Green Refractories Co. v. Peerless Boiler & Eng'r Co., 303 F. Supp. 275 (E.D. Mo. 1969); Travelers Ins. Co. v. Williams, 164 F. Supp. 566 (W.D.N.C. 1958).

[55] 28 U.S.C. § 1472(2). See 11 U.S.C. § 101(2) for the definition of "affiliate."

[56] Denver & R.G.W.R.R. v. Brotherhood of R.R. Trainmen, 387 U.S. 556 (1967).

[57] American Airlines, Inc. v. Airline Pilots Ass'n Int'l, 169 F. Supp. 777, 783 (S.D.N.Y. 1958).

[58] Penrod Drilling Co. v. Johnson, 414 F.2d 1217 (5th Cir. 1969), *cert. denied* 396 U.S. 1003 (1970).

govern the residence of entities of these types that file voluntary bankruptcy petitions will remain an open question until new Bankruptcy Rules or future case law clarifies the meaning of "residence" in the Bankruptcy Reform Act. Until these matters are resolved, petitions on behalf of unincorporated associations and partnerships should be filed in the district where the debtor has its principal place of business or its principal assets.

Alternatively, a petition on behalf of a partnership entity may be filed in any district where the bankruptcy case of a general partner is already pending.[59]

A general partner who wishes to file a petition as an individual bankrupt may do so in the district of the partner's domicile, residence, principal place of business, or principal assets. In addition, a partner has the choice of filing an individual petition in any district in which the bankruptcy case of the partnership entity or of any other general partner is already pending.[60] Suppose that a partnership's residence, domicile, principal place of business, and principal assets are in New Jersey. Partner A filed a bankruptcy petition as an individual in Maryland because his personal assets are located there. Partner B, who has no connection with Maryland, may file his own individual petition in Maryland nonetheless.

¶ 1.05 TRANSFER OF CASES

[1] Improper Venue

When a petition is filed in the wrong district, the court has two options made available by the Bankruptcy Reform Act. The judge has the discretion either to retain the case despite improper venue or to transfer it to another district. The court must base its decision on the "interest of justice" and "convenience of the parties."[61] Such factors as the location of the debtor, corporate officers, major creditors, business records, counsels' offices, and many other personal considerations relate to the convenience of the debtor and creditors.[62]

The treatment of cases with improper venue under the Bankruptcy Reform Act differs in one significant way from the treatment under the

---

[59] 28 U.S.C. § 1472(2), *as amended by* B.R.A. § 241(a).

[60] *Id.*

[61] 28 U.S.C. § 1477(a), *as amended by* B.R.A. § 241(a). See B. Rule 116(b)(2). See also *In re* Commonwealth Oil Ref. Co., 5 Bankr. Dec. 480 (5th Cir. 1979).

[62] See ¶ 1.05[2] for a discussion of these factors.

former Act. Bankruptcy Rule 116, which governed venue problems prior to the Reform Act, gave the court a third option when dealing with petitions filed in the wrong district: The court had the right to dismiss such cases.[63] The Reform Act does not permit the dismissal of such cases.[64]

It is interesting to note that the bankruptcy court may transfer a case to *any* other district or division. Accordingly, the court has the discretion to transfer a case even if venue does not lie in the district to which the case is transferred.[65] This flexibility is necessary, particularly in reorganization cases, because a corporate bankruptcy often involves numerous creditors and the multi-state location of assets.

The procedural requirements for objecting to improper venue are governed by the Bankruptcy Rules. The court may retain or transfer a case filed without proper venue on motion by a party in interest or on its own initiative if it acts prior to or at the meeting of creditors. After the meeting of creditors, the judge may dismiss or transfer the case only upon a timely motion by an interested party. In any event, the court must hold a hearing prior to dismissal or transfer. If no objection to venue is raised, the court may retain the case without a hearing.[66]

[2] Proper Venue

Even if there is proper venue, a court has the discretion to transfer a case to another district in the interest of justice and for the convenience of the parties.[67] In fact, the judge may transfer the case to another district even if there is improper venue in the receiving district.

The Bankruptcy Rules provide that such a transfer may be made upon motion by an interested party or on its own initiative at or before the meeting of creditors. After the meeting of creditors, it may transfer a case only upon motion of a party. No transfer may take place unless the petitioner is afforded a hearing.[68] These procedural rules govern cases that are commenced under the Bankruptcy Code.

Factors that are usually considered by bankruptcy judges in determining whether a transfer will be "in the interest of justice" and "for the convenience of the parties" are: (1) proximity to the court of

---

[63] B. Rule 116(b)(2).

[64] See 28 U.S.C. § 1477(a).

[65] 28 U.S.C. § 1477(a). See B. Rule 116(b)(2).

[66] See 28 U.S.C. § 1477(b); B. Rule 116(b)(2).

[67] 28 U.S.C. § 1475, *as amended by* B.R.A. § 241(a). See B. Rule 116(b)(1).

[68] B. Rule 116(b)(1).

creditors of every kind; (2) proximity of the debtor to the court; (3) proximity to the court of the witnesses necessary to the administration of the estate; (4) location of the assets; (5) the economical and efficient administration of the estate; and (6) intertwined relationships of debtors, such as when several partners commence bankruptcy cases in the district.[69]

[3] Two or More Petitions

Suppose that an involuntary petition is filed against a debtor in one district and the same debtor files a voluntary petition in a different district. Because there are several bases for venue, it is possible that both courts have proper venue. Or, suppose that two involuntary petitions are filed against a partnership by two general partners in two different courts, both courts having proper venue. These problems are resolved by giving the court in which the first petition was filed the power and obligation to determine the court in which the case will proceed. The court that received the first petition will hold a hearing and apply the "interest of justice" and "convenience of the parties" tests to determine the proper court to handle the case. The other courts involved must stay all proceedings until the first court makes a determination, which is binding on all other courts.[70]

¶ 1.06 DOCUMENTS TO BE FILED

[1] The Petition

A voluntary bankruptcy case is commenced by the filing of a petition[71] in the office of the bankruptcy judge.[72] The petition should conform to the official form.[73] Unless a local court rule provides other-

---

[69] For illustrations of how these factors have been applied, see *In re* Bankers Trust, 403 F.2d 16 (7th Cir. 1968); *In re* Fairfield Puerto Rico, Inc., 333 F. Supp. 1187 (D. Del. 1971); *In re* Commonwealth Oil Ref. Co., note 61 *supra*.

[70] B. Rule 116(c).

[71] B. Rule 109 requires that the petition be verified. However, Suggested Interim Bankruptcy Form No. 1 permits an unsworn statement in lieu of verification. See 28 U.S.C. § 1746. See also Sugg. Int. B. Form No. 5 in Appendix B for an unsworn declaration on behalf of a corporation or partnership.

[72] 11 U.S.C. § 301.

[73] Sugg. Int. B. Form No. 1, which is set forth in Appendix B, should be used unless a local court rule provides otherwise.

wise, the debtor should file with the court clerk an original petition plus three copies,[74] and the caption of the petition must contain all names used by the debtor within the previous six years.[75] The petition is referred to the bankruptcy judge who presides over the case.

[2] List of Creditors

The debtor is required to file a list of creditors with the court.[76] The list should include names and addresses of *all* creditors and should be filed together with the petition.

[3] Schedules of Assets and Liabilities

Unless the court orders otherwise, the debtor must file schedules of assets and liabilities.[77] Because the Bankruptcy Code does not deal with specific details concerning content and time limits relating to the schedules, the Bankruptcy Rules should be followed until new rules are promulgated.[78] The petitioner should file an original plus three copies of the schedules, which should conform to the official form.[79] "Schedule A" contains lists of creditors with priority, secured creditors, and unsecured nonpriority creditors. "Schedule B" contains separate lists of the debtor's real property, personal property, property not otherwise scheduled, and property claimed as exempt.[80]

The schedules should be filed together with the petition. However, it is often necessary to file a petition as soon as possible, and there may not be enough time to prepare the schedules. The Bankruptcy Rules, therefore, permit the debtor to file the schedules within ten days after

---

[74] Sugg. Int. B. Rule 1002(b)(1). In reorganization cases under chapter 11, an original plus six copies must be filed. Sugg. Int. B. Rule 1002(b)(2).

[75] B. Rule 106; Sugg. Int. B. Rule 1005.

[76] 11 U.S.C. § 521(1). See 11 U.S.C. § 101(9) for the definition of "creditor."

[77] 11 U.S.C. § 521(1).

[78] See B. Rule 108. These matters are not covered by the Suggested Interim Bankruptcy Rules.

[79] B. Rule 108(a) provides that the number of copies to be filed corresponds to the number of copies of the petition. Sugg. Int. B. Rule 1002 (b)(1) requires an original plus three copies of the petition. See Sugg. Int. B. Form No. 6 in Appendix B.

[80] See Chapter 4 *infra* for a discussion on exempt property.

the petition is filed if the debtor files a list of the names and addresses of creditors along with the petition. The court may grant up to ten additional days to file the schedules or it may extend the deadline even further for good cause. If a debtor fails to file schedules, the court may order the debtor, the trustee, or another interested party to file the schedules.[81]

It cannot be overemphasized that these schedules must be drawn with the utmost care. Although the consequences of neglect or carelessness may at times be overcome, the borderline between carelessness and falsity is sometimes so difficult to define that grave consequences ensue. Failure to set forth the correct address of a creditor, for example, may result in a claim not being discharged.[82] Knowingly omitting a creditor's name or failing to list all assets may result in the commission of a crime.[83] When preparing schedules, therefore, follow these suggestions:

(1) Consult with the debtor and the debtor's accountant. The accountant very often will have a better understanding of the debtor's affairs, particularly as to contingent liabilities, maintenance of books and records, financial statements, and inventories.

(2) Conduct a judgment search to ascertain judgments of record that may have been forgotten by the debtor.

(3) After the court mails notices of the meeting of creditors, check with the clerk to determine if any notices sent to creditors were returned. Try to ascertain correct addresses of each of these creditors and send a registered letter to each so as to give the creditor notice of the bankruptcy in time to participate in it and file a proof of claim.

(4) List all claims, even if the debtor intends to pay certain creditors when financially able. Otherwise, there may be an objection to discharge and the debtor may be guilty of making a false oath.[84]

---

[81] B. Rule 108(b).

[82] See Chapter 3 *infra*.

[83] See 18 U.S.C. § 152. See also *In re* Turner, 185 F. Supp. 790 (M.D.N.C. 1960), in which the denial of a discharge was affirmed where the bankrupt failed to list a stock interest in a newly organized corporation, such failure constituting a false oath punishable by imprisonment under 18 U.S.C. § 152. The bankrupt's explanation that "he did not think of it" was characterized by the court as "incredible." *Id.* at 793.

[84] 11 U.S.C. § 727(a)(4); *In re* Haydu, 105 F. Supp. 859 (E.D.N.Y.

(5) List assignees of claims as creditors.

(6) List all property regardless of value. Otherwise, such failure to schedule may constitute a false oath.

[4] Statement of Affairs

In addition to the petition and schedules, the debtor is required to file a statement of financial affairs.[85] An original plus three copies of a statement that conforms to the appropriate official form should be filed.[86] The statement of affairs is a series of questions and answers relating to the debtor's financial history and previous transactions.

It is customary for the petition, schedules, and statement of affairs to be filed together. However, the Bankruptcy Rules relating to time limits and time extensions for filing schedules also apply to filing the statement of financial affairs.[87] If the debtor fails to file the statement, the court may order the debtor, the trustee, or another interested party to file it.

The same care that goes into the preparation of the schedules should be observed in preparing the statement of affairs. Here again, failure to answer correctly may, if done knowingly and willfully, constitute a crime and may be the basis for denial of a discharge. Each question should be answered or the failure to answer should be explained. If the answer is "none," this should be stated.

[5] Amendments and Supplemental Schedules

The Bankruptcy Code leaves procedures for amending documents and filing supplemental schedules to the Bankruptcy Rules. The present Rules permit a debtor to amend a voluntary petition, schedule, or statement of affairs as a matter of course at any time before the case is closed. In addition, the court may order an amendment upon motion by any interested party.[88] If a schedule is amended to add the name of

---

1952), in which the court held that failure to set forth a debt in schedules was a false oath and precluded a discharge. See also Stim v. Simon, 284 F.2d 58 (2d Cir. 1960).

[85] See Sugg. Int. B. Forms No. 7 (debtor not engaged in business), No. 8 (debtor engaged in business) set forth in Appendix B.

[86] See also Sugg. Int. B. Rule 1002(b)(1) and B. Rule 108(a), which, when read together, require the filing of an original plus three copies.

[87] See B. Rule 108, and ¶ 1.06[3].

[88] B. Rule 110. These matters are not covered by the Suggested Interim Bankruptcy Rules.

a creditor when it is too late for the creditor to file a timely proof of claim, the amendment may not affect the nondischargeability of the claim.[89]

Certain postbankruptcy acquisitions of property by the debtor pass to the trustee to become part of the estate.[90] The debtor, therefore, is required to file supplemental schedules within ten days after acquiring such property. If the debtor wishes to claim any of this property as exempt, it must be so indicated on the supplemental schedules. These supplemental schedules must be filed notwithstanding the close of the bankruptcy case.[91]

¶ 1.07 FILING FEES

The petitioner must pay a filing fee of $60 to the clerk when the petition is filed.[92] If a debtor is unable to pay the fee at one time, an application for permission to pay it in installments may accompany the petition.[93] The application, which should be filed in duplicate, must contain the proposed terms of the installment payments and must state that the debtor is unable to pay the fee except in installments and that the debtor has paid no money and transferred no property to a lawyer for services in connection with the case.[94] After a hearing and before the meeting of creditors, the court may order that installment payments are permitted and may set the amount and due date of each installment. However, the number of installments may not exceed four, and the final payment must be made within four months after the commencement of the case. The court may extend the time for the payment of any installment to a date within six months after the filing of the petition, but such extension must be based on cause shown.[95]

The bankruptcy court has no power to waive the filing fee and permit a debtor to proceed in forma pauperis. In *United States v.*

---

[89] See 11 U.S.C. § 523(a)(3).

[90] See 11 U.S.C. § 541 on postpetition property which becomes part of the bankruptcy estate. See Chapter 4 *infra.*

[91] B. Rule 108(e).

[92] 28 U.S.C. § 1930(a)(1), *as amended by* B.R.A. § 246(a). See Sugg. Int. B. Rule 1006(a).

[93] 28 U.S.C. § 1930(a), *as amended by* B.R.A. § 246(a). See Sugg. Int. B. Rule 1006(b)(1).

[94] Sugg. Int. B. Rule 1006(b)(1). See Sugg. Int. B. Form No. 3 in Appendix B.

[95] Sugg. Int. B. Rule 1006(b)(2); B. Rule 107(b)(2). See Sugg. Int. B. Form No. 4 in Appendix B.

Kras,[96] the Supreme Court held that an indigent debtor had no right to obtain a discharge of debts under the former Act unless the debtor pays the filing fee in full. Under the Bankruptcy Reform Act, courts still may not permit debtors to proceed in forma pauperis.[97]

¶ 1.08 JOINT PETITIONS, JOINT ADMINISTRATION, AND CONSOLIDATION

[1] Husband and Wife

When the petitioning debtor is married, careful consideration should be given to determine whether a bankruptcy petition should be filed by the debtor's spouse. Petitions by both spouses may not be advisable in a particular situation so that at least one spouse may preserve his or her assets. The effects of bankruptcy of one spouse on the property rights of the other will be determined not by state law, as under the former Act, but by the provisions of the Bankruptcy Code. The legal ramifications of joint property interests, community property laws, and exemptions must be examined when deciding whether the debtor's spouse should commence a bankruptcy case.[98]

It is often necessary for a husband and wife to file petitions because of heavy indebtedness of both spouses. For example, it is common for one spouse to guarantee debts of the other spouse, especially when the debts are business loans. Because the discharge of one spouse will not relieve the other of liability, it may be necessary to obtain discharges for both spouses.

The Bankruptcy Code permits a husband and wife to file a joint petition, which commences a joint case.[99] The joint case is designed primarily for convenience in administration of the bankruptcy. It is common for spouses to have jointly held property and joint obligations for which a joint administration will usually result in less expense for both the creditors and the debtors. In addition, the petitioners will pay

---

[96] 409 U.S. 434 (1973). The Court reasoned that a debtor has no constitutional right to obtain relief from indebtedness.

[97] See 28 U.S.C. § 1930(a), *amended by* B.R.A. § 246(a), which requires the payment of the filing fee "notwithstanding section 1915 of this title." Section 1915 is the part of Title 28 that permits fees to be waived in federal court. Accordingly, it appears that 28 U.S.C. § 1915 is not applicable in bankruptcy cases.

[98] Property interests of the debtor and the debtor's spouse are discussed in Chapter 4 *infra.*

[99] 11 U.S.C. § 302(a).

only one filing fee. Because a joint case must be voluntary, it is necessary for both spouses to consent to join in the petition. The mere filing of a joint petition does not, in and of itself, result in the consolidation of the estates of both spouses. After the petition is filed, the court will determine the extent, if any, to which the estates will be consolidated by combining assets and liabilities of the spouses.[100]

[2] Joint Petitions for Other Debtors Prohibited

The Bankruptcy Code contains no provision for the filing of a joint petition other than for debtors who are husband and wife. Accordingly, single petitions must be filed by all other entities who wish to commence a bankruptcy case. When general partners want to proceed as individual debtors and also desire to file a petition on behalf of the firm, separate petitions must be filed by each partner and the partnership entity. Likewise, when parent and subsidiary corporations want to become debtors under the Code, it is necessary for each corporate entity to file a separate petition.

[3] Joint Administration and Consolidation

Although debtors who are not married to each other may not file a joint petition, the court may order cases involving two or more related debtors, such as a partnership and one or more general partners or a corporation and one or more affiliates, to be administered jointly.[101] Joint administration may include the use of a single docket for administrative matters, a joint listing of filed claims, and the combining of notices to creditors. It also permits application for relief and the issuance of orders applicable to more than one case, such as an order authorizing the retention of counsel in two cases. The purpose of administering the cases jointly is to avoid unnecessary costs and delay and for administrative convenience. Substantive rights of creditors, however, may not be adversely affected by a joint administration.

The Bankruptcy Rules also permit the consolidation of cases, which must be distinguished from joint administration.[102] Consolidation is of greater significance than joint administration because it may affect the substantive rights of debtors and creditors. When two or more

---

[100] 11 U.S.C. § 302(b).

[101] B. Rule 117.

[102] B. Rule 117. See Chemical Bank N.Y. Trust Co. v. Kheel, 369 F.2d 845 (2d Cir. 1966).

cases are consolidated, there is a merging of assets and assumption of liabilities by all debtors involved. Consolidation occurs in situations where the assets and liabilities of parent and subsidiary corporations, or of other debtors that are closely related, are so intermingled that the court cannot separate them.[103]

¶ 1.09 AUTOMATIC STAY

[1] Purpose

The typical debtor has already been sued or threatened with legal action by creditors by the time that a voluntary petition is filed. The debtor may have been subjected to wage garnishments and other judicial processes employed in the collection efforts of creditors. In order to relieve the financial pressures that drove the debtor into bankruptcy in the first place, the Bankruptcy Code provides that the filing of the petition results in an automatic stay of actions against the debtor.[104] This stay, which arises by operation of law and requires no judicial action, halts the collection of claims and protects the debtor from further harassment by creditors.

Another purpose of the automatic stay is to prevent a creditor from pursuing remedies against the debtor's assets to the detriment of other creditors. If the speediest creditors were permitted to continue to grab the debtor's property after the bankruptcy case had commenced, an orderly liquidation and fair and equal distribution of the estate to creditors would be frustrated.

It should be kept in mind that the automatic stay is not intended to alter the substantive rights of creditors, but merely stops collection efforts pending a determination of the creditors' and debtor's rights by the bankruptcy court.

[2] Scope of the Stay Against Collection Efforts

The Bankruptcy Code makes it clear that the automatic stay is not confined to judicial actions and is very broad in scope. The following acts are subject to the stay:

---

[103] See James Talcott, Inc. v. Wharton, 517 F.2d 997 (2d Cir. 1975), on consolidation of assets and liabilities of two debtors, except for secured claims, in a reorganization plan. Consolidation is discussed more fully in ¶ 8.16.

[104] 11 U.S.C. § 362.

(1) The commencement or continuation of a proceeding against the debtor that was or could have been commenced before the filing of the bankruptcy petition.[105] This includes any judicial, administrative, and arbitration proceeding, whether or not it is before a governmental tribunal. It also applies to every step of the proceeding, including the issuance of process, levy, garnishment, and supplemental proceedings.

(2) The enforcement of a judgment obtained before the petition was filed, either against the debtor personally or against property of the bankruptcy estate. Creditors may not proceed with levy or execution to satisfy the prebankruptcy judgment.[106]

(3) Efforts to obtain possession of property *of* the estate or property *from* the estate.[107] Property of the estate includes the debtor's property as of the date of the petition.[108] Property from the estate includes all property that the estate controls or possesses, whether or not the bankruptcy estate has lawful title. The stay covers these acts so as to give the trustee ample time to discover and evaluate the respective rights in the property before creditors start grabbing.

(4) Any attempt to collect or recover on a claim against the debtor that arose before the bankruptcy petition was filed.[109] Creditors may not telephone or otherwise communicate with the debtor to encourage the payment of these obligations.

(5) The setoff of any debt that a creditor owes to a debtor against the debtor's liability to the creditor.[110] Thus, if a creditor owes the debtor $100 and the debtor owes the creditor $100 from a separate transaction, the creditor is stayed from offsetting the mutual debts. However, it is important to emphasize that the creditor's substantive right of setoff may not be affected. In fact, the creditor may be treated as a secured creditor to protect setoff rights.[111]

---

[105] 11 U.S.C. § 362(a)(1).

[106] 11 U.S.C. § 362(a)(2).

[107] B.R.A. § 362(a)(3), 11 U.S.C. § 362(a)(3) (1978).

[108] See Chapter 4 *infra* for a discussion of property of the estate.

[109] 11 U.S.C. § 362(a)(6).

[110] 11 U.S.C. § 362(a)(7). See ¶ 5.10 on the right of setoff in bankruptcy.

[111] See 11 U.S.C. § 506(a).

(6) The commencement or continuation of a proceeding before the U.S. Tax Court concerning the debtor.[112]

[3] Scope of the Stay Against Lien Enforcement

The automatic stay under prior bankruptcy law was extremely limited as applied to liens. The stay only applied to acts or court proceedings to *enforce* a lien against property in the custody of the bankruptcy court or a judicial lien obtained within four months of bankruptcy against the debtor's property.[113]

The Bankruptcy Code enlarged the scope of the automatic stay so as to prohibit the creation and perfection, as well as the enforcement, of any liens against property of the bankruptcy estate and, to the extent that a lien secures a claim arising prior to filing the petition, against the debtor's property that is exempt or that does not otherwise pass to the trustee.[114] The stay applies to judicial, statutory, and consensual liens, such as real estate mortgages and security interests in personal property. Creditors are even prohibited from filing a financing statement to perfect a security interest in accordance with the Uniform Commercial Code, except a purchase money security interest as set forth below.

[4] Exceptions to the Automatic Stay

There are eight exceptions to the automatic stay rule: [115]

(1) Bankruptcy laws are not intended to shield debtors from criminal prosecution, and therefore criminal actions against the debtor may proceed despite the bankruptcy.

(2) The collection of alimony, maintenance, and support is not affected by the automatic stay to the extent that it is from property which is not part of the bankruptcy estate. This exception should be of no consequence to the bankruptcy case because the property used to pay these claims is not subject to liquidation and the claims are not discharged.[116] Also, staying the collection of these claims could possibly cause extreme hardship to the protected spouse or children.

---

[112] 11 U.S.C. § 362(a)(8).

[113] See B. Rule 601(a).

[114] 11 U.S.C. §§ 362(a)(4), 362(a)(5).

[115] These exceptions are contained in 11 U.S.C. § 362(b).

[116] See 11 U.S.C. § 523(a)(5). However, creditors with claims that are nondischargeable on other grounds are subject to the automatic stay.

(3) Perfection of a lien or property interest to make it effective against the bankruptcy trustee under Section 546(b) of the Bankruptcy Code is permitted. That section allows postbankruptcy perfection of only certain liens, such as purchase money security interests within ten days of attachment.[117]

(4) Governments may proceed to enforce their police or regulatory powers, such as by prosecuting actions to prevent violations of health, consumer protection, environmental, or other similar laws.

(5) Governments may also take steps to enforce injunctions or judgments, other than money judgments, obtained prior to bankruptcy in the exercise of their police or regulatory powers. Although it may enter a money judgment, the governmental unit may not enforce a prebankruptcy money judgment against the debtor by execution, levy, wage garnishment, or otherwise.

(6) The automatic stay does not cover certain setoffs of mutual debts and claims relating to commodity transactions.

(7) Despite the automatic stay, the Secretary of Housing and Urban Development may commence an action to foreclose on a mortgage insured under the National Housing Act. This exception applies only when the property in question consists of five or more living units.

(8) The automatic stay does not apply to the issuance of a notice of tax deficiency issued by a governmental unit.

Actions not covered by the automatic stay, either because they are outside the scope of the stay or are within the enumerated exceptions, may be stayed nonetheless by a court after a proceeding commenced by the trustee or other interested party. The power to enjoin these actions is conferred on the court by virtue of its power to issue any order "that is necessary or appropriate" to carry out the provisions of the Bankruptcy Code.[118] Of course, the moving party will be required to show that there is a need for the requested stay to protect the rights of the parties.

---

[117] See ¶ 7.01.

[118] 11 U.S.C. § 105(a). A bankruptcy judge, as an adjunct of the district court, has all the injunctive powers of a court of equity and may enjoin a creditor from proceeding, although he may not enjoin another court. See 28 U.S.C. § 1481, *as amended by* B.R.A. § 241(a). The Bankruptcy Rules require that the party seeking an injunction must commence an adversary proceeding. B. Rule 701(5). See Chapter 6 *infra* for a discussion on bankruptcy courts.

[5] Adequate Protection of Property Rights

Persons who have interests in property of the debtor or of the bankruptcy estate and who are unable to enforce their property interests because of the automatic stay may request protection against decreasing value of the property pending the stay.[119] For example, a secured party who is stayed from foreclosing on collateral that is depreciating in value will be damaged and deprived of the benefits of the security interest to the extent of the depreciation and should be adequately protected against such loss. Likewise, a consignor is stayed from recovering goods from a bankrupt consignee while the stay is pending. In these situations, the trustee must, whenever possible, propose and provide an adequate protection method.[120] The trustee may protect the rights of the secured creditor or other holder of the property interest by making periodic cash payments from the estate to the interest holder in an amount that would compensate for depreciation.[121] Alternatively, the trustee may give the interest holder an additional or replacement lien on other property to the extent of depreciation.[122] The trustee may grant the interest holder an administrative expense priority when it is fairly certain that there are enough assets to pay administrative expenses.[123] These protection methods are not exclusive, and the parties may fashion other means of protection to fit the situation.[124]

[6] Automatic Termination

The automatic stay is not permanent. To the extent that the stay covers acts against property of the bankruptcy estate, it terminates auto-

---

[119] See 11 U.S.C. §§ 361, 362(d).

[120] 11 U.S.C. § 361.

[121] 11 U.S.C. § 361(1).

[122] 11 U.S.C. § 361(2).

[123] 11 U.S.C. § 361(3).

[124] Although the former Act was silent on giving these kinds of protections, courts were concerned with protecting the rights of secured parties who were stayed from foreclosure in arrangement and reorganization cases. See *In re* Blazon Flexible Flyer, Inc., 407 F. Supp. 861 (N.D. Ohio 1976), in which a secured party who was owed $1.34 million and who had a security interest in assets worth $5.73 million was stayed from foreclosing on accounts receivable and inventory needed for rehabilitation. The court instituted safeguards to protect the secured party, including an assurance that financial information about the debtor be transmitted to the secured party and the court on a regular basis. See also *In re* American Kitchen Foods, Inc., 2 Bankr. Dec. 715 (D. Me. 1976).

matically when the property is no longer a part of the estate because of sale, abandonment, exemption, or otherwise.[125] However, if property leaves the estate and passes to the debtor, the debtor remains protected to the extent that the stay applies to property of the debtor. For example, suppose that a secured party wishes to enforce a lien against property the debtor owned at the time of the commencement of the bankruptcy case. This property is part of the estate, and therefore enforcement of the lien is stayed. Suppose further that the debtor obtains the property by claiming that it is exempt under state law.[126] May the secured creditor foreclose on the security interest? If the secured debt arose *before* bankruptcy, the stay would continue because it applies to protect the debtor's own property. But if the secured debt arose *after* bankruptcy, the stay terminates and the secured party is free to foreclose because the automatic stay does not apply to the enforcement of liens against the debtor's property (as opposed to property of the estate) if it secures a postpetition debt.[127]

The stay of any act other than acts against property of the estate ceases upon the occurrence of any one of the following events: (1) the close of the case, (2) dismissal of the case, or (3) denial or grant of a discharge.[128]

[7] Relief From the Stay on Request

A person may seek earlier relief from the automatic stay by commencing an adversary proceeding for such relief.[129] Upon the request of any interested party, the judge may terminate, annul, modify, or condition the stay or otherwise grant appropriate relief to protect the rights of the moving party. The judge must base the relief upon good cause shown at a hearing.[130] For example, if a secured party shows that the collateral held by the estate is depreciating in value and that the trustee

---

[125] 11 U.S.C. § 362(c)(1). See 11 U.S.C. § 541(a), and Chapter 4 *infra*, dealing with property of the estate.

[126] See 11 U.S.C. § 522, and Chapter 4 *infra*, on exemptions.

[127] 11 U.S.C. § 362(a)(5).

[128] 11 U.S.C. § 362(c)(2). See 11 U.S.C. § 350, governing the closing of bankruptcy cases. The third event does not apply in corporation or partnership bankruptcies because discharge is not available in these cases. See ¶ 1.02[1][b].

[129] B. Rule 701(6) requires the party seeking relief from the stay to commence an adversary proceeding. See ¶ 6.04[2], dealing with adversary proceedings.

[130] 11 U.S.C. § 362(d).

has made no provision to adequately protect the secured party against such depreciation,[131] the bankruptcy judge should grant relief from the stay, such as by conditioning the stay to require the trustee to make periodic cash payments to the secured party as adequate protection or by any of the other protective devices discussed above.[132] Also, the court should grant relief from the stay if the debtor and the estate have no equity in the property that is the subject of the stay.[133] If a $1,000 debt is secured by collateral worth only $500, there is usually no justification for preventing the secured party from foreclosing on the collateral in a liquidation case since the estate has no equity interest in the property, but the relief may be different in a reorganization case if there is a danger that foreclosure would interfere with reorganization.[134] Another situation in which relief from a stay may be granted occurs when the debtor is a party to a lawsuit in a representative capacity only, such as when the debtor is acting as the executor of an estate in a probate proceeding or as guardian of a minor in a civil action involving rights of the minor. If the act that is stayed does not interfere with the bankruptcy case and is unrelated to the debtor's harassment by creditors, which is the purpose of the automatic stay rule, the court should grant appropriate relief from the stay.

The Bankruptcy Code requires that the court make its determination after a hearing on notice to the parties. The hearing is limited in scope to the issues of whether there is cause to grant relief from the stay and, if cause is shown, the form of relief appropriate to the situation. Other issues and all counterclaims may not be decided on the merits because of the summary nature of the hearing, but the existence of other issues and counterclaims may be considered by the court in its determination of whether the stay should be continued.[135] Although the party seeking relief from the stay must initiate the request as the moving party, the burden of proof on all issues is on the party opposing the requested relief, except that the party requesting the relief has the burden of proof on the issue of the debtor's equity in the property.[136] Accordingly, when a secured party requests relief from a stay so as to

---

[131] See 11 U.S.C. § 361.

[132] See ¶ 1.09[5].

[133] 11 U.S.C. § 362(d)(2)(A).

[134] See Chapter 8 *infra* on reorganization cases.

[135] A motion seeking relief from the stay is not the assertion of a claim, and, therefore, it does not give rise to the right or obligation to assert counterclaims. *In re* Essex Properties, Ltd., 430 F. Supp. 1112 (N.D. Cal. 1977).

[136] 11 U.S.C. § 362(g).

foreclose on his collateral, the trustee, the debtor, or other party wishing the stay to continue may have to prove that the secured party is adequately protected against depreciation.

A problem that existed under prior bankruptcy law was that the court was under no time pressure to decide a request for relief from a stay. Court delays in holding the hearing or making a decision seriously jeopardized the rights of secured creditors and other property interest holders. The Bankruptcy Code is designed to avoid these judicial delays by providing for specific time restrictions. If the court does not make a ruling within thirty days after the request for relief is made, the stay will terminate automatically as applied to the moving party. If it is impractical to make a final determination within thirty days because of the complexity of the case, the court may order the stay continued if it is shown at a preliminary hearing that there is a reasonable likelihood that the trustee or other party opposing relief from the stay will prevail at a subsequent final hearing. Therefore, the court is required to make either a final ruling or a preliminary ruling pending a final hearing within the thirty-day period, or else the stay is automatically terminated. If a preliminary ruling is made during the thirty-day period in favor of maintaining the stay, the final hearing must be commenced within thirty days after the preliminary hearing.[137] Moreover, the Suggested Interim Bankruptcy Rules provide that the stay terminates automatically thirty days after the commencement of the final hearing unless within that time period the court makes a final ruling that the stay should be continued.[138]

[8] Ex Parte Relief From the Stay

If an interested party will suffer irreparable injury because of the stay before there is an opportunity for prior notice and hearing, the Code permits the court to grant ex parte relief.[139] It should be emphasized, however, that the granting of relief without notice and a prior hearing is rare.

The Suggested Interim Bankruptcy Rules set forth the procedure to be followed in obtaining such ex parte relief from the stay.[140] Upon filing a complaint seeking relief, the court may grant the relief without

---

[137] 11 U.S.C. § 362(e).

[138] Sugg. Int. B. Rule 4001(a).

[139] 11 U.S.C. § 362(f).

[140] See Sugg. Int. B. Rule 4001(b).

written or oral notice to the adverse party only if "(1) it clearly appears from specific facts shown by affidavit or by a verified complaint that immediate and irreparable injury, loss, or damage will result to the plaintiff before the adverse party or his attorney can be heard in opposition, and (2) the plaintiff's attorney certifies to the court in writing the efforts, if any, which have been made to give the notice and the reasons supporting his claim that notice should not be required." The party obtaining ex parte relief must give both written and oral notice thereof as soon as possible to the trustee and the debtor and also must mail to them a copy of the order granting relief. On two days' notice to the party who obtained ex parte relief, or on such shorter notice as the court may prescribe, the adverse party may appear and move for reinstatement of the stay, and the court is required to hear and determine such motion "as expeditiously as the ends of justice require." [141]

[9] Enforcing the Stay

The automatic stay will not protect the debtor or the estate unless creditors are aware of it. It is important, therefore, to notify creditors as soon as possible after the filing of the petition. Within a reasonable time after the petition is filed, the clerk of the bankruptcy court sends a notice to all creditors listed by the debtor. This notice, which is usually not received until several weeks after the petition is filed, informs creditors of the bankruptcy case, the automatic stay, the first meeting of creditors, and the deadlines for filing objections to discharge and complaints for determining dischargeability of certain debts.[142]

If the debtor needs the protection of the automatic stay immediately after the petition is filed against a creditor who has a pending lawsuit, the debtor's attorney should notify the creditor's attorney by mail or telegram instead of waiting for the clerk to send out notices. Notification should contain information concerning the filing of the petition, the court, and the index number and make reference to the automatic stay.

In the event that the creditor ignores the automatic stay, the debtor or the trustee may commence an adversary proceeding to obtain a specific injunction against the violator and a temporary stay pending the

---

[141] *Id.*

[142] See 11 U.S.C. § 342(a); B. Rule 203. See also Sugg. Int. B. Form No. 13 in Appendix B.

hearing on the injunction.[143] This step should not be necessary because the "injunction" is automatic under the bankruptcy laws. Nevertheless, a specific injunction by court order is often more convincing than an automatic stay. Alternatively, the debtor or the trustee may seek a contempt order to punish the violator.[144]

¶ 1.10 DEBTOR'S PROTECTION AGAINST LOSS OF UTILITY SERVICES

In addition to being protected by the automatic stay, as discussed above, the debtor is protected against the loss of telephone, electric, gas, and other utility services. The Bankruptcy Code prohibits a utility from refusing or discontinuing service to a debtor or the trustee because of the failure to pay for prebankruptcy service. The utility company, however, may refuse or discontinue service if the company is not provided, within twenty days after the petition is filed, with adequate assurance of payment for service to be rendered after the filing of the petition. This assurance may be in the form of a cash deposit or other security. After notice and a hearing, the court may order reasonable modification of the amount of the deposit or security.[145]

¶ 1.11 PROCEDURE AFTER THE CASE IS COMMENCED

[1] Order for Relief

The filing of a voluntary petition for liquidation does not commence an adversarial litigation. Until a dispute arises within the bankruptcy case, the procedure is more administrative than judicial. There is no respondent or defendant who is required to "answer" the petition. In fact, the Bankruptcy Code provides that the filing of a petition itself constitutes an "order for relief." [146]

---

[143] See B. Rule 701(5), which provides that a moving party must commence an adversary proceeding to obtain an injunction.

[144] See ¶ 6.03 on contempt power of the court.

[145] 11 U.S.C. § 366.

[146] The Bankruptcy Code uses the phrase "order for relief" to replace the term "adjudication." In fact, there is no actual "adjudication" by a court in a voluntary bankruptcy case. 11 U.S.C. § 301; Sugg. Int. B. Rule 1001 (a)(2). Compare former B.A. § 18 on adjudication.

[2] Appointment of an Interim Trustee

Promptly after the petition is filed, the bankruptcy judge will appoint an interim trustee to represent the estate until the regular trustee is elected or designated to serve.[147] The interim trustee has all of the powers of a regular trustee.[148] The debtor should cooperate with the interim trustee by surrendering property of the estate and by otherwise permitting the interim trustee to perform the official duties. If the debtor is in business, the interim trustee may seek a court order to continue the operation of the business for a brief time prior to liquidation if that will benefit the estate.[149] For example, if the debtor is in the manufacturing business, the court may permit the interim trustee to run the business so as to complete the manufacture of unfinished goods in order to increase the resale value of such merchandise upon liquidation.

[3] Meeting of Creditors

Before filing the petition, a debtor should be informed about the public nature of a bankruptcy case. The debtor should be aware that the petition, schedules, statement of affairs, and other documents filed in the case will be open to the public for inspection.[150] Also, the debtor is required to appear for an examination under oath at a public meeting of creditors in the bankruptcy court.[151] The Suggested Interim Bankruptcy Rules provide that the meeting shall be held between twenty and forty days after the petition is filed.[152] Unless creditors vote to designate a presiding officer, the clerk of the bankruptcy court presides at the meeting of creditors.[153] The purpose of the meeting is to give credi-

---

[147] 11 U.S.C. § 701(a). The availability of a procedure for appointing an interim trustee makes it unnecessary to appoint a receiver. Accordingly, a bankruptcy court does not have the power to appoint a receiver. 11 U.S.C. § 105(b).

[148] See Chapter 6 *infra* for a discussion of this subject.

[149] 11 U.S.C. § 721.

[150] See 11 U.S.C. § 107. However, the court may protect trade secrets or confidential research, development or commercial information and may protect a person with respect to scandalous or defamatory matter contained in filed documents. *Id.*

[151] 11 U.S.C. § 343; B. Rule 205(b).

[152] Sugg. Int. B. Rule 2003(a). A later time may be set if there is an appeal from or a motion to vacate the order for relief or if there is a motion to dismiss the case. See Sugg. Int. B. Form No. 13 in Appendix B.

[153] Sugg. Int. B. Rule 2003(b)(1). Only creditors who are eligible to

tors and the trustee an opportunity to examine the debtor in respect to the debtor's acts, conduct, or property, or in respect to any other matter that may affect the administration of the estate or the debtor's right to a discharge.[154] The meeting, which may be held in the bankruptcy court or at any other place within the district convenient for the parties in interest,[155] is investigatory in nature, and no party has a burden of proof on any issue. The debtor will be asked questions concerning the location of assets and any transfers of property that the debtor may have made. The scope of the examination is broad and, in effect, puts the debtor's financial affairs under a public microscope. Moreover, the meeting is recorded by electronic sound-recording equipment.[156]

The debtor should be prepared by his attorney prior to the meeting of creditors. The debtor should read the petition, schedules, and statement of affairs carefully because detailed questions will be asked about them. It is advisable to have available the debtor's business books, records, tax returns, stocks and bonds, accounts receivable ledger, cancelled checks, and other financial documents. If the debtor does not have these records available or is unable to answer questions satisfactorily because of lack of preparation, the meeting will in all likelihood be adjourned to a future date. False testimony may give rise to the denial of a discharge as well as to other penalties for perjury.[157] If the debtor answers questions adequately and is prepared with adequate documentation, it is likely that further appearances in the bankruptcy court will not be necessary. It is not necessary for the debtor's attorney to examine the debtor at the meeting. Counsel should, however, pose questions that enable the debtor to explain or clear up ambiguities in prior testimony, so that it will not be considered an admission against interest in another case or proceeding.

In addition to the debtor's examination, another purpose of the meeting of creditors is the election of a regular trustee and, when appropriate, a creditors' committee.[158]

---

vote for a trustee may vote for a presiding officer. That vote of eligible creditors holding a majority in amount of claims that actually vote governs the designation of the presiding officer. See 11 U.S.C. § 702(a), and ¶ 6.07[2], on eligibility for voting. The U.S. Trustee presides if there is one in the applicable district. See ¶ 6.08.

[154] B. Rule 205(d).

[155] Sugg. Int. B. Rule 2003(a).

[156] Sugg. Int. B. Rule 2003(c).

[157] 11 U.S.C. § 727(a)(4).

[158] See B. Rule 204(a)(2); Sugg. Int. B. Rule 2003(b)(1). See also

[4] Examination of Witnesses

The Bankruptcy Code is silent on the examination of persons other than the debtor. Therefore, the Bankruptcy Rules on this subject remain in effect. Upon application of any interested party, the bankruptcy court may order the examination of any witness.[159] The scope of the examination is broad in that it extends to the "acts, conduct, or property of the bankrupt, or to any matter which may affect the administration of the bankrupt's estate, or to his right to discharge." [160]

[5] Meeting of Equity Security Holders

Limited partners of a debtor partnership, shareholders of a debtor corporation, or other equity security holders may wish to have their own meeting. The court has the power to order such a meeting and may order the debtor to appear to be examined.[161] According to the Suggested Interim Bankruptcy Rules, the clerk of the bankruptcy court presides at the meeting.[162]

¶ 1.12 SELF-INCRIMINATION AND IMMUNITY

The former Bankruptcy Act gave automatic blanket immunity for all testimony that the debtor was compelled to give, except for testimony given at a hearing on an objection to discharge. The former Act provided that any testimony, or any evidence that was directly or indirectly derived from testimony, may not be used against the debtor in any criminal proceeding. This provision constituted "use" immunity, not "transactional" immunity.[163]

The Bankruptcy Code provision on immunity is a radical departure from the prior law. There is no longer a blanket immunity that

---

11 U.S.C. §§ 702 and 705, and Chapter 6 *infra*, on the election of a trustee and creditors' committee.

[159] See B. Rules 205(a), 916. Federal Rule of Evidence 501 applies common-law rules on witness privileges to federal cases. Because of the silence of the Bankruptcy Code on spousal privileges, the common-law rule is applied to bankruptcy cases through the Federal Rules of Evidence. See B. Rule 917. Compare with Section 21(a) of the former Bankruptcy Act, which removed the privilege for confidential communication between husband and wife with regard to certain business transactions.

[160] B. Rule 205(d).

[161] 11 U.S.C. § 341(b).

[162] Sugg. Int. B. Rule 2003(b)(2).

[163] Former B.A. § 7(a)(10).

arises automatically. Under the Code, immunity is governed by the Organized Crime Control Act of 1970, which governs immunity for witnesses before grand juries and other federal tribunals.[164] The debtor or other witness receives no immunity by merely testifying. The witness who does not want the testimony to be used against him or her must refuse to answer based on the constitutional privilege against self-incrimination. In that event, the U.S. attorney for the district in which the court sits may request an immunity order from the district court. If the district court grants the immunity order, which is limited to "use" instead of "transactional" immunity,[165] the witness is required to testify.[166] The debtor's refusal to testify after being informed of the immunity order may result in the denial of a discharge as well as other contempt penalties.[167] If the district court does not issue an immunity order, the witness has the right to refuse to answer, claiming the privilege against self-incrimination. If the witness is the debtor, the right to a discharge will not be lost.[168]

¶ 1.13 DUTIES OF THE DEBTOR

Several of the debtor's duties have been discussed earlier in this chapter. The debtor must file a list of creditors, schedules of assets and liabilities, and a statement of financial affairs.[169] The debtor is also required to appear and to submit to an examination at the meeting of creditors as well as to other examinations as directed by the bankruptcy court.[170]

In addition, the debtor must cooperate with the trustee to enable the trustee to perform official duties as a representative of the estate.[171] For example, the debtor may be required to assist the trustee in determining which claims against the estate are valid and meritorious. The debtor may also be required to cooperate in the preparation of an in-

---

[164] 11 U.S.C. § 344. The Organized Crime Control Act of 1970 is contained in 18 U.S.C. §§ 6001-6005. See Note, 4 J. L. Ref. 546, 577-585 (1970-1971); McClellan, "The Organized Crime Act (S-30) or Its Critics: Which Threatens Civil Liberties?" 46 Notre Dame Law. 55, 82-86 (1970).

[165] Tierney v. United States, 409 U.S. 1232 (1972).

[166] 18 U.S.C. §§ 6002, 6003.

[167] See 11 U.S.C. § 727(a)(6)(B).

[168] *Id.*

[169] See ¶ 1.06.

[170] See ¶ 1.11[3].

[171] See 11 U.S.C. § 521(2), and Chapter 6 *infra*, on the trustee's duties.

ventory of business assets.[172] The debtor must surrender to the trustee all property of the estate and any recorded information, including books, documents, records, and papers, relating to the property of the estate.[173]

Failure to fulfill these duties or noncompliance with any lawful order of the bankruptcy court may subject the debtor to punishment for contempt[174] as well as to the denial of a discharge.[175]

When the debtor is a corporation, the court may direct any or all of its officers, directors, controlling shareholders, or any other person in control to fulfill the debtor's duties under the bankruptcy laws. It is common for the officers and other persons connected with the bankrupt corporation to shirk responsibility for filing schedules or performing other duties on the corporation's behalf. In such event, the court may designate the persons who must perform this function. The court has similar discretion to direct a general partner or other person in control of a partnership entity that filed a petition for liquidation to perform the duties of the debtor.[176]

¶ 1.14 DISMISSAL OR WITHDRAWAL OF THE PETITION AND CONVERSION OF THE CASE

The debtor should be told that there is no absolute right to withdraw a voluntary petition after it is filed. Before commencing a bankruptcy case, the debtor should understand that there may not be an opportunity to retreat from the jurisdiction of the bankruptcy court.

Prior to the enactment of the Bankruptcy Reform Act, courts have held that the dismissal of a bankruptcy case at the debtor's request was within the court's discretion.[177] When a debtor moved to dismiss or withdraw a petition, the court considered factors such as the possible prejudicial effects on the parties involved, the debtor's good faith or lack thereof, laches on the part of the debtor, and whether creditors consented or objected to the dismissal.[178] At least one court denied a

---

[172] See B. Rule 402(5).

[173] 11 U.S.C. § 521(3).

[174] See ¶ 6.03 on contempt powers of the court.

[175] 11 U.S.C. § 727(a). See ¶ 3.03.

[176] See B. Rule 901(6).

[177] Stern v. Barnett, 452 F.2d 211 (7th Cir. 1971); Goodrich v. England, 262 F.2d 298 (9th Cir. 1958). In *Stern*, the court refused to dismiss a bankruptcy case when two creditors objected despite the fact that the other twenty creditors consented.

[178] See Note, "Bankruptcy: Right of Withdrawal of Voluntary Petition for Bankruptcy," 29 Okla L. Rev. 114 (1976).

debtor's motion to dismiss a voluntary petition because dismissal would have been highly prejudicial and inequitable to persons who had contracted for the purchase of property from the trustee.[179]

The Bankruptcy Code is not more generous to debtors who wish to dismiss or withdraw their voluntary petitions for liquidation. The Code permits a court to dismiss a liquidation case "only for cause."[180] The Code cites two examples of when the court would find cause to dismiss: unreasonable delay by the debtor, which is prejudicial to creditors, and nonpayment of fees.[181] These illustrations indicate that dismissals for cause will usually result from the trustee's or a creditor's motion to dismiss based on some wrongful conduct by the debtor.[182] It is difficult to anticipate the situations in which a court will dismiss a voluntary liquidation case "for cause" upon the debtor's motion.

A motion or application to dismiss a voluntary petition may not result in a dismissal until after a hearing on notice to all creditors.[183] If the petition is dismissed by the court, the dismissal is without prejudice and will not prevent the debtor from obtaining a discharge in a subsequent bankruptcy case, unless the court orders otherwise for cause.[184]

Although the debtor does not have the absolute right to withdraw a petition, the debtor may at any time convert a liquidation case to a chapter 11 reorganization or a chapter 13 debt adjustment, whichever is appropriate under the circumstances.[185] This right is protected under the Bankruptcy Code in that any waiver of the right to convert is unenforceable.[186] A conversion of the case upon request of a party other than the debtor is not as automatic. When a creditor or another person who is not the debtor requests conversion to chapter 11, the request

---

[179] *In re* Strunks, Lane & Jellico Mountain Coal & Coke Co., 64 F. Supp. 731 (E.D. Ky. 1946). The court denied the motion to dismiss despite the consent of all creditors.

[180] 11 U.S.C. § 707.

[181] *Id.*

[182] Under the former Bankruptcy Act, creditors did not have standing to oppose the adjudication in a voluntary case. See, e.g., Commercial Creditor Corp. v. Skutt, 341 F.2d 177 (8th Cir. 1965). The new Code is silent on creditor standing to seek dismissal of a voluntary petition, but in view of Section 707 permitting dismissal for cause such as unreasonable delay, creditors should be allowed to move for such dismissal.

[183] See B. Rule 120(a); 11 U.S.C. § 707.

[184] 11 U.S.C. § 349(a); B. Rule 120(c).

[185] 11 U.S.C. §§ 706(a), 706(d). This right does not apply, however, if the case was previously converted to chapter 7 from chapter 11 or chapter 13. 11 U.S.C. § 706(a).

[186] 11 U.S.C. § 706(a).

must be made on notice and the court must afford all interested parties an opportunity to be heard before ordering the conversion.[187] Moreover, the court may not convert a liquidation case involving an individual to a chapter 13 debt adjustment unless the debtor makes the request.[188]

---

[187] 11 U.S.C. § 706(b).
[188] 11 U.S.C. § 706(c).

Chapter 2

LIQUIDATION AS A CREDITOR'S REMEDY: THE INVOLUNTARY CASE

¶ 2.01 BANKRUPTCY AS A CREDITOR'S REMEDY

In the previous chapter, bankruptcy was discussed from the standpoint of the honest debtor seeking a discharge of debts. Statistics have shown that 199 bankruptcy liquidation cases out of every 200 are commenced by the debtor filing a voluntary petition.[1] It is not surprising,

---

[1] See Administrative Office of the U.S. Courts, *Tables of Bankruptcy Statistics* 6 (1978).

therefore, that bankruptcy is often viewed as being for the primary benefit of debtors.

It should be kept in mind, however, that bankruptcy can also be an effective remedy for creditors. In fact, bankruptcy in Anglo-American law began exclusively as a creditor's remedy for the orderly distribution of the debtor's assets.[2] Modern bankruptcy laws may be used either as a debtor's remedy to achieve relief from indebtedness or as a creditor's remedy to compel a reorganization or liquidation of the debtor's estate. The Bankruptcy Code, as well as the former Bankruptcy Act, permits creditors to take the initiative to force a debtor into bankruptcy by filing an involuntary petition. As we will discuss later,[3] a significant modification in the law as a result of the Bankruptcy Code is the relaxation of the requirements necessary for creditors to successfully commence an involuntary bankruptcy case. It is likely that the liberalization of these requirements will produce an increase in the number of involuntary petitions in the future.

As discussed in the Introduction, there are four types of bankruptcy cases available under the Bankruptcy Code. Only two types, however, may be commenced by an involuntary petition: liquidation under chapter 7 and reorganization under chapter 11.[4] Although many of the same rules apply in liquidation and reorganization cases concerning involuntary petitions, the emphasis in this chapter is on liquidation cases.[5]

¶ 2.02 ALTERNATIVES FOR CREDITORS

This section is designed to assist the general creditor and the creditor's counsel to make a choice of whether or not to commence an involuntary liquidation case against a debtor. This decision cannot be

---

[2] See MacLachlan, *Handbook of the Law of Bankruptcy* §§ 25-27 (1956). See also Donnelly, "The New (Proposed?) Bankruptcy Act: The Development of its Structural Provisions and Their Impact on the Interests of Consumer-Debtors," 18 Santa Clara L. Rev. 291, 295-296 (1978), for a discussion of the history of bankruptcy law in America.

[3] See ¶ 2.08.

[4] 11 U.S.C. § 303(a). An involuntary petition may not be filed against a municipality for relief under chapter 9 of the Bankruptcy Code because to permit such filings would infringe on state sovereignty rights under the Constitution. It would also be unwise to permit involuntary petitions against individuals with regular income under chapter 13 because the unwilling debtor should not be compelled to continue working to repay his creditors. See Chapter 9 *infra* on individual debt adjustments.

[5] See Chapter 8 *infra* for a detailed discussion of reorganization cases.

made without exploring alternative courses of action available to general creditors.

[1] No Legal Action

It is advisable to take legal action to collect a debt only if the prospect of recovery outweighs the inconvenience and expense of the collection effort. Unfortunately for creditors, the ability to recover payment is limited to the amount of the debtor's nonexempt assets.[6] Also, our system of debt collection is based on grab law pursuant to which the first creditors to acquire liens in the debtor's property succeed to the detriment of the remaining creditors who are left empty-handed.[7] Therefore, if a debtor is "judgment proof" because he is without nonexempt assets and is unlikely to receive significant income or property in the future and he did not fraudulently convey property or make preferential payments to other creditors, it will often be in the creditor's best interest to refrain from further collection efforts.

[2] State Collection Remedies

If the debtor has assets sufficient to pay at least a portion of the total indebtedness, the unsecured creditor may effectuate collection by pursuing judicial remedies under state law. The creditor should obtain a lien on the debtor's property by judicial process and levy before other creditors do the same or the debtor becomes the subject of a bankruptcy case. In addition, if the creditor does not know about the existence or location of the debtor's assets, state laws provide for postjudgment discovery for this purpose. State law also provides for provisional remedies, orders of attachment, receiverships, and other procedures for protecting a creditor from dissipation of the debtor's assets while an action for a money judgment is pending.[8]

[3] Debtor Rehabilitation

It may be in the creditors' best interests for the debtor to be rehabilitated. The insolvent debtor who can pay only a small fraction of

---

[6] See Chapter 4 *infra* on exemptions.

[7] See MacLachlan, *Handbook of the Law of Bankruptcy* 3 (1956); Countryman, "The Bill of Rights and The Bill Collector," 15 Ariz. L. Rev. 521 (1973).

[8] See, e.g., N.Y. Civ. Prac. Law Art. 52 (McKinney) for New York's procedures for the collection of a money judgment.

total debts if all assets are liquidated but who has the ability to improve a dim financial situation and to make periodic payments of a greater amount should be given the opportunity to do so. In accordance with this policy, a reorganization case under chapter 11 of the Bankruptcy Code may be commenced by an involuntary petition to compel the debtor to attempt such a rehabilitation.[9]

Under the former Bankruptcy Act, involuntary petitions were permitted in Chapter X reorganization cases[10] but not in Chapter XI arrangement cases or Chapter XII real property arrangements. Since a complex statement of facts had to be alleged in an involuntary petition for relief under former Chapter X[11] and creditors often preferred a simple arrangement under former Chapter XI, insolvent debtors were usually allowed to continue their businesses until a levy of execution, foreclosure of a security interest, or bank setoff against a deposit resulted in a voluntary petition for relief under former Chapter XI. This delay, however, reduced the likelihood that the debtor could be rehabilitated successfully.

The Bankruptcy Code now makes this waiting unnecessary. The allegations for an involuntary petition for reorganization under the new chapter 11 are the same as the allegations made in an involuntary petition for liquidation.[12] Also, the relief available under Chapters X, XI, and XII of the former Act are now available under chapter 11 of the Code.[13] Therefore, petitioning creditors can commence an involuntary case for reorganization as easily and as quickly as they can for liquidation.

The benefits of pursuing a reorganization under the Bankruptcy Code, or a more informal extrajudicial arrangement for debt adjustment, will be discussed in Chapter 8 of this book.

[4] Involuntary Petition for Liquidation

There are situations in which a creditor will benefit from the debtor's bankruptcy under chapter 7 of the Bankruptcy Code, despite the debtor's discharge of debts. These situations are discussed below.

---

[9] 11 U.S.C. § 303(a).

[10] Former B.A. § 126.

[11] Former B.A. § 130.

[12] See Sugg. Int. B. Form No. 9, which applies in both chapter 7 and chapter 11 cases, set forth in Appendix B.

[13] See Chapter 8 *infra* on reorganizations.

¶ 2.03 PURPOSES FOR FILING AN INVOLUNTARY PETITION FOR LIQUIDATION

The main purpose for filing an involuntary petition for liquidation is to achieve an equal distribution of the debtor's property among each class of creditors without preferential treatment. Also, an involuntary petition should result in the maximization of the debtor's estate by the accumulation of property and possibly the elimination of certain voidable liens and encumbrances. Basically, these purposes are accomplished by the appointment of a trustee in bankruptcy who is given extraordinary powers with which to represent the class of general creditors. It is important, therefore, to understand the trustee's powers before determining whether to file an involuntary petition.[14]

Suppose, for example, that a debtor has only nominal assets, but that a sizable payment of money to Creditor *A* was made within the previous ninety days. Under state law, Creditor *B* would be unable to effectuate collection because of the debtor's lack of assets on which to levy. By filing an involuntary petition, however, Creditor *B* will commence a bankruptcy case and a trustee will be appointed who may be able to recover the preferential payment from Creditor *A* to be shared among the class of general creditors.[15] Under state law, Creditor *B* would be without power to compel the return of the preferential payment.

Consistent with the trustee's power to avoid certain liens and to recover certain property in order to increase the size of the estate, the trustee also has powers that facilitate an investigation of the debtor's affairs so as to discover preferences, fraudulent transfers, and vulnerable liens.[16]

An involuntary bankruptcy case may also be justified when the debtor has chosen a different method of liquidation, such as a state court receivership or assignment for the benefit of creditors.[17] Here the

---

[14] See Chapter 7 *infra* for a discussion of the trustee's avoiding powers.

[15] See 11 U.S.C. § 547 on voidable preferences.

[16] See Chapter 6 *infra* for a discussion of these powers.

[17] Pendency of state or federal equity receivership proceedings does not prevent the filing of a voluntary or involuntary bankruptcy petition. *In re* Allied Constr., Inc., 79 F. Supp. 141 (W.D. Pa. 1948); *In re* American & British Mfg. Corp., 300 F. 839 (D. Conn. 1924). However, a federal court injunction may be issued in connection with a federal receivership proceeding to prohibit the filing of a voluntary or involuntary petition when such extreme relief is necessary. See Jordan v. Independent Energy Corp., 446 F. Supp. 516 (N.D. Tex. 1978).

creditors wish to accomplish a different goal, namely, substitution of a disinterested trustee for an assignee or receiver who may be friendly to the debtor. The creditor wants an impartial trustee who will investigate the debtor zealously to discover and expose fraudulent or other dishonest conduct. Moreover, the power of an assignee or receiver is often curtailed by statute, and the right to recover preferential or fraudulent transfers under state law is not always as broad as the avoiding powers of a bankruptcy trustee.[18]

If it appears, however, that the debtor is without nonexempt assets and that a trustee will be unable to recover preferences or fraudulent conveyances or otherwise accumulate assets for the estate, the filing of an involuntary petition will probably be a fruitless exercise that may only accomplish a discharge for the debtor. It is not unusual, therefore, for defunct corporations and other business debtors to go out of business without ever being the subject of a bankruptcy case.

¶ 2.04 DEBTORS AGAINST WHOM AN INVOLUNTARY PETITION MAY BE FILED

[1] Debtors Who May File Voluntary Petitions

Any person who may file a voluntary petition for liquidation may become the subject of an involuntary bankruptcy case,[19] except for farmers and not-for-profit corporations.[20] Accordingly, an involuntary petition may be filed against a natural person, partnership, corporation, or unincorporated organization. As in a voluntary bankruptcy, the debtor in an involuntary case must have either a residence, domicile, place of business, or property located in the United States.[21] The fact that the debtor was in bankruptcy in the recent past does not prohibit the commencement of an involuntary case, even though the previous bankruptcy may prevent another discharge.[22]

Those debtors who are ineligible to file voluntary petitions for liquidation may not be forced into involuntary bankruptcy. Therefore, the foreign and domestic insurance companies, banking institutions, and credit unions, as well as municipalities and railroads, that are excluded

---

[18] See Chapter 7 *infra*.

[19] See ¶ 1.03.

[20] See 11 U.S.C. § 303(a).

[21] 11 U.S.C. § 109(a).

[22] See 11 U.S.C. § 727(a)(8).

from eligibility for voluntary liquidation under the Code need not be concerned about being subjected to an involuntary petition.[23]

[2] Debtors Against Whom an Involuntary Petition May Not Be Filed

[a] Farmers

As under the former Bankruptcy Act, the only way that a farmer may go into bankruptcy today is by filing a voluntary petition. The Bankruptcy Code continues to protect farmers from involuntary bankruptcy by expressly providing that they may not be the subject of an involuntary petition.[24] The policy behind this exclusion is to protect farmers when they are experiencing temporary periods of financial distress due to the cyclical nature of the farming business. The farmer who is unable to pay creditors because of a period of low prices or drought may not be pushed into bankruptcy.

Several changes in the exclusion for farmers were made by using a new definition of "farmer" in the Bankruptcy Code. The former Act limited the definition of "farmer" to an "individual" who is "personally" engaged in farming.[25] By contrast, the Code expands the scope of the farmer exclusion to cover partnerships, corporations, and other entities whose income is from a "farming operation" that is "owned or operated" by the entity.[26] Therefore, a large corporation or conglomerate engaged in a multimillion dollar agribusiness may now receive the same protection from involuntary bankruptcy as does the individual who operates a small family farm. In addition, "farming operation" is defined broadly so as to include dairy farming, ranching, and the production of poultry or livestock products in an unmanufactured state, as well as the traditional raising of crops.[27]

Whether a debtor is a farmer for the purpose of this exclusion depends on the portion of income received from farming operations. The former Act granted the exclusion to individuals whose "principal part of his income" was from farming.[28] The vagueness of this standard resulted in much time-consuming and costly litigation.[29] The Code

[23] See ¶ 1.03[6].

[24] 11 U.S.C. § 303(a).

[25] Former B.A. § 1(17).

[26] 11 U.S.C. § 101(17).

[27] 11 U.S.C. § 101(18).

[28] Former B.A. § 1(17).

[29] See *In re* Hinrichs, 314 F.2d 384 (7th Cir. 1963), where the court

contains a more definite standard, however, by limiting the farmer exclusion to persons who received more than 80 percent of their gross income from a "farming operation" during the taxable year immediately preceding the taxable year in which the petition is filed.[30]

When an involuntary petition is filed against a debtor who claims an exemption as a farmer, the petitioning creditors have the burden of proving that the debtor is not a farmer.[31]

[b] Not-for-Profit Corporations

Although it may file a voluntary petition, a debtor corporation that is not a "moneyed, business or commercial corporation" may not be the subject of an involuntary bankruptcy case.[32] This category of excluded debtors includes all corporations and unincorporated associations that are not organized for the purpose of earning a profit. The general nature and purpose of the entity must be examined to determine whether it is primarily charitable or benevolent so as to be protected from involuntary bankruptcy.

Cooperative associations organized to benefit its members may be considered business or commercial corporations despite their organization under membership or nonprofit corporation laws, if the ultimate result is financial profit to the members of the cooperative.[33] However, a not-for-profit corporation that engages in incidental money-making activities still qualifies for this exclusion from involuntary bankruptcy if its primary purpose relates to benevolent activities. Accordingly, a

---

found that the debtor's principal source of income was from a farm implement business, so that he was not a farmer and could be the subject of an involuntary bankruptcy petition, despite the fact that he worked as a farmer in the evenings and on weekends and vacations on the 870 acres of farmland that he owned. See also *In re* White, 238 F. Supp. 454 (D. Colo. 1965), where the court held that a partner in a farming operation was not a "farmer" because his personal participation in the farming activities was negligible.

[30] 11 U.S.C. § 101(17).

[31] See *In re* Brais, 15 F.2d 693 (7th Cir. 1926); *In re* White, 238 F. Supp. 454 (D. Colo. 1965).

[32] 11 U.S.C. § 303(a).

[33] See Missco Homestead Ass'n v. United States, 185 F.2d 280 (8th Cir. 1950), where the purpose of the Cooperative Society's formation was to use money borrowed from the government to lease real estate for division and subletting to tenant farms so as to help rehabilitate needy farm families. Despite this purpose, the court held that the society was a "moneyed, business or commercial corporation." See also *In re* American Grain & Cattle, Inc., 415 F. Supp.. 270 (N.D. Tex. 1976).

university organized as a nonprofit educational corporation may not be the subject of an involuntary petition, even though it operates a day care center and university apartments and offers printing services to the public for a fee.[34]

[3] Minimum Debt Requirement

The former Bankruptcy Act provided that a debtor could not become an involuntary bankrupt unless the total debts owed amounted to at least $1,000.[35] The Bankruptcy Code eliminates this requirement. However, as will be discussed later in ¶ 2.05[2], the petitioning creditors must have claims aggregating at least $5,000 more than the value of liens securing their claims.[36] Therefore, it would be impossible for creditors to force a debtor into bankruptcy unless the debtor owes at least $5,000 in debts above the value of any security. The requirement that petitioning creditors have $5,000 in unsecured claims is significant because it will protect many low-income consumers from involuntary bankruptcy.

[4] Dissolved Corporations; Insane or Deceased Debtors

The pendency of dissolution proceedings, liquidation of a corporation under state statutes, or cessation of business neither defeats bankruptcy jurisdiction nor prevents the filing of an involuntary petition, because the corporation still exists as an entity. Some question exists as to the jurisdiction of the bankruptcy court when the bankruptcy case is commenced after the state dissolution proceedings have been terminated.[37] But in any event, once instituted the bankruptcy case is not terminated by a subsequent corporate dissolution. Similarly, a bankruptcy case does not terminate if an individual debtor dies or becomes insane during the pendency of the case.[38] Of course, an involuntary petition

---

[34] *In re* Allen Univ., 497 F.2d 346 (4th Cir. 1974).

[35] Former B.A. § 4(b).

[36] 11 U.S.C. § 303(b). See 11 U.S.C. § 104, providing for the adjustment of dollar amounts every six years.

[37] See *In re* Peer Manor Bldg. Corp., 134 F.2d 839 (7th Cir.), *cert. denied sub. nom.* Nicholas v. Witter, 320 U.S. 211 (1943), where the court held that the bankruptcy court has no jurisdiction over a dissolved corporation. Compare *In re* Thomas, 78 F.2d 602 (6th Cir.), *cert. denied* 296 U.S. 626 (1935).

[38] See B. Rule 118.

cannot be filed against an insolvent decedent's estate, but can be filed against the estate of a living incompetent.[39]

¶ 2.05 WHO MAY FILE AN INVOLUNTARY PETITION AGAINST THE DEBTOR?

[1] Requisite Number of Petitioning Creditors

An involuntary petition must be executed by a specified number of creditors or indenture trustees.[40] These moving parties will be referred to in this book as the "petitioning creditors."

One petitioning creditor is sufficient to commence an involuntary bankruptcy if the debtor has fewer than twelve creditors or indenture trustees.[41] But, to determine whether there are fewer than twelve of such creditors, the following creditors are not counted: (1) any employees of the debtor who are also creditors, (2) any "insiders"[42] of the debtor who are creditors, and (3) any creditors who received a preference, fraudulent conveyance, statutory lien, postpetition transfer, or any other lien or interest in the debtor's property that is voidable by a trustee in bankruptcy.[43] The reason for not counting these creditors is that they probably would not want the debtor to go into bankruptcy because of their special relationship with the debtor. The employee will lose a job if the debtor is liquidated in bankruptcy; the insider is likely to be too closely connected to the debtor, so as to be biased in favor of protecting the debtor against others; and the creditor who has a voidable lien or who received a voidable transfer does not want to be subjected to the trustee's extraordinary powers because of the creditor's own self-interest.[44] Therefore, only creditors without these special rea-

---

[39] See Chapter 1 *supra.*

[40] In general, an indenture trustee is a trustee under a mortgage, deed of trust, or other instrument under which securities, either debt or equity, of the debtor are outstanding. See 11 U.S.C. §§ 101(22), 101(23). See also Chapter 5 *infra* on claims.

[41] 11 U.S.C. § 303(b).

[42] *Id.* The term "insider," which is new in bankruptcy, includes relatives, general partners and relatives of general partners, partnerships in which the debtor is a general partner, and corporations of which the debtor is a director, officer, or person in control. In the case of corporate debtors, a director, officer, or person in control is an insider. Managing agents or "affiliates" of a business debtor are also insiders. See 11 U.S.C. §§ 101(2), 101(25).

[43] See 11 U.S.C. § 303(b)(2).

[44] See Chapter 7 *infra* on the trustee's avoiding powers.

sons for wanting to avoid bankruptcy are counted to determine if there are fewer than twelve creditors. The exclusion of these types of creditors makes it easier for a single creditor to commence an involuntary case. However, although employees, insiders, and holders of voidable liens or transfers are not counted to determine whether there are fewer than twelve creditors, these special types of creditors may act as petitioning creditors if they wish to force an involuntary bankruptcy.[45]

If there are twelve or more creditors, the petition must be executed by at least three petitioning creditors. Suppose that an insolvent debtor has fewer than twelve creditors, but decides to discontinue its usual practice of paying small incidental bills on a monthly basis for the purpose of intentionally increasing the number of creditors to twelve or more and thereby preventing an involuntary petition by fewer than three petitioning creditors. For example, the debtor does not pay small monthly utility or telephone bills. It has been held that such manipulation by the debtor to increase the number of creditors will not prevent a single creditor with a large claim from filing an involuntary petition.[46]

[2] Requisite Amount of Claims

The petitioning creditors, regardless of their number, must have claims against the debtor that are not contingent as to liability and that aggregate to at least $5,000 above the value of any security interests, mortgages, or other liens the petitioning creditors have on the debtor's property.[47] Accordingly, the petitioning creditors must have claims that

---

[45] See *In re* J.J.S. Co., 445 F.2d 138 (7th Cir. 1971), in which an active manager who was also an officer, director, and owner of 50 percent of the shares of the debtor corporation was qualified to be a petitioning creditor against the corporation.

[46] Denham v. Shellman Grain Elevator, Inc., 444 F.2d 1376 (5th Cir. 1971).

[47] 11 U.S.C. § 303(b). Compare with Section 59(b) of the former Bankruptcy Act, which required that petitioners' claims amount to the aggregate of only $500. Also, the former Bankruptcy Act provided that unliquidated claims could not be counted in computing the number and aggregate amount of the claims of petitioning creditors if the court was unable to estimate the value of the total claims as aggregating to $500 without unduly delaying the decision on the merits of the involuntary petition. Former B.A. § 59(b). The Bankruptcy Code requires the court to convert a claim into a dollar value regardless of how unliquidated it is. See 11 U.S.C. § 502(c). In addition, the requirement under the former Act that the claims of petitioners must be "provable" no longer applies because the concept of provability was eliminated by the new Code. See Former B.A. § 59(b).

are unsecured to the extent of $5,000 collectively. Fully-secured creditors may not commence an involuntary bankruptcy case, but a partially-secured creditor may act as a petitioning creditor to the extent of the deficiency over and above the value of the collateral.[48]

The claims of petitioning creditors may not be contingent as to liability. When a claim of fraud against the debtor was reduced to judgment in state court, the mere fact that the debtor was appealing the fraud judgment at the time the creditor executed an involuntary petition did not make the creditor's fraud claim contingent.[49] However, when the debtor is indorser of an unmatured promissory note, the holder of the note should not qualify as a petitioning creditor because it cannot be shown that the principal obligor on the note had defaulted. Such claim against the indorser is too contingent as to liability because the debtor may never be required to pay the note if the maker does not default.[50]

The fact that a creditor's claim is entitled to a priority in distribution does not disqualify the creditor from acting as a petitioner and does not affect priority rights.[51] In fact, priority creditors often file involuntary petitions when the debtor makes an assignment for the benefit of creditors or otherwise liquidates under state law so as to take advantage of priority rules under federal bankruptcy laws.

[3] Transfers of Claims

It is the policy of the Bankruptcy Rules to discourage the transfer or acquisition of claims for the sole purpose of qualifying as a petitioning creditor to force a debtor into bankruptcy. A person who transfers or acquires a claim for this purpose is not eligible to be a petitioning creditor. To assist the debtor and the court in policing this rule, any petitioning creditor who is a transferor or transferee of a claim is required, regardless of the reason for the transfer, to annex to the petition copies of all documents evidencing the transfer together with a signed statement setting forth the consideration and terms of the transfer. The statement must also contain an assertion that the claim was not transferred for the purpose of commencing a bankruptcy case. This report-

---

[48] See *In re* Hayes, 127 F. Supp. 514 (D. Alaska 1955).

[49] Denham v. Shellman Grain Elevator, Inc., 444 F.2d 1376 (5th Cir. 1971).

[50] See *In re* Gibraltor Amusements, Ltd., 187 F. Supp. 931 (E.D.N.Y. 1960), *aff'd* 291 F.2d 22 (2d Cir. 1961), for a case that held that a claim was too contingent for other reasons.

[51] See Chapter 5 *infra* on priority claims.

ing requirement must be met even if the claim was assigned by or to the petitioning creditor only as security.[52]

[4] Joinder of Petitioning Creditors After Filing

Suppose that three creditors execute and file a petition and that the debtor has twelve or more creditors. Then, after the filing, the claim of one of the petitioning creditors is not recognized because it is contingent as to liability or for another reason. Does the court have to dismiss the petition? The Bankruptcy Code follows the Bankruptcy Rule, which permits creditors other than the petitioning creditors to join in the petition after filing with the same effect as if the joining creditor had been one of the original petitioners.[53] If another creditor joins in the petition, therefore, the petition will not be dismissed for want of three qualified petitioning creditors.

If a petition is executed and filed by only one or two petitioning creditors because they believe that the debtor has fewer than twelve creditors, the debtor may allege in its answer that there are twelve or more creditors. In such event, however, the debtor must file with the answer a list of all creditors with their addresses and a brief statement of the amounts and nature of their claims. If it appears that there are twelve or more creditors, the court must give the petitioning creditors a reasonable opportunity to have other creditors join in the petition before it is dismissed for want of the requisite number of creditors.[54] This rule, which is designed to allow petitioning creditors to cure a defective petition, may not be used by a creditor who acted in bad faith. For example, if a single petitioning creditor falsely alleges that there are fewer than twelve creditors, knowing that there are actually twelve or more, the petitioner will not be entitled to have other creditors subsequently join in the petition and the petition will be dismissed.[55]

---

[52] B. Rule 104(d); Sugg. Int. B. Rule 1003(b). A creditor who assigns a claim may be a petitioner if the claim is assigned as security and exceeds the amount of the debt secured thereby. *In re* 69th & Crandon Bldg. Corp., 97 F.2d 392 (7th Cir.), *cert. denied sub nom.* Eastholm-Melvin Co. v. Hoffman, 305 U.S. 629 (1938).

[53] 11 U.S.C. § 303(c); B. Rule 104(e).

[54] B. Rule 104(e). A petitioning creditor may solicit other creditors to join in filing an involuntary petition. *In re* Kootenai Motor Co., 41 F.2d 403 (D. Idaho 1930). It is advisable that the creditor, instead of the creditor's attorney, make such solicitations, so as to avoid a possible violation of the American Bar Association Code of Professional Responsibility.

[55] See *In re* Crofoot, Nielson & Co., 313 F.2d 170, 171 (7th Cir. 1963), where the court said that "if a single creditor files a petition with knowledge

[5] Partnerships

There are special rules governing the commencement of an involuntary bankruptcy case against a partnership entity. In addition to institution by means of an involuntary petition filed by petitioning creditors, an involuntary case may be instituted by any one or more of the general partners without regard to the amount of claims or number of petitioners.[56] If all the general partners join in the petition, however, it is treated as a voluntary petition.[57]

Why would a general partner want to file an involuntary petition against the partnership entity? A partner who wants a discharge of his debts may be sufficiently protected by filing a voluntary petition as an individual. A partner who files a voluntary petition as an individual may receive a discharge from both his personal and partnership debts.

There are situations, however, in which a partner would want to have a petition filed against the firm. Suppose that a general partner has reason to believe that other partners embezzled partnership property, causing the insolvency of the firm. When the innocent but insolvent partner files a voluntary petition as an individual, filing another petition against the firm may be advisable so that a partnership trustee can be appointed to investigate and recover fraudulently transferred property.[58] The partnership trustee may succeed in recovering enough assets to pay at least a portion of the innocent petitioning partner's personal debts that are nondischargeable.[59] Likewise, a partner may file an involuntary petition against the partnership to have the partnership trustee recover voidable preferences or to invalidate voidable liens.[60] Another reason for a partner to file an involuntary petition

---

that the allegation (fewer than twelve creditors) is false, the petition will be dismissed as a fraudulent attempt to confer jurisdiction upon the court where none exists and intervention 'presumably' will be denied." But see *In re* Crown Sportswear, Inc., 4 Bankr. Dec. 476 (1st Cir. 1978), where the burden of proof to establish bad faith was not met.

[56] 11 U.S.C. § 303(b)(3)(A). The requirement that petitioning creditors have claims aggregating to at least $5,000 does not apply when fewer than all of the general partners file an involuntary petition.

[57] See ¶ 1.03[2] for a discussion of voluntary petitions filed on behalf of partnerships.

[58] See Chapter 7 *infra* for a discussion of the trustee's power to avoid fraudulent conveyances.

[59] See Chapter 3 *infra* for a discussion of nondischargeable debts.

[60] See Chapter 7 *infra* for a discussion of the trustee's power to recover voidable preferences or to invalidate liens.

against the firm is to achieve a reorganization under chapter 11 of the Bankruptcy Code.[61]

If all the general partners are in personal bankruptcy, a general partner, the bankruptcy trustee of any general partner, or the holder of any claim against the partnership may commence an involuntary case against the partnership without regard to the amount of claims or number of petitioners.[62] The purpose of this rule is to facilitate the administration of partnership assets when all general partners are in personal bankruptcy.

[6] Foreign Proceedings

If a debtor's estate is the subject of a judicial liquidation or reorganization in a foreign country, the representative of that estate may file an involuntary petition against the debtor in the United States to permit the administration of assets located in this country.[63]

As an alternative to the filing of an involuntary petition commencing a full bankruptcy case against a debtor involved in a foreign proceeding, the Bankruptcy Code provides that a foreign representative may commence a case "ancillary to a foreign proceeding." [64] A petition to commence an ancillary case is involuntary in nature and may be contested by the debtor. Such an ancillary case gives the bankruptcy court jurisdiction to facilitate the administration of assets located in the United States. The court has flexible powers to handle ancillary cases so as to give appropriate weight to principles of international comity and to cooperate with and recognize the insolvency laws of the foreign nation.

The importance of having sufficient flexibility in administering cases ancillary to foreign insolvency proceedings was shown in *Banque de Financement v. First National Bank of Boston.*[65] The debtor was a Swiss bank involved in a rehabilitation proceeding under Swiss law. The debtor had substantial bank deposits in the United States that were being attached by American creditors. To avoid the dissipation of assets located here pending reorganization efforts abroad, the debtor filed a petition under Chapter XI of the former Bankruptcy Act. However,

---

[61] See Chapter 8 *infra* on reorganization.

[62] 11 U.S.C. § 303(b)(3)(B).

[63] 11 U.S.C. § 303(b)(4).

[64] 11 U.S.C. § 304.

[65] 568 F.2d 911 (2d Cir. 1977). See also Nadelmann, "Rehabilitating International Bankruptcy Law: Lesson Taught by Herstatt and Company," 52 N.Y.U.L. Rev. 1 (1977), and Nadelmann, *"Israel-British Bank (London) Ltd:* Yet Another Trans-Atlantic Crossing," 52 Am. Bankr. L.J. 369 (1978),

because Swiss criminal law prohibits public disclosure of a bank's creditors, the debtor did not file the required list of creditors.[66] Nonetheless, the court of appeals reversed the dismissal of the petition and suggested alternative procedures that may be used to effectuate an orderly administration while protecting the rights of local creditors. The bankruptcy court could exercise jurisdiction to set aside preferential attachments under U.S. bankruptcy law, transfer the assets located here to Geneva to be administered in the Swiss proceeding, and suspend the bankruptcy case here. A second alternative is to administer fully the estate in this country in coordination with the Swiss proceeding. In either event, the Swiss court, which has a confidential list of creditors, could notify depositors and local creditors, who then may decide whether to file claims in the bankruptcy case here. Pro rata distribution could be achieved by marshalling the assets in Switzerland, which could take into account the dividends paid to local creditors who filed claims in the U.S. bankruptcy court. Such flexibility to effectuate an equitable administration in international bankruptcy situations is provided by the Bankruptcy Code.[67]

When an involuntary petition for liquidation, reorganization, or the commencement of an ancillary case is filed, the foreign representative of the estate in the foreign proceeding may make a limited appearance in connection with the petition without being subjected to the general jurisdiction of the bankruptcy court or of any other court in this country.[68]

¶ 2.06 JURISDICTION, VENUE, AND TRANSFER OF CASES

The U.S. district court and the bankruptcy judge as an adjunct of the district court have jurisdiction to entertain involuntary petitions.[69] The involuntary case should be commenced by filing a petition with the clerk of the court where there is proper venue.

The venue rules in involuntary cases are the same as those in voluntary bankruptcies.[70] Accordingly, the proper judicial district for

---

for discussions of two other cases that presented problems because of insolvency proceedings pending abroad.

[66] Under Section 7a(8) of the former Bankruptcy Act, the debtor was required to file a list of creditors. This requirement was similar to the debtor's duty to file a list of creditors under the Bankruptcy Code. 11 U.S.C. § 521(l).

[67] See 11 U.S.C. § 304(c).

[68] 11 U.S.C. § 306.

[69] 28 U.S.C. § 1471. See Chapter 6 *infra* on bankruptcy courts.

[70] See ¶ 1.04.

commencing an involuntary case depends on the debtor's residence, domicile, or place of business, or on the location of the principal assets. In addition, a petition may be filed in a district in which the bankruptcy case of an affiliate of the debtor is pending. Likewise, the liberal rules that permit the retention of cases despite improper venue and the transfer of cases in the interest of justice and the convenience of the parties in voluntary cases apply equally to involuntary cases.[71]

¶ 2.07 THE PETITION

An involuntary case is instituted by filing an involuntary petition, executed by the petitioners, in the office of the clerk of the bankruptcy court.[72] The petitioners must pay a $60 filing fee at the time of the filing in liquidation cases. In reorganization cases, the fee is $200.[73] An original petition plus three copies of the petition must be filed unless local court rules provide otherwise.[74] The petition should conform to the official form.[75]

It is important to understand and appreciate that an involuntary petition is a pleading that commences a legal action and should contain allegations made in the form of a pleading. The petitioner must identify the debtor in the caption of the petition by inserting the debtor's name, as well as all other names used by the debtor within the previous six years according to the petitioners' best information.[76] The petition should contain the names and addresses of the petitioners and an assertion that petitioning creditors have claims against the debtor, not contingent as to liability, amounting in the aggregate to $5,000 or more in excess of the value of securities held by them.[77] The nature and amount of the petitioners' claims should be described briefly. The petition

---

[71] See ¶ 1.05 for a detailed discussion of these rules, as well as of the problem that arises when two or more petitions are filed against or on behalf of the debtor.

[72] 11 U.S.C. § 303(b). Verification of the petition is not required if it contains an unsworn declaration. 28 U.S.C. § 1746.

[73] 28 U.S.C. § 1930(a). If the petition is filed against a railroad seeking reorganization under chapter 11 of the Act, the filing fee is $500.

[74] Sugg. Int. B. Rules 1002(b)(1), 1003(a).

[75] See Sugg. Int. B. Form No. 9, which is set forth in Appendix B.

[76] B. Rule 106; Sugg. Int. B. Rule 1005.

[77] If petitioners are not creditors, such as when a general partner files a petition against a partnership, no allegation is necessary concerning petitioner's claims against the debtor.

should allege the basis of jurisdiction and venue and should state that the debtor is a person against whom an order for relief may be entered under the Code. In addition, the petition must allege that at least one of the grounds for an order for relief [78] is satisfied. Since an involuntary petition may be filed to seek either liquidation or reorganization, the petition should specify whether it is for relief under chapter 7 or chapter 11 of the Bankruptcy Code.

¶ 2.08 REQUIREMENTS FOR AN ORDER OF RELIEF: ACTS OF BANKRUPTCY ABOLISHED

When the former Bankruptcy Act was enacted in 1898, Congress was concerned about the prospect of creditors pushing a debtor into bankruptcy without sufficient justification. Involuntary bankruptcy was not intended as a remedy that creditors can invoke at any time and without good reason. To protect debtors against an unwarranted involuntary petition, the former Act permitted an involuntary bankruptcy adjudication only if the debtor had committed one of the six "acts of bankruptcy" within four months prior to the filing of the petition.[79]

The acts of bankruptcy, which had to be pleaded in the petition with sufficient particularity to identify the specific occurrence,[80] were as follows: (1) The debtor made a fraudulent transfer or concealment of property while insolvent; (2) the debtor made a voidable preference to a creditor while insolvent; (3) a creditor obtained a judicial lien on the debtor's property while the debtor was insolvent which was not vacated or discharged within thirty days after the date of the lien or at least five days before the date set for the sale; (4) the debtor made a general assignment for the benefit of creditors; (5) a receiver or trustee was appointed to take charge of the debtor's property while the debtor was insolvent or unable to pay his debts; and (6) the debtor admitted in writing the inability to pay debts and the willingness to be adjudged a bankrupt.[81]

The necessity of alleging and proving an act of bankruptcy was most frustrating to creditors. Many of the acts, if committed, were not notorious and could only have been ascertained through an examination

---

[78] See ¶ 2.09 for a discussion of the grounds for an order for relief.

[79] Former B.A. § 3(b).

[80] B. Rule 104(c).

[81] Former B.A. § 3(a).

of the debtor's books and records. The debtor's books were not readily available to creditors except through the medium of judicial proceedings to enforce a money judgment under state law.[82] Unless a creditor was able to identify and prove a specific act of bankruptcy, the creditor was powerless to commence an involuntary bankruptcy case, despite the debtor's dilatory tactics or inability to pay bills.

The requirement of alleging an act of bankruptcy was further complicated by the fact that the petition had to be filed within four months of the act.[83] If a creditor discovered that the debtor had made a preferential payment five months previously, there was no basis for filing a petition against the debtor. Moreover, in addition to obtaining facts as to several of these acts, which was difficult because they were often clandestine (e.g., preferences and fraudulent conveyances), the creditor had to obtain evidence in most instances that the debtor was insolvent. Under the former Act, insolvency required that the aggregate of the debtor's property at a fair valuation not be sufficient in amount to pay all debts.[84] It was difficult for creditors to have information sufficient to determine whether the debtor met this "balance sheet" insolvency test.

The need to plead and prove an act of bankruptcy had been severely criticized as contributing to unnecessary delay between the time a debtor first becomes unable to pay debts and the time of filing the involuntary petition.[85] The difficulty of discovering and proving an act of bankruptcy after the debtor defaulted on monetary obligations resulted in further deterioration of the debtor's assets by the time of liquidation or reorganization. The need to establish an act of bankruptcy by competent evidence made it extremely difficult to commence an involuntary bankruptcy case.

The Bankruptcy Code abolishes the concept of acts of bankruptcy and replaces it with grounds for relief that make it easier for creditors to file an involuntary petition promptly after the debtor first experiences serious financial difficulties. By commencing the bankruptcy case at an earlier date, creditors should be able to protect the debtor's assets from further dissipation and, in reorganization cases, to increase the likelihood that rehabilitation will be successful.

---

[82] See, e.g., N.Y. Civ. Prac. Law §§ 5223, 5224 (McKinney).

[83] Former B.A. § 3(b).

[84] See Former B.A. § 1(19).

[85] See, e.g., MacLachlan, *Handbook of the Law of Bankruptcy* Ch. 6 (1956); Trost & King, "Congress and Bankruptcy Reform Circa 1977," 33 Bus. Law. 489 (1978).

¶ 2.09 GROUNDS FOR RELIEF UNDER THE BANKRUPTCY CODE

If an involuntary petition is controverted by a timely answer, the court may not order the relief sought unless at least one of the following grounds exists: (1) the debtor is generally not paying debts as they become due, or (2) within 120 days before the date of the filing of the petition, a custodian was appointed or took possession of substantially all of the debtor's property.[86]

[1] General Failure to Pay Debts

The Bankruptcy Code does not recognize mere balance sheet insolvency as a ground for an involuntary petition.[87] The fact that the debtor's total indebtedness is greater than the fair value of all of the debtor's nonexempt assets does not, in and of itself, justify the commencement of an involuntary case. This is due to the recognition that a debtor, although technically insolvent, may be able to pay current bills nonetheless. Moreover, a debtor could have total assets worth more than total liabilities but still have a serious cash-flow problem that stands in the way of paying debts as they mature. For these reasons, the Code adopts as a ground for involuntary bankruptcy the so-called equity insolvency test, which is based on a general failure to pay debts as they become due regardless of what the debtor's balance sheet looks like.[88]

What is a "general" failure to pay debts? Apparently, nonpayment of only a small number or amount of debts will not constitute a general failure to pay. But at what point do the debtor's defaults justify an involuntary petition? Courts will have to deal with this question on a

---

[86] 11 U.S.C. § 303(h).

[87] See 11 U.C.C. § 101(26) for the definition of "insolvent." See also former B.A. § 1(19).

[88] 11 U.S.C. § 303(h)(1). The equity insolvency test is not new in bankruptcy legislation. It was used in the former Bankruptcy Act as an alternative to balance sheet insolvency in Chapter X reorganization cases. See former B.A. § 130(1). Also, the equity insolvency test is used in the Uniform Commercial Code. U.C.C. § 1-201(23). One court has held that petitioners must offer evidence of what constitutes the debtor's "regular course of business" in order to show a nonpayment of debts when due, regardless of the due dates agreed upon when the obligations arose. *In re* Trans-High Corp., 1 Coll. B.C.2d. 509 (S.D.N.Y. 1980).

case-by-case basis, taking into consideration an analysis of the relationship of past-due debts to total liabilities.

An involuntary petition should set forth specific facts that support the allegation that the debtor is generally not paying debts as they become due.[89] In a recent case, an involuntary petition filed under chapter 7 of the Code alleged that the debtor had sent a letter to its creditors stating that the debtor did not have sufficient working capital to continue operations and intended to liquidate its assets and distribute the remaining funds pro rata to creditors.[90] Although this petition was not contested, it is interesting to speculate whether such an allegation is sufficient to withstand a motion to dismiss the petition on its face. Of course, it is conceivable that the debtor had not ceased paying its debts generally at the time the petition was filed, despite the intention to liquidate. Nonetheless, the likelihood that the debtor who sends such a letter is failing to pay current liabilities is so great that the petitioners should have their day in court to prove general nonpayment of debts. Similarly, a statement in a petition that the debtor convened a meeting of creditors at which the debtor sought a composition of debts should also be sufficient to support the allegation that the debtor is generally not paying debts as they become due.

When an involuntary petition alleges that the debtor is generally not paying debts as they become due, the debtor may file an answer denying the allegation. Upon such denial, the debtor is required to appear in court at the trial and must bring its books, papers, and accounts. In addition, the debtor may be required to appear for a pretrial examination on this issue.[91]

[2] Appointment of a Custodian

There are several reasons for permitting involuntary bankruptcy upon the appointment of a custodian to take over the debtor's assets. First, if a custodian of all or substantially all of the debtor's property is appointed, it is a clear indication that the debtor is having serious financial difficulties. Ordinarily, custodians are appointed as the result of a state court receivership, an assignment for the benefit of creditors,

---

[89] See Sugg. Int. B. Form No. 9, which is set forth in Appendix B.

[90] *In re* Great Shapes Leotard, Inc., Dkt. No. 79-10025-1979 (S.D.N.Y. 1979).

[91] Sugg. Int. B. Rule 1008.

or some other liquidation mechanism. Therefore, the Bankruptcy Code essentially recognizes the appointment of a custodian as creating an irrebuttable presumption that the debtor is unable to pay debts as they mature.

Second, the appointment of a custodian is usually made to facilitate a liquidation of assets outside the context of a federal bankruptcy case. Once such a liquidation process is commenced by the custodian's appointment, the creditors who are affected by the liquidation should have the absolute right to have it proceed in bankruptcy court with the benefit of all the protections afforded by federal bankruptcy law. In essence, the creditors have a right to convert the state liquidation proceeding to a federal bankruptcy case. Also, creditors may believe that it is in their best interests to force a reorganization under the bankruptcy laws to rehabilitate the debtor instead of having a liquidation.

Creditors may rely on the appointment of a custodian as a ground for relief in bankruptcy only if the petition is filed within 120 days of either the date of the appointment or the date on which the custodian took possession.[92] Because of the notoriety of the appointment of a custodian, this time period is adequate to protect creditors. Of course, if the petition is filed more than 120 days after the custodian is appointed or takes possession, the petitioning creditors may rely on the debtor's general failure to pay debts as they become due as the ground for the petition without the time limitation.

Custodian, within the meaning of the Bankruptcy Code, includes trustees, receivers, assignees, and liquidators, whether or not they are judicially appointed.[93] However, the appointment of a trustee, receiver, or agent appointed or authorized to take charge of less than substantially all of the debtor's property for the purpose of enforcing a lien is not sufficient.[94] For example, foreclosure of a mortgage on the debtor's real estate involving the appointment of a receiver to take charge of the property is not grounds for involuntary bankruptcy if the real estate is not substantially all of the debtor's assets.

---

[92] 11 U.S.C. § 303(h)(2).

[93] 11 U.S.C. § 101(10). Compare *In re* Blair & Co., 471 F.2d 178 (2d Cir. 1972), *cert. granted* 411 U.S. 930, *remanded* 414 U.S. 212, *vacated as moot* 495 F.2d 299 (2d Cir. 1974), in which it was held that the appointment of a liquidator by the New York Stock Exchange to take control of the debtor stockbroker's assets was not enough to trigger the creditors' right to commence an involuntary bankruptcy petition under the former Bankruptcy Act.

[94] 11 U.S.C. § 303(h)(2).

¶ 2.10 PROCEDURE AFTER FILING AN INVOLUNTARY PETITION

[1] Service of the Summons and Petition

Upon the filing of an involuntary petition, the clerk of the bankruptcy court issues a summons to be served on the debtor together with a copy of the petition.[95] The petitioners have the choice of serving the summons and petition either by personal service or by mail.[96] In either case, service must be made within ten calendar days from the issuance of the summons. Otherwise, the petitioner will have to obtain a new summons from the clerk.[97] When service is made by mail, it must be made by first-class mail. A signed receipt from the debtor is not necessary as long as the person who mails it certifies that the mailing took place.[98] However, in order to avoid any contention that the papers were not served, it is advisable to serve the summons and complaint by certified or registered mail with a return receipt requested.

Rules governing service of a summons and involuntary petition are extremely liberal.[99] Personal service may be made by anyone who is an adult and not a party.[100] The attorney for the petitioner or the attorney's clerk often serves them by mail. If personal service or service by mail cannot be made, the court may order that the summons and petition be served by mailing copies to the last known address, if any, and by publication in the manner and form as directed by the judge.[101] As long as there is no material prejudice to the debtor caused thereby, an error in the manner or proof of service or in the papers served will not affect the validity of the service, and the bankruptcy case will commence nonetheless.[102]

If an involuntary petition is filed against a partnership, the Suggested Interim Bankruptcy Rules require that within five days after the

---

[95] See Sugg. Int. B. Form No. 10, the official summons form, set forth in Appendix B; B. Rule 111.

[96] B .Rules 111, 704(b), 704(c). See B. Rule 704(c) to determine to whom the summons and petition are to be mailed.

[97] B. Rules 111, 704(e). The ten-day period includes Saturdays, Sundays, and legal holidays, unless the tenth day is a Saturday, Sunday, or legal holiday, in which event it will not count. See B. Rule 906; Fed. R. Civ. P. 6(a).

[98] B. Rules 111, 704(c), 704(g).

[99] B. Rule 111.

[100] *Id.;* B. Rule 704(b).

[101] B. Rule 111.

[102] *Id.;* B. Rule 704(h).

filing the petitioning creditors or partners send a copy of the petition by first-class mail to the last known address of each general partner who has not joined in the petition or who has not been served. In lieu of mailing, however, a copy of the petition may be delivered to each general partner.[103]

[2] The Answer to the Petition

The debtor or, in the case of a petition against a partnership, any general partner who is not a petitioner may file and serve an answer to the petition.[104] Creditors and other persons may not file an answer to contest the petition.[105] The answer will usually challenge the standing of the petitioning creditors or the alleged grounds for involuntary bankruptcy. The answer should be in the same form and may contain defenses in the same manner as answers in other types of civil actions in federal district courts.[106] However, the answer may include the statement of a claim against a petitioning creditor *only* for the purpose of defeating the petition, because an affirmative judgment cannot be sought by way of a counterclaim in a bankruptcy case.[107] The answer must be served and filed within twenty calendar days after the issuance of the summons, unless a different time limit is stated in a court order for service by publication.[108] No other pleadings are permitted after an answer is filed and served, except for the rare occasion when the court orders the petitioners to reply to the answer.[109]

As in other federal civil actions, the debtor may make any one or more of a number of motions, some of which may be made prior to the answer. For example, the debtor may make a motion to dismiss

---

[103] Sugg. Int. B. Rule 1004(b).

[104] 11 U.S.C. § 303(d). See B. Rule 112.

[105] Prior to 1938, creditors had standing to question the sufficiency of an involuntary petition. The former Bankruptcy Act was amended in 1938 to preclude creditors from challenging the petition, and this preclusion is continued under the Bankruptcy Code. See former B.A. § 18(b). It was held that a creditor may not challenge the petition, even when it is so inadequate as to deprive the bankruptcy court of jurisdiction. *In re* Ludlum Enterprises, Inc., 510 F.2d 996 (5th Cir. 1975).

[106] B. Rule 112. See Rule 12 of the Federal Rules of Civil Procedure on the requirements for an answer in federal civil actions.

[107] B. Rule 112. See Georgia Jewelers, Inc. v. Bulova Watch Co., 302 F.2d 362 (5th Cir. 1962). See also Harris v. Capehart-Farnsworth Corp., 225 F.2d 268 (8th Cir. 1955).

[108] B. Rule 112.

[109] *Id.*

the petition for lack of jurisdiction, or for failure to state a claim upon which relief can be granted because the petition fails to adequately state a ground for an involuntary petition. The debtor may also make a motion for a more definite statement, although this will be a rare occurrence under the Bankruptcy Code because of the elimination of the need to plead an act of bankruptcy. The debtor may make any of the motions that are permitted by Rule 12 of the Federal Rules of Civil Procedure.[110] The timely service of a motion may have the effect of extending the time to answer pending a decision on the motion. If the court denies a motion or postpones its disposition until the trial on the merits, the answer need not be served until five days after the debtor receives notice of the court's action.[111]

If the answer alleges that one or more of the petitioning creditors is ineligible to be a petitioner or if such an allegation is made in a pre-trial motion, the court must give the other petitioners reasonable time to have other creditors join in the petition before dismissing the bankruptcy case. If the petition is executed by fewer than three creditors and the debtor alleges that there are twelve or more creditors, thus requiring at least three petitioning creditors to commence an involuntary case, the debtor must file and serve with the answer a list of all of the creditors.[112]

[3] The Trial on Factual Issues

If a petition is contested, the court is required to determine the issues at the "earliest practicable time" and either order relief, dismiss the case, or enter other appropriate orders.[113] If there are genuine triable issues of fact, the court may not dispose of them without conducting a trial.[114] The Bankruptcy Code departs from prior law by permitting the judge to order that the issues in an involuntary case be tried without a jury.[115]

In preparation for the trial, all parties may resort to all discovery

---

[110] *Id.*

[111] *Id.;* B. Rule 712(a).

[112] B. Rule 104(e).

[113] Sugg. Int. B. Rule 1009(a).

[114] 11 U.S.C. § 303(h). For a discussion of the debtor's rights against self-incrimination and immunity in a bankruptcy case, see Chapter 1 *supra.*

[115] 28 U.S.C. § 1480(b). Under the former Bankruptcy Act, the debtor had a right to a jury trial on the issues of insolvency and presence of an act of bankruptcy. Former B.A. § 19.

methods that are applicable to other federal civil actions as contained in the Federal Rules of Civil Procedure.[116]

[4] Order for the Relief Requested in the Petition

The court will order the relief requested in the petition or enter other appropriate orders if the debtor defaults by failing to controvert the petition within the applicable time limits.[117] If the petitioners sought relief under chapter 7 of the Bankruptcy Code, the court will order the liquidation of the debtor. If the relief requested is a reorganization, the court will order it under chapter 11.

If the petition is controverted and a trial is held, the court will order the requested relief only if it is found that one of the grounds for involuntary bankruptcy is present, that is, that the debtor is generally not paying debts as they become due or that a custodian was appointed or took possession of the debtor's assets within 120 days before the filing of the petition.[118]

[5] List of Creditors, Schedules, and Statement of Affairs

The debtor's duty to file a list of creditors, schedules, and statement of affairs, which was discussed in the previous chapter, applies in involuntary cases.[119] These documents must be filed within ten days after the order for relief in an involuntary bankruptcy. The court may on application grant up to ten additional days for filing these documents, but any further extension may be granted only for cause and on notice as directed by the court.[120] Rules dealing with supplemental schedules are also applicable in involuntary cases.[121]

When a partnership is the subject of an involuntary petition, the list of creditors, schedules, and statement of affairs must be prepared and filed by the general partners. Every general partner who is not in bankruptcy as an individual must also file a statement of personal assets

---

[116] B. Rules 121, 726; Fed. R. Civ. P. 26.

[117] 11 U.S.C. § 303(h). See Sugg. Int. B. Rule 1009(b), requiring that the court order relief upon default "on the next day, or as soon thereafter as practicable." An order for relief should conform to Sugg. Int. B. Form No. 11, set forth in Appendix B.

[118] See ¶ 2.09. See also note 88 *supra*.

[119] See 11 U.S.C. § 521, and ¶ 1.06.

[120] See B. Rule 108(b).

[121] B. Rule 108(e). See ¶ 1.06[5].

and liabilities with the trustee of the partnership within ten days of the trustee's qualification or within a time period set by the court.[122] The purpose of this requirement is to facilitate the marshalling of assets by the trustee when necessary.

If the debtor is a corporation, the duty to file these documents is imposed on the person or persons designated by the court to perform these functions.[123]

If the debtor fails to file the required documents within the time permitted by the Rules or by court order, the court may direct the trustee or petitioning creditors, or anyone else who is an interested party, to prepare and file the list of creditors, schedules, and statement of affairs.[124] In such a situation, it is often necessary for the trustee or petitioning creditors to employ accountants or other assistants in preparing the documents. The trustee or petitioning creditors should petition the court to authorize such employment so that these expenses will constitute a claim against the estate that has priority as an administrative expense.[125] Moreover, in such a situation it is possible that the debtor's failure to file these documents may result in punishment for contempt and the denial of a discharge.[126]

[6] Meeting of Creditors

After an order for relief is entered under the Bankruptcy Code, notice is sent by the clerk of the bankruptcy court to creditors and the debtor informing them of the date set for the meeting of creditors. The same rules that relate to meetings in voluntary cases are equally applicable in involuntary bankruptcies. The debtor has the duty to attend the meeting to be examined. In addition, the court may order a separate meeting of equity holders, which the debtor must attend.[127]

After the order of relief is entered and the list of creditors, schedules, and statement of affairs is filed, the involuntary case follows essentially the same procedures as are followed in a voluntary case.[128]

---

[122] B. Rule 108(c). See *In re* Ira Haupt & Co., 240 F. Supp. 369 (S.D.N.Y. 1965).

[123] See B. Rule 901(6), and ¶ 1.13.

[124] B. Rule 108(d).

[125] See B. Rules 215, 219; 11 U.S.C. §§ 503, 507(a)(1). See also Chapter 5 *infra* on claims.

[126] See 11 U.S.C. § 727(a)(6), and Chapter 3 *infra*, on discharge.

[127] See ¶ 1.11[3].

[128] See Chapter 1 *supra*.

¶ 2.11 JOINT PETITIONS, JOINT ADMINISTRATION, AND CONSOLIDATION

The Bankruptcy Code permits joint petitions to be filed only against husbands and wives.[129] However, in appropriate cases separate involuntary petitions may be filed against related corporations or other debtors who are closely connected, followed by either a joint administration of assets or a complete consolidation of the bankruptcy cases.[130]

¶ 2.12 APPOINTMENT OF AN INTERIM TRUSTEE

After an involuntary petition is filed but before the court orders relief for liquidation or reorganization, continued possession of the property of the estate by the debtor could jeopardize the rights of creditors. For example, it is not unlikely that a business debtor served with an involuntary petition for liquidation will not continue to devote full energies to the business and may even permit the wasting of assets. In such a situation, any party in interest may request the appointment of an interim trustee to take possession of the debtor's property in order to preserve it or prevent loss to the estate.[131] The court may appoint an interim trustee only after notice to the debtor and such other parties in interest as the court may designate, and after a hearing to determine whether the appointment is necessary to preserve the estate or to prevent such loss.[132] In a rare case, an interim trustee may be appointed without notice upon a showing that irreparable loss to the estate would otherwise result.[133] The order appointing an interim trustee must set forth the specific duties to be carried out, and copies of the order must be delivered or mailed to the debtor or to other persons as the court may designate.[134]

---

[129] 11 U.S.C. § 302(a).

[130] See ¶ 1.08 for a discussion of the concepts of joint administration and consolidation.

[131] 11 U.S.C. § 303(g). Suggested Interim Bankruptcy Rule 2001(b) requires that the application for the appointment of an interim trustee state specific facts showing the necessity for the appointment. Because of the availability of procedures for the appointment of an interim trustee, the court does not have the power to appoint a receiver. 11 U.S.C. § 105(b).

[132] 11 U.S.C. § 303(g); Sugg. Int. B. Rule 2001(a). Suggested Interim Bankruptcy Rule 2001(c) requires that the applicant furnish a bond sufficient to indemnify the debtor for the costs, attorney's fee, expenses, and damages allowable upon dismissal of the petition. See 11 U.S.C. § 303(i).

[133] Sugg. Int. B. Rule 2001(a).

[134] Sugg. Int. B. Rule 2001(d).

The interim trustee, who may continue to operate the debtor's business, serves while the trial is pending and until the selection of a trustee at the meeting of creditors.[135] Until the interim trustee is appointed, the debtor may operate the business in the ordinary course, but persons who extend credit to the debtor during that time will not have first priority in distribution as an administrative expense; instead, the creditor will have a second-priority claim.[136]

A debtor who wants to regain possession of the business or other property from an interim trustee prior to the order for relief may do so by posting a sufficient bond. The amount of the bond will be set by the court to assure that such property, or its monetary equivalent, is delivered to the trustee in the event that an order for liquidation is granted.[137] Regaining possession by posting a bond will probably be a rare occasion because the collateral needed to obtain such a bond must come from sources outside the estate assets.

In some instances, the creditors may not have to request the appointment of an interim trustee or the protection of a bond. For example, in *In re Louis Marx, Inc.*,[138] creditors filed an involuntary petition against a debtor under chapter 11 of the Code. For a few days thereafter the debtor continued its operations, but then consented to be reorganized under chapter 11, thereby avoiding the necessity for any protective measures at that time.

¶ 2.13 ALLOWANCE OF PETITIONER'S EXPENSES AS A PRIORITY CLAIM

Petitioning creditors must incur expenses in commencing an involuntary case. If the involuntary petition results in an order for relief and ultimate distribution to creditors, the petitioning creditors may recoup at least some of their expenses as administrative expense claims entitled to priority above the claims of other creditors. Specifically, the Code provides that petitioning creditors may claim as an administrative expense their "actual, necessary expenses," [139] as well as reasonable compensation for professional services rendered to the petitioners by an

---

[135] See 11 U.S.C. § 702, and Chapter 6 *infra*, on the appointment of trustees. Upon the appointment of a regular trustee, the interim trustee must turn over all records and property of the estate and, within thirty days thereafter, file a final report and account. Sugg. Int. B. Rule 2001(e).

[136] See 11 U.S.C. §§ 502(f), 507(a)(2).

[137] 11 U.S.C. § 303(g).

[138] Dkt. No. B10150 (S.D.N.Y. 1980).

[139] 11 U.S.C. § 503(b)(3)(A).

accountant or attorney.[140] Such expenses include the filing fee, cost of serving the summons and petition, attorney's fees, and other related expenses. The rationale for permitting creditors to recoup expenses as a priority claim is that the actions of the petitioners benefit all general creditors, and therefore the petitioners should be reimbursed for such expenses from the estate before a pro rata distribution is made to all general creditors.[141]

¶ 2.14 PROTECTING THE DEBTOR AFTER THE INVOLUNTARY PETITION IS FILED

In the period between the filing of an involuntary petition and either the order of relief or the dismissal of the bankruptcy case, the debtor is given certain protections designed to minimize the disruptive impact on the debtor's business and financial affairs.

The most important protection given by the Bankruptcy Code is the debtor's right to continue to operate the business prior to an order for relief as if the involuntary petition had never been commenced. The debtor may continue to use, acquire, or dispose of property unaffected by the bankruptcy case.[142] Debts incurred in the ordinary course of business after the petition is filed but before the order for relief or appointment of a trustee are treated as claims against the estate and will receive priority in distribution so as to encourage persons to continue dealing with the debtor, but it should be noted that these gap claims have only a second priority.[143]

As discussed in the previous section, however, when there is evidence that the debtor is likely to abscond with assets, waste property, or sell goods for less than fair market value, the debtor may be deprived of possession of assets. The court may grant appropriate orders to control or limit the debtor's powers, or, upon application by an interested party, an interim trustee may be appointed if necessary to preserve the estate.[144] In fact, it can be expected that creditors will generally seek the appointment of an interim trustee to remove possession from the debtor in liquidation cases under chapter 7.

Another protection that benefits the debtor is the automatic stay.[145]

---

140 11 U.S.C. § 503(b)(4).

141 See Chapter 5 *infra* on claims against the estate.

142 11 U.S.C. § 303(f).

143 See Chapter 5 *infra* on priority claims; 11 U.S.C. §§ 502(f), 507(a)(2).

144 11 U.S.C. § 303(g).

145 11 U.S.C. § 362.

While the involuntary case is pending, the debtor will be free from further harassment and judicial process by creditors. The automatic stay becomes effective upon the filing of the involuntary petition so as to preserve the estate from the earliest possible time in the bankruptcy case. The automatic stay facilitates an orderly administration of the estate and therefore is for the benefit of general creditors as well as the debtor. The rules that apply to automatic stays in voluntary cases apply equally in involuntary cases. (The scope, exceptions, termination, and procedures for relief from the stay, as well as the required safeguards for the protection of property rights and security interests, were discussed in detail in Chapter 1.[146]

¶ 2.15 WITHDRAWAL OF, ABSTENTION FROM, OR DISMISSAL OF AN INVOLUNTARY CASE

[1] Withdrawal of the Petition

As discussed in the previous chapter, a debtor who files a voluntary petition does not have an absolute right to withdraw it to terminate a bankruptcy case.[147] Similarly, petitioners in an involuntary case may not withdraw their petition as a matter of right. Suppose, for example, that after the creditors file and serve an involuntary petition alleging the debtor's general failure to pay debts the petitioning creditors receive payment of their claims in full. May the petitioners merely withdraw their petition? Obviously, if voluntary dismissal by the petitioners is possible in such a situation, the door would be open for collusive settlement among the debtor and the petitioners. A creditor who files a petition against a debtor would have extraordinary powers to compel the debtor to make a preferential payment in order to avoid liquidation. Therefore, the Bankruptcy Code protects other creditors by not giving the petitioners the absolute right to withdraw a petition either before or after an answer is interposed.

The only way for a petitioner to withdraw an involuntary petition is to do so by motion, with notice to all creditors, followed by a hearing. The court may then dismiss the case if that would be in the best interests of creditors and the debtor. The requirement for notice to all creditors and a hearing applies even when the debtor and all petitioners consent to withdraw the petition or dismiss the case. Based on the same rationale, the Code provides that an involuntary case may not even be dis-

---

[146] See ¶ 1.09.

[147] See ¶ 1.14.

missed for want of prosecution or nonpayment of the required filing fees unless the court holds a hearing on notice to all creditors and determines that such dismissal will best serve the interests of the debtor and creditors in general.[148]

[2] Abstention

Even when the court has an adequate basis for jurisdiction and venue and there is a sufficient ground for ordering relief under the bankruptcy laws, it may still be in the best interests of the parties for the court to decline jurisdiction over a case. The Bankruptcy Code expressly gives the court the right to abstain by either dismissing a case or suspending all proceedings in a case if such dismissal or suspension would best serve the interests of the debtor and the creditors generally.[149] A dismissal or suspension may be warranted, for example, when an out-of-court arrangement is being worked out among creditors and the debtor that is followed by an involuntary petition for liquidation filed by a few petitioning creditors who wish to upset the settlement because of dissatisfaction with the arrangement. If the court is satisfied that the extrajudicial arrangement will be in the best interests of the debtor and creditors generally, it will be appropriate to dismiss or suspend the bankruptcy case pending the arrangement. Suspension may even aid the out-of-court arrangement by giving the debtor an opportunity to work out a settlement with creditors and, if the recalcitrants do not consent, consummate the arrangement through chapter 11 of the Bankruptcy Code.[150]

Dismissal or suspension of a bankruptcy case pursuant to the court's abstention powers may occur at any time, and the judge's decision, either to abstain or not abstain, is not reviewable on appeal.[151] Abstention powers apply in both voluntary and involuntary cases.

[3] Dismissal

The court may dismiss the petition after trial for any one of a variety of reasons in addition to the exercise of abstention powers. If the petitioners are unable to establish a ground for involuntary bank-

---

[148] 11 U.S.C. §§ 303(j), 305(a), 707.

[149] 11 U.S.C. § 305. See 11 U.S.C. § 1112(b), which gives the court the discretion to dismiss or convert a reorganization case in the best interests of creditors.

[150] See Chapter 8 *infra* on reorganization.

[151] 11 U.S.C. § 305(c). See also note 88 *supra*.

ruptcy, or if the petitioners cannot prove that they have claims against the debtor aggregating $5,000, a contested petition will be dismissed.[152] In addition, a case may be dismissed prior to the trial on the merits of the petition if the debtor makes a pretrial motion to dismiss pursuant to the Federal Rules of Civil Procedure.[153] Lack of jurisdiction, for example, may be raised in a motion to dismiss. Also, the petition may be dismissed for want of prosecution.[154] When the case is dismissed by pretrial motion or after trial on the merits of the petition, no order of relief is entered in the case.

Unless the court orders otherwise, the dismissal of a bankruptcy case is without prejudice and will not stand in the way of a subsequent petition and discharge for the debtor.[155] In addition, after dismissal the rights of parties are put back to their positions prior to the filing of the petition. Any liens or transfers that were voided are reinstated, and property of the estate revests in the persons who owned the property prior to commencement of the bankruptcy case.[156]

¶ 2.16 CONVERSION OF THE CASE

Suppose that a meritorious involuntary petition seeks a liquidation under chapter 7. Suppose further that, although the debtor would like to avoid bankruptcy altogether, the debtor would rather be subjected to a reorganization under chapter 11 than a liquidation under chapter 7 which ends the business. In this situation, the debtor has the absolute right to convert the case from a liquidation to a reorganization.[157] The rationale for giving the debtor this right is that the debtor should always be given the opportunity to rehabilitate and repay debts. The conversion may be made at any time, either before or after the default or trial, and the debtor's right to convert may not be waived.[158] Similarly, an

---

[152] 11 U.S.C. § 303(h). See ¶ 2.09.

[153] See ¶ 2.10[2].

[154] Before dismissing an involuntary petition for want of prosecution, the court must conduct a hearing upon notice to all creditors. 11 U.S.C. § 303(j)(3).

[155] However, if the debtor received a discharge before dismissal that is not revoked by the court, the debtor may not seek another discharge in a liquidation case for six years. 11 U.S.C. § 727(a)(8). See Chapter 3 *infra* on discharge.

[156] 11 U.S.C. § 349.

[157] 11 U.S.C.§ 706(a).

[158] *Id.*

individual debtor with regular income may convert the case to achieve an adjustment of debts under chapter 13.[159] As soon as a conversion is made, it becomes an order for relief under the chapter to which the case is transferred. Accordingly, a debtor may contest an involuntary petition for liquidation and, if unsuccessful, may convert the case to accomplish a rehabilitation instead of liquidation. If the involuntary petition originally seeks a reorganization, however, the debtor does not have the right to convert it to a case for liquidation, except that upon notice and a hearing the reorganization case may be converted by the court for cause if it is in the best interests of creditors and the estate.[160]

¶ 2.17 RISKS ASSUMED BY PETITIONERS IN INVOLUNTARY BANKRUPTCY CASES

Petitioning creditors should carefully consider the risks incurred when an involuntary petition is filed. Before the filing, creditors should understand their exposure to possible liability in the event that the petition is dismissed.

Dismissal of a petition on consent of the debtor and all petitioning creditors will not result in liability for costs, expenses, or damages, even though notice to all creditors and a hearing is required. However, when an involuntary petition is dismissed for any other reason, the court may award the debtor costs and a reasonable attorney's fee to be paid by the petitioners, unless the debtor waives the right to recover such costs and expenses. In addition, if an interim trustee took possession of the debtor's assets prior to the dismissal, the debtor may recover damages proximately caused by such taking of possession.[161]

The petitioner's exposure to liability is generally limited to costs, an attorney's fee, and damages caused by loss of possession to an interim trustee. The unsuccessful petitioner who acted in good faith is not liable for loss resulting from damaged reputation or defamation. But, if the court finds that the petition was filed in bad faith, the petitioning creditors may be required to compensate the debtor for all damages proximately caused by the filing.[162] If the debtor's reputation is damaged because of the involuntary petition, and such damage results in the loss of business either before or after the dismissal, the debtor would have

---

[159] *Id.* See Chapter 9 *infra* on debt adjustments for individuals with regular income.

[160] 11 U.S.C. §§ 1112(a)(2), 1112(b).

[161] 11 U.S.C. § 303(i)(1).

[162] 11 U.S.C. § 303(i)(2).

a claim for such loss against the petitioners who acted in bad faith. In addition, the court may award punitive damages against any petitioner who filed an involuntary petition in bad faith.[163]

A case that exemplifies a debtor's rights against creditors who caused an involuntary petition to be filed in bad faith is *Sachs v. Weinstein*.[164] After the involuntary petition was dismissed upon a jury verdict in the bankruptcy court, the debtor instituted a state court action for malicious prosecution against his creditors who had been instrumental in having the bankruptcy petition filed against him. The debtor alleged that, among other things, the creditors assigned their claim to their lawyer's stenographer and conspired to have the involuntary petition filed in her name in the hope that the real creditors would be protected against liability for malicious prosecution. The debtor alleged that the involuntary petition was filed, among other reasons, "to extort from plaintiff payment of said debt of approximately $650" [165] and that it was filed upon false allegations of insolvency and fabricated acts of bankruptcy. The debtor, who was a retailer, sought damages including counsel fees, loss of customers due to the inability to supervise the business during the pendency of the involuntary petition, and injury to his reputation and credit among his customers and suppliers. Moreover, he also sought exemplary damages. The appellate court agreed with the trial court that the complaint was sufficient and should not be dismissed, and it expressly held that exemplary damages may be given in such a case.

The Bankruptcy Code gives the bankruptcy court jurisdiction to award the debtor a judgment against the unsuccessful petitioners who filed in bad faith for proximate and punitive damages.[166] Therefore, there is no need for the debtor to sue in a different forum to recover against the malicious petitioners. However, it is questionable whether the bankruptcy court may grant judgment against persons who conspired to cause the petition to be filed but who were not the named petitioners. In such a situation, if the court abstains, the debtor may have to resort to a different forum.

The Bankruptcy Code permits the debtor in an involuntary case to request that a bond be posted to indemnify the debtor for its potential claim against the petitioners in the event of dismissal. The court may require the petitioners to file such a bond, but only if cause is shown at

---

[163] 11 U.S.C. § 303(i)(2)(B).

[164] 208 App. Dir. 360, 203 N.Y.S. 449 (1st Dep't 1924).

[165] *Id.* at 450.

[166] 11 U.S.C. § 303(i).

a hearing upon notice to the interested parties.[167] Whenever the debtor plans to contest an involuntary petition, the protection of a bond should be requested.

If the court exercises its abstention powers to dismiss or suspend a bankruptcy petition in the best interest of the debtor and creditors in general, the debtor will not have a claim for damages.

---

[167] 11 U.S.C. § 303(e).

Chapter 3

DISCHARGE OF DEBTS IN LIQUIDATION CASES

¶ 3.01 THE GOAL OF THE DEBTOR

As we discussed in Chapter 1, the primary purpose of bankruptcy from the debtor's standpoint is to obtain relief from indebtedness. In both voluntary and involuntary bankruptcy cases, a discharge from debts is the ultimate goal of individual debtors. The Bankruptcy Code makes discharge available to individuals in chapter 7 liquidation cases, chapter 11 reorganizations, and chapter 13 debt adjustment cases. The focus of this chapter of the book, however, is on discharge in liquidations only.[1]

¶ 3.02 OBJECTIONS TO DISCHARGE

Although most liquidation cases result in a discharge, the debtor contemplating bankruptcy should not take discharge for granted. Discharge in bankruptcy is a privilege, not a right.[2] The policy underlying the discharge provisions of the Code is to give financial relief and a fresh start to the poor but honest debtor who is willing to cooperate with the court in the orderly liquidation of assets. Accordingly, certain dishonest or uncooperative acts may give rise to grounds for the denial of a discharge. Also, there are grounds for objection that are unrelated to dishonesty or the failure to cooperate.

It is of utmost importance that the debtor and the debtor's counsel carefully consider whether facts exist that may give rise to an objection to discharge. This consideration should take place *prior* to filing a liquidation petition. The presence of such grounds may be a sufficient deterrent to filing the petition in the first place. If an objection is made successfully, the debtor will be subjected to the loss of nonexempt assets without receiving the benefit of a discharge of any debts. However, at this juncture the debtor may consider the benefits to be derived from chapter 13, which grants the debtor a discharge from most debts provided for in the plan despite the existence of an objection to discharge under chapter 7.[3]

¶ 3.03 TEN GROUNDS FOR DENIAL OF DISCHARGE

The Bankruptcy Code sets forth ten grounds for the denial of a discharge, which are discussed below.

---

[1] See Chapter 8 *infra* for a discussion of discharge in reorganizations, and Chapter 9 *infra* for a discussion of discharge in debt adjustments for individuals with regular income.

[2] See United States v. Kras, 409 U.S. 434, 446 (1973) ("There is no constitutional right to obtain a discharge of one's debts in bankruptcy"); *In re* Tabibien, 289 F.2d 793, 795 (2d Cir. 1961) ("It is true that a discharge is a privilege granted the honest debtor and not a right accorded all bankrupts").

[3] See 11 U.S.C. § 1328, and ¶ 9.17.

[1] First Ground: Discharge Is for Individuals Only

The former Bankruptcy Act provided for discharges for all types of debtors in liquidation cases, including individuals, corporations, and partnerships.[4] Discharges for partnership entities and corporations, however, were usually not important because it was rare for the bankrupt entity to continue to do business in the same form. Bankrupt corporations are often dissolved or remain dormant after liquidation. In the case of close corporations, it is easy for the principals to form a new corporation after bankruptcy.

It is for this reason that the Bankruptcy Code does not permit discharges for corporations and partnership entities in liquidation cases.[5] As a congressional report had indicated, this "change in policy will avoid trafficking in corporate shells and in bankrupt partnerships."[6] Accordingly, only individuals may receive a discharge. Of course, if general partners file petitions as individuals, with or without a partnership petition, each partner so filing will obtain a discharge from both business and personal debts.[7]

[2] Second Ground: Fraudulent Transfers or Concealment of Property

The discharge benefits of bankruptcy are not intended to help debtors who have taken certain steps to purposely frustrate the orderly distribution of their assets. Specifically, the Bankruptcy Code provides that the debtor is not entitled to a discharge if, with intent to defraud, hinder, or delay creditors or a custodian of the bankruptcy estate, the debtor "transferred, removed, destroyed, mutilated, or concealed" property of the debtor or of the estate.[8] The debtor may be precluded from obtaining a discharge whether the debtor actually committed any of these acts or merely permitted somebody else to do so.[9]

---

[4] Former B.A. § 14(a). The Act provided that "any person," which included partnership entities, may receive a discharge. Former B.A. § 1(23).

[5] 11 U.S.C. § 727(a)(1).

[6] H.R. Rep. No. 95-595, 95th Cong., 1st Sess. 384 (1977) (hereinafter cited as H.R. Rep. No. 95-595).

[7] Failure of a general partner to file a petition as an individual may result in the turnover of the partner's personal assets to the trustee of the partnership for marshalling. Therefore, unlike a corporation in bankruptcy, which causes the principals little concern, a liquidating partnership may have an impact upon the assets of the general partners.

[8] 11 U.S.C. § 727(a)(2). This ground for objection to discharge derives from Section 14(c)(4) of the former Bankruptcy Act.

[9] *Id.*

There are two limitations that are relevant to the second ground for objecting to a discharge. First, if the prohibited conduct occurs prior to the filing of the petition, it must have taken place not more than one year prior to that time.[10] If the debtor fraudulently conceals or transfers property more than one year prior to the petition, it will not bar a discharge.[11] Second, if the fraudulent conduct occurs after the petition is filed, the property affected must belong to the bankruptcy estate to constitute an objection to discharge.[12] Thus, if exempt property is transferred after the exemption is claimed, the debtor may nonetheless obtain a discharge because the property no longer belongs to the estate.

Great care should be taken in preparing the statement of affairs and schedules of assets for the bankruptcy court so as to avoid the appearance of fraud. Even the concealment of property that has insignificant value may result in the denial of a discharge. *In re Zidoff*[13] illustrates this problem. The debtor in that case failed to list a deep freeze, a hi-fi set, and an air-conditioning unit on the schedule of assets. These items, most of which were exempt, were worth not more than $400. In fact, the trustee did not even bother to take possession and sell this property after he discovered them. Nonetheless, the debtor's discharge was denied because of the fraudulent concealment. In a similar case, *In re Mascolo,*[14] a discharge was revoked because the debtor swore in his statement of affairs that he had maintained no bank accounts within two years preceding the filing of the petition. In fact, he had maintained two accounts involving $150 and $350 that were closed more than six months prior to bankruptcy.

Although the concealment or transfer of a small amount of property is enough to bar a discharge, the necessity of fraudulent intent must not be underestimated. An accidental omission in the debtor's schedule of assets is not sufficient to deny a discharge.[15] Furthermore, constructive fraud does not meet the required level of intent. For example, the mere fact that a debtor gave $500 as a gift to each of her two daughters within a year of bankruptcy was not sufficient for a finding of actual

---

[10] 11 U.S.C. § 727(a)(2)(A).

[11] Although a fraudulent transfer more than one year prior to bankruptcy does not bar a discharge, the trustee may still be able to avoid the transfer and recover the property. See 11 U.S.C. § 544(b), and ¶ 7.03.

[12] 11 U.S.C. § 727(a)(2)(B). See Chapter 4 *infra* for a discussion relating to property of the estate.

[13] 309 F.2d 417 (7th Cir. 1962).

[14] 505 F.2d 274 (1st Cir. 1974).

[15] Avallone v. Gross, 309 F.2d 60 (2d Cir. 1962).

fraud. Such evidence may create a presumption of fraud, but the debtor may rebut the presumption by proving that the gifts were made to help meet her daughters' living expenses, that at the time of the gifts she was unaware that a suit had been instituted against her, and that she was accustomed to making such gifts.[16] As explained by one court, "it is not so much the acts of the bankrupt that will prevent his discharge, as it is the intent with which he acts."[17]

[3] Third Ground: Failure to Keep Books and Records

Adequate books and records relating to the debtor's financial history are important to facilitate an orderly liquidation and distribution to creditors. Accordingly, the Bankruptcy Code continues the practice of denying a discharge to a debtor who has concealed, destroyed, mutilated, falsified, or failed to keep or preserve any records from which the debtor's financial condition or business transactions and may be ascertained.[18] Such records may include books, documents, receipts, ledgers, cancelled checks, or other recorded information. Fraudulent intention is not a necessary element of this objection; negligence or sloppiness in keeping records may be enough to bar a discharge.

This ground for objection does not apply, however, if the debtor's failure to have adequate records is justified under the particular circumstances of the case. For example, if records are in the possession of a creditor or sheriff as a result of a levy, or if they were destroyed by an act of God, the debtor will not lose the benefit of a discharge because of the failure to produce them.[19]

The nature, type, form, and extent of business records required depends on many different factors, including the specific occupation or business of the debtor. Generally, so long as the debtor keeps records in the customary way, using acceptable accounting procedures for the size, type, and complexity of the particular business, there is no need to worry.[20] The bankruptcy court has broad discretion to determine the standards for keeping and preserving adequate records with respect to a particular business.[21] A case that involved a debtor who was engaged

---

[16] *In re* Nemerov, 134 F. Supp. 678 (S.D.N.Y. 1955).

[17] *In re* Pioch, 235 F.2d 903, 906 (3d Cir. 1956).

[18] 11 U.S.C. § 727(a)(3). See former B.A. § 14(c)(2).

[19] See *In re* Tucker, 399 F. Supp. 660 (S.D. Fla. 1975); *In re* Williams, 66 F. Supp. 157 (E.D. Pa. 1946).

[20] See *In re* Halpern, 387 F.2d 312 (2d Cir. 1968).

[21] See Johnson v. Bockman, 282 F.2d 544, 546 (10th Cir. 1960) ("But reasonably wide discretion is lodged in the bankruptcy court in determining whether the books of account or records in a given case are sufficient to meet

in a building supply business with assets and liabilities each exceeding $100,000 illustrates the danger in keeping records carelessly.[22] In that case, the bankruptcy court's findings that books and records were inadequate and the resulting denial of a discharge were affirmed by the district court. Although the debtor's records were voluminous and filled ten boxes, they were so disorganized that the trustee was unable to understand from them the debtor's business transactions. There were missing payroll records, missing checks, missing invoices, and missing accounts receivable records. The ledger which would organize the receipts and disbursements information was absent.

> A mass of unorganized, mixed and miscellaneous records could be as confusing as no records. The bankrupt cannot fill his burden of proof by dumping a great volume of miscellaneous papers upon the trustee and leaving completely to the trustee the responsibility for fitting the jigsaw together and determining if all of the pieces are there. Some organization of voluminous records can be as much a part of record keeping as the existence of the records themselves.[23]

[4] Fourth Ground: Commission of a Bankruptcy Crime

There are four specific acts, which, in addition to constituting federal crimes, may give rise to an objection to discharge when committed by the debtor in connection with the debtor's own bankruptcy case.[24] These acts are treated as felonies under Title 18 of the U.S. Code and are punishable by a fine of not more than $5,000 or imprisonment of not more than five years, or both.[25] Of course, there must be proof beyond a reasonable doubt to convict the debtor of these so-called "bankruptcy crimes." However, the standard of proof that must be met to block a discharge is only a fair preponderance of the evidence.[26] It

---

the requirements of the statute, and the determination of that question will not be disturbed on appeal unless it is plainly erroneous").

[22] *In re* Romano, 196 F. Supp. 954 (E.D. Tenn. 1961).

[23] *Id.* at 958-959.

[24] 11 U.S.C. § 727(a)(4).

[25] 18 U.S.C. § 152.

[26] See *In re* Mascolo, 505 F.2d 274 (1st Cir. 1974), in which the court applied the fair preponderance of the evidence standard of proof to deny a discharge on the basis of the debtor's perjury. Although *Mascolo* was decided under the former Bankruptcy Act, the legislative history of the Bankruptcy Code indicates that it remains applicable under the new law. H.R. Rep. No. 95-595, note 6 *supra*, at 384.

should be emphasized, therefore, that conviction of one of these crimes is not necessary for the objection. The four crimes are as follows:

[a] Knowingly and Fraudulently Making a False Oath or Account

During the course of a bankruptcy case, there are instances when the debtor is required to make statements or to give testimony under oath.[27] As discussed previously, the debtor's schedules of assets and liabilities and statement of financial affairs either must be verified or must contain an unsworn statement in lieu of verification so that an intentional false statement therein will constitute perjury.[28] Likewise, at the meeting of creditors or in other proceedings, the debtor must submit to an examination under oath.[29]

If the debtor intentionally makes a false statement under oath, whether in the petition, schedules, statement of affairs, or testimony, the debtor may later find that a discharge will not be granted.[30] Because the debtor is required to attest to the completeness and accuracy of the schedules, an intentional omission of any property or debt may also result in a bar to discharge. As the court of appeals stated in *In re Mascolo* when a debtor's discharge was revoked because he intentionally failed to list bank accounts as assets, even though they had been closed six months before bankruptcy, "successful functioning of the Bankruptcy Act hinges both upon the bankrupt's veracity and his willingness to make a full disclosure."[31]

Although a knowing and fraudulent false oath or account may bar a discharge, an honest mistake will not. In response to a question in her statement of affairs as to what property she transferred within a year prior to the filing of the bankruptcy petition, a debtor failed to mention the transfer of her automobile. The court found that this omission was not knowingly and fraudulently made because she believed, *on advice of counsel,* that she only had to list transfers of real estate and not items of personal property.[32] It is important to understand, however, that the

---

[27] See 11 U.S.C. § 521 for a list of the debtor's duties.

[28] See ¶ 1.06. See also B. Rule 109; Sugg. Int. B. Forms Nos. 6 and 7, set forth in Appendix B; 28 U.S.C. § 1746, concerning unsworn statements under penalty of perjury.

[29] See ¶¶ 1.11-1.13; 11 U.S.C. § 343.

[30] 11 U.S.C. § 727(a)(4)(A). See *In re* Semel, 479 F.2d 1269 (3d Cir.) *cert. denied* 415 U.S. 931 (1973), for an illustration of a denial of discharge based on false testimony concerning the debtor's assets.

[31] 505 F.2d 274, 278 (1st Cir. 1974).

[32] *In re* German, 193 F. Supp. 948, 953 (S.D. Ill. 1961).

debtor who has made a misrepresentation in the statement of affairs or schedules has the burden of proving that it was the result of a mistake. Once it reasonably appears that the oath is false, the burden falls upon the debtor to come forward with evidence to prove that it was not an intentional misrepresentation. Otherwise, the court may infer fraudulent intent from the unexplained false statement.[33] For this reason, the debtor and the debtor's attorney should exercise extreme care in the preparation of schedules and the statement of affairs. The conferences at which the attorney and the client prepare these documents should not be treated lightly.

[b] Knowingly and Fraudulently Presenting or Using a False Claim

If the debtor engages in a scheme involving the knowing and fraudulent filing or use of a false claim against the bankruptcy estate, such conduct may give rise to an objection to discharge.[34]

[c] Knowingly and Fraudulently Giving or Receiving a Bribe

A debtor may be barred from obtaining a discharge if the debtor gave or received a bribe in connection with the bankruptcy case. Specifically, the Code provides that if a debtor knowingly and fraudulently "gave, offered, received, or attempted to obtain money, property, or advantage, or a promise of money, property, or advantage, for acting or forbearing to act," a discharge will not be granted.[35] Although this ground for objection is rarely asserted in bankruptcy cases, in at least one old case a court had denied a discharge pending further proceedings to determine whether the debtor did anything illegal to induce creditors to withdraw their previous opposition to his discharge on other grounds.[36] If creditor opposition to a debtor's discharge is withdrawn because the creditor is "bought off" by the debtor, such conduct will bar a discharge as well as constitute a crime.[37]

[d] Knowingly and Fraudulently Withholding Records

The debtor is not entitled to a discharge if the debtor intentionally withholds any records, books, documents, or other papers relating to

---

[33] *In re* Mascolo, 505 F.2d 274, 276 (1st Cir. 1974).

[34] 11 U.S.C. § 727(a)(4)(B).

[35] 11 U.S.C. § 727(a)(4)(C).

[36] *In re* Sanborn, 131 F. 397 (W.D.N.Y. 1904). See also *In re* Luftig, 162 F. 322 (D. Mass. 1905).

[37] *In re* Sanborn, 131 F. 397, 398 (W.D.N.Y. 1904).

the debtor's property or financial affairs.[38] The debtor has the duty to surrender to the trustee all recorded information relating to property of the estate and is also obligated to cooperate with the trustee by, among other things, providing the trustee with all relevant documents and papers.[39] Therefore, the knowing and fraudulent withholding of these materials from the trustee constitutes an objection to discharge.

[5] Fifth Ground: Failure to Explain Loss of Assets

It is often difficult to prove that a debtor fraudulently concealed or transferred property prior to bankruptcy. The evidence may show nothing more than the disappearance of assets without even a hint as to what happened to them. Such evidence, nonetheless, may give rise to the fifth ground for objection. The Bankruptcy Code provides for a denial of discharge if the debtor has failed to explain satisfactorily any loss or deficiency of assets to meet liabilities.[40] Thus, if a creditor proves that the debtor no longer has assets that the debtor previously owned, the burden is on the debtor to explain the loss.[41] The objection may be sustained even if the debtor's failure to explain is not accompanied by fraudulent intent.

Debtors should be counseled to keep careful records concerning assets, especially if they are on the eve of financial distress. If a substantial sum of money or property is lost, it may not be satisfactory for the debtor to give an explanation in general terms. For example, in *In re Solari Furs,*[42] debtors were each denied a discharge when they explained in general terms that assets were lost because of "sales of merchandise below cost."[43] Although the court did not question the fact that such sales were made, the debtors "failed to demonstrate the verity of their explanation with sufficient particularity."[44]

The court has a great deal of leeway in determining whether an explanation is satisfactory so as to defeat the objection. In *Baum v.*

---

[38] 11 U.S.C. § 727(a)(4)(D).

[39] 11 U.S.C. § 521. See ¶ 1.13 for a discussion of the trustee's duties.

[40] 11 U.S.C. § 727(a)(5).

[41] See McBee v. Sliman, 512 F.2d 504, 506 (5th Cir. 1975) ("[The debtor's burden] is to convince the referee either by direct or circumstantial evidence that the money was in fact lost and the gambling explanation was not merely a ruse to evade creditors").

[42] 263 F. Supp. 658 (E.D. Mo. 1967).

[43] *Id.* at 669.

[44] *Id.*

Earl Milliken, Inc.,[45] the debtor submitted a financial statement to Dun and Bradstreet disclosing a net worth of $309,359. Twenty-one months later, the debtor's bankruptcy schedules indicated that assets were worth $57,381.26 less than liabilities. What happened to cause a loss of $366,740.26 in assets in such a short period of time? The court denied the debtor's discharge because it was not satisfied with his explanation that the loss was due to "shrinkage" of assets. "A 'satisfactory explanation' of a loss of assets to meet liabilities . . . must consist of more than the vague, indefinite, and uncorroborated hodgepodge of financial transactions. . . ."[46] The court added that the judge has "reasonably broad discretion to accept or reject an explanation designed to satisfy an objection made under this section."[47]

Another interesting illustration of this concept is the case of *McBee v. Sliman*,[48] in which the court dealt with objections to discharge based on failure to maintain books and records to satisfactorily explain the loss of $14,000 in assets. The joint debtors, who were husband and wife, testified that the wife's separate fund of $14,000 was placed in a closet in their home for two weeks. The husband testified that he, without his wife's knowledge, took the money on a gambling junket to Las Vegas in an attempt to recoup his debts. He claimed that he lost all at the blackjack tables and flew home with only airline ticket stubs and hotel receipts. He remembered the name of the hotel casino where he allegedly gambled and that the dealer had a mustache, but could testify as to nothing more. His memory with respect to particular bets and losses was vague. As the court pointed out, "Who hit whom or with what and when was never revealed."[49] Although the court recognized that gambling records by their nature are hard to come by, the debtor still must produce "some kind of direct evidence in order to defeat an objection . . . based on a failure to explain loss of assets."[50] Moreover, the wife was also denied a discharge despite the fact that nobody contradicted the husband's testimony that his wife did not know about or participate in the gambling spree. "[T]he burden under the bankruptcy law to explain the loss and justify the absence of records applies as evenly to Marilyn McBee as it does to her husband."[51]

---

[45] 359 F.2d 811 (7th Cir. 1966).

[46] *Id.* at 814.

[47] *Id.*

[48] 512 F.2d 504 (5th Cir. 1975).

[49] *Id.* at 506.

[50] *Id.*

[51] *Id.*

[6] Sixth Ground: Refusal to Obey Lawful Court Order or to Answer Questions

A discharge may be denied if the debtor refuses to obey any lawful order of the court.[52] During the case, the bankruptcy judge, on application of the trustee or a party in interest, may issue numerous orders to compel the debtor to turn over assets or to appear in court. A refusal to obey such an order, which may be in the form of a subpoena, gives rise to the sixth ground for objection.[53]

It should be emphasized that the court's order must be lawful. An order that exceeds the court's jurisdiction, for example, may not be the basis for this objection. In addition, an accidental or inadvertent failure to comply with an order is not enough to give rise to an objection to discharge. When a debtor failed to comply with the judge's order to complete and file his schedules within ten days because of his attorney's carelessness, the court granted the discharge nonetheless because the debtor's failure to comply with the order was not due to willful disobedience. "There was no evidence of any intent to harm creditors or insult the authority of the court."[54] Moreover, cases under the former Bankruptcy Act have held that the refusal to obey a court does not *require* the denial of a discharge, but merely permits the court to exercise its discretion as to whether or not to grant a discharge.[55] It is unclear as to whether the new Bankruptcy Code makes the denial of a discharge on this ground discretionary, as opposed to mandatory.[56]

---

[52] 11 U.S.C. § 727(a)(6), derived from former B.A. § 14(c)(6).

[53] Failure to appear in court to give testimony also may be considered an implied waiver of a discharge. See B. Rule 406; *In re* Shapiro, 110 F. Supp. 288, 292 (W.D. Pa. 1953). In addition, see ¶ 3.03[10] for a discussion concerning implied waivers.

[54] *In re* Jones, 490 F.2d 452, 456 (5th Cir. 1974). See also Maggio v. Zeitz, 333 U.S. 56 (1947), where the Court held that a debtor should not be held in contempt if it appears that the debtor is presently unable to comply with the judge's order. On remand the district court after evaluating the testimony found that the debtor had no ability to comply . See *In re* Luma Camera Serv., Inc., 84 F. Supp. 839 (S.D.N.Y. 1949). Compare *In re* California Motors, Inc., 122 F. Supp. 885 (E.D.N.Y. 1954), holding a debtor in contempt of court for refusal to obey a turnover order and directing that he be sent to prison.

[55] *In re* Kokoszka, 479 F.2d 990 (2d Cir. 1973), *aff'd* 417 U.S. 642 (1974). The Second Circuit wrote: "[B]efore denying a discharge, the referee should weigh the detriment to the proceedings and the dignity of the court against the potential harm to the debtor if the discharge is denied." *Id.* at 997-998. See also *In re* Jones, 490 F.2d 452 (5th Cir. 1974).

[56] The Code provides that the court "shall grant the debtor a discharge, unless . . . the debtor has refused, in the case . . . to obey any lawful

The Bankruptcy Code departs from prior law with respect to the effect of the debtor's refusal to testify or answer questions. Under the former Act, a refusal to answer a material question approved by the court gave rise to an objection to discharge.[57] This same rule applied even when the debtor refused to answer based on the constitutional privilege against self-incrimination.[58] Pursuant to the Code, however, the refusal to answer a question on the ground of the privilege against self-incrimination may not bar a discharge unless the debtor has been granted immunity prior to the refusal.[59] By asserting the Fifth Amendment privilege, therefore, the debtor will not have to give up the right to a discharge in bankruptcy. Of course, if the debtor refuses to answer a material question approved by the court after immunity has been granted, or based on some ground other than the privilege against self-incrimination, a discharge may be denied.[60]

[7] Seventh Ground: Prohibited Acts in Connection with an Insider's Bankruptcy

If at any time during the debtor's own bankruptcy case, or within one year prior to filing the debtor's own petition, the debtor commits certain acts in connection with a separate bankruptcy case of an insider, the debtor may be barred from obtaining a discharge. The prohibited conduct that would give rise to this ground for objection is the same acts that constitute the second, third, fourth, fifth, and sixth grounds for objection stated above.[61] For example, if the debtor participates in a fraudulent concealment of an insider's property, intentionally commits perjury, or gives an illegal bribe in connection with an insider's bankruptcy, there will be grounds to object to a discharge if the debtor files a liquidation petition within one year thereafter.

This ground for objection is limited to situations in which an insider is the subject of a separate bankruptcy case. The term "insider" is a term of art. In the case of an individual debtor, insiders include relatives, general partners, partnerships in which the debtor is a general

---

order. . . ." 11 U.S.C. § 727(a)(6)(A). This language is substantially similar to the language in Section 14(c) of the former Bankruptcy Act.

[57] Former B.A. § 14(c)(6).

[58] *In re* Bayknight, 14 F.2d 674 (S.D. Fla. 1926).

[59] 11 U.S.C. § 727(a)(6)(B).

[60] 11 U.S.C. § 727(a)(6)(C).

[61] 11 U.S.C. § 727(a)(7). This ground for objection to discharge is new

partner, and corporations of which the debtor is a director, officer, or person in control.[62]

[8] Eighth Ground: Prior Discharge Within Six Years

Chapter 7 of the Bankruptcy Code continues the practice of permitting discharge only once within a six-year period.[63] Specifically, the debtor is not entitled to a discharge in a liquidation case if one had been granted within six years under chapter 7 or chapter 11 of the Code or under the "straight bankruptcy" sections, Chapter XI or Chapter XII of the former Bankruptcy Act.[64] The six-year period begins to run from the time that the previous bankruptcy case was commenced by the filing of a petition. A new liquidation petition should not be filed, therefore, until at least six years after the previous petition was filed if this ground is to be avoided. It is this rule that gave rise to the inaccurate but often spoken comment that a person may go bankrupt only once every six years. In truth, a debtor may file a liquidation petition despite a recent discharge, and the bankruptcy case will proceed. The six-year rule applies only to discharge, not to any other aspect of the bankruptcy case.

[9] Ninth Ground: Prior Chapter 13 Discharge

The eighth ground for objection to discharge discussed above is limited to situations in which the debtor received a discharge in a prior liquidation or reorganization case. A different rule applies when the debtor was discharged in a previous Chapter XIII wage earner's plan under the former Bankruptcy Act or chapter 13 adjustment of debts under the new Code.

In general, the debtor who received a discharge in a Chapter XIII wage earner or chapter 13 debt adjustment case commenced within the previous six years may not obtain a discharge in a subsequent liquidation case.[65] In essence, the one-discharge-every-six-years rule applies. However, there are two exceptions. First, if the payments in the earlier case totaled at least 100 percent of the allowed unsecured claims, the

---

[62] 11 U.S.C. § 101(25)(A).

[63] See former B.A. § 14(c)(5).

[64] 11 U.S.C. § 727(a)(8). But see 11 U.S.C. § 1328, and ¶ 9.17, indicating that the debtor may receive a discharge under chapter 13 despite a discharge within the previous six years.

[65] 11 U.S.C. § 727(a)(9).

debtor will not be barred from obtaining a discharge in a liquidation case commenced within six years thereafter.[66] This would be an "extension-type" plan because it accomplishes only an extension of payment without a reduction of debt. Although the debtor receives a discharge under chapter 13,[67] the debts have been paid in full and should not stand in the way of a discharge in a subsequent liquidation.

The second exception deals with "composition-type" plans which provide for payment of less than 100 percent of the unsecured debts. If the plan provides for payments totaling at least 70 percent of allowed unsecured claims, was proposed by the debtor in good faith, and was the debtor's "best effort," the discharge obtained in the case will not bar another discharge in a liquidation case within the next six years.[68] Congress anticipated that a debtor in a chapter 13 case will be permitted to request a determination of whether a plan is the debtor's "best effort" prior to confirmation of the plan so that the debtor will know if it will bar a discharge in a future liquidation case commenced within six years. The court may consider many factors in determining whether the plan was the debtor's "best effort," including but not limited to assets, income, retirement benefits, insurance, foreseeable living expenses, dependents, stability of employment, and age. As stated by Congressman Don Edwards on the floor of the House of Representatives: "Different facts and circumstances in cases under chapter 13 operate to make any rule of thumb of limited usefulness." [69] This second exception also applies to plans not fully executed by the debtor but under which the debtor has made payments equal to at least 70 percent of the allowed unsecured claims, so long as the "good faith" and "best effort" requirements are met.

[10] Tenth Ground: Waiver

Can a debtor waive the privilege to receive a discharge? In general, a waiver of a discharge is not enforceable in a subsequent bankruptcy case.[70] The Bankruptcy Code provides, however, that a discharge shall be denied if (1) the debtor executes a written waiver of discharge, (2) the waiver was made after the order for relief under chapter 7, and (3)

[66] 11 U.S.C. § 727(a)(9)(A). This section follows case law that applied the former Act. See Perry v. Commerce Loan Co., 383 U.S. 392 (1966); Barnes v. Maley, 360 F.2d 922, 924 (7th Cir. 1966).

[67] See 11 U.S.C. § 1328; former B.A. §§ 660, 661.

[68] 11 U.S.C. § 727(a)(9)(B).

[69] 124 Cong. Rec. H11098 (daily ed., Sept. 28, 1978).

[70] See Fallick v. Kehr, 369 F.2d 899, 904 (2d Cir. 1966).

the waiver is approved by the court.[71] Other express waivers will not be effective. These restrictions are intended to protect the individual debtor who may be coerced by economic duress into signing a waiver while under financial stress. Otherwise, it would be too easy for creditors to influence the debtor unduly to waive a discharge when the desperate debtor is seeking an extension of credit.

The Bankruptcy Rules of Procedure, which predate the Bankruptcy Code, provide for an implied waiver of discharge upon the debtor's failure to attend and submit to examination at the meeting of creditors, at any meeting specially called for the debtor's examination, or at the trial on a complaint objecting to a discharge. The court may entertain a motion to declare an implied waiver of discharge or may do so on its own initiative. Prior to declaring such a waiver, however, the court must hold a hearing upon notice on the implied waiver issue.[72] It is not clear whether the implied waiver rule survives the adoption of the Bankruptcy Code. The Code is silent on implied waivers, and therefore, until new rules are promulgated, this question will remain unanswered. Nevertheless, the debtor's failure to appear at the meeting of creditors or any other meeting or trial in the case after being ordered to do so may constitute the sixth ground for objection.[73]

¶ 3.04 PROCEDURES RELATING TO OBJECTIONS TO DISCHARGE

The Bankruptcy Code was designed to deal with substantive bankruptcy law and therefore does not deal with procedures relating to discharge. It is anticipated that new Bankruptcy Rules of Procedure will be promulgated in the future to deal with the method for granting or objecting to a discharge.[74] 'Until that time, the present Rules which predate the Code remain effective to the extent that they are consistent with the new statute.[75]

[1] In the Absence of an Objection

Generally speaking, an individual debtor will receive a discharge automatically and without the need to plead for one. The mere absence

---

[71] 11 U.S.C. § 727(a)(10). This section of the Code supersedes B. Rule 405.

[72] B. Rule 406.

[73] 11 U.S.C. § 727(a)(6). See ¶ 3.03[6].

[74] See H.R. Rep. No. 95-595, note 6 *supra*, at 300.

[75] B.R.A. § 405(d). See Sugg. Int. B. Rule 4002; B. Rule 404.

of an objection will usually result in a discharge as a matter of course.

There are a few instances, however, in which the court may deny the individual debtor a discharge in the absence of an objection. First, if the court approved a written waiver of discharge the debtor will not receive one. Second, if it appears that the debtor has failed to attend and submit to an examination at the meeting of creditors or at any meeting specially called for that purpose, the judge may on the court's own initiative hold a hearing to determine whether the debtor waived a discharge by implication.[76]

A third exception to the automatic discharge rule that may cause confusion under the Code relates to the failure to pay the filing fee. The former Bankruptcy Act and the present Bankruptcy Rules provide for a denial of discharge on the basis of the debtor's failure to pay the required filing fee.[77] This ground may be raised by the court itself. In *United States v. Kras,*[78] the Supreme Court held that an indigent debtor who was unable to afford paying the fee was not entitled to a discharge. The former Act and the Rules do not provide for in forma pauperis cases, which are cases in which poor persons may proceed without paying court fees. It is interesting to note that the new Code does not list the nonpayment of the filing fee as a ground for objection to discharge, but the Bankruptcy Reform Act of 1978 seems to continue the policy of not permitting in forma pauperis bankruptcy cases.[79] Also, the Reform Act continues the practice of allowing debtors to pay such fees in installments over a period of time.[80] May a debtor receive a discharge if the filing fee is not paid in full? Although the new Code does not enumerate nonpayment of the fee as an objection, it is likely that courts will continue to apply Bankruptcy Rule 404(d) to deny a discharge on that basis on its own initiative, especially in view of the Suggested Interim Bankruptcy Rules, which provide that Bankruptcy Rule 404 applies in cases filed under chapter 7 of the Code.[81]

---

[76] B. Rule 404(d).

[77] Former B.A. § 14(c)(8); B. Rule 404(d)(4).

[78] 409 U.S. 434 (1973).

[79] In forma pauperis proceedings in federal courts are authorized by 28 U.S.C. § 1915. Section 246(a) of the Bankruptcy Reform Act creates 28 U.S.C. § 1930(a), which requires the payment of filing fees in bankruptcy cases "notwithstanding section 1915" of Title 28. Accordingly, it appears that fees in bankruptcy cases must be paid regardless of Section 1915.

[80] B.R.A. § 246(a); 28 U.S.C. § 1930(a).

[81] Sugg. Int. B. Rule 4002.

[2] Who May Object to Discharge?

The only persons who have standing to object to the debtor's discharge are the trustee and the creditors.[82] In jurisdictions that have the U.S. Trustee Pilot Program, the U.S. Trustee also may object to a discharge.[83] On request of any party in interest, the court may order the trustee to examine the debtor's conduct to determine whether a ground exists for denial of a discharge.[84]

[3] Time for Making an Objection

The party in interest who desires to block the debtor's discharge must act promptly. After the filing of a voluntary petition or the order for liquidation in an involuntary case, the court sends notice to creditors to inform them of the meeting of creditors.[85] Usually in the same notice, the court sets forth the deadline for filing objections to discharge. The time for making objections may not be less than thirty days nor more than ninety days after the first date set for the meeting of creditors, and the creditors are entitled to receive written notice of this time limit at least thirty days prior thereto.[86] If it appears from the schedule of assets and statement of financial affairs filed by the debtor that there are no assets from which a distribution to creditors can be made, and notice to that effect is given to creditors, the court may set the deadline for objecting as early as the date set for the meeting of creditors and may give only ten days' notice of it.[87] The reason for permitting such an early deadline in "no asset" cases is to expedite their administration.

Despite these time limits, the court has the discretion to extend the deadline for cause, either on request of a party in interest or on its own initiative.[88] For example, if the debtor's examination at the meeting of creditors is adjourned to a date past the deadline for filing objections, the trustee or creditors may apply for an extension of the deadline. One of the purposes for compelling the debtor to appear at the meeting is to give the trustee and creditors an opportunity to examine the debtor

---

[82] 11 U.S.C. § 727(c)(1). See *In re* Meredith, 4 Bankr. Dec. 652 (S.D. Ohio 1978), which held that a state has no standing to object to discharge if it is not a creditor.

[83] 11 U.S.C. § 15727(a)(1). See Chapter 6 infra on the U.S. Trustee Pilot Program.

[84] 11 U.S.C. §§ 727(c)(2), 15727(a)(2).

[85] See Sugg. Int. B. Form No. 13, set forth in Appendix B.

[86] B. Rules 404(a), 404(b).

[87] *Id.*

[88] B. Rule 404(c).

to discover facts that may give rise to a ground for objecting to a discharge.

[4] How to Object to Discharge

A person who wants to object to discharge must commence an adversary proceeding by filing a complaint before the deadline set by the court.[89] A summons will be issued by the clerk of the bankruptcy court together with a notice for trial or for a pretrial conference.[90] The complaint must state a ground for objection to discharge,[91] and, if the debtor contests the complaint by filing an answer, a trial will be held. The debtor may make motions, such as a motion to dismiss or for a more definite statement of the objections,[92] and the parties may engage in discovery.[93] The Federal Rules of Evidence apply, as well as the Bankruptcy Rules governing adversary proceedings.[94] In essence, the complaint seeking an objection to discharge starts a full-fledged lawsuit within the bankruptcy case. At the trial, the plaintiff (objector) has the burden of proving all facts essential to the objection.[95]

[5] The Order of Discharge

If the court grants a discharge upon the expiration of the time limit in which to file objections, or after an objection is unsuccessfully made and the adversary proceeding is over, the court will issue an order of discharge.[96] The order will be mailed to all creditors and to the trustee.[97] The discharge order may be registered in any other district by filing a certified copy with the clerk of the district court in that district.[98]

Let us assume that a creditor files a complaint to challenge the dis-

---

[89] See B. Rules 404(e), 701(4), 703, and Chapter 6 *infra*, on adversary proceedings.

[90] B. Rule 704.

[91] But see *In re* Sturdevant, 415 F.2d 465 (5th Cir. 1969), in which the court allowed a creditor to amend the specifications of grounds for an objection to discharge. See B. Rule 715 on amended and supplemental pleadings.

[92] B. Rule 712(b).

[93] B. Rule 726.

[94] See Chapter 6 *infra* for a discussion concerning adversary proceedings.

[95] B. Rule 407.

[96] See Sugg. Int. B. Form No. 19, set forth in the Appendix B.

[97] B. Rule 404(h). Copies of the order must be mailed within forty-five days after the discharge order becomes final.

[98] B. Rule 404(g).

chargeability of a particular debt but does not raise an objection to the discharge of remaining debts.[99] In such a situation, the Code gives the debtor an opportunity to settle the challenge by entering into a binding reaffirmation agreement with the creditor. However, as will be discussed later in this chapter, a reaffirmation agreement is not binding unless it is made before the granting of a discharge.[100] Thus, it may be in the debtor's best interest to delay the entry of a discharge order so that the parties will have time to negotiate and execute a reaffirmation agreement. For this reason, the Suggested Interim Bankruptcy Rules provide that the entry of a discharge order may be deferred for forty-five days on application of the debtor. Moreover, upon an application made within the forty-five-day period, the court may for cause further defer entry of the discharge order to a specified date.[101]

¶ 3.05 THE EFFECTS OF DISCHARGE

Denial of a discharge means that each and every debt will survive the bankruptcy case. On the other hand, a discharge order has the effect of relieving the debtor of almost all of the debtor's liabilities, thus allowing the fresh start to begin.

Except with respect to certain nondischargeable debts specified in the Bankruptcy Code,[102] a discharge in a liquidation case applies to debts that arose before the filing of the voluntary petition. In an involuntary case the discharge applies to those debts that arose prior to the order for liquidation.[103] In the event that the debtor is involved in a chapter 11 reorganization or chapter 13 debt adjustment that is subsequently converted to a chapter 7 liquidation, the discharge applies to the debts that accrued prior to the time of conversion.[104] Discharge also applies to postpetition liabilities that arise out of the rejection of executory contracts, the continuation of the debtor's ordinary course of business between the filing of an involuntary petition and the order for relief, and other postpetition obligations of the type normally allowable as if they were prepetition claims.[105] Accordingly, in the usual case most debts that arise after the date of the order for relief under chapter 7,

---

[99] See ¶ 3.09 on nondischargeable debts.
[100] See ¶ 3.07.
[101] Sugg. Int. B. Rule 4002.
[102] 11 U.S.C. § 523. See ¶ 3.09.
[103] 11 U.S.C. § 727(b).
[104] See 124 Cong. Rec. H11098 (daily ed., Sept. 28, 1978).
[105] 11 U.S.C. §§ 502(f), 502(g), 727(b).

which is the date on which the petition is filed in a voluntary case, will be unaffected by the discharge.

It is important to note that a creditor's failure to file a proof of claim in the case is irrelevant with respect to discharge of the debt.[106] Otherwise, it would be too easy for a creditor who expects a small dividend in liquidation merely to refrain from filing a proof of claim for the sole purpose of avoiding the effects of discharge. Likewise, even if a claim is filed but is not allowed, the debt is discharged.[107] For example, a claim for unmatured interest on a loan may not be allowed, and therefore the creditor may not receive a dividend based on that claim.[108] However, the debt will be discharged nonetheless.

The Bankruptcy Code is specific with respect to the effect of discharge on these discharged debts. First, discharge voids any judgment to the extent that it is a determination of the debtor's personal liability, regardless of when the judgment was obtained or whether the debtor waived the discharge of that debt.[109] Second, discharge operates as an injunction against the enforcement of any discharged debt, including the continuation of legal process, offsets, or other collection efforts against the debtor or the debtor's property, even if the debtor waived the right to discharge with respect to the debt.[110] Third, the Code provides that a discharge enjoins a creditor from acting to collect a discharged debt against certain community property.[111] In short, the practical effect of a discharge is to extinguish discharged obligations of the debtor.

The Code continues the policy of the former Bankruptcy Act with respect to sureties or codebtors who are not discharged in bankruptcy.[112] With a limited exception concerning community claims against spouses, the debtor's discharge does not affect the liability or

---

[106] 11 U.S.C. § 727(b). See Chapter 5 *infra* on proofs of claims.

[107] 11 U.S.C. § 727(b). See Chapter 5 *infra* on allowability of claims.

[108] 11 U.S.C. § 502(b)(2).

[109] 11 U.S.C. § 524(a)(1). See ¶ 3.07 for a discussion on waivers of discharge.

[110] 11 U.S.C. § 524(a)(2). It appears that this provision of the Code follows *In re* Malone, 4 Bankr. Dec. 1186 (D.N.J. 1978), in which a landlord was permanently enjoined by a bankruptcy court from proceeding in state court with a dispossess action based on the debtor's failure to pay prebankruptcy rent payments. Since "the real purpose of a summary dispossess action based upon non-payment of rent is to compel payment of the rent due," the discharge of the debt in bankruptcy justifies the permanent injunction against the landlord. *Id.* at 1187.

[111] 11 U.S.C. §§ 524(a)(3), 524(b). See 11 U.S.C. § 541(a)(2), concerning community property that is part of the bankruptcy estate.

[112] See Former B.A. § 16.

property of any other entity.[113] Therefore, to the extent that a creditor has a deficiency after receiving a distribution in bankruptcy, the creditor is free to proceed against codebtors or guarantors, even if the creditor has filed a proof of claim or accepted a debtor's plan of reorganization.

¶ 3.06 PROTECTION AGAINST DISCRIMINATORY TREATMENT

When two debtors filed bankruptcy petitions in 1967, there was a tort judgment against them arising out of an automobile accident in which others were personally injured. Although the judgment was discharged in bankruptcy, their driver's licenses were suspended pursuant to an Arizona statute because of their failure to pay the judgment. The state statute specifically provided that mandatory suspension of driving privileges for nonpayment of a tort judgment applies even if the judgment is discharged in bankruptcy.[114] In *Perez v. Campbell,*[115] the U.S. Supreme Court found that the sole purpose of the statute was to provide leverage for the collection of debts despite a discharge and that it therefore conflicted with the fresh start policy of the bankruptcy laws. Accordingly, the Court held that the Arizona statute was an unconstitutional violation of the Supremacy Clause.[116]

In a similar case, a state university prevented a student from registering or obtaining her college transcript because she defaulted on her student loan, despite the fact that the debt was discharged in bankruptcy. She was unable to pay her loan and was hopelessly insolvent because of high medical bills due to a recent and serious illness. She obtained a bankruptcy discharge of her debts, including the student loan, before attempting to register for further studies at the university. Nonetheless, the university refused to permit registration or to provide her with a transcript because of nonpayment of the student loan. Relying on *Perez,* the bankruptcy court in *Handsome v. Rutgers University*[117] held that the university's actions were unconstitutional in that they violated the Supremacy Clause.

The Bankruptcy Code follows the results in *Perez* and *Handsome* by making it unlawful for a state or other governmental unit to discriminate against persons because of nonpayment of a debt discharged

---

[113] 11 U.S.C. § 524(e).
[114] Ariz. Rev. Stat. Ann. § 28-1163(B).
[115] 402 U.S. 637 (1971).
[116] U.S. Const., Art. VI, Cl. 2.
[117] 445 F. Supp. 1362 (D.N.J. 1978).

in bankruptcy.[118] Congress was concerned about the possibility that government bodies might coerce people to pay or reaffirm previously discharged debts by withholding certain privileges and rights, such as by suspending driving privileges or preventing attendance at a public university. Specifically, the Code provides that a governmental unit may not "deny, revoke, suspend, or refuse to renew a license, permit, charter, franchise" or other similar grant to a person solely because the person was in bankruptcy or is associated with a person who was in bankruptcy. Also, the government may not discriminate against a person solely because of the person's insolvency either before the bankruptcy petition was filed or during the case, or because the person received a discharge and did not pay a dischargeable debt. Similarly, a person may not be discriminated against with respect to employment on the basis of a previous bankruptcy or nonpayment of discharged debts. The legislative history of the Code indicates that this list of discriminatory practices is not exhaustive. "The enumeration of various forms of discrimination against former bankrupts is not intended to permit other forms of discrimination." [119]

Discriminatory treatment by state bar associations and medical societies with respect to the licensing of professionals is covered by this provision. The prohibition of discriminatory treatment, however, does not prevent a bar association character committee from investigating and considering the circumstances surrounding an applicant's bankruptcy to determine whether there is independent evidence of bad moral character. This point was illustrated in *In re Gahan,*[120] in which the Minnesota Supreme Court affirmed the decision of the Board of Law Examiners denying an application for membership to the bar. The applicant filed a bankruptcy petition to obtain a discharge of approximately $14,000 of student loan obligations incurred while he was in college and law school. Because he was healthy, single, and not subject to any unusual hardship when he filed the bankruptcy petition, the Board of Law Examiners found that procuring a discharge of student loans "with so little effort to repay or extend" them demonstrated a "lack of good moral character having a rational connection with appli-

---

[118] 11 U.S.C. § 525. This section does not apply with respect to discriminatory treatment resulting from the Perishable Agricultural Commodities Act (7 U.S.C. §§ 499a-499s), the Packers and Stockyards Act (7 U.S.C. §§ 181-229), and Section 1 of a 1944 Department of Agriculture appropriations act (7 U.S.C. § 204).

[119] H.R. Rep. No. 95-595, note 6 *supra*, at 367.

[120] 5 Bankr. Dec. 512 (Minn. 1979). See also Florida Bd. of Bar Examiners, 364 So. 2d 454 (Fla. 1978).

cant's fitness or capacity to practice law."[121] The Minnesota Supreme Court carefully noted, however, that "the fact of his bankruptcy may not be considered,"[122] although the circumstances surrounding the bankruptcy may be relevant. The court characterized the filing of the bankruptcy petition to obtain a discharge of student loans while the debtor was able to repay as a "flagrant financial irresponsibility . . . reflecting adversely on his fitness for the practice of law."[123]

The anti-discriminatory provision in the Code is not without limitations. First, it only applies to conduct by governmental units. Purely private discrimination based on bankruptcy is not prohibited and does not violate the Constitution.[124] Second, as shown in the *Gahan* case, government bodies may continue to consider certain factors surrounding bankruptcy and insolvency, so long as the person is not discriminated against merely because the person sought the protection of the bankruptcy laws. For example, future financial responsibility, as well as the ability to administer a business, may still be considered in evaluating an application for a government contract or loan.[125]

¶ 3.07 WAIVER OF DISCHARGE OF A PARTICULAR DEBT: THE REAFFIRMATION PROBLEM

Prior to the enactment of the Bankruptcy Reform Act of 1978, it was not uncommon for debtors to reaffirm particular debts despite the fact that they were discharged in bankruptcy. Such a reaffirmation was effective as a waiver and, in essence, revived the enforceability of such debts.[126] The reasons for which consumer debtors reaffirmed discharged debts are numerous, including the need to satisfy former creditors when seeking new postbankruptcy loans or to induce secured creditors to permit the debtor to keep possession of collateral. Sometimes

---

[121] *In re* Gahan, note 120 *supra*, at 513.

[122] *Id.*

[123] *In re* Gahan, note 120 *supra*, at 515.

[124] This limitation follows prior case law. For example, Girardier v. Webster College, 563 F.2d 1267 (8th Cir. 1977), held that a private college has the right to refuse to furnish transcripts to students who have received discharges of student loans. See also McLellan v. Mississippi Power & Light Co., 545 F.2d 919 (5th Cir. 1977).

[125] See H.R. Rep. No. 95-595, note 6 *supra*, at 367.

[126] Several states, including New York, require that the new promise to pay the debt must be in writing. See, e.g., N.Y. Gen. Obl. Law § 5-701(a)(5) (McKinney); Jelliffe v. Thaw, 67 F.2d 880 (2d Cir. 1933).

debts were reaffirmed as a result of scare tactics when creditors unscrupulously continued collection efforts or threatened loss of employment. Threats to the debtor's reputation and property and offers of additional cash were also used to induce reaffirmations.[127]

Congress took steps in 1978 to remedy this reaffirmation problem. The Bankruptcy Code provides that reaffirmation agreements are not enforceable against the debtor unless certain requirements are met.[128] These requirements are applicable whenever a creditor and the debtor enter into an agreement, the consideration for which, in whole or in part, is based on a dischargeable debt. Therefore, it applies when a new debt or advance is based on revival of a discharged debt. The requirements for reviving the discharged debt are as follows:

(1) The reaffirmed debt may be enforced only to the extent that it is enforceable under applicable nonbankruptcy law.[129] This limitation is not a significant obstacle because reaffirmed debts are generally enforceable under state law.[130]
(2) The reaffirmation agreement must have been made before the granting of the discharge to be enforceable. The Code prohibits reaffirmation agreements made after the debt is discharged.[131]
(3) The debtor has the right to rescind the reaffirmation agreement within thirty days after it becomes enforceable.[132] This provision is intended to give the debtor a cooling-off period to reconsider the agreement.
(4) Whenever the case involves an individual, and a discharge is either granted or denied, the court is required to hold a hearing at which the debtor must be either informed that a dis-

---

[127] See Stanley & Girth, *Bankruptcy: Problem, Process, Reform* 59-62 (1971); Donnelly, "The New (Proposed?) Bankruptcy Act: The Development of Its Structural Provisions and Their Impact on the Interests of Consumer Debtors," 18 Santa Clara L. Rev. 291, 321-322 (1978).

[128] 11 U.S.C. § 524(c).

[129] *Id.*

[130] See Zavelo v. Reeves, 227 U.S. 625, 629 (1913), where the Supreme Court wrote that "a discharge, while releasing the bankrupt from legal liability to pay a debt that was provable in bankruptcy, leaves him under a moral obligation that is sufficient to support a new promise to pay the debt."

[131] 11 U.S.C. § 524(c)(1). For this reason, the Suggested Interim Bankruptcy Rules provide for a delay in the entry of the discharge order of at least forty-five days upon the debtor's request. Sugg. Int. B. Rule 4002.

[132] 11 U.S.C. § 524(c)(2).

charge has been granted or given the reason why a discharge has not been granted. If a discharge has been granted and the debtor wishes to reaffirm a discharged debt, the Code obliges the judge to inform the debtor at that hearing (a) that such reaffirmation is not required under any law or agreement, and (b) of the legal effect of such reaffirmation and the consequences of a default.[133] This requirement is designed to make sure that the debtor is fully informed concerning a reaffirmation.

(5) In the case of reaffirmation of an individual's consumer debt, except for obligations secured by a real estate mortgage, the reaffirmation agreement is not enforceable unless the court determines that it does not impose an undue hardship on the debtor or the debtor's dependents and that it is in the debtor's best interest, or, alternatively, that it was entered into as part of a good-faith settlement of a litigation concerning the issue of whether the debt was nondischargeable.

¶ 3.08 REVOCATION OF DISCHARGE

The debtor who was guilty of the type of misconduct that gives rise to a ground for objection to discharge, but who was granted a discharge nonetheless because nobody raised the objection, may not be free from indebtedness for long. The Code continues the practice of the former Bankruptcy Act with respect to permitting the revocation of a discharge in certain situations.[134]

The court may revoke a discharge only upon the request of a creditor or a trustee,[135] as well as of the U.S. Trustee in jurisdictions that have the U.S. Trustee Pilot Program.[136] The judge may revoke the discharge only if, after a hearing on notice, the judge finds that at least one of the three grounds for revocation exists.

---

[133] 11 U.S.C. § 524(d). This procedural requirement is applicable in chapter 7, chapter 11, or chapter 13 cases when an individual debtor is involved. The Suggested Interim Bankruptcy Rules provide that the hearing must be held within thirty days after the entry of the order either granting or denying a discharge and must be on at least ten days' notice to the debtor and the trustee. Applications by the debtor for approval of reaffirmation agreements must be filed before or at the hearing. Sugg. Int. B. Rule 4004.

[134] 11 U.S.C. § 727(d). See former B.A. § 15.

[135] 11 U.S.C. § 727(d).

[136] 11 U.S.C. § 15727(b). See Chapter 6 *infra* for a discussion of the U.S. Trustee Pilot Program.

[1] Three Grounds for Revocation

[a] Fraud by the Debtor

The first ground for revocation is that the discharge was obtained through the debtor's fraud and the requesting party did not discover such fraud until after the discharge was granted.[137] In *Keeble v. Sulmeyer,*[138] for example, a discharge was revoked under the former Bankruptcy Act upon the findings (1) that the oaths made by the debtor in his schedules, his statement of affairs, and his testimony were false and therefore constituted objections to discharge, (2) that material misrepresentations and concealment of facts relating to a certain deed of trust and note resulted in the debtor obtaining his discharge through fraud, and (3) that the trustee was denied an opportunity to object to discharge during the case because of the debtor's fraud in concealing the true facts. In essence, any fraud that would have constituted a ground for objection to discharge if raised in the case will justify a subsequent revocation if not discovered until after the discharge is granted.

[b] Concealing the Acquisition of Property of the Estate

The second ground for revocation of discharge relates to the concealment of acquired property. If the debtor acquires or is entitled to acquire property that would belong to the estate and therefore is subject to liquidation and distribution among creditors, the discharge may be revoked if the debtor knowingly and fraudulently fails to report that fact or to deliver such property to the trustee.[139] The debtor should be counseled to inform the trustee whenever the debtor receives property belonging to the estate, especially when such property is of the type that becomes part of the estate even though obtained after bankruptcy.[140]

[c] Refusal to Obey Orders or to Answer Questions

The third ground for revocation is the commission of the sixth ground for objection: the refusal to obey a lawful court order or to

---

[137] 11 U.S.C. § 727(d)(1).

[138] 290 F.2d 127 (9th Cir. 1961).

[139] 11 U.S.C. § 727(d)(2).

[140] See 11 U.S.C. § 541(a)(5), and Chapter 4 *infra,* for a discussion concerning property that becomes part of the estate after the case is commenced.

answer questions.[141] The reader should consult the portion of this chapter dealing with this ground for objection.[142]

[2] Time Limitations

There are strict time limitations with respect to a request for revocation of discharge. Such request must be made within one year after the granting of discharge if the ground for revocation is that the debtor obtained it through fraud.[143] If the second or third ground for revocation is asserted, the request may be made before the bankruptcy case is closed or before one year after the granting of the discharge, whichever is later.[144]

The Bankruptcy Rules provide that a request to revoke a discharge must be made by commencing an adversary proceeding.[145] The moving party must file a complaint and comply with the procedural requirements contained in Part VII of the Rules.[146]

¶ 3.09 NONDISCHARGEABLE DEBTS

The Bankruptcy Code provides for a discharge of debts as an important element in furnishing the debtor with a new opportunity in life without the burden of financial pressures. The debtor would be deprived of a fresh start without such relief. There are, however, several nonbankruptcy policies that justify the continuation of certain financial obligations despite the debtor's general discharge. In weighing the need for a fresh start against these other policies for preserving certain debts, Congress has carved out nine categories of nondischargeable debts, or "exceptions to discharge." [147]

It is important to distinguish between the so-called "objections to discharge" and these "exceptions to discharge." The former relates to the complete bar of a discharge; if an objection is successfully made the debtor will not be relieved of any debts. On the other hand, the pres-

---

[141] 11 U.S.C. § 727(d)(3).

[142] See ¶ 3.03[6].

[143] 11 U.S.C. § 727(e)(1).

[144] 11 U.S.C. § 727(e)(2).

[145] B. Rule 701(4).

[146] See Chapter 6 *infra* for a discussion concerning adversary proceedings.

[147] 11 U.S.C. § 523(a). Compare former B.A. § 17(a), which provided that only "provable" debts were discharged. The concept of provability has been eliminated by the Bankruptcy Code.

ence of an exception to discharge has the less drastic effect of allowing one or more particular debts to survive bankruptcy despite the discharge of remaining liabilities. The nine exceptions to discharge will be discussed separately.[148]

[1] First Exception: Taxes

The debtor who thinks the payment of taxes can be escaped by filing a petition for liquidation is often surprised to learn that most taxes are nondischargeable. As stated in a recent congressional report, "An open-ended dischargeability policy would provide an opportunity for tax evasion through bankruptcy."[149] For this reason, Congress provided that certain tax obligations are exceptions to discharge.[150] In order to soften the blow of excepting these taxes from a discharge, the Bankruptcy Code gives the taxing authority priority in distribution, which often reduces the amount the debtor must pay after the bankruptcy case.[151]

There are three categories of nondischargeable taxes. First, any tax obligation of the type normally entitled to a priority in distribution above general creditors is excepted from discharge.[152] This includes taxes that become due in the ordinary course of the debtor's business after the petition is filed but before the appointment of a trustee or order for relief in an involuntary case. Taxes that may receive a sixth-level priority are also included. In general, this means that income tax claims for which a return was due within three years of the bankruptcy petition are not dischargeable. Certain property, employment, excise, withholding, and other taxes and customs duties are also nondischargeable because they are of the type entitled to priority.[153]

The second class of nondischargeable tax claims relates to those taxpayers with respect to which a required tax return either was not filed at all or was filed late but within two years prior to the bankruptcy petition.[154] The purpose of this exception is to give tax authorities

---

[148] But see 11 U.S.C. § 1328, and Chapter 9 *infra*, indicating that most of these nondischargeable debts may be discharged in a chapter 13 case.

[149] H.R. Rep. No. 95-595, note 6 *supra*, at 190.

[150] 11 U.S.C. § 523(a)(1). Compare former B.A. § 17(a)(1).

[151] 11 U.S.C. §§ 507(a)(6), 507(a)(2).

[152] 11 U.S.C. § 523(a)(1)(A). These tax claims will be discharged whether or not claims were filed or allowed. See Newberg v. United States, 296 F.2d 152 (2d Cir. 1961).

[153] See Chapter 5 *infra* for a detailed discussion of priority tax claims.

[154] 11 U.S.C. § 523(a)(1)(B).

ample time to collect taxes or achieve a secured status by obtaining a tax lien on the taxpayer's property. The taxing authority is not given enough time to effectuate such collection if the taxpayer fails to file a return or files it late and then goes bankrupt shortly thereafter. This provision gives the taxing authority two years to act after the late filing of a return.

Finally, a tax obligation or customs duty may not be discharged if the debtor made a fraudulent return or otherwise made a willful attempt to evade or defeat the tax, regardless of when the debtor committed the wrongful act.[155]

These categories of tax claims excepted from discharge are so broad that it is not surprising that most taxes are nondischargeable in a typical liquidation case.

[2] Second Exception: Debts Incurred by Fraud

The second exception to discharge is based on the premise that bankruptcy is designed to benefit only the honest debtor. The lender or supplier who extends credit based on fraudulent information communicated by a dishonest debtor should be protected against the effects of a bankruptcy discharge. Accordingly, the Bankruptcy Code specifically provides for the nondischargeability of such debts.[156]

The debts covered by this exception are those for which the debtor obtained money, property, services, or an extension renewal or refinance of credit by false pretense, false representation, or actual fraud.[157] The exception also includes any situation in which the debtor used a materially false financial statement in writing respecting the debtor's financial condition that was made or published with intent to deceive and on which the creditor reasonably relied.[158]

The legislative history of the Bankruptcy Code makes it clear that

---

[155] 11 U.S.C. § 523(a)(1)(C).

[156] 11 U.S.C. § 523(a)(2), derived from former B.A. § 17(a)(2). The debtor guilty of fraud, however, may resort to chapter 13 for a discharge. See 11 U.S.C. § 1328, and Chapter 9 *infra.*

[157] 11 U.S.C. § 523(a)(2)(A). This exception also applies when the debtor fraudulently misrepresents an insider's financial condition. See 11 U.S.C. § 101(25) for the definition of "insider."

[158] 11 U.S.C. § 523(a)(2)(B). Compare Section 14(c)(3) of the former Act, which provided that this type of fraud gave rise to an objection to discharge when committed in connection with a business loan. The Bankruptcy Code eliminates this fraud as an objection to discharge, but retains it as a reason for excepting the debt from discharge.

Congress intended to codify *In re Danns* [159] with respect to the refinancing or renewal of debts.[160] In *Danns,* a debtor who already owed $2,019.37 to a consumer finance company obtained an additional loan of $483. State law required that the finance company consolidate the old debt with the new loan, and the debtor accordingly signed a new promissory note for $3,261.96 (which included finance charges).[161] When he applied for the new loan, the debtor intentionally misrepresented that he only had one other debt for $50, when in actuality he was indebted to other creditors in the sum of $14,000. A year later, when the balance owed to the finance company was $2,622, the debtor filed a bankruptcy petition. The finance company maintained that the entire debt was nondischargeable under the former Bankruptcy Act because of the false financial statement submitted in renewing the loan.[162] The court disagreed, holding that only that portion of the loan obtained fraudulently (i.e., $483 plus finance charges) was excepted from discharge. It did not "seem equitable for a bankrupt to be deprived of discharge on all his indebtedness to a particular creditor simply because a small portion of it was procured dishonestly." [163] The creditor failed to prove that the original loan was renewed in reliance on the false statement. In fact, it was renewed (instead of the creditor's making a separate additional loan) only because state law required it. Thus, the only credit extended *in reliance* on the misrepresentation was the additional $483.[164]

The Bankruptcy Code provides that the debtor may receive a reasonable attorney's fee and costs from a creditor who makes an unsuccessful attempt to obtain a judicial determination of nondischargeability of a consumer debt, unless such awarding of fees and costs would be clearly inequitable. This Code provision reduces the pressure placed on the honest debtor to settle a nondischargeability claim for the sole purpose of avoiding attorney's fees and costs of litigation.[165] If the court finds that the creditor's allegations of fraud are not supported by the

---

[159] 558 F.2d 114 (2d Cir. 1977).

[160] 124 Cong. Rec. H11096 (daily ed., Sept. 28, 1978).

[161] N.Y. Banking Law § 352(b) prohibits a small loan company from having more than one loan contract in effect with the same borrower at any one time.

[162] Former B.A. § 17(a)(2).

[163] Note 159 *supra* at 116.

[164] See Townsend, " 'Fresh Cash'—Another Element of a Bankrupt's 'Fresh Start,' " 31 U. Miami L. Rev. 275, 281-286 (1977).

[165] 11 U.S.C. § 523(d). The purpose of this provision is best understood in view of the history of consumer dealings with finance companies. See H.R. Rep. No. 95-595, note 6 *supra,* at 130-131.

evidence, the debtor may recover from the creditor a reasonable attorney's fee and costs. The Code does not, however, give the debtor the right to receive other pecuniary damages, such as loss of a day's work, that the debtor may have suffered as a result of the litigation.[166]

[3] Third Exception: Unscheduled Debts

In a bankruptcy case, the debtor has the duty to file a list of creditors and, unless the court orders otherwise, a schedule of assets and liabilities and a statement of financial affairs.[167] One reason for imposing this duty on the debtor is to provide a mechanism by which the court may identify all creditors so as to provide them with notice of the case. As a matter of course, notice of the case and of deadlines for filing proof of claim forms and for objecting to discharge are sent to creditors by the clerk of the bankruptcy court soon after the petition is filed.[168] Thus, if a debt is not listed or scheduled by the debtor, it is likely that the creditor will not receive notice and may be deprived of the right to participate in the case.

In fairness to creditors who are not listed or scheduled and to encourage debtors to be careful and complete when preparing these papers for the court, the Bankruptcy Code excepts from discharge unlisted and unscheduled debts.[169] To be discharged, a debt must be listed or scheduled with the name, if known to the debtor, of the creditor to whom such debt is owed, within certain specified time periods. In general, if the debt is neither listed nor scheduled in time to permit the timely filing of a proof of claim, it is nondischargeable.[170] Moreover, if the debt would have been nondischargeable because it is based on fraud (the second exception), misconduct of a fiduciary or embezzlement or larceny (the fourth exception), or willful and malicious injury (the sixth exception), but the creditor failed to challenge dischargeability on these grounds because the creditor did not know about the bankruptcy case and the debt was unlisted and unscheduled within the time limit for making such a challenge, the failure to list or schedule the debt consti-

---

[166] A former version of H.R. 8200, the bill to establish the Bankruptcy Code, provided for recovery of actual monetary damages. This provision was removed prior to passage of H.R. 8200. See 124 Cong. Rec. H11096 (daily ed., Sept. 28, 1978).

[167] 11 U.S.C. § 521(1).

[168] See Sugg. Int. B. Rule 2003; Sugg. Int. B. Form No. 13, set forth in the Appendix B; ¶ 3.04[3].

[169] 11 U.S.C. § 523(a)(3). This provision derives from Section 17(a)(3) of the former Act.

[170] See Chapter 5 *infra* for a discussion on the filing of a proof of claim.

tutes, in and of itself, sufficient grounds for rendering the debt nondischargeable.[171]

Since the purpose of this exception is based on fairness to creditors who are not notified of the bankruptcy case, a debt will be discharged despite the failure to list or schedule it if the creditor involved has received notice in some other manner or has actual knowledge of the case in time to file a proof of claim or, if applicable, a timely complaint to declare a debt nondischargeable on the grounds mentioned above.[172] Thus, if a creditor hears about the debtor's bankruptcy through the grapevine or reads about it in a newspaper and, with reasonable diligence, is able to file a timely proof of claim or complaint for determination of dischargeability, the question of whether or not the debt was listed or scheduled will be irrelevant, and the third exception to discharge will not apply. Of course, if the creditor learns of the bankruptcy after the deadline for filing a proof of claim, the debt will not be discharged.[173]

It should be pointed out that the timely listing or scheduling of the debt is all that is required of the debtor. If the court fails to send notice to the creditor or if, for some reason, the creditor is not actually informed of the bankruptcy, the debt will be discharged nonetheless. The question of actual notice becomes relevant only when the debtor fails to list or schedule the debt.

[4] Fourth Exception: Embezzlement, Larceny, and Fiduciary's Fraud

The fourth exception to discharge includes any debts arising out of the debtor's embezzlement or larceny, whether or not the debtor was acting in a fiduciary capacity at the time of the misconduct.[174] Congress

---

[171] 11 U.S.C. § 523(a)(3)(B).

[172] 11 U.S.C. § 523(a)(3). Verbal notice to the creditor is sufficient to establish that the creditor has actual knowledge. Lincoln Rochester Trust Co. v. Pearl, 60 Misc. 2d 631, 303 N.Y.S.2d. 200 (Sup. Ct. Monroe County 1969). The burden of establishing actual notice is on the debtor, and the burden may not be met by proving the mere publication of notice in a newspaper. Michigan Consol. Gas Co. v. Wilson, 4 Mich. App. 188, 144 N.W.2d 682 (1966).

[173] The Bankruptcy Code follows Birkett v. Columbia Bank, 195 U.S. 345 (1904), in that the actual knowledge must have been obtained in time for the creditor to participate in the bankruptcy case.

[174] 11 U.S.C. § 523(a)(4). Compare Section 17(a)(4) of the former Bankruptcy Act, which included in this exception only embezzlement and larceny committed by a fiduciary. See Crawford v. Burke, 195 U.S. 176 (1904), in which the Supreme Court construed former Seciton 17(a)(4) as being limited to fiduciary's acts.

intended to include in this category willful and malicious conversions of property, even if the debtor intends wrongfully to borrow property for only a short period of time with no intent to inflict injury.[175] Although the debtor may not intend to cause injury by temporarily using the converted property, any liability that does result from actual injury to the rightful owner will be a nondischargeable debt. Such willful misconduct by the debtor which injures another and causes damage justifies permitting the debtor's liability to survive a bankruptcy case.

Also included in the fourth exception is certain misconduct by fiduciaries. The Code provides that debts based on fraud or defalcation by a person acting in a fiduciary capacity shall not be discharged.[176] The kind of fiduciary relationship covered by this exception is illustrated in *In re Romero,*[177] which was based on a similar provision of the former Bankruptcy Act.[178] A contractor was advanced funds by the property owner for the specific purpose of paying laborers, materialmen, and subcontractors. The contractor intentionally misrepresented that he used the funds to make such payment, and, relying on this statement, the owner made further advances for the same purpose. New Mexico law requires a contractor to use advanced funds in accordance with the purpose for which the advancement is made.[179] "That Romero was acting in a fiduciary capacity imposed by law . . . is evidenced by the fact that his obligation not to divert advances is imposed by statute."[180] When the contractor filed a bankruptcy petition, his debt to the owner arising out of the failure to pay laborers, materialmen, and subcontractors was declared nondischargeable on the ground that it was based on fraud by a person acting in a fiduciary capacity.[181]

A debt based on defalcation by a fiduciary is also covered by this exception. Courts have been struggling for years to define defalcation, which is used in the former Bankruptcy Act as well as in the new Code.

---

[175] See H.R. Rep. No. 95-595, note 6 *supra*, at 364.

[176] 11 U.S.C. § 523(a)(4).

[177] 535 F.2d 618 (10th Cir. 1976).

[178] Former B.A. § 17(a)(4).

[179] N.M. Stat. Ann. § 67-35-26 (1953).

[180] Note 177 *supra* at 621-622.

[181] Compare *In re* Thornton, 544 F.2d 1005 (9th Cir. 1976), in which the court held that an employer's obligation to hold certain deducted amounts from employees' wages for an employee benefit fund did not create a fiduciary relationship despite a state statute that mandates the creation of a trust. "While Oregon law may impose a trusteeship upon an employer who misappropriates the monies he is contractually obligated to deduct, such a trust does not convert the employer's status to that of a fiduciary for the purposes of § 17(a)(4) of the Bankruptcy Act." *Id.* at 1007.

"A defalcation clearly requires acts amounting to misconduct or reflecting bad faith, and not merely inadvertence, mistake or negligence. . . . But the conduct does not have to be criminal or malicious, only willful and wrongful."[182] For example, when a receiver in a mortgage foreclosure withdrew and spent funds in accordance with a lower court order, he was guilty of defalcation, and his obligation to repay the funds after the court order was modified on appeal was declared nondischargeable. The receiver knew that the order might be appealed and therefore should not have withdrawn the funds until the time for appeal expired or the higher court ruled on the appeal.[183] As another court had indicated, defalcation is not a synonym for fraud, embezzlement, or misappropriation, but has a broader meaning relative to the failure of a fiduciary to account for money received in a fiduciary capacity as a result of misconduct.[184]

[5] Fifth Exception: Alimony, Maintenance, and Support

The policy in favor of giving the poor but honest debtor a fresh start in bankruptcy is subordinate to the more compelling interests of the debtor's family members in continuing to receive financial support. This ranking of priorities is manifested in the fifth exception to discharge, which applies to any debt owed to a spouse, former spouse, or child of the debtor, for alimony, maintenance, or support in connection with a separation agreement, divorce decree, or property settlement agreement.[185]

The exception for alimony, maintenance, and support obligations does not apply if such an obligation is assigned to another entity by the debtor's family member.[186] The Bankruptcy Code rejects such cases as *Williams v. Department of Social and Health Services,*[187] in which the court declared nondischargeable the claim of a government agency based on the recoupment of public assistance funds used for the benefit of the debtor's dependent children. The court focused on the govern-

---

[182] Kadish v. PHX.-Scotts. Sports Co., 466 P.2d 794, 798 (Ariz. 1970).

[183] Central Hanover Bank & Trust Co. v. Herbst, 93 F.2d 510 (2d Cir. 1937).

[184] Ivy v. Plyler, 246 Cal. App. 2d 678, 54 Cal. Rptr. 894 (1966). See also Western Sur. Co. v. Reed, 79 N.M. 647, 447 P.2d 672 (1968).

[185] 11 U.S.C. § 523(a)(5). This exception derives from Section 17(a)(7) of the former Bankruptcy Act. It is interesting to note that this is the only type of debt that may not be discharged in a chapter 13 debt adjustment case. See 11 U.S.C. § 1328, and Chapter 9 *infra.*

[186] 11 U.S.C. § 523(a)(5)(A).

[187] 529 F.2d 1264 (9th Cir. 1976).

ment agency's right to be subrogated to the welfare recipient's right to support from his parents and, accordingly, viewed the agency's claim against the debtor as one for "support" within the meaning of the former Bankruptcy Act. Under the new Code, a debt for alimony, maintenance, or support is dischargeable unless it is owed *directly* to a spouse, former spouse, or child of the debtor.[188]

The Bankruptcy Code makes it clear that the mere labeling of an obligation as one for alimony, maintenance, or support will not, in and of itself, render it nondischargeable. This will probably lead to litigation concerning the fine distinction between nondischargeable alimony obligations and dischargeable property settlement obligations, an issue that has been puzzling the courts for many years. For example, in *Goggins v. Osborn,*[189] the Court of Appeals for the Ninth Circuit had to decide whether a particular agreement between spouses which was later incorporated into a divorce decree gave rise to alimony obligations or was merely a property settlement. The court held that the debt arising from the agreement was discharged because the agreement dealt primarily with the division of property consisting of the family home and a partnership business operated by the spouses. The court discussed the difference between alimony and a property settlement:

> Alimony is an allowance which a husband is required to pay his wife for her maintenance following or pending her divorce or legal separation from him. It may also include an award made for the support of minor children. Although parties may contract as between themselves concerning the amount of alimony the allowance of alimony is incidental to the divorce procedure and requires the court's intervention to give it validity.
>
> A decree providing for alimony, whether or not based upon a contract, may be modified or terminated upon the death of the husband, the remarriage of the wife or a change in the financial condition of the parties. Bankruptcy will not relieve a husband of his obligation to make alimony payments. For the willful refusal of the husband to pay alimony, contempt proceedings will lie. . . .
>
> A property settlement agreement deals with the division of property belonging to a husband and wife. A wife is free to settle her claims against her husband's property by private agreement.

---

[188] Consistent with this provision, the Bankruptcy Reform Act of 1978 repealed 42 U.S.C. § 656(b) (Social Security Act § 456(b)), which provided that a child-support obligation assigned to a state under the Social Security Act could not be released in bankruptcy. B.R.A. § 328.

[189] 237 F.2d 186 (9th Cir. 1956).

> For a consideration, she may waive all claims for support. A decree incorporating a property settlement agreement gives rise to legal consequences which are different from those involving alimony.
>
> The provisions of a property settlement agreement are governed by the law of contracts. When approved by the court, they may not be modified without the consent of the parties unless there was fraud or collusion. The rights and obligations they create survive the parties and are not affected by changing conditions such as the remarriage of the wife or inability of the husband to pay. They may be discharged by bankruptcy. The payments cannot be enforced by contempt proceedings.[190]

Legislative history relating to the Bankruptcy Code indicates that federal bankruptcy law will govern the determination of whether a debt is in the nature of alimony, maintenance, or support.[191] This is a departure from the previous practice of resorting to state law on this issue.[192] Consequently, it may be difficult to rely on prior case law to predict the outcome of future litigation. For example, it remains to be seen whether bankruptcy courts will follow those cases that have included as alimony a husband's obligation to pay his former wife's attorney's fees incurred during the divorce proceeding.[193] Congress did express the thought, however, that an obligation of a spouse to a third party assumed by the debtor in connection with a separation agreement, property settlement agreement, or divorce proceeding, is dischargeable to the extent that payment of it by the debtor is not in the nature of alimony, maintenance, or support.[194]

[6] Sixth Exception: Willful and Malicious Injury

The Bankruptcy Code continues the policy of the former Act with respect to debts for willful and malicious injury caused by the debtor.[195] When a person or entity is injured or property is damaged as a result of willful and malicious conduct of the debtor, the debtor's liability

---

[190] *Id.* at 188-189 (footnotes omitted).

[191] See H.R. Rep. No. 95-595, note 6 *supra*, at 364.

[192] See, e.g., *In re* Waller, 494 F.2d 447 (6th Cir. 1974), in which the federal court looked to Ohio law to determine whether a particular obligation was one to pay alimony.

[193] See, e.g., *In re* Nunnally, 506 F.2d 1024 (5th Cir. 1975).

[194] 124 Cong. Rec. H11096 (daily ed., Sept. 28, 1978).

[195] See former B.A. § 17(a)(8).

arising therefrom is not dischargeable.[196] This exception covers debts arising out of willful and malicious conversions of property.[197]

In 1904, the Supreme Court in *Tinker v. Colwell*[198] construed "willful and malicious" under the former Bankruptcy Act so as to include the situation in which the debtor committed criminal conversation with the claimant's wife despite the absence of personal malevolence toward the husband.[199] The debtor's conduct "itself necessarily implies" malice sufficient to bring it within the scope of the exception to discharge; "it is not necessary that the cause of action be based upon special malice."[200] This case set the trend toward the application of the loose standard of reckless disregard for determining whether an act was malicious. The use of this standard is illustrated in *Den Haerynck v. Thompson,*[201] which involved a liability arising out of an automobile accident in which a minor was killed. The child's death was caused by the debtor's negligence while under the influence of liquor. The debtor was speeding with a wanton disregard for the safety of others, and therefore his liability to the child's father was based on "willful and malicious injury." The fact that the debtor had no intention to injure was considered irrelevant.

Although the same words, "willful and malicious," are used in the Bankruptcy Code, it is important to note that Congress expressed an intention to reject any broad interpretation of these words in connection with the new law. A congressional report on the Bankruptcy Reform Act of 1978 states that "to the extent that *Tinker v. Colwell* . . . held that a looser standard is intended, and to the extent that other cases have relied on *Tinker* to apply a 'reckless disregard' standard, they are

---

[196] 11 U.S.C. § 523(a)(6).

[197] Debts arising from the willful conversion of property were excepted from discharge under Section 17(a)(2) of the former Bankruptcy Act. In the Code, the sixth exception for willful and malicious injury to another entity or property of another is intended to include any willful and malicious conversion. See 124 Cong. Rec. H11096 (daily ed., Sept. 28, 1978). For an illustration of a nondischargeable debt arising from conversion of property, see McIntyre v. Kavanaugh, 242 U.S. 138 (1916), in which a stockbroker wrongfully sold securities held as collateral for a loan and converted the proceeds.

[198] 193 U.S. 473 (1904).

[199] Criminal conversation is a cause of action based on the seduction of the plaintiff's spouse by a third party. See generally Prosser, *Handbook of the Law of Torts* § 118 (3d ed. 1964).

[200] 193 U.S. at 485.

[201] 228 F.2d 72 (10th Cir. 1955). See also Note, "Bankruptcy—Survival of Liability for Willful and Malicious Injury," 38 N.C.L. Rev. 384 (1960).

overruled."[202] It will be interesting to see how courts interpret "willful and malicious" in future cases.

[7] Seventh Exception: Fines and Penalties

A person should not be permitted to avoid penal sanctions for wrongdoing by filing a petition for liquidation. Accordingly, any obligation to pay a fine, penalty, or forfeiture owed to a governmental unit will remain unaffected by the case.[203] Liabilities to pay traffic fines, for example, are not dischargeable. This exception to discharge does not apply to liabilities to compensate government bodies for actual pecuniary loss.

A penalty relating to a tax is nondischargeable only to the extent that the tax itself is nondischargeable.[204] Moreover, tax penalties imposed with respcct to an event or transaction that occurred more than three years before the filing of the bankruptcy petition will be discharged.[205]

[8] Eighth Exception: Student Loans

The Federal Higher Education Act was amended in 1976 to provide that federally guaranteed student loans may not be discharged during the first five years of the repayment period unless a court determines that payment of the loan during that period will impose "an undue hardship" on the debtor or the debtor's dependents.[206] This statute was a reaction to a sharp increase in bankruptcies among recent college graduates that had resulted in the discharge of many student loans.[207]

The Bankruptcy Reform Act repealed this section of the Higher Education Act[208] and replaced it with a similar provision contained in

---

[202] H.R. Rep. No. 95-595, note 6 *supra* (citation omitted).

[203] 11 U.S.C. § 523(a)(7).

[204] 11 U.S.C. § 523(a)(7)(A). See ¶ 3.09[1] for a discussion of nondischargeable tax claims.

[205] 11 U.S.C. § 523(a)(7)(B).

[206] 20 U.S.C. § 1087-3. This provision was effective with respect to bankruptcy cases that commenced on or after September 30, 1977.

[207] In Hayman v. Wilmington Trust Co., 4 Bankr. Dec. 932 (S.D. Fla. 1978), a bankruptcy judge reported that bankruptcies involving student loans, which totalled 760 in the years 1968-1970, increased to 8,641 in 1976. "It has been reported that the Department of Health, Education and Welfare has paid over $500 million to banks for nearly 350,000 student defaults." *Id.*

[208] B.R.A. § 317.

the Bankruptcy Code.[209] The Code provision is broader in scope, however, because it applies to debts owed to any nonprofit institution of higher education, as well as to governmental units, based on education loans.[210]

Pursuant to the Code, an education loan covered by the exception may be discharged only if it first became due more than five years prior to the filing of the bankruptcy petition or if survival of the obligation to pay will impose an undue hardship on the debtor or the debtor's dependents. Courts have wide discretion in determining on a case-by-case basis when repayment will impose undue hardship.[211] After considering a debtor's monthly expenses and income in a case under the former Higher Education Act provision, a bankruptcy judge rejected the government's argument that "undue hardship" requires "exceptional circumstances":

> If the Congress had meant to limit discharges within the five-year period to only exceptional circumstances, they would have said so and offered concrete examples of what those exceptional circumstances were. Instead they used the words "undue" which means inappropriate or unsuitable or not right and not extraordinary. They also used the words "hardship" which simply means that which is hard to bear. In essence, Congress is saying to the Bankruptcy Courts that they are Courts of Equity and if they are satisfied that the repayment of student loans within the purview of the statute would work an inappropriate, inequitable burden upon the bankrupt or their dependents [*sic*] then a discharge should be granted.
>
> In the present case, taking into account the efforts made to obtain work; the jobs attained; the present level of employment; the lack of income to sustain her present style of living, which is at the poverty level, this court is convinced that the bankrupt cannot repay the loan without "undue hardship" to herself.[212]

Does the court have the discretion to discharge only a portion of the debt while allowing the remaining part to survive bankruptcy? In

---

[209] 11 U.S.C. § 523(a)(8).

[210] See 11 U.S.C. § 101(21), which defines "governmental unit." In essence, federal, state, and local government bodies are included within this term.

[211] See, e.g., *In re* Moore, 4 Bankr. Dec. 791 (W.D.N.Y. 1978); *In re* Glover, 4 Bankr. Dec. 786 (E.D. Pa. 1978); *In re* Hayman, 4 Bankr. Dec. 932 (S.D. Fla. 1978).

[212] *In re* Moore, 4 Bankr. Dec. 791, 792 (W.D.N.Y. 1978).

at least one case, a court found that it would create an undue hardship on the debtor to require repayment of the entire student loan. However, it would not be too great a burden for the debtor to repay only the principal of the loan in monthly installments. Relying on its equitable powers, the court ordered the interest discharged, but the principal had to be repaid at the rate of $25 per month.[213]

[9] Ninth Exception: Multiple Bankruptcies: Debts From a Previous Bankruptcy in Which Discharge Was Denied

If the debtor was denied a discharge in an earlier bankruptcy case or if the debtor made an effective waiver of a previous discharge, those debts that existed before the prior bankruptcy case may not be discharged in a subsequent liquidation.[214] Otherwise, the debtor who is denied a discharge will be able to file liquidation petitions in the future until a discharge is obtained. In essence, this exception is merely a recognition of res judicata principles with respect to the denial of discharge in a previous bankruptcy case. This exception applies whether the subsequent bankruptcy is commenced before or after the six-year waiting period.

This exception does not apply, however, if the previous denial of discharge was based solely on the six-year bar.[215] In addition, this exception does not apply to debts that were only exceptions to the general discharge the debtor received in a previous case. In fact, certain kinds of debts excepted from the discharge in a previous case may be rendered dischargeable in a subsequent bankruptcy. For example, if a tax claim is nondischargeable because it accrued within three years of bankruptcy, it may be discharged in another liquidation case filed more than three years after the accrual of the tax claim.[216] Also, unscheduled debts that survive a bankruptcy may be discharged in a later bankruptcy case in which the debt is properly scheduled.[217] Of course, the six-year waiting period must be observed between bankruptcy petitions in order for the debtor to receive any discharge in the subsequent liquidation case.[218]

---

[213] *In re* MacPherson, 4 Bankr. Dec. 950 (W.D. Wis. 1978).

[214] 11 U.S.C. § 523(a)(9). But see ¶ 9.17, and 11 U.S.C. § 1328, indicating that these debts may be discharged in a subsequent chapter 13 case.

[215] See 11 U.S.C. §§ 727(a)(8), 727(a)(9).

[216] 11 U.S.C. § 523(b). See 77 U.S.C. § 523(a)(1).

[217] 11 U.S.C. § 523(b). See 11 U.S.C. § 532(a)(3).

[218] 11 U.S.C. §§ 727(a)(8), 727(a)(9). See ¶¶ 3.03[8], 3.03[9].

¶ 3.10 PROCEDURES FOR EXCEPTING DEBTS FROM DISCHARGE

Soon after a bankruptcy case is commenced, notice is sent to listed or scheduled creditors informing them of, among other things, the first meeting of creditors and the deadline for filing objections to discharge.[219] In addition, the notice sets forth a deadline for commencing a proceeding for challenging the dischargeability of any particular debt with respect to certain grounds.[220] Specifically, a creditor who wishes to have a debt declared nondischargeable as falling within the second exception (false pretenses or fraudulent statements), the fourth exception (embezzlement, larceny, or fiduciary's misconduct), or the sixth exception (willful and malicious injury), must act within the time limit set by the court.[221] Generally, the time limit is between thirty and ninety days after the first meeting of creditors.[222] If no proceeding for this purpose is commenced before the deadline, the debt in question will be discharged and the creditor will be forever time-barred from raising the dischargeability issue either in or out of bankruptcy court.[223]

If a debt is nondischargeable for reasons other than the second, fourth, and sixth exceptions, there is no time limit for seeking a determination that it survives bankruptcy. Any creditor, as well as the debtor, may seek a bankruptcy court determination concerning dischargeability.[224] Even if a bankruptcy case is closed, upon request it can always be reopened to consider the dischargeability of a particular debt.[225] Alternatively, state courts may decide the dischargeability question when a creditor seeks to enforce a claim and the debtor raises discharge as a defense.[226]

The debtor or creditor who wishes to obtain a determination of dis-

---

[219] See Sugg. Int. B. Rule 2003; Sugg. Int. B. Form No. 13, set forth in Appendix B; ¶ 3.04[3].

[220] B. Rule 409(a)(2). Sugg. Int. B. Rule 4003 provides that B. Rule 409(a) applies in liquidation cases under the Bankruptcy Code.

[221] 11 U.S.C. § 523(c).

[222] B. Rule 409(a)(2).

[223] Of course, the failure to commence the proceeding will not prevent a creditor from subsequently seeking a determination of dischargeability if the reason for the delay is that the debt was not scheduled and the creditor did not have actual knowledge of the bankruptcy. 11 U.S.C. §§ 523(a)(3)(B), 523(c).

[224] B. Rule 409(a)(1).

[225] See 11 U.S.C. § 350(b).

[226] 28 U.S.C. § 1471(b). Bankruptcy courts have exclusive jurisdiction, however, to determine dischargeability with respect to the second, fourth, and sixth exceptions. 11 U.S.C. § 523(c).

chargeability in the bankruptcy court must file a complaint to commence an adversary proceeding.[227] The rules with respect to adversary proceedings are applicable and should be consulted by the practitioner involved with a dischargeability problem. If a judgment on the nondischargeable debt has not been obtained prior to bankruptcy, the creditor may request a judgment in the complaint and the court has the power to grant this request.[228]

¶ 3.11 EVIDENCE THAT MAY BE CONSIDERED AT THE DISCHARGEABILITY TRIAL: THE RES JUDICATA PROBLEM

Assume that a debtor committed fraud and deceit to induce a lender to extend credit. Upon the debtor's default, the lender commences a lawsuit in state court to collect the balance due. Although the lender is aware of the debtor's fraud, the complaint in the state court action is based solely on the debtor's default on the loan agreement and does not mention the debtor's fraudulent conduct. Assume further that a judgment is rendered in the lender's favor and the debtor subsequently files a petition for liquidation. In an adversary proceeding commenced to challenge the dischargeability of this debt, may the creditor introduce evidence that is not contained in the judgment or record of the prior state action?

Prior to 1979, courts have not been in agreement on whether the doctrine of res judicata[229] prevents a bankruptcy court from considering evidence that is extrinsic to the record of a prior state court action when determining whether a debt previously reduced to judgment is dischargeable in bankruptcy. In *In re Nicholas,*[230] the Court of Appeals for the Tenth Circuit held that the bankruptcy court must limit its review to the record and judgment in the prior state proceeding. Thus, if the state court record does not contain evidence that would support the allegation of nondischargeability, such as fraudulent conduct or

---

[227] B. Rules 409(a)(1), 701(7). See Chapter 6 *infra* for a discussion of adversary proceedings.

[228] See B. Rule 409(b); 11 U.S.C. § 105(a).

[229] Under the doctrine of res judicata, a final judgment on the merits bars further claims by the same parties based on the same cause of action. In general, the doctrine prevents litigation of all grounds for, or defenses to, recovery that were previously available to the parties, regardless of whether they were asserted or determined in the prior proceeding. See Chicot County Dist. v. Bank, 308 U.S. 371, 378 (1940).

[230] 510 F.2d 160 (10th Cir.), *cert. denied* 421 U.S. 1012 (1975).

willful and malicious conversion, the debt must be discharged. On the other hand, courts in other circuits have allowed bankruptcy courts to go beyond the state court record to find evidence that a debt is nondischargeable.[231]

This conflict among courts was settled by the Supreme Court in *Brown v. Felsen.*[232] The Court held that the bankruptcy court is not confined to a review of the judgment and record in the prior state court proceeding when considering the dischargeability of a debt. The Court recognized that considerations material to dischargeability are often irrelevant to the ordinary collection proceeding. In state actions, the creditor usually sues on the instrument that created the debt despite the existence of misconduct by the debtor. Therefore, questions regarding the debtor's wrongful conduct usually are not in issue until a bankruptcy petition is filed. "They are the type of question Congress intended that the bankruptcy court would resolve." [233] The Court added, however, that the bankruptcy court may "take into account whether or not petitioner's failure to press these allegations at an earlier time betrays a weakness in his case on the merits." [234]

---

[231] See, e.g., *In re* Wright, 584 F.2d 83, 84 (5th Cir. 1978); *In re* Houtman, 508 F.2d 651, 653-654 (9th Cir. 1978).

[232] 99 S. Ct. 2205 (1979).

[233] *Id.* at 231.

[234] *Id.*

Chapter 4

PROPERTY OF THE ESTATE AND EXEMPTIONS

Page

¶ 4.01 CREATION OF THE ESTATE

An *estate* is created by operation of law as soon as a voluntary or involuntary petition is filed commencing a case under the Bankruptcy Code.[1] In general, only property of the estate is administered in the bankruptcy case.[2] Whether or not certain property is part of the estate

---

[1] 11 U.S.C. § 541(a). This section is derived from Section 70(a) of the former Bankruptcy Act. An estate is created in all types of cases, including cases under chapters 7, 9, 11, and 13 of the Bankruptcy Code.

[2] But see 11 U.S.C. § 362(a)(5), which applies the automatic stay to property of the debtor that is not part of the estate. See ¶ 1.09[2].

is especially significant in liquidation cases because only property of the estate is reduced to cash for distribution to creditors.[3]

¶ 4.02 WHAT IS "PROPERTY"?

Before discussing the rules with respect to the inclusion of property in the estate, it is necessary to discuss the meaning of the term "property" as used in the bankruptcy context. Obviously, if something is not "property," it may not become property of the estate and will not be subjected to a bankruptcy administration.[4]

In *Segal v. Rochelle,*[5] the U.S. Supreme Court decided that loss-carryback tax refund claims due the debtor on the date of bankruptcy constituted "property" that became part of the estate under the former Bankruptcy Act. In its opinion, however, the Court noted that the term "property" is limited by the purposes of the Bankruptcy Act: "[O]ne purpose which is highly prominent . . . is to leave the bankrupt free after the date of his petition to accumulate new wealth in the future."[6] Four years later, the Court, in *Lines v. Frederick,*[7] again emphasized that "property" must be defined in connection with the policies of the bankruptcy laws when it held that accrued vacation pay owed to the debtor employee on the date of bankruptcy was *not* "property" and therefore remained with the debtor. The Court noted:

> The most important consideration limiting the breadth of the definition of "property" lies in the basic purpose of the Bankruptcy Act to give the debtor a "new opportunity in life and a clear field for future effort, unhampered by the pressure and discouragement of pre-existing debt." . . . The wage-earning bankrupt who must take a vacation without pay or forego a vacation altogether cannot be said to have achieved the "new opportunity in life and [the] clear field for future effort . . . ."[8]

In *Segal* and *Lines,* the Supreme Court made it clear that state law did not control with respect to a determination of whether a particular asset is property that becomes part of the bankruptcy estate. In essence,

---

[3] See 11 U.S.C. § 726(a).

[4] 11 U.S.C. § 541(a) provides that the "estate is comprised of all the following *property* . . ." (emphasis added).

[5] 382 U.S. 375 (1966).

[6] *Id.* at 379.

[7] 400 U.S. 18 (1970).

[8] *Id.* at 19-20.

assets that are needed for the debtor's fresh start were not considered property.[9]

It is interesting that the Bankruptcy Code is similar to the former Act in that it provides, in essence, that the debtor's property becomes the estate, but fails to define the word "property." It could be argued, therefore, that the restricted definition used in *Segal* and *Lines* is still applicable and that courts may continue to exclude assets needed for the debtor's fresh start. However, this argument is weak in view of a brief statement in the legislative history of the Bankruptcy Reform Act that announces that the Code "has the effect of overruling *Lines v. Frederick.*"[10] Accordingly, it appears that the word "property" under the Code is intended to be broad and includes even those assets needed to give the debtor a new opportunity in life.

¶ 4.03 PROPERTY INCLUDED IN THE ESTATE

The estate is comprised of all of the property in which the debtor has an interest on the date of the commencement of the bankruptcy case, wherever such property is located.[11] This provision is extremely broad and includes equitable as well as legal interests of the debtor with respect to property.[12]

Property that becomes part of the estate may be in many forms. The estate includes both tangible and intangible property. Of course, cash and bank accounts are included. The debtor's interests in copyrights, patents, trademarks, accounts receivable, causes of action, documents, books and records, contingent remainders, future interests, life insurance policies, leaseholds, rights of entry to real property, and other

---

[9] See also Kokoszka v. Belford, 417 U.S. 642, 647 (1974), in which the Supreme Court held that an income tax refund was property of the estate because "it does not relate conceptually to future wages and it is not the equivalent of future wages for the purpose of giving the bankrupt a 'fresh start' "; *In re* Schmeltzer, 480 F.2d 1074 (6th Cir. 1973), where the court indicated that, based on the reasoning of *Lines v. Frederick*, an unliquidated claim for personal injury suffered from an automobile accident was not part of the bankruptcy estate; Nunnally v. Nunnally, 506 F.2d 1024 (5th Cir. 1975), where the court relied on *Lines v. Frederick* when it held that Navy retirement benefits due after the bankruptcy petition was filed were not "property."

[10] H.R. Rep. No. 95-595, 95th Cong., 1st Sess. 368 (1977) (hereinafter cited as H.R. Rep. No. 95-595).

[11] 11 U.S.C. § 541(a).

[12] See H.R. Rep. No. 95-595, note 10 *supra*, at 367.

kinds of interests are included.[13] The debtor's goodwill[14] and trade secrets[15] may also constitute property that becomes part of the estate. Security interests or liens held by the debtor, vested rights in pension plans, accrued vacation pay,[16] and accrued tax refunds attributable to prebankruptcy income or losses are also included.

The scope of the bankruptcy estate under the Code is broader than its scope under the former Act in several important ways. First, as discussed above, the term "property" as used in the Code is broader than that used in the former Act so as to include even those assets needed for a fresh start.[17] Second, exempt property was not considered part of the estate under the former Act,[18] but is included under the Code.[19] By including exempt property as part of the estate, bankruptcy courts have greater control over those assets. In essence, exempt property automatically becomes part of the estate and subject to the administration and jurisdiction of the bankruptcy court until the debtor claims the exemption. If there is no objection to the debtor's claim or if the court declares property as exempt, it is then removed from the estate.[20] A third significant change in the law is the deletion of the old requirement that property be transferable by the debtor or subject to judicial levy under state law in order to pass to the bankruptcy estate.[21] Under the Bankruptcy Code, whether the property can be transferred or levied

---

[13] Many of these forms of property were expressly included in the estate under Section 70(a) of the former Act. Compare Section 541(a) of the Code, which does not list any specific forms of property.

[14] See Mutual Life Ins. Co. v. Menin, 115 F.2d 975 (2d Cir.), *cert. denied* 313 U.S. 578 (1941), which held that a bankruptcy court has the power to sell the debtor's goodwill along with other property of the estate; Merry Hull & Co. v. Hi-Line Co., 243 F. Supp. 45, 51 (S.D.N.Y. 1965), indicating that the test used to determine if the purchaser at the bankruptcy sale is entitled to the goodwill is whether the assets purchased with the name are sufficient to enable the purchaser to "go on in real continuity with its past" (quoting from *Mutual Life Ins. Co. v. Menin*). See also Kripke, "A Good Look at Goodwill in Corporate Acquisition," 78 Banking L.J. 1028 (1961).

[15] See *In re* Uniservices, Inc., 517 F.2d 492 (7th Cir. 1975), holding that a laundry's customer information is property.

[16] See ¶ 4.02. It appears that Congress intended to include all types of property, whether or not they are needed for the debtor's fresh start. Therefore, accrued vacation pay would become part of the estate despite the decision in Lines v. Frederick, note 7 *supra.*

[17] See ¶ 4.02.

[18] See Lockwood v. Exchange Bank, 190 U.S. 294 (1903).

[19] See H.R. Rep. No. 95-595, note 10 *supra*, at 368.

[20] 11 U.S.C. § 522 (*l*).

[21] See former B.A. § 70(a)(5).

upon is irrelevant. In sum, "these changes will bring anything of value that the debtors have into the estate." [22]

It should be emphasized that the property interests that pass to the estate are no greater than the interests held by the debtor when the petition is filed. If the debtor had an equitable interest only, the estate's interest is similarly limited. For example, if the debtor contracted to purchase real estate prior to bankruptcy, but the deed did not yet pass, the estate's interest in the land is no greater than the debtor's equitable interest under nonbankruptcy law. On the other hand, if the debtor had only bare legal title but no equitable interest, the estate gets the same bare legal title.[23] Thus, if the debtor's right to property in the debtor's possession was the subject of a constructive trust for somebody else's benefit, the estate's interest is also subject to the trust. To illustrate, if the debtor had incurred medical bills that were covered by insurance, and the insurance company had sent payment to the debtor before the medical bills were paid, the payment would actually be held in a constructive trust for the person to whom the bill was owed. If the debtor filed a bankruptcy petition while holding this payment, the estate's interest in the payment would be limited by the constructive trust.[24]

[1] The Debtor's Powers

Let us assume that the debtor is a trustee of a testamentary trust at the time the bankruptcy petition is filed. Does the principal or income of the trust become part of the bankruptcy estate for distribution to creditors? The answer to this question depends on whether the debtor has on the date of bankruptcy the right to exercise the trustee powers for the debtor's own benefit. For example, if the debtor has the power pursuant to the trust document to distribute income or the principal of the trust for the debtor's own benefit, the bankruptcy estate receives the same power, and, accordingly, the bankruptcy trustee may exercise the power and obtain the assets of the trust. However, the Bankruptcy Code provides that such powers of the debtor do not pass to the bankruptcy estate if they may only be exercised solely for the benefit of an entity other than the debtor.[25] Therefore, if the terms of the testamentary trust prevent the debtor from exercising the trust

---

[22] H.R. Rep. No. 95-595, note 10 *supra*, at 176.

[23] 11 U.S.C. § 541(d).

[24] This illustration was used in a congressional report on the Code. H.R. Rep. No. 95-595, note 10 *supra*, at 368.

[25] 11 U.S.C. § 541(b). This section is derived from Section 70(a)(3) of the former Bankruptcy Act.

powers to distribute the income or principal for the debtor's personal benefit, these powers do not become part of the bankruptcy estate. The rationale behind this distinction is that creditors of the debtor have no interest in a trust when the debtor as trustee has no power to receive the benefits of it.[26]

The same rule applies to other types of powers the debtor has when the bankruptcy case commences. A power of appointment, for example, also passes to the estate unless it must be exercised solely for the benefit of someone other than the debtor.

[2] Interests in Community Property

Several states have community property laws that make acquisitions by one spouse after the marriage the community property of both husband and wife.[27] These laws have created complex problems in cases under the former Bankruptcy Act involving only one spouse. In essence, community property acquired after the bankruptcy and discharge of one spouse could have been subjected to levy by a discharged creditor if the nonbankrupt spouse was also liable on the debt. Because the postbankruptcy property of the bankrupt spouse becomes community property, the bankrupt spouse was not effectively released from discharged debts so long as creditors could reach this property by relying on their rights against the nonbankrupt spouse. For this reason a bankruptcy discharge for a debtor residing in a community property state did not give adequate relief from indebtedness.[28]

The Bankruptcy Code takes three steps to clear up this confusion and to protect the bankrupt spouse in community property states. First, the community property interests of both the debtor and the nonbank-

---

[26] See Parker v. Klochko Equip. Rental Co., 590 F.2d 649 (6th Cir. 1979). Building construction funds due a subcontractor on a public construction project were subject to a statutory trust fund for the benefit of materialmen. After the subcontractor filed a bankruptcy petition, the court held that the trust funds were not part of the bankruptcy estate because the materialmen owned the equitable interests in the fund and the debtor as trustee of the fund had no power to use it for its own benefit. Accordingly, payments from the fund to materialmen within four months of bankruptcy could not constitute a preference.

[27] At the time the Bankruptcy Code was enacted, there were eight states with such laws. The states are Arizona, California, Idaho, Louisiana, Nevada, New Mexico, Texas, and Washington. H.R. Rep. No. 95-595, note 10 *supra*, at 176 n.18.

[28] See Pedlar, "The Implications of the New Community Property Laws for Creditors' Remedies and Bankruptcy," 63 Cal. L. Rev. 1610 (1975).

rupt spouse are now included in the bankruptcy estate and may be liquidated for distribution.[29] Second, community creditors of *both* spouses may share in the community property of the estate in accordance with special rules that require a marshalling of assets.[30] Third, after the discharge, community creditors of the nonbankrupt spouse are barred from moving against community property acquired after bankruptcy. In essence, these creditors may proceed in the future only against separate property of the nonbankrupt spouse.[31] The practical effect of these three provisions of the Code is to give the debtor a meaningful discharge.[32]

[3] Property Acquired by the Debtor After the Commencement of the Case

In general, any property acquired by the debtor after the commencement of the case does not become part of the estate.[33] The rationale underlying this rule is that the debtor should be encouraged to be productive and to begin a new financial life at the earliest possible time. Once the debtor makes the crucial decision to seek the protections afforded by the Bankruptcy Code, or once creditors force the debtor into bankruptcy, there is no reason to delay the fresh start.[34] On the other hand, if the debtor would lose assets obtained during or after the bankruptcy case, there would be no incentive to acquire property.

---

[29] 11 U.S.C. § 541(a)(2). For a community property interest to become part of the estate, it must be either (1) under the sole, equal, or joint management and control of the debtor, or (2) liable for an allowable claim against the debtor or for both an allowable claim against the debtor and an allowable claim against the debtor's spouse.

[30] 11 U.S.C. § 726(c).

[31] See 11 U.S.C. §§ 524(a)(3), 524(b). See also Chapter 3 *supra* for a discussion of the effects of a discharge.

[32] This approach is known as the "split discharge." See H.R. Rep. No. 95-595, note 10 *supra*, at 177.

[33] 11 U.S.C. § 541(a)(1). This section follows Section 70(a) of the former Act. For an illustration of this concept, see *In re* Commodore, 262 F. Supp. 30 (D. Kan. 1966), in which the court held that accrued severance pay did not become property of the estate, since it was not vested in the debtor at the time he filed a bankruptcy petition because he did not terminate his employment until after that time.

[34] Nonetheless, caution may dictate that an individual debtor await the granting of a discharge before acquiring property, because otherwise the property will become vulnerable to levy by creditors in the event that a discharge is denied. See 11 U.S.C. § 362(c)(2)(C), which provides for the termination of the automatic stay when a discharge is denied.

This principle may be subject to abuse in certain situations. If an insolvent debtor is able to predict a fortuitous acquisition of property in the near future, a careful and deliberate timing of the petition may result in depriving creditors of such property while giving the debtor a discharge of debts. Congress was not unmindful of this possible abuse when it enacted the Bankruptcy Code. The Code provides for inclusion in the estate of postbankruptcy property in three specific situations. Unless one of these situations is present, however, any property obtained after the petition is filed will remain with the debtor, unaffected by the bankruptcy case.[35]

[a] Property Inherited Within 180 Days After the Filing of the Petition

Any property that the debtor receives by means of a bequest, devise, or inheritance within the 180-day period following the filing of the petition goes to the bankruptcy estate, whether or not the debtor expected the inheritance and regardless of motive.[36]

An interesting problem arises when the debtor attempts to renounce an inheritance within this 180-day period for the purpose of depriving the estate of such property. *In re Estate of Danker*[37] illustrates how renunciation had been used effectively by bankrupt heirs. Shortly after William Danker filed a bankruptcy petition, his father died without a will. William filed with the surrogate's court a renunciation of his intestate share pursuant to a New York statute permitting such renunciations. The bankruptcy trustee claimed the right to receive the intestate share under the former Bankruptcy Act.[38] However, because the state statute in effect at that time provided that renunciation was retroactive to the date of the decedent's death and had the same effect as

---

[35] It is important to distinguish between property that is acquired after the case is commenced and property that merely changes in form. For example, if the debtor has an account receivable at the time the petition is filed, cash received in payment of the account after the case is commenced becomes part of the estate. See ¶ 4.03[5] on proceeds and income from the estate.

[36] See 11 U.S.C. § 541(a)(5)(A), which is derived from Section 70(a) of the former Bankruptcy Act.

[37] 86 Misc. 2d 1081, 384 N.Y.S.2d 683 (1976). For comments on the decision, see "1976 Survey of New York Law," 28 Syracuse L. Rev. 346, 377-378 (1977).

[38] Former B.A. § 70(a) provides that property that vests in the debtor within six months after the petition is filed by bequest, devise, or inheritance becomes part of the bankruptcy estate.

though the renouncing person predeceased the decedent,[39] the surrogate's court treated the situation as if no inheritance ever passed to William Danker. Accordingly, the bankruptcy trustee had no right to receive the inheritance. At least one federal district court, however, disagreed with the result in *Danker*. In *In re Detlefsen,*[40] the debtor became the beneficiary of a testamentary trust within two months after he filed a bankruptcy petition. He disclaimed his interest in the trust that was effective against his creditors pursuant to Illinois law at that time.[41] Nonetheless, the court held that the disclaimer was not effective against the bankruptcy trustee because Congress intended for inherited property to become part of the bankruptcy estate. State laws "would permit individuals who have filed for bankruptcy to divert legacies from creditors to persons with whom the bankrupt is usually on more amiable terms. The supremacy clause requires that such laws yield to apparent congressional intent." [42]

[b] Life Insurance or Death Benefit Proceeds Acquired Within 180 Days After Filing the Petition

If the debtor is the beneficiary of a life insurance policy or a death benefit plan, the bankruptcy estate is entitled to the proceeds if the insured or owner of the plan dies within 180 days after the debtor's petition is filed.[43] Whether the debtor anticipated the time of the insured's death when the bankruptcy petition was filed is irrelevant. Although this may seem harsh when applied to a debtor who was financially dependent on the insured and who must rely on insurance or death benefits for support in the future, it should be kept in mind that life insurance proceeds and death benefits are often exempt and therefore will ultimately remain with the debtor despite inclusion in the estate.[44]

---

[39] N.Y. Est., Powers & Trusts Law § 4-1.3, which was repealed in 1977 and replaced by N.Y. Est., Powers & Trust Law § 2-1.11.

[40] 4 Bankr. Dec. 1241 (D. Minn. 1979).

[41] Ill. Ann. Stat., Ch. 3, § 15, *as amended;* Ill. Ann. Stat. Ch. 110 ½, § 2-7.

[42] Note 40 *supra* at 1243.

[43] 11 U.S.C. § 541(a)(5)(C). Compare the former Bankruptcy Act, which contained no similar provision. Moreover, it was held that, under the former Act, life insurance proceeds that vest after the petition is filed do not constitute a "bequest, devise or inheritance" and, therefore, do not become part of the estate. Klebanoff v. Mutual Life Ins. Co. of N.Y., 362 F.2d 975 (2d Cir. 1966).

[44] See ¶¶ 4.07[1][b], 4.07[2]. See also Vukowich, *"Debtors' Exemption Rights,"* 62 Geo. L.J. 779, 807 (1974).

[c] Property Settlements and Divorce Decrees Within 180 Days After Filing the Petition

Any property interest that the debtor acquires within 180 days after the petition is filed becomes part of the bankruptcy estate if it is obtained as a result of a property settlement agreement with the debtor's spouse or as a result of a divorce decree.[45] This rule applies whether the divorce decree is interlocutory or final. The motive for filing the bankruptcy petition and the question of whether the property settlement or divorce was anticipated in advance are irrelevant.

[4] Property Recovered Pursuant to the Trustee's Powers

The Bankruptcy Code gives the trustee certain powers to recover property for the estate.[46] These powers often give the trustee *greater* rights than the debtor has on the date the petition is filed. The trustee has powers to recover property in the hands of an assignee for the benefit of creditors, a receiver, or other custodian.[47] The trustee has the power to avoid preferential transfers[48] and fraudulent conveyances[49] made prior to bankruptcy. In addition, certain security interests, mortgages, and statutory and judicial liens may be avoided by the trustee despite the validity of these interests as against the debtor.[50] Such voided liens may be preserved for the benefit of the estate.[51] The trustee may invalidate certain setoffs made by creditors before or after bankruptcy.[52] In partnership cases, the trustee may have the power to reach the nonbusiness assets of a general partner.[53]

Accordingly, the Code provides that any property reached by the trustee pursuant to these or other powers becomes part of the estate.[54]

---

[45] 11 U.S.C. § 541(a)(5)(B). This provision is a departure from the former Bankruptcy Act, which contained no similar provision.

[46] See Chapter 7 *infra* for a detailed discussion of these powers.

[47] 11 U.S.C. § 543. See 11 U.S.C. § 101(10) for the definition of "custodian."

[48] 11 U.S.C. § 547.

[49] 11 U.S.C. § 548.

[50] See 11 U.S.C. § 544.

[51] 11 U.S.C. § 551.

[52] 11 U.S.C. § 553.

[53] 11 U.S.C. § 723.

[54] 11 U.S.C. §§ 541(a)(3), 541(a)(4). This provision also applies with respect to liens that are transferred to the estate when a claim is subordinated on equitable grounds. 11 U.S.C. § 510(c).

The same principle applies when the debtor in possession uses these powers in reorganization cases.[55]

[5] Proceeds and Income of the Estate

Income earned from services performed by the debtor after the petition is filed does not become part of the estate. However, the estate does reap the benefit of any income from property of the estate that accrues after the commencement of the case and does not arise from postpetition services performed by the debtor.[56] For example, if the debtor owns an office building on the date on which a petition is filed, rents collected from tenants for use of the premises after the date of the petition belong to the estate because the building itself is part of the estate.

Proceeds of property of the estate also belong to the estate.[57] Accounts receivable owned by the debtor when the case commences, for example, are part of the estate, as is the cash received in payment of the accounts while the case is pending. If property of the estate is destroyed or damaged, insurance proceeds become part of the estate.

Although it is uncommon in liquidations, property of the estate may be used to acquire other property. In a reorganization, for example, the debtor in possession often spends cash of the estate to purchase new assets needed for successful rehabilitation. In essence, the estate is buying new property, not the debtor. Therefore, the new property acquired becomes part of the estate.[58]

[6] Special Provision for Postpetition Acquisitions in Chapter 13 Cases

As discussed above, income earned from the debtor's services after the petition is filed does not become part of the estate. This rule is modified, however, when the debtor is the subject of a chapter 13 adjustment of debts. In such cases, earnings from services performed by the debtor after the commencement of the chapter 13 case but before the case is closed, dismissed, or converted to a liquidation or reorganization become part of the estate.[59] Similarly, the property that the debtor acquires after the commencement of the case and before it is

---

[55] See Chapter 8 *infra* for a discussion of the powers of a debtor in possession in reorganization cases.

[56] 11 U.S.C. § 541(a)(6).

[57] *Id.* This provision also applies when animals owned by the estate produce offspring.

[58] 11 U.S.C. § 541(a)(7).

[59] 11 U.S.C. § 1306(a)(2).

closed, dismissed or converted becomes part of the estate.[60] The reason for this special rule is based on the fact that the debtor in a chapter 13 case is expected to pay creditors using income earned after the petition is filed. It is appropriate, therefore, to make postpetition earnings and assets subject to the bankruptcy administration.[61]

[7] Provisions Restricting or Conditioning Transfers of the Debtor's Property

When enacting the Bankruptcy Code, Congress was concerned that a transferor of property may restrict or condition a transfer in such a way that, in the event of a subsequent bankruptcy by the transferee, the property would not become part of the estate. For example, a donor of a gift or testator of a will may expressly provide that if the donee or beneficiary becomes the subject of a bankruptcy case or becomes insolvent, title to the property shall revert to the donor or the testator's estate. Similarly, it is common for a real estate lease to have a forfeiture clause, which purports to terminate the leasehold upon the tenant's bankruptcy or insolvency. Such provisions that restrict or condition a transfer would, if effective, deprive the bankruptcy estate of assets it would otherwise have.

In response to this problem, the Bankruptcy Code expressly includes in the estate the debtor's property interests despite any provision that restricts or conditions the transfer of property by the debtor, as well as any provision that is conditioned on the insolvency or financial condition of the debtor.[62] Provisions that are conditioned on the filing of a bankruptcy petition, appointment of a trustee, or the taking of possession by a custodian will not deprive the estate of any property it would otherwise acquire in the absence of such provisions.[63] These kinds of provisions will not succeed in shielding property from the effects of bankruptcy, even if they purport to give somebody an option to effect a forfeiture, modification, or termination of the debtor's interest in the property. Accordingly, bankruptcy forfeiture clauses in contracts and leases are invalid.[64]

---

[60] 11 U.S.C. § 1306(a)(1).

[61] See Chapter 9 *infra.*

[62] 11 U.S.C. § 541(c)(1).

[63] *Id.*

[64] Compare Former B.A. § 70(b), which gave effect in leases to termination clauses triggered by the tenant's bankruptcy. See also 11 U.S.C. § 363(*l*), which provides, in essence, that these clauses will not prevent a sale of property by the estate. See Chapter 7 *infra* for a discussion of executory leases and contracts.

There is one important exception, however, whereby a provision restricting transfer by the debtor *is* effective in depriving a transferee's bankruptcy estate of property. This exception is limited to cases involving spendthrift trusts, which may not be reached under state law by the beneficiary's creditors. A spendthrift trust established for the debtor's benefit does not become part of the bankruptcy estate.[65] This recognition of spendthrift trusts in bankruptcy cases should be considered when a donor or testator fears that the donee or beneficiary may become the subject of a bankruptcy case.

¶ 4.04 LIMITATIONS ON THE TRUSTEE'S POWERS FOR OBTAINING POSSESSION OF PROPERTY OF THE ESTATE

The trustee has the right to obtain possession of property of the estate from any entity, including the debtor or a bailee.[66] Any entity in possession of such property during the bankruptcy case is obligated to deliver to the trustee and account for either the property itself or the value of such property.[67] Similarly, any entity that owes a debt to the debtor that is property of the estate must pay such debt to the trustee if it is either matured, payable on demand, or payable on order.[68]

There are several limitations with respect to the trustee's right to recover possession of property or payment of debts belonging to the estate. These limitations are designed to protect the rights of others in the following specified situations.

[1] Property of Inconsequential Value or Benefit

A person in possession of property of the estate is not obligated to turn it over to the trustee if it is of inconsequential value or benefit to the estate.[69] It is important to note that monetary value is not the sole consideration. If property is beneficial to the estate without having significant market value, it must be delivered to the trustee.[70] For ex-

---

[65] 11 U.S.C. § 541(c)(2). The recognition of spendthrift trusts in bankruptcy is not new. See, e.g., Danning v. Lederer, 232 F.2d 610 (7th Cir. 1956); *In re* Nicks, 366 F.2d 754 (6th Cir. 1966).

[66] 11 U.S.C. § 704(1).

[67] 11 U.S.C. § 542(a).

[68] 11 U.S.C. § 542(b).

[69] 11 U.S.C. § 542(a).

[70] See H.R. Rep. No. 95-595, note 10 *supra*, at 369.

ample, certain records and documents may be useful in the administration of the estate despite their lack of any market value.

[2] Setoffs

A person who owes money to the debtor on the date the petition is filed is obligated to make payment to the trustee when it is due. Nonetheless, in most situations the Code permits the person to offset the amount of his own claim, if any, against the debtor,[71] subject, however, to the restraint of the automatic stay.[72] When the debtor and another entity have mutual debts, offsetting is usually permitted to protect the party who is not in bankruptcy. It must be kept in mind, however, that the right of setoff is limited by the trustee's avoiding powers in certain situations.[73]

[3] Good-Faith Transfers or Payment to Another Entity

Generally, the person in possession of property of the estate or an obligor on a debt owed to the estate is required to transfer the property or pay the debt to the trustee. This rule, however, may result in unfair hardship to the person who transfers the property or pays the debt to another entity in good faith and without actual knowledge of the bankruptcy case.

Bank of Marin v. England[74] is a well-known illustration of this problem. The debtor in that case had issued checks prior to bankruptcy. These checks were presented to the bank for payment after the bankruptcy petition was filed. Because the bank was unaware of the drawer's bankruptcy, it paid the checks and charged the appropriate amounts to the debtor's account. The trustee claimed that the bank had no right to pay the checks and charge the account because, as of the date of the filing, the account became property of the estate.[75] In essence, when the bank paid the checks it was converting the estate's property. Nevertheless, the Supreme Court relied on equitable principles when it held that the bank, which paid the money in good faith and without notice of the bankruptcy, was protected and was not liable to the trustee for the amount of the checks paid.

---

[71] 11 U.S.C. §§ 542(b), 553.

[72] See 11 U.S.C. § 362(a)(7), and ¶ 1.09, on the automatic stay.

[73] 11 U.S.C. § 553. See Chapter 5 *infra* for a discussion of the trustee's power to avoid setoffs under particular circumstances.

[74] 385 U.S. 99 (1966).

[75] The case focused on Section 70(a) of the former Bankruptcy Act.

The Bankruptcy Code adopts the Court's position in *Bank of Marin* by providing that any entity that has no actual knowledge of the bankruptcy case may transfer property or pay a debt to a person other than the trustee. So long as the transfer or payment is made in good faith, it will have the same legal effect as if the bankruptcy case never commenced.[76]

It is important to realize, however, that this protection does not apply to the *transferee* or *payee,* but protects only the *transferor* or *payor.* In the kind of situation illustrated in *Bank of Marin,* for example, the trustee may have the right to recover the payments from the payees of the checks as postpetition transfers.[77]

[4] Life Insurance Companies

The Code contains a special protective provision for life insurance companies. If an insurance company is required to make automatic premium loans from property that would otherwise be part of the bankruptcy estate, it may do so without liability to the trustee as long as it acts in good faith.[78] It is common for whole life insurance policies to require the company to apply part of the cash surrender or loan value to the payment of premiums if the owner of the policy fails to pay them otherwise. This use of the cash surrender value, which belongs to the estate as soon as the policy owner commences a bankruptcy case, does not jeopardize the rights of the insurance company.

[5] Privileged Information in the Hands of a Professional

As discussed above, the debtor's books and records are part of the bankruptcy estate, and therefore the trustee has the right to take possession of them. However, the Code contains certain safeguards designed to give effect to valid claims of privilege with respect to records held by professionals. Specifically, an attorney, accountant, or other person who holds recorded information relating to the debtor's property or financial affairs is not obligated to turn it over to the trustee unless

---

[76] 11 U.S.C. § 542(c). "This subsection codifies the result of *Bank of Marin v. England* . . . but does not go so far as to permit bank setoff in violation of the automatic stay, proposed 11 U.S.C. § 362(a)(7), even if the bank offsetting the debtor's balance has no knowledge of the case." H.R. Rep. No. 95-595, note 10 *supra*, at 369.

[77] But see 11 U.S.C. §§ 549 and 550, which protect transferees of certain postpetition transfers. These protections are discussed in ¶ 4.05.

[78] 11 U.S.C. § 542(d).

the court orders the person to do so after a hearing on notice. In addition, the duty to turn over such records is subject to any applicable privilege, such as the doctor-patient or attorney-client privilege. The recorded information may be in the form of books, documents, records, or papers.[79]

Although the Code is silent on the question, legislative history indicates that the duty to turn over recorded information is not subject to a professional's lien arising from nonpayment of services. The Code "deprives accountants and attorneys of the leverage . . . under State law lien provisions, to receive payment in full ahead of other creditors when the information they hold is necessary to the administration of the estate." [80]

[6] Property Held by a Custodian

In many cases, the property of the debtor is in the hands of a receiver, nonbankruptcy trustee, assignee for the benefit of creditors, or other custodian when the bankruptcy petition is filed. Except for actions necessary to preserve the property, the custodian with knowledge of the bankruptcy petition is prohibited from continuing with the administration or disbursement of such property or its proceeds.[81] The custodian is required to deliver the property and its proceeds to the bankruptcy trustee and also must file an accounting with the bankruptcy court as soon as the custodian acquires knowledge of the bankruptcy.[82] Until such notice is received, however, the custodian is not liable for administering the property pursuant to nonbankruptcy law.

When a custodian turns property over to the trustee, the court is required to protect any obligations incurred by the custodian, to provide for the payment of reasonable compensation for services, costs, and expenses of the custodian, and to surcharge the custodian for improper or excessive disbursements.[83] These orders, however, may not be made unless the court conducts a hearing on notice to give interested persons the right to be heard.[84] In addition, the bankruptcy court may exercise

---

[79] 11 U.S.C. § 542(e).

[80] H.R. Rep. No. 95-595, note 10 *supra*, at 369-370. See Browy v. Brannon, 527 F.2d 799 (7th Cir. 1976), where the court ordered that a trustee may examine the debtor's books and records while preserving the unpaid attorney's priority afforded by the attorney's statutory lien.

[81] 11 U.S.C. § 543(a). This section is derived from former B.A. § 69(d).

[82] 11 U.S.C. § 543(b). See B. Rule 604.

[83] 11 U.S.C. § 543(c).

[84] *Id.*

abstention powers by permitting the custodian to administer property if to do so would better serve the interests of creditors.[85]

¶ 4.05 RIGHTS OF TRANSFEREES IN POSTPETITION TRANSFERS

The trustee has the right to avoid any transfer of property of the estate that occurs after the petition is filed if it is not authorized by the court or the Bankruptcy Code.[86] The practical effect of this avoiding power is that a person who purchases property from the debtor after the bankruptcy petition is filed does so with considerable risk. If, for example, an innocent person buys the debtor's equipment without knowing that the debtor is in bankruptcy and therefore no longer has the right to sell the equipment, the purchaser may be required to turn over the equipment to the trustee.[87]

The Bankruptcy Code softens the harshness of this avoiding power by protecting certain transferees who purchase estate assets in good faith. These special protections are as follows:

[1] Involuntary Gap Transferees

During the period between the filing of an involuntary petition and the order of relief, the debtor may continue to operate a business and use or dispose of property as if the case was not commenced.[88] The rationale for allowing the debtor such freedom in using property of the

---

[85] 11 U.S.C. § 543(d). This provision is consistent with the general abstention policy set forth in 11 U.S.C. § 305(a). If the debtor is solvent, the interests of equity security holders must be considered in determining whether the custodian should continue to administer the estate.

[86] 11 U.S.C. §§ 549(a), 550(a). Transfers that occur in the ordinary course of the debtor's business before an order for relief in an involuntary case, as well as transfers in which the good faith transferor is protected pursuant to 11 U.S.C. § 542(c), are also voidable by the trustee under this section. This provision follows Section 70(d) of the former Bankruptcy Act.

[87] See Lake v. New York Life Ins. Co., 218 F.2d 394, 399 (4th Cir.), *cert. denied* 349 U.S. 917 (1955), where the court noted that "there is almost always some injustice or hardship which attends transactions occurring after the filing of a petition in bankruptcy between the bankrupt, acting wrongfully, and an innocent third person, because the loss must fall either upon the third person or upon the creditors of the bankrupt. Whether the line which has been drawn is the best possible solution of the problem is not for the courts to say."

[88] 11 U.S.C. § 303(f). See Chapter 2 *supra* on involuntary liquidation cases.

estate is that, prior to the order for relief, the subject of an involuntary petition should not be adversely affected by the case. Consistent with this policy, persons who deal with the debtor should also be protected. Otherwise, debtors may be damaged because persons would be fearful of dealing with them during "involuntary gap" periods.

For this reason, the Code provides that a transfer between the filing of the petition and the granting of an order for relief is valid and may not be avoided to the extent that value is given for it after the commencement of the involuntary case.[89] Value may be in the form of money, goods, or services, but may not include the satisfaction or securing of a prepetition debt. The transferee is entitled to this protection whether or not there is knowledge concerning the involuntary petition.

[2] Bona Fide Purchasers of Real Estate

A good-faith purchaser of real estate who buys without knowledge of the seller's pending bankruptcy case and who either pays fair equivalent value or buys at a judicial sale may keep the real estate free of the trustee's rights if: (1) the real property is not located in the county in which the bankruptcy case was commenced, and (2) a copy of the petition was not filed prior to perfection of the sale in the office where a deed would be recorded to make a conveyance of such real estate effective against a bona fide purchaser.[90] In sum, a purchaser of real estate is expected to check the place where real estate conveyances are recorded concerning the relevant property, as well as the bankruptcy court in the county in which the property is located, for the purpose of discovering whether the seller or record owner of the real estate is the subject of a bankruptcy petition. If a good-faith purchaser qualifies for protection under this provision but does not pay fair equivalent value, the Code offers some protection by giving the purchaser a lien on the real estate to the extent of the value given.

It is interesting to note that there is no analogous protection for bona fide purchasers who buy personal property from the debtor after the case is commenced.

[3] Subsequent Transferees

Let us assume that the debtor wrongfully conveys a car to a good-faith purchaser after the bankruptcy case is commenced. The pur-

---

[89] 11 U.S.C. § 549(b), which is derived from Section 70(d) of the former Bankruptcy Act.

[90] 11 U.S.C. § 549(c), which is derived from Section 21(g) of the former Bankruptcy Act.

chaser, of course, is liable to the estate for the car or its value. Suppose, however, that the good-faith purchaser resells the car to a second buyer. Is the second buyer liable to the trustee? Although the first transferee is not protected from liability for receiving estate assets, the Code protects the secondary transferee who takes for value in good faith and without knowledge of the voidability of the initial transfer.[91] The secondary transferee, who would not have reason to know that the seller of the car acquired title from a debtor in bankruptcy, is beyond the reach of the trustee.

[4] The Single Satisfaction Rule

It is possible that several transferees will be liable to the trustee based on the unauthorized receipt of property of the estate. If the debtor, for example, conveys personal property of the estate after commencing the case, and the transferee then conveys it as a gift to a second transferee, the trustee would have the right to recover the value of the property from either the initial transferee or the second transferee (who did not take for value).[92] The Code provides, however, that the trustee is entitled to only one recovery so as to avoid giving the estate a windfall.[93]

[5] Lien for Improvements

If an innocent transferee of estate assets wrongfully conveyed by the debtor spends money to improve the property, certain protection is given in the event that the transferee becomes liable to the estate. Any good-faith transferee of the estate's property is given a lien on such property to secure the net cost of improvements made by the transferee.[94] The lien may not, however, exceed the increase in the value of the property as a result of such improvement.

---

[91] 11 U.S.C. § 550(b). Value in this context may consist of the satisfaction of an antecedent debt. 11 U.S.C. § 550(b)(1).

[92] 11 U.S.C. § 550(a).

[93] 11 U.S.C. § 550(c).

[94] 11 U.S.C. § 550(d). Net cost means the actual cost of improvements less the amount of any profit realized by the transferee from the property. 11 U.S.C. § 550(d)(1)(A). Improvements may include physical changes or additions to the property, repairs and preservation, payment of any tax on the property or of a debt secured by a lien on the property, or discharge of a lien that is superior or equal to the rights of the trustee. 11 U.S.C. § 550(d)(2).

[6] Statute of Limitations for Recovering Transferred Property

The Code contains two statutes of limitations related to the avoidance of postpetition transfers and the liability of transferees. A proceeding to avoid a transfer of property of the estate may not be commenced more than two years after the transfer in question. If the bankruptcy case is closed or dismissed prior to the expiration of the two-year period, any proceeding to avoid the transfer must be commenced before the close or dismissal of the case.[95] Usually, the trustee will proceed against the transferee of the property to declare the transfer void *and* to recover the property or its value. However, in the event that a separate proceeding is commenced to recover property or its value *after* the postpetition transfer is avoided, such separate proceeding must be commenced prior to the close or dismissal of the case and within one year after the avoidance of the transfer.[96]

¶ 4.06 ABANDONMENT OF PROPERTY

It is sometimes in the best interests of the creditors and the debtor for the estate to deliberately abandon certain property. If, for example, property is of insubstantial or no value or is heavily encumbered by liens and security interests so that upon liquidation there will be little or no proceeds for distribution to general creditors, the trustee may decide that the expenses of collecting, preserving, and disposing of it may outweigh any benefit to the estate. In such circumstances, it makes no sense to require the trustee to administer the property.

The former Bankruptcy Act did not deal expressly with the abandonment of property by the estate, but courts permitted abandonment in appropriate cases nonetheless.[97] In an attempt to codify such case law, Congress included certain provisions in the Bankruptcy Code dealing with the question of abandonment.[98]

There are two ways in which property of the estate may be abandoned. First, after notice and a hearing and on request of the trustee or any party in interest, the court may order the trustee to abandon any

---

[95] 11 U.S.C. § 549(d).

[96] 11 U.S.C. § 550(e).

[97] See, e.g., First Nat'l Bank of Jacksboro v. Lasater, 196 U.S. 115, 118 (1905) ("trustees in bankruptcy are not bound to accept property of an onerous or unprofitable character"). But see Ottenheimer v. Whitaker, 198 F.2d 289 (4th Cir. 1952), in which the court refused to allow the trustee to abandon deteriorated floating barges because otherwise they would sink and obstruct the passage of other vessels. See also B. Rule 608.

[98] 11 U.S.C. § 554.

property that is burdensome or that is of inconsequential value to the estate.[99] The second method of abandonment is by the trustee's failure to administer property before the close of the case that was properly scheduled by the debtor. Unless the court orders otherwise, such failure to administer scheduled assets operates as an abandonment.[100] This second method of abandonment, however, does not apply to unscheduled property of the estate. The trustee's failure to administer unscheduled property will not operate as an abandonment, even if the case is closed. Of course, in such a situation the debtor or any other interested party may seek an order to deem the property abandoned.

What happens to abandoned property? Normally, property is abandoned to the debtor as if the bankruptcy case never commenced.[101] However, if a person other than the debtor has a possessory interest in the property, it may be abandoned to that person.[102]

¶ 4.07 EXEMPTIONS

Every state has exemption laws that are designed to shield individual debtors from complete destitution by keeping certain property out of the reach of their creditors.[103] Similarly, there are numerous federal nonbankruptcy statutes that provide that particular property or government benefits shall be immune from judicial process initiated by creditors.[104] Recognition of these state and federal exemption laws in bankruptcy cases is consistent with the underlying policy of affording the debtor a fresh start and new financial opportunity. Accordingly, the former Bankruptcy Act, which did not contain specific exemptions for debtors, expressly preserved the debtor's right to benefit from these state and federal exemption laws.[105]

The Bankruptcy Code departs from the prior act with respect to exemptions. The most significant change is that the Code gives an individual debtor a choice between two exemption systems. The debtor may

---

[99] 11 U.S.C. §§ 554(a), 554(b).

[100] 11 U.S.C. § 554(c).

[101] See, e.g., Port of Walla Walla v. Sun-Glo Producers, Inc., 8 Wash. App. 51, 504 P.2d 324 (1972); Kaplan v. Ringland, 66 Misc. 2d 448, 321 N.Y.S.2d 405 (1971).

[102] See H.R. Rep. No. 95-595, note 10 *supra*, at 377, which notes that "abandonment may be to any party with a possessory interest in the property abandoned."

[103] See Vukowich, "Debtors' Exemption Rights," 62 Geo. L.J. 779 (1974).

[104] See ¶ 4.07[1][a].

[105] Former B.A. § 6.

elect either the exemptions permitted by the laws of the state of domicile and by federal nonbankruptcy law, or may choose the newly created exemptions set forth in the Bankruptcy Code.[106] Any state may, however, prevent its citizens from choosing the Bankruptcy Code exemptions by passing legislation that specifically prohibits such an election.[107] As a result, unless the state legislature provides otherwise, the Bankruptcy Code establishes a minimum exemption level to protect debtors domiciled in any state that has less generous exemption statutes. State exemption laws will continue to play an important role in the few states that have more favorable exemptions than those contained in the Code, such as Texas, Florida, and California,[108] and in states that enact legislation prohibiting the use of the new Bankruptcy Code exemptions.

Before filing a liquidation petition, the debtor and the debtor's lawyer should carefully weigh the benefits of both exemption systems available under the Code to determine which system is most advantageous for the debtor. It is important to realize, however, that the debtor is not permitted to pick and choose several state law exemptions and several federal bankruptcy exemptions. The choice is between exemption *systems,* and the mixing of systems is prohibited. In joint cases, each spouse is entitled to his or her exemptions, and there is nothing to prevent them from using different exemption systems so as to maximize the amount of combined exemptions.

[1] The First Alternative: State Exemptions

The debtor who chooses state exemptions instead of the exemptions contained in the Bankruptcy Code is entitled to keep the following: (1) any property that is exempt under federal statutes other than the Bankruptcy Code, (2) any property that is exempt under state or local law in effect on the date the petition is filed in the place of the

---

[106] 11 U.S.C. §§ 522(b), 522(d). See Donnelly, "The New (Proposed?) Bankruptcy Act: The Development of its Structural Provisions and their Impact on the Interests of Consumer Debtors," 18 Santa Clara L. Rev. 291 (1978).

[107] 11 U.S.C. § 522(b)(1).

[108] Under the homestead law of Texas, a debtor may keep a rural ranch of 200 acres regardless of value. Tex. Const., Art. 16, § 51 (Vernon 1955); Tex. Rev. Civ. Stat. Ann. Art. 3833(a)(1) (Vernon Supp. 1978). The Florida Constitution provides for a 160-acre homestead exemption for land located outside a municipality and a one-half acre exemption for land located within a municipality. Fla. Const., Art. 10, § 4(a)(1). Fla. Stat. Ann. Vol. 26A, 1968 Rev. (West). California allows a $30,000 homestead exemption. Cal. Civ. Code § 1260 (West).

debtor's domicile,[109] and (3) the debtor's interest in property as a tenant by the entirety or joint tenant to the extent that such interest is exempt from judicial process under state law.[110]

[a] Federal Exemptions Not Contained in the Bankruptcy Code

Exemptions granted under federal nonbankruptcy legislation are very limited in scope and do not benefit the majority of debtors. Most federal exemptions relate to monetary benefits and pensions, such as payments made under the Foreign Service Retirement and Disability System,[111] the Social Security Act,[112] and the Longshoremen's and Harbor Workers' Compensation Act.[113] Benefits from the Veterans Administration[114] and Railroad Unemployment Insurance[115] are also exempt, as are retirement pensions for civil service employees of the United States.[116]

[b] Exemption Laws Vary From State to State

It is difficult to generalize about state exemptions because of the wide disparity among exemption laws from state to state and region to region caused by many historical and political factors. Many of the northeastern states adopted restrictive exemption laws similar to those then in effect in England. The English exemptions were limited to such necessities for survival as clothing, bedding, and tools of trade. In several states, legislatures granted more generous exemptions after economic depressions in the eighteenth and nineteenth centuries that made people realize that anyone could be economically hurt by fortuitous events. More liberal exemption laws were passed in some states in response to widespread impoverishment following the Civil War. In several western and southern states, extremely liberal exemption laws were enacted to attract settlers, who were permitted to keep their homesteads

---

[109] The state or local law that applies is the one in effect on the date of the filing of the petition at the place where the debtor's domicile has been located either for the 180-day period immediately preceding the commencement of the case or for a longer portion of such 180-day period than in any other place. 11 U.S.C. § 522(b)(2)(A).

[110] 11 U.S.C. § 522(b)(2)(B).

[111] 22 U.S.C. § 1104.

[112] 42 U.S.C. § 407.

[113] 33 U.S.C. § 916.

[114] 38 U.S.C. § 3101.

[115] 45 U.S.C. § 228(*l*) (1970 and Supp. IV 1974).

[116] 5 U.S.C. § 8346(a). This list is not exclusive.

and other property free from creditors' claims. Politics and lobbying efforts by various interest groups also had an impact on state exemption laws. It is difficult to ascertain any other reason for several states to have exempted shares of stock in building and loan associations or cash deposits in savings and loan associations without exempting other types of stock or cash deposit accounts in other financial institutions. The result of these historical and political influences is that among the fifty states there are extreme variations with respect to exemptions.[117]

Another factor that makes it hard to generalize about state exemption laws is that few states have attempted to modernize their exemption policies, while most continue to use antiquated exemption laws enacted decades or even centuries ago.[118] Some obsolete exemption laws still on the books were designed for a rural society that no longer exists. Extreme obsolescence is exemplified in the state of Maine where, even after statutory revision in 1977, five tons of anthracite coal, fifty dollars' worth of wood, and ten sheep remain exempt for any individual debtor.[119]

Another manner in which exemption laws differ from state to state is in the amount or ceiling of each exemption. Some attach fixed-dollar limitations on exempt property. For example, New York exempts "a watch not exceeding thirty-five dollars in value." [120] Other exemption laws have quantity limits, such as in California, where "one vehicle" is exempt.[121] Some quantity limits are extremely high, the most notable example being found in the homestead law of Texas, which exempts a rural ranch of two hundred acres regardless of worth.[122]

Despite the difficulty in generalizing about state exemption laws,

---

[117] For a discussion of these historical and political factors, see Resnick, "Prudent Planning or Fraudulent Transfer? The Use of Nonexempt Assets to Purchase or Improve Exempt Property on the Eve of Bankruptcy," 31 Rutgers L. Rev. 615, 620-621 (1978); Note, "Bankruptcy Exemptions: A Full Circle Back to the Act of 1800?" 53 Cornell L. Rev. 663, 668 (1968).

[118] See Countryman, "Consumer Bankruptcy—Some Recent Changes and Some Proposals," 19 U. Kan. L. Rev. 165, 167 (1971); Joslin, "Debtors' Exemption Laws: Time for Modernization," 34 Ind. L. J. 355, 366 (1959); Kennedy, "Limitations of Exemptions in Bankruptcy," 45 Iowa L. Rev. 445, 448 (1960).

[119] Me. Rev. Stat. Ann., Tit. 14, § 4401(8) (Supp. 1978-1979).

[120] N.Y. Civ. Prac. Law § 5205(a)(6) (McKinney 1978).

[121] Cal. Civ. Proc. Code § 690.2(a) (West Supp. 1978).

[122] Tex. Const., Art. 16, § 51 (Vernon 1955); Tex. Rev. Civ. Stat. Ann. Art. 3833(a)(1) (Vernon Supp. 1978). For a discussion of a debtor who succeeded in keeping nearly 200 acres of land, a $250,000 house, and a $175,000 "party barn" despite his bankruptcy, see Note, note 117 *supra*, at 664-665.

it is possible to mention several categories of exemptions that exist in most states.[123] Every state exempts certain property needed for basic survival. The most common exemptions that serve this purpose are those for food, wearing apparel,[124] household furniture, and homes. Many states have exemption laws designed to protect those items that have significant sentimental, cultural, or religious value that greatly outweighs their monetary worth. For example, Bibles, family pictures, wedding rings, books, seats occupied in places of worship, and domestic pets are often exempt. Other common exemption laws, which are designed to enable the debtor to be financially rehabilitated, are for tools of trade and machinery, books used in business, and farming implements. Most states also have exemption laws designed to benefit family dependents of the debtor. For example, life insurance policies and proceeds are usually exempt under state law.

[c] Interest as a Tenant by the Entirety or Joint Tenant

The Bankruptcy Code makes it clear that if the state exemption system is chosen, the debtor's interest in property as a tenant by the entirety or joint tenant is exempt in bankruptcy to the same extent that the interest is exempt against judicial process under nonbankruptcy law.[125]

It is common for a husband and wife to own their home or other real estate as tenants by the entirety. If only one spouse files a liquidation petition and elects the state exemption system, the trustee's right to liquidate the debtor's interest or to oust the married couple from possession of the property is subject to the same limitations that state law places on the rights of judgment creditors.[126]

[2] The Second Alternative: Federal Bankruptcy Exemptions

In lieu of the state exemption system, the debtor may take advantage of the federal exemptions set forth in the Bankruptcy Code.[127] In

---

[123] These categories are discussed in more detail in Resnick, note 117 *supra*, at 621-627.

[124] See *In re* Westhem, 4 Bankr. Dec. 863 (C.D. Cal. 1978), where the district judge held that a four-carat diamond engagement ring qualifies as an "item of necessary wearing apparel" and, accordingly, is exempt.

[125] 11 U.S.C. § 522(b)(2)(B).

[126] For a discussion of the rights of creditors against property held as tenant by the entirety, see Miller, "Rights of a Tenant by the Entireties," 51 N.Y. St. B.J. 199 (1979).

[127] These exemptions are listed in 11 U.S.C. § 522(d).

most situations, the bankruptcy exemptions will be the better choice because they are much more generous than the exemption laws of most states. The Bankruptcy Code exemptions include the following:

(1) The debtor's total interest up to $7,500 in value [128] in property used as a residence of the debtor or a dependent.[129] The residence may be either personal or real property. Accordingly, a mobile home, condominium apartment, or shares in a cooperative that owns a residence qualifies for this exemption. Burial plots also qualify for this exemption.

(2) The debtor's interest up to $1,200 in value in one motor vehicle.

(3) The debtor's interest in all household goods and furnishings, wearing apparel, appliances, books, animals, crops, or musical instruments held primarily for personal or family use by the debtor or a dependent. The exemption may not, however, exceed $200 in value in any particular item.

(4) An interest in jewelry held by the debtor or a dependent for personal or family use. The total value of this exemption may not exceed $500.

(5) In addition to all other exemptions, the debtor may claim as exempt an interest in any property, including cash, that does not exceed $400 in value. The debtor also may exempt up to $7,500 worth of cash or property if a residence or burial plot exemption is not claimed. If the debtor claims an exemption for an interest in a residence or burial plot, but the interest is worth less than $7,500, the debtor may exempt other property that equals in value the difference between the residence or burial plot exemption and $7,500. The purpose of this provision is to avoid discriminating against the debtor who does not own a home or burial plot.

(6) The debtor's interest up to $750 in value in implements, tools, or professional books used in the trade of the debtor or a dependent.

(7) Any unmatured life insurance policy owned by the debtor, regardless of value or face amount, other than a credit life insurance contract. In addition, any accrued dividends, interest, or cash surrender value of any unmatured life insurance policy is exempt if the insured under the policy is the debtor or a dependent. However, the total value of the exempt dividends, interest, or cash surrender value may not ex-

---

[128] "Value" means fair market value as of the date of the filing of the bankruptcy petition. 11 U.S.C. § 522(a)(2).

[129] For the purpose of determining exemptions, "dependent" includes the debtor's spouse, whether or not actually dependent. 11 U.S.C. § 522(a)(1).

ceed $4,000.[130] For example, if the debtor owns a $100,000 life insurance policy that has a $10,000 loan value, the debtor may keep $4,000 of the loan value as exempt. The trustee has the right to use the remaining $6,000 for distribution to creditors. This may reduce the amount of insurance, but will not deprive the debtor of the policy and will not deprive dependents of insurance protection.

(8) Professionally prescribed health aids for the debtor or a dependent of the debtor.

(9) Many governmental benefits are exempt regardless of value. The debtor may claim as exempt a social security benefit, unemployment compensation, or a local public assistance benefit. A veteran's benefit, as well as a disability, illness, or unemployment benefit, qualifies as exempt property.

(10) Certain rights to receive income are exempt, but only to the extent that they are reasonably necessary for the support of the debtor and any dependent. This exemption applies to alimony, support, or maintenance payments. It also applies to payment under a stock bonus, pension, profit sharing, annuity, or similar plan on account of illness, disability, death, age, or length of service. However, payment under a retirement plan is not exempt if the plan was established by or under the auspices of an insider[131] who employed the debtor at the time the debtor's rights in the plan arose, and if the retirement plan does not qualify for certain deferred tax benefits.[132]

(11) The debtor's rights to receive several other types of payments are exempt. Included in this category are crime victim compensation awards without limitation. If the debtor was dependent on another person who is deceased, the debtor's rights to life insurance proceeds and wrongful death payments relating to the decedent are exempt to the extent reasonably necessary for support. If the debtor suffered personal bodily injury, payments arising from the injury are exempt up to $7,500, but this exemption does not cover awards on settlements for pain and suffering, loss of past wages, medical expenses, or other pecuniary loss. However, to the extent necessary for support, payments for the loss of future earnings are exempt. All of the exemptions mentioned

---

[130] If the insurance company automatically applied part of the cash surrender value to pay a premium, the $4,000 ceiling must be reduced to that extent. 11 U.S.C. §§ 522(d)(8), 542(d).

[131] "Insiders" includes any relative or general partner of the debtor, or any relative of a general partner. It also includes any partnership in which the debtor is a general partner or any corporation of which the debtor is a director, officer, or person in control. See 11 U.S.C. § 101(25).

[132] See 11 U.S.C. § 522(d)(10)(E).

in this paragraph apply to any property traceable to the proceeds of the payments, as well as to the actual payments. Thus, if a debtor receives a $10,000 crime victim compensation award and purchases a new boat, the boat would qualify for this exemption.[133]

The reader will notice that there are monetary limitations on several of the bankruptcy exemptions. It is important to emphasize that these limits apply to the debtor's equity in the property. In essence, if the debtor's equity above liens and mortgages exceeds the monetary exemption limit, the trustee may liquidate the property for the purpose of realizing the excess value for the estate. For example, let us assume that the debtor owns a home worth $30,000 which is subject to a $15,000 mortgage. The trustee may sell the home, pay off the mortgage, pay the debtor $7,500, and use the remaining proceeds for distribution to creditors.[134]

¶ 4.08 PROVISIONS DESIGNED TO PROTECT THE DEBTOR'S EXEMPTIONS

The Bankruptcy Code contains several provisions that are intended to give the debtor reasonable protection with respect to exempt property. Most of these protections are new in bankruptcy law and are not derived from the former Bankruptcy Act.

[1] Protection Against Nondischargeable Debts

Let us assume that the debtor chooses the new Bankruptcy Code exemption system and, accordingly, claims an exemption for an automobile valued at $1,200. After the liquidation case is commenced, several debts are declared nondischargeable. When the case is closed, may nondischarged creditors resort to state judicial process to levy on the automobile if state law does not grant a motor vehicle exemption? It is easy to see that if property that is exempt under the Bankruptcy Code but not under state law is available to creditors with nondischargeable claims, the effect of the exemption may be wiped out.

Congress was aware of this problem, and for this reason, the Code provides that exempt property may not be levied upon for any prepeti-

---

[133] For a discussion of the tracing of proceeds of exempt property, see Dunham, "Tracing the Proceeds of Exempt Assets in Bankruptcy and Non-Bankruptcy Cases," S. Ill. U.L.J. 317 (1978).

[134] See H.R. Rep. No. 95-595, note 10 *supra,* at 360-361.

tion debt, whether or not the debt is discharged.[135] There are, however, several exceptions. Exempt property may be seized to pay nondischargeable tax liabilities and obligations to pay alimony, maintenance, or support.[136] Moreover, valid liens that may not be avoided under the trustee's powers and even certain avoidable tax liens in exempt property will not be affected by the bankruptcy.[137]

[2] Judicial Liens

The debtor may avoid any judicial lien on exempt property to the extent that it impairs the exemption.[138] For example, if the debtor who elects the federal Bankruptcy Code exemptions owns a residence worth $10,000 which is subject to judicial lien for $10,000 on the date of bankruptcy, the debtor may reduce the lien to $2,500 so as to preserve the $7,500 homestead exemption.[139]

[3] Nonpurchase Money Security Interests

The debtor may avoid security interests in exempt household and personal items, tools of the trade, and health aids to the extent that the exemption is impaired.[140] The purpose of this provision is to avoid a practice that was common prior to the enactment of the Code. Creditors making consumer loans often insisted on security interests in all of the debtor's belongings, as well as on a waiver of exemptions. After the debtor incurred financial difficulties, the creditor often used threats of repossession of essential household goods as a means of obtaining payment. Creditors rarely repossessed, however, because of the absence of significant resale value. As noted in a congressional report, in this manner consumer debtors, "ignorant of the creditors' true intentions, are coerced into payments they simply cannot afford to make." [141]

This protection for consumer debtors, however, does not apply to purchase-money security interests. Instead, the debtor is given a right of redemption with respect to purchase-money security interests in exempt property.[142] Also, if the nonpurchase-money secured party had

---

[135] 11 U.S.C. § 522(c).
[136] 11 U.S.C. § 522(c)(1). See 11 U.S.C. §§ 523(a)(1), 523(a)(5).
[137] 11 U.S.C. § 522(c)(2).
[138] 11 U.S.C. § 522(f)(1).
[139] See 11 U.S.C. § 522(d)(1) for the homestead exemption.
[140] 11 U.S.C. § 522(f)(2).
[141] H.R. Rep. No. 95-595, note 10 *supra*, at 127.
[142] See 11 U.S.C. § 722, and ¶ 4.08[4].

taken possession of the exempt property prior to bankruptcy, the debtor may not use this provision to avoid the lien.

[4] Redemption Rights

In liquidation cases, the debtor has the right to redeem exempt personal property intended for personal, family, or household use from any lien securing a dischargeable consumer debt by paying the creditor the amount of the allowed secured claim.[143] In essence, this gives the debtor the right of first refusal to purchase the property. The redemption right extends to the whole property, not just to the debtor's interest, and applies to purchase-money or nonpurchase-money security interests, as well as to other types of liens. For example, if the debtor owns a $2,000 car subject to a $1,200 purchase-money security interest, the $800 equity interest may be exempt under the Bankruptcy Code exemption system.[144] The debtor may also redeem and keep the *entire* car by paying $1,200 to the lienor, even though the automobile exemption has a $1,200 limit.[145] Because the allowed secured claim may not exceed the value of the collateral, this provision also assures that the consumer will not have to pay more than the present value of the exempt property in order to retain it.

[5] Using the Trustee's Avoiding Powers

The trustee has the power to avoid certain transfers and liens.[146] For example, preferential transfers[147] and fraudulent conveyances[148] may be avoided, as well as unperfected security interests.[149] If the debtor voluntarily transferred otherwise exempt property to prefer a creditor or as part of a scheme to defraud creditors, the trustee may recover the property for the estate and the debtor will not be able to claim it as exempt.[150] However, the Code gives the debtor the benefits

---

[143] 11 U.S.C. § 722. In addition to exempt property, this right of redemption applies to abandoned property. See ¶ 4.06. The reader should note, however, that nonpossessory, nonpurchase money security interests and judicial liens may be avoided totally pursuant to 11 U.S.C. § 522(f). See ¶ 4.08[3]. Therefore, in most cases the right of redemption will be exercised in situations involving purchase-money security interests.

[144] 11 U.S.C. § 522(d)(2) exempts the debtor's interest, not to exceed $1,200, in a motor vehicle.

[145] See H.R. Rep. No. 95-595, note 10 *supra*, at 381.

[146] The trustee's avoiding powers are discussed in Chapter 7 *infra*.

[147] 11 U.S.C. § 547.

[148] 11 U.S.C. § 548.

[149] 11 U.S.C. § 544(a).

[150] See 11 U.S.C. § 522(g). Compare Rutledge v. Johansen, 270 F.2d

of the trustee's avoiding powers with respect to exempt property that was *involuntarily* seized from the debtor and not concealed by the debtor.[151] For example, if the debtor's automobile was taken pursuant to a judicial levy within ninety days before the commencement of a bankruptcy case, and the trustee recovered the car as a voidable preference, the debtor may claim it under an applicable motor vehicle exemption. Likewise, if the trustee does not pursue an avoiding power to recover otherwise exempt assets, the debtor may pursue it to recover the property so long as the debtor did not voluntarily convey or conceal the property.[152] It must be kept in mind that the debtor's right to recover property or avoid liens under this provision is no greater than that of the trustee.[153] Also, the total amount of property exempted, including property recovered for the debtor's benefit pursuant to the trustee's avoiding powers, may not exceed applicable monetary limitations on exemptions.[154]

In general, exempt property may not be used to pay administrative expenses of the estate. However, costs and expenses incurred by the trustee in avoiding transfers or liens for the benefit of the debtor with respect to exempt property must be paid by the debtor or from the exempt property.[155]

[6] Waivers

Any waiver of exemptions is not enforceable if it is executed in favor of an unsecured creditor.[156] It is irrelevant whether the waiver is executed before or after bankruptcy. By limiting this ban on waivers to unsecured claims, the Code recognizes by implication that a security interest or mortgage in exempt property is valid unless the debtor or the trustee avoids it under one of the protections discussed above.[157]

Any waiver of the debtor's avoiding powers with respect to exempt property is also not effective.[158]

---

881 (10th Cir. 1959), in which the court held that the transfer of exempt property may not constitute a preference under the former Bankruptcy Act.

[151] 11 U.S.C. § 522(g).

[152] 11 U.S.C. § 522(h).

[153] 11 U.S.C. § 522(i)(1).

[154] 11 U.S.C. § 522(j).

[155] 11 U.S.C. § 522(k).

[156] 11 U.S.C. § 522(e).

[157] See ¶ 4.08[2]-4.08[5].

[158] 11 U.S.C. § 522(e).

¶ 4.09 PURCHASING EXEMPT PROPERTY ON THE EVE OF BANKRUPTCY [159]

A debtor who faces bankruptcy is naturally tempted to salvage as much property as possible. It is not surprising, therefore, that a debtor may purchase or improve exempt property on the eve of bankruptcy for the purpose of maximizing the benefits available under exemption statutes. The difficult question for debtors and their lawyers is whether it is lawful for an insolvent person to use nonexempt assets to acquire or improve exempt property in contemplation of bankruptcy. Unfortunately for those lawyers who must advise their debtor clients, there is no clear answer to this question.

Exemption laws are not intended to benefit dishonest debtors who are guilty of fraudulent conduct that relates to the property claimed as exempt.[160] Accordingly, courts have disallowed exemptions when the debtor committed such a fraud. In *Miguel v. Walsh,*[161] for example, an exemption was denied because the property was purchased with funds that were fraudulently obtained. The question that arises, therefore, is whether the purchase of exempt property with nonexempt funds is fraudulent solely because the debtor intends to file a bankruptcy petition in the immediate future.

It is well settled that the conversion of nonexempt to exempt property by an insolvent debtor is not, in and of itself, a fraud on creditors.[162] *In re Dudley* [163] is a case in point. The State of California granted an exemption for $1,000 worth of stock in a building and loan association.[164] One week before filing a bankruptcy petition, and while

---

[159] For a more detailed discussion of the problem with respect to purchasing exempt property on the eve of bankruptcy, see Resnick, "Prudent Planning or Fraudulent Transfer? The Use of Nonexempt Assets to Purchase or Improve Exempt Property on the Eve of Bankruptcy," 31 Rutgers L. Rev. 615 (1978).

[160] See, e.g., *In re* Gerber, 186 F. 693, 696 (9th Cir. 1911); *In re* Prestien, 427 F. Supp. 1003, 1008 (S.D. Fla. 1977).

[161] 447 F.2d 724 (9th Cir. 1971).

[162] See, e.g., *In re* Adlman, 541 F.2d 999 (2d Cir. 1976); *In re* Jackson, 472 F.2d 589 (9th Cir. 1973). Also, the legislative history of the Code indicates that the debtor may convert nonexempt property into exempt property prior to bankruptcy and that this is not, in and of itself, fraudulent. See H.R. Rep. No. 95-595, note 10 *supra*, at 361.

[163] 72 F. Supp. 943 (S.D. Cal. 1947), *aff'd sub nom.* Goggin v. Dudley, 166 F.2d 1023 (9th Cir. 1948).

[164] Former Cal. Civ. Proc. Code § 690.21, *repealed by* 1970 Cal. Stats., Ch. 1523, § 43, at 3075 (1970).

he was "heavily in debt and clearly insolvent,"[165] the debtor used $1,000 of his nonexempt funds to buy such stock. The court rejected the trustee's argument that the exemption should be denied because the stock was purchased for the sole purpose of maximizing exemptions. The deliberate conversion of nonexempt to exempt assets was permitted in the absence of a showing of extrinsic fraud. In similar cases, courts have held that insolvent debtors may make mortgage payments on exempt homesteads in contemplation of bankruptcy, thereby maximizing the amount of equity free from creditors' claims.[166]

Although the mere purchase of exempt property in contemplation of bankruptcy is not fraudulent, courts have denied exemptions when the purchase of exempt assets is accompanied by *actual fraud*.[167] For example, in *In re White*,[168] copartners consulted with counsel and received advice as to possible exemptions under California law. Despite their intention to terminate their business and commence bankruptcy proceedings, the partners continued to purchase goods on credit and resell them for cash in the ordinary course of business. The proceeds of those sales were not used to pay for the goods, but were used instead to enable each debtor to deposit $1,000 in a federal savings and loan association account and $1,500 in a credit union account, the maximum amounts of such deposits exempt under state law.[169] The court held that there was factual support for a finding of actual fraud in that the debtors acquired credit without intending to repay. Because the fraud was committed to enable the debtors to take advantage of state exemption laws, the trustee was permitted to seize the funds in the exempt accounts.

Several courts have indicated that the *purpose* for which the exempt property was acquired is an important factor in determining whether there is actual fraud.[170] *In re Majors*[171] is an early case in

---

[165] Note 163 *supra*, 72 F. Supp. at 944.

[166] See, e.g., *In re* Wilson, 123 F. 20 (9th Cir. 1903); Gray v. Brunold, 140 Cal. 615, 74 P. 303 (1903). But see *In re* Boston, 98 F. 587 (D. Neb. 1899), where the trustee was given a lien upon an exempt homestead for an amount paid by the debtor to reduce the balance due on the mortgage in contemplation of bankruptcy.

[167] See, e.g., Kangas v. Robie, 264 F. 92 (8th Cir. 1920); *In re* Martin, 217 F. Supp. 937 (D. Ore. 1963).

[168] 221 F. Supp. 64 (N.D. Cal. 1963).

[169] Cal. Fin. Code § 11000 (West 1968); 1935 Cal. Stats., Ch. 723, § 21. The current version of this statute is at Cal. Civ. Proc. Code § 690.7 (West Supp. 1978).

[170] See, e.g., Shanks v. Hardin, 101 F.2d 177 (6th Cir. 1939); *In re* Martin, note 167 *supra*.

[171] 241 F. 538 (D. Ore. 1917).

which a court denied an exemption on the sole ground that the insolvent debtor acquired the exempt property with the motive to deprive creditors of assets. The debtor had purchased certain exempt farm equipment and livestock prior to filing a voluntary bankruptcy petition. The court found that the debtor was not motivated by a desire to own such property but was instead interested in depriving his creditors of assets. The court relied on the testimony of the debtor to prove that his "direct and especial reason . . . for purchasing the property was, as he has expressed it, that otherwise his creditors would have taken everything he had."[172] Based on the debtor's motive, the court found actual fraud so as to deprive him of the exemption.

The use of the debtor's motive to distinguish between those acquisitions of exempt property that are fraudulent and those that are permitted causes problems for the debtor and counsel. It is often difficult to determine the purpose for which a debtor obtains exempt property prior to bankruptcy. This determination is further complicated by the likelihood that the debtor is acting upon multiple motives. Assume that a debtor purchases a television set prior to bankruptcy with the knowledge that the television would be exempt under applicable law. Was the debtor motivated by a desire to own a new television set, or was the sole purpose to deprive creditors of assets and to preserve as much property as possible? It is likely that the debtor was motivated by both desires.

Given that the debtor may well have multiple motives, the outcome may be affected by the skillful preparation and questioning by the debtor's attorney. To illustrate this point, consider a debtor with $500 of nonexempt cash who is about to file a liquidation petition. Assume further that the debtor plans to elect the state exemption system. The debtor's attorney, while preparing the schedules that must be filed, asks if the debtor owns a television set, which is exempt under state law. When the debtor gives a negative reply, the attorney advises, "If you would like to own a television set, you have the right to purchase one now and you will be permitted to keep it after bankruptcy." The debtor, knowing that the $500 will be lost in bankruptcy, uses the money to purchase a television set. The exemption would probably be allowed pursuant to prevailing case law. Let us assume, however, that the attorney has asked whether the debtor would like to keep as much of his assets as possible in bankruptcy and suggests that, "if so, you should buy a television set." This advice might influence the debtor's own

---

[172] *Id.* at 540.

perception of the primary motive for the purchase, despite the real desire to own a television set. It might also affect the debtor's testimony in bankruptcy court when asked about the motive for buying the television set.[173]

This problem is further illustrated in *In re Martin,*[174] in which a debtor was denied an exemption for a rifle purchased prior to bankruptcy on the advice of counsel. The debtor testified that he had consulted with his attorney about conserving his $400 of nonexempt cash and that the attorney "told me I was allowed the rifle and a pistol and a whole bunch of exempt articles."[175] Knowing that he had to spend $200 for other purposes, the debtor spent the remaining $200 on a rifle. The bankruptcy judge found that the purchase was "effected with a conscious effort to convert nonexempt assets into exempt assets with the purpose of making them unavailable to the trustee."[176] The outcome might have been different had the debtor's attorney first asked his client whether he had a desire to own a rifle, which happened to be exempt under state law. It is unclear how far a lawyer may go in preparing a client for testimony on this issue. Unless the debtor acted with malice toward creditors, it is highly doubtful that there was not at least some desire to own a rifle. It can be argued that the debtor's attorney had a duty to help the client manifest a true desire to own the rifle even though the client had the dual motives of preserving as much of his assets as possible and of owning a rifle.

Judicial treatment of this issue has made it extremely difficult for the debtor's lawyer to give specific and complete advice to the debtor. Lack of uniformity and use by some courts of the nebulous purpose test to determine the nature of the debtor's conduct hampers the attorney's ability to predict with certainty when actual fraud relating to a particular conversion of nonexempt to exempt property will be found.

It must also be emphasized that the debtor who purchases exempt property in contemplation of bankruptcy may be gambling with very high stakes. Although the usual sanction for crossing the murky line between permissible purchases and fraudulent conduct is denial of the exemption, at least one court denied the debtor's discharge for engaging in a fraudulent transfer of nonexempt assets for the purpose of acquiring exempt property.[177] When uncertainty is combined with risk that

---

[173] See Resnick, note 159 *supra*, at 637-646, for a discussion of the ethical problems confronting the debtor's lawyer.

[174] 217 F. Supp. 937 (D. Ore. 1963).

[175] *Id.*

[176] *Id.*

[177] *In re* Schwingle, 4 Bankr. Dec. 434 (W.D. Wis. 1978). See also *In re*

a court may deprive the debtor of a discharge of debts, the result is a chilling effect on the debtor's counsel in advising the client. A cautious lawyer may be reluctant to advise a debtor to purchase exempt property, even when the purchase is justified by the debtor's genuine need for the property. On the other hand, a lawyer who does advise a debtor to acquire exempt property may be exposing the client to serious risks.

¶ 4.10 PROCEDURE FOR CLAIMING EXEMPTIONS

The debtor is required to file with the court a list of property that is claimed as exempt.[178] If the debtor fails to file such a list, a dependent of the debtor may file it on behalf of the debtor. The rationale for permitting a dependent to claim exemptions is that many exemption laws are designed to protect the family as well as the debtor. Unless a creditor, the trustee, or another party in interest objects, the property on the list is exempt.[179]

Since there are two alternative exemption systems under the Code, at some point in time the debtor must make a choice. It is anticipated that new Bankruptcy Rules will be promulgated to govern the time and manner of making this choice. A congressional report indicates that the new Rules will provide for the situation where the debtor's choice of exemptions proves to be improvident and should be changed. For example, when the court rules against the debtor with respect to a major exemption, the debtor will be given an opportunity to reconsider the choice of exemption systems.[180]

¶ 4.11 LIQUIDATION OF THE ESTATE

In liquidation cases, the property interests of the estate that are available for distribution to creditors must be reduced to cash. The trustee, however, may not sell property of the estate out of the ordinary course of the debtor's business unless the court approves the sale after

---

Adlman, note 162 *supra*, where there was an unsuccessful attempt to bar a discharge.

[178] The list of property claimed as exempt is contained in Schedule B-4 of the Schedule of Assets and Liabilities. See Sugg. Int. B. Form No. 6, set forth in Appendix B.

[179] 11 U.S.C. § 522(*l*). See B. Rule 403, which is superseded by Section 522 (*l*) of the Code.

[180] H.R. Rep. No. 95-595, note 10 *supra*, at 360. It is interesting to note, however, that the Suggested Interim Bankruptcy Rules do not address this matter.

a hearing on notice.[181] The court may approve either a public or private sale and may impose certain conditions. For example, the court may approve a public sale on condition that it produce a bid equal to or greater than a specified percentage of the appraised value of the property.[182] The court may approve either a bulk sale of substantially all of the assets in one transaction or separate sales on a piecemeal basis. If there are others who have valid interests in the property, such as secured parties or lienors, the court must provide them with adequate protection when approving the sale.[183]

In an attempt to maximize the monetary return of estate assets, the Bankruptcy Code gives the court the power to authorize the sale of property free and clear of liens and other interests under certain limited circumstances.[184] When applicable nonbankruptcy law permits the sale of such property free and clear or when the lienor or holder of the other interest consents, the court may authorize a sale free of those interests.[185] In addition, the Code permits the court to authorize a sale free and clear of any lien if the price for which the property is to be sold is greater than the amount secured by the lien.[186] If the proceeds of the sale exceed the value of the lien, there will be enough cash to compensate the lienor adequately. The court may also permit a sale free and clear of another's property interest if the other interest is in bona fide dispute.[187] Finally, whenever the lienor could be compelled in a legal or equitable proceeding to accept a money satisfaction for its in-

---

[181] 11 U.S.C. § 363(b), which is derived from former B.A. § 70(f) and B. Rule 606. See 11 U.S.C. § 363(*l*), which provides that forfeiture or termination clauses in a contract or lease that is conditioned on bankruptcy or insolvency does not prevent the sale of property by the trustee. See also ¶ 4.03[7].

[182] Compare former B.A. § 70(f), which required that property of the estate be appraised and that the court set a minimum "upset price" of at least 75 percent of value, below which a sale may not be consummated. The Code contains no similar provision. See B. Rule 606.

[183] 11 U.S.C. §§ 363(d), 363(e). See 11 U.S.C. § 363(c)(2), and ¶ 8.11[3] *infra*, with respect to special limitations on the sale of "cash collateral," including negotiable instruments, documents of title, securities, and other forms of cash equivalents.

[184] 11 U.S.C. § 363(f). Bankruptcy Rule 606(b)(3) provides that a proceeding to obtain authorization to sell property free and clear of a lien or other property interest is an adversary proceeding governed by Part VII of the Bankruptcy Rules. See Chapter 6 *infra* for a discussion of adversary proceedings.

[185] 11 U.S.C. §§ 363(f)(1), 363(f)(2).

[186] 11 U.S.C. § 363(f)(3).

[187] 11 U.S.C. § 363(f)(4).

terest, the bankruptcy court may authorize a sale free of the lien.[188] Of course, after the sale the lien or other property interest usually attaches to the sales proceeds or to some other property so that the rights of the other entity are not jeopardized by the sale. It is also common in such situations for the lienor to bid at the sale and, if successful, to offset the amount of the secured claim against the purchase price and pay the trustee the balance remaining.[189]

The Bankruptcy Code contains specific provisions that relate to the sale of property of which a spouse or another person is co-owner.[190] In limited situations, the court may authorize the sale of both the estate's interest and the co-owner's interest when the debtor owns an undivided interest as a joint tenant, tenant by the entirety, or tenant in common. Such a sale may be authorized only if three conditions are met: partition of the property would be impractical, the sale of the estate's interest by itself would realize significantly less than a sale of the property free of the co-owner's interest, and the benefit to the estate from such a sale would outweigh the detriment to the co-owner.[191] Moreover, the court may authorize the sale of property free and clear of dower or curtesy rights, whether vested or contingent, without meeting these three conditions.[192] For the purpose of adequately protecting spouses with dower or curtesy rights and others who are co-owners of property, the Code gives them the first right to purchase the property from the estate at the same price and terms as in an approved proposed sale.[193] Also, the spouse's or co-owner's interest in the property attaches to the appropriate share of the sales proceeds after deduction of the costs and expenses of the sale.[194]

Let us assume that the bankruptcy court approves the sale of estate assets and that the sale is consummated. Thereafter, a party in interest appeals the sale authorization, and the appellate court reverses the bankruptcy court's decision. Is the sale rescinded? If so, it is not difficult to imagine the predicament that the good-faith purchaser might be in, especially if the purchaser used or resold the property. In fact, the

---

[188] 11 U.S.C. § 363(f)(5).

[189] 11 U.S.C. § 363(k) permits this offset.

[190] 11 U.S.C. § 363(h). Compare former B.A. § 2a(7).

[191] 11 U.S.C. §§ 363(h)(1), 363(h)(2), 363(h)(3). A fourth condition that must be met, but that will not be a factor in most cases, is that the property is not used in the gas or electric energy business. See 11 U.S.C. § 363(h)(4).

[192] 11 U.S.C. § 363(g).

[193] 11 U.S.C. § 363(i). The right of first refusal also applies to spouses in community property states.

[194] 11 U.S.C. § 363(j).

possibility of a reversal would probably result in lower bids for the property because of the increased risk to the purchaser. For this reason, the Bankruptcy Code provides that the validity of the sale to a good-faith purchaser is not affected by the reversal or modification on appeal, whether or not the purchaser knew of the pendency of the appeal.[195] This protection does not apply, however, if the sale was stayed pending the appeal.

¶ 4.12 TRUSTEE'S POWERS CONCERNING MONEY OF THE ESTATE

The debtor's cash and bank accounts that the debtor has at the time of the commencement of the case become part of the estate. In addition, cash is produced when the trustee liquidates the other property of the estate. While the case is pending, what does the trustee do with all of this cash?

The Bankruptcy Code permits the trustee to deposit or invest money of the estate in a manner that will yield "the maximum reasonable net return on such money, taking into account the safety" of the deposit or investment.[196] Trustees may deposit or invest funds in savings and loan accounts or government bonds, or may make other appropriate investments. The trustee is put in the position or making judgments with respect to the safety of depositories and investments.[197] Of course, speculative ventures must be avoided.

The trustee is required to take certain precautions to protect money of the estate and to minimize the risk of loss. Unless the deposit or investment is insured or guaranteed by the United States or a federal agency such as the Federal Deposit Insurance Corporation, the trustee must require from the depository a bond by a court-approved corporate surety issued in favor of the United States.[198] The bond must be conditioned on a proper accounting and return with respect to all money deposited or invested.[199]

---

[195] 11 U.S.C. § 363(m).

[196] 11 U.S.C. § 345(a).

[197] Under the former Bankruptcy Act, funds had to be deposited in banking institutions specifically designated by the court. See former B.A. §§ 47(a)(2), 61; B. Rules 512, 605(b).

[198] 11 U.S.C. § 345(b). See also 11 U.S.C. § 15345(a), with respect to U.S. Trustees. In lieu of a bond, the depository may deposit security of the kind specified in 6 U.S.C. § 15, which governs the posting of security by banks that receive public funds for deposit.

[199] 11 U.S.C. §§ 345(b)(1)(C), 15345(a)(1)(C).

Ordinarily, the trustee will deposit money of the estate in one or more interest-bearing bank accounts. The trustee must avoid, however, the comingling of funds that are subject to a lien or security interest. Specifically, any cash collateral must be segregated from the remainder of the estate.[200] This segregation requirement applies to money, negotiable instruments, documents of title, securities, deposit accounts, and any other cash equivalents in which another entity has an interest.[201]

---

[200] 11 U.S.C. § 363(c)(4).
[201] 11 U.S.C. § 363(a).

Chapter 5

CREDITORS, CLAIMS, AND INTERESTS

When a bankruptcy case is commenced and an order for relief is granted, creditors will want to make sure that their interests are protected. In liquidation cases, creditors are primarily interested in sharing in the distribution of estate assets. Creditors in reorganization cases want to have the right to vote to accept or reject a plan and to benefit from dividends payable under the plan.[1] Likewise, partners of debtor partnerships, stockholders of debtor corporations, and other equity

[1] See Chapter 8 *infra* on reorganizations.

security holders may wish to participate in the bankruptcy, especially in reorganization cases. This chapter focuses on the rights of creditors and equity security holders to participate in the bankruptcy case.

¶ 5.01 PROVABILITY CONCEPT ELIMINATED

The former Bankruptcy Act employed the concept of *provability* of claims to determine whether particular creditors might participate in the bankruptcy case.[2] If a claim was not provable, the creditor was not permitted to play any significant role in the case. A creditor with a nonprovable claim was not entitled to share in a distribution of the estate[3] or to file an involuntary bankruptcy petition.[4] Moreover, a creditor without a provable claim was not affected by the debtor's discharge.[5] Whether or not a claim was provable depended on the nature of the claim; provability did not relate to ability to prove the claim by competent evidence. The former Act listed nine categories of debts that qualified as provable claims.[6]

To illustrate, let us assume that the debtor caused injury to a person as a result of negligence prior to the debtor's bankruptcy. Did the injured party have the right to share in the debtor's estate? Did the person have the right to file an involuntary petition? Was the debt dischargeable? The answers to these questions depended, under the former Act, on whether the negligence claim was provable. The Act provided that negligence claims were provable only if the claimant commenced a negligence action that was pending when the bankruptcy petition was filed.[7] If no action was commenced at that time, the injured party would not be affected by the bankruptcy and could not participate in the case. Other examples of nonprovable claims were intentional tort claims that were not reduced to judgment[8] and contingent or unliquidated claims

---

[2] See former B.A. § 63(a).

[3] The former Act provided that dividends be distributed only on "allowed" claims, and that a claim could not be allowed unless it was provable. See former B.A. §§ 65(a), 57(d).

[4] See former B.A. § 59(b).

[5] See former B.A. § 17(a).

[6] See former B.A. § 63(a).

[7] Former B.A. § 63(a)(7).

[8] There were exceptions to the rule that intentional tort claims were not provable in bankrupcty. Tort claims that also gave rise to quasi-contractual claims, such as when a person was unjustly enriched by wrongfully converting property of another, were provable. Torts committed by persons in contractual relationships, such as a doctor-patient relationship, were considered provable. See Schall v. Camors, 251 U.S. 239 (1920).

not capable of liquidation or reasonable estimation without undue delay.[9]

Today, the concept of provability is eliminated. The Bankruptcy Code does not even mention the concept and therefore makes it possible for more creditors to be affected by, and to participate in, the bankruptcy case. Whether a creditor may share in a distribution of the estate or otherwise participate in the case depends on whether its claim is *allowed*—not whether it is provable.

¶ 5.02 WHAT IS A CLAIM?

An entity is not considered a creditor for bankruptcy purposes unless it holds a *claim*.[10] The Bankruptcy Code defines "claim" in a manner that makes the term broader than the term "debt" or "claim" under the former Bankruptcy Act.[11] Any right to payment, whether or not it is reduced to judgment, is a claim that may enable the holder of it to participate in the bankruptcy case. It does not matter if the right to payment is liquidated or unliquidated, fixed or contingent, matured or unmatured, disputed or undisputed, or secured or unsecured. In addition, if the debtor's breach of performance results in the right to an equitable remedy, the creditor has a claim so long as the breach also gives rise to a right to payment.[12] For example, in certain states a judgment for specific performance may be satisfied by an alternative right to payment in the event performance is refused. In these states, the person who is entitled to specific performance will have a claim for bankruptcy purposes if the debtor files a petition. However, a right to an equitable remedy that does not give the holder a right to the payment of money is not a "claim" in the context of the Bankruptcy Code.

The practical consequence of having such a broad definition of "claim" in the Bankruptcy Code is to permit the most comprehensive relief in the bankruptcy court.

---

[9] See former B.A. §§ 57(d), 63(d); Thompson v. England, 226 F.2d 488 (9th Cir. 1955). See also State v. Wilkes, 41 N.Y.2d 655, 394 N.Y.S.2d 849 (1977), in which the court held that a student loan was not provable or dischargeable because of various conditions attached to the repayment provisions of the loan that made it too contingent. See ¶ 5.05[4] for a discussion of contingent and unliquidated claims.

[10] See 11 U.S.C. § 101(9) for the definition of "creditor."

[11] Compare the definition of "claim" in 11 U.S.C. § 101(4) with the definitions of "claim" and "debt" in former B.A. §§ 1(14), 106(1), 307(2), 406(2), 606(1).

[12] U.S.C. § 101(4).

¶ 5.03 EQUITY SECURITY HOLDERS AND THEIR INTERESTS

Creditors are not the only ones who may wish to participate in a bankruptcy case. Equity security holders, including those persons who hold shares of stock in a debtor corporation, interests of a limited partner in a limited partnership debtor, or warrants or other rights to purchase, sell, or subscribe to such securities, may also wish to participate in the case.[13] This is especially true in reorganization cases in which equity security holders will want to vote on, and benefit from, the reorganization plan. The Bankruptcy Code permits equity security holders to participate in the case according to their *allowed interests*.[14]

¶ 5.04 FILING A PROOF OF CLAIM OR INTEREST

The Bankruptcy Code gives creditors the right to file proofs of claims in a bankruptcy case.[15] Although the provision is permissive and not mandatory, any creditor who wishes to have an allowed claim in a liquidation case or in a chapter 13 debt adjustment must file a proof of claim with the court.[16] Otherwise, the creditor may be unable to share in the distribution of the estate.

There are certain situations in which filing a proof of claim may not be warranted. In no-asset liquidation cases or when the estate is so insubstantial that priority creditors will consume the estate,[17] there may be no need for the general creditors to file proof-of-claim forms. Likewise, if a creditor is fully secured and wishes to rely solely on the value of the collateral, there will be no purpose in filing a proof of claim unless a party in interest requests that the secured claim be allowed or disallowed.[18] It is important to note, however, that creditors may not

---

[13] See 11 U.S.C. §§ 101(15) and 101(16) for definitions of "equity security" and "equity security holder." A convertible debenture that is convertible into an equity security, but that was not so converted, is itself not an equity security for bankruptcy purposes. See also H.R. Rep. No. 95-595, 95th Cong., 1st Sess. 311 (1977) (hereinafter cited as H.R. Rep. No. 95-595).

[14] See 11 U.S.C. § 1126(a).

[15] 11 U.S.C. § 501(a). An indenture trustee also has the right to file a proof of claim. See 11 U.S.C. §§ 101(22) and 101(23) for definitions of "indenture" and "indenture trustee."

[16] See 11 U.S.C. § 502.

[17] See 11 U.S.C. § 507, and ¶ 5.13, dealing with priority claims.

[18] See 11 U.S.C. § 506(d)(1), which provides, in effect, that a lien securing a claim that is not an allowed secured claim is valid nonetheless if a party in interest has not requested that the court rule on its allowability.

avoid the debtor's discharge by failing to file proofs of claims, since unfiled claims are dischargeable in the same manner as allowed claims.[19] Thus, in the usual case, general creditors, partially-secured creditors, secured creditors requested to file, creditors seeking a priority, and creditors with postpetition allowable claims[20] will file proofs of claims in order to protect their rights against the estate in a liquidation case.

Although a proof of claim must be filed before a claim will be allowed in a liquidation case or in a chapter 13 debt adjustment, a different rule governs reorganization cases. Chapter 11 of the Code provides that a proof of claim is "deemed filed" if the claim appears on the schedules filed by the debtor or the trustee, unless it is scheduled as disputed, contingent, or unliquidated.[21] Accordingly, only creditors who are not listed on the schedules or those listed as having disputed contingent or unliquidated claims need file a proof of claim to have the claim allowed so as to permit participation in the case. If a proof of claim is executed and filed in accordance with the Bankruptcy Rules, it will supersede any listing.[22] Moreover, even though the listing may be correct, an attorney-in-fact may want to file a proof of claim so that notices and dividends will be sent directly to the attorney-in-fact.

A creditor's failure to file a timely proof of claim may unfairly jeopardize the rights of other parties in certain situations. For example, a person who guaranteed an obligation owed by the debtor would benefit by having the creditor receive as much money as possible from the estate. If the creditor's claim is not allowed because of the failure to file a proof of claim, the guarantor may be liable for the entire debt.[23] Similarly, if the creditor has a nondischargeable claim, the debtor has an interest in having that creditor receive a distribution in bankruptcy. If the creditor receives no distribution because of the failure to file a proof of claim, the entire nondischargeable debt will survive bankruptcy

---

[19] See Chapter 3 *supra* on discharge.

[20] See ¶ 5.07 for a discussion on allowable postpetition claims.

[21] 11 U.S.C. § 1111(a), which is derived from B. Rules 10-401 and 12-30. See Sugg. Int. B. Rule 3001, on the proof of claim or interest in a chapter 11 reorganization case.

[22] See B. Rule 301(b), and Sugg. Int. B. Rule 3001(b)(4), on the evidentiary effect of the filing. Note that Sugg. Int. B. Rule 3001 applies only in cases filed under chapter 11. Sugg. Int. B. Rule 3001(g).

[23] The Bankruptcy Code follows Section 16 of the former Act by providing that the liability of codebtors is unaffected by the debtor's discharge. 11 U.S.C. § 524(e). However, see 11 U.S.C. § 1301, and Chapter 9 *infra*, for a discussion concerning the stay of actions against codebtors in chapter 13 cases.

to be collected against the debtor at some future date. For these reasons, the Bankruptcy Code and the Suggested Interim Bankruptcy Rules provide that a codebtor,[24] as well as a person who secured the debtor's obligation, may file a proof of claim if the creditor fails to do so within applicable time limits.[25] In addition, the debtor or the trustee may file a proof of claim if the creditor does not.[26]

The Bankruptcy Rules of Procedure and, where applicable, the Suggested Interim Bankruptcy Rules govern the form and procedural requirements for filing a proof of claim.[27] The proof must be in writing and executed by the creditor or by an authorized agent of the creditor,[28] unless it is filed by either a trustee, a debtor, or a codebtor upon the creditor's failure to file. The official proof-of-claim forms should be utilized for filing purposes.[29] If the creditor wishes to appoint an attorney-in-fact in the case, a general or special power of attorney may be filed together with the proof of claim.[30] When the claim or a security interest in connection with the claim is founded on a writing, such as when the debt is evidenced by a promissory note, the original or duplicate of the writing must be filed with the proof of claim. However, if the writing was lost or destroyed, a statement explaining the loss or destruction must be filed instead. In the case of a secured claim, satisfactory evidence that the security interest was perfected, such as a copy of a financing statement stamped as a receipt by the Secretary of State, must accompany the proof-of-claim form.[31]

A proof of claim is filed timely in a liquidation case if it is filed within six months after the first date set for the first meeting of credi-

---

[24] The term "codebtor" means any entity that is liable to the creditor with the debtor, whether it has primary liability with the debtor (e.g., a comaker of a promissory note) or secondary liability as a guarantor only.

[25] 11 U.S.C. § 501(b); Sugg. Int. B. Rule 3002. See B. Rule 304.

[26] 11 U.S.C. § 501(c). See B. Rule 13-303. See also Sugg. Int. B. Rule 3004, which applies to cases under chapters 7 and 11. An indenture trustee may also file for all holders of securities, known or unknown, issued pursuant to the instrument under which it is trustee. Sugg. Int. B. Rule 3001(b)(6).

[27] See B. Rules 301 and 302; Sugg. Int. B. Rules 3001-3004; Sugg. Int. B. Form Nos. 14 and 15, which are set forth in Appendix B.

[28] B. Rule 301(a). See B. Rule 302(d) for special rules dealing with claims that are assigned either unconditionally or as security.

[29] See Official Form No. 15, which should be used until new official forms are promulgated. For wage claims, Suggested Interim Bankruptcy Form No. 14 or 15 should be used. These forms are set forth in Appendix B.

[30] Official Form No. 13 or 14, set forth in Appendix B, should be used for this purpose. It is customary for the power of appointment to be added to the end of the proof-of-claim form.

[31] B. Rule 302(c).

tors.[32] The Suggested Interim Bankruptcy Rules provide as to reorganization cases that a proof of claim is filed timely as long as it is filed prior to the approval of the disclosure statement.[33] This requirement appears to be sound since that is the first time creditor identification is important. It would also appear that an earlier date should be required for disputed, contingent, or unliquidated claims so that they may be resolved prior to the approval of the disclosure statement.[34] In Chapter 13 debt adjustment cases, the creditor should file a claim within six months after the first date set for the first meeting of creditors, unless it is a secured claim, in which case it should be filed before the conclusion of the first meeting of creditors.[35]

In liquidation cases, limited partners or shareholders of the debtor will usually not participate in a distribution of the estate. Nonetheless, the Code permits such equity security holders to file proofs of interest to obtain allowed interests.[36] In the unlikely event that there are assets remaining after all allowed claims of creditors are paid in full, a distribution may be made to allowed interest holders. It is advisable, therefore, for a limited partner or shareholder to file a proof of interest when the debtor is solvent or when the estate has substantial assets.

In contrast to liquidation cases, in reorganization cases it is *always* advisable for equity security holders to have their interests allowed. Only those equity security holders who have allowed interests may vote to accept or reject a plan of reorganization.[37] If the interest was scheduled by the debtor or the trustee, filing a proof of interest form is not necessary for allowance unless it was scheduled as disputed, contingent, or unliquidated.[38]

---

[32] B. Rule 302(e). The rule contains several exceptions to the six month rule. For example, the court may grant an extension to an infant or an incompetent person, or to the United States or other government body.

[33] Sugg. Int. B. Rule 3001(b)(3), but note that the court on notice may fix a different time. See Sugg. Int. B. Rule 2002. See also Sugg. Int. B. Rule 3001(b)(2), which provides that any creditor that fails to file a claim before approval of the disclosure statement or other time fixed by the court is not to be treated as a creditor for voting or distribution purposes. See Chapter 8 *infra*, and 11 U.S.C. § 1125, on disclosure statements in reorganization cases.

[34] If a creditor in this group does file a proof of claim, of course, a hearing should be held prior to approval of the disclosure statement to estimate the dollar amount of the claim. See ¶ 5.05[4] on contingent and unliquidated claims.

[35] B. Rule 13-302(e). See the rule for several exceptions to these time limits.

[36] 11 U.S.C. § 501(a).

[37] 11 U.S.C. § 1126(a).

[38] 11 U.S.C. § 1111(a).

The Suggested Interim Bankruptcy Rules permit a creditor to withdraw a claim as of right unless certain events have occurred. Specifically, once an objection is filed, a complaint is filed against the creditor in an adversary proceeding, or the creditor has accepted or rejected a reorganization plan or otherwise has participated significantly in the case, the claim may not be withdrawn unless the court orders it withdrawn after a hearing on notice.[39]

¶ 5.05 ALLOWANCE OF CLAIMS OR INTERESTS

If a proof of claim or interest is filed, it will be deemed allowed automatically unless a party in interest objects.[40] In essence, the mere filing of the proof of claim or interest constitutes prima facie evidence of its validity and amount. In reorganization cases, this automatic allowability rule also applies to any scheduled claim and interest without the filing of a proof if the claim or interest is not listed as disputed, contingent, or unliquidated.[41]

It is the duty of the trustee to examine proofs of claims and to object to the allowance of improper ones.[42] The debtor is obligated to assist the trustee in this endeavor.[43] In reorganization cases in which the debtor remains in possession, the debtor has the duty to object to improper claims or interests.[44] Any objection to a claim or interest must be made in writing, and a copy of the objection and at least ten days' notice of a hearing must be mailed or delivered to the claimant.[45] The court, after the notice and a hearing, will determine the validity and amount of the claim or interest as of the date of the filing of the petition.[46] Since the claim will be allowed for the amount owed as of the

---

[39] Sugg. Int. B. Rule 3003, which is derived from B. Rule 10-404.

[40] 11 U.S.C. § 502(a); B. Rule 306(b).

[41] See 11 U.S.C. § 1111(a).

[42] See 11 U.S.C. §§ 704(4), 1106(a)(1), 1302(b)(1).

[43] See 11 U.S.C. § 521(2).

[44] See 11 U.S.C. § 1107(a).

[45] B. Rule 306(c). If the claim is for taxes, at least thirty days' notice of a hearing must be given. See Sugg. Int. B. Rules 3001(d), 3001(f).

[46] 11 U.S.C. § 502(b). Before a case is closed, however, a claim that has been allowed may be reconsidered for cause, and reallowed or disallowed according to the equities of the case. See 11 U.S.C. § 502(j), which is derived from former B.A. § 57(k). See also B. Rule 307; Sugg. Int. B. Rule 3001(e).

date the petition is filed, postpetition debts will not generally give rise to allowable claims.[47]

[1] Grounds For Disallowance

The Bankruptcy Code contains several grounds for disallowance of a claim in whole or in part. To the extent that any of the grounds are found to exist, the court will not allow the claim.

[a] Unenforceability Against the Debtor

To the extent that the claim is unenforceable against the debtor and the debtor's property under nonbankruptcy law or by virtue of an agreement, the claim will not be allowed.[48] For example, if the claim is unenforceable pursuant to applicable usury law or because of failure of consideration, it may not be allowed. The same rule applies to claims barred by the statute of frauds or the statute of limitations as of the date the petition was filed. Any claim for a deficiency by a partially secured creditor on a nonrecourse loan must be disallowed because it is unenforceable against the debtor personally or the debtor's property.[49] In short, any defense that the debtor could have raised against the claimant immediately before the bankruptcy case commenced may be raised as an objection to allowance of the claim.

There are two situations, however, in which a claim will be allowed despite unenforceability against the debtor. The first situation deals with contingent claims that are not enforceable under nonbankruptcy law. If, for example, an obligation is conditioned on the occurrence of an event that has not yet occurred, the claimant will not have a cause of action to enforce it until the condition is satisfied. Nonetheless, the Bankruptcy Code provides that such contingent obligations are allowable in bankruptcy even though they are not enforceable in the absence of bankruptcy.[50] Second, claims that are unenforceable against the

---

[47] 11 U.S.C. § 502(b). But see ¶ 5.07 for a discussion of allowable postpetition claims.

[48] 11 U.S.C. § 502(b)(1). Compare the approach of Section 70(c) of the former Act, which gave the trustee the benefit of the defenses available to the debtor.

[49] However, see 11 U.S.C. § 1111(b), and Chapter 8 *infra*, with respect to nonrecourse claims in reorganization cases.

[50] 11 U.S.C. §§ 502(b)(1), 502(c)(1). See ¶ 5.05[4] for a more detailed discussion of contingent claims.

debtor because they have not matured, such as a debt that is not due until several years after the petition is filed, are allowable in bankruptcy nonetheless.[51] In essence, the debtor's obligations are accelerated upon the filing of a bankruptcy petition.

[b] Claims for Unmatured Interest

The creditor's allowable claim may include interest that accrues on the obligation up to the date when the petition is filed. For purposes of allowability, however, interest stops accruing at that time. The Code provides that any claim for interest that is unmatured as of the date the case commences may not be allowed.[52] The legislative history of the Code makes it clear that whether interest is matured or unmatured on the date of bankruptcy is to be determined without reference to any clause in an agreement calling for acceleration of the debt upon bankruptcy of the debtor.[53] These so-called ipso facto or bankruptcy clauses do not affect the allowability of the claim for interest.

Unmatured interest includes postpetition interest that is not due and payable at the time the petition is filed. It also includes that portion of prepaid interest that results from discounting the debt at the time the credit is originally advanced. To illustrate, let us assume that the debtor signed and delivered a $1,000 promissory note the day before filing a bankruptcy petition. The allowability of the claim represented by the note will depend on the amount of cash actually advanced by reason of a discount rate. If the original discount was 10 percent, so that the cash advanced was only $900, then only $900 will be allowed as the claim. The remaining $100 of the face amount of the note represents prepaid but unmatured interest. If $900 was advanced several months or years prior to bankruptcy, the interest portion of the note would have to be prorated and disallowed to the extent that it is for interest accruing after the petition is filed.[54]

It is important to understand that the commencement of the bankruptcy case automatically accelerates the total amount of principal due

---

[51] 11 U.S.C. § 502(b)(1).

[52] 11 U.S.C. § 502(b)(2), which derives from former B.A. §§ 63(a)(1), 63(a)(5). See New York v. Saper, 336 U.S. 328 (1949), which held that tax claims bear interest only until the date of bankruptcy and not until payment. Note, however, that claims for postpetition interest may be paid in liquidation cases at the legal rate if all allowed claims are paid in full. See 11 U.S.C. § 726(a)(5), and ¶ 5.15.

[53] H.R. Rep. No. 95-595, note 13 *supra,* at 352.

[54] See H.R. Rep. No. 95-595, note 13 *supra,* at 352-353.

on the obligation.[55] The entire principal, whether due in the past or future, is allowable despite the fact that the unmatured interest is not.

[c] Claims Subject to Offset

In certain situations, the creditor may offset against his claim any debt that the creditor owes to the debtor from a separate transaction.[56] For example, if the debtor owes $1,000 to the bank on an unsecured loan, and the debtor has $1,000 in his checking account at the same bank, the bank as creditor may offset the balance of the account (which the bank "owes" the debtor) from the claim based on the loan. Since the creditor may offset the debt owed to the debtor against the creditor's claim, resulting in a zero balance, the creditor's claim may not be allowed.[57] The disallowance of the claim to the extent that the creditor may offset it against the debt owed to the debtor prevents double recovery by the creditor. The claim may be allowed only to the extent of the balance remaining due to the creditor after the creditor's obligations to the debtor are offset.

[d] Excess Property Tax

Claims for property taxes are not allowable to the extent that they exceed the value of the estate's interest in the property that is the subject of the tax.[58] This disallowance rule only applies when the tax is ad valorem, which means that the tax obligation is based on the value of the property.[59]

[e] Services of an Insider or Attorney

Claims of the debtor's attorney are subject to close scrutiny by the bankruptcy court. The Bankruptcy Code expressly provides that a claim for attorney's fees is not allowable to the extent that such claim exceeds the reasonable value of the legal services.[60] Claims for services ren-

---

[55] See 11 U.S.C. § 502(b)(1), and ¶ 5.05[1][a].

[56] See 11 U.S.C. § 553, and ¶ 5.10, for a more detailed analysis of the right of setoff and its limitations.

[57] 11 U.S.C. § 502(b)(3).

[58] 11 U.S.C. § 502(b)(4).

[59] See H.R. Rep. No. 95-595, note 59 *supra*, at 353.

[60] 11 U.S.C. § 502(b)(5). See Chapter 6 *infra* for a discussion of attorney compensation in bankruptcy cases.

dered by an insider are also subject to close examination by the court and may be disallowed to the extent that they are found unreasonable.[61] Insiders include relatives or partners of the debtor and officers or directors of a debtor corporation, as well as others who have a sufficiently close relationship with the debtor.[62] The purpose of requiring disallowance of unreasonable claims of insiders is to prevent collusive conduct as a means of diverting assets from the estate to a person who is close to the debtor.

[f] Postpetition Alimony, Maintenance, and Support

As discussed above, the filing of a bankruptcy petition accelerates the principal due on an obligation, so that an unmatured debt is allowable.[63] However, an exception to this rule is contained in the Bankruptcy Code for the purpose of disallowing claims for unmatured alimony, maintenance, or support, which are excepted from discharge.[64] Since these claims are not dischargeable, they are to be paid from property to be acquired by the debtor after bankruptcy and not from the bankruptcy estate. Claims for alimony, maintenance, and support that are payable prior to the filing of the petition are allowable despite the fact that they are nondischargeable.

[g] Employment Tax Claims Against Employers

A debtor who is an employer may have an obligation to the federal government arising out of a reduction of the Federal Unemployment Tax Act credit on account of a tardy contribution to a state unemployment fund. If state unemployment insurance taxes are paid late, the federal tax credit is reduced or disallowed.[65] In such cases, however, the federal claim against the employer's bankruptcy estate will be disallowed as if the federal tax credit had been granted in full.[66] By providing for the disallowance of this claim, the bankruptcy estate will not be penalized for the debtor's tardy payment of state unemployment insurance taxes.

---

[61] 11 U.S.C. § 502(b)(5).

[62] See 11 U.S.C. § 101(25) for the definition of "insider."

[63] See ¶ 5.05[1][a].

[64] 11 U.S.C. § 502(b)(6). See 11 U.S.C. § 523(a)(5), and ¶ 3.09[5], for a discussion of the alimony exception to discharge.

[65] See I.R.C. § 3302; 124 Cong. Rec. H11110 (daily ed., Sept. 28, 1978); 124 Cong. Rec. S17426 (daily ed., Oct. 6, 1978).

[66] 11 U.S.C. § 502(b)(9).

[2] Allowance of Landlords' Claims

The Bankruptcy Code follows the policy of the former Act [67] by limiting the allowability of a landlord's claim for damages resulting from breach or termination of a lease. Congress is concerned about landlords with long-term leases submitting huge claims for unpaid rent that accrues in the future. If a landlord on a twenty-year lease, for example, had the right to recover damages for unpaid rent for the remainder of the lease, say sixteen years, the landlord would receive a substantial portion of the estate at the expense of other creditors.[68]

A landlord's claim for loss of future rent resulting from the termination of a lease on real estate may be allowed for an amount not to exceed the rent reserved by the lease for the greater of one year or 15 percent of the remaining lease term, not to exceed three years.[69] The one-year or three-year period begins to run on the date the petition is filed, when the landlord repossesses the premises, or when the tenant surrenders the lease, whichever occurs first. For the purpose of determining the amount of rent reserved in the lease for this period, any acceleration clause is to be ignored.[70] It should be remembered, however, that this formula provides only a ceiling on the allowability of a claim for future rent and that the claim may be reduced further if the landlord's actual damages are less.

For example, assume that there is a lease with ten years remaining at an annual rental of $100,000 or a total rental of $1 million. Expert testimony estimates the value of the premises over ten years at $600,000, leaving a claim for damages of $400,000. This claim, however, is further reduced by the Code to one year of rent ($100,000) or 15 percent of $1 million ($150,000), whichever is greater, but not exceeding three years' rent ($300,000). The landlord's claim will therefore be allowed for $150,000. If the value of the remaining ten-year lease is $950,000, however, the allowed claim would be only $50,000.

In addition to the allowance of the claim for future rent subject to these limits, the court may also allow the landlord's claim based on any

---

[67] See former B.A. §§ 63(a)(9), 202, 353, 458.

[68] See 11 U.S.C. § 365, and chapter 7 *infra*, dealing with the right to reject an unexpired lease and the landlord's rights upon termination of an unexpired lease. Se also 11 U.S.C. § 502(b)(1), and ¶ 5.05[1][a], dealing with the allowability of unmatured claims that may be applicable to claims for future rent.

[69] 11 U.S.C. § 502(b)(7). The term "lease" as used in this context means a "true" or "bona fide" lease, not a lease intended solely as security or as a financing device. See 124 Cong. Rec. S17410 (daily ed., Oct. 6, 1978).

[70] 11 U.S.C. § 502(b)(7)(A).

unpaid rent that accrued, without acceleration, prior to the time when either the petition is filed, the landlord repossesses, or the lease is surrendered, whichever is earliest.[71] In sum, the landlord's allowable claim is limited to any rent due prior to bankruptcy or loss of possession of the premises, plus rent that accrues after that time for a period not to exceed one year or 15 percent of the remaining term up to three years.

It is worth noting at this point that a landlord's statutory lien pursuant to state law will not help the landlord in bankruptcy. Any statutory lien for rent may be avoided by the trustee.[72]

In the usual case, the landlord may be holding a security deposit pursuant to the lease. What effect does the security deposit have on the landlord's claim? May the landlord keep the security deposit when the tenant files a bankruptcy petition? These questions were discussed and answered in *Oldden v. Tonto Realty Corp.*[73] If the security deposit is less than the amount of the landlord's allowable claim, the claim will be considered a secured claim to the extent of the security deposit and an unsecured claim for the balance of the landlord's allowable claim. The security deposit must be applied, however, in satisfaction of the total allowable claim. For example, if the total allowable claim in the above illustration is $150,000 and the landlord holds a $25,000 security deposit, the allowed secured claim will be $25,000 and the allowed unsecured claim will be $125,000. In the unlikely event that the security deposit exceeds the total allowed claim, the landlord must pay the excess into the estate.

In many situations, the debtor or trustee will remain in possession of the leased premises after the bankruptcy petition is filed. This is especially common in reorganization cases. The debtor in possession or trustee may elect to assume the lease or to continue using the premises until a decision is made with respect to assuming or rejecting the unexpired lease.[74] In either event, the landlord is entitled to be paid for use and occupation of the premises accruing after the date the petition is filed as an administrative expense.[75] Ordinarily, the rental rate in the lease will be used to determine the amount of the claim. Aside from

---

[71] 11 U.S.C. § 502(b)(7)(B).

[72] 11 U.S.C. §§ 545(3) and 545(4), which are derived from former B.A. § 67(c)(1)(C). See Chapter 7 *infra* on the trustee's avoiding powers in connection with liens for rent.

[73] 143 F.2d 916 (2d Cir. 1944). See H.R. Rep. No. 95-595, note 13 *supra*, at 353-354.

[74] See 11 U.S.C. § 365, and Chapter 7 *infra*, on executory contracts and unexpired leases.

[75] See 11 U.S.C. § 503(b)(1)(A), and ¶ 5.08[1].

obtaining an administrative expense priority in distribution, the landlord's claim for postpetition occupancy of the premises is not subject to the limitations on allowability applicable to other landlord's claims. Moreover, the cost of removing debris from the premises after the petition is filed may be allowed as an administrative expense.[76]

[3] Allowance of Employees' Claims

Claims of employees who have long-term employment contracts with the debtor present the same potential problems as do claims based on long-term leases. Under the former Bankruptcy Act, there were no limitations on employees' claims. If an employee with several years remaining on a favorable employment contract was unable to mitigate damages caused by termination because of the inability to find other employment, the resulting claim against the estate might have been so large as to unduly limit the distribution to other creditors.

The Bankruptcy Code departs from the former Act by restricting the allowability of any claim for damages resulting from termination of an employment contract.[77] The employee's allowable claim may include all unpaid compensation that accrues under the contract prior to the filing of the petition or termination of employment, whichever occurs first.[78] However, any claim based on the loss of earnings that accrue after the date of bankruptcy or termination of employment may not be allowed for more than a one-year period at the rate of compensation provided in the contract.[79] Damages resulting from loss of earnings for more than one year after bankruptcy or termination of employment may not be included in the employee's claim. Of course, acceleration clauses in employment contracts are not effective for the purpose of computing the employee's allowable claim. It should be remembered that these restrictions are ceilings on an employee's claims and that these claims may be reduced further if the employee mitigates the damages by obtaining other employment.

[4] Contingent or Unliquidated Claims

Certain claims are very difficult to convert to specific dollar amounts. Obligations may be contingent on the occurrence of a future event or may be difficult to liquidate for other reasons. For example,

---

[76] See *In re* Furniture-in-the-Raw, Inc., 4 Bankr. Dec. 519 (S.D.N.Y. 1978).

[77] 11 U.S.C. § 502(b)(8).

[78] 11 U.S.C. § 502(b)(8)(B).

[79] 11 U.S.C. § 502(b)(8)(A).

if the debtor is the guarantor on a $1,000 promissory note that has not matured, what is the amount of the claim against the debtor? Of course, if the principal obligor is solvent at the time of the debtor's bankruptcy, there is a good chance that the debtor will never be required to pay the note because it is unlikely that the maker will default. In any event, the debtor's liability may not be determined with certainty until the maturity of the note, which may not occur for several years.

The former Bankruptcy Act dealt with the problem of contingent or unliquidated claims by recognizing them as provable and allowable unless the court determined either that they were not capable of liquidation or of reasonable estimation, or that liquidation or estimation would unduly delay the administration of the estate.[80] The result of this approach was that some contingent or unliquidated claims were discharged and others were not. Consequently, some creditors with these claims were permitted to share in the distribution of the estate and others were deprived of that right.

The treatment of contingent or unliquidated claims under the former Act is illustrated in *Thompson v. England.*[81] A wife loaned her husband $12,000, to be repaid from the proceeds of his business "as soon as said business is in a sound financial position."[82] When the husband filed a bankruptcy petition, the wife filed a claim. The court held that the claim was not subject to reasonable estimation and that therefore the wife could not participate in a distribution of the estate. The appellate court noted that, to allow this claim, the bankruptcy judge would have to estimate the probability that the debtor would start his business anew after bankruptcy and would arrive at a sound financial condition. That event was so fortuitous that there was no way to determine whether liability would ever attach in the future.

The Bankruptcy Code rejects the approach taken in the former Act with respect to contingent and unliquidated claims. The Bankruptcy Code requires that the court *estimate* the dollar amount of any claim that is disputed, contingent, or unliquidated, even if the administration of the estate or the closing of the case would be delayed.[83] An estimate is possible in contingencies that mathematical computation can resolve,

---

[80] See former B.A. §§ 57(d), 63(d). Paradoxically, if a Chapter XI arrangement were confirmed, creditors with these nonprovable and nondischargeable claims would collect in full from the reorganized debtor.

[81] 226 F.2d 488 (9th Cir. 1955). See also Maynard v. Elliott, 283 U.S. 273 (1931); State v. Wilkes, 41 N.Y.2d 655, 394 N.Y.S.2d 849 (1977).

[82] Thompson v. England, note 81 *supra*, at 490.

[83] 11 U.S.C. § 502(c)(1). But see 28 U.S.C. § 1471(d), and Chapter 6 *infra*, for a discussion of the court's right to abstain from hearing a proceeding that may result in a delay of the allowance.

but it is difficult to perceive how an estimate can be made, for example, in cases involving disputed allegations of negligence, antitrust, or stockholder class actions.[84] The court is required to put a dollar value on every claim, including any claim that gives the claimant the alternative right to an equitable remedy as well as monetary relief.[85]

This requirement is consistent with the Code's general policy of expanding the bankruptcy court's jurisdiction and ability to give complete relief in bankruptcy cases. For example, if the facts of *Thompson v. England* occurred under the Bankruptcy Code, the court would be required to hold a hearing to arrive at an estimation of the present value of the wife's claim against the debtor despite the realization that the husband's debt may never mature. Apparently, this task involves a difficult analysis of many factors, but at least one court in a case under the former Act found a method of making a determination of the value of a contingent claim. In *In re Frederick N. Zucker,*[86] the court held that a note that was guaranteed by the debtor and that obligated the debtor to pay "solely and only in the event of the death of the maker" was not too contingent to be reasonably estimated despite the fact that the maker was alive and well at the time of the bankruptcy.

[5] Transferees of Voidable Transfers

The Bankruptcy Code gives the trustee or debtor in possession the right to avoid certain transfers of property. Property belonging to the estate may be recovered from the hands of a custodian or other third party.[87] Postpetition transfers of estate assets may be reversed.[88] In addition, fraudulent conveyances, voidable preferences, and some other kinds of transfers and liens may be avoided by the trustee or debtor in possession.[89] Certain setoffs are also voidable.[90] The effect of avoiding

---

[84] Conceivably, bankruptcy rules will be promulgated to provide a method of procedure, such as arbitration or preferences on calendars, to expedite the estimation of contingent and unliquidated claims. Of course, settlement is always available as a means of resolving the dispute. Abstention is also possible, but expedition is important in moving towards confirmation in a reorganization case. See Sugg. Int. B. Rule 3001(b)(3), requiring the filing of a proof of claim prior to approval of the disclosure statement.

[85] 11 U.S.C. §§ 502(c)(1), 502(c)(2).

[86] 5 Bankr. Dec. 433 (S.D.N.Y. 1979). Although this case was decided under Section 57(d) of the former Act, the court referred to Section 502(c) of the Code.

[87] See 11 U.S.C. §§ 542 and 543, and ¶ 4.04[6].

[88] See 11 U.S.C. § 549, and ¶ 4.05 *supra.*

[89] See Chapter 7 *infra* on the trustee's avoiding powers.

[90] See 11 U.S.C. § 553, and ¶ 5.10.

or reversing such transfers is the creation of an obligation on the part of the transferee to return property or to pay money to the estate.[91]

It is not uncommon for creditors or equity security holders to be on the receiving end of voidable transfers or to be otherwise obligated to restore property to the estate. To compel such persons to fulfill their obligations to the estate, the Code follows the policy of the former Act by requiring the disallowance of their claims until they perform their obligations.[92] The Code provides that the court must disallow any claim of a creditor or equity security holder from whom property is recoverable by the estate or who has received a voidable transfer, unless the claimant has paid an amount or turned over property in full compliance with the Code.[93]

The purpose of this disallowance provision is to achieve restoration to the estate—not to punish the transferee.[94] Moreover, the Code requires total disallowance regardless of the magnitude of the voidable transfer or the amount of the claim.[95] If a creditor receives a voidable preference worth $25,000 and thereafter files a claim for $100,000, the entire claim will be disallowed unless $25,000 is paid back to the estate. Of course, the trustee will file an objection to the claim. However, the objection may also be joined with a demand for relief against the claimant based on the claimant's liability to the estate. If such a demand is interposed, the matter becomes an adversary proceeding and triggers the procedural requirements of Part VII of the Bankruptcy Rules of Procedure.[96]

¶ 5.06 RIGHTS OF CODEBTORS

As previously discussed, a codebtor has the right to file a proof of claim if the creditor fails to do so.[97] This rule benefits codebtors be-

---

[91] See 11 U.S.C. § 550.

[92] 11 U.S.C. § 502(d), derived from former B.A. § 57(g).

[93] In addition, this provision applies when a claimant is holding property that is recoverable by the debtor, or by the trustee acting on the debtor's behalf, on the ground that there was a preferential transfer of exempt property. See 11 U.S.C. §§ 502(d), 522(f), 522(g), and ¶ 4.08[5].

[94] See *In re* George M. Hill Co., 130 F. 315, 321 (7th Cir. 1904), in which the court stated that "restoration, not punishment, is the object of this law."

[95] See H.R. Rep. No. 95-595, note 13 *supra*, at 354.

[96] B. Rules 306(c) and 701. See Chapter 6 *infra* for a discussion of adversary proceedings.

[97] See 11 U.S.C. § 501(b); B. Rule 304; ¶ 5.04. The term "codebtors"

cause it ensures that creditors will realize as much money as possible from the estate so as to diminish the balance due or secured by the codebtor. The codebtor may file the claim if the creditor does not do so by the first date set for the first meeting of creditors or, in reorganization cases, at any time prior to the approval of the disclosure statement.[98] If the creditor files a proof of claim after the codebtor files, the creditor's proof of claim supersedes the previous one.[99]

Problems often arise with respect to a codebtor's rights against the debtor for contribution or reimbursement. For example, a joint obligor who cosigned a promissory note with the debtor may be called upon to pay the entire amount of the note to the holder. What right to contribution or reimbursement will the cosigner have if the debtor files a bankruptcy petition? What right to contribution is there if the codebtor has not been called upon to pay the note because it matures after the debtor's bankruptcy?

The Bankruptcy Code has specific provisions dealing with the rights of codebtors and the allowance of their claims. Basically, the codebtor has the choice of seeking reimbursement or contribution by filing a proof of claim for it, or of being subrogated to the rights of the original creditor.[100]

There are certain restrictions on the allowance of a codebtor's claim for contribution or reimbursement. First, if the creditor's claim is disallowed for a reason other than payment, the codebtor's claim must be disallowed also.[101] The policy behind this provision is that the codebtor's claim for contribution or reimbursement is entitled to no better status than the principal claim. Second, the codebtor's claim is allowed only to the extent that the principal claim has been paid by the codebtor.[102] If a guarantor has paid $10,000 of a $30,000 debt and is entitled to 100 percent reimbursement pursuant to an agreement with the debtor, the guarantor will have an allowable claim for $10,000 and the original creditor will have an allowable claim for $20,000.

---

is used to include comakers, guarantors, sureties, and persons who secured the debtor's obligations. See also Sugg. Int. B. Rule 3002 on claims by codebtors in chapter 11 cases.

[98] Sugg. Int. B. Rule 3001(b)(3).

[99] B. Rule 304.

[100] See 11 U.S.C. §§ 502(e), 509. See also 124 Cong. Rec. H11094 (daily ed., Sept. 28, 1978).

[101] 11 U.S.C. § 502(e)(1)(A).

[102] See 124 Cong. Rec. H11094 (daily ed., Sept. 28, 1978), where it is reported that a "surety or codebtor is generally permitted a claim for reimbursement or contribution to the extent the surety or codebtor has paid the assured party at the time of allowance."

As an alternative to filing a proof of claim for reimbursement or contribution, the codebtor may elect to be subrogated to the rights of the original creditor to the extent of the payments made by the codebtor.[103] The codebtor is subrogated automatically subject to certain exceptions.[104] The codebtor will not be subrogated to the rights of the creditor to the extent that a claim for contribution or reimbursement was allowed. In essence, the codebtor may enjoy either subrogation or reimbursement/contribution—but not both. Also, if the court disallows the codebtor's claim for reimbursement or contribution, such as when the surety's rights against the debtor are not enforceable under applicable nonbankruptcy law, subrogation is not permitted. Moreover, if the court exercises its equitable powers to subordinate the codebtor's claim for contribution or reimbursement, the codebtor may not elect to be subrogated to the creditor's rights because subrogation would defeat the purpose of subordination.[105] Finally, the codebtor is not entitled to be subrogated to the creditor's rights to the extent that the codebtor received the consideration for the creditor's claim. The purpose of this final restriction is to prevent the "real" debtor, who is ultimately liable on the debt and who received the consideration for it, from recovering against the codebtor, who winds up in bankruptcy. This situation may arise when the debtor's partner, who received all of the consideration for a loan, tries to be subrogated to the rights of the creditor against the debtor who cosigned on the loan but who received none of the consideration.

In general, giving the codebtor an allowable claim for contribution or reimbursement or, in the alternative, giving the codebtor the right to be subrogated to the creditor's claim to the extent of the amount paid to the creditor appears to be equitable to other creditors. For example, let us assume that a surety paid $10,000 of a $30,000 debt and is entitled to 100 percent reimbursement from the debtor pursuant to an agreement between them. The surety may have an allowed claim of $10,000 for reimbursement, and the creditor would have an allowed claim of $20,000. The rights of other creditors are not affected unfairly. However, this approach could create inequities between the creditor on the loan and the surety. It would be unjust to give the surety's $10,000 claim the same priority as the creditor's $20,000 claim. After all, the surety guaranteed the debt and therefore should not be

---

[103] 11 U.S.C. § 509(a).

[104] These exceptions are contained in 11 U.S.C. § 509(b).

[105] See 11 U.S.C. § 510, and ¶ 5.14, dealing with the subordination of claims.

permitted to diminish the creditor's distribution by sharing equally in the estate. Likewise, the surety should not obtain equal priority by asserting the rights of the creditor through subrogation. The Code deals with this problem by treating the codebtor's allowed claim or right of subrogation as being equal in priority with other unsecured claims, but subordinated to the claim of the original creditor until the creditor is paid in full from the bankruptcy estate or elsewhere.[106] In the above example, therefore, the surety's claim for $10,000 is subordinated to the $20,000 claim of the creditor until the creditor is paid in full.

When should a codebtor elect subrogation instead of filing a proof of claim for contribution or reimbursement? The answer to this question may depend on whether there is collateral securing the claim. If the creditor's claim is secured by the debtor's assets, the codebtor will be put in a more favorable position by asserting subrogation rights. Since the creditor's claim is secured, the codebtor may obtain through subrogation a secured claim against the estate. Assume, however, that the creditor's claim is unsecured but that the surety's rights against the debtor are secured; that is, the debtor and the surety have agreed that the debtor's assets will secure the surety's right to reimbursement. In this situation, the surety should file a proof of claim seeking allowance of a secured claim for reimbursement. If the surety relied on the right of subrogation alone, the surety would have only the unsecured claim of the creditor.[107]

¶ 5.07 POSTPETITION CLAIMS

In general, only those claims that exist at the time the petition is filed may be allowed.[108] The commencement of the bankruptcy case marks the beginning of the debtor's fresh start, and claims that first arise after the petition is filed are accordingly not affected by the bankruptcy.

There are several exceptions, however, to the general bar on allowability of postpetition claims. Specifically, the following postpetition claims may be allowed:

[1] Gap Claims in Involuntary Cases

In an involuntary bankruptcy case, there is a period of time between the filing of the petition and the order for relief. The debtor in

---

[106] 11 U.S.C. § 509(c).

[107] See 124 Cong. Rec. H11094 (daily ed., Sept. 28, 1978).

[108] See 11 U.S.C. § 502(b), which provides that the court shall allow a

the involuntary case is entitled to defend against the petition and has the right to a trial on questions of fact. In order to protect the debtor prior to the order for relief in an involuntary case, the Bankruptcy Code permits the debtor to continue to operate in business pending trial.[109] It will be pointless, however, to permit the debtor to continue to do business if trade suppliers and others who extend credit to the debtor during that time in the ordinary course of business are not permitted to share in the estate or to participate in the case. Those creditors who are aware of the pending case are not likely to do business with the debtor on a credit basis, and those creditors who are unaware of it will be unfairly discriminated against if their postpetition claims are disallowed unless some priority position is afforded these claims.

For this reason, the Code provides that claims arising in the ordinary course of the debtor's business or financial affairs after the commencement of an involuntary case but before the order of relief or appointment of a trustee may be allowed the same as if they had arisen before the date of the filing of the petition.[110] In addition to allowing these claims, the Code gives them priority over all other unsecured claims except for administrative expenses.[111] By allowing and giving priority to these involuntary gap claims, the Code permits the debtor to continue doing business in the usual way without much damage to its credit until the trial on the petition is over and a ruling is made.

[2] Claims Arising From the Rejection of Executory Contracts or Unexpired Leases

The Bankruptcy Code gives the trustee or debtor in possession the right to reject executory contracts and unexpired leases.[112] Alternatively, an executory contract or lease may be rejected as part of a plan of reorganization in a chapter 11 case[113] or a debt adjustment plan in a chapter 13 case.[114] When such rejection occurs, damages may be caused that give rise to a claim against the debtor. Since these claims

---

claim in the "amount of such claim as of the date of the filing of the petition. . . ."

[109] See 11 U.S.C. § 303(f), and Chapter 2 *supra*, on involuntary cases.

[110] 11 U.S.C. § 502(f), derived from former B.A. § 63(b). This provision does not apply to the extension of credit while a voluntary case is pending. See Lignacraft, Inc. v. Automation Servs., Inc., 37 A.D.2d 786, 324 N.Y.S.2d 521 (3d Dep't 1971).

[111] 11 U.S.C. § 507(a)(2). See ¶ 5.13[2].

[112] See 11 U.S.C. § 365, and Chapter 7 *infra*.

[113] 11 U.S.C. § 1123(b)(2).

[114] 11 U.S.C. § 1322(b)(7).

for damages first arise when the contract or lease is rejected, they are postpetition claims.

It would be unjust to permit rejection of executory contracts and leases without permitting persons who are damaged thereby to participate in the bankruptcy case. For this reason, claims arising out of such rejection may be allowed the same as if they had arisen before the date of the filing of the petition.[115]

[3] Claims Arising From the Recovery of Property

During the pendency of the bankruptcy case, it is common for the trustee or debtor in possession to recover property for the estate.[116] For example, the trustee may recover property transferred prior to bankruptcy as a voidable preference or fraudulent conveyance. Whenever the recovery of property gives rise to a claim against the estate, the claim will be treated and allowed the same as if it had arisen prior to bankruptcy.[117]

Let us assume, for example, that a creditor who was owed $50,000 received payment in full as a voidable preference. As of the date of bankruptcy, the creditor has no claim because of the payment. If the trustee recovered the $50,000 payment as a preference after the bankruptcy petition was filed, it would be unfair to deprive the creditor of the original $50,000 claim. Accordingly, the creditor's $50,000 claim would be allowed as a prepetition claim as if the preference was never made.

[4] Priority Tax Claims

Certain unsecured tax claims that are entitled to priority may arise after the filing of the petition.[118] A discussion of these priority tax claims will be found later in this chapter.[119] For the purpose of allowability, however, it is important to note that those priority tax claims that arose before but are assessable after the petition is filed are treated as prepetition claims.[120]

---

[115] 11 U.S.C. § 502(g).
[116] See 11 U.S.C. §§ 522(i), 550, 553.
[117] 11 U.S.C. § 502(h).
[118] 11 U.S.C. § 507(a)(6).
[119] See ¶ 5.13[6].
[120] 11 U.S.C. § 502(i).

[5] Postpetition Claims in Chapter 13 Cases

When an individual debtor files a petition for debt adjustment under chapter 13, the debtor usually retains possession of all assets while a trustee distributes a portion of future income to creditors. What rights do creditors have when a new debt is incurred after the petition is filed but while the case is still pending? The Bankruptcy Code provides that only two types of postpetition claims may be allowed. First, a government body may file a proof of claim for taxes that first become payable after the case was commenced and while it is still pending.[121] Second, postpetition consumer debts are allowable if they are liabilities for property or services necessary for the debtor's performance under the plan.[122] For example, liabilities incurred in connection with repairing the debtor's automobile are allowable if the car is needed for job-related transportation. Postpetition medical bills that relate to an injury of the debtor may be allowed if the debtor was incapacitated. Persons who extend consumer credit to the chapter 13 debtor while the case is pending must, however, obtain the trustee's approval in advance whenever feasible. The Code mandates the disallowance of postpetition consumer debt claims if the creditor knew or should have known that prior approval by the trustee was practicable and was not obtained.[123]

¶ 5.08 ADMINISTRATIVE EXPENSES

During the course of a bankruptcy proceeding, the trustee or debtor in possession may find it necessary to expend money or incur indebtedness for the purpose of administering the estate. These expenses and liabilities arise after the case is commenced. The Code permits any entity to file a request for payment or reimbursement of these administrative expenses from the bankruptcy estate.[124]

The court may not allow a claim for an administrative expense unless it first conducts a hearing on notice to determine allowability.[125] The Bankruptcy Code enumerates several types of administrative expenses that may be allowed. It is important to note, however, that involuntary gap claims that arise in the ordinary course of business between the filing of the petition and the order for relief in involuntary

---

[121] 11 U.S.C. § 1305(a)(1), derived from B. Rules 13-305(1) and 13-305(2), and from former B.A. § 680.

[122] 11 U.S.C. § 1305(a)(2), derived from B. Rule 13-305(3).

[123] 11 U.S.C. § 1305(c).

[124] 11 U.S.C. § 503(a), derived from former B.A. § 62.

[125] 11 U.S.C. § 503(b).

cases are not treated as administrative expenses because of their separate treatment elsewhere in the Code.[126]

The following types of administrative expense claims may be allowed by the court:

[1] Expenses of Preserving the Estate

The actual and necessary costs and expenses of preserving the estate may be allowed as administrative expenses.[127] The cost of storing, repairing, or towing property of the estate, for example, may be included in this category.

The Code expressly includes in this category wages, salary, and commissions for services rendered after the commencement of the case for the purpose of preserving the value of estate assets.[128] In fact, actual payments to an individual debtor for services rendered to the estate are administrative expenses and may be retained as such by the debtor. If the debtor is the sole proprietor of a going concern, upon filing a petition for reorganization the debtor would actually be employed by the estate and would be entitled to compensation for running the business while it is in chapter 11.[129] The corporate debtor in possession also may hire personnel to operate the business while the case is pending, thereby giving rise to an administrative expense.[130]

Another common expense that is necessary to preserve the estate in most bankruptcy cases is rent. If the trustee or debtor in possession rejects an unexpired lease but continues in possession, the reasonable value of the actual use and occupation of the premises is an expense of administration.[131] Similarly, if the trustee or debtor in possession elects

---

[126] See 11 U.S.C. §§ 502(f) and 503(b), and ¶ 5.07[1].

[127] 11 U.S.C. § 503(b)(1)(A). See former B.A. § 64(1).

[128] 11 U.S.C. § 503(b)(1)(A). Severance pay that is allocable to the postpetition period also qualifies as an administrative expense, but not severance pay based on prepetition employment. Compare *In re* Unishops, Inc., 553 F.2d 305 (2d Cir. 1977), which is overruled by the Code.

[129] See H.R. Rep. No. 95-595, note 13 *supra*, at 355. See also Local Loan Co. v. Hunt, 292 U.S. 234, 243 (1933), in which the Court quoted: "The wages earned after the adjudication became the property of the bankrupt clear of the claims of all creditors."

[130] See *In re* Patterson-MacDonald Shipbuilding Co., 288 F. 546 (9th Cir. 1923), in which the court allowed a $20,000 administrative expense claim in favor of the former vice-president and manager of the debtor corporation for services rendered to the trustee during the case.

[131] The amount of rent recoverable as an administrative expense is determined by the reasonable value of the trustee's actual use and enjoyment. Usually, the amount of rent specified in the lease agreement is presumed to be

to assume the lease as an asset of the estate, the rent payable to the landlord during the case becomes an administrative expense.

[2] Taxes Incurred by the Estate

In general, tax obligations incurred by the estate, as opposed to by the debtor, may be allowed as an administrative expense.[132] For example, withholding taxes attributable to wages earned by employees during the postpetition period are administrative expenses.[133] Also, tax obligations caused by overestimation of a tentative loss carryback adjustment that the estate received after the petition was filed may be allowed as an administrative expense.[134] Fines, penalties, or reduction of credit relating to these administrative tax expenses are also allowable as costs of administration.[135]

[3] Compensation of Officers

Professionals, including attorneys, accountants, appraisers, and auctioneers, who render services to the trustee or to a creditors' committee during the case are entitled to reasonable compensation as administrative expenses.[136] The court may also award to the trustee, the examiner, and the debtor's attorney reasonable compensation for their services.[137] Moreover, the Bankruptcy Code expressly permits the awarding of compensation to paraprofessionals employed by these officials.[138] The amount of compensation that may be paid to these persons is supervised by the court and is subject to strict limitations.[139]

---

the reasonable value. However, the court may determine, if circumstances warrant, that the fair and reasonable worth of the premises is higher or lower than the rent specified in the rejected lease. See *In re* First Research Corp., 457 F.2d 331 (5th Cir. 1972); S&W Holding Co. v. Kuriansky, 317 F.2d 666 (2d Cir. 1963).

[132] See 11 U.S.C. § 503(b)(1)(B). However, priority tax claims specified in 11 U.S.C. § 507(a)(6) are not considered administrative expenses.

[133] See Otte v. United States, 419 U.S. 43 (1974), where the Court said that "the withholding taxes are, in full effect, part of the claims themselves and derive from and are carved out of the payment of those claims." See also H.R. Rep. No. 95-595, note 13 *supra*, at 355.

[134] 11 U.S.C. § 503(b)(1)(B)(ii).

[135] 11 U.S.C. § 503(b)(1)(C).

[136] See 11 U.S.C. §§ 327, 330, 503(b)(2), and 1103(a). See also B. Rules 215 and 606(c).

[137] See 11 U.S.C. § 330(a)(1).

[138] *Id.*

[139] See Chapter 6 *infra* for a discussion of these limitations. See also 11 U.S.C. § 504, which restricts the sharing of compensation by professionals.

The court may also order the reimbursement of the actual and necessary expenses incurred by such officers and professional persons.[140]

[4] Expenses of Certain Creditors and Other Entities

It is not uncommon for certain creditors to incur expenses by performing a service that benefits the estate or the other creditors. In order to encourage creditors to take certain actions that further the policies of the Bankruptcy Code, certain expenditures may be recouped as administrative expenses.[141] Specifically, the expenses incurred by a creditor who files an involuntary petition against the debtor may be allowed.[142] Similarly, expenses of a creditor who, after the court's approval, recovers for the estate property concealed or transferred by the debtor are allowable.[143] Expenses of a creditor incurred in connection with the prosecution of a criminal offense relating to the case or to the business or property of the debtor also qualify as administrative expenses.[144]

The Code contains a separate catch-all category that gives administrative expense status to any expenditures that are incurred by a creditor, an indenture trustee, an equity security holder, or a committee representing any of these groups (other than a committee appointed under chapter 11), in making a "substantial contribution" in a reorganization case.[145] For the contribution to be "substantial," it is not necessary that it lead to confirmation of a plan. In fact, the discovery of fraud or of some other fact that results in denial of confirmation may be substantial enough.[146] When an indenture trustee makes a "substantial contribution" in the case, the court may award reasonable compensation for services as well as expenses.[147]

Wherever these expenses of creditors, committees, or others are allowed as administrative expenses, the court may also award as administrative expenses reasonable compensation for services rendered by

---

[140] 11 U.S.C. § 330(a)(2).

[141] These provisions are derived from former B.A. § 64(1).

[142] 11 U.S.C. § 503(b)(3)(A).

[143] 11 U.S.C. § 503(b)(3)(B).

[144] 11 U.S.C. § 503(b)(3)(C).

[145] 11 U.S.C. § 503(b)(3)(D).

[146] See H.R. Rep. No. 95-595, note 13 *supra*, at 355.

[147] The compensation payable to the indenture trustee must be based on the time, the nature, the extent, and the value of such services, and the cost of comparable services if performed in a nonbankruptcy setting. See 11 U.S.C. § 503(b)(5).

their attorneys or accountants. However, the compensation must be based on the time, nature, extent, and value of such services and the cost of comparable services in nonbankruptcy cases.[148] These expenses must, of course, be actual and necessary to qualify as administrative expenses.[149]

[5] Compensation and Expenses of a Custodian

When the bankruptcy petition is filed, the debtor's estate may be in the hands of an assignee for the benefit of creditors, a court-appointed receiver, or some other person designated as a custodian. The Code requires the custodian in the usual case to deliver estate assets to the bankruptcy trustee or debtor in possession and to file an accounting with respect to the property or its proceeds.[150] The court, after notice and hearing, may order the payment of reasonable compensation for services rendered and for costs and expenses incurred by the custodian before or after the petition. The compensation and expenses of the custodian are allowable as administrative expenses.[151]

[6] Witness Fees and Mileage

Federal law provides for fees and mileage to be paid to witnesses in U.S. courts.[152] These expenses are treated as administrative expenses in bankruptcy cases.[153]

¶ 5.09 DETERMINATION OF TAX LIABILITIES

Debtors in financial trouble are usually burdened with substantial tax liabilities. The ordinary tax problems of the debtor, especially the business debtor, may become even more complex once a bankruptcy petition is filed.[154] If the trustee or debtor in possession cannot determine with relative certainty and swiftness the amount of tax liabilities

---

[148] See 11 U.S.C. § 503(b)(4). See also 11 U.S.C. § 504, which restricts the sharing of fees paid to professionals.

[149] 11 U.S.C. § 503(b), overruling United Merchants & Mfrs., Inc. v. J. Henry Schroeder Bank & Trust Co., 597 F.2d 348 (2d Cir. 1979).

[150] See 11 U.S.C. § 543.

[151] 11 U.S.C. §§ 543(c)(2), 503(b)(3)(E). See Randolph v. Scruggs, 190 U.S. 533 (1903).

[152] See 28 U.S.C. §§ 1821-1825.

[153] 11 U.S.C. § 503(b)(6).

[154] See the special tax provisions of the Bankruptcy Code contained in 11 U.S.C. §§ 346, 728, 1146. Further reform with respect to tax aspects of

of the estate, it is not difficult to imagine that the administration of the estate or formulation of a plan of reorganization may be unduly delayed. The Internal Revenue Service procedures, Tax Court litigation, audit procedures of various taxing authorities, and other administrative and judicial activity may hold up a final determination of tax liability for a substantial period of time.

The Bankruptcy Code is sensitive to this problem. Accordingly, it contains provisions that are designed to expedite the determination of tax liability of the debtor or the estate. One of these provisions follows the former Bankruptcy Act practice of giving the bankruptcy court jurisdiction over certain tax questions.[155] The court may determine the amount or legality of any tax or tax-related fine or penalty, unless the issue was contested and fully adjudicated by an administrative or judicial tribunal of competent jurisdiction, such as the U.S. Tax Court, prior to bankruptcy.[156] The bankruptcy court's jurisdiction over such tax issues is broad and exists whether or not the tax was previously assessed or paid. Furthermore, if the debtor files a bankruptcy petition while a tax case is pending before the U.S. Tax Court, the automatic stay provisions of the Code require that the Tax Court proceeding be halted until the stay is lifted.[157] If the bankruptcy court decides to permit the Tax Court proceeding to continue, the trustee may desire to intervene in the Tax Court.[158]

The bankruptcy court also has jurisdiction to determine any right that the estate may have to a tax refund. However, for the purpose of giving the taxing authorities time to act on a refund request, the bankruptcy court may not determine the tax refund question until at least 120 days after the trustee properly requests the tax refund from the

---

bankruptcy was anticipated during the Ninety-Fifth Congress, but that process was not completed. It is expected that a special bankruptcy tax bill will be enacted in the near future. See Hearings on H.R. 9973 Before the Joint Comm. on Taxation, 95th Cong., 2d Sess. (1978). See also Plumb, "The Tax Recommendations of the Commission on the Bankruptcy Laws Tax Procedures," 88 Harv. L. Rev. 1360 (1975); H.R. Rep. No. 95-595, 274-284; Newton, "Tax Planning Factors to Be Considered by Debtors and Creditors—In and Out of Court," 83 Com. L.J. 513 (1978).

[155] 11 U.S.C. § 505(a), derived from former B.A. § 2(a)(2A).

[156] 11 U.S.C. § 505(a)(2)(A).

[157] 11 U.S.C. § 362(a)(8).

[158] The Bankruptcy Code follows Arkansas Corp. Comm'r v. Thompson, 313 U.S. 132 (1941), by permitting the bankruptcy court to abstain where uniformity of assessment by appropriate tax authorities is of significant importance. See 11 U.S.C. § 362(d)(1) with respect to termination of the automatic stay. See also H.R. Rep. No. 95-595, note 13 *supra*, at 356.

appropriate governmental authorities. If the governmental unit makes a determination on the request before the 120-day period expires, the bankruptcy court may rule on this issue at that time.[159]

Another provision of the Bankruptcy Code gives the trustee the right to request that the taxing authorities make a determination with respect to tax liability of the estate. The trustee may request a determination of the estate's liability for any unpaid tax obligation incurred during the bankruptcy administration. The trustee makes this request by submitting a tax return to the appropriate governmental authorities and asking them to determine the estate's liability.[160] Unless the tax return is fraudulent or contains material misrepresentations, the debtor, any successor to the debtor, and the trustee will be discharged from any liability for such tax if any one of three events occurs.

First, if the taxing authority determines the amount of tax due, the payment of that amount results in a discharge. Second, there is a discharge upon payment of the amount set by the bankruptcy court as the amount of tax due after an audit is completed and after notice and a court hearing. The third event that results in a discharge of these tax obligations is the most important one for the purpose of expediency. If the trustee pays the sum shown on the return as the amount due and the taxing authorities do not notify the trustee within sixty days after the trustee's request for a determination that the return has been selected for an audit, the tax obligation is discharged. Moreover, if the governmental unit notifies the trustee that there will be an audit, but does not complete the audit and give notice of the tax due within 180 days after the trustee first made the request for a determination, the tax is discharged nonetheless unless the court extends the 180-day period for cause.[161]

It is important to note that the filing of a bankruptcy petition automatically stays any act to collect or assess any claim against the debtor.[162] Accordingly, tax authorities may not assess a tax during the bankruptcy case. The stay, however, does not prevent the determination of tax liability upon the trustee's request or the adjudication of tax claims in bankruptcy court. Moreover, if the bankruptcy court renders a final judgment with respect to a tax obligation, the taxing authority

---

[159] 11 U.S.C. § 505(2)(B).

[160] With respect to federal taxes, this request should be made to the district director in the district where the bankruptcy case is pending. See 124 Cong. Rec. H11111 (daily ed., Sept. 28, 1978).

[161] 11 U.S.C. § 505(b).

[162] 11 U.S.C. § 362(a)(6).

may disregard the stay and may make an assessment as otherwise permitted by law.[163]

¶ 5.10 THE RIGHT TO SETOFF

Let us assume that a creditor has a $10,000 unsecured claim against the debtor for manufactured goods sold and delivered. Assume that, as a result of a separate transaction, the debtor sold other goods to the creditor on credit for $4,000. In essence, the creditor owes the debtor $4,000 and the debtor owes the creditor $10,000. If the debtor files a bankruptcy petition, the Bankruptcy Code permits the offsetting of prepetition mutual debts so that the creditor will have, in essence, a $6,000 unsecured claim against the debtor. This general recognition of the right to set off mutual debts is not new in bankruptcy law, although the Bankruptcy Code makes several changes with respect to setoffs.[164]

It is important to understand at the outset why the right to set off mutual debts is to the advantage of the creditor. Assume that the debtor's estate is large enough to pay only 10 percent of all nonpriority unsecured claims in liquidation. If the creditor discussed above did not have the right of setoff, the unsecured claim allowable in bankruptcy would be $10,000 and, accordingly, the creditor would receive $1,000 as a dividend. Also, since the debtor's $4,000 claim against the creditor would become property of the estate, the trustee would be able to recover $4,000 from the creditor. The net effect of this would be a loss of $3,000 for the creditor. On the other hand, because the Bankruptcy Code permits a setoff, the real net effect is that the creditor has an unsecured claim for $6,000 and would receive $600 as a dividend without having to pay anything to the estate. As one court commented: "A setoff has the effect of paying one creditor more than another. Despite the preferential advantages bestowed upon certain creditors by virtue of section 68 [of the former Bankruptcy Act], setoffs are accepted and approved because they are based upon long-recognized rights of mutual debtors." [165]

It is not surprising that most rights of setoff are exercised by banks. In a typical case, the debtor has funds on deposit in a checking or savings account at a certain bank. In addition, the debtor has an outstand-

---

[163] 11 U.S.C. § 505(c).

[164] See 11 U.S.C. § 553, derived from former B.A. § 68, and ¶ 5.05(1)(c). See also Loyd, "The Development of Setoff," 64 U. Pa. L. Rev. 541 (1916), for a discussion of the historical roots of the right of setoff.

[165] *In re* Bohack Corporation, 599 F.2d 1160, 1165 (2d Cir. 1979).

ing loan from the same bank. Even if the bank does not require the debtor to maintain a compensating balance in the accounts to secure the loan, the bank may succeed in setting off the balance of the debtor's accounts against the balance due on the loan if the debtor files a bankruptcy petition. Courts have viewed bank account balances as debts owed by the bank to its customers. Accordingly, this "debt" owed to the customer may be set off against the loan.[166]

[1] When the Right of Setoff Is Denied

Despite the general recognition of the right of banks and other creditors to set off mutual debts, there are certain situations in which the right of setoff may be denied by the court. First, the right only applies to mutual debts that arose prior to the commencement of the bankruptcy case. Thus, the creditor may not improve its position by buying goods from the debtor on credit after the petition is filed.[167] Second, the right to set off a mutual debt may not be exercised to the extent that the creditor's claim against the debtor is disallowed.[168] For example, if the creditor's claim violates the statute of frauds or is otherwise unenforceable, there is no right of setoff and the trustee may recover payment on the debt owed by the creditor to the debtor. Third, the right of setoff will be denied if the creditor received the claim against the debtor by means of an assignment by someone else after the petition is filed or within ninety days prior to the filing while the debtor was insolvent.[169] The reason for this limitation is to prevent the person who

[166] The leading case that supports the bank's right to set off the balance of a bank account is New York County Nat'l Bank v. Massey, 192 U.S. 138 (1903). See also *In re* Applied Logic Corp., 576 F.2d 952 (2d Cir. 1978), in which a bank was permitted to set off certificates of deposit held by the bank against a debt owed to it. Of added interest is the discussion of special accounts and the application of the debtor's payments where the creditor has secured or guaranteed open accounts. Compare, however, Goldstein v. Franklin Square Nat'l Bank, 107 F.2d 393 (2d Cir. 1939), which held that the deposit of funds by the insolvent debtor in a checking account for the deliberate purpose of permitting the bank to offset the deposit against an antecedent debt constituted a voidable preference and was not protected by the setoff provision of the Bankruptcy Act.

[167] 11 U.S.C. § 553(a).

[168] 11 U.S.C. § 553(a)(1). Of course, this limitation does not apply if the claim was disallowed solely because the creditor has the right of setoff. See 11 U.S.C. § 502(b)(3).

[169] 11 U.S.C. § 553(a)(2). The debtor is presumed to have been insolvent during the ninety-day period prior to bankruptcy. 11 U.S.C. § 553(c).

owes money to the debtor from buying for nominal consideration almost worthless claims against the debtor on the eve of bankruptcy for the purpose of effectuating a setoff.

The final ground for the denial of the right to set off mutual debts also involves deliberate manipulation by the creditor. To illustrate, let us assume that the creditor has an unsecured claim against the debtor for $10,000. The creditor, knowing that the debtor is insolvent, orders $10,000 worth of goods from the debtor on credit. The creditor does not need the goods, but wants to have the right to set off mutual debts in case the debtor files a bankruptcy petition. When bankruptcy becomes a reality, the creditor has $10,000 worth of goods instead of a $10,000 claim against a hopelessly insolvent estate. Similarly, an insolvent debtor may adhere to a bank's request to deliberately build up the balance of a bank account so that the bank may obtain a greater setoff upon the debtor's bankruptcy. The Code deals with these situations by providing for the denial of a setoff to the extent that the debt owed to the debtor was incurred by the creditor within ninety days prior to the commencement of the case, while the debtor was insolvent, for the purpose of obtaining a right of setoff against the debtor.[170]

[2] Trustee's Power to Recover Certain Setoffs Made Within Ninety Days of Bankruptcy

Another limitation on the right of setoff relates to the creditor who exercised the right of setoff before the commencement of the bankruptcy case and whose position was improved within the ninety-day period prior to the filing of the petition. Specifically, if the creditor offsets mutual debts on or within ninety days before the commencement of the case, the trustee may recover from the creditor the amount set off to the extent that any insufficiency on the date of the setoff is less than the insufficiency ninety days before the petition is filed or, if there is no insufficiency ninety days before bankruptcy, when there is an insufficiency for the first time within the ninety-day period.[171] The term *insufficiency* means the amount by which a claim against the debtor exceeds the amount of the mutual debt owed to the debtor.[172] The ratio-

---

[170] 11 U.S.C. § 553(a)(3). This provision follows Goldstein v. Franklin Square Nat'l Bank, note 166 *supra*. Notice that the trustee is aided by the fact that the debtor is presumed to have been insolvent during the ninety-day period prior to bankruptcy. 11 U.S.C. § 553(c).

[171] 11 U.S.C. § 553(b)(1). For a good discussion of this provision, see Orr & Klee, "Secured Creditors Under the New Bankruptcy Code," 11 U.C.C.L.J. 312, 335-338 (1979).

[172] 11 U.S.C. § 553(b)(2). A similar concept is used to determine the

nale for giving the trustee the power to recover these setoffs is to prevent creditors from effectuating a preference by making a prepetition setoff. This apparently complicated rule, which is new in bankruptcy law, should not be left without illustration.

Illustration 1. The debtor owed the bank $10,000 at all times during the past year. Ninety days before the petition was filed, the debtor had $6,000 in a bank account at the same bank. The insufficiency at that time was $4,000 ($10,000 less $6,000). Prior to the commencement of the case, the bank set off the account balance, which was $5,000 at that time. Because the insufficiency ninety days prior to bankruptcy ($4,000) was less than the insufficiency when the setoff occurred ($5,000), the trustee may not recover any of it. In essence, the bank's position did not improve during the ninety-day period because it could have set off more ($6,000) if it made the setoff ninety days prior to bankruptcy.

Illustration 2. The debtor owed the bank $10,000 at all times during the past year. Ninety days before the petition was filed, the debtor had $6,000 in a bank account. Immediately before bankruptcy, the bank set off the balance of the debtor's account, which was $7,000 at that time. The insufficiency ninety days prior to bankruptcy was $4,000 ($10,000 less $6,000), and was $3,000 ($10,000 less $7,000) on the day of the setoff. The trustee may recover $1,000 from the bank because the bank's position improved by $1,000 during the ninety-day period.

Illustration 3. The debtor owed the bank $10,000 at all times during the past year. Ninety days before bankruptcy the debtor had $13,000 in a bank account. Thirty days prior to bankruptcy, the debtor withdrew funds for the first time, which reduced the account balance to $6,000. Ten days prior to the filing of the petition the bank set off $7,000, which was the account balance at that time. The trustee may recover $1,000 from the bank. The first time during the ninety-day period when there was an insufficiency was thirty days before the petition was filed. The insufficiency then ($4,000) was less than the insufficiency at the time of the setoff ($3,000). Accordingly, the bank's position improved by $1,000 during that time.[173]

---

extent of a preference with respect to inventory and accounts receivable financing. See Chapter 7 *infra* for a discussion on preferences.

[173] For similar illustrations, see Orr & Klee, note 171 *supra*.

If the trustee recovers a setoff because of the improved position of the creditor within the ninety-day period prior to bankruptcy, the creditor's unsecured claim against the estate will be increased accordingly.[174]

[3] Setoffs and the Automatic Stay Rule

There are procedural hurdles that affect the creditor's exercise of a valid right of setoff once the bankruptcy petition is filed. Of course, if the creditor has already exercised the right of setoff prior to bankruptcy, the creditor may simply submit a proof of claim for the deficiency owed. If the trustee has the right to recover all or part of the amount of the prepetition setoff because of the improvement of position within the crucial ninety-day period, a proceeding may be commenced by the trustee for that purpose or the creditor's claim for a deficiency may be disallowed until recovery is made.[175]

Assume, however, that the creditor who has a valid right of setoff has not exercised it prior to bankruptcy. What are the rights of the bank that has the right to set off the balance of a bank account against an unsecured loan balance? The bank or other creditor who wants to exercise setoff rights is confronted by the automatic stay provision of the Bankruptcy Code that applies to setoffs.[176]

The rationale behind the automatic stay of setoff rights is to prevent the situation in which the debtor's cash flow problem becomes fatal to its operations because of the loss of bank accounts and accounts receivable. This is especially important in reorganization cases. If the bank could freeze all bank accounts upon the filing of the petition, whatever chances the debtor may have had for rehabilitation would probably vanish without the use of its bank balances. Even in liquidation cases, the continuation of business for a temporary period of time may be appropriate to maintain the value of the business as a going concern. The use of cash deposits and the collection of accounts receivable without interruption can be important for the preservation of the estate.

The automatic stay rule does not, however, strip the creditor of the substantive right of setoff. The creditor whose right of setoff is stayed is entitled to adequate protection.[177] This protection may be in the form of periodic cash payments by the trustee, giving the creditor a lien

---

[174] 11 U.S.C. § 502(h).

[175] 11 U.S.C. § 502(d).

[176] 11 U.S.C. § 362(a)(7). See Chapter 1 *supra* for a discussion of the automatic stay provisions of the Code.

[177] See 11 U.S.C. §§ 361, 362(d)(1).

on specific assets, granting an administrative expense priority in asset cases, or any other appropriate mechanism. If the creditor wants relief from the stay or believes that there is no adequate protection to secure the right of setoff, an adversary proceeding may be instituted for that purpose.[178]

When the unsecured creditor's right of setoff is stayed, the creditor's claim will be allowed as a secured claim to the extent of the setoff.[179] For example, the creditor who has a $10,000 unsecured claim and a $2,000 right of setoff may be treated as having a secured claim for $2,000 and an unsecured claim for $8,000. This treatment further protects the setoff rights of the unsecured creditor.

¶ 5.11 SECURED CLAIMS

There are three types of liens that creditors may have obtained with respect to the debtor's property prior to bankruptcy. The first type of lien is the consensual lien, which is created by agreement between the debtor and the creditor and which includes real estate mortgages and security interests in personal property.[180] Second, creditors may have judicial liens, which are those created by judgment, levy, sequestration, or other legal or equitable judicial proceeding.[181] The third category includes statutory liens, which arise solely by force of a statute on specific circumstances.[182] Examples of statutory liens are the landlord's lien for rent, the garageman's lien, the artisan's lien, the warehouseman's lien,[183] and the tax lien.[184]

The Bankruptcy Code gives the trustee or debtor in possession the power to avoid liens in certain situations. For example, liens obtained

---

[178] See Chapter 6 *infra* for a discussion of the procedures for these proceedings.

[179] 11 U.S.C. § 506(a).

[180] These consensual liens are included in the definition of "security interest" in 11 U.S.C. § 101(37). Article 9 of the Uniform Commercial Code contains the body of state law that governs security interests in personal property in every state except Louisiana.

[181] 11 U.S.C. § 101(27) defines "judicial lien."

[182] 11 U.S.C. § 101(38) defines "statutory lien."

[183] See Sections 7-209 and 7-210 of the Uniform Commercial Code, which govern the warehouseman's lien. Section 7-210 was upheld by the Supreme Court in a recent constitutional attack. Flagg Bros., Inc. v. Brooks, 436 U.S. 149 (1978). Compare Sharrock v. Dell Buick, 45 N.Y.2d 152 (1978), in which the court of appeals held that the New York garageman's lien statute is unconstitutional with respect to its sales provisions.

[184] For a discussion of tax liens with respect to federal income taxes, see

as voidable preferences or fraudulent conveyances may be avoided. Statutory liens may be avoided to the extent that they first become effective upon the filing of a bankruptcy petition. These are only a few of the numerous situations in which liens may be avoided under the Code.[185]

The policy of the Bankruptcy Code is to recognize and give effect to those liens that are not avoided by the trustee or debtor in possession.[186] In fact, most liens will remain effective against the estate in the typical bankruptcy case. To the extent that a claim is secured by a valid consensual, judicial, or statutory lien, the Code treats it as a *secured claim*.[187] As discussed above, to the extent that an unsecured creditor has a right of setoff, the creditor's claim also is treated as a secured claim.[188]

A creditor with a secured claim does not have to file a proof of claim to maintain its lien.[189] However, the creditor that does not file a proof of claim may lose its lien if one of two possible actions occurs. First, if the trustee or debtor in possession commences a proceeding to invalidate the lien pursuant to an avoiding power, the lien may become void. Second, if any party in interest requests that the court determine and allow or disallow the creditor's claim, the lien will survive only to the extent that the secured claim is allowed by the court.[190] Of course, if the creditor's claim is disallowed, the lien will not survive.[191]

[1] Allowance of the Secured Claim and Valuation

Although the secured creditor may take a "wait and see" attitude without filing a proof of claim, the failure to have the claim allowed

---

Maule, "Collection of Federal Income Taxes by Levy," 64 A.B.A.J. 1439 (1978). See 11 U.S.C. § 724(b), derived from former B.A. § 67(c)(3), which subordinates tax liens to the rights of certain unsecured priority claims.

[185] See Chapter 7 *infra* for a more detailed discussion of the trustee's avoiding powers.

[186] See 11 U.S.C. § 506, which follows the policy of the former Act in recognizing valid liens in bankruptcy. See also Straton v. New, 283 U.S. 318 (1930). For a discussion concerning priorities among secured claims, see Jackson & Kronman, "Secured Financing and Priorities Among Creditors," 88 Yale L.J. 1143 (1979).

[187] 11 U.S.C. § 506(a).

[188] *Id.* See ¶ 5.10.

[189] See Orr & Klee, note 171 supra, at 315.

[190] See 11 U.S.C. § 506(d)(1).

[191] However, if a secured claim held by a codebtor is disallowed on certain grounds, the lien may still remain effective. See 11 U.S.C. §§ 502(e), 506(d)(2).

may deprive the creditor of an opportunity to participate in the bankruptcy case. For example, assume that a creditor has a $10,000 claim secured by collateral worth $6,000. The creditor whose claim is not allowed is not permitted to share in the distribution of the estate upon liquidation with respect to the $4,000 deficiency.[192] Similarly, in a reorganization case the secured creditor may not vote to accept or reject a plan if its claim is not allowed.[193] Therefore, the secured creditor who wants to participate in the bankruptcy case will have to file a proof of claim to have the claim allowed. As discussed earlier, the proof of claim is "deemed filed" in a reorganization case if it is properly scheduled, unless it is scheduled as disputed, contingent, or unliquidated.[194]

Once the creditor's claim is allowed under the Code, it becomes a secured claim to the extent of the value of the collateral or the amount subject to setoff. To the extent that the value of the collateral or right of setoff is less than the total allowed claim, the creditor is deemed to have an unsecured claim.[195] In essence, the undersecured creditor whose collateral is worth less than the debt is treated as having two claims, one secured and one unsecured. For the purpose of determining the value of the collateral, the court will usually hold a hearing.[196] Valuation must be determined on a case-by-case basis and in light of the purpose of the valuation and the proposed disposition or use of the collateral. The value placed on the collateral for this purpose is not binding with respect to any other purpose. For example, valuation to determine the extent of adequate protection needed to continue the automatic stay against lien foreclosure does not preclude a subsequent valuation for the purpose of a "cram down" confirmation in a reorganization case or for the purpose of determining the extent of a partially secured creditor's lien.[197]

---

[192] See ¶ 5.15.

[193] 11 U.S.C. § 1126(a). In addition, if the secured claim is not allowed, the creditor in a reorganization case may not elect to be treated as a fully secured creditor under 11 U.S.C. § 1111(b)(2).

[194] 11 U.S.C. § 1111(a). See ¶ 5.04.

[195] 11 U.S.C. § 506(a). However, see 11 U.S.C. § 1111(b)(2), and Chapter 8 *infra*, with respect to the right of partially secured creditors to be treated as fully secured creditors in reorganization cases.

[196] See B. Rule 306(d), and former B.A. § 57(h), which dealt with valuation of collateral.

[197] See 11 U.S.C. § 506(a); H.R. Rep. No. 95-595, note 13 *supra*, at 356. The court has considerable discretion in determining the appropriate method of valuation. See, e.g. *In re* American Kitchen Foods, Inc., 2 Bankr. Dec. 715 (D. Me. 1976).

[2] What Happens to the Collateral During the Case

The secured creditor is stayed automatically from the enforcement of its lien and therefore may not proceed to foreclose on the collateral after the petition is filed.[198] The stayed creditor, however, is entitled to adequate protection to assure that it will not be damaged by the stay. The secured creditor's right to adequate protection, as well as the creditor's right to relief or modification of the stay, is discussed in more detail in Chapter 1 of this book.

While the secured creditor is stayed from lien enforcement, the trustee or debtor in possession may use the collateral in the ordinary course of business or, if the court approves, not in the ordinary course of business.[199] The only collateral that may not be used without either consent or court approval is "cash collateral."[200] Furthermore, collateral may be sold free and clear of liens under certain circumstances.[201] However, whether collateral is used or sold during the case, the creditor's right to adequate protection may not be jeopardized.[202]

[3] Expenses Relating to the Collateral

It is not uncommon for the trustee to incur expenses with respect to protecting the collateral. When this occurs, the secured creditor is often the beneficiary of these expenses. For this reason, the Bankruptcy Code gives the trustee the right to recover from the collateral the reasonable and necessary costs and expenses of preserving or disposing of the collateral to the extent of any benefit to the secured creditor.[203]

[4] Interest on Secured Claims

As a general proposition, interest that accrues after the petition is filed is not allowable in bankruptcy. The running of interest stops when the case is commenced.[204] However, the Code contains an exception whereby postpetition interest may be recovered by the holder of a secured claim. Whenever the value of the collateral, after the deducting of expenses that may be recovered from the property, exceeds the amount of the allowed claim, the claimant is entitled to an allowable

---

[198] 11 U.S.C. § 362(a)(4).

[199] 11 U.S.C. §§ 363(b), 363(c). See Chapter 4 *supra* for a discussion of the use of estate assets during the case.

[200] 11 U.S.C. §§ 363(a), 363(c).

[201] 11 U.S.C. § 363(f).

[202] 11 U.S.C. § 363(e).

[203] 11 U.S.C. § 506(c).

[204] See ¶ 5.05[1][b].

claim for postpetition interest to the extent of the excess collateral value. In addition, such oversecured creditors may receive an allowance for any reasonable fees, costs, or charges, including attorneys fees, as provided in the security agreement.[205] In no event, however, may the creditor's claim for interest and fees exceed the excess value of the collateral over the amount of the claim.[206]

[5] Security Interests on After-Acquired Property

Article 9 of the Uniform Commercial Code provides that a security agreement may give the creditor a lien on after-acquired property.[207] For example, a creditor may obtain a security interest on "all inventory presently owned and hereafter acquired." Because the lien attaches to new collateral as soon as the debtor acquires it, this type of security interest is commonly referred to as a "floating lien."[208] Due to the frequent turnover of inventory and accounts receivable, after-acquired property clauses are common in security agreements dealing with these types of collateral.

The Bankruptcy Code limits the effect of such after-acquired property clauses by making them inoperative with respect to postpetition property of the estate or the debtor.[209] Accordingly, the inventory financer whose security interest is in after-acquired inventory may not assert a lien in any inventory purchased after the petition is filed. The effect of the bankruptcy petition is to stop the lien from floating to new collateral.

This limitation with respect to after-acquired collateral purchased after the case commences does not, however, apply to the secured party's lien on proceeds, rents, or profits from the original collateral.[210] Let us assume that the creditor has a security interest in the debtor's

---

[205] See Textile Banking Co. v. Widener, 265 F.2d 446 (4th Cir. 1959), in which the court stated that the trustee's expenses incurred in selling the collateral may be charged against the proceeds, but such charge may not exceed the costs of selling the collateral through a state court foreclosure proceeding.

[206] 11 U.S.C. § 506(b). See *In re* Black Ranches, Inc., 362 F.2d 8 (8th Cir. 1966).

[207] U.C.C. § 9-204.

[208] See, e.g., 1 Coogan, Hogan & Vagts, *Secured Transactions Under the Uniform Commercial Code* Ch. 2 (1978); White & Summers, *Uniform Commercial Code* 876-883 (1972); DuBay v. Williams, 417 F.2d 1277 (9th Cir. 1969).

[209] 11 U.S.C. § 552(a), codifying *In re* Sequential Information Sys., Inc., CCH Bankr. Dec. 63848 (S.D.N.Y. 1970).

[210] 11 U.S.C. § 552(b). Whether or not the security interest attaches to

inventory and its proceeds.[211] After the bankruptcy petition is filed, the debtor's inventory is sold on credit, thus creating accounts receivable. Since the accounts receivable are proceeds of the inventory, the creditor has a lien on the accounts, which may be worth more than the inventory. Similarly, if the inventory is destroyed by fire after the case is commenced, proceeds of the fire insurance policy will become the collateral. The security interest may also attach to postpetition profits, rents, produce, or offspring of the collateral to the same extent that it would attach in the absence of bankruptcy. Accordingly, if a mortgage agreement gives the creditor a lien on rents to be collected from an office building, the creditor's claim is deemed secured by future rents. It is important to note, however, that postpetition proceeds, profits, rents, offspring, and produce are subject to the lien only if they derive from prepetition collateral.[212]

The extension of the prepetition security interest to postpetition proceeds, profits, rents, offspring, and produce is not absolute and automatic. The Code provides that the court may, after a notice and hearing and based on the equities of the case, order that proceeds and profits shall not be subject to the lien.[213] It is anticipated that the court will take into account any related expenses of the estate that may have depleted funds available for unsecured creditors. For example, if the trustee converts raw materials into inventory at considerable expense, it is doubtful that the creditor with a lien on the raw materials will be given a lien on all of the inventory as proceeds or on the profits on the sale of the inventory without an adjustment made to avoid depletion of funds for unsecured claimants because of the related expenses.[214]

¶ 5.12 THE SELLER'S RIGHT TO RECLAIM GOODS

At common law, the unpaid seller who was defrauded into extending unsecured credit to a buyer had the right to rescind the sale and recover the goods. The mere purchase of goods on credit was considered as an implied representation that the buyer was solvent and able to pay for the goods. Accordingly, when a buyer ordered goods on credit while

---

rents depends on state law. See Butner v. United States, 440 U.S. 48 (1979). This provision does not apply, however, where it would be inconsistent with other sections of the Bankruptcy Code. See 11 U.S.C. §§ 363, 506(c), 544, 545, 547, 548.

[211] Section 9-306 of the UCC governs the secured party's rights with respect to proceeds.

[212] 11 U.S.C. § 552(b).

[213] *Id.*

[214] See S. Rep. No. 95-989, 95th Cong. 2d Sess. 91 (1978).

insolvent, the seller had the right to rescind on the grounds of fraud upon discovery of the insolvency.[215]

The Uniform Commercial Code codifies and limits the unpaid seller's right to reclaim goods. Section 2-702(2) provides as follows:

> Where the seller discovers that the buyer has received goods on credit while insolvent he may reclaim the goods upon demand made within ten days after the receipt, but if misrepresentation of solvency has been made to the particular seller in writing within three months before delivery the ten day limitation does not apply. Except as provided in this subsection the seller may not base a right to reclaim goods on the buyer's fraudulent or innocent misrepresentation of solvency or of intent to pay.

Let us assume that the seller delivers goods to a buyer on credit. Within ten days after delivery, the seller discovers that the buyer is insolvent and demands the return of the goods. Pursuant to the UCC, the seller has the right to reclaim the goods. However, assume that the buyer files a bankruptcy petition before the seller takes possession of the goods. Is the seller's right to reclaim the goods effective against the trustee in bankruptcy?

This issue had been litigated extensively under the former Bankruptcy Act. Trustees have argued that Section 2-702 of the UCC creates a statutory lien that is effective upon the buyer's insolvency only, thereby creating an invalid statutory lien.[216] It has also been argued that Section 2-702 is an improper interference with the priority rules under the former Act.[217] Despite these arguments, most courts have held that the seller's right to reclaim was effective against the trustee under the former Act because it created a valid right of rescission.[218] Several courts, however, refused to allow the unpaid seller to reclaim.[219]

---

[215] See Gordon v. Spalding, 268 F.2d 327 (5th Cir. 1959); Braucher, "Reclamation of Goods From a Fraudulent Buyer," 65 Mich. L. Rev. 1281, 1282-84 (1967).

[216] See 11 U.S.C. § 545(1); former B.A. § 67(c)(1)(A).

[217] See, e.g., Sebert, "The Seller's Right to Reclaim: Another Conflict Between the Uniform Commercial Code and the Bankruptcy Act," 52 Notre Dame Law. 219 (1976); Weintraub & Edelman, "Seller's Right to Reclaim Property Under Section 2-702(2) of the Code Under the Bankruptcy Act: Fact or Fancy," 32 Bus. Law. 1165 (1977).

[218] See *In re* Federal's, Inc., 553 F.2d 509 (6th Cir. 1977); *In re* Telemart Enterprises, Inc., 524 F.2d 761 (9th Cir. 1975), *cert. denied* 424 U.S. 969 (1976); *In re* PFA Farmers Mkt. Ass'n, 4 Bankr. Dec. 747 (8th Cir. 1978).

[219] See *In re* Wetson's Corp., 17 U.C.C. Rep. 423 (S.D.N.Y. 1975); *In re* Giltex, 17 U.C.C. Rep. 887 (S.D.N.Y. 1975).

The Bankruptcy Code clears up any confusion with respect to the rights of the unpaid seller by expressly adopting, in part, Section 2-702 of the UCC. Specifically, the Bankruptcy Code provides that the trustee's avoiding powers are subject to any reclamation rights of the seller who sold goods to the debtor in the ordinary course of business while the debtor was insolvent.[220] The seller's right to reclaim may derive from the common law or from a statute, such as the Uniform Commercial Code. There are, however, strict limitations on the seller's right to reclaim in bankruptcy. First, the sale of goods must have been in the ordinary course of the seller's business. Second, the seller may not reclaim goods unless reclamation is demanded in writing within ten days after the debtor received the goods.[221] It is important to note that Section 2-702 of the UCC relieves the seller of the ten-day demand rule if the buyer made a written misrepresentation as to solvency within three months. The Bankruptcy Code, however, does not adopt this part of Section 2-702. Despite any written misrepresentation, the seller's right to reclaim is lost against a debtor in bankruptcy if demand is not made within ten days.

The bankruptcy court is given a choice with respect to the treatment of the seller's right to reclaim goods when a proper demand is made within the ten-day period.[222] The court may grant the seller's request for possession of the goods. Alternatively, the court may deny reclamation and grant the seller's claim as an administrative expense priority.[223] A third way to treat the right of reclamation is to grant the seller a lien on the goods or on some other property of the estate. The reason for allowing the court to deny reclamation by giving the seller an administrative expense priority or lien is to accommodate a debtor in possession who requires the use of the goods in reorganization cases. Permitting the debtor to use the goods purchased on credit may benefit the estate or increase the likelihood of a successful rehabilitation.

¶ 5.13 PRIORITY CLAIMS

The Bankruptcy Code sets forth certain types of unsecured claims and expenses that are entitled to priority in distribution over other unsecured claims. It is important to appreciate, however, that on the

---

[220] 11 U.S.C. § 546(c).
[221] 11 U.S.C. § 546(c)(1).
[222] This choice is set forth in 11 U.S.C. § 546(c)(2).
[223] See ¶ 5.13[1] with respect to the administrative expense priority.

priority ladder these claims and expenses rank below allowed secured claims[224] but above all other unsecured claims. Moreover, the six categories of priorities are ranked among themselves. For example, administrative expenses rank as the first priority and therefore must be paid in full upon the debtor's liquidation before the second priority, involuntary gap claims, receives any dividend. Similarly, involuntary gap creditors must be paid in full before the third priority, wage claims, receives a dividend, and so on.[225]

[1] First Priority: Administrative Expenses

It is important that the estate pay for expenses of bankruptcy administration. Thus, the Code continues the policy of the former Act in giving administrative expenses a first priority.[226] In addition to including administrative expenses, which are discussed in detail earlier in this chapter,[227] the first priority also includes any court fees and charges assessed against the estate.[228]

[2] Second Priority: Involuntary Gap Claims

As discussed above, claims that arise in the ordinary course of the debtor's business after an involuntary case is commenced but before the order for relief or appointment of a trustee are allowable as if they arose prior to the petition.[229] In order to encourage persons to do business as usual with the debtor who has not had a day in court to challenge the involuntary petition, these unsecured "involuntary gap claims" are given a second priority.[230]

---

[224] However, see 11 U.S.C. § 724(b), which provides for the subordination of tax liens to certain unsecured priority creditors. See also former B.A. § 67(c)(3).

[225] It should be noted, however, that an entity that is subrogated to the rights of a holder of a third-, fourth-, fifth-, or sixth-level priority claim is not entitled to benefit from the priority status. 11 U.S.C. § 507(d).

[226] 11 U.S.C. § 507(a)(1). See former B.A. § 64(1). Notice that the Code gives the court authority to grant superpriority status over other administrative expenses to encourage new postpetition financing. 11 U.S.C. § 364(c). Compare *In re* Texlon Corp., 596 F.2d 1092 (2d Cir. 1979).

[227] See ¶ 5.08.

[228] 11 U.S.C. § 507(a)(1). See 28 U.S.C. Ch. 123, which governs court fees and charges.

[229] See ¶ 5.07[1]; 11 U.S.C. § 502(f).

[230] 11 U.S.C. § 507(a)(2).

[3] Third Priority: Wage Claims

The Bankruptcy Code follows the former Act in that it gives a priority to certain unsecured claims for wages, salary, or commissions earned by the debtor's employees who suffer by a loss of their jobs as a result of the filing of a bankruptcy petition.[231] As Judge Learned Hand once commented: "The statute was intended to favor those who could not be expected to know anything of the credit of their employer, but must accept a job as it comes. . . ."[232]

The wage priority includes claims for vacation, severance, and sick leave pay as well as claims for basic wages, salary, and commissions. However, this priority is not without limits. The wage priority applies to claims for compensation earned by an individual within ninety days before the filing of the petition or the cessation of the debtor's business, whichever occurs first. Moreover, the priority may not exceed $2,000 for each employee.[233] Thus, an employee who is owed $5,000 for wages earned during the ninety-day period plus $5,000 for wages earned more than ninety days before bankruptcy may obtain a $2,000 priority claim and an $8,000 nonpriority claim.

[4] Fourth Priority: Contributions to Employee Benefit Plans

Under the former Bankruptcy Act, courts have not granted wage priority status to claims based on employees' rights to fringe benefits, such as claims for unpaid contributions to employee annuity plans. The Supreme Court construed the wage priority provision of the former Act very narrowly.[234] When enacting the new Code, however, Congress recognized the realities of modern labor contract negotiations that result in increased fringe benefits as a substitute for substantial wage demands. Accordingly, the Bankruptcy Code now gives employees certain protection with respect to their fringe benefits. Specifically, claims for

---

[231] 11 U.S.C. § 507(a)(3). See former B.A. § 64(2). See also Sugg. Int. B. Form Nos. 14, 15, set forth in Appendix B, for proof of claims for wages.

[232] *In re* Lawsam Elec. Co., 300 F. 736 (S.D.N.Y. 1924).

[233] Compare former B.A. § 64(2), which limited the employee's priority claim to $600.

[234] See Joint Indus. Bd. v. United States, 391 U.S. 224 (1968); United States v. Embassy Restaurant, Inc., 359 U.S. 29 (1959). But see *In re* E. Moore of Cal., Inc., 447 F.2d 1106 (9th Cir.), *cert. denied* 404 U.S. 995 (1971), in which the court afforded wage priority status to amounts required to be paid by the debtor, a painting contractor, into a union's vacation pay trust fund.

unpaid contributions to employee benefit plans, such as pension, health, or life insurance plans are given a fourth priority.[235]

The priority given to claims for unpaid contributions to employee benefit plans are not unlimited. First, the claims for unpaid contributions must arise from services rendered by employees within 180 days before the commencement of the case or cessation of the debtor's business, whichever occurs first.[236] Second, there is a monetary limitation on this priority. For each benefit plan, the priority may not exceed the number of employees covered by the plan multiplied by $2,000, minus the total amount paid to other benefit plans or to employees under the wage priority.[237] The effect of this limitation is that the aggregate amount of claims paid to or for the benefit of employees for wages and fringe benefits pursuant to the third and fourth priorities shall not exceed $2,000 per employee. Of course, the balance of these types of claims are allowable as general unsecured claims without priority.

[5] Fifth Priority: Consumer Deposits

It is common for consumers to pay money to a retailer as a deposit for merchandise to be delivered at a future date. Similarly, customers often prepay for services, such as when a consumer buys a contract for dance lessons or a health club membership. If the business does not deliver the goods or services, these consumers have nothing but unsecured claims against the business. Moreover, many consumers who make such deposits or prepayments are under the mistaken belief that their money becomes part of a trust fund and that they will be protected in the event of insolvency.[238]

The Bankruptcy Code departs from prior law in that it gives each of these consumer creditors a fifth priority status to the extent of $900 to cover any deposit made prior to the bankruptcy of the retail establishment.[239] To benefit from this priority, the consumer's claim must be based on a cash deposit in connection with either the purchase, lease, or rental of property or the purchase of services that were not delivered or provided. Furthermore, it is required that the property or services be for personal, family, or household use—not for use in a commercial

---

[235] 11 U.S.C. § 507(a)(4).

[236] 11 U.S.C. § 507(a)(4)(A).

[237] 11 U.S.C. § 507(a)(4)(B).

[238] See Schrag & Ratner, "Caveat Emptor, Empty Coffer: The Bankruptcy Law Has Nothing to Offer," 72 Colum. L. Rev. 1147 (1972).

[239] 11 U.S.C. § 507(a)(5).

context. It is clear, therefore, that this priority is for the protection of consumers only.

[6] Sixth Priority: Tax Claims

Government claims for taxes are given a preferred status in bankruptcy in several ways. Tax liens are recognized and give rise to a secured claim in favor of the government.[240] If the taxing authority has not obtained a lien prior to the filing of the petition, the tax claim will be entitled to only a sixth-level priority.[241] Furthermore, most tax claims in a typical bankruptcy case will survive as nondischargeable debts in the event that there are not sufficient assets to pay these priority claims in full.[242] In fact, the reason for giving the tax claimant a priority above other unsecured creditors is to benefit the debtor. Since these tax claims are nondischargeable, it is in the debtor's best interest to maximize the amount distributed to the tax claimant.[243]

Not all tax claims are entitled to the sixth priority, although most federal, state, and local tax obligations in the usual bankruptcy case are included. The categories of taxes entitled to a sixth priority are set forth with specificity in the Bankruptcy Code.[244] In general, the following kinds of tax claims are included in the priority:

(1) Income or gross receipts tax, if any one of the following conditions is met: (a) it is for a taxable year that ends on or before the filing of the bankruptcy petition, and the tax return is last due either after the commencement of the bankruptcy case or three years before that time; (b) the tax is assessed within 240 days before the filing of the bankruptcy petition;[245] or (c) the tax is not assessed before, but is assessable under applicable tax law, the statute of limitations, or by agreement after, the filing of the bankruptcy petition.

---

[240] However, see 11 U.S.C. § 724(b) with respect to the subordination of tax liens to certain priority claims.

[241] 11 U.S.C. § 507(a)(6), which derives from former B.A. § 64(4). Certain tax claims are entitled to a first priority as administrative expenses. See ¶ 5.13[1].

[242] See 11 U.S.C. § 523(a)(1), and Chapter 3 *supra*, on nondischargeability of tax claims.

[243] See H.R. Rep. No. 95-595, note 13 *supra*, at 190.

[244] See 11 U.S.C. § 507(a)(6).

[245] See 11 U.S.C. § 507(a)(6)(A)(ii), which provides for a greater period of time in cases when a settlement offer is made within the 240-day period.

(2) Property tax that is assessed before the filing of the bankruptcy petition and last payable without penalty within one year before the petition is filed.
(3) Tax that the debtor is required to collect or withhold for which the debtor is liable, such as income taxes and social security taxes that the debtor employer is required to withhold from employees' paychecks. This category covers the so-called "trust fund" taxes.
(4) Employment tax on the wages that are entitled to a third priority and that were earned before bankruptcy if a tax return for them is last due within three years before the commencement of the case.
(5) Excise tax on a prepetition transaction that occurs within three years prior to the bankruptcy if no return is required, or on any prepetition transaction for which a return is due within three years before the bankruptcy.
(6) Customs duty arising out of the importation of merchandise under certain circumstances.[246]
(7) Penalties related to any of these priority tax claims in compensation for actual pecuniary loss.

¶ 5.14 SUBORDINATION OF CLAIMS

There are three situations that may result in the subordination of a claim to others of the same type. The most common situation involves the subordination agreement among creditors. When a debtor is experiencing financial difficulty and needs additional credit, it is not uncommon for the new lender to insist on an agreement with existing creditors under which other claims are voluntarily subordinated to that of the new lender. Existing creditors may be willing to subordinate their claims for the purpose of encouraging the new lender to furnish needed capital. Subordination agreements among creditors are enforceable in bankruptcy to the same extent that they are valid in nonbankruptcy situations.[247] Of course, the senior creditor may waive the right to full

---

[246] See 11 U.S.C. § 507(a)(6)(F).

[247] 11 U.S.C. § 510(a). For a discussion of the effect of subordination on the requirements for a "cram down" confirmation in reorganization cases, see Chapter 8 *infra.* See also *In re* National Discount, 212 F. Supp. 929 (W.D.S.C.), *aff'd* 322 F.2d 928 (4th Cir. 1963), holding subordination by creditors in common-law settlement binding in a subsequent bankruptcy;

payment above subordinated claims by accepting a reorganization plan that provides for equal treatment.

The second situation that may give rise to subordination of claims occurs when an equity security holder has a claim against the debtor for rescission or damages. For example, if a shareholder was defrauded into purchasing shares in violation of the securities laws,[248] and if the corporation files a bankruptcy petition, the shareholder may attempt to bootstrap his status by filing a claim as a general creditor based on fraud and rescission. The problem with permitting the defrauded shareholder to rise to the level of a general creditor is that all other creditors would be adversely affected. Congress examined existing case law on this issue, which generally favored the rescinding shareholder,[249] but decided to adopt the position that such shareholders should not be able to improve their status. The Code provides that any rescission or damage claim of a security holder shall be subordinated to all claims or interests that are senior or equal to the interest represented by the security.[250] Thus, a defrauded stockholder or limited partner who rescinds the purchase of the security based on fraud may not share in a distribution of the estate on equal footing with general creditors. The rationale for this provision relates to the allocation of risk with respect to the unlawful issuance of securities. "While both security holders and general creditors assume the risk of insolvency, . . . the risk of illegality in securities issuance should be borne by those investing in securities and not by general creditors."[251]

Golin, "Debt Subordination as a Working Tool," 7 N.Y.L.F. 370 (1961); Rome, "The Business Workout—A Primer for Participating Creditors," 11 U.C.C.L.J. 183 (1978).

[248] See the antifraud provisions of federal securities laws contained in Section 17(a) of the Securities Act (15 U.S.C. § 77q) and in Rule 10b-5 of the Securities and Exchange Commission (17 C.F.R. § 240.10b-5).

[249] See Oppenheimer v. Harriman Nat'l Bank & Trust Co., 301 U.S. 206 (1937). But see *In re* Stirling Homex Corp., 579 F.2d 206 (2d Cir. 1978), in which claims of rescinding shareholders were subordinated. See also *In re* Cartridge Television, Inc., 535 F.2d 1388 (2d Cir. 1976), in which fraud claims were denied because their liquidation would unduly delay administration of the estate.

[250] 11 U.S.C. § 510(b).

[251] H.R. Rep. No. 95-595, note 13 *supra*, at 195. For an historical analysis of this issue and the policies involved, see Slain & Kripke, "The Interface Between Securities Regulation and Bankruptcy—Allocating the Risk of Illegal Securities Issuance Between Securityholders and the Issuer's Creditors," 48 N.Y.U.L. Rev. 261 (1973). See also Note, "Securities Claims in Bankruptcy: Provability and Priority," 53 N.Y.U.L. Rev. 1056 (1978).

The third situation that may lead to the subordination of claims involves the principle of *equitable subordination.* The bankruptcy court may either subordinate a claim below other claims of the same type or order that a lien securing a claim be transferred to the estate when there exists conduct by the claimant that makes it inequitable to permit a pro rata sharing with others.[252]

An illustration of the equitable subordination doctrine is found in the case of *In re Trimble Co.*[253] The controlling shareholders of a close corporation loaned $85,000 to the business and received demand promissory notes. At the time of the loan banks were unwilling to extend credit, and the business was found to be a "hopelessly insolvent corporate structure."[254] Upon the bankruptcy of the corporation, the shareholders who were holding the notes asserted claims as general creditors for the sum of $85,000. The court refused to permit the shareholders to participate as general creditors despite the fact that they held promissory notes. Because of the poor financial condition of the corporation when the loan was made, the court relied on equitable powers to categorize these advances as contributions of capital—not loans. "In such a situation, a test which may be used to decide whether a contribution by a proprietary interest is a loan or an additional injection of capital is whether the advance was made at a time when a bank or other ordinary commercial agency would be willing to lend it funds."[255]

Despite the result in *Trimble,* most courts have held that equitable subordination of an insider's claim is not justified unless there is evidence of fraud, inequitable conduct, or unjust enrichment; the extention of loans to a failing business is usually not, in and of itself, sufficient to justify subordination.[256] Nonetheless, insiders[257] who are desirous of

---

[252] 11 U.S.C. § 510(c). See Herzog & Zweibel, "The Equitable Subordination of Claims in Bankruptcy," 15 Vand. L. Rev. 83 (1961).

[253] 479 F.2d 103 (3d Cir. 1973). See also Pepper v. Litton, 308 U.S. 295 (1939).

[254] *In re* Trimble Co., note 253 *supra*, at 118.

[255] *Id.* at 116.

[256] See, e.g., *In re* Mid-Town Produce Terminal, Inc., 5 Bankr. Dec. 759 (10th Cir. 1979); *In re* Ultimate Corp. 207 F.2d 427, 429 (2d Cir. 1953), citing *In re* Madelaine, Inc., 164 F.2d 419 (2d Cir. 1947), which stated: "In the absence of fraud or unfair advantage it is not wrongful for an officer or director of a corporation to lend money to it."

[257] Although the doctrine of equitable subordination is not limited to claims of insiders, most subordination cases involve such claims. The Code defines "insider" so as to include an individual, partnership, or corporation "in control of the debtor." 11 U.S.C. § 101(25). See *In re* Prima Co., 98 F.2d 952 (7th Cir. 1938), *cert. denied* 305 U.S. 658 (1939), involving an unsuccessful attempt to hold a bank liable for what creditors alleged was the

lending money to a troubled business may have second thoughts about making such loans. Rather than risk subordination, insiders often consider making loans with court approval after the business files a petition for reorganization. By proceeding in this manner, insiders not only avoid the risk of subordination, but also may obtain a first priority as an administrative expense [258] or even a superpriority above all other administrative expenses.[259] In addition, the utilization of funds during the reorganization may be more conducive as an aid to rehabilitation.

¶ 5.15 DISTRIBUTION OF THE ESTATE IN A LIQUIDATION CASE

Creditors who have valid liens against property of the estate are entitled to the value of their allowed secured claims in liquidation cases.[260] The remaining property of the estate is to be distributed in accordance with the scheme set forth in the Bankruptcy Code.[261] The following order of distribution must be adhered to in liquidation cases, except to the extent that claims are subordinated by the court:

(1) Priority claims must be paid in order of their respective rank.[262]

(2) Allowed unsecured claims must be paid, but only with respect to those claims that were timely filed by the creditor, an indenture trustee, a codebtor, or the trustee. Also, an allowed unsecured claim that was filed late is included in this category if the creditor had no notice or actual knowledge of the bankruptcy in time to make a timely

---

bank's control over the affairs of the debtor. It is conceivable, however, that a lender that exercises control over the management of the debtor may be considered an insider and, accordingly, may risk equitable subordination.

[258] 11 U.S.C. § 507(a)(1). See ¶ 5.13[1].

[259] 11 U.S.C. § 364(c).

[260] See ¶ 5.11. See also 11 U.S.C. § 725. However, tax liens may be subordinated to certain priority claims pursuant to 11 U.S.C. § 724(b).

[261] This scheme is set forth in 11 U.S.C. § 726. For special rules on the order of distribution with respect to community property, see 11 U.S.C. § 726(c). A creditor's right to payment may be affected by a distribution in a foreign proceeding or payment by a nonbankrupt general partner. See 11 U.S.C. § 508.

[262] See ¶ 5.13 for a discussion of priority claims. If the case was converted from chapter 11 or chapter 13, administrative expenses incurred in the liquidation case have priority over administrative expenses incurred prior to the conversion. 11 U.S.C. § 726(b). In addition, administrative expenses caused by the inadequate protection of a secured creditor have priority over all other administrative expense claims. 11 U.S.C. § 507(b).

filing and if the proof of the claim is filed in time to permit payment of the claim.

(3) Allowed unsecured cliams that are not timely filed are then paid if the creditor had notice or actual knowledge of the case in time to file a timely proof of claim but failed to do so.

(4) Payment is made on allowed secured or unsecured claims that are for the recovery of fines, penalties, forfeitures, or exemplary or punitive damages arising before the order for relief or appointment of a trustee. Multiple damage awards, such as a treble damage recovery in an antitrust action, are also in this category to the extent that they are not compensation for actual pecuniary loss. By subordinating these penalty awards, which include prepetition tax penalties, to other classes of claims, the Code makes sure that they are paid out of estate assets only to the extent that there is a surplus after paying those claims that are based on actual pecuniary loss.

(5) To the extent that there remains a surplus after the above claims are paid in full, creditors may be paid interest on their claims that accrues after the petition is filed. Although postpetition interest is generally not allowable, it will be paid before returning a surplus to the debtor. It is important to note, however, that postpetition interest is paid at the legal rate, not at the agreed rate.

(6) In the rare case where there is a surplus remaining after all of the above claims are paid, the surplus must be paid to the debtor.

In the event that there are inadequate funds to pay the holders of claims of a particular class in full, the claims within that class are paid on a pro rata basis.[263]

---

[263] 11 U.S.C. § 726(b).

Chapter 6

BANKRUPTCY COURTS AND OFFICERS

The Bankruptcy Reform Act of 1978 made sweeping changes with respect to bankruptcy court jurisdiction and the administration of bankruptcy cases. The Reform Act also made significant changes in connection with trustees and other court officials. It is important for the practitioner to be familiar with the new court structure, the powers of bankruptcy judges, and the role of court officers.

¶ 6.01 BANKRUPTCY COURTS UNDER THE FORMER ACT

A brief discussion of the characteristics of bankruptcy courts under the former Bankruptcy Act is necessary for the reader to appreciate the reforms made by the 1978 Act. Since 1898, when the former Act became law, bankruptcy courts were arms of the U.S. district courts.[1] The Act vested jurisdiction over bankruptcy cases in the district courts, and district court judges appointed referees to preside over such cases.[2] Referees, who were selected by district court judges to serve for six-year terms,[3] were always subject to review by the district court.[4] The salaries of referees were much lower than those of district court judges,[5] and they had no law clerks or other research support to assist them on complex legal questions. It was not until the Bankruptcy Rules of Procedure were promulgated in 1973 that referees were given the title of "bankruptcy judge."[6]

The old bankruptcy court system came under attack as having two basic deficiencies: The jurisdiction of bankruptcy courts was extremely limited, and bankruptcy judges were forced to serve both administrative and judicial functions.

The jurisdiction of the bankruptcy court under the former Act was

---

[1] Former B.A. § 1(10) defined "courts of bankruptcy" to include U.S. district courts.

[2] Former B.A. § 34(a).

[3] *Id.*

[4] Former B.A. § 38.

[5] See former B.A. § 40.

[6] B. Rule 901(7).

limited to "summary jurisdiction." [7] This means, in essence, that courts had jurisdiction only over that property which was either actually or constructively possessed by the debtor on the date of bankruptcy.[8] Also, the court had personal jurisdiction over the debtor and other persons who consented to the court's jurisdiction.[9] By basing jurisdiction on possession or consent, however, many disputes that arose in bankruptcy cases fell outside the scope of the bankruptcy court's jurisdiction and therefore had to be adjudicated in nonbankruptcy state or federal courts. For example, when a trustee filed a complaint in a bankruptcy court charging that the estate owned an easement adjoining the debtor's real estate and that he was entitled to construct improvements there, the court of appeals held that the bankruptcy court lacked jurisdiction to deal with the issue.[10] Similarly, a bankruptcy court had no jurisdiction to determine whether a discharged debt had been reaffirmed.[11] As a result, bankruptcy judges were unable to preside over many significant issues that had a direct impact on the bankruptcy case.

The second flaw of the court system under the former Act was caused by the dual role of the bankruptcy judge. The judge served as the administrator of the case and performed supervisory and ministerial roles. In this administrative capacity, the judge often held informal conferences and presided over the relatively informal first meeting of creditors. At the meeting, the judge usually engaged in a comprehensive examination of the debtor with respect to the conveyance of assets, financial dealings, and the like. This testimony was exploratory and in many instances laid the foundation for future action by the trustee. Later, when a real dispute arose, the same judge was called upon to preside over the issues and make decisions with respect to the same testimony. Although rules of evidence often resulted in the exclusion of inadmissible testimony, it was feared that the judge's objectivity might have been influenced by the unsubstantiated testimony at the first meet-

---

[7] Weidhorn v. Levy, 253 U.S. 268 (1920). See Gendel, "Summary Jurisdiction in Bankruptcy Related to Possible Referee Disqualification," 51 Calif. L. Rev. 755 (1963).

[8] Cline v. Kaplan, 323 U.S. 97 (1944); Thompson v. Magnolia Petroleum Co., 309 U.S. 478 (1940).

[9] See Katchen v. Landy, 382 U.S. 323 (1966), in which the Supreme Court held that the filing of a proof of claim constituted consent to the summary jurisdiction of the bankruptcy court when the trustee sought to recover a voidable preference.

[10] Bel Marin Keys Community Servs. Dist. v. Bel Marin Enterprises, Inc., 582 F.2d 477 (9th Cir. 1978), *cert. denied* 99 S. Ct. 1230.

[11] Glass v. Miller & Kearney, — F.2d —, 4 Bankr. Dec. 874 (9th Cir. 1978).

ing of creditors. In any event, the object of relieving the bankruptcy judge from burdensome administrative chores was salutary.[12]

¶ 6.02 THE NEW U.S. BANKRUPTCY COURT: AN OVERVIEW

The Reform Act creates in each judicial district, as of April 1, 1984, a new U.S. bankruptcy court that will have broad jurisdiction over virtually all aspects of bankruptcy cases.[13] Although these courts will be "adjuncts" of the U.S. district courts,[14] there is no doubt that they will exist as separate departments and will function as autonomous units. The Reform Act increases bankruptcy judge salaries substantially, and new bankruptcy judges added to these courts will be appointed to fourteen-year terms by the President upon the recommendation of circuit panels and with the consent of the Senate.[15] Commensurate with their expanded jurisdiction, bankruptcy judges may appoint law clerks and support staff to assist them in the same manner that clerks assist district court judges.[16] In sum, the Reform Act substantially elevates the role and the status of the bankruptcy judge.

The problems associated with the dual administrative-judicial role of the bankruptcy judge are also addressed by the Reform Act. The most obvious attempt to separate these functions is a provision that forbids the judge to preside at, or even to attend, a meeting of creditors.[17]

The clerk of the bankruptcy court (which is a new position designed to handle the details of court administration)[18] presides at the

---

[12] See, e.g., Treister, "Bankruptcy Jurisdiction: Is it Too Summary?" 39 S. Calif. L. Rev. 78 (1966); H.R. Rep. No. 95-595, 95th Cong., 1st Sess. 88-91 (1977) (hereinafter cited as H.R. Rep. No. 95-595). Compare the remark of Bankruptcy Judge Asa S. Herzog: "[T]he trained judicial mind is quite capable of disregarding information which was extrajudicially acquired as well as the evidence offered during the trial and excluded for one reason or another." Herzog, "Bankruptcy Law—Modern Trends," 38 Ref. J. 23, 26 (1964).

[13] Section 201(a) of Title II of the Bankruptcy Reform Act amended Title 28 of the U.S. Code to create the U.S. bankruptcy courts. 28 U.S.C. § 151; B.R.A. § 201(a).

[14] 28 U.S.C. § 151(a).

[15] 28 U.S.C. §§ 152, 153(a), 154. Compare former B.A. § 34(a), which provided that bankruptcy judges be appointed by district court judges for six-year terms.

[16] B.R.A. § 233(a); 28 U.S.C. § 772.

[17] 11 U.S.C. § 341(c). Compare B. Rule 204(a)(2), which is superseded by the Bankruptcy Code.

[18] B.R.A. § 233(a), 28 U.S.C. § 771.

meeting of creditors unless a different presiding officer is elected in a liquidation case.[19] In districts that have a U.S. Trustee, the U.S. Trustee or a designate of that office presides at the meeting.[20] Moreover, ex parte communications between the bankruptcy judge and an interested party, attorney, or accountant are prohibited.[21]

Although the new U.S. Bankruptcy Courts will not come into existence until 1984, the Reform Act gives present bankruptcy judges the same expanded powers and jurisdiction over bankruptcy cases during the transition period between October 1, 1979 and April 1, 1984.[22] Accordingly, the new court powers and jurisdictional rules are effective immediately.

¶ 6.03 JURISDICTION AND POWERS OF BANKRUPTCY COURTS UNDER THE BANKRUPTCY REFORM ACT

As of October 1, 1979, bankruptcy judges have pervasive jurisdiction over almost every aspect of bankruptcy cases.[23] Bankruptcy cases are commenced by filing a petition with the clerk of the bankruptcy court. From that time until the case is closed, bankruptcy courts have original, but not exclusive, jurisdiction over all civil proceedings arising under the Bankruptcy Code or arising in or relating to the bankruptcy case.[24] The bankruptcy court also has exclusive jurisdiction over all of the debtor's property wherever located.[25] Accordingly, the bankruptcy court has jurisdiction over all adversary proceedings commenced to recover property for the estate, regardless of who possesses the property. Similarly, the bankruptcy court has jurisdiction over all claims

---

[19] Sugg. Int. B. Rule 2003(b)(1). Creditors who are eligible to vote for a trustee and who hold a majority in amount of claims that vote may designate a presiding officer in a liquidation case. See 11 U.S.C. § 702(a), and ¶ 6.07[2].

[20] Sugg. Int. B. Rule X-1003(b)(1). See ¶ 6.08 on the U.S. Trustee Pilot Program.

[21] Sugg. Int. B. Rule 5001.

[22] Title IV of the Bankruptcy Reform Act governs the transition period. See B.R.A. §§ 404, 405.

[23] B.R.A. § 241(a) added Chapter 90 to Title 28 of the U.S. Code to deal with jurisdiction, venue, appeals, and other aspects of bankruptcy courts. See 28 U.S.C. § 1471. Chapter 90 is applicable to courts during the transition period. B.R.A. § 405(b).

[24] The Reform Act actually gives this jurisdiction to district courts and then provides that bankruptcy courts "shall exercise all of the jurisdiction conferred by this section on the district courts." 28 U.S.C. § 1471.

[25] 28 U.S.C. § 1471(e).

against the debtor. For example, if a creditor files a proof of claim for damages caused by the negligence of the debtor, the bankruptcy court may hold the trial on the underlying negligence claim.

Consistent with the broad jurisdiction of the bankruptcy court, the Reform Act gives the court the power to issue any order, process, or judgment that is necessary or appropriate to carry out the provisions of the Bankruptcy Code.[26] The powers of the court are not, however, without limitation. The Code strips the judge of the power to appoint a receiver.[27] This limitation is imposed because the role of the receiver in bankruptcy cases was replaced by the interim trustee. Moreover, bankruptcy judges do not have the power to enjoin another court or punish a criminal contempt unless the contemptuous act is committed in the judge's presence and does not warrant a punishment of imprisonment.[28]

It is important to note that the bankruptcy court has the powers of a court of equity as well as the powers of a law court.[29] Historically, bankruptcy courts have not been shy in exercising their equitable powers. The most notable example is *Bank of Marin v. England,*[30] in which the Supreme Court relied on equitable powers to disregard, in a sense, the wording of the former Bankruptcy Act. In *Bank of Marin,* a bank honored checks drawn before the depositor's bankruptcy but presented for payment after the depositor had filed a voluntary bankruptcy petition. The lower courts granted the trustee's application directing the bank to pay the trustee the amount of the checks because payment of them constituted a postpetition transfer of estate assets.[31] The Supreme Court considered the unequivocal language of Section 70(d)(5) of the former Act, which provided that "no transfer by or on behalf of the bankrupt after the date of bankruptcy shall be valid against the trustee." However, the Court held in favor of the bank, and, in an effort to overcome a harsh doctrine, Justice Douglas wrote the following frequently cited comment: "[W]e do not read these statutory words with

---

[26] 11 U.S.C. § 105(a). This section is similar in effect to the All Writs Statute, 28 U.S.C. § 1651, which applies to bankruptcy courts under 28 U.S.C. § 451. See 28 U.S.C. § 2256, which gives bankruptcy courts the authority to issue writs of habeas corpus.

[27] 11 U.S.C. § 105(b).

[28] 28 U.S.C. § 1481. The same rule is effective during the transition period under B.R.A. § 405(a).

[29] 28 U.S.C. § 1481, derived from former B.A. § 2(a). The Reform Act also gives bankruptcy courts the power of courts of admiralty.

[30] 385 U.S. 99 (1966).

[31] See Bank of Marin v. England, 352 F.2d 186 (9th Cir. 1963).

the ease of a computer. There is an overriding consideration that equitable principles govern the exercise of bankruptcy jurisdiction." [32]

¶ 6.04 BANKRUPTCY COURT PROCEEDINGS

A bankruptcy case is a unique kind of legal matter. The voluntary case is not, in and of itself, a contested proceeding. In fact, the mere filing of the voluntary petition automatically acts as the order for relief under the appropriate chapter of the Bankruptcy Code.[33] The involuntary case may be a contested proceeding in which the debtor may file an answer and dispute the allegations made in the petition.[34] However, after the order for relief is granted in the involuntary case, the matter is no longer a legal contest between adverse parties. The order for relief actually sets into motion the administrative steps required for either the liquidation or rehabilitation of the debtor.

[1] Motion Practice

Although the bankruptcy case is not a contested matter after the order for relief is granted, there are several events that may require judicial action. For example, an interested party may request that the court abstain from entertaining the bankruptcy case,[35] or that the court remove a trustee for cause.[36] The trustee may object to a proof of claim filed by a creditor.[37] The trustee may also wish to seek court approval of compensation to be paid to the attorney or accountant for services to the estate,[38] or for permission to use property of the estate outside the ordinary course of the debtor's business.[39] In a liquidation case, a creditor may seek conversion to a chapter 11 reorganization.[40] Credi-

---

[32] Bank of Marin v. England, note 30 *supra*, at 103. For other Supreme Court decisions in which the Court relied on equitable powers in a bankruptcy case, see Pepper v. Litton, 308 U.S. 295 (1939); SEC v. U.S. Realty & Improvement Co., 310 U.S. 434 (1940).

[33] 11 U.S.C. § 301, which is derived from former B.A. § 18(f).

[34] 11 U.S.C. § 303. See Chapter 2 supra for a discussion of involuntary petitions.

[35] 11 U.S.C. § 305.

[36] 11 U.S.C. § 324.

[37] 11 U.S.C. § 502(a).

[38] 11 U.S.C. § 330.

[39] 11 U.S.C. § 363(b).

[40] 11 U.S.C. § 706(b).

tors in a chapter 11 case may seek the appointment of a trustee for cause.[41] Similarly, the debtor may seek an extension of time to file a reorganization plan.[42] These are only a few of the numerous types of requests that may be made by motion during the bankruptcy case and that require the court to hold a hearing on notice to interested parties.[43]

The Bankruptcy Rules of Procedure govern motion practice in the bankruptcy courts. Unless made during a hearing or trial, a motion must be made in writing, must conform substantially to a pleading in form, and must state the relief sought and the grounds for it with sufficient particularity.[44] Motion papers must be served in the same manner that a summons and complaint are served.[45] No responsive pleading is required unless the court orders an answer to a motion.[46] Motions may become complex and time-consuming contested matters, and elemental requisites of due process must be afforded all parties to the dispute. The Federal Rules of Civil Procedure apply to motions with respect to misjoinder and nonjoinder of parties,[47] substitution of parties,[48] discovery,[49] depositions,[50] interrogatories,[51] requests for admissions,[52] dismissals,[53] consolidations,[54] summary judgment,[55] defaults, and many other aspects of civil procedure.

---

[41] 11 U.S.C. § 1104(a).

[42] 11 U.S.C. § 1121(d).

[43] The Code requires that the notice and opportunity to be heard be "appropriate in the particular circumstances." A hearing may be dispensed with if it is not requested by a party in interest after appropriate notice is given or if there is insufficient time for a hearing because of the urgency of the matter. See 11 U.S.C. § 102(1).

[44] B. Rule 901(9). See *In re* J. & M. Doyle Co., 130 F.2d 340 (3d Cir. 1942), which held that an oral motion for extension of time for filing a petition to review an allowance of a claim was insufficient; *In re* Long Island Properties, Inc., 125 F.2d 206 (2d Cir. 1942), which held that a motion for approval of a contract was insufficient because of lack of particularity.

[45] B. Rules 704, 914. See Fed. R. Civ. P. 4(d) on service of process requirements.

[46] B. Rule 914.

[47] B. Rules 721, 914. See Fed. R. Civ. P. 21.

[48] B. Rules 725, 914. See Fed. R. Civ. P. 25.

[49] B. Rules 726, 914. See Fed. R. Civ. P. 26.

[50] B. Rules 728, 914. See Fed. R. Civ. P. 28.

[51] B. Rules 731, 914. See Fed. R. Civ. P. 31.

[52] B. Rules 736, 914. See Fed. R. Civ. P. 36.

[53] B. Rules 741, 914. See Fed. R. Civ. P. 41.

[54] B. Rules 742, 914. See Fed. R. Civ. P. 42.

[55] B. Rules 756, 914. See Fed. R. Civ. P. 56.

[2] Adversary Proceedings

The typical bankruptcy case, although itself an uncontested matter, may be characterized as an umbrella under which numerous related lawsuits may be litigated. As discussed above, interested parties may make various motions within the bankruptcy case. However, there are certain types of disputes that may not be resolved merely by making a motion. The Bankruptcy Rules require that any party who desires to obtain any one of seven specific forms of relief in a bankruptcy case must proceed by initiating an *adversary proceeding*.[56]

Specifically, an adversary proceeding must be commenced to: (1) recover money or property, except if it is from an attorney as excessive fees or from a prior custodian of the estate; (2) determine the validity, priority, or extent of a lien or other interest in property; (3) sell property free of a lien or other interest for which the holder can be compelled to take a money satisfaction; (4) object to or revoke a discharge; (5) obtain an injunction; (6) obtain relief from a stay;[57] or (7) determine the dischargeability of a debt.

In view of the expanded jurisdiction of the bankruptcy court under the Bankruptcy Reform Act, the Suggested Interim Bankruptcy Rules provide that *any* proceeding before a bankruptcy judge for legal, equitable, or declaratory relief that arises under nonbankruptcy law is an adversary proceeding.[58] Thus, the seven categories of adversary proceedings set forth in the Bankruptcy Rules are not exclusive.

An adversary proceeding is, in a sense, a complete civil lawsuit within a bankruptcy case. It is commenced by filing a complaint with the court.[59] A trial or pretrial conference date is set by the bankruptcy judge, and a summons and notice of trial or pretrial conference are issued.[60] The summons and notice must be served within ten days after issuance.[61] The Bankruptcy Rules incorporate by reference many of the Federal Rules of Civil Procedure with respect to the form of pleadings,[62]

---

[56] These seven forms of relief are set forth in B. Rule 701.

[57] See 11 U.S.C. § 362(e), which provides for a speedy hearing on requests for relief from a stay.

[58] Sugg. Int. B. Rule 7001.

[59] B. Rule 703. See Sugg. Int. B. Form Nos. 24 and 25 for the caption required on all pleadings. Sugg. Int. B. Rule 7002 provides that a pleading setting forth a claim for relief must contain a statement of the grounds of the bankruptcy court's jurisdiction.

[60] B. Rule 704(a).

[61] B. Rule 704 (e).

[62] B. Rules 707-710. See Fed. R. Civ. P. 7-10. But see Sugg. Int. B. Rule 7001, requiring jurisdictional allegations; Sugg. Int. B. Form Nos. 24 and 25, for the caption of pleadings.

answers, counterclaims,[63] third-party practice,[64] pretrial procedure,[65] joinder of claims and remedies,[66] class actions,[67] shareholder derivative suits,[68] general discovery,[69] injunctions,[70] and numerous other aspects of civil procedure.[71] The Bankruptcy Rules of Procedure, as well as local court rules, should be consulted with respect to the procedural aspects of an adversary proceeding.[72]

[3] Evidence

Practitioners who are unfamiliar with bankruptcy practice sometimes have the mistaken impression that proceedings in a bankruptcy case are relatively informal. Such lawyers are often surprised to find that bankruptcy courts are as exacting as other courts with respect to rules on the admissibility of evidence.[73] In fact, the Bankruptcy Rules expressly provide that the Federal Rules of Evidence are applicable to motions and adversary proceedings in bankruptcy cases.[74]

[4] Venue of Proceedings

The appropriate place for filing a petition to commence a bankruptcy case is discussed in detail in the first chapter of this book.[75] The Bankruptcy Reform Act, however, contains separate provisions that govern venue problems with respect to proceedings, including adversary proceedings and other contested matters, that relate to a pending bankruptcy case.

---

[63] B. Rule 713. See Fed. R. Civ. P. 13.

[64] B. Rule 714. See Fed. R. Civ. P. 14.

[65] B. Rule 716. See Fed. R. Civ. P. 16.

[66] B. Rule 718. See Fed. R. Civ. P. 18.

[67] B. Rule 723. See Fed. R. Civ. P. 23.

[68] B. Rule 723.1. See Fed. R. Civ. P. 23.1.

[69] B. Rule 726. See Fed. R. Civ. P. 26.

[70] B. Rule 765. See Fed. R. Civ. P. 65.

[71] See generally Moore, *Moore's Federal Practice* (2d ed. 1978).

[72] Each bankruptcy court may promulgate local court rules that govern bankruptcy practice. See 28 U.S.C. §§ 156, 157, 1471(c), which were added by B.R.A. §§ 201, 241. Compare B. Rule 927, which gave district courts the power to promulgate local bankruptcy court rules.

[73] See Treister, "Bankruptcy Jurisdiction: Is it Too Summary?" 39 S. Calif. L. Rev. 78 (1966).

[74] B. Rule 917. See Norton, Jr. & Russell, *Evidence in Trials Under the Bankruptcy Act* (1978). See generally Weinstein & Berger, *Weinstein's Evidence* (1977).

[75] See ¶ 1.04.

As a general rule, any proceeding may be commenced in the bankruptcy court in which the related bankruptcy case is pending.[76] The Reform Act, however, sets forth four exceptions to this general rule. First, a trustee may commence a proceeding to recover either a money judgment of less than $1,000 or property worth less than $1,000, or to enforce a consumer debt of less than $5,000, *only* in a bankruptcy court in the judicial district in which a defendant resides.[77] The rationale for this exception is that the defendant in a proceeding for such a small sum should not be compelled to travel great distances to defend.

Another category of proceedings that may be commenced in a bankruptcy court where the main bankruptcy case is not pending includes situations in which the trustee acts to recover property as statutory successor to the debtor or a creditor. Specifically, the trustee may recover property that belongs to the estate, or may seek to avoid a transfer of property that is voidable by an actual unsecured creditor, by commencing a proceeding in the bankruptcy court in any district where the state or federal court sits in which the action for this relief may have been commenced by the debtor or a creditor in the absence of bankruptcy.[78] For example, if a bankruptcy case is pending in the Southern District of New York, and if a person residing in the Northern District of Illinois possesses the debtor's personal property, the trustee may recover that property by commencing a proceeding in the bankruptcy court in the Northern District of Illinois because the debtor, in the absence of bankruptcy, would have been able to sue the converter of property in Illinois based on nonbankruptcy venue rules. Of course, the trustee has the alternative of commencing the proceeding in the bankruptcy court in which the main bankruptcy case is pending.

A third exception to the general rule that proper venue lies only where the bankruptcy case is pending relates to claims by the trustee that arise from the operation of the debtor's business after the petition is filed. Let us assume, for example, that during a case the trustee continues to operate the business and purchases goods from a supplier. If the goods are defective and the trustee wants to pursue a cause of action against the seller based on a breach of implied warranty of merchantability, the trustee may commence the proceeding against the creditor *only* in the bankruptcy court for the district where a state or federal court sits in which the breach of warranty action could have been com-

---

[76] 28 U.S.C. § 1473(a), added by B.R.A. § 241(a).

[77] 28 U.S.C. § 1473(b). However, this limitation does not apply to proceedings based on postpetition claims. See 28 U.S.C. § 1473(d).

[78] 28 U.S.C. § 1473(c). See 11 U.S.C. §§ 541, 544(b).

menced in the absence of bankruptcy.[79] The reason for limiting venue with respect to postpetition claims against persons who deal with the trustee is to reduce the adverse effects of the bankruptcy on persons who do business with the estate during the case. If, for example, a California dealer sells goods in California to a trustee in connection with a bankruptcy case in New York, it will be unfair and prejudicial to give the trustee the right to sue the seller for breach of warranty in a New York bankruptcy court unless there is an independent nonbankruptcy basis for venue in New York.

For the same reason, a proceeeding *against* the estate may be commenced to enforce a postpetition claim arising from the operation of the debtor's business in a bankruptcy court in the district where the state or federal court sits in which the claim could have been enforced in the absence of bankruptcy. When the trustee is the defendant, however, the plaintiff has the alternative of commencing the proceeding in the bankruptcy court where the main bankruptcy case is pending.[80] In the above hypothetical, therefore, the California seller as plaintiff may commence a proceeding against the trustee for payment of the price either in the New York bankruptcy court where the case is pending or, alternatively, in the bankruptcy court of the judicial district in California where venue would lie in a nonbankruptcy situation. In sum, the party who deals with the debtor's business after the bankruptcy case commences may be sued on a postpetition claim *only* in the bankruptcy court in the district where venue will be in the absence of bankruptcy, but may sue as plaintiff in the bankruptcy court *either* where the case is pending or where venue will be in the absence of bankruptcy.

These venue rules are designed to further administrative convenience and fairness among the parties in bankruptcy proceedings. It is common knowledge, however, that inflexible rules designed for fairness often result in inequities in certain situations. For this reason, the Reform Act gives bankruptcy judges the right to transfer a proceeding to a bankruptcy court in a different district. The court may always grant a motion for change of venue "in the interest of justice and for the convenience of the parties," which is the same standard used by the court in determining whether an entire bankruptcy case should be transferred.[81]

---

[79] 28 U.S.C. § 1473(d).

[80] 28 U.S.C. § 1473(e).

[81] 28 U.S.C. § 1475, which is derived from B. Rule 782. See ¶ 1.05[2]. See also Downey, Ferriell & Pfeiffer, "The Proposed Bankruptcy Reorganization Provisions: A Comparison of the Current Law With Chapter 11 of H.R. 8200 and S. 266," 18 Santa Clara L. Rev. 567, 572 n.24 (1978), where the authors commented: "It would be no surprise if section 1475 becomes a well-

[5] Removal to the Bankruptcy Court

Consistent with the pervasive jurisdiction of bankruptcy courts, a party to a civil action pending in a nonbankruptcy court may remove the cause of action to the bankruptcy court for the district where the civil action is pending, provided that bankruptcy courts have jurisdiction over the cause of action.[82] Thus, if the plaintiff in a pending civil action files a bankruptcy petition, the trustee as successor to the debtor may remove the action to the bankruptcy court for that district.

The Suggested Interim Bankruptcy Rules contain provisions dealing with the procedures for removal.[83] A party desiring to remove a civil action or proceeding to a bankruptcy court must file a verified application in the bankruptcy court for the district and division in which the action is pending. The application must contain a brief statement of facts that justify removal and must be accompanied by a copy of all process and pleadings in the action and by a sufficient bond to assure the payment of costs and disbursements in the event that removal is improper.[84] If an action is within the bankruptcy court's jurisdiction when it is commenced, then only the defendant may remove by filing an application within thirty days after the defendant receives a copy of the initial pleading.[85] If an action first becomes removable after it is initiated, then either the plaintiff or the defendant may remove by filing an application within thirty days after the order for relief in the bankruptcy case.[86] For example, if a corporation is a plaintiff in a pending state court action at the time it files a bankruptcy petition, the action may be removed to the bankruptcy court by the plaintiff within thirty days after the filing of the bankruptcy petition.

The party filing an application for removal is required to give

---

spring of pyrrhic victories. Counsel for debtors and creditors will agree that the ability to bring contested claims from around the country before a single forum is of enormous practical importance. Many debtor decisions to initiate reorganization cases may turn on this jurisdictional windfall."

[82] 28 U.S.C. § 1478(a), added by B.R.A. § 241(a). However, a proceeding before the U.S. Tax Court or a civil action by a governmental unit to enforce police or regulatory powers may not be removed to the bankruptcy court.

[83] See Sugg. Int. B. Rule 7004.

[84] A bond is not required, however, if a trustee, debtor in possession, or the United States is the applicant. Sugg. Int. B. Rule 7004(b).

[85] The application must be filed within thirty days after service of the summons upon the defendant if the initial pleading has then been filed in court and is not required to be served on the defendant. Sugg. Int. B. Rule 7004(a)(2).

[86] Sugg. Int. B. Rule 7004(a)(3).

written notice of it to all adverse parties and to file a copy of the application with the clerk of the state or federal court from which the action was removed. Once a copy of the application is so filed, the parties may not proceed further in that court unless the action is subsequently remanded.[87]

In all actions removed, the bankruptcy court has the power to issue all necessary orders and processes to bring all parties and records before it.[88] Part VII of the Bankruptcy Rules, which governs adversary proceedings, also applies to civil actions removed to the bankruptcy court. Repleading after removal is not necessary unless the court orders it. If the defendant has not answered prior to removal, an answer may be filed within twenty days after the receipt of a copy of the initial pleading, or within twenty days after the service of a summons, or within five days after the filing of the application for removal, whichever period is longest.[89] All bonds, security, injunctions, and court orders in effect prior to removal remain in effect unless modified or dissolved by the bankruptcy court.[90] The Suggested Interim Bankruptcy Rules also provide for the filing of a demand for a jury trial after removal.[91]

It is not difficult to imagine a situation in which removal will cause undue delay and inconvenience. For example, assume that there is a pending antitrust suit in which the jury was selected over a long period of time and that the trial is already in its fifth month. Upon the plaintiff's bankruptcy, shall the trustee be permitted to remove the suit which is in midstream to the bankruptcy court? To provide for such situations, the Reform Act gives bankruptcy courts the right to remand civil actions "on any equitable ground."[92] Furthermore, the bankruptcy court may remand a proceeding to a state or federal court at any time prior to a final judgment if it appears that it was removed to the bankruptcy court improvidently or without justification. Upon remand, the bankruptcy court may order the payment of costs. The court in which the action was originally commenced may proceed with the case upon receipt of a certified copy of the remand order.[93] An order remanding an action is not reviewable on appeal.[94]

---

[87] Sugg. Int. B. Rule 7004(c).
[88] Sugg. Int. B. Rule 7004(d), 7004(e).
[89] Sugg. Int. B. Rule 7004(f).
[90] Sugg. Int. B. Rule 7004(i); 28 U.S.C. § 1479.
[91] See Sugg. Int. B. Rule 7004(g).
[92] 28 U.S.C. § 1478(b), added by B.R.A. § 241(a).
[93] Sugg. Int. B. Rule 7004(j).
[94] 28 U.S.C. § 1478(b).

[6] Abstention

The substantial broadening of the bankruptcy court's jurisdiction is not intended to restrict the court's power to abstain from entertaining a dispute when circumstances so warrant. The Bankruptcy Reform Act makes it clear that "in the interest of justice" the court may refuse to hear a particular proceeding that relates to the bankruptcy case as long as there is another forum that has jurisdiction over the dispute. A decision to abstain is not reviewable on appeal.[95]

Thompson v. Magnolia Petroleum Co.[96] is a good focal point for a discussion of the court's abstention powers. In that case, a railroad reorganization trustee claimed the right to recover oil found beneath the railroad's right-of-way across certain lands. Although the trustee claimed a fee simple in the right-of-way, other parties claimed that the right-of-way was only an easement and that the owner of the fee to the land was entitled to the oil. The Supreme Court ruled that, because of the trustee's possession of the right of way, the bankruptcy court had summary jurisdiction to hear the proceeding. Nonetheless, the Court decided that it was more desirable to have the litigation proceed in state court:

> A court of bankruptcy has an exclusive and nondelegable control over the administration of the estate in its possession. But the proper exercise of that control may, where the interests of the estate and the parties will best be served, lead the bankruptcy court to consent to submission to state courts of particular controversies involving unsettled questions of state property law and arising in the course of bankruptcy administration.[97]

In *Thompson,* the Court found that the underlying issue of the proceeding required the interpretation of conveyance instruments in accordance with unclear Illinois law. Therefore, it was more appropriate for the bankruptcy court to abstain.

---

[95] 28 U.S.C. § 1471(d), added by B.R.A. § 241(a). Bankruptcy courts may not abstain, however, when no other court, either federal, state, or local, has jurisdiction over the proceeding: "That clearly would not be in the interest of justice." H.R. Rep. No. 95-595, note 12 *supra*, at 446. See 11 U.S.C. § 305, and ¶ 2.15[2], for a discussion of the court's power to abstain from entertaining an entire bankruptcy case, as opposed to a proceeding within a case.

[96] 309 U.S. 478 (1940).

[97] *Id.* at 483.

¶ 6.05 TRIAL BY JURY

Prior to the enactment of the Bankruptcy Reform Act, debtors in an involuntary case had the right to a trial by jury with respect to the issues of insolvency and the commission of an act of bankruptcy.[98] The Reform Act departs from the former law in that the court now has the power to order that all issues arising with respect to the grounds for an involuntary petition be tried without a jury.[99] Indeed, debtors do not have a constitutional right to a jury trial on issues raised by an involuntary bankruptcy petition because there was no such right at common law and, moreover, there is no longer a statutory right to a jury trial on these issues.[100]

The right to a jury trial in contested matters arising within the bankruptcy case is a much more complex subject. Whether or not a party is entitled to a jury trial in the contested matter or adversary proceeding arising under the Reform Act depends on whether that party would have been entitled to a jury trial under the former Act. Specifically, the Reform Act preserves the same right to a trial by jury that existed before its enactment, except with respect to the issues raised by an involuntary petition.[101] This provision is likely to cause considerable confusion because of the change in the court's jurisdiction. Under the former Act, any issue raised in the bankruptcy court, except for certain issues in connection with the involuntary petition and the nondischargeability of a debt,[102] was triable without a jury because contested matters falling within the bankruptcy court's summary jurisdiction were considered equitable in nature. For example, a hearing upon an objection to discharge did not have to be tried by a jury despite a demand for it. On the other hand, plenary actions heard in nonbankruptcy federal courts that related to the bankruptcy case afforded the right to a jury trial whenever a legal remedy was being sought. Accordingly, a defendant was entitled to a jury trial in a plenary suit in federal district

---

[98] Former B.A. § 19(a); B. Rule 115. See Moore v. Yampa Mercantile Co., 287 F. 629 (8th Cir. 1923).

[99] 28 U.S.C. § 1480(b), added by B.R.A. § 241(a).

[100] Bankruptcy cases are equitable in nature and therefore do not afford a constitutional right to jury trial.

[101] 28 U.S.C. § 1480(a), added by B.R.A. § 241(a), provides that the Bankruptcy Code does not affect any right to trial by jury that is provided by any statute in effect on September 30, 1979.

[102] Former B.A. § 17(c); B. Rule 409(c). However, the right to a jury trial in a nondischargeability hearing existed only with respect to issues to which the right to jury trial applied under nonbankruptcy law. See *In re* Swope, 466 F.2d 936 (7th Cir. 1972); Countryman, "The New Dischargeability Law," 45 Am. Bankr. L.J. 1, 34 (1971).

court initiated to recover a money judgment against a person who received a preference.[103]

Of course, under the Reform Act all these matters are now heard in the bankruptcy court.[104] Therefore, despite the broadened jurisdiction of the bankruptcy court, the practitioner may still have to determine whether the party would have had a right to a jury trial if the matter had been heard in a plenary suit under the former Act. As a general rule of thumb, however, when a contested matter or adversary proceeding involves the recovery of a money judgment instead of equitable relief, the right to a jury trial exists. Also, because the former Act afforded the right to a jury trial at nondischargeability hearings with respect to legal issues, as opposed to equitable issues, that right continues also.[105]

The Suggested Interim Bankruptcy Rules provide that the party desiring a jury trial as of right must serve a written demand therefor at any time after the commencement of the case or proceeding, but not later than ten days after the service of the last pleading directed to the triable issue. The demand, which may be contained in a pleading of the party, may specify the issues to be tried by a jury. If no such specification is made, the demand is construed to cover all issues triable by a jury as of right. If a demand specifies only some of the issues, any other party may serve a separate demand for trial by jury on any or all other issues so triable. The separate demand must be made, however, within ten days after service of the original demand, unless a shorter time is ordered by the court. Failure to make a timely demand and to file it with the court constitutes a waiver of the right to trial by jury. Once a demand is made, however, it may not be withdrawn without the consent of the parties.[106]

¶ 6.06 APPEALS

The Bankruptcy Reform Act establishes three separate routes for appealing a decision of a bankruptcy judge.[107]

---

[103] Schoenthal v. Irving Trust Co., 287 U.S. 92 (1932). But see Hummel v. Wells Petroleum Co., 111 F.2d 883 (7th Cir. 1940), in which the court denied the right to a jury trial when the trustee sought to set aside a preference by way of an equitable remedy voiding an assignment of accounts because there was no adequate remedy at law.

[104] See ¶ 6.03 for a discussion of the expanded jurisdiction of bankruptcy courts.

[105] See note 102 *supra.*

[106] These provisions are contained in Sugg. Int. B. Rule 9001. See also Fed. R. Civ. P. 47-51, which apply to jury trials in bankruptcy cases.

[107] The three routes for appealing a decision apply during the transition

[1] Appellate Panels of Bankruptcy Judges

Each federal circuit has a judicial council, which is comprised of all circuit court judges in regular active service. The councils meet at least twice each year to discuss and decide various administrative matters.[108] The Bankruptcy Reform Act gives to each judicial council the power to order the chief judge of the respective circuit to designate panels of three bankruptcy judges to hear appeals from judgments, orders, and decrees of the bankruptcy court for a particular district. The panels are to be composed of bankruptcy judges from the district in which the appeal arises.[109] Of course, a three-judge panel may not hear an appeal from a decision of a member of the panel.[110]

If bankruptcy judge panels are appointed for a particular district, they have jurisdiction over all appeals from final judgments, orders, and decrees of bankruptcy courts located in that district.[111] In addition, panels have jurisdiction to hear appeals from interlocutory judgments, orders, and decrees, but only if the panel receiving the appeal grants leave for that purpose.[112] Appeals from a decision of an appellate panel of bankruptcy judges may be taken to the court of appeals.[113]

[2] Appeals to the District Court

If the judicial council for the circuit does not order the creation of bankruptcy judge appellate panels, the U.S. district court has jurisdiction to hear appeals from final judgments, orders, and decrees from a bankruptcy court in the same district.[114] The district court may also

---

period between October 1, 1979 and March 31, 1984. B.R.A. § 405(c). Compare former B.A. § 39(c); Part VIII of the Bankruptcy Rules of Procedure. Prior to the Reform Act, bankruptcy court decisions were appealed to the district court. A notice of appeal must be filed within ten days of the date of the entry of the order or judgment appealed from. B. Rule 802(a). Procedures for appeals are governed by Part VIII of the Bankruptcy Rules to the extent that they do not conflict with the Bankruptcy Reform Act. See also Sugg. Int. B. Rules 8001-8007, and local court rules governing procedures for appeals.

[108] 28 U.S.C. § 332.

[109] 28 U.S.C. § 160(a), added by B.R.A. § 201(a).

[110] 28 U.S.C. § 160(b), added by B.R.A. § 201(a).

[111] 28 U.S.C. § 1482(a), added by B.R.A. § 241(a).

[112] 28 U.S.C. § 1482(b), added by B.R.A. § 241(a).

[113] 28 U.S.C. § 1293(a), added by B.R.A. § 236(a).

[114] 28 U.S.C. § 1334(a), added by B.R.A. § 238(a). A district court judge must decide the appeal and may not refer it to a magistrate or special master. 28 U.S.C. § 1334(c).

grant leave to appeal from an interlocutory order or decree of a bankruptcy court.[115] Accordingly, the district courts sit as one-judge appellate courts in the absence of bankruptcy judge panels. District court decisions are reviewable by appeal to the court of appeals.[116]

[3] Direct Appeals to the Circuit Court

Appeals from final judgments, orders, and decrees of the bankruptcy court may be taken directly to the court of appeals if all of the parties to the appeal so agree.[117] By appealing directly to the circuit court of appeals, the district court or appellate panel of bankruptcy judges may be bypassed. It should be pointed out, however, that an appeal from an interlocutory order, such as a temporary injunction, may not be taken directly to the court of appeals despite the parties' agreement. Of course, decisions of the court of appeals may be appealed to the Supreme Court if certiorari is granted.

¶ 6.07 TRUSTEES

The trustee is the officer who represents the estate in a bankruptcy case.[118] After a case is commenced, the estate is treated as a separate entity that must be distinguished from the debtor. The person who sues or who may be sued on behalf of the estate is the trustee.[119]

In general, the trustee undertakes to act in the best interest of general creditors in collecting and preserving estate assets. To assist in this task, the trustee is given extraordinary powers to avoid certain transfers, executory contracts, and liens so as to enlarge the value of the estate

---

[115] 28 U.S.C. § 1334(b), added by B.R.A. § 238(a).

[116] 28 U.S.C. § 1293(b), added by B.R.A. § 236(a).

[117] *Id.*

[118] 11 U.S.C. § 323(a). The former Act, although not explicitly identifying the trustee as the representative of the estate, certainly treated the trustee as such. See, e.g., former B.A. §§ 47, 70(a). In a joint case or joint administration of cases, one trustee may represent both estates. See B. Rule 210(a). See also *In re* International Oil Co., 427 F.2d 186 (2d Cir. 1970), where one trustee had been elected for a corporate debtor and three wholly-owned subsidiaries in arrangement proceedings under Chapter XI, and, when bankruptcy liquidation ensued, an application was made to have four separate trustees elected. The court of appeals denied the application because no showing had been made for the appointment of separate trustees.

[119] 11 U.S.C. § 323(b), derived from former B.A. § 11 and B. Rule 610. If there is a vacancy in the office of trustee, pending actions and proceedings are not abated. 11 U.S.C. § 325, derived from former B.A. § 46.

available to general creditors.[120] The precise role and method of selection of the trustee may vary depending on the type of bankruptcy case.

[1] Who May Serve as Trustee

Any individual who is competent to perform the duties of a trustee is eligible to serve in that capacity.[121] However, in chapter 7 liquidations or chapter 13 debt adjustments, the individual who is the trustee must reside or have an office in either the judicial district where the case is pending or in any district adjacent to it.[122]

A corporation is also eligible to serve as a trustee, but only if its charter or by-laws specifically authorize it to act in that role and if, in a chapter 7 or chapter 13 case, it has an office in the judicial district where the case is pending or in a district adjacent to it.[123]

In addition to being eligible to serve as a trustee, the person must qualify for the position by filing a bond to secure the faithful performance of official duties. The bond must be posted within five days after the trustee's selection and before beginning the official duties.[124] The amount of the bond and sufficiency of the surety is determined by the court.[125] A proceeding on a trustee's bond may not be commenced after two years from the date of the trustee's discharge.[126]

Appointment of trustees in a particular district should not center among a small select group of individuals unless circumstances indicate that it is objectively warranted. In order to avoid the concentration of appointments to only a few persons, the Suggested Interim Bankruptcy Rules provide that appointments of trustees, except standing trustees in

---

[120] These extraordinary powers of the trustee are discussed in Chapter 7 *infra*.

[121] 11 U.S.C. § 321(a)(1), derived from former B.A. § 45. However, a person who served as an examiner in a reorganization case may not serve as trustee. 11 U.S.C. § 321(b).

[122] 11 U.S.C. § 321(a)(1), derived from former B.A. § 45.

[123] 11 U.S.C. § 321(a)(2), derived from former B.A. § 45.

[124] 11 U.S.C. § 322. The trustee also has five days to advise the court in writing of acceptance or rejection of the office from the date the trustee receives notice of the appointment. Sugg. Int. B. Rule 2004.

[125] When a trustee is elected in a liquidation case, the creditors may recommend the amount of the trustee's bond to be fixed by the court. Sugg. Int. B. Rule 2003(b)(1).

[126] 11 U.S.C. § 322, derived from former B.A. § 50 and B. Rule 212. The trustee is not personally liable on the bond in favor of the United States, however, in connection with any penalty or forfeiture incurred by the debtor. 11 U.S.C. § 322(c).

chapter 13 cases, shall be made so that the annual aggregate compensation of any person shall not be disproportionate or excessive, giving proper regard to geographic constraints. Moreover, the clerk of the bankruptcy court must maintain public records listing fees paid to trustees and professionals.[127]

The selection and qualification of a person as trustee does not prevent a subsequent replacement. The Bankruptcy Code follows the former Bankruptcy Act by providing for the trustee's removal for cause after the court conducts a hearing on notice.[128]

The Bankruptcy Reform Act created the U.S. Trustee Pilot Program to operate on an experimental basis until April 1, 1984 in eighteen judicial districts. This program is discussed in more detail later in this chapter.[129] It is important to mention at this point, however, that in those districts that have the pilot program, the U.S. Trustee for the judicial district in which the case is pending is eligible to serve as a trustee without the need to qualify by posting a bond.[130] Moreover, the U.S. Trustee may not be removed by the court.[131] If there is cause for removal, the Attorney General may exercise his administrative powers to remove the U.S. Trustee. In addition, the U.S. Trustee has the task of determining the amount and sufficiency of the bond filed by any private trustee in the relevant judicial district.[132]

[2] The Trustee in a Liquidation Case

Promptly after the filing of a voluntary petition for liquidation, a disinterested person is appointed as interim trustee to perform temporarily all of the functions and duties of a trustee until a permanent trustee is selected and qualified.[133] Between the filing of a voluntary petition and the first meeting of creditors, the interim trustee begins

---

[127] Sugg. Int. B. Rule 2005. See also B. Rule 213.

[128] 11 U.S.C. § 324, derived from former B.A. § 2(a)(17) and B. Rule 221(a).

[129] See ¶ 6.08.

[130] 11 U.S.C. § 15322(a).

[131] 11 U.S.C. § 15324.

[132] 11 U.S.C. § 15322(b).

[133] 11 U.S.C. § 701(a). The former Act did not provide for the appointment of an interim trustee, although a receiver could have been appointed for cause under the prior law. See former B.A. §§ 2(a)(3), 2(a)(5); B. Rule 201. The reason for providing for the appointment of an interim trustee in all liquidation cases is to expedite the administration of the estate. Since the appointment of an interim trustee is mandatory, the Code does not give the court the power to appoint a receiver. 11 U.S.C. § 105(b).

preliminary investigations regarding assets and the debtor's financial affairs.[134] An interim trustee is appointed in an involuntary case shortly after the order for relief, unless the court grants a request to appoint an interim trustee prior to the order for relief to preserve the estate or to operate the debtor's business pending trial on the involuntary petition. The early appointment of an interim trustee prior to the order for relief, however, requires a hearing on notice and may be vacated upon the filing of a bond by the debtor.[135]

In making the actual selection of the interim trustee, the court must appoint a member of a panel of private trustees established and maintained in each judicial district by the Director of the Administrative Office of the U.S. Courts.[136] If the case is pending in a district that has the U.S. Trustee Pilot Program, the U.S. Trustee appoints the interim trustee from a panel of private trustees established and supervised by the U.S. Trustee.[137] If none of the members of the panel is willing to serve as interim trustee, the U.S. Trustee must serve in that role.[138]

The creditors in a liquidation case have the right to elect a trustee at the meeting of creditors, but only if an election is requested by, and votes are cast by, creditors who are eligible to vote and who hold at least 20 percent in amount of all the allowable claims that are unsecured, undisputed, and liquidated.[139] A creditor is not eligible to vote unless the creditor holds a claim that is allowable, unsecured, undisputed, and liquidated.[140] The creditor who desires to vote must file a proof of claim at or before the creditors' meeting. If an objection to the claim is made, the court may temporarily allow it for the sole purpose of permitting the creditor to vote for a trustee.[141] A creditor who

---

[134] See H.R. Rep. No. 95-595, note 12 *supra*, at 102.

[135] 11 U.S.C. §§ 303(g), 15303.

[136] 28 U.S.C. § 604(f), added by B.R.A. § 225(b). See 11 U.S.C. § 701(a).

[137] See 28 U.S.C. § 586(a)(1), added by B.R.A. § 224(a); 11 U.S.C. § 15701(a). See also ¶ 6.08 for a discussion on the U.S. Trustee Pilot Program.

[138] 11 U.S.C. § 15701(b).

[139] 11 U.S.C. § 702(b). Compare former B.A. § 44(a) and B. Rule 209, which provided for the election of a trustee in all cases, regardless of how many creditors voted, unless the creditors failed to elect one. When a trustee is elected, the creditors also may recommend the amount of the trustee's bond to be fixed by the court. Sugg. Int. B. Rule 2003(b)(1).

[140] 11 U.S.C. § 702(a)(1). However, creditors who have priority claims or claims for interest accruing after the commencement of the case may not vote. See 11 U.S.C. §§ 702(a)(1), 726(a)(1), 726(a)(5). The rationale for excluding these creditors is that their interests are often adverse to those of general creditors.

[141] See B. Rule 207(a); Sugg. Int. B. Rule 2003(b)(3).

holds a priority or secured claim may vote only with respect to the amount by which the claim exceeds the amount of priority or value of security.[142] Proxies may be used for the purpose of voting at the creditors' meeting.[143] A trustee must be elected by a majority in amount of claims that are held by those who vote.[144]

The Code follows the practice under the Bankruptcy Rules of Procedure by denying the right to vote to creditors who have an interest that is materially adverse to that of general creditors.[145] Whether an interest is materially adverse depends on various factors, such as the nature, size, and degree of the adverse interest. For example, a creditor who has a large equity interest in the debtor corporation may not be permitted to vote. However, if the equity interest is insubstantial in relation to the creditor's allowable unsecured claim, the creditor may vote for a trustee.[146] Furthermore, voting rights are denied to any insider, including relatives, partners, controlling shareholders, officers, directors, or others in a close relationship with the debtor.[147]

If an election is disputed, the presiding officer at the meeting of creditors is required to so inform the court in writing, and the interim trustee continues in office until the dispute is resolved. However, if an application for a resolution of the dispute is not made within ten days after the date of the creditors' meeting, the interim trustee becomes the permanent trustee and the dispute will never be resolved.[148]

In view of the fact that an election will not be held unless creditors who are eligible to vote and who hold at least 20 percent of the claims discussed above request an election and vote, it is unlikely that an election will occur in cases that involve no assets or small estates. Creditors are not likely to spend the time and money to appear at a meeting to vote unless there are enough scheduled assets to make the effort worthwhile or there exists the potential of avoiding transfers of property. The

---

[142] See B. Rule 207(c).

[143] See B. Rule 208.

[144] 11 U.S.C. § 702(c)(2). See 11 U.S.C. § 703, which provides for the same election process for successor trustees in the event that the office of trustee becomes vacant.

[145] 11 U.S.C. § 702(a)(2). See B. Rule 207(d).

[146] See H.R. Rep. No. 95-595, note 12 supra, at 378. "An insubstantial equity interest does not disqualify a creditor from voting for a candidate for trustee." 124 Cong. Rec. H11098 (daily ed., Sept. 28, 1978).

[147] 11 U.S.C. § 702(a)(3). See 11 U.S.C. § 101(25) for the definition of "insider."

[148] Sugg. Int. B. Rule 2003(d).

Code anticipates this by providing that the interim trustee shall become the permanent trustee in the event that a trustee is not elected.[149]

Once a person qualifies as a trustee in a liquidation case, there are numerous duties that must be performed. The role of the trustee may be summarized by the following list: [150]

(1) The trustee must collect and reduce to cash the property of the estate.[151]

(2) When appropriate to preserve the value of the estate, the trustee should seek authorization to continue to operate the debtor's business temporarily.[152]

(3) The trustee may examine the debtor at the meeting of creditors.[153]

(4) In partnership liquidations, the trustee sues general partners for any deficiency after the distribution of estate assets.[154]

(5) The trustee must be accountable for all property received. This duty includes the filing of a complete inventory, keeping records of receipts and of the disposition of money and property, and making reports to the court every three months with respect to the financial condition of the estate and progress of the administration.[155]

(6) The trustee conducts an investigation of the debtor's financial affairs.[156]

(7) If appropriate, the trustee examines proofs of claims and objects to the allowance of any claim that is improper.[157]

(8) If advisable, the trustee may oppose the discharge of the debtor.[158]

(9) The trustee must furnish information relating to the bank-

---

[149] 11 U.S.C. § 702(d).

[150] See former B.A. § 47(a) with respect to the trustee's duties under the previous law.

[151] 11 U.S.C. § 704(1). In the performance of this duty, the trustee is aided by certain voiding powers discussed in Chapter 7 *infra.*

[152] 11 U.S.C. § 721.

[153] 11 U.S.C. § 343.

[154] 11 U.S.C. § 723. See *In re* Ira Haupt & Co., 240 F. Supp. 369 (S.D.N.Y. 1965), where a court directed a solvent partner to turn over personal assets to the trustee of a bankrupt partnership. See also B. Rule 108(c), requiring filing of schedules by each general partner not in bankruptcy.

[155] 11 U.S.C. § 704(2); B. Rule 218.

[156] 11 U.S.C. § 704(3).

[157] 11 U.S.C. § 704(4).

[158] 11 U.S.C. § 704(5).

ruptcy as requested by a party in interest, unless the court orders otherwise.[159]

(10) If the business continues to operate, the trustee must file with the court and appropriate taxing authorities periodic reports and summaries of the operation of the business.[160]

(11) The trustee must make a final report and file a final account of the administration of the estate. The report and final account must be filed with the court and, if there is a U.S. Trustee in the district, with the U.S. Trustee.[161]

[3] The Trustee in a Reorganization Case

A trustee must be elected or appointed in every liquidation case. In contrast, however, a trustee is not appointed in a chapter 11 reorganization case unless the court, after notice and a hearing, determines that there is cause for such an appointment.[162] For example, the court may appoint a trustee if the debtor in possession proves to be incompetent or dishonest. In the usual case, the debtor in possession performs the trustee's functions during a reorganization.

If the court orders the appointment of a trustee in a reorganization case, creditors do not have the right to elect one. The court appoints "one disinterested person" to serve as trustee.[163] Because of the complexity of certain reorganizations and the demand for experienced business leadership and managerial skills, the Code does not limit the court's ability to choose the best person to serve as trustee. Accordingly, the selected person does not have to be a member of the panel of private trustees maintained by the Director of the Administrative Office of the U.S. Courts, but must be eligible to serve as a trustee in bankruptcy and must qualify for the office.[164] If the U.S. Trustee Pilot Program is in effect in the district, the U.S. Trustee selects the trustee after consultation with parties in interest and subject to the court's approval. However, the U.S. Trustee may not serve as the trustee in a reorganization case.[165]

---

[159] 11 U.S.C. § 704(6).

[160] 11 U.S.C. § 704(7).

[161] 11 U.S.C. §§ 704(8), 15704.

[162] 11 U.S.C. § 1104(a). If the court does not order the appointment of a trustee, it may order the appointment of an examiner to investigate the debtor's business. See 11 U.S.C. § 1104(b).

[163] 11 U.S.C. § 1104(c).

[164] See 11 U.S.C. §§ 321, 322.

[165] 11 U.S.C. § 151104(c).

Chapter 8 of this book contains a detailed discussion concerning the appointment, as well as the duties, of a trustee in a reorganization case. The reader interested in this subject is referred to that chapter.

[4] The Trustee in a Chapter 13 Debt Adjustment

A trustee must be appointed in every chapter 13 case to serve as the principal administrator.[166] The role of the chapter 13 trustee is different from the trustee's role in liquidations and reorganizations.[167]

Creditors do not have the right to elect a trustee in a chapter 13 case. Instead, the court selects and appoints one. Whenever the number of cases filed under chapter 13 in a judicial district so warrants, the court may appoint one or more individuals to serve as standing trustee in all chapter 13 cases pending in that district.[168]

In a judicial district that is subject to the U.S. Trustee Pilot Program, the U.S. Trustee may, with the Attorney General's approval, appoint one or more persons to serve as standing trustee under the U.S. Trustee's supervision if the number of chapter 13 cases warrants such appointment. In the absence of a standing trustee, however, the U.S. Trustee serves as trustee in chapter 13 cases.[169]

[5] Compensation of Trustees

Trustees, including interim trustees, are entitled to receive from the estate reasonable compensation for their services.[170] The payment of fees to a trustee is granted priority in distribution as an administrative expense.[171] The court sets the trustee's compensation after a hearing on notice to parties in interest.[172]

The Bankruptcy Code contains several provisions limiting the amount of compensation that may be awarded to a trustee. The limitation that is the most flexible and that calls upon the court's discretion is that the fee must be "reasonable compensation for actual, necessary services . . . based on the time, the nature, the extent, and the value of

---

[166] See 11 U.S.C. § 1302(a).

[167] See Chapter 9 *infra* for a detailed discussion of the role of the chapter 13 trustee.

[168] 11 U.S.C. §§ 1302(a) and 1302(d), derived from B. Rule 13-205(a).

[169] See 11 U.S.C. § 151302. See also 28 U.S.C. § 586(b), added by B.R.A. § 224(a). See ¶ 6.08 on the U.S. Trustee Pilot Program.

[170] See 11 U.S.C. § 330(a).

[171] See 11 U.S.C. §§ 503(b)(2), 507(a)(1).

[172] 11 U.S.C. § 330(a).

such services, and the cost of comparable services [in nonbankruptcy cases]." [173] This reasonableness standard, which also applies to compensation for attorneys, accountants, and other professionals who are employed by the estate, is discussed in greater depth later in this chapter.[174]

Aside from the reasonableness standard, the Code contains maximum ceilings on trustee compensation. In a case under either chapter 7 or chapter 11, the fee may not exceed 15 percent on the first $1,000 or less, 6 percent on any amount from $1,000 to $3,000, 3 percent on any amount from $3,000 to $20,000, 2 percent on any amount from $20,000 to $50,000, and one percent on any amount in excess of $50,000, based upon all money disbursed or turned over in the case by the trustee to parties of interest. To determine the amount of money for this purpose, money distributed to secured creditors is included, but sums distributed to the debtor are excluded.[175]

The maximum compensation payable to a trustee in a chapter 13 case also depends on the amount of funds distributed. A chapter 13 trustee, other than a standing trustee, may not receive more than 5 percent of all payments under the plan.[176] A standing trustee may collect a percentage fee up to 10 percent based on a maximum annual compensation set by the court and any necessary expenses.[177] The maximum annual compensation and percentage fee payable to a standing trustee in districts that have a U.S. Trustee is determined by the Attorney General after consultation with the U.S. Trustee.[178] If a U.S. Trustee serves as trustee in a chapter 13 case, however, a fee may not be awarded.[179]

In addition to receiving fees, trustees are entitled to be reimbursed

---

[173] 11 U.S.C. § 330(a)(1).

[174] See ¶ 6.10[3].

[175] 11 U.S.C. § 326(a). Compare the fee schedule under former B.A. § 48(c). Although the former Act assured the trustee of a minimum of $150, the Code fixes only $20 as a minimum because the former Act "has too often been used to pay trustees while leaving nothing for the creditors." H.R. Rep. No. 95-595, note 12 *supra*, at 327. See 11 U.S.C. § 330(b), which provides that $20 be paid to the trustee from the filing fee.

[176] 11 U.S.C. § 326(b), derived from former B.A. § 659(3).

[177] See 11 U.S.C. § 1302(e). Note, however, that the Code appears to be inconsistent in that Section 1302(e) provides for a fee for the standing trustee, and Section 326(b) provides that "the court may not allow compensation for services or reimbursement of expenses of a standing trustee."

[178] See 28 U.S.C. § 586(e), added by B.R.A. § 224(a).

[179] 11 U.S.C. § 15326. But see 11 U.S.C. § 15330, which permits the court to award fees to the U.S. Trustee in other bankruptcy cases. The fees must be paid, however, to the Treasury.

for actual expenses that are necessary to the performance of official duties.[180]

In order to avoid double compensation when there are two or more trustees in a case, the Code provides that the maximum fee limits apply to the aggregate compensation.[181] For example, if an interim trustee performs services before an elected trustee assumes office, the total compensation paid may not exceed the statutory ceiling. The Code also prohibits the sharing of fees by a trustee and other persons, unless the fee is shared with partners, corporations, or associates of the trustee.[182] Moreover, a trustee may be denied compensation if, without making a diligent inquiry, the trustee employes an attorney or other professional who has a conflict of interest.[183]

The Suggested Interim Bankruptcy Rules contain provisions designed to make public the fees paid to trustees and other professionals in bankruptcy cases. Specifically, the clerk of the bankruptcy court is required to keep a public record listing fees paid from estates to trustees, attorneys, accountants, and other professionals employed by the trustee, as well as fees paid to examiners and appraisers appointed by the court. The record includes the name and docket number of each case, the name of the individual or firm receiving the fee, and the amount of the fee paid. At the close of each annual period, the clerk must prepare a summary of the public record by individual and firm name to reflect total fees paid during the preceding year.[184] This public record provides a means for monitoring the appointment process. Bankruptcy cases often last for several years before they are finally closed. For this reason, the Code permits a trustee to apply for interim compensation once every 120 days or, if the court permits, even more often. The court may award interim compensation for services performed prior to the application, but only after a hearing on notice to parties in interest.[185]

---

[180] 11 U.S.C. § 330(a)(2).

[181] 11 U.S.C. § 326(c). See H.R. Rep. No. 95-595, note 12 *supra,* at 327-328.

[182] See 11 U.S.C. § 504. This section is derived from B. Rule 219(d), which permitted a sharing of compensation between an attorney for the debtor or for a petitioning creditor and any other attorney contributing to the services rendered. Section 504 of the Code, however, permits sharing of compensation with a petitioning creditor only. Of course, a court order is necessary for the retention of any professional person. See Rule 2-107 of the Code of Professional Responsibility adopted by the American Bar Association.

[183] See 11 U.S.C. §§ 326(d), 328(c). See ¶ 6.10[2] on the employment of professionals and the conflict of interest problem.

[184] Sugg. Int. B. Rule 2005.

[185] 11 U.S.C. § 331. This provision also applies to examiners seeking

¶ 6.08 THE U.S. TRUSTEE PILOT PROGRAM

As discussed earlier, a major criticism of the bankruptcy court system under the former Act was that bankruptcy judges performed both administrative and judicial functions.[186] Although Congress agreed that the judge should be free from the burdens of supervising and managing bankruptcy cases, there was sharp disagreement as to who should substitute for the judge with respect to administrative tasks. The House of Representatives wanted to create the Office of U.S. Trustee in every judicial district as an arm of the Department of Justice to supervise the administration of bankruptcy cases.[187] On the other hand, the Senate wanted private trustees to assume the primary role in estate administration without the need for a supervising governmental official.[188] As a compromise, the Bankruptcy Reform Act created a pilot program in ten selected areas covering eighteen judicial districts to experiment with U.S. Trustees for a five-year period.[189]

Specifically, there are ten U.S. Trustees appointed by the Attorney General under the pilot program. There is one U.S. Trustee for each of the following areas:

(1) District of Maine, District of New Hampshire, District of Massachusetts, and District of Rhode Island.
(2) Southern District of New York.
(3) District of Delaware and District of New Jersey.
(4) Eastern District of Virginia and District of District of Columbia.
(5) Northern District of Alabama.
(6) Northern District of Texas.
(7) Northern District of Illinois.
(8) District of Minnesota, District of North Dakota, and District of South Dakota.

---

interim compensation in reorganization cases. Although the former Act did not provide for interim compensation, courts have permitted it nonetheless. See *In re* Imperial "400" Nat'l, Inc., 324 F. Supp. 582 (D.N.J. 1971), in which the court granted an application for a fourth interim allowance of $30,000 to the trustee in a reorganization case that commenced five years prior to the application.

[186] See ¶ 6.01.

[187] See H.R. Rep. No. 95-595, note 12 *supra*, at 100.

[188] See S. Rep. No. 95-989, 95th Cong., 2d Sess. 4 (1978).

[189] The pilot program is governed by Chapter 15 of Title 11 and by Chapter 39 of Title 28 of the U.S. Code. Part X of the Suggested Interim Bankruptcy Rules contains procedural rules applicable to U.S. Trustees.

(9) Central District of California.
(10) District of Colorado and District of Kansas.[190]

The U.S. Trustee is not a substitute for private trustees in pilot program districts. Instead, the U.S. Trustee performs appointing and supervisory functions previously reserved for bankruptcy judges. Each U.S. Trustee establishes and supervises a panel of private trustees who are eligible and available to serve in chapter 7 cases as interim trustee or, if a different trustee is not elected, as trustee.[191] In a liquidation case, the U.S. Trustee is the one who appoints a member of the panel to serve as interim trustee in each case; or, if no member is willing to serve, the U.S. Trustee serves as interim trustee.[192] If the court orders the appointment of a trustee or examiner in a reorganization case, the U.S. Trustee appoints a private trustee or examiner after consulting with parties in interest.[193] In chapter 13 cases, the U.S. Trustee either appoints a standing trustee or serves as the trustee.[194] In sum, the U.S. Trustee never assumes the role of trustee in reorganization cases and rarely serves as trustee in liquidation cases involving sufficient assets to warrant the election of a private trustee.

In addition to maintaining a panel of private trustees and making appointments, the U.S. Trustee supervises the administration of cases and trustees in all bankruptcies.[195] The U.S. Trustee monitors the performance of private trustees and determines the amount and sufficiency of bonds filed by private trustees to qualify.[196] The U.S. Trustee may examine the debtor at the meeting of creditors [197] and may object to a discharge.[198] The U.S. Trustee also appoints the creditors' committee in reorganization cases.[199] The Suggested Interim Bankruptcy Rules give the U.S. Trustee the additional tasks of calling and presiding at the first meeting of creditors as well as any other creditors' or equity security

---

[190] 28 U.S.C. § 581(a), added by B.R.A. § 224(a), and 11 U.S.C. § 1501.

[191] 28 U.S.C. § 586(a)(1); 11 U.S.C. § 15701(a). See also 11 U.S.C. § 702(d), which provides that the interim trustee becomes the trustee in the absence of an election.

[192] 11 U.S.C. § 15701(b).

[193] 11 U.S.C. § 151104(c). The appointment by the U.S. Trustee is subject to the court's approval. *Id.*

[194] 11 U.S.C. § 151302(a).

[195] 28 U.S.C. § 586(a)(3).

[196] 11 U.S.C. § 15322(b).

[197] 11 U.S.C. § 15343.

[198] 11 U.S.C. § 15727(a)(1).

[199] 11 U.S.C. § 151102.

holders' meetings.[200] The U.S. Trustee also has the right to raise and be heard on any issue relating to the responsibilities of the office in any bankruptcy case.[201]

The Attorney General is required to evaluate the feasibility and effectiveness of the U.S. Trustee Pilot Program and to make annual reports to Congress, the President, and the Judicial Conference.[202] It is anticipated that Congress will study the results of the pilot program to determine whether the U.S. Trustee system should be adopted in all judicial districts. However, unless Congress acts to expand or extend the U.S. Trustee system by future legislation, the pilot program terminates automatically on April 1, 1984.[203]

¶ 6.09 COMMITTEES

In liquidation cases, creditors who are eligible to vote for a trustee may elect a creditors' committee to consult with the trustee, make recommendations, and submit questions to the court concerning the administration of the estate.[204] In essence, the committee acts as an advisory body and watchdog for the general creditors. The size of the committee is governed by the Bankruptcy Code; it may have no fewer than three and not more than eleven members. Each committee member must hold an allowable, unsecured, nonpriority claim.[205] It is unlikely that creditors will bother to elect such a committee, however, unless there are substantial assets in the estate or there exists the potential of avoiding transfers of property. In a substantial liquidation the committee often retains counsel and other professionals at its own expense, but the Code does not permit the committee or its counsel to obtain compensation or reimbursement for expenses from the estate.[206]

The rules relating to committees in reorganization cases are significantly different in several respects from those applicable in liquidations. First, although the election of a creditors' committee in a liquidation case is optional, the creation of a creditors' committee is mandatory in

---

[200] Sugg. Int. B. Rule X-1003. A final meeting of creditors may be called if the net proceeds realized exceed $250. Sugg. Int. B. Rule X-1003(f).

[201] Sugg. Int. B. Rule X-1005.

[202] B.R.A. §§ 408(a), 408(b).

[203] B.R.A. § 408(c).

[204] 11 U.S.C. § 705, which is derived from former B.A. § 44(b) and B. Rule 214.

[205] 11 U.S.C. § 705(a).

[206] "There is no provision for compensation or reimbursement of [the committee's] counsel." H.R. Rep. No. 95-595, note 12 *supra*, at 380.

every reorganization case. Second, creditors may elect committee members in a liquidation case but not in a reorganization case. In a chapter 11 case, the court selects and appoints all committee members. The court may also order the appointment of other committees, including a committee of equity security holders.[207] In districts that are subject to the U.S. Trustee Pilot Program, the U.S. Trustee appoints committee members in chapter 11 cases.[208] Finally, attorneys and other professionals employed by a committee may receive compensation from the estate under chapter 11, but not under chapter 7.[209]

The formation and functions of committees in reorganization cases are discussed in greater detail in chapter 8 of this book.

¶ 6.10 EMPLOYMENT OF ATTORNEYS, ACCOUNTANTS, AND OTHER PROFESSIONALS

[1] Who May Hire Professionals

In the course of performing official duties, the trustee may need the services of certain professionals. For example, the trustee may need a lawyer to sue a creditor for the recovery of a preferential payment or to compel a person to turn over estate assets. An accountant may be needed to interpret the debtor's books and records, an auctioneer may have to be hired to liquidate estate assets, or an appraiser may be required to determine the value of certain collateral. Moreover, in cases where the trustee is authorized to continue the operation of the debtor's business, professionals are often needed to deal with the day-to-day affairs of the company. In view of the need for such services, the Bankruptcy Code gives the trustee the power to hire professionals to represent the estate or to assist in carrying out official duties. However, court approval is required before a professional may be hired.[210]

The debtor in possession in reorganization cases is required to perform most of the trustee's functions, such as the recovery of fraudulent conveyances and preferential payments. In addition, the debtor in possession continues the business pending confirmation of a plan. Committees of creditors or equity security holders also play active roles as

---

[207] 11 U.S.C. §§ 1102(a)(1), 1102(a)(2).

[208] 11 U.S.C. § 151102(a). There is no similar provision with respect to liquidation cases. See ¶ 6.08 on the U.S. Trustee Pilot Program.

[209] See 11 U.S.C. §§ 1103(a), 330(a).

[210] 11 U.S.C. § 327, which is derived from B. Rules 215(a) and 606(c). See also Sugg. Int. B. Rule 2006 with respect to the application for an order approving the employment of a professional.

advisers and watchdogs in chapter 11 cases, especially in the absence of a trustee. In view of these complex functions, debtors in possession and committees in reorganization cases also may employ professionals to assist them, subject to prior court approval.[211]

The procedures for obtaining court approval to retain a professional are governed by the Bankruptcy Rules.[212] An application must be made that states the specific facts showing the necessity for such employment, the name of the attorney or other professional to be retained, the reasons for the selection of that professional, and the services to be rendered. In addition, the application must set forth, to the best of the applicant's knowledge, all of the professional's connections with the debtor, the creditors, or any other party in interest and their respective attorneys and accountants. If the court is satisfied that the employment is necessary and that the professional is eligible to serve, it may issue an order authorizing such employment.

[2] Who May Serve as Attorney or Other Professional

The court may not authorize the trustee to employ any professional who holds or represents an interest that is adverse to the estate.[213] Moreover, only "disinterested persons" may be retained by the trustee, which means that the person is not a creditor, equity security holder, relative, insider, or investment banker for the debtor's securities.[214] In a chapter 11 case, the trustee is not permitted to hire any professional who served as examiner in the same case.[215] By requiring that the attorney, accountant, or other professional be disinterested, the Code assures that the professional's judgment will not be compromised by a conflict or potential conflict of interest.[216]

---

[211] See 11 U.S.C. § 1107(a), which gives the debtor in possession the same rights and powers as a trustee in reorganization cases. 11 U.S.C. § 1103(a), which is derived from B. Rule 11-29(b), gives committees the power to employ professionals. For the committee to do so, however, there must be an affirmative vote at a scheduled meeting at which a majority of members is present.

[212] These procedures are contained in B. Rule 215(a), as well as in Sugg. Int. B. Rule 2006.

[213] 11 U.S.C. § 327(a).

[214] 11 U.S.C. § 327(a), which is derived from B. Rule 10-206(b). See 11 U.S.C. § 101(13) for the definition of "disinterested person."

[215] 11 U.S.C. § 327(f).

[216] If a conflict of interest is found with respect to a professional serving the estate, the court may deny the professional's fee request. 11 U.S.C. § 328(c). Moreover, the court may deny the *trustee's* fee if the trustee appointed a professional who has a conflict of interest. See 11 U.S.C. § 326(d).

There are specific instances, however, when the Code permits the employment of a professional who has or had some connection with the debtor. For example, if the trustee or debtor in possession is authorized to continue the operation of the debtor's business, the trustee or debtor in possession may either retain or replace the attorneys, accountants, and others who were regularly employed by the debtor prior to bankruptcy.[217] Otherwise, the automatic removal of competent professionals most familiar with the debtor's business would cause disruption and might contribute to the deterioration of the business.

There are other situations in which the Code tolerates the employment of interested persons. The fact that a professional formerly represented a creditor is not a bar to employment by a trustee as long as the professional does not represent a creditor while representing the trustee.[218] Also, the court may authorize the trustee to act as attorney or accountant for the estate if such appointment is in the estate's best interest.[219]

Ordinarily, the debtor's attorney may not be retained to represent the trustee because of a conflict of interest. For example, the trustee's attorney may be called upon to commence litigation against the debtor to recover fraudulently concealed assets. However, the Code permits the trustee to hire the debtor's attorney for a "specified special purpose" only.[220] To illustrate, if the debtor is a plaintiff in a complex antitrust case that has been pending prior to bankruptcy, the trustee as successor to the debtor's antitrust claim may retain the debtor's lawyer to continue the lawsuit. This would be in the best interest of the estate because of the delay and expense of switching antitrust counsel so late in the case.

[3] Compensation of Professionals

When the court authorizes the employment of a professional to serve the trustee, the debtor in possession, or a reorganization committee, the court may award reasonable compensation for such services and the reimbursement of expenses.[221] In fact, professional compensation and expenses qualify for priority as administrative expenses.[222]

---

[217] 11 U.S.C. §§ 327(b), 1107(b).

[218] 11 U.S.C. § 327(c), which is derived from former B.A. § 44(c).

[219] 11 U.S.C. § 327(d), which is derived from B. Rule 215(e).

[220] 11 U.S.C. § 327(e).

[221] 11 U.S.C. § 330. See Sugg. Int. B. Rule 2005, and ¶ 6.07[5], with respect to public records of fees paid to professionals in bankruptcy cases.

[222] 11 U.S.C. §§ 503(b)(2), 507(a)(1).

The awarding of fees, however, may not occur unless the court holds a hearing on notice to determine the appropriate fee.[223]

Compensation may be allowed only for services actually performed that were necessary under the circumstances. The Code specifically authorizes compensation for work performed by paralegals as well as other paraprofessionals who are employed.[224] This provision is designed to induce attorneys to use paralegals when appropriate so as to reduce the costs of administrating the estate. Fees in a bankruptcy case may be set by agreement between the parties on any reasonable terms of employment, such as by making a down payment on account with the balance to be fixed by the court, or by retainer with an attorney setting an hourly rate or contingent fee. However, even though the court initially authorizes such fee arrangement, the court will nevertheless ultimately approve fees based on the time, nature, extent, and value of the services.[225] Accordingly, the court may disregard a fee agreement if its terms prove to be improvident and unanticipated at the time the fee was fixed.[226]

The Bankruptcy Code departs from prior law by providing that fees for professionals must be based on "the cost of comparable services" in nonbankruptcy cases.[227] Prior to the enactment of the Code, courts often set arbitrary limits on attorneys' fees based on the amount of a judge's salary or on some vague notions of conservation of the estate and economy of administration. For example, in *Finn v. Childs*

---

[223] 11 U.S.C. § 330(a).

[224] 11 U.S.C. § 330(a)(1).

[225] *Id.* Compare B. Rule 219(c)(1), which included the "conservation of the estate" and the "interests of creditors" as factors to be considered in allowing compensation.

[226] 11 U.S.C. § 328(a). Compare B. Rule 215, which did not authorize retainers or agreements fixing fees. In fact, the Bankruptcy Reform Act repealed the Borah Act, 18 U.S.C. § 155, which made fee agreements illegal. See B.R.A. § 314(f). Under the Reform Act, fee agreements are illegal only if they are fraudulently made.

[227] 11 U.S.C. § 330(a)(1). Compare York Int'l Bldg., Inc. v. Chaney, 527 F.2d 1061, 1069 (9th Cir. 1975), in which the court commented that "trustees and their attorneys, being regarded as public servants, should not expect as much for their services in bankruptcy proceedings as they might in private employment." See also *In re* Paramount Merrick, Inc., 252 F.2d 482 (2d Cir. 1958), in which the court wrote, with respect to an attorney's compensation: "The principal factors which enter into a determination of what is reasonable are the time spent, the intricacy of the questions involved, the size of the estate, the opposition encountered, the results obtained and the 'economic spirit' of the Bankruptcy Act to curtail unnecessary expenses." *Id.* at 485.

Co.,[228] the court of appeals reduced an attorney's fee below the amount the attorney would have received in a nonbankruptcy case, stating that attorneys cannot expect to be paid fees at the "same rate as in litigation of the usual kind. . . ."[229]

The approach taken in *Finn* was overruled by the Code so that attorneys and other professionals may receive fees that are similar to the fees received in other types of cases. The rationale for this change is that Congress wants bankruptcy specialists to remain in the bankruptcy field instead of turning to other areas because of a marked discrepancy in fee levels.[230]

As previously discussed,[231] a trustee may be authorized to act as attorney or accountant for the estate. In such situations the trustee may receive compensation as attorney or accountant, but based only on actual legal or accounting services rendered.[232]

It cannot be overemphasized that the attorney retained in a bankruptcy case should keep detailed time records and other documentation of services performed. Without adequate time records, courts may deny the application.[233] Similarly, records should distinguish between actual legal services and ministerial or clerical services because the amount of the fee awarded may depend on such an allocation of the time spent.[234] Moreover, the Code prohibits fee sharing unless it is being shared by firms or partners of the professional retained.[235]

The court does not award professional fees for work that is per-

---

[228] 181 F.2d 431 (2d Cir. 1950). See also Massachusetts Mutual Life Ins. Co. v. Brock, 405 F.2d 429 (5th Cir. 1968).

[229] Finn v. Childs Co., note 228 *supra*, at 436.

[230] See H.R. Rep. No. 95-595, note 12 *supra*, at 330.

[231] See ¶ 6.10[2].

[232] 11 U.S.C. § 328(b).

[233] See, e.g., *In re* Hardwick & Magee Co., 355 F. Supp. 58 (E.D. Pa. 1973), in which the court reversed a referee's award of fees because the attorney did not keep time records. "[R]esults achieved, no matter how good, will not support an award without consideration of time spent as well, and the demonstration of some reasonable nexus between the two." *Id.* at 70. Compare *In re* Borgenicht, 470 F. 2d 283 (2d Cir. 1972), where the court held that an estimate of time was inadequate, but remanded the proceeding to the bankruptcy court to allow submission of reconstructed records. The court stated in a footnote: "We do not suggest that the amount of time spent is the only—or even the most important—factor in granting an allowance."

[234] See *In re* Mabson Lumber Co., 394 F.2d 23 (2d Cir. 1968), in which the court denied compensation for services that did not require legal expertise, such as the general management of the estate. See also Pickels, "Attorneys' Fees in Bankruptcy Proceedings," 54 Texas L. Rev. 762 (1976).

[235] 11 U.S.C. § 504. See note 182 *supra*.

formed prior to the application. However, in fairness to professionals who serve for a long period of time, the Code permits application for interim fees and reimbursement once every 120 days, or more frequently if so order by the court.[236]

[4] The Debtor's Attorney

Whether it is paid prior to bankruptcy or during the case, the debtor's attorney must file with the court a statement of the compensation paid or agreed to be paid within one year prior to the commencement of the case. A statement must be filed as long as the legal services were rendered in connection with, or in contemplation of, the bankruptcy. Prepetition services are included, and the statement must identify the source of any compensation.[237] If fees exceed the reasonable value of the services rendered, the court may, after a hearing on notice, cancel the retainer or order the return of excessive compensation.[238]

If the debtor's attorney does not receive a fee prior to the filing of the petition, compensation may be awarded by the court as an administrative expense entitled to a priority in distribution.[239]

---

[236] 11 U.S.C. § 331.

[237] 11 U.S.C. § 329(a), derived from former B.A. § 60(d) and B. Rules 219, 220.

[238] 11 U.S.C. § 329(b).

[239] 11 U.S.C. §§ 330(a), 503(b)(2), 507(a)(1).

Chapter 7

THE TRUSTEE'S POWERS

The Bankruptcy Code gives the trustee certain extraordinary powers to assist in the performance of official duties. These powers are exercised to benefit general creditors by maximizing the size of the bankruptcy estate and the distribution to creditors.[1] In chapter 11 and chap-

---

[1] If a trustee initiates an action or proceeding to avoid a transfer under one of these powers, the action or proceeding must be commenced within two

ter 13 cases, the trustee's powers play an important role in facilitating rehabilitation. Specifically, these powers enable the trustee to set aside certain liens, recover property for the estate, avoid certain transfers, and reject or assume executory contracts and unexpired leases.

It should be kept in mind that the debtor in possession in a reorganization has the same powers as a trustee.[2] Accordingly, the powers discussed in this chapter may be exercised by the debtor in possession under chapter 11.

¶ 7.01 TRUSTEE AS HYPOTHETICAL LIEN CREDITOR

The Code follows the "strong arm" clause of the former Act by giving the trustee the rights and powers of a judicial lien creditor as of the date of bankruptcy.[3] Specifically, the trustee may avoid any transfer of property or obligation incurred by the debtor that would be voidable by a creditor on a simple contract who, at the time of the commencement of the case, extends credit and obtains a judicial lien on all of the debtor's property, whether or not such a creditor exists. The Code also gives the trustee the powers of a creditor with a writ of execution that is returned unsatisfied on the date the petition is filed.[4] In order to determine the extent of these powers, state law must be consulted to ascertain whether a particular transfer or obligation is voidable by such creditors.[5]

The trustee's status as a hypothetical lien creditor is often used to defeat unperfected security interests. Pursuant to Article 9 of the Uniform Commercial Code, a judicial lien creditor has priority over an unperfected security interest.[6] As a result, the trustee may avoid a security interest that has not been properly perfected in accordance with the requirements of Article 9.[7] If an unperfected security interest is

---

years after the appointment of the trustee or before the time when the case is closed or dismissed, whichever is earlier. 11 U.S.C. § 546(a).

[2] 11 U.S.C. § 1107(a). See Chapter 8 *infra* on reorganization.

[3] 11 U.S.C. § 544(a)(1), derived from former B.A. § 70(c). Section 544 (a)(1) overrules Pacific Fin. Corp. v. Edwards, 304 F.2d 224 (9th Cir. 1962), by making it clear that the trustee has the status of a creditor who extended credit immediately before the filing of the petition. See 124 Cong. Rec. H11097 (daily ed., Sept. 28, 1978).

[4] 11 U.S.C. § 544(a)(2).

[5] If the rights of a judicial lien creditor under state law depend on the creditor's knowledge, the trustee may exercise this avoiding power regardless of any knowledge of the trustee or of any actual creditor.

[6] U.C.C. § 9-301(1)(b).

[7] See, e.g., *In re* Leggett, 505 F.2d 120 (5th Cir. 1974). See also Appeal of Copeland, 531 F.2d 1195 (3d Cir. 1976), in which a security interest in

avoided by the trustee, the secured creditor loses the lien and is reduced to the status of a general unsecured creditor.

The Bankruptcy Code contains a special provision designed to protect certain liens that, although not perfected prior to bankruptcy, may be perfected under state law to protect the creditor against other interests acquired prior to perfection.[8] For example, assume that a debtor purchases equipment on credit and gives the seller a purchase-money security interest. Less than ten days after the sale but before the seller perfects the security interest, the debtor files a bankruptcy petition. Assume further that the seller files a financing statement to perfect the security interest immediately after the bankruptcy petition is filed. Although the security interest is not perfected prior to bankruptcy, the seller's security interest may not be avoided by the trustee. The UCC provides that a purchase-money security interest that is perfected within ten days after delivery of the goods takes priority over the rights of a creditor who obtains a lien between the time of the delivery of the goods and the time of perfection of the purchase-money security interest.[9] In essence, perfection relates back to defeat an earlier lien. Accordingly, such perfection enables the seller to defeat the trustee who is a hypothetical judicial lien creditor who obtained the lien on the date of bankruptcy.

In light of the trustee's power to avoid unperfected security interests, creditors should be cautious in perfecting their liens. A noteworthy case that should concern creditors is *In re Raymond F. Sargent, Inc.*[10] A financing statement was filed to perfect a security interest in the tractor, loader, and rake of the debtor whose actual name is "Raymond F. Sargent, Inc." After the debtor filed a bankruptcy petition, the trustee discovered that the financing statement listed the debtor's name as "Raymond F. Sargent Co., Inc." and challenged the validity of the security interest on the ground that the debtor's true name was not contained in the statement. The bankruptcy judge, agreeing with the trustee, held that the security interest was not perfected properly and that the trustee, as a hypothetical lien creditor, could avoid it. The secured creditor lost its lien only because it was careless in inserting the debtor's name on the financing statement.[11]

---

stock was sufficiently perfected by delivery to an escrow agent prior to bankruptcy.

[8] See 11 U.S.C. § 546(b). See also H.R. Rep. No. 95-595, 95th Cong., 1st Sess. 371 (1977) (hereinafter cited as H.R. Rep. No. 95-595).

[9] U.C.C. § 9-301(2).

[10] 8 U.C.C. Rep. 583 (D. Me. 1970).

[11] Compare a decision of the same court twenty days later holding that

¶ 7.02 TRUSTEE AS HYPOTHETICAL BONA FIDE PURCHASER OF REAL ESTATE

Whether or not such a purchaser actually exists, the trustee has the rights of a bona fide purchaser of the debtor's real property as of the time of the commencement of the bankruptcy case. The consequence of this status is that any transfer of real estate by the debtor that is not perfected as against bona fide purchasers prior to bankruptcy may not be effective as against the trustee.[12]

Why does the Code depart from the former Bankruptcy Act by giving the trustee the powers of a bona fide purchaser of real estate in addition to the powers of a judicial lien creditor? The answer to this question reflects the differences between real estate mortgages and security interests in personal property in relation to priority disputes in many states. In New York, for example, a judicial lien on personal property has priority over an unperfected secured interest pursuant to Article 9 of the Uniform Commercial Code. Therefore, the trustee does not need the additional status of a bona fide purchaser in order to avoid unperfected security interests. The trustee may defeat the interest while wearing the hat of a judicial lien creditor.[13] In contrast, however, a judicial lien creditor may not always defeat an unrecorded real estate mortgage because real property recording acts in some states were designed to protect bona fide purchasers—not judicial lien creditors. Thus, the trustee wearing the hat of a judicial lien creditor may not avoid an unrecorded mortgage in New York.[14] By granting the trustee the additional rights of a bona fide purchaser of real estate, mortgages that are unrecorded on the day of bankruptcy may be avoided under the new Code even in those states that give the unrecorded mortgage priority over judicial lien creditors.

¶ 7.03 TRUSTEE AS SUCCESSOR TO ACTUAL CREDITORS

The trustee, as the representative of general creditors, is given all of the rights and powers that actual creditors have when the bankruptcy

---

a different financing statement that listed the debtor's name as "Sargent Raymond F. Inc." was not seriously misleading and therefore was sufficient to properly perfect the security interest. 8 U.C.C. Rep. 746 (D. Me. 1970).

[12] 11 U.S.C. § 544(a)(3). This section is not derived from the former Bankruptcy Act.

[13] See ¶ 7.01.

[14] See, e.g., Savings & Loan Ass'n of Kingston v. Berberich, 24 A.D.2d 187, 264 N.Y.S2d (3d Dept. 1965); Suffolk County Fed. Sav. & Loan Ass'n v. Geiger, 291 N.Y.S.2d 982 (Sup. Ct. Suffolk Co. 1968).

petition is filed. Specifically, the Bankruptcy Code provides that the trustee may avoid any transfer of the debtor's property or any obligation incurred by the debtor that is voidable under nonbankruptcy law by an actual unsecured creditor who has an allowable claim.[15]

It is important to understand the difference between the trustee's status as a hypothetical judicial lien creditor and the trustee's status as a successor to actual creditors. As an imaginary judicial lien creditor as of the date of bankruptcy, the trustee may not be able to avoid security interests or other transfers that are perfected prior to bankruptcy.[16] For example, assume that the debtor fraudulently transfers a security interest two years before the filing of the bankruptcy petition. As long as the security interest is perfected prior to bankruptcy, the trustee as a judicial lien creditor as of the commencement of the case may not prevail over the fraudulent security interest. Furthermore, because the transfer occurred more than one year prior to bankruptcy, it is not vulnerable pursuant to the fraudulent transfer section of the Code.[17] However, the trustee may avoid the security interest by identifying any unsecured creditor who has the right to defeat the interest as a fraudulent transfer under applicable state law. Many states have adopted the Uniform Fraudulent Conveyance Act, which gives actual creditors the right to avoid such fraudulent transfers.[18]

The trustee's power to assert the rights of actual creditors to avoid transfers has been used effectively under the former Act to reverse bulk transfers that did not satisfy the requirements of the Bulk Sales Act. In *Danning v. Daylin, Inc.*,[19] the trustee of a corporate debtor successfully avoided a prebankruptcy bulk transfer by the corporation of approximately 25 percent of its inventory and fixtures in exchange for other inventory and fixtures. The transfer was voidable by an actual unsecured creditor because of the failure to notify the debtor's creditors in accordance with the bulk sale provisions of the California Commercial Code.[20] Since the bulk transfer was voidable as against at least one

---

[15] 11 U.S.C. § 544(b), derived from former B.A. § 70(e). The trustee may not use this power to assert the rights of secured creditors. See H.R. Rep. No. 95-595, note 8 *supra*, at 370. The trustee may assert the rights of an unsecured creditor whose claim is disallowed, but only if the disallowance is based on the fact that the claim belongs to a codebtor or guarantor and is one for reimbursement or contribution. See 11 U.S.C. §§ 502(e), 544(b).

[16] See ¶ 7.01.

[17] See 11 U.S.C. § 548(a) and ¶ 7.06.

[18] For example, see N.Y. Debt. & Cred. Law Art. 10 (McKinney), which is based on the Uniform Fraudulent Conveyance Act.

[19] 488 F.2d 185 (9th Cir. 1973).

[20] Cal. Com. Code §§ 6101 et. seq. (West 1964). This statute is based

actual creditor, the trustee was able to avoid it for the benefit of the estate.

Although this power depends upon the existence of a creditor who has the right to avoid the transfer, the extent of the trustee's power is often greater than that of the actual creditor. For example, the trustee may avoid *in toto* a fraudulent transfer of assets worth $1 million if the transfer is voidable as against one actual creditor who has only a $1,000 claim.[21] Moreover, the transfer is avoided by the trustee for the benefit of the estate—not of the actual creditor.[22] In fact, the actual creditor who has the right to avoid the fraudulent transfer is in no better position than other general creditors who would not be able to avoid it in the absence of bankruptcy. It is not surprising, therefore, that a court characterized the position of the trustee as standing "in the overshoes of the creditors" as well as "in the shoes of the bankrupt." [23]

¶ 7.04 STATUTORY LIENS

State and federal statutes often provide for the creation of liens upon specified events or conditions and in favor of certain types of creditors. For example, many states grant liens that arise solely by force of state legislation to garagemen, artisans, landlords, mechanics, and others. Similarly, both state and federal laws provide for the creation of tax liens. These statutory liens should not be confused with security interests and real estate mortgages, which are created by agreement of the parties, or judicial liens, which arise by levy, execution, or other legal or equitable process.[24]

In general, statutory liens are valid as against a bankruptcy

---

on Article 6 of the Uniform Commercial Code. For a discussion of Article 6 and its application in bankruptcy cases, see Coogan, Hogan & Vagts, Secured Transactions Under the Uniform Commercial Code Ch. 22 (1978).

[21] See Moore v. Bay, 284 U.S. 4 (1931); Roscoe Moss Co. v. Duncan, 336 F.2d 670 (9th Cir. 1964).

[22] See Mallagh v. Bank of America, 300 F.2d 679, 681 (9th Cir. 1962), in which the court noted that "the rights of a single creditor, however minor his claim, rebound to the benefit of all creditors in bankruptcy."

[23] Schneider v. O'Neal, 243 F.2d 914, 918 (8th Cir. 1957).

[24] Compare the definition of "statutory lien" in 11 U.S.C. § 101(38) with the definitions of "security interest" in 11 U.S.C. § 101(37) and "judicial lien" in 11 U.S.C. § 101(27). See Selby v. Ford Motor Co., 590 F.2d 642, (6th Cir. 1979), holding that a statutory trust fund is not a statutory lien.

trustee.[25] These liens are recognized as valid property interests of the lienholders and, as such, are protected in a bankruptcy case. Accordingly, the claims of statutory lienors usually are allowed as secured claims.[26]

Despite the general recognition of statutory liens, however, the trustee may avoid such liens for the benefit of the estate in three specified circumstances: [27]

[1] Liens That First Become Effective Upon Financial Disaster

The general recognition of statutory liens presents a danger that state legislatures will enact liens for the sole purpose of altering the order of distribution in bankruptcy cases. The scheme of priorities in bankruptcy cases is governed by the Code,[28] and therefore states should not be permitted to alter it. On the other hand, legitimate liens and property rights under state law should not be overlooked in bankruptcy administration. In order to balance these concerns, the Code attempts to identify and invalidate only those statutory liens that are enacted for the sole purpose of affecting a distribution in bankruptcy. The distinguishing characteristic of those liens that are obviously designed to alter bankruptcy distributions is that they first become effective, by their own terms, upon the financial disaster of the debtor.[29]

In particular, the Code gives the trustee the power to avoid statutory liens to the extent that they first become effective against the debtor upon the occurrence of any one of the following events:

(1) A bankruptcy case concerning the debtor is commenced;
(2) An insolvency proceeding other than a bankruptcy case is commenced;
(3) A custodian is appointed or takes possession of the debtor's assets;

---

[25] Notice that a statutory lien may not create a voidable preference. See 11 U.S.C. § 547(c)(6). The general recognition of statutory liens derives from Section 67(b) of the former Act.

[26] See 11 U.S.C. § 506 and ¶ 5.11.

[27] The three grounds for invalidating statutory liens are derived from former B.A. § 67(c). See King, "Statutory Liens—1966 Amendment of Section 67 of the Bankruptcy Act," 55 Ky. L.J. 542 (1967); Comment, "Statutory Liens Under Section 67c of the Bankruptcy Act; Some Problems of Definition," 43 Tul. L. Rev. 305 (1969).

[28] See 11 U.S.C. § 507.

[29] See former B.A. § 67(c)(1)(A). See also *In re* Federal's Inc., 553 F.2d 509, 516 (6th Cir. 1977).

(4) The debtor becomes insolvent;
(5) The debtor's financial condition fails to meet a specified standard;
(6) A creditor, other than the statutory lienor, causes an execution to be levied against the debtor's property.[30]

[2] The Bona Fide Purchaser Test

The trustee may avoid a statutory lien to the extent that it fails to pass a hypothetical bona fide purchaser test as of the date the petition is filed. If a statutory lien is not perfected or enforceable against a bona fide purchaser who purchases the property at the time the case is commenced—whether or not such a purchaser actually exists—it is not valid in bankruptcy.[31]

The power to avoid statutory liens that are not enforceable against bona fide purchasers is significant with regard to tax liens. Federal tax liens are not valid as against a bona fide purchaser until notice of the lien is filed in the proper place.[32] Moreover, federal tax liens on certain types of property, such as securities and motor vehicles, are not enforceable against bona fide purchasers despite perfection by filing.[33]

State tax liens are also not valid in bankruptcy if a bona fide purchaser could have defeated them under state law on the date of bankruptcy. *In re Perry*[34] is an interesting case that held a state tax lien for unpaid personal income taxes to be invalid in bankruptcy despite the prebankruptcy recording of the lien. Under California law, a recorded tax lien gives the state the status of a judicial lienor. The court reasoned that a bona fide purchaser may defeat a prior judicial lien creditor with respect to personal property unless a levy is made, such as by seizing the property. Thus, the mere recording of the California tax lien did not perfect it as against a subsequent bona fide purchaser.

---

[30] 11 U.S.C. § 545(1).

[31] 11 U.S.C. § 545(2). This section is based substantially on former B.A. § 67(c)(1)(b). See Phillips Constr. Co., Inc. v. Limperis, 579 F.2d 431 (7th Cir. 1978), which upheld the validity of a subcontractor's mechanic's lien because it was enforceable under Illinois law.

[32] 26 U.S.C. § 6323(a). See United States v. Speers, 382 U.S. 266 (1965), holding that an unrecorded federal tax lien was invalid as against a bankruptcy trustee under the former Act.

[33] 26 U.S.C. § 6323(b).

[34] 487 F.2d 84 (9th Cir. 1973), *cert. denied* 415 U.S. 978 (1974).

[3] Landlords' Liens

Many states give landlords statutory liens on property located on their premises to secure the payment of rent.[35] Because it is common for debtors in financial trouble to locate some of their assets in a rented area, the recognition of statutory landlords' liens would deprive other creditors of the right to share in the distribution of assets in liquidation.

In order to prevent landlords from consuming a substantial part of the estate by virtue of statutory liens, the Bankruptcy Code gives the trustee the power to avoid all liens for rent and liens in distress for rent, whether they are statutory or common-law liens.[36] A landlord, therefore, is treated as a general creditor in the absence of a security interest created by agreement of the parties prior to bankruptcy.[37]

¶ 7.05 PREFERENCES

A basic policy that underlies the Bankruptcy Code is equality of treatment among creditors. In order to achieve equality, the Code gives the trustee the power to avoid a preferential transfer made shortly before bankruptcy that gives one creditor unfair advantage over others.[38] Another benefit that results from the power to avoid preferences is that creditors are discouraged from racing to levy on the debtor's assets by judicial process on the eve of bankruptcy.

In Code terms, a *preference* is any transfer of the debtor's property to or for the benefit of a creditor, for or on account of an antecedent debt owed by the debtor, and made while the debtor is insolvent and within ninety days (one year in the case of an insider who had reasonable cause to believe that the debtor was insolvent) before the filing of the petition that enables the transferee to receive more than such creditor would receive in a liquidation case if the transfer had not been made.[39] Such transfers may be avoided by the trustee for the benefit of the estate.

---

[35] For example, see Fla. Stat. Ann. § 83.08 (West), which creates the Florida landlord's lien.

[36] 11 U.S.C. §§ 545(3) and 545(4), derived from former B.A. § 67(c)(1)(C).

[37] If the landlord's lien is not predicated on a statute or on common law, but is the result of a security agreement, the trustee may not use 11 U.S.C. §§ 545(3) and 545(4) to avoid it. See *In re* King Furniture City, Inc., 240 F. Supp. 453 (E.D. Ark. 1965), where a court distinguished between statutory liens and contractual liens in favor of landlords.

[38] 11 U.S.C. § 547, derived from former B.A. § 60.

[39] 11 U.S.C. § 547(b).

[1] When a Transfer Occurs: The Delayed Perfection Problem

There cannot be a voidable preference unless there is a transfer of the debtor's property. The Bankruptcy Code defines "transfer" in broad terms so as to include both the voluntary and involuntary disposition of property.[40] A preference may take place, for example, when a creditor obtains a judicial lien on the debtor's assets by means of an execution and levy. The granting of a mortgage, as well as the retention of a security interest by the seller of goods, also constitutes a transfer by the debtor.[41]

In order to know whether a transfer constitutes a preference, it is necessary to determine the time when a transfer is made.[42] For preference purposes, a transfer occurs at the time it becomes effective between the transferor and the transferee *if* the transfer is perfected within ten days after such time.[43] If perfection occurs after the ten-day period, the transfer is deemed to occur at the time of perfection.[44] If the transfer is not perfected at all before bankruptcy or within the ten-day period, it is deemed to occur immediately before the date of the filing of the petition.[45] Because the time of the transfer depends on when it is perfected, the Code contains guidelines for determining when perfection occurs.

A transfer of an interest in real estate other than fixtures is perfected when a bona fide purchaser of the property cannot acquire an interest that is superior to the interest of the transferee.[46] For example, a transfer of a real estate mortgage or the conveyance of land is perfected when it is recorded. A transfer of personal property or of a fix-

---

[40] 11 U.S.C. 101(40). But note that it must be a transfer of the *debtor's* property interest. See Parker v. Klochko Equip. Rental Co., 590 F.2d 649 (6th Cir. 1979), holding that the debtor's payment of funds from a statutory trust fund to materialmen was not a transfer of the debtor's property.

[41] See Glessner v. Massey-Ferguson, Inc., 353 F.2d 986 (9th Cir. 1965), *cert. denied* 384 U.S. 970 (1966), which held that repossession of the debtor's equipment pursuant to a conditional sales contract was a transfer for preference purposes under the former Act.

[42] A transfer may not be a preference unless it takes place after the debt is incurred and within a specified time period prior to bankruptcy. See ¶ 7.05[2][b], 7.05[2][d].

[43] 11 U.S.C. § 547(e)(2)(A). Compare former B.A. § 60(a)(7), which provided for a twenty-one-day period, instead of the new ten-day period, for perfection.

[44] 11 U.S.C. § 547(e)(2)(B).

[45] 11 U.S.C. § 547(e)(2)(C).

[46] 11 U.S.C. § 547(e)(1)(A), derived from former B.A. § 60(a)(2).

ture is perfected when a creditor on a simple contract cannot acquire a judicial lien that is superior to the interest of the transferee.[47]

Assume that the debtor borrows money from a creditor on June 1. At the same time, the debtor executes loan documents that grant a security interest in the debtor's equipment to secure the debt. On June 25, the creditor perfects the security interest by filing a financing statement. If the debtor files a bankruptcy petition on September 15, may the trustee avoid the security interest as a preference? Because perfection of the security interest occurred more than ten days after it first became effective between the debtor and the creditor, the transfer was made at the time of perfection on June 25. The transfer was to secure a debt that arose on June 1, thus being an antecedent debt, and it occurred within ninety day of the commencement of the bankruptcy case. Accordingly, the delayed filing of the financing statement leaves the security interest vulnerable to attack as a voidable preference. On the other hand, if the security interest was perfected by filing on June 9, the transfer would be deemed to occur on June 1, and, as a result, it would fall outside the crucial ninety-day prebankruptcy period and would not be a transfer to secure an antecedent debt. In view of this grace period for perfecting security interests and mortgages, a creditor should make sure that all steps necessary for perfection are completed within ten days after the lien is created by agreement.

Regardless of the time of recording or filing, a "transfer" cannot occur for preference purposes until the debtor acquires rights in the property transferred.[48] For example, on August 1 the debtor gives the secured party a security interest on "all equipment now owned and hereafter acquired." Although a financing statement is filed within ten days—say on August 5—the security interest that attaches to after-acquired collateral is not a transfer until the debtor obtains the new equipment. If the debtor purchases equipment on October 1, the transfer occurs at that time, and, in the event that a bankruptcy petition is filed within ninety days after October 1, the security interest in the new equipment may be avoided as a preference.

---

[47] 11 U.S.C. § 547(e)(1)(B), derived from former B.A. § 60(a)(2).

[48] 11 U.S.C.§ 547(e)(3). This section overrules DuBay v. Williams, 417 F.2d 1277 (9th Cir. 1969), and Grain Merchants of Ind., Inc. v. Union Bank & Savs. Co., 408 F.2d 209 (7th Cir.), *cert. denied* 396 U.S. 827 (1969), which held that the transfer of a security interest in after-acquired collateral relates back to the time that the financing statement was filed. See ¶ 7.05[8] for an exception with respect to floating liens in after-acquired inventory or accounts receivable.

[2] Elements of a Preference

The mere fact that a transfer of the debtor's property took place within the ninety-day preference period is not enough for the trustee to avoid it. The Bankruptcy Code sets forth the following five elements that must be present to constitute a preference:

[a] The Transfer Must Have Been to or for the Benefit of a Creditor [49]

A preference involves favoring one creditor over others. Thus, a transfer of property to someone who is not a creditor cannot constitute a voidable preference. For the purpose of determining whether a transfer constitutes a preference, the Bankruptcy Code and the courts define "creditor" broadly.[50] The Code expressly provides that a governmental unit is a creditor, so that the payment of an old tax claim may constitute a preference.[51] Courts have held that a guarantor of the debtor's obligations can be the recipient of a voidable preference.[52] Moreover, transfers that benefit a creditor only indirectly may be a preference. For example, when an insolvent debtor conveyed real estate to his wife, who subsequently conveyed a mortgage to the husband's creditor, a court held that the transfer to the debtor's wife was actually for the benefit of the creditor and therefore constituted a voidable preference.[53]

[b] The Transfer Must Have Been for or on Account of an Antecedent Debt Owed by the Debtor [54]

Transfers for new consideration are not preferences. For example, if the debtor pays $10,000 for machinery worth $10,000 contemporaneously, during the ninety-day prebankruptcy period, there is no preference because new value is received in exchange for cash. In effect,

---

[49] 11 U.S.C. § 547(b)(1).

[50] See 11 U.S.C. § 101(9).

[51] 11 U.S.C. § 106(c)(1). See 124 Cong. Rec. H11097 (daily ed., Sept. 28, 1978).

[52] See, e.g., Joseph F. Hughes & Co., v. Machen, 164 F.2d 983 (4th Cir.), *cert. denied* 333 U.S. 881 (1947); Cooper Petroleum Co. v. Hart, 379 F.2d 777 (5th Cir. 1967).

[53] See Carroll v. Mansell, 251 F. Supp. 992 (W.D. Okla. 1966), *aff'd* 379 F.2d 682 (10th Cir. 1967).

[54] 11 U.S.C. § 547(b)(2).

the estate is not diminished because of the transaction. In contrast, transfers that secure or pay an antecedent debt may constitute a preference. For this reason, it is important to determine both the time that the debt was incurred and the time of the transfer in order to ascertain whether there is a preference.[55]

[c] The Debtor Must Have Been Insolvent at the Time of the Transfer[56]

If the debtor has sufficient assets to pay all obligations, creditors have no cause to complain when the debtor makes a payment. The equal treatment of creditors is affected only when the sum of all liabilities exceeds the value of the debtor's nonexempt assets.

The need to prove the debtor's insolvency at the time of the alleged preferential transfer was a serious impediment to the effective application of preference policies under the former Bankruptcy Act. The trustee's task was extremely difficult in light of the poor state of the books and records of most debtors on the eve of bankruptcy. As stated in a congressional report, "[T]he preference section [of the former Act] requires the trustee to prove a fact that nearly always exists yet never can be proved with certainty."[57]

In order to remedy this problem, a presumption of insolvency is contained in the new Bankruptcy Code to assist the trustee.[58] For preference purposes only, the debtor is presumed to have been insolvent on and during the ninety days immediately preceding the date of the filing of the petition. This presumption does not remove the burden of proof on the insolvency issue from the trustee. Instead, the presumption merely requires the creditor who received the alleged preference to go forward and present some evidence to overcome the presumption. The ultimate burden of proof remains with the trustee if the creditor rebuts the presumption.[59]

---

[55] See ¶ 7.05[1] for a discussion of the time of the transfer for preference purposes.

[56] 11 U.S.C. § 547(b)(3). See 11 U.S.C. § 101(26) for the definition of "insolvent."

[57] H.R. Rep. No. 95-595, note 8 *supra,* at 178.

[58] 11 U.S.C. § 547(f).

[59] See H.R. Rep. No. 95-595, note 8 *supra,* at 178-179, 375. See also Fed. R. Evid. 301, which is made applicable to bankruptcy cases by B.R.A. §§ 251 and 252.

[d] The Transfer Must Have Been Made Within Ninety Days or, in the Case of an Insider Who Had Reasonable Cause to Believe That the Debtor Was Insolvent, Within One Year Before Bankruptcy [60]

This element represents a significant departure from the preference section of the former Bankruptcy Act in several ways. First, the four-month preference period under the former Act [61] is reduced to ninety days under the Code.

Second, in order to avoid any preference under the former Act, it was necessary for the trustee to prove that the creditor receiving the transfer had reasonable cause to believe that the debtor was insolvent at the time of the transfer.[62] The insurmountable task of proving the creditor's state of mind was an obstacle in avoiding many preferences. In addition, the creditor's state of mind is unrelated to the policy of equality of distribution. For these reasons, under the new Code it is not necessary for the trustee to prove that the creditor had reason to believe that the debtor was insolvent.[63]

The reduction of the preference period from four months to ninety days would, standing alone, make it easier for a controlling shareholder, director, relative, partner, or other insider [64] who is also a creditor to receive a preference and then cause a delay in the filing of the debtor's bankruptcy petition for at least three months. For this reason, the Code provides that a transfer may constitute a voidable preference if made between ninety days and one year prior to bankruptcy to an insider who has reasonable cause to believe that the debtor was insolvent at the time of the transfer.[65] Accordingly, the state of the creditor's mind remains relevant in the case of a transfer to an insider before the crucial ninety-day preference period.

[e] The Transfer Must Enable the Creditor to Receive More Than the Creditor Would Have Received in a Liquidation Case [66]

A prebankruptcy payment on account of an antecedent debt does not adversely affect other creditors unless the transferee receives more

---

[60] 11 U.S.C. § 547(b)(4).

[61] Former B.A. § 60(a)(1).

[62] Former B.A. § 60(b). See, e.g., Hoppe v. Rittenhouse, 279 F.2d 3 (9th Cir. 1960).

[63] See H.R. Rep. No. 95-595, note 8 *supra*, at 178, 179.

[64] See 11 U.S.C. § 101(25) for a definition of "insider."

[65] 11 U.S.C. § 547(b)(4)(B).

[66] 11 U.S.C. § 547(b)(5), derived from former B.A. § 60(a)(1).

than it would have received as a distribution in liquidation. Thus, the trustee must establish that a creditor received more than it would have received if there were liquidation under chapter 7 of the Code. In order to determine the amount that the creditor would have received in liquidation, it must be assumed that the alleged preference had not been made. This element necessitates a determination of the allowability of the creditor's claim,[67] as well as of the priority accorded to it.[68] For example, if the creditor's claim were to be disallowed in total, this element would be satisfied because the creditor would have received nothing in liquidation. On the other hand, it is not a preference if the creditor receiving the transfer had received the same amount in a liquidation case by virtue of a priority.

[3] Exception: Contemporaneous Exchanges for New Value

A transaction between the debtor and a creditor does not result in a preference to the extent that it was intended by them to be, and was in fact, a "substantially contemporaneous exchange." [69] For example, assume that the debtor purchases equipment and, at the time of the sale, gives the seller a personal check in payment of the price. If the seller deposits the check three weeks later while the debtor is insolvent and within ninety days of bankruptcy, does payment of the check constitute a voidable preference? Although payment by personal check is often viewed as a credit transaction, such payment is "intended to be contemporaneous" and is treated as a cash transaction for preference purposes. The Code considers payment to be made when the check is delivered, unless it is dishonored.[70]

[4] Exception: Payment in the Ordinary Course of Business or Financial Affairs

The preference provision of the Code is designed to prevent *unusual* payments or transfers, which unfairly benefit some creditors at the expense of others on the eve of bankruptcy. Normal business relations should not be disturbed. For this reason, the Code departs from the former Act by protecting against attack certain payments that are made in the ordinary course of business.

---

[67] See 11 U.S.C. § 502 and ¶ 5.05, with respect to the allowability of claims.

[68] See 11 U.S.C. § 507 and ¶ 5.13, with respect to priorities.

[69] 11 U.S.C. § 547(c)(1). See generally Countryman, "Bankruptcy Preferences—Current Law and Proposed Changes," 11 U.C.C.L.J. 95 (1978).

[70] See 124 Cong. Rec. H11097 (daily ed., Sept. 28, 1978).

Specifically, a transfer in payment of an antecedent debt is not a voidable preference to the extent that it meets the following four requirements: (1) It was in payment of a debt incurred in the ordinary course of business or financial affairs [71] of the debtor and the transferee; (2) payment was made not later than forty-five days after the debt was incurred; [72] (3) payment was made in the ordinary course of business or financial affairs of the debtor and the transferee; and (4) payment was made according to ordinary business terms.[73]

Let us assume that the debtor ordered goods on credit payable in thirty days. Within ninety days prior to filing a bankruptcy petition and within thirty days after purchasing the goods, the debtor pays the bill. Assuming that such a purchase on credit and payment within thirty days are normal business practices in the industry, this payment would not constitute a preference. On the other hand, if the credit term called for payment within sixty days of the billing and if payment was made on the sixtieth day, the payment would be a preference because it would be outside the forty-five day period.

Furthermore, assume that forty-five day credit terms are established by the parties, but that the debtor consistently pays bills in more than forty-five days. Then, within the ninety-day period prior to bankruptcy, the debtor pays a bill not later than forty-five days after the debt was incurred. This payment may very well be considered a payment that was not made in the ordinary course of business of the parties and not according to ordinary business terms, because the practice between the parties was to ignore the original credit terms.

The exception for debts paid in the ordinary course of business or financial affairs is important in connection with tax payments. If the debtor pays a tax obligation when it becomes due, either originally or

---

[71] The term "financial affairs" is used to refer to a consumer's non-business activities, such as the payment of monthly utility bills. H.R. Rep. No. 95-595, note 8 *supra*, at 373.

[72] This requirement makes it necessary for the court to determine the time when the debt is "incurred" and the time when "payment" is made. It may be argued that a debt is incurred when the first bill or demand for payment is received by the debtor. In the usual sales situation, it may make sense to recognize that the debt is incurred when the debtor obtains a property interest in goods purchased unless a different time for payment is agreed upon by the parties. See Section 2-501 of the Uniform Commercial Code, which deals with the time when the buyer obtains an insurable interest in goods. As to the interpretation of "payment," see Henson, "The Uniform Commercial Code and the New Bankruptcy Act: Some Problem Areas," 35 Bus. Law. 83, 95-96 (1979).

[73] 11 U.S.C. § 547(c)(2).

under an extension, or within forty-five days thereafter, such payment does not constitute a voidable preference. However, if the tax is paid after the imposition of a penalty for late payment, such payment would be neither in the ordinary course of business nor on ordinary business terms and would constitute a preference, whether or not it is paid within the forty-five day exception period.[74]

[5] Exception: Security Interests in Connection With Enabling Loans

As discussed above, a security interest is not a "transfer" for preference purposes until the debtor acquires rights in the collateral.[75] Thus, if the debtor purchases during the ninety-day preference period equipment to which a lien attaches by virtue of an after-acquired collateral clause contained in a preexisting security agreement, the creditor's interest in the new property may be vulnerable as a preference. However, in order to encourage the extension of credit that enables debtors to acquire new assets, the Code contains an exception that protects certain security interests against preference attack.[76]

If the debtor gives a creditor a purchase-money security interest that is perfected within ten days after it attaches, the transfer may not be avoided as a preference, regardless of when the collateral is acquired. This protection applies only to security interests given in connection with new extensions of credit. The security interest must have been given at or after the signing of a security agreement that describes as collateral the property that the debtor then acquires with the loan proceeds. In essence, this exception protects sellers and lenders who extend credit to enable the debtor to purchase the property that becomes the collateral for the extension of credit.

[6] Exception: Subsequent Advances and the Net Result Rule

It is common for a debtor to have numerous exchanges with a creditor within the crucial ninety-day preference period. For example, assume that on May 1 an insolvent debtor made a preferential payment to a creditor for the sum of $20,000; on May 10 the creditor gave the debtor an unsecured advance in the sum of $12,000; on May 20 the debtor made a preferential payment in the sum of $4,000; on May 30 the creditor advanced another $2,000 to the debtor; and on June 10 the debtor filed a bankruptcy petition. How much can the trustee recover from the creditor as a voidable preference?

---

[74] See H.R. Rep. No. 95-595, note 8 *supra*, at 373.

[75] See ¶ 7.05[1].

[76] 11 U.S.C. § 547(c)(3).

During the ninety-day preference period, the debtor made two preferential payments: one for $20,000 and one for $4,000, for a total of $24,000. However, after each preferential payment, the creditor restored property to the debtor by making other unsecured advances. The Code follows the former Act by permitting the creditor to set off the subsequent advances from the amount recoverable by the trustee as a voidable preference.[77] Thus, the $12,000 advance may be set off against the first preference of $20,000, and the $2,000 advance may be set off against the second preference of $4,000. The net result is that the trustee may recover $10,000 from the creditor.

A preferred creditor may not set off a subsequent advance that is secured or for which the debtor made any other transfer to the creditor.[78] The rationale behind the net result rule is that the creditor who gives the debtor new value, usually in the form of a cash advance or delivery of goods on credit, is restoring property to the debtor that becomes part of the bankruptcy estate. For example, the creditor who receives a $20,000 preference is depriving the estate and other creditors of that amount of money. However, by giving the debtor a subsequent advance of $12,000 that remains unpaid at the time of bankruptcy, the creditor is restoring $12,000 to the estate for distribution to other creditors. Fairness dictates that the creditor have the right to deduct the $12,000 advance from the $20,000 preference. Compare the situation in which the creditor's subsequent advance is secured. In liquidation, the creditor would receive either full payment or the value of the collateral that secures the $12,000 advance. Thus, to the extent that the subsequent advance is secured, it does not benefit other creditors or the estate. For this reason, the Code does not permit the creditor to set off a subsequent advance to the extent that it is secured. Similarly, if the debtor gave the creditor property in exchange for the new advance, the advance may not be set off against the preference.

The net result rule is not limited to subsequent cash advances or the delivery of goods on credit. Any new value, including property or services, given to the debtor by the preferred creditor raises the possibility of an offset. *In re Ira Haupt & Co.*[79] is a good illustration of the type of new value that may result in a reduction of a voidable preference. Within the preference period and while insolvent, the debtor paid $20,700 to a firm of attorneys and accountants for services rendered as

---

[77] 11 U.S.C. § 547(c)(4), derived from former B.A. § 60(c).

[78] 11 U.S.C. § 547(c)(4)(B). See *In re* Hygrade Envelope Corp., 393 F.2d 60 (2d Cir. 1968).

[79] 424 F.2d 722 (2d Cir. 1970).

tax advisors for the debtor in the past. Subsequently, the firm performed further services for which it received no payment. When the trustee sought to recover $20,700 from the firm as a voidable preference, the court of appeals held that the amount recoverable by the trustee must be reduced by the value of services rendered to the debtor after the preferential payment.

[7] Exception: Statutory Liens

As previously discussed, statutory liens may be avoided by the trustee in certain situations.[80] Section 545 of the Bankruptcy Code governs the validity and avoidance of such liens. For this reason, the Code expressly excepts statutory liens from the realm of the preference section.[81] In essence, a statutory lien is not subject to attack by the trustee unless it is vulnerable under Section 545.

[8] Floating Liens in Inventory or Accounts Receivable

It is common for a lender to obtain a valid security interest in all of the debtor's inventory "presently owned and hereafter acquired." Indeed, the Uniform Commercial Code is designed to enable creditors to have such *floating liens* in collateral that turn over continuously.[82] In essence, the security interest attaches to new inventory automatically as soon as the debtor acquires it. These floating liens are also common when the collateral consists of accounts receivable, since accounts, like inventory, usually turn over many times during the life of a loan. Floating liens in inventory, accounts, or other types of collateral raise interesting questions relating to preference law.

Let us assume that a lender has a valid security interest in the debtor's inventory. Ninety days prior to the date on which the debtor files a bankruptcy petition, the debtor is insolvent, the loan balance is $500,000, and the inventory is worth $300,000. Assume further that on the day the petition is filed, the loan balance remains at $500,000, but the inventory is worth $400,000. Did the creditor receive a voidable preference?

Under the former Act, trustees have argued that such a floating lien creates a preference to the extent that new collateral was acquired during the crucial preference period. A security interest does not attach to property until the debtor requires it. Accordingly, trustees have

---

[80] See ¶ 7.04.

[81] 11 U.S.C. § 547(c)(6), derived from former B.A. § 67(b).

[82] See U.C.C. § 9-204.

argued that a lien on any inventory purchased within the preference period resulted in a transfer to secure an antecedent debt. Moreover, trustees contended that secured creditors with floating liens were preferred unfairly over other creditors to the extent that the value of the collateral increased during the preference period. Nonetheless, courts rejected these arguments and protected floating liens against preference attack.[83] A floating lien was viewed as a single entity that fluctuated in value but did not result in a new transfer upon the acquisition of new collateral. As one court wrote, quoting Professor Hogan: "The secured creditor's interest is in the stream of accounts flowing through the debtor's business, not in any specific accounts. As with the Heraclitean river, although the accounts in the stream constantly change, we can say it is the same stream." [84]

The Bankruptcy Code departs from prior law in several ways with respect to the treatment of floating liens. One significant change is that the Code distinguishes between floating liens in inventory or accounts receivable, and floating liens in other types of collateral.

Security interests in after-acquired collateral other than inventory or accounts receivable may be vulnerable as preferences to the extent that new collateral is acquired within ninety days of bankruptcy. For example, assume that a lender has a security interest in "all of the debtor's equipment presently owned and hereafter acquired." Ninety days before a petition is filed by the debtor, the debtor owns machinery worth $100,000, which secures the loan balance of $150,000. During the ninety-day preference period, the debtor, with consent of the lender, disposes of the machinery because of obsolescence and purchases new replacement machinery worth $300,000. Upon the debtor's bankruptcy, the trustee may avoid the security interest in the new machinery *in toto*. The Code expressly provides that, for preference purposes, a transfer is not made until the debtor has acquired rights in the collateral.[85] Accordingly, the transfer occurred within the preference period to secure an antecedent debt. Whether a financing statement was filed covering

---

[83] DuBay v. Williams, 417 F.2d 1277 (9th Cir. 1969); Grain Merchants of Ind., Inc. v. Union Bank & Savs. Co., 408 F.2d 209 (7th Cir.), *cert. denied* 396 U.S. 827 (1969). See Queenan, "The Preference Provision of the Pending Bankruptcy Law," 82 Com. L.J. 465, 470-472 (1977).

[84] Grain Merchants of Ind., Inc. v. Union Bank & Savs. Co., note 83 *supra*, at 215-216, quoting from Hogan, "Games Lawyers Play With the Bankruptcy Preference Challenge to Accounts and Inventory Financing," 53 Cornell L. Rev. 553, 560 (1968).

[85] 11 U.S.C. § 547(e)(3). See ¶ 7.05[1]. But see 11 U.S.C. § 547(c)(3), and ¶ 7.05[5], with respect to an exception for enabling loans.

the after-acquired equipment prior to the ninety-day period is irrelevant. In the above hypothetical, the creditor may lose the benefit of the security interest entirely, except to the extent that the creditor gives new value when the new machinery is purchased. In this way, the Code creates a possible pitfall for lenders with security interests in after-acquired equipment.

Floating liens in inventory or accounts receivable are not treated the same as other types of collateral. In essence, the Code protects such liens from attack to the extent that the creditor's position is not improved at the expense of other creditors during the preference period. However, to the extent that an increase in the value of the collateral gives the secured party an advantage over unsecured creditors in general, the floating lien creates a voidable preference.[86]

In order to determine whether and to what extent a secured creditor's position was improved during the preference period, a two-point test is used. In general, if the unsecured deficiency decreases during the ninety-day preference period (or one year in the case of an insider), the creditor receives a preference. The value of the collateral and the balance of the secured debt both at the time the petition is filed and ninety days prior to that time must be ascertained in order to apply the two-point test. If the secured loan is incurred after the beginning of the ninety-day preference period, then the date on which the loan was first given under the security agreement is substituted as the first point in the two-point test. Other fluctuations in value between these two points in time are irrelevant.[87]

There are two ways in which collateral may increase in value during the preference period. First, the debtor may purchase new collateral. Such acquisitions may result in a voidable preference in accordance with the two-point test. Second, the market value of the debtor's property may increase in value without the debtor acquiring new items. For example, inventory may increase in value because of seasonal market fluctuations. The first type of increase in value prejudices the rights of other creditors because the debtor expends unencumbered assets to acquire new collateral, thus depleting the estate. However, the second type of increase in value does not adversely affect the rights of other creditors because it does not diminish the estate. In fact, an increase in value due solely to market fluctuations improves the position of other unsecured creditors because it reduces the size of the secured

---

[86] 11 U.S.C. § 547(c)(5).

[87] See H.R. Rep. No. 95-595, note 8 *supra*, at 374. See also Queenan, note 83 *supra*, at 472.

party's allowable unsecured claim. For this reason, the Code provides that the improvement of the secured creditor's position during the pre-bankruptcy preference period due to an increase in the value of collateral results in a voidable preference only if it is "to the prejudice of other creditors holding unsecured claims." [88] Accordingly, an increase in the value of the collateral that is not caused by the acquisition of new collateral does not usually create a voidable preference.[89] However, if the debtor expends funds on labor, materials, and machinery in the process of finishing existing goods, so that unsecured creditors suffer due to the loss of funds available to the estate, the court may be justified in treating the improvement of the secured party's position with respect to the inventory collateral as a voidable preference.

The treatment of floating liens in inventory and accounts receivable is too complex to be left without illustration. Consider the following examples:

> *Illustration 1.* The debtor owed $100,000 to the lender at all times during the ninety-day period prior to bankruptcy, and the debt is secured by a floating lien on all of the debtor's accounts receivable. Ninety days prior to the date on which the petition was filed, the aggregate value of the accounts was $75,000. Sixty days prior to bankruptcy, the accounts were worth $60,000. On the date the petition was filed, the accounts were worth $90,000. Assume that the increase in value was due to a turnover of accounts and to the expansion of the debtor's business. Assuming that the other elements of a preference exist, the amount that may be avoided by the trustee is $15,000. According to the two-point test, the lender's position was improved from $75,000 to $90,000 during the ninety-day preference period. The fact that the lender's position improved by $25,000 during the sixty-day period prior to bankruptcy is irrelevant.

> *Illustration 2.* Assume the same facts as in Illustration 1, except that the lender first extended credit and took the security interst only thirty days prior to bankruptcy, when the collateral was worth $40,000. Thus, there was no debt ninety days before bankruptcy. On the date the petition was filed, the accounts were worth $90,000. The lender may retain the floating lien to the extent of

---

[88] 11 U.S.C. § 547(c)(5).

[89] See Orr & Klee, "Secured Creditors Under the New Bankruptcy Code," 11 U.C.C.L.J. 312, 334 note 209 (1979); H.R. Rep. No. 95-595, note 8 *supra*, at 377.

$40,000, but the remaining $50,000 of accounts is a voidable preference.

Illustration 3. Assume the same facts as in Illustration 1, except that the value of the accounts ninety days prior to bankruptcy was $125,000 and the value on the date of bankruptcy was $90,000. Because the lender's position did not improve, there is no preference.

[9] Transfers to Reimburse a Surety

Let us assume that a creditor acquires a judicial lien by obtaining an order of attachment on the debtor's property that constitutes an involuntary transfer within ninety days before bankruptcy. Prior to the commencement of the case, the debtor arranges for a surety to post a bond to dissolve the judicial lien so that the debtor may use the property. In order to secure reimbursement of the surety in the event that the debtor fails to pay a final judgment, the debtor gives the surety a security interest in certain assets. In view of the fact that the judicial lien was a preferential transfer, what are the consequences of replacing the lien with a surety bond secured by other assets?

The Bankruptcy Code follows the former Act with respect to the trustee's and the surety's rights.[90] Basically, the security interest transferred to the surety may be avoided if it secures the surety's reimbursement on a bond furnished to dissolve a preferential judicial lien. Thus, the security interest in the above hypothetical is invalid as against the trustee. Of course, the surety's rights would be jeopardized unfairly by the loss of its security interest. For this reason, the Code provides that the surety's liability under the bond shall be discharged to the extent that the security interest is invalidated. The result of these provisions is that the trustee's right to avoid a preferential judicial lien is not affected adversely by a prebankruptcy dissolution of the lien and transfer of a security interest to a surety. In essence, the trustee may avoid the surety's security interest instead of the dissolved judicial lien.

---

[90] See 11 U.S.C. § 547(d), derived from former B.A. § 67(a). See also B. Rule 612, which remains applicable under Suggested Interim Bankruptcy Rule 6001, for the procedural requirements for avoiding the surety's security interest. See also *In re* General Steel Tank Co., 478 F.2d 294 (4th Cir. 1973), holding that the rights of attaching creditors against an unindemnified (unsecured) surety on bonds given to release the debtor's property from judicial liens voidable in bankruptcy are not affected.

[10] Transfers of Exempt Property

The Bankruptcy Code departs from cases decided under the former Act by giving the trustee or the debtor the right to avoid preferential transfers of exempt property.[91] Although such transfers do not deprive other creditors of assets for distribution, the policies of equality among creditors and the protection of the debtor's exempt assets are facilitated by applying the trustee's avoiding powers to transfers of exempt property.[92]

¶ 7.06 FRAUDULENT TRANSFERS AND OBLIGATIONS

The Bankruptcy Code follows the approach of the former Act by giving the trustee two separate avenues for attacking fraudulent conveyances and obligations. The first avenue the trustee may use to defeat fraudulent transfers is the application of state law through Section 544(b).[93] That section gives the trustee the right to avoid transfers that are voidable by an actual unsecured creditor under state law. Many states have adopted the Uniform Fraudulent Conveyance Act (UFCA), which provides for the avoidance of fraudulent transfers by creditors in nonbankruptcy situations. The specific provisions of the UFCA are similar to the provisions set forth in Section 548 of the Code. However, because of the one-year limitation contained in Section 548, the trustee should use Section 544(b) together with state law to attack fraudulent transfers occurring more than one year before the filing of the petition.

The second avenue available to the trustee is Section 548 of the Code, which contains comprehensive provisions for the avoidance of fraudulent transfers and obligations. Section 548 is similar to Section 67(d) of the former Act in that it describes several types of transfers and obligations that are characterized as fraudulent and that may be avoided by the trustee.

It is important to note that a transfer may not be avoided under Section 548 unless it takes place within one year prior to the filing of the bankruptcy petition. For the purpose of determining the time of the transfer when applying Section 548, a transfer is made when it becomes so far perfected that it would defeat a subsequent bona fide purchaser

---

[91] See, e.g., Rutledge v. Johansen, 270 F.2d 881 (10th Cir. 1959).

[92] See ¶ 4.08[5] for a more extensive discussion of the application of avoiding powers to exempt assets.

[93] See ¶ 7.03.

from the debtor.[94] For example, a mortgage in real estate becomes a transfer when it is recorded. If such perfection does not occur prior to the commencement of the case, the transfer is deemed to occur immediately before the date of the filing of the petition. Moreover, the Code defines "transfer" broadly so as to include an involuntary taking of the debtor's property by levy and execution.[95]

There are several types of transfers and obligations that are considered fraudulent under Section 548:

[1] Transfers with Actual Fraudulent Intent

A transfer of property or an obligation incurred by the debtor "with actual intent to hinder, delay, or defraud" any past or future creditor may be avoided by the trustee.[96] The state of mind of the debtor must be examined in order to determine whether this type of fraud took place. Although the debtor's financial condition may be relevant in determining state of mind, a transfer may be fraudulent despite the debtor's solvency.[97]

The most obvious example of a transfer with actual intent to defraud creditors takes place when the debtor, while insolvent and contemplating liquidation, gives nonexempt property to friends and relatives for the sole purpose of placing assets out of the reach of creditors.

Transfers other than gifts may also be considered fraudulent in certain situations. For example, in *In re Allied Development Corp.,*[98] a financially troubled debtor gave a second mortgage to secure a new loan. The debtor and the mortgagee agreed that the mortgage would not be recorded because of fear that public notice of it would taint the credit rating of the debtor. The mortgagee, who was also the debtor's attorney, testified that the debtor "was in a cash liquid bad position and I did not record it [the second mortgage] because . . . I didn't want the Chamber of Commerce report to pick up the fact that [the debtor] granted a mortgage. . . ."[99] Although the mortgage was recorded prior to the debtor's bankruptcy and only three weeks after it was granted, the court held that the mortgage transaction constituted a fraudulent

---

[94] 11 U.S.C. § 548(d)(1). Compare the rules for determining the time of a transfer for preference purposes. See ¶ 7.05[1].

[95] 11 U.S.C. § 101(40).

[96] 11 U.S.C. § 548(a)(1), derived from former B.A. § 67(d)(2)(D).

[97] See McConnico v. Third Nat'l Bank in Nashville, 499 S.W.2d 874 (Tenn. 1973).

[98] 435 F.2d 372 (7th Cir. 1970).

[99] *Id.* at 374.

conveyance because of the debtor's actual intent to hinder or delay future creditors by concealing the existence of the mortgage.[100]

Does an intentional preference constitute a fraudulent transfer? Assume that the debtor, in contemplation of filing a bankruptcy petition, prefers a favorite unsecured creditor and then waits more than ninety days before filing the petition. If the creditor is not an insider, the payment is not voidable as a preference.[101] Is it voidable as a fraudulent conveyance?

In general, courts have held that the making of a preference is not, in and of itself, a fraudulent transfer.[102] The application of the debtor's assets to the payment of one group of creditors instead of another group is not fraudulent as long as the debtor acts in good faith. However, if evidence supports a finding that the debtor's primary purpose in making the preference was to prejudice other creditors, the transaction may be avoided as a fraudulent transfer.[103] For example, a preference to a friendly creditor with the understanding that the debtor will retain possession and use of the property is a transfer to hinder, delay, or defraud creditors.[104]

The purchase of exempt property with nonexempt assets may also constitute a fraudulent transfer if the debtor's primary motive is to keep property out of the reach of creditors in contemplation of bankruptcy.[105] The effects of the conversion of nonexempt to exempt assets on the eve of bankruptcy are discussed in greater detail earlier in this book.[106]

[2] Transfers for Less Than Reasonably Equivalent Value While Insolvent

The Bankruptcy Code follows the former Act by characterizing as fraudulent any transfer by an insolvent debtor for less than reasonably

---

[100] The intentional delay of the recording of a mortgage does not always result in a fraudulent transfer. See Rankin v. Cox, 71 F.2d 56 (8th Cir. 1934), which held that there was no fraud when the delay was for the purpose of avoiding a run in 1929 on a bank of which the debtor was president.

[101] See ¶ 7.05[2][d].

[102] See Van Iderstine v. National Discount Co., 227 U.S. 575 (1913); Richardson v. Germania Bank, 263 F. 320 (2d Cir. 1919).

[103] See *In re* Cushman Bakery, 526 F.2d 23, 33 (1st Cir. 1975), *cert. denied* 425 U.S. 937 (1976).

[104] See Shelley v. Boothe, 73 Mo. 74 (1880).

[105] See Resnick, "Prudent Planning or Fraudulent Transfer? The Use of Nonexempt Assets to Purchase or Improve Exempt Property on the Eve of Bankruptcy," 31 Rutgers L. Rev. 615 (1978).

[106] See ¶ 4.09.

equivalent value.[107] This type of fraud is not based on the debtor's state of mind or bad faith. Instead, the Code recognizes that creditors' rights are jeopardized whenever a debtor whose assets are not sufficient to pay liabilities disposes of property for less than fair consideration, regardless of the debtor's motive.[108] Similarly, a transfer for less than reasonably equivalent value that causes the debtor to become insolvent first is also voidable by the trustee as a fraudulent conveyance.

Steph v. Branch [109] provides an interesting illustration of a transfer of property for less than reasonably equivalent value. A controlling shareholder of a corporation that was engaged in the lumber business sold all of his shares to a buyer for the sum of $5,000 in cash plus $23,000 represented by a promissory note. It was agreed that the seller could purchase construction materials from the corporation at the special discount rate of cost plus 20 percent and that the price of materials so purchased would be deducted from the balance of the promissory note. While the corporation was insolvent, the seller of the shares purchased almost $20,000 worth of building materials from the corporation and, instead of paying cash for it, deducted the price from the balance of the promissory note as agreed. The effect of the transaction was that the insolvent corporation transferred property to the seller of the stock without consideration flowing back to the corporation. The buyer of the corporation actually used corporate assets to pay most of the balance of the promissory note on which he was personally obligated. Accordingly, the court held that the transfer constituted a fraudulent conveyance regardless of the parties' intentions.[110]

---

[107] 11 U.S.C. § 548(a)(2)(A). See 11 U.S.C. § 548(d)(2)(A), and ¶ 7.06[8], for a discussion of the meaning of "value."

[108] 11 U.S.C. § 548(a)(2). Compare the Code with former B.A. § 67(d)(2)(a), which used the term "fair consideration" instead of "reasonably equivalent value." The concept of "fair consideration" under the former Act required both fair equivalent value and good faith, whereas the concept of "reasonably equivalent value" under the Code requires only economic equivalence. See former B.A. § 67(d)(1)(e). See also Bullard v. Aluminum Co. of America, 468 F.2d 11 (7th Cir. 1972), which held that, despite the equivalent value received by the insolvent debtor in exchange for a transfer of funds, the transfer was not for "fair consideration" under the former Act because of the absence of good faith.

[109] 255 F. Supp. 526 (E.D. Okla. 1966), *aff'd* 389 F.2d 233 (10th Cir. 1968).

[110] For another case holding that a stockholder of an insolvent corporation may not use corporate funds to pay his personal obligations in connection with the purchase of stock, see Pemberton v. Longwire, 151 P.2d 410 (Okla. 1944).

[3] Transfers for Less Than Reasonably Equivalent Value With Intent to Incur Debts Beyond the Ability to Pay

Insolvency is defined in the Bankruptcy Code to mean the financial condition when the debtor's obligations are greater than the fair value of all assets, except exempt assets and property fraudulently conveyed.[111] It is possible for a debtor to be solvent pursuant to the Code's "balance sheet" test, but to be unable to pay liabilities as they mature. For example, a debtor who has all nonexempt assets tied up in real estate or long-term accounts receivable may have a serious cash-flow problem that prevents the payment of current bills.

As discussed earlier, a transfer of property by an insolvent debtor is fraudulent if reasonably equivalent value is not received. The Code also provides that, whether or not the debtor is insolvent, a transfer for less than reasonably equivalent value is fraudulent if the debtor intended to incur, or believed that it would incur, liabilities that would be beyond the debtor's ability to pay as they mature.[112] This provision is designed to give the trustee the power to avoid a transfer for less than fair consideration while the debtor, although solvent, is aware that payment of current debts is unlikely because of the lack of liquid assets.

[4] Transfers for Less Than Reasonably Equivalent Value When Undercapitalized

Although the debtor may be solvent, the rights of creditors may be jeopardized if the debtor's assets are transferred for less than reasonably equivalent value while the debtor's business is undercapitalized. For this reason, the Code provides that a transfer for less than reasonably equivalent value while the debtor was engaged in business, or was about to engage in a business transaction, is fraudulent if the property remaining with the debtor after the transfer is an unreasonably small capital.[113] Whether the debtor has fraudulent intent and whether the business is

---

[111] See 11 U.S.C. § 101(26).

[112] 11 U.S.C. § 548(a)(2)(B)(iii), derived from former B.A. § 67(d)(2)(c). See *In re* Farmers Fed'n Coop., Inc. 242 F. Supp. 400 (W.D.N.C. 1965), holding that chattel morgtages were invalid as against the mortgagor's trustee because at the time they were executed the mortgagor's indebtedness on open accounts exceeded its ability to pay upon maturity.

[113] 11 U.S.C. § 548(a)(2)(B)(ii), derived from former B.A. § 67(d)(2)(b). See *In re* Atlas Foundry Co., 155 F. Supp. 615 (D.N.J. 1957), in which a mortgage given by a corporation was invalid as against the mortgagor's trustee because it left the business with unreasonably small capital and was without fair consideration.

insolvent are not relevant questions for the purpose of detecting this type of fraud.

[5] Transfers of Partnership Property

A transfer of property by an insolvent partnership to a general partner adversely affects the rights of business creditors, despite the fact that general partners remain personally liable for firm obligations. For this reason, the Bankruptcy Code follows the former Act by giving the trustee the power to avoid any transfer of partnership property or any obligation incurred by the firm to a general partner within one year before the filing of the partnership petition if the firm either was insolvent or became insolvent as a result of the transfer or obligation.[114] The trustee may recover the property so transferred from the general partner who received it, or from an agent or employee who disbursed funds to individual partners with knowledge of the firm's poor financial condition.[115]

It is not uncommon for the general partners of a failing business to withdraw funds from the firm in order to take advantage of exemption laws. In *In re Reese,*[116] for example, funds and proceeds of the inventory of a partnership of a husband and wife were deposited in the wife's name in a savings and loan association and credit union. The reason for making this transfer was to take advantage of the California exemption statute that exempts these deposits from the reach of creditors. Despite the exemption law, however, the court ordered his wife to turn over the funds to the trustee of the partnership firm because at the time of the transfer to the wife the business was insolvent.[117]

[6] Transfers With Intent to Make a Preference: The Abolition of Dean v. Davis

An early Supreme Court case that became a landmark decision in American bankruptcy law is *Dean v. Davis.*[118] While insolvent, a debtor feared that he would be arrested because he forged endorsements

---

[114] 11 U.S.C. § 548(b), derived from former B.A. § 67(d)(4).

[115] See McNeill v. Sideman, 377 F. Supp. 792 (E.D. Wis. 1974), holding that the debtor's employee who disbursed funds to the individual partners was liable to the trustee despite the fact that he received no benefit from the transaction.

[116] 223 F. Supp. 626 (N.D. Cal. 1963).

[117] See Resnick, note 105 *supra,* at 635-636.

[118] 242 U.S. 438 (1917).

on the back of promissory notes that he discounted at a bank. He appealed to his brother-in-law to loan him the $1,600 that he needed to buy back the notes from the bank, thus satisfying the bank and, hopefully, avoiding criminal prosecution. His brother-in-law advanced the needed funds to him but took a mortgage on the debtor's assets to secure the new loan. The proceeds of the loan were used to pay the bank and, shortly thereafter, an involuntary bankruptcy petition was filed against the debtor. Although the mortgage was not voidable as a preference because it secured a new loan, the Supreme Court agreed with the trustee that the mortgage was invalid as a fraudulent conveyance. The Court held that the transfer of a mortgage to secure an advance that was made to enable the debtor to make a preferential payment in contemplation of bankruptcy "presents an element upon which fraud may be predicated." [119] Because the debtor and the brother-in-law knew that the bank would be preferred, the mortgage constituted a fraudulent transfer.

The doctrine of *Dean v. Davis* was codified by an amendment to the former Act in 1938.[120] In essence, the Act deemed fraudulent any transfer by an insolvent debtor within four months of bankruptcy if made in contemplation of liquidation and with intent to use the consideration obtained for the transfer to make a preference *and* if the transferee knew that the consideration would be so used. In essence, this doctrine penalized secured lenders who advanced money to a troubled debtor for the purpose of enabling the debtor to pay off some of its creditors. In addition, although a preference is not, in and of itself, a fraud on creditors, *Dean v. Davis* treats the funding of a preference as fraudulent. As one commentator wrote: "Preferences have commonly been considered as one degree less obnoxious than fraudulent conveyances and, from this point of view, it seems anomalous to stigmatize as fraudulent actions merely accessory to a preference." [121]

In view of this criticism, the doctrine of *Dean v. Davis,* as codified in the former Act, is not contained in the new Code. The omission of the doctrine was deliberate. Thus, transfers to secure advances for the purpose of enabling debtors to make preferential payments are no longer fraudulent per se.

---

[119] *Id.* at 444.

[120] Former B.A. § 67(d)(3). See Corker, "Hazards of Doing Business With an Insolvent: The *Dean v. Davis* Amendment in the Chandler Act," 1 Stan. L. Rev. 189 (1949).

[121] MacLachlan, *Handbook of the Law of Bankruptcy* § 243 (1956).

[7] Rights of Good-Faith Transferees

A good-faith purchaser who buys property for less than a reasonably equivalent value may not realize that the seller is a financially troubled debtor or that the transaction jeopardizes the rights of creditors. It would be unjust, therefore, to permit a trustee to recover fraudulently transferred property from a transferee who paid at least some value for it in good faith.

In order to protect such persons, the Code provides that a transferee or obligee who takes for value and in good faith has a lien on any property transferred or may enforce any obligation incurred, as the case may be, to the extent of the value given.[122] If the fraudulent transfer consists of a mortgage or security interest, the good-faith transferee may retain the interest.

For example, assume that an insolvent debtor sold property worth $50,000 to a bona fide purchaser for $40,000. Upon the debtor's bankruptcy, the purchaser is given a lien on the property to secure repayment of $40,000. Accordingly, the trustee must return $40,000 in order to obtain the property worth $50,000. The practical effect of avoiding the fraudulent conveyance is the rescission of the initial transfer, thus depriving the transferee of the benefit of the bargain.

[8] What is "Value"?

The concept of value plays an important role in the area of fraudulent conveyances. As discussed above, transfers by insolvent debtors, undercapitalized businesses, and debtors who are unable to pay current bills may be characterized as fraudulent if they are for less than reasonably equivalent value.[123] In addition, good-faith transferees are given certain protections to the extent of value exchanged.[124] In view of the significance of determining value in this context, the Code contains a special definition of "value" applicable only to fraudulent conveyance problems.[125]

"Value" may consist of property or the satisfaction or securing of

---

[122] 11 U.S.C. § 548(c), derived from former B.A. § 67(d)(6). However, the purchaser may not be protected by this section if the transfer is voidable on other grounds, such as when it constitutes a voidable preference. For a discussion of the rights of good-faith transferees in relation to all of the trustee's avoiding powers, see ¶ 7.07.

[123] See ¶ 7.06[2]-7.06[5].

[124] See ¶ 7.06[7].

[125] 11 U.S.C. § 548(d)(2)(A).

either a present or an antecedent debt. Thus, an insolvent debtor receives value by paying an old obligation.[126] For this reason, making a preference in good faith is not a fraudulent conveyance because value is exchanged by the cancellation of the antecedent debt. The Code expressly provides, however, that an unperformed promise to furnish support to the debtor or to a relative of the debtor is not value. Accordingly, if an insolvent debtor transfers property to another person in exchange for a promise to support the debtor in the future, such a promise is not value and the transfer may be avoided by the trustee. Other executory promises, however, may constitute value.

¶ 7.07 LIABILITY OF THE TRANSFEREE OF AN AVOIDED TRANSFER

In general, the avoidance of a transfer pursuant to the trustee's avoiding powers gives the trustee the right to recover, for the benefit of the estate, the property transferred. Instead of the actual property, however, the value of the property may be recovered if the court so orders.[127] The property or its value may be recovered from the initial transferee, the entity for whose benefit the transfer was made, or the immediate or mediate transferee of the initial transferee.[128] Of course, the trustee is entitled to only a single satisfaction.[129]

The Code contains several provisions that protect transferees of avoided transfers in certain instances. The protection of good-faith transferees of fraudulent conveyances to the extent that value is given is discussed above.[130] The other protections, which are discussed in this section, are applicable to the transferees regardless of the basis for the avoidance of the transaction.

A trustee may not recover property or its equivalent value from a secondary transferee that takes the property for value, in good faith, and without knowledge of the voidability of the transfer.[131] In this con-

---

[126] See Strongin v. International Acceptance Bank, Inc., 70 F.2d 248 (2d Cir.), *cert. denied* 293 U.S. 575 (1934).

[127] See Welsch v. Palumbo, 73 N.E.2d 844 (Mass. 1947), holding that the measure of value is not necessarily determined by the price for which the transferee sold it.

[128] 11 U.S.C. § 550(a).

[129] 11 U.S.C. § 550(c). See Steel Structures, Inc. v. Star Mfg. Co., 466 F.2d 207 (6th Cir. 1972), limiting the trustee to a single recovery under the former Bankruptcy Act.

[130] See note 124 *supra.*

[131] 11 U.S.C. § 550(b)(1).

text, value may consist of the satisfaction or securing of a present or antecedent debt. Once such a good-faith transferee for value exists, all subsequent good-faith transferees receive the same protection.[132] For example, assume that the debtor transfers property that results in a voidable preference to a creditor, and, subsequently, the creditor transfers the property to a good-faith purchaser for value. So long as the purchaser is unaware of the preferential character of the initial transfer, the trustee may not recover from the purchaser. Moreover, if the secondary transferee (the good-faith purchaser) conveys the property to a relative as a gift, the good-faith donee is also protected. It is important to note, however, that this protection applies only to secondary transferees. The initial transferee, such as the creditor in the above hypothetical, is liable to the trustee for the value of the property regardless of its good faith.

Let us assume that a transferee is liable to a trustee because of the avoidability of the transfer. Prior to the avoidance, however, the transferee expends funds to preserve or improve the property in good faith. For example, a creditor who is unaware of the debtor's insolvency receives equipment as a preference and, subsequently, makes needed repairs to the equipment that increase its value significantly. Should the estate reap the benefits of the repairs at the expense of the transferee? The Code answers this question negatively.

Specifically, the Code protects good-faith transferees by giving them liens on the property recoverable by the trustee to secure reimbursement of the cost of any improvement, less any profit realized by the transferee from the property.[133] However, the lien may not exceed the increase in the value of the property as a result of the improvement. For example, assume that a creditor receives equipment worth $100,000 as a preference and subsequently spends $25,000 to repair it. The creditor earns a $10,000 profit from the use of the equipment in its business. Furthermore, the value of the equipment increases to $110,000 after the repairs. The trustee may recover the equipment, but the creditor has a lien to secure reimbursement. The $25,000 cost of repairs, less the $10,000 profit from using the equipment, leaves a balance of $15,000. However, because the increase in the value of the equipment was only $10,000, the creditor's lien is limited to secure the reimbursement of only $10,000.

The Code defines "improvement" very broadly. An improvement may consist of physical additions or changes, repairs, preservation, or

---

[132] 11 U.S.C. § 550(b)(2).
[133] 11 U.S.C. § 550(d)(1).

payment of any tax on the property. The payment of any debt secured by a lien on the property, as well as the discharge of any lien that is superior or equal to the rights of the trustee, also qualifies as improvement.[134]

Finally, transferees of avoided transfers are protected by a brief statute of limitations. An action or proceeding to recover property from a transferee of an avoided transfer must be commenced, if at all, within one year after the avoidance of the transfer or before the case is closed or dismissed, whichever occurs first.[135]

¶ 7.08 AUTOMATIC PRESERVATION OF AVOIDED TRANSFERS

Let us assume that on May 1 a debtor sells and conveys title to certain real estate worth $100,000. The deed is recorded on May 5, but on May 4 an unsecured creditor of the debtor acquires a judicial lien on the property by virtue of an order of attachment to secure payment of a $150,000 debt. Pursuant to state law, the lien of the attaching creditor is valid as against the purchaser of the real estate. Assume further that the debtor files a bankruptcy petition on June 1 and that the trustee avoids the order of attachment on the grounds that it constitutes a preference.[136] As a result of the avoidance of the judicial lien that has priority over the purchaser, is the purchaser's title now unencumbered? Does the purchaser benefit from the trustee's actions?

Pursuant to the former Act, a transfer that was avoided by the trustee became null and void unless the trustee took affirmative action to obtain a court order to preserve it.[137] In the above illustration, unless the court orders otherwise, the judicial lien would have become null and void and, accordingly, the purchaser of the property would keep it unencumbered. In that case, the consequence of the trustee's avoiding power would be to benefit the purchaser instead of the estate. The distribution to general creditors would not be increased at all by avoiding the transfer. For this reason, trustees often commenced ad-

---

[134] 11 U.S.C. § 550(d)(2).

[135] 11 U.S.C. § 550(e). Moreover, any action to avoid a transfer must be commenced within two years after the appointment of the trustee or before the time the case is closed or dismissed, whichever is earlier. 11 U.S.C. § 546(a).

[136] See ¶ 7.05.

[137] See B. Rule 611, which derives from former B.A. §§ 60(b), 67(a)(3), 67(c)(2), 67(d)(6), 70(e)(2).

versary proceedings to obtain an order to preserve the transfer for the benefit of the estate.[138]

What is the effect of preserving an avoided transfer? In the above example, the mere avoidance of the judicial lien benefits the purchaser of the property. However, if the avoided judicial lien is preserved for the benefit of the estate, then the trustee stands in the shoes of the judicial lienor to give the estate priority over the purchaser. The general creditors receive a greater distribution because, although the lien is avoided, it becomes property of the estate. In essence, the preservation of an avoided lien prevents a junior lienor from improving its position when a senior lien is avoided. The avoidance of a senior security interest does not improve the position of a junior security interest because the estate takes the place of the senior lienor.

The Bankruptcy Code departs from the former Act by providing for the automatic preservation of avoided transfers for the benefit of the estate.[139] Thus, the trustee need not take any steps to preserve liens or other transfers. Of course, if preservation of a transfer does not benefit the estate, the trustee has the right to abandon it.[140]

¶ 7.09 SETOFFS

The trustee's right to recover the amount of a prebankruptcy setoff is discussed in detail in Chapter 5 of this book.[141]

¶ 7.10 EXECUTORY CONTRACTS AND UNEXPIRED LEASES

The Bankruptcy Code follows the former Act by giving the trustee the power to either reject or assume executory contracts and unexpired leases subject to court approval.[142] The rationale underlying this power

---

[138] See, e.g., Egyptian Supply Co. v. Boyd, 117 F.2d 608 (6th Cir. 1941); *In re* Conant, 10 F. Supp. 273 (D. Me. 1935).

[139] 11 U.S.C. § 551.

[140] See 11 U.S.C. § 554 and ¶ 4.06.

[141] See ¶ 5.10.

[142] 11 U.S.C. § 365, derived from former B.A. §§ 70(b), 116(1), 313(1). For information concerning the rejection of executory contracts and leases under the former Act, see Countryman, "Executory Contracts in Bankruptcy: Part I," 57 Minn. L. Rev. 439 (1973); Countryman, "Executory Contracts in Bankruptcy: Part II," 58 Minn. L. Rev. 479 (1974); Silverstein, "Rejection of Executory Contracts in Bankruptcy and Reorganization," 31 U. Chi. L. Rev. 467 (1964). For a discussion of executory con-

is that the trustee should be insulated from contracts that impose burdensome liabilities upon the bankruptcy estate, but should also be able to take advantage of favorable contracts that benefit the estate.[143] The power to assume or reject executory contracts is especially important in reorganization cases where it is used to relieve the debtor in possession of unperformed obligations that would otherwise hamper the debtor's opportunity to make a fresh start.

[1] What is an Executory Contract?

The Code does not contain a definition of "executory contract." Therefore, court decisions that have construed this term in the context of the former Act continue to be applicable to new cases.

In general, an executory contract is one pursuant to which the obligations of *both* parties are so far unperformed that the failure of either party to complete performance would constitute a material breach.[144] A contract is not executory if it is fully performed on one side prior to bankruptcy. For example, a promissory note executed by the debtor is not an executory contract, despite the fact that it matures at a future date, if the only obligation remaining is payment of the note.[145] Similarly, an agreement to guarantee the debts of another is not an executory contract if the debtor is to obtain no future benefit from the transaction.[146] In contrast, contracts to build and operate shopping centers,[147] contracts to sell goods to be delivered in the future,[148] and options to purchase land are executory contracts.[149] Moreover, courts have permitted debtors in possession under Chapter XI of the former Act to reject stock warrants or convertible debentures issued

---

tracts and leases under the Code, see Shanker, "The Treatment of Executory Contracts and Leases in the 1978 Bankruptcy Code," 25(7) Prac. Law. 11 (Oct. 1979).

[143] See *In re* Mercury Homes Dev. Co., 4 Bankr. Dec. 837, 839 (N.D. Cal. 1978).

[144] See Jenson v. Continental Fin'l Corp., 591 F.2d 477 (8th Cir. 1979); *In re* Knutson, 563 F.2d 916, 917 (8th Cir. 1977); Countryman, note 142 *supra*, 57 Minn. L. Rev. at 460-462.

[145] See H.R. Rep. No. 95-595, note 8 *supra*, at 347.

[146] See *In re* Unishops, Inc., 422 F. Supp. 75 (S.D.N.Y. 1975), holding that a parent corporation's guaranty of a subsidiary's lease of shopping center property is not executory. See also *In re* Grayson-Robinson Stores, Inc., 321 F.2d 500 (2d Cir. 1963).

[147] Workman v. Harrison, 282 F.2d 693 (10th Cir. 1960).

[148] Di Lauro v. Electronic Wholesalers, Inc., 239 A.2d 162 (D.C. 1968).

[149] *In re* Jackson Brewing Co., 567 F.2d 618 (5th Cir. 1978).

prior to arrangement proceedings.[150] Pension plans of a debtor, as well as collective bargaining agreements, have also been rejected as executory contracts.[151]

An interesting decision that explores the question of whether an airline ticket is an executory contract is *In re Knutson*.[152] Prior to filing a bankruptcy petition, the debtor purchased two round-trip airline tickets to Hawaii. The price of $1,450.52 was charged on an airline credit card and the tickets were received. Three days prior to the filing of the petition, the debtor was billed for the tickets and was given twenty-five days to pay. When the debtor failed to pay, the airline commenced a proceeding in bankruptcy court against the trustee to have the tickets declared executory contracts and to force the trustee to either affirm them by paying the price in full or to reject them so that the airline might resell the tickets to other customers. The bankruptcy court held that the tickets were property of the estate, not executory contracts, and ordered the airline to pay the cash value of the tickets. That order left the airline with nothing but an unsecured claim against the estate for the price after paying the full value of the tickets. However, the decision was reversed on appeal. The court of appeals held that the tickets were executory contracts because both parties had to perform in the future: The airline was obligated to perform transportation services at some future date, and the debtor had not yet paid the price when the petition was filed. As a result, the trustee had either to pay for the tickets in full or to reject them and leave the airline free to sell them to others.

[2] When Will a Court Approve Rejection?

The trustee's power to assume or reject executory contracts and unexpired leases is not absolute. The Bankruptcy Code requires court

---

[150] See *In re* Sequential Info. Sys., Inc., CCH Bankr. Rep. ¶ 64,401 (S.D.N.Y. 1972); *In re* Flora Mir Candy Corp., CCH Bankr. Rep. ¶ 64,175 (2d Cir. 1971).

[151] See *In re* Alan Wood Steel Co., 4 Bankr. Dec. 850 (E.D. Pa. 1978), holding that pension plans by a debtor that is not operating are onerous and may be rejected. For decisions that have permitted the rejection of collective bargaining agreements, see Brotherhood of Ry., Airline and S.S. Clerks v. REA Express, Inc., 523 F.2d 164 (2d Cir.), *cert. denied* 423 U.S. 1017 (1975); Shopmen's Local Union No. 455 v. Kevin Steel Prods., Inc., 519 F.2d 698 (2d Cir. 1975); Bohack Corp. v. Truck Drivers Local Union No. 807, 541 F.2d 312 (2d Cir. 1976), *on remand*, 431 F. Supp. 646 (E.D.N.Y. 1977).

[152] 563 F.2d 916 (8th Cir. 1977).

approval for rejection or assumption, but contains no guidelines for determining when such approval should be granted.[153]

In general, courts have approved the rejection of executory contracts or unexpired leases only when they are "burdensome" to the estate.[154] This standard is based on the assumption that the power to reject executory contracts grows out of the doctrine that a trustee may abandon burdensome property. The difficult problem for the courts, however, is in determining when an executory contract or unexpired lease is burdensome.

An executory contract may be rejected as burdensome despite the fact that the debtor would receive a net financial benefit by assuming it. Thus, the mere fact that a profit could be made under the contract does not prevent rejection.[155] Furthermore, the debtor in possession or trustee in a reorganization case is not required to show that rejection will aid in the debtor's rehabilitation.[156] Instead, courts have used the broad "business judgment" test, which permits rejection if, as a matter of business judgment, rejection of the contract or lease may in some way benefit the estate. As the Supreme Court has stated, "the question whether a lease should be rejected and, if not, on what terms it should be assumed is one of business judgment." [157]

[3] Requirements for the Assumption of Executory Contracts and Leases

The Code contains certain limitations on the trustee's power to assume executory contracts and unexpired leases. These limitations are designed to protect the rights of the parties other than the debtor.

---

[153] 11 U.S.C. § 365(a).

[154] See, e.g., *In re* Minges, 602 F.2d 38 (2d Cir. 1979); *In re* Tilco, Inc., 408 F. Supp. 389 (D. Kan. 1976), *rev'd on other grounds*, 558 F.2d 1369 (10th Cir. 1977).

[155] See, e.g., Group of Inst'l Investors v. Chicago, M., St. P. & Pac. R.R., 318 U.S. 523 (1943); *In re* Minges, note 154 *supra*.

[156] See *In re* Minges, note 154 *supra*, at 457.

[157] Group of Inst'l Investors v. Chicago, M., St. P. & Pac. R.R., note 155 *supra*, at 549-550. See *In re* Minges, note 154 *supra*, where the court held that, although a lease was profitable for the debtor landlord, the trustee was governed by the "business judgment" standard in determining whether burdensome lease provisions should be rejected. "The lessor's covenants to provide utilities and janitorial services consume what has come to be a very large portion of the rental income." *Id* at 456. The case was remanded to ascertain whether "there is a reasonable likelihood that general creditors will derive substantial or significant benefit from the proposed lease rejection."

It is common for the debtor to be in default with respect to a contract or lease at the time of the filing of the bankruptcy petition or while the case is pending. In such a situation, the trustee may not assume the contract or lease unless, at the time of assumption, the trustee either cures the default or provides adequate assurance that cure will occur promptly.[158] If any party to the contract or lease other than the debtor has suffered any actual pecuniary loss as a result of the default, the trustee is required either to compensate or provide adequate assurance of prompt compensation to the injured party.[159] Moreover, the trustee must provide adequate assurance of future performance under the contract or lease before assumption will be permitted.[160] What constitutes adequate assurance must be determined on a case-by-case basis, depending on the particular facts and equities of the situation.

Many contracts and leases contain bankruptcy clauses that, in essence, provide that the debtor is deemed in default in the event that the debtor suffers certain financial difficulty or becomes the subject of a bankruptcy case. However, for the purpose of assuming or rejecting executory contracts and leases, these bankruptcy clauses are not effective. Accordingly, if default of the contract or lease is nothing more than a breach of a provision relating to the insolvency or financial condition of the debtor, the commencement of a bankruptcy case, or the appointment or taking possession by a custodian, the trustee may assume it nevertheless without the need to cure this default or provide assurance of future performance.[161]

There is another limitation on the trustee's power to assume executory contracts that applies when another party is obligated to extend credit to the debtor. Of course, these business transactions are usually based on the debtor's financial strength. For example, a loan or other financing arrangement that involves future advances is probably based on the debtor's present and anticipated future financial condition. If the debtor files a bankruptcy petition, another party's contractual commitment to extend new credit to the debtor in the future may be unfairly onerous to that party. In order to deal with this situation, the Code expressly prohibits the trustee's assumption of an executory contract that requires the other party to make a loan to the debtor, to extend other debt-financing or financial accommodations for the debtor's benefit, or

---

[158] 11 U.S.C. § 365(b)(1)(A).
[159] 11 U.S.C. § 365(b)(1)(B).
[160] 11 U.S.C. § 365(b)(1)(C).
[161] 11 U.S.C. § 365(b)(2).

to issue a security of the debtor.[162] In essence, a contracting party may not be required to extend new credit to the debtor after the commencement of the case.

Similarly, the trustee may not assume or assign a contract or lease if applicable state law excuses the nonbankrupt party from accepting or rendering performance to a trustee or assignee, unless the party consents to the assumption or assignment.[163] Thus, certain personal service contracts that require the unique skill of the debtor, such as for the painting of a portrait, may not be assumed and performed by the trustee or a delegatee upon the painter's bankruptcy.[164] The presence or absence of a clause prohibiting or restricting assignment of rights or delegation of duties is irrelevant in this context so long as state law excuses the other party from performance.[165]

[4] The Assumption of Shopping Center Leases

The Code contains a provision that limits the trustee's power to assume an unexpired lease of real estate located in a shopping center under which the debtor is a tenant. As discussed above, the trustee must provide adequate assurance of performance if the debtor is in default of the lease.[166] Although the Code does not define "adequate assurance," it does contain several requirements that must be met in order to adequately assure the performance of shopping center leases. These requirements are based on the recognition that a shopping center is a carefully planned enterprise consisting of a particular tenant mix designed to attract higher patronage of stores. These requirements are also based on the fact that the lease agreement in a shopping center often gives the landlord a percentage of the tenant's gross receipts as the rental. In order to protect the investments of the shopping center owner, the financier, and the other tenants, it is necessary to provide

---

[162] 11 U.S.C. § 365(c)(2). See H.R. Rep. No. 95-595, note 8 *supra,* at 348.

[163] 11 U.S.C. § 365(c)(1).

[164] See Taylor v. Palmer, 31 Cal. 240 (1866), where the court noted that "all painters do not paint portraits like Sir Joshua Reynolds, nor landscapes like Claude Lorraine, nor do all writers write dramas like Shakespeare or fiction like Dickens. Rare genius and extraordinary skill are not transferable, and contracts for their employment are therefore personal, and cannot be assigned."

[165] 11 U.S.C. § 365(c).

[166] See ¶ 7.10[3].

assurance that the tenant mix will not be adversely affected by a tenant's bankruptcy.[167]

Specifically, the trustee or debtor in possession may not assume a shopping center lease under which the debtor is a tenant unless there is adequate assurance: (1) of the source of future rent and any other consideration due under the lease; (2) that any percentage rent due under the lease will not decline substantially; (3) that assumption or assignment of the lease will not be in substantial breach of any provision, such as a radius, location, use, or exclusivity provision, in any other lease, financing agreement, or master agreement relating to the shopping center; and (4) that assumption or assignment of the lease will not substantially disrupt any tenant mix or balance in the shopping center.[168] If any of these assurances cannot be made, the landlord may insist on rejection of the lease so that the premises may be rented to a new tenant who is in a position to make such assurances.

[5] Protection for Lessors Prior to Assumption or Rejection

What are the rights of a lessor who is obligated to provide future services for the benefit of a tenant after the tenant files a bankruptcy petition? As discussed below, the trustee does not have to act immediately either to reject or assume an unexpired lease.[169] Does the lessor have to continue to provide services in the hope that the trustee will eventually assume the lease and cure a default?

The Code deals with these questions by protecting the lessor against further losses that may arise out of the performance of an obligation to provide services or supplies during the pendency of the case. In particular, if there has been a default in an unexpired lease under which the debtor is the tenant, the trustee or the debtor may not require the lessor to provide services or supplies before the lease is assumed unless the lessor is compensated under the terms of the lease for any services and supplies provided.[170] By giving lessors the right to insist on assumption, which requires adequate assurance of cure and future performance, or full compensation before rendering services or delivering supplies, they do not have to rely on their priority status as an unsecured administrative expense.[171] This limitation applies to both real estate and personal property leases.

---

[167] See H.R. Rep. No. 95-595, note 8 *supra*, at 348-349.

[168] 11 U.S.C. § 365(b)(3).

[169] See ¶ 7.10[6].

[170] 11 U.S.C. § 365(b)(4).

[171] See ¶ 5.13[1] for a discussion of the administrative-expense priority.

[6] Time Limits on Assumption and Rejection

Parties to unperformed contracts and leases should not be kept in doubt for too long concerning the status of their rights against the estate. For this reason, the Code imposes time limits for assumption or rejection.[172]

In a liquidation case, the trustee has sixty days from the order for relief either to assume or reject a contract or lease. The court may, however, extend this time before the original sixty-day period expires. If a contract or lease is not assumed or rejected within this time period, it is deemed rejected automatically.[173]

The sixty-day time limitation does not apply in cases under chapters 11 or 13. Instead, the trustee or debtor in possession under chapter 11 or 13 may assume or reject at any time before the confirmation of the plan, unless the court, on request of a party to the contract or lease, orders the trustee or debtor in possession to determine within a specified time period whether to assume or reject.[174]

[7] The Effect of Bankruptcy Termination Clauses

As discussed above, bankruptcy clauses in contracts or leases that provide that a party is deemed in default in the event of financial difficulty or bankruptcy are not recognized as causing default. Thus, the presence of such a clause does not trigger the trustee's duty to cure or provide adequate assurance of future performance prior to assumption of the contract or lease.[175]

The Bankruptcy Code takes another step to invalidate the effect of certain clauses that relate to a party's bankruptcy. It is common for a contract or lease to contain a bankruptcy termination clause, sometimes referred to as an ipso facto clause, which provides that the financially secure party has the right to terminate or modify a contract or lease automatically upon the other party's bankruptcy or insolvency, or upon the appointment of, or loss of assets to, a custodian. Under the former Act, these bankruptcy termination clauses were generally effective and allowed the nonbankrupt party to prevent the assumption of the contract or lease by exercising the right to terminate or modify.[176]

---

[172] These time limits are contained in 11 U.S.C. § 365(d), which supersedes B. Rule 607.

[173] 11 U.S.C. § 365(d)(1).

[174] 11 U.S.C. § 365(d)(2).

[175] See ¶ 7.10[3].

[176] Former B.A. § 70(b). See *In re* D.H. Overmyer Co., 510 F.2d 329 (2d Cir. 1974). But see Queens Boulevard Wine & Liquor Corp. v. Blum,

An adverse consequence of giving the nonbankrupt party the right to prevent assumption based on such a clause is that rehabilitation efforts may be hampered in reorganization cases. Also, favorable leases and contracts that are otherwise assignable in liquidation cases lose their value entirely. The loss of these leases and contracts is especially frustrating in view of the many protections afforded to the nonbankrupt party in the event of assumption, such as the adequate assurance of future performance.[177] For these reasons, the Bankruptcy Code provides that an unexpired lease or executory contract may not be terminated or modified after bankruptcy solely because of a provision that is conditioned on the insolvency or financial condition of the debtor, the commencement of a bankruptcy case, or the appointment of or taking possession by a trustee or custodian before or after the filing of a bankruptcy petition.[178]

The Code does contain, however, limited exceptions to the invalidation of ipso facto clauses. When the contract or lease obligates the nonbankrupt party to extend new credit for the benefit of the debtor or to issue a security of the debtor after the commencement of the case, ipso facto clauses that trigger the termination or modification of the contract or lease are effective. In addition, if state law excuses the nonbankrupt party from accepting performance from or rendering performance to an assignee, then the lease or contract may be terminated pursuant to an ipso facto clause. These exceptions are designed to protect the nonbankrupt party from being compelled to extend credit or to deal with the trustee or an assignee when the contract, such as a personal service contract, may not be assigned or delegated under applicable law.[179]

[8] The Assignment of Assumed Contracts and Leases

Trustees often assume favorable contracts and leases with a view toward assignment to a third party. In a reorganization case, it is not uncommon for the debtor in possession to assume favorable leases on

---

503 F.2d 202 (2d Cir. 1974), barring the enforcement of a lease termination clause because termination would have been grossly inequitable and contrary to the policy underlying Chapter XI of the former Act. See also *In re* M & M Transp. Co., 437 F. Supp. 821 (S.D.N.Y. 1977), in which the court enjoined the lessor from terminating an equipment lease based on the reasoning in *Queens Boulevard.*

[177] See ¶ 7.10[3].

[178] 11 U.S.C. § 365(e)(1).

[179] 11 U.S.C. § 365(e)(2).

many of its locations so that they can be sold for capital needed to finance the remaining locations. Because the sale of contract rights and leases benefits the estate and facilitates rehabilitation, the policy of the Code is to permit assignment whenever possible.

The Code contains two provisions designed to assure free assignability of executory contracts and leases. First, unless the contract or lease requires the extension of new credit in the future or is not assignable pursuant to applicable nonbankruptcy law, any clause that prohibits, restricts, or conditions the assignment of the lease or contract is ineffective.[180] Second, any clause that provides for the termination or modification of an executory contract or lease on account of an assignment is also null and void.[181] Accordingly, the trustee's right to assign and sell contracts and leases is not affected by language in them that purports to restrict such assignments.

It is important to note, however, that the Code does not ignore the interests of nonbankrupt parties in connection with the assignment of contracts and leases. In fact, there are restrictions imposed on the trustee who wants to make such an assignment. A contract or lease may not be assigned unless the trustee first assumes it by complying with the requirements for assumption. Thus, defaults must be cured and compensation must be paid to persons who suffered pecuniary loss due to any default.[182] Moreover, adequate assurance of future performance by the assignee must be provided, whether or not there has been a default.[183] Accordingly, if there is a likelihood that the proposed assignee is too weak financially to perform in the future, the court should not permit the assignment. Once the assignment is made, however, the trustee and the estate are relieved from liability for any breach that occurs after the assignment.[184]

[9] The Effect of Rejection

In general, the rejection of an executory contract or unexpired lease constitutes a breach that gives the nonbankrupt party a claim for damages against the estate. The Code treats this right to recover damages as a prepetition claim by creating the fiction that a rejection results in a breach immediately before the date of the filing of the bankruptcy

---

[180] 11 U.S.C. § 365(f)(1).
[181] 11 U.S.C. § 365(f)(3).
[182] 11 U.S.C. § 365(f)(2)(A). See ¶ 7.10[3].
[183] 11 U.S.C. § 365(f)(2)(B).
[184] 11 U.S.C. § 365(k).

petition.[185] Thus, the claim is allowable.[186] In the event that a contract or lease is assumed but subsequently rejected, the breach is deemed to occur at the time of the rejection and accordingly becomes a post-petition claim.[187]

[10] Special Provisions That Protect Parties to Real Estate Contracts and Leases Upon Rejection

The Bankruptcy Code contains several safeguards for the protection of nonbankrupt parties to leases and sales contracts involving real estate.

The first protection applies to rejected leases under which the debtor is the lessor. In general, the Code protects the tenant from eviction upon the rejection of a lease by the trustee. The tenant is given the option either to treat the lease as terminated by the rejection or to remain in possession of the premises for the balance of the lease term, including any renewal or extension of the term that would be enforceable without the lessor's consent under nonbankruptcy law. Accordingly, rejection of the lease does not deprive the tenant of the right to remain in possession.[188] If the tenant remains in possession after the lease is rejected, the rent reserved under the lease may be offset against any damages occurring after rejection caused by the nonperformance of the lessor's obligations under the lease.[189] For example, damages caused by the lessor's failure to provide certain services or supplies may be offset against the rent. However, the tenant does not have the right to obtain an affirmative judgment against the estate based on such damages.

Purchasers of real estate who are in possession of the premises are

---

[185] 11 U.S.C. § 365(g)(1).

[186] See ¶ 5.05 on the allowability of claims.

[187] 11 U.S.C. § 365(g)(2)(A). The Code contains different rules for dealing with cases that are converted from one chapter to another. If the contract or lease is assumed, the case is converted from chapter 11 or chapter 13 to a liquidation case, and a rejection takes place after the conversion, the breach is deemed to occur immediately before the date of the conversion. But if the contract or lease is assumed *after* the conversion and is then rejected, the breach occurs when the rejection takes place. See 11 U.S.C. § 365(g)(2)(B).

[188] 11 U.S.C. § 365(h)(1). This provision is consistent with former B.A. § 70(b). See *In re* Penn Cent. Transp. Co., 458 F. Supp. 1346-1356 (E.D. Pa. 1978); Silverstein, "Rejection of Executory Contracts in Bankruptcy and Reorganization," 31 U. Chi. L. Rev. 467, 484-497 (1964).

[189] 11 U.S.C. § 365(h)(2).

given similar protection under the Code. If the trustee rejects an executory contract for the sale of land under which the debtor is the seller, the purchaser in possession either may treat the contract as terminated or may remain in possession.[190] This protection is especially important in installment sales contracts, which require the transfer of title after the payment of all installments. On the other hand, a purchaser who is not in possession may not compel specific performance of the sales contract.[191]

If the purchaser remains in possession, the trustee must deliver title in accordance with the terms of the sales contract. However, the seller is relieved of all other contractual obligations. The purchaser remaining in possession is required to make all payments due under the agreement but has the right to offset damages arising after rejection that are caused by nonperformance of the seller's obligations. In no event, however, may the purchaser obtain affirmative relief against the estate on account of such damages.[192]

The Code also protects the purchaser's right to the return of funds in the event of termination of the contract, whether or not the purchaser is in possession. A purchaser in possession who treats the sales contract as terminated, as well as a purchaser who is not in possession at the time of rejection, is given a lien on the debtor's interest in the property to secure the repayment of any portion of the purchase price that was paid.[193]

---

[190] 11 U.S.C. § 365(i)(1). See *In re* Mercury Homes Dev. Co., 4 Bankr. Dec. 837 (N.D. Cal. 1978).

[191] See *In re* New York Investors Mut. Group, 143 F. Supp. 51 (S.D.N.Y. 1956), in which the court held that a buyer did not have the right to compel specific performance under the former Act.

[192] 11 U.S.C. § 365(i)(2).

[193] 11 U.S.C. § 365(j).

Chapter 8

REORGANIZATION

¶ 8.01 WHAT IS REORGANIZATION?

A basic assumption that underlies American bankruptcy law is that it is often preferable to encourage and facilitate rehabilitation of businesses in financial trouble instead of providing for liquidation only. From a broad perspective, rehabilitation is better for the economy because it minimizes unemployment and waste of business assets.[1] It is much more productive to use assets in the industry for which they were designed instead of selling them as distressed merchandise at liquidation sales. Also, rehabilitating a business is in the best long-term interest of creditors and shareholders.[2]

Chapter 11 of the Bankruptcy Code provides a means by which a financially distressed business may restructure its finances so that it may continue its operation and avoid the auctioneer's hammer.

¶ 8.02 BUSINESS REHABILITATION UNDER THE FORMER BANKRUPTCY ACT

An understanding of business rehabilitation under the former Bankruptcy Act helps us to appreciate the policies and rules of the new Bankruptcy Code. The former Act had three chapters dealing with business rehabilitation: Chapter X entitled "Corporate Reorganizations,"

---

[1] See, "Philosophically Opposed, A.M.C. Asks Chrysler Aid," N.Y. Times, Sept. 19, 1979, at D1, quoting the chairman of a competitor of the ailing Chrysler Corporation who was philosophically opposed to federal assistance for the company: "However, we have hundreds of thousands of people whose livelihoods are tied up with a very large company, and . . . 'no' [to Chrysler's request for aid] would hurt those people and conceivably go contrary to our social objectives."

[2] See H.R. Rep. No. 95-595, 95th Cong., 1st Sess. 220 (1977), where these purposes of business reorganization are discussed.

Chapter XI entitled "Arrangements," and Chapter XII designated "Real Property Arrangements."[3] Each chapter had different rules anu procedures governing business rehabilitation, which often resulted in rigidity, confusion, and unnecessary litigation.

Former Chapter X was designed to permit a thorough investigation and extensive reorganization of a corporation. Administration of a Chapter X case was time-consuming and complicated. An independent receiver or trustee replaced management and operated the business pending the outcome of the case.[4] The plan for reorganization, which was formulated by the trustee, had to be evaluated by the court and the Securities and Exchange Commission regardless of how long this process took.[5] Although Chapter X was designed to benefit and protect public investors, it contained the inflexible requirement that the reorganization plan be "fair and equitable." This meant that the plan had to recognize absolute priority by giving full compensation to senior classes of creditors before the juniors (subordinated public debt or stockholders) could share in the estate.[6] The insolvency of the debtor meant the elimination of stockholder interests and little, if any, payment to public subordinated creditors if the value of the enterprise was not adequate to reach them.[7] Moreover, the very interests that SEC participation was designed to protect (public security holders) could be eliminated in a Chapter X case, but specific provisions of former Chapter XI preserved such interests.[8] Obviously, this paradox of Chapter X made law reform necessary.

---

[3] Former B.A. §§ 101, 301, 401 et seq. These chapters deal with various types of businesses. A fourth rehabilitation chapter under the former Act was Chapter VIII (Section 77), which is now incorporated in Subchapter IV of chapter 11, dealing solely with railroad reorganizations. Because Section 77 is limited to railroads, which are not covered in this book, it will not be used as a basis for comparing or contrasting the provisions of the new chapter 11.

[4] The appointment of a trustee was mandatory if the liquidated and noncontingent debt was $250,000 or more, and was optional when the indebtedness was less than $250,000. Former B.A. § 156; B. Rule 10-202.

[5] Former B.A. § 172; B. Rule 10-303(b). The former Act required that the plan be submitted to the SEC if indebtedness exceeded $3,000,000. The court had discretion to submit the plan to the SEC if the scheduled indebtedness did not exceed $3,000,000.

[6] Former B.A. § 221(2). For a discussion of the "fair and equitable" requirement under the new chapter 11, see ¶ 8.23[4].

[7] Former B.A. § 216(8).

[8] Rep. Don Edwards (D. Calif.), who sponsored the Bankruptcy Reform Act (H.R. 8200), remarked that "the application of the absolute priority rule under Chapter X leads to the exclusion, rather than the protection, of the public." 124 Cong. Rec. H11101 (daily ed. Sept. 28, 1978).

Chapter XI, which was available for individuals and partnerships as well as corporations, was less formal and permitted existing management to continue operation of the business as a "debtor in possession." [9] It differed from Chapter X in many other respects as well. In contrast to Chapter X, which effectuated a complete restructuring of a corporation, the less drastic Chapter XI resulted in an extension or reduction of unsecured debt only.[10] A Chapter XI debtor in possession could affect secured creditors only by negotiating with them.[11] Furthermore, Chapter XI did not even provide for the discharge of all unsecured indebtedness.[12] Objections to confirmation or nondischargeability of claims presented a serious problem for debtors, even though the plan of arrangement could provide for a separate class of nondischargeable claims; [13] such creditors were reluctant to compromise their claims that survived confirmation. Additionally, such claims could result in the court's finding a plan not to be feasible and thereby denying confirmation.[14] Moreover, Chapter XI did not affect equity structure and therefore was not a total remedy for financially distressed businesses. Consistent with the speed and informality of Chapter XI, the SEC was not a party in the case and did not necessarily evaluate the plan of arrangement.

The difference between the financial standards used for valuation purposes in Chapter X and Chapter XI cases was without justification. In reorganization cases, the "absolute priority rule" required that senior interests receive full compensation before junior interests received anything.[15] This rule required a "going concern" valuation of the business to determine the worth of new securities issued to creditors as part of the reorganization plan. The court estimated the value of the going business by predicting the future earnings of the financially distressed debtor, a technique often criticized as mere guesswork.[16] The financial standard used in Chapter XI cases, however, was that the proposed plan must be in the "best interests of creditors," which meant that the credi-

---

[9] Former B.A. § 342.

[10] Former B.A. §§ 306(1), 357(1).

[11] See R.I.D.C. Indus. Dev. Fund v. Snyder, 539 F.2d (5th Cir. 1976), *cert. denied* 429 U.S. 1095 (1977), where a Chapter XI plan incorporated provisions affecting a secured creditor which were accepted by it.

[12] Former B.A. §§ 371, 17.

[13] Former B.A. § 351. However, classifications and different treatment of creditors had to be just and reasonably necessary to effectuate the Chapter XI arrangement. See Bartle v. Markson Bros., 314 F.2d 303 (2d Cir. 1963).

[14] See Former B.A. § 366(2) and B. Rule 11-38(e).

[15] See ¶ 8.23[4] for a discussion of the absolute priority rule.

[16] See ¶ 8.23[4][b] for a discussion of "going concern" valuation.

tors must receive at least what they would have received had the business been liquidated in straight bankruptcy.[17] As long as creditors received that much, shareholders and subordinated interests were able to retain something in Chapter XI cases. The method of valuation in Chapter XI cases, therefore, consisted of determining present liquidation value of the assets instead of predicting future earnings.

Chapter XI suffered from several procedural problems. First, creditors were unable to compel a business debtor, even a corporation, to attempt an informal arrangement under Chapter XI because a voluntary petition was required.[18] In contrast, Chapter X provided for involuntary petitions.[19] Second, the debtor had the exclusive right to propose a plan in Chapter XI cases that creditors had either to accept or reject.[20] A rejection often led to bankruptcy liquidation for the debtor and loss of going-concern value for the creditors, or to an equally unattractive conversion to Chapter X. Moreover, the lack of investigative examination and the method of election of creditors' committees presented problems relating to an absence of thoroughness in the Chapter XI case.[21]

The availability of Chapter X and Chapter XI with different sets of rules and procedures resulted in a good deal of litigation on the issue of the proper chapter for a particular case.[22] The former Act was designed to compel the use of Chapter XI whenever appropriate.[23] It was

---

[17] Former B.A. § 366(2). For a discussion of the liquidation method of valuation, see ¶ 8.23[2].

[18] Former B.A. § 321; B. Rule 11-3. Of course, an involuntary petition for straight bankruptcy often resulted in the debtor filing under Chapter XI and obtaining a stay of adjudication. See Former B.A. § 321.

[19] Former B.A. § 126; B. Rule 10-105.

[20] Former B.A. § 306(1); B. Rule 11-36(a).

[21] See *Report of the Comm. on the Bankruptcy Laws of the United States,* Part I, H.R. Doc. No. 93-137, 93d Cong., 1st Sess. 244 (1973) for a discussion of the differences between Chapter X and XI with respect to the effectiveness of investigations into the debtor's affairs.

[22] See, e.g., Securities & Exchange Comm'n v. American Trailer Rentals Co., 379 U.S. 594 (1965). See Weintraub, Levin & Novick, "Chapter X or Chapter XI: Coexistence for the Middle-Sized Corporation," 24 Fordham L. Rev. 616 (1956); Weintraub & Levin, "A Sequel to Chapter X or Chapter XI: Coexistence for the Middle-Sized Corporation," 26 Fordham L. Rev. 292 (1957); Weintraub & Levin, "Reorganization or Arrangement: An Analysis of Contemporary Trends in Recent Cases," 37 Nat'l Ass'n of Ref. in Bankr. 103 (1963).

[23] Section 130(7) of the former Act required that every petition for Chapter X reorganization specify facts showing why adequate relief cannot be obtained under Chapter XI.

common for a corporate debtor to file a petition under Chapter XI instead of Chapter X so as to retain control. Then, generally the SEC or, in rare instances, creditors would attempt to convert the case to Chapter X to accomplish a thorough investigation and to oust existing management.[24] This litigation resulted in additional delay, slackening of credit, uncertainty of confirmation, and expense.

Chapter XII of the former Bankruptcy Act provided for real property arrangements and had the best features of Chapter XI as well as the "cram down" provision of Chapter X that permitted the imposition of a plan on nonconsenting secured creditors and equity holders.[25] Institutional lender dissatisfaction with Chapter XII came to a climax when a court held that the "cram down" rule could be applied in a Chapter XII case in which the only creditor, a mortgagee of real property, had its claim reduced to the market value of the real property without any compensation as an unsecured claimant for the amount of the reduction and without the necessity of the mortgagee's accepting the plan.[26]

In view of the numerous problems with Chapters X, XI, and XII of the former Act, it is not surprising that Congress made substantial modifications in the law regarding business rehabilitation. Congress regarded former Chapter X as being too rigid, time-consuming, and unworkable in its procedures and financial standards. Chapter XI was regarded as inadequate for complete rehabilitation because of the dominant position occupied by the debtor and its limited scope in dealing only with unsecured creditors. Chapter XII was found to constitute a windfall for the debtor as the real estate market improved without any benefit for the mortgagee. Accordingly, the design of the Bankruptcy Code was to alleviate these shortcomings.

---

[24] See Former B.A. § 328 and B. Rule 11-15(b) which gave the SEC standing to seek conversion of a Chapter XI case on the grounds that it should have been brought under Chapter X. See, e.g., Securities & Exchange Comm'n v. American Trailer Rentals, note 22 *supra*. This case also cited with approval Securities & Exchange Comm'n v. Canandaigua Enterprises Corp., 339 F.2d 14 (2d Cir. 1964), which contained a discussion contrasting the benefits and weaknesses of the respective chapters and indicated that the SEC had a role to play in Chapter XI notwithstanding an absence of statutory language.

[25] Former B.A. §§ 461(11), 468.

[26] *In re* Marietta Cobb Apartments Co., 3 Bankr. Dec. 720 (S.D.N.Y. 1977). But see Gardens of Cortez v. John Hancock Mutual Life Ins. Co., 585 F.2d 975 (10th Cir. 1978) and *In re* Stillbar Constr. Co., 4 Bankr. Dec. 1110 (N.D. Ga. 1978) which reject *Marietta Cobb*.

¶ 8.03 THE NEW CHAPTER 11: AN OVERVIEW

Probably the most important transformation of bankruptcy law made by the Bankruptcy Reform Act of 1978 was the consolidation of former Chapters X, XI, and XII into a single chapter of the Bankruptcy Code. All business rehabilitation now comes under the umbrella of chapter 11 of the Bankruptcy Code.[27] By consolidating the three chapters of the prior Act, Congress gave bankruptcy courts much more leeway in dealing with the business in distress, not only by preserving the best features of each of the former chapters, but also by remedying the deficiencies described in the previous section.

A significant characteristic of the new chapter 11 is flexibility and speed. Congress recognized that the business community for many years preferred the quickness and economy of the former Chapter XI and Chapter XII negotiation process between the debtor and creditors as a far more satisfactory resolution of the problems of an insolvent business.[28] Rigid imposition of a court-appointed trustee and expensive formalities made debtors and creditors reluctant to pursue a remedy under Chapter X. It is not surprising that only ninety-six Chapter X cases were commenced in 1977 as compared with 3,046 Chapter XI cases, and that the total number of Chapter X cases each year had been declining since 1975.[29]

It is understandable that even large publicly held corporations, such as United Merchants and Manufacturers, Inc., which conducted a large international manufacturing, retailing, and factoring business with several hundred million dollars in debts and a balance sheet showing more than one billion dollars in assets, chose the informal Chapter XI route instead of Chapter X.[30] As debtor in possession, it sold a factoring subsidiary after notice and a hearing and closed numerous retail units, selling the inventory, fixtures, and leaseholds at auction. These

---

[27] 11 U.S.C. §§ 1101 et seq.

[28] Rep. Don Edwards commented that "[O]ne cannot overemphasize the advantages of speed and simplicity to both creditors and debtors." 124 Cong. Rec. H11102 (daily ed. Sept. 28, 1978).

[29] Administrative Office of the U.S. Courts, *Tables of Bankruptcy Statistics* 6 (1978). This report is based on cases commenced between July 1, 1976 and June 30, 1977.

[30] Dkt. No. 77-B-1513 (S.D.N.Y. 1977). Other large corporations that filed Chapter XI petitions are listed in H.R. Rep. No. 95-595, note 2 *supra*, at 253 n.31. See also, 124 Cong. Rec. H11102 (daily ed. Sept. 28, 1978). Of course, the proverbial "corner drug store" may also find relief under chapter 11 of the Code even though assets and liabilities may amount to only several thousand dollars.

sales had a beneficial effect in enabling the debtor in possession to reach confirmation: First, the closing of the retail stores eliminated substantial losses and burdensome leases; second, numerous good leases were sold at a profit; third, the sales produced cash that made a plan of extension attractive. All of this activity was accomplished in less than a year. It is anticipated that chapter 11 will offer the same relief to the multimillion dollar corporation as well as to the smaller entities.

In addition to preserving simplicity, speed, and economy when meshing the former chapter proceedings, Congress incorporated in the new chapter 11 the benefits of the "cram down" provisions of former Chapters X and XII so that a plan of reorganization could be imposed on nonassenting classes of creditors or equity holders.[31] The Code eliminated the automatic appointment of a trustee, but provides for a reasonable amount of control over the activities of a debtor in possession.[32] Also, the role of the SEC was significantly reduced from the supervisory role played in former Chapter X cases.[33]

The financial standards required for confirmation of a reorganization plan under the new chapter 11 integrate aspects of both the "best interests of creditors" rule of Chapter XI and the "absolute priority rule" of Chapter X. When every member of a class of creditors or equity holders does not agree to a plan, the plan must be in the "best interests" of that class (i.e., the class must receive a distribution equal to the dividend it may have received in a hypothetical liquidation under chapter 7.) If a class of creditors or interest holders does not accept the plan by a vote of a minimum percentage of its members, the plan may still be imposed or "crammed down" on that class and on other classes junior to it so long as the absolute priority requirement is met as to the nonassenting class.[34]

Another significant aspect of the new chapter 11 relates to the proposal of a plan. Unlike former Chapter X, the debtor has a right to propose the plan under the new chapter 11. Also, in contrast to former Chapter XI, the creditors may propose a plan under the new law after a certain time period following the commencement of the case.[35]

Considerable administrative expenses and time-consuming litigation will be alleviated by virtue of the consolidation of the former rehabilitation chapters. This factor alone makes the reform of bankruptcy laws worthwhile. There are no conversion procedures to worry about

---

[31] See ¶ 8.23[3].
[32] See ¶¶ 8.08, 8.12, 8.13.
[33] See ¶ 8.15.
[34] See ¶ 8.23[4].
[35] See ¶ 8.19[1].

because of the single rehabilitation chapter, except conversion of a reorganization case to one of liquidation under chapter 7.[36]

The remainder of this chapter will discuss these and other features of chapter 11 of the Bankruptcy Code in detail.

¶ 8.04 STRUCTURE OF CHAPTER 11

Familiarity with the structure of chapter 11 of the Bankruptcy Code will help the practitioner locate appropriate sections, as well as giving the reader a broad overview of a reorganization case.

It is important to know that chapter 11 does not contain all of the provisions applicable to reorganization cases. Chapter 1, entitled "General Provisions," contains definitions and other provisions that are applicable in all cases commenced under the Bankruptcy Code.[37] Chapter 3, entitled "Case Administration," deals with the commencement of the case, trustees and other officers, automatic stays, meetings, and many other administrative matters that are applicable in reorganization cases.[38] Chapter 5, "Creditors, the Debtor, and the Estate," deals with claims, priorities, debtor's duties, exemptions, property of the estate, and numerous other aspects of all bankruptcy cases.[39] In sum, chapters 1, 3, and 5 contain the meat that covers the bare bones of chapter 11, as well as of chapters 7, 9, and 13.

Chapter 11, which itself deals with reorganization cases only, contains four subchapters. Subchapter I is entitled "Officers and Administration,"[40] subchapter II deals with "The Plan,"[41] and subchapter III consists of "Postconfirmation Matters."[42] Subchapter IV of chapter 11 governs "Railroad Reorganization."[43] To keep the size of this book within the confines of a handbook within easy reach of the lawyer's or executive's swivel chair, it is necessary to omit a discussion of this subchapter. The text of subchapter IV is set forth in Appendix A.

¶ 8.05 ELIGIBILITY FOR REORGANIZATION

One of the problems with the former Bankruptcy Act was the inability of certain business entities to achieve complete financial relief

[36] See ¶ 8.17.
[37] 11 U.S.C. §§ 101 et seq.
[38] 11 U.S.C. §§ 301 et seq.
[39] 11 U.S.C. §§ 501 et seq.
[40] 11 U.S.C. §§ 1101 et seq.
[41] 11 U.S.C. §§ 1121 et seq.
[42] 11 U.S.C. §§ 1141 et seq.
[43] 11 U.S.C. §§ 1161 et seq., derived from former B.A. § 77.

under Chapter X. Sole proprietors and partnerships were not permitted to file Chapter X petitions and therefore were unable to achieve a restructuring of secured indebtedness, a "cram down" on nonassenting classes of creditors, or a complete discharge.[44] Also, corporations could not seek relief under Chapter XII for real property arrangements.[45] The meshing of Chapters X, XI, and XII into chapter 11 of the Bankruptcy Code solved these problems of access.

Under the new chapter 11, any entity that can file a voluntary petition for liquidation is eligible to file a petition for reorganization. Accordingly, a corporation, partnership, sole proprietor, business trust, or unincorporated association with a residence, domicile, place of business, or property located in the United States may seek relief under chapter 11.[46]

There are certain entities that may not file a petition under chapter 11. Those entities that are ineligible for liquidation under chapter 7 of the Bankruptcy Code are also ineligible for chapter 11 relief. This category includes domestic and foreign insurance companies, banking institutions, and credit unions engaged in business in the United States.[47] Likewise, government bodies and municipalities may not seek chapter 11 relief,[48] but may seek relief under chapter 9.

Railroads, which may not seek liquidation under chapter 7, are eligible for reorganization under chapter 11.[49] However, railroad reorganization is governed by a separate body of rules contained in subchapter IV of chapter 11[50] and therefore may not be subject to the same principles that will be discussed in connection with reorganization in general.

Another category of businesses that receives special treatment under the Bankruptcy Code consists of stockbrokers and commodity brokers. These businesses are eligible for liquidation under subchapters III and IV of chapter 7,[51] but are not eligible for reorganization.[52] The

---

[44] Former B.A. § 106(5) defines "debtor" as a corporation only.

[45] Former B.A. § 406(6) defines "debtor" so as to exclude the corporation.

[46] 11 U.S.C. § 109(d). See Chapter 1 *supra* for a discussion on the eligibility to file a petition for liquidation.

[47] 11 U.S.C. § 109(d).

[48] Only a "person" may become a debtor under chapter 11 and "person" is defined so as to exclude governmental units. 11 U.S.C. §§ 109(d), 101(30).

[49] 11 U.S.C. § 109(d).

[50] 11 U.S.C. §§ 1161-74, derived from former B.A. § 77.

[51] See 11 U.S.C. §§ 741-752, 761-766. See also White," The Commodity-Related Provisions of the Bankruptcy Act of 1978," 34 Record 262 (No. 4, April 1979).

[52] 11 U.S.C. § 109(d).

special rules relating to stockbroker and commodity broker liquidations are designed to give preferential protection to customers. Congress recognized that an application of these customer protection features to the complex reorganization rules of chapter 11 would be unworkable. Therefore, liquidation is the only option available to stockbrokers and commodity brokers under the Bankruptcy Code.

Farmers and nonprofit organizations are eligible to file voluntary petitions for reorganization. However, they may not be compelled to reorganize because of their immunity from all involuntary bankruptcy petitions.[53]

¶ 8.06 CONDITIONS LEADING TO A CHAPTER 11 PETITION[54]

Doomsday appears to be at hand. Short-term loans are overdue and have already been extended. Covenants in bank agreements setting ratios of debts to equity have been breached. Compensating balances have not been maintained. Credit has virtually dried up. Finally, letters, visitors, and telephone calls demand payment.

This foreboding of financial misfortune does not necessarily mean disaster because it may still be possible to reverse the downhill financial trend. In some instances, institutional investors may be asked to restructure their outstanding debt, adjust the interest rate, subordinate part of their debt, or convert part of their debt to an equity security.

However, institutional lenders are not apt to adjust such extensions and waivers unless the debtor is prepared to show sound financial projections indicating a turnaround in financial prospects, generally based on such factors as economies in operations, possible sales of nonprofitable units, limitation of expansion and the like. Indeed, institutional lenders may even insist, as a condition of granting relief, that one or more subsidiaries or divisions be sold and the proceeds applied in reduction of heavy outstanding debt. Moreover, it is not unusual for institutional lenders to insist upon receiving collateral security, such as the shares of stock of subsidiary corporations of the debtor and security interests in fixed assets, particularly if fresh advances or subordinations of present debt for such advances are sought.[55] Inventory is rarely

---

[53] 11 U.S.C. § 303(a). See Chapter 1 *supra*.

[54] This section is adapted with modifications and footnotes from Weintraub, "Guiding the Insolvent Company Through Chapter XI," 4 EXECUTIVE, 38 (NO. 1) (1977), published by and copyright of the Graduate School of Business Admin., Cornell University; reprinted with permission.

[55] See Musselman, *Non-Bankruptcy Work-Outs*, N.Y. State Bar Ass'n

sought as security from a debtor, since some suppliers who extend credit to a debtor often have prior legal rights in the inventory. Moreover, most suppliers consider the inventory a resource for the collection of their debts if the debtor becomes insolvent.[56]

When bank credit has dried up, there is still the possibility that a debtor's problems may be solved by commercial financing—namely, by pledging accounts receivable, inventory, and fixed assets to the finance company. This "collateralized borrowing is not only the primary but often the sole source of working capital."[57] If lesser funds are necessary, factoring of receivables alone may provide a cash flow that will tide the debtor over during a period when the regular banking sources no longer offer unsecured loans.

Often closely interlinked with the problems of institutional lenders is the disappearance of credit from suppliers. However, buttoning up institutional investors may give confidence to the suppliers and keep the flow of credit close to normal; but, if credit disappears, negotiations with creditors to extend the time of payment of past due debt generally requires the convening of creditors.

At this juncture in the affairs of a company, the chief executive and, in the case of a corporation, the board of directors must look squarely at the rehabilitation features offered by the new Bankruptcy Code. What can chapter 11 of the Code do for the beleaguered debtor? The succeeding sections will indicate that the citadel of despair may be stormed by the utilization of the reorganization process afforded by the Code.[58] Of course, chapter 11 is not the only resort a debtor may have

---

Addresses at annual meeting of Banking, Corporation and Business Law Section, Jan. 29, 1970. See also, Rome, "The Business Workout—A Primer for Participating Creditors," 11 U.C.C.L.J. 183 (1979).

[56] Purchase money security interests in inventory may have priority over all other security interests. See U.C.C. § 9-312(3). See also *In re* W.T. Grant Co., Dkt. No. 75B-1735 (S.D.N.Y. 1975), where the trustee applied for approval of a compromise of bank claims and subordinated debentures. The latter claimed, among other allegations, that "the granting of security interests . . . [caused] Grant's trade suppliers to stop or restrict credit extensions to Grant . . . and that the disruption of the flow of goods and services to Grant's after the security interests and/or liens were granted to the Bank claimants impaired the prospects of a successful reorganization of Grant's."

[57] Miller, "Taking A Look At The Commercial Finance Contract," 65 A.B.A.L.J. 628 (1979).

[58] Cf., Weintraub & Levin, "Three Alternatives in Search of a Lawyer: An Analysis of Corporate Rehabilitation for the Middle-Sized Corporation," 7 N.Y.L.F. 394 (1961), analyzing White, *The View from the Fortieth Floor,*

in an effort to reorganize: it may also attempt to effectuate an out-of-court arrangement.

The out-of-court arrangement is a cooperative venture of both debtor and creditors whose basic objective is to endeavor to work out plans of extension or composition of creditors' liabilities without the necessity of resorting to chapter 11. To consummate this objective, a meeting of creditors must be convened so that their representatives may negotiate with the debtor.[59] These meetings and the proposed settlement should not be organized casually because an adherence to certain rules may be of great advantage to the debtor and creditors in the event such arrangement cannot be consummated and it is necessary to employ chapter 11. Specifically, the Code provides that the holder of a claim or interest who accepts or rejects an out-of-court plan prior to the chapter 11 petition is deemed to have accepted or rejected the plan under chapter 11 if solicitation of the acceptance complies with applicable rules and regulations governing adequacy of disclosure.[60] It is advantageous, therefore, for the debtor to follow these disclosure requirements.

It is common for a committee of unsecured creditors of all types to be formed to facilitate negotiations for an out-of-court arrangement. In the event that it becomes necessary to file a chapter 11 petition, the court may appoint the members of the existing committee to serve on the committee in the chapter 11 case if such committee is "fairly chosen."[61] Accordingly, care should be taken to make sure that committees are chosen fairly so as to maintain continuity of existing committees created prior to the filing of the reorganization petition. Adequate written notice to creditors should be given prior to the elec-

---

in which the novelist's erroneous conclusion of former Chapter X as a skeleton in the closet never gave the advertising company an opportunity to rehabilitate. See also White, *In Search of History* 432 (1978), in which the author writes: "When money runs out and a corporation cannot pay its debts, its creditors take over and its investors are wiped out. . . ."

[59] However, occasionally an offer will be made without a meeting. See the advertisement in the April 25, 1976 issue of the New York Times (at F-9) in which an investment trust invited tenders from 7 percent subordinated debenture holders at an exchange rate of $22 cash net for $100 principal amount. The advertisement stated: "Management of the Trust believes that a successful restructuring of the Trust's subordinated Debentures is critical to the Trust's viability."

[60] 11 U.S.C. § 1126(b). See ¶ 8.20. See also *In re* NJB Prime Investors, 4 Bankr. Dec. 1219 (S.D.N.Y. 1979), where a bankruptcy court rejected prepetition acceptances of a plan since the prospectus soliciting acceptances of the plan made no reference to their use in a subsequent Chapter XI case.

[61] 11 U.S.C. § 1102(b). See ¶ 8.12[1].

tion of committees and proxies should be solicited fairly. Bankruptcy Rules 208 and 11-28, which deal with solicitation of proxies, are good guides to follow. To insure orderly parliamentary proceedings at creditors' meetings, the registration of those appearing and the taking and preservation of written minutes are required. This procedure will be of extreme significance if the out-of-court arrangement cannot be consummated and the debtor becomes the subject of a chapter 11 case, and the debtor and creditors wish to preserve the benefits derived by obtaining the prepetition acceptances.

The debtor and creditors should bear in mind that a failure to consummate an out-of-court arrangement still leaves open the alternative of seeking reorganization under chapter 11. If it appears that an out-of-court settlement cannot be reached because of unwilling creditors or taxing authorities who continue to pursue collection remedies to the point of interfering with the debtor's ability to do business, or because executory contracts, such as long-term leases, are a heavy burden on the debtor, a petition for relief under chapter 11 may be the only way to save the business.[62] The remainder of this chapter will deal with the features of chapter 11 which are designed to protect the debtor and to help the business recover from financial distress.

¶ 8.07 COMMENCING A CHAPTER 11 CASE

The debtor may commence a chapter 11 case by filing a voluntary petition.[63] Reorganization may be viewed, therefore, as a business debtor's remedy for relief from financial distress. Procedures for commencing the case are the same in liquidation and reorganization cases. The Code provisions which govern jurisdiction, abstention, limited appearances, venue, and transfer applicable in liquidation cases are also

---

[62] See Proxmire, "The Case Against Bailing Out Chrysler," N.Y. Times Magazine, Oct. 21, 1979, at 30, 94: "Our bankruptcy laws have always been . . . designed . . . to give a failing company a breathing spell while it works out its problems. In fact, a revised law that took effect October 1 makes it even easier to reorganize and continue functioning . . . [t]he plants keep operating, management stays in place and most workers kept on the job." See also Statements of Epstein and Weintraub submitted at the Hearings on H.R. 5805 on "The Chrysler Corporation Financial Situation" Before the Subcomm. on Economic Stabilization of the House Comm. on Banking, Finance and Urban Affairs, 96th Cong., 1st Sess. 855 (Oct. 30, 1979).

[63] 11 U.S.C. § 301. See Sugg. Int. B. Rule 1002(b)(2) requiring the filing of an original and six copies of the petition. Two copies are forwarded by the clerk of the court to the SEC, one copy to the district director of the IRS, and one copy to the Secretary of the Treasury.

applied in reorganization cases. The debtor seeking chapter 11 relief has an obligation to file certain documents, including lists of creditors and equity security holders, schedules of assets and liabilities, and a statement of financial affairs.[64]

Chapter 11 is also available as a creditor's remedy in that a reorganization may be commenced by an involuntary petition.[65] The procedures and requirements for commencing an involuntary reorganization under the Bankruptcy Code are substantially different from those of the former Act. Former Chapter X required complex factual allegations in involuntary petitions which caused unnecessary delay and may have deterred creditors from pursuing involuntary reorganization.[66] In contrast to the former Chapter X, an involuntary case under the new chapter 11 may be instituted with ease. The allegations necessary for an involuntary petition for reorganization are the same as the allegations involved in an involuntary liquidation case, namely, that the three petitioning creditors (or, if there are less than twelve creditors, the one petitioning creditor) have unsecured claims of at least $5,000; and either that the debtor: (1) generally is not paying its debts as they become due; or (2) has suffered the appointment of a custodian within 120 days prior to the filing date.[67] The only difference is the request for relief, namely, that the petitioner's request that an order for relief under chapter 11 be granted.

---

[64] These matters are discussed in detail in Chapter 1 *supra*. The filing fee for a chapter 11 debtor other than a railroad is $200. 28 U.S.C. § 1930(a); for a railroad the fee is $500. 28 U.S.C. § 1930(a)(4). See Sugg. Int. B. Rule 1007 which requires the filing of three lists: First, a list of the ten largest unsecured creditors excluding insiders; second, a list of creditors of each class showing amounts and character of their claims and securities, their names and addresses, and statements as to whether each claim is disputed, contingent or unliquidated; third, a list of equity security holders of each class showing the number and kind of interests registered in the name of each holder, and the last known address or place of business of each holder. These documents must be filed with the petition or, if the petition is accompanied by a list of all creditors and their addresses, within fifteen days thereafter. In an involuntary case, they must be filed within fifteen days after entry of the order for relief. Sugg. Int. B. Rule 1007(d).

[65] 11 U.S.C. § 303(a). Compare former Chapter XI which did not provide for involuntary petitions and former B.A. § 321 which authorized a debtor's filing under Chapter XI after an involuntary petition for liquidation was filed.

[66] Former B.A. § 130.

[67] 11 U.S.C. § 303. See Chapter 2 *supra* for a discussion on the requirements for an involuntary petition. See also 11 U.S.C. § 101(10) for the definition of "custodian."

Chapter 2 of this book contains a detailed discussion of involuntary bankruptcies which is applicable in reorganization cases as well as liquidations. Reference should, therefore, be made to that discussion with regard to the requisite number of petitioners, the amount of claims for an involuntary petition, transfer of claims, joinder of petitioning creditors, special rules relating to petitions against partnerships, petitions against entities involved in foreign insolvency proceedings, grounds for involuntary relief, postpetition procedures and trials, dismissals, abstention, and liability of creditors for improper petitions.

¶ 8.08 THE DEBTOR IN POSSESSION

An important characteristic of chapter 11 is that the debtor usually will remain in control of its business after a reorganization is commenced. The debtor remaining in control is referred to as a "debtor in possession." The first section of chapter 11 defines "debtor in possession" as meaning the debtor in a reorganization case except when a trustee is appointed and qualifies to serve by posting a bond.[68]

A debtor in possession is given all of the extraordinary rights and powers of a trustee, except that the debtor in possession does not receive a trustee's compensation. A debtor in possession is also obligated to perform the functions and duties of a chapter 11 trustee, except that there is no requirement to perform investigative functions. Likewise, the debtor in possession is subject to the limits that bankruptcy law imposes on trustees and also may be subjected to court-imposed limitations. In essence, the debtor in possession is the debtor who wears the hat of a reorganization trustee during the chapter 11 case.[69]

¶ 8.09 THE MEETINGS OF CREDITORS

Soon after the reorganization case is commenced, an official meeting of creditors will be scheduled to be held in court in the same fashion as in liquidation cases.[70] The Code provides that the judge will not preside at the meeting and the Suggested Interim Bankruptcy Rules add that either the clerk of the bankruptcy court or a designee of the creditors who have the right to vote shall preside.[71] The debtor must attend

---

[68] 11 U.S.C. § 1101(1).

[69] See 11 U.S.C. § 1107 and ¶ 8.13[2].

[70] 11 U.S.C. § 341(a). See ¶¶ 11.1[3], 6.09.

[71] 11 U.S.C. § 341(c). A presiding officer may be designated by creditors who may vote under 11 U.S.C. § 702(a) and who hold a majority in

the meeting and submit to an examination.[72] The rules concerning self-incrimination and immunity apply equally in liquidation and reorganization cases.[73] Upon request of a party in interest and after notice and a hearing, additional committees of equity security holders, including limited partners, may be appointed and the court may change the membership or size of a committee if the membership of such committee is not representative of the different kinds of claims or interests to be represented.[74] Prior to this official meeting, it is likely that the debtor will convene an unofficial meeting of creditors for the purpose of acquainting creditors with its financial condition and obtaining support for its rehabilitation.[75] In all likelihood the creditors' committee will be appointed by this time and their participation at this meeting will supply a helpful forum for a discussion of the debtor's problems.

What are creditors likely to ask at this meeting when they have the first opportunity to conduct a dialogue with the debtor? Sophisticated creditors do not really anticipate that a complete investigation can take place within an hour or two during which this meeting takes place. Nonetheless, creditors may be expected to ask questions concerning bank setoffs and how they will be treated.[76] Vendors often ask about the status of payments for merchandise recently shipped to the debtor on credit.[77] Will the goods be returned or will payment be made? Trade creditors will want to know about future dealings and priority of future debts as administrative expenses. Plans for the immediate future in connection with cash flow problems will be discussed, particularly with reference to the debtor's ability to pay for future shipments of goods and services. The discussion may involve the quick sale of assets or subsidiaries, loans to be obtained within the near future, intercompany loans and cross guarantees, and the disposition of unprofitable units. The current status of assets and liabilities, activities of committees, and retention of independent consultants to assist the debtor may likewise be discussed.[78] Preparation is important for this meeting. Presentations

---

amount of claims. Sugg. Int. B. Rule 2003(b)(1). Where a U.S. Trustee Pilot Program is in effect, the U.S. Trustee presides at the meeting. Sugg. Int. B. Rule X-1003(b)(1). See ¶¶ 6.07[2], 6.08. Compare former B.A. § 334. The Code is designed to eliminate administrative work and prejudice of the judge hearing *ex parte* testimony.

[72] 11 U.S.C. § 343. See Chapter 1 *supra.*

[73] 11 U.S.C. § 344. See ¶ 1.12.

[74] 11 U.S.C. §§ 1102(a)(2), 341(b).

[75] See ¶ 8.06.

[76] See ¶ 5.10.

[77] See ¶ 5.12.

[78] For example, most of these problems were discussed at the meeting

are to be made at least by the debtor's counsel, the chief executive officer and its accountant. Each is to present the debtor's plight and the remedies which will make the debtor a viable entity, giving special attention to analyzing the problems which are discussed in the succeeding sections.

¶ 8.10 THE AUTOMATIC STAY

An important benefit which the troubled business receives upon the filing of the petition is the automatic stay of debt collection and lien enforcement.[79] The rules pertaining to automatic stays in liquidations apply equally in reorganization cases.[80] A detailed discussion of the scope of the automatic stay, exceptions to the stay, requirements for the adequate protection of lienholders and property rights, termination and relief from the stay, and enforcement is contained in Chapter 1 of this book and should be consulted by practitioners involved in reorganization cases.

Although the automatic stay provision of the Bankruptcy Code applies in both liquidation and reorganization cases, the stay has added significance in reorganizations. The purposes of providing for an automatic stay in liquidations under chapter 7 are: (1) to prevent harassment and financial pressures of indebtedness; and (2) to avoid the dissipation of assets and the interference with the orderly administration of the estate. In reorganizations, however, the automatic stay serves a third purpose: to help the debtor in possession or trustee to rehabilitate the business by using all of its assets in its ongoing operations free from financial pressures. Old obligations are frozen by this protective shield which permits the debtor to concentrate its resources on nursing the business back to health.[81]

---

of creditors in *In re* J. M. Fields, Inc., Dkt. No. 78-B-1764 (S.D.N.Y. 1978), whose parent company is Food Fair, Inc., one of the largest conglomerates to file a Chapter XI petition.

[79] 11 U.S.C. § 362.

[80] For a discussion of the use of these rules in former Chapters X, XI, XII and XIII, see Countryman, "Treatment of Secured Claims in Chapter Cases," 82 Com. L.J. 349 (1977); Kennedy, "The Automatic Stay in Bankruptcy," 11 U. Mich. J.L. Ref. 177 (1978).

[81] Moreover, see *In re* Equity Funding Corp. of America, 396 F. Supp. 1266 (C.D. Cal. 1975), where the court assumed jurisdiction to stay a suit against an insurance subsidiary which was not in a Chapter X proceeding, holding that the suit would interfere with the reorganization of the parent company.

A major problem, which often resulted in litigation under the former Bankruptcy Act, concerned the rights of secured parties, including real estate mortgagees, when the defaulting debtor filed a petition for reorganization.[82] If a secured party is stayed from foreclosing on collateral, there exists the possibility of the secured party losing the benefit of the security interest. The collateral may depreciate in value or be consumed by the debtor.[83] On the other hand, to permit secured parties to foreclose on collateral will often make it impossible for debtors to be rehabilitated because of the loss of assets which are necessary for continuing the business. How does the Bankruptcy Code deal with this problem?

The secured party is subjected to the automatic stay against lien enforcement and, therefore, may not use self-help or ordinary judicial process to effectuate foreclosure.[84] Instead, relief from the stay must be sought under the Bankruptcy Code. Chapter 1 of this book contains a discussion of the procedures for obtaining relief from the stay. In essence, the secured party may obtain relief from the stay "for cause," including the lack of adequate protection of its property interest against depreciation or consumption.[85] Thus, if the collateral will depreciate rapidly and if no measures are taken to give the secured party additional collateral or periodic cash payments, appropriate relief or modification of the stay may be obtained to protect the collateral. Additionally, the Code expressly provides that relief should be given to the secured party when the debtor has no equity in the collateral and the collateral "is not necessary to an effective reorganization."[86]

What factors will be used by bankruptcy courts in determining when there is cause to permit a secured party to foreclose on collateral? There is a mass of case law decided under the rehabilitation chapters of the former Bankruptcy Act which focuses on several factors used by the courts:[87] (1) the likelihood that the reorganization will succeed but if a hopeless situation exists the court should permit foreclosure;[88] (2)

---

[82] See B. Rules 11-44, 10-601 which provide for automatic stays against lien enforcement in cases under former Chapters X and XI.

[83] See Peitzman & Smith, "The Secured Creditor's Complaint: Relief From the Automatic Stays in Bankruptcy Proceedings," 65 Calif. L. Rev. 1216 (1977).

[84] 11 U.S.C. § 362.

[85] 11 U.S.C. § 362(d)(1).

[86] 11 U.S.C. § 362(d)(2).

[87] For a discussion of these factors, see Kennedy, note 80 *supra*, at 239-253.

[88] See *In re* Hunterbrook Bldg. Corp., 276 F.2d 190 (2d Cir. 1960), in which creditors in a Chapter X proceeding involving the reorganization of

the necessity of keeping the collateral to continue the debtor's business and achieve rehabilitation;[89] (3) the probable injury to the secured party caused by delaying foreclosure, such as by depreciation or loss of assets, and provisions made for adequately protecting the value of security;[90] (4) the debtor's diligence, or lack of diligence, in effectuating a reorganization;[91] (5) the congressional policy of favoring and encouraging rehabilitation as opposed to liquidation;[92] and (6) balancing the potential injury to the secured party who is denied reclamation of collateral against the potential injury to the debtor who is denied the use and going-concern value of the assets.[93] These factors were used in varying degrees in Chapters X, XI, and XII of the former Act and will probably be used in reorganization cases under the Bankruptcy Code.

---

a real estate development corporation successfully moved to dismiss the petition on the ground that it was unreasonable to expect that reorganization could be achieved. The debtor's property consisted of unfinished homes which had little value until completion and the debtor had no chance of procuring funds to complete construction. Compare *In re* Bermac Corp., 445 F.2d 367 (2d Cir. 1971), in which the creditors' motion to dismiss was denied. The court in *Bermac* was "conscious of the deep concern of the manufacturing secured creditors lest their security depreciate beyond adequate salvage. . . ." However, the prospect of reorganization was not "so hopeless" as to dismiss despite the secured creditors' intention to reject any plan. "Creditors have been known to change their minds when a plan is actually put on the table." *Id.* at 369.

[89] See *In re* Yale Express Sys., Inc., 370 F.2d 433 (2d Cir. 1966) ("the courts have been fairly consistent in denying reclamation where the petitioner only had a lien on the property . . . and repossession would, in the court's opinion, jeopardize the reorganization"). *Id.* at 436. But see Associated Midwest, Inc. v. White Birch Park, Inc., 443 F. Supp. 1342 (E.D. Mich. 1978).

[90] If the value of the collateral exceeds the balance of the debt owed to the secured creditor, thus giving the debtor equity in the property, continuation of the stay is less likely to injure the secured party's position. See Kennedy, note 80 *supra*, at 177, 244, 245.

[91] See Lincoln-Alliance Bank & Trust Co. v. Dye, 115 F.2d 234 (2d Cir. 1940), a Chapter X case in which the court permitted foreclosure because the debtor did not even propose a plan during the fourteen-month stay.

[92] See *In re* Nevada Towers Assocs., 14 Collier Bankr. Cas. 146, 151 (S.D.N.Y. 1977) where the bankrupcty judge stated that the "foremost consideration is the rehabilitative purpose of Chapter XII" where a mortgagee seeks relief from the automatic stay.

[93] See *In re* Castle Village Co., 13 Collier Bankr. Cas. 452, 463 (S.D.N.Y. 1977), in which the court balanced the "disastrous" effect which foreclosures would have on the debtor against injury to the mortgagee likely to result from continuation of the stay in the Chapter XII case.

A case which illustrates the problems of the secured creditor in a rehabilitation situation is *In re Blazon Flexible Flyer, Inc.,*[94] a Chapter XI case under the former Bankruptcy Act. A creditor had a perfected security interest in all accounts receivable and inventory of the debtor to secure a $1.34 million loan when the Chapter XI petition was filed. The accounts receivable were worth $2.7 million and the inventory was worth $1 million. Also, the secured creditor had a security interest in the other assets of the debtor worth $5.73 million. The accounts receivable and inventory were necessary for the survival of the debtor's business and the court permitted the debtor in possession to continue using them in the ordinary course of business. However, the court instituted a number of safeguards to protect the secured creditor, including an assurance that financial information about the debtor's operations was to be transmitted to the secured party and the court. "As long as it appears that the [secured party's] interests in the $1,340,000 are more than adequately protected it is this Court's determination that the Chapter XI proceedings must enable a company to attempt its rehabilitation."[95] The court also held that continuation of the stay against foreclosure did not violate the Fifth Amendment of the Constitution because the security interest was to continue, the use of the collateral was being directed towards the creation of new inventory and accounts receivable, and the secured party maintained a first and best lien on the newly acquired inventory and accounts receivable which greatly exceeded the amount of the secured debt.[96] The rationale of *Blazon Flexible Flyer* is applicable to reorganization cases under chapter 11 of the new Bankruptcy Code.[97]

The Bankruptcy Code also contains special protections for lessors and conditional vendors of certain aircraft equipment and vessels in chapter 11 cases.[98]

---

[94] 407 F. Supp. 861 (N.D. Ohio 1976). See also *In re* American Kitchen Foods, Inc., 2 Bankr. Dec. 715 (D. Me. 1976), where the court, in continuing the stay and considering adequate protection, evaluated the collateral on a standard based on commercial reasonableness following Sections 9-504(3) and 9-507(2) of the Uniform Commercial Code. This case may very well have been a harbinger of the "adequate protection" rule set forth in 11 U.S.C. §§ 361, 362, 363.

[95] See 407 F. Supp. at 865.

[96] *Id.* at 864.

[97] As to the debtor's use, sale or lease of the secured creditor's collateral, see ¶ 8.11[3]. As to the ultimate status of the secured creditor's collateral as affected by the cram down provisions of the Bankruptcy Code, see ¶ 8.23[4][a].

[98] 11 U.S.C. § 1110.

¶ 8.11 CONTINUED OPERATION OF THE BUSINESS

It is essential that the debtor in a reorganization case be able to continue to operate the business without unnecessary interruption. Chapter 11 provides that the business may continue to operate in the ordinary course without the necessity of obtaining a court order permitting such operation.[99] Although the Code gives a trustee the power to operate the business, the debtor in possession has this same right in the absence of the appointment of a trustee.[100] The debtor in possession will operate the business with the protections of the automatic stay and with the extraordinary powers given to trustees to avoid certain transfers, such as voidable preferences and fraudulent transfers, and to reject burdensome executory contracts.[101] This combination of powers and protections creates the optimum environment for the rehabilitation of a financially distressed business. The debtor in possession, or trustee if one is appointed, is required to file written reports on a periodic basis concerning the financial condition of the business, receipts and disbursements and other data relating to the continued operations so as to give the court and creditors a capsule view of the debtor's financial condition throughout the reorganization case.[102]

[1] Problems With Landlords

The financially distressed debtor in need of reorganization is often worried about the landlord. Termination of the debtor's lease and eviction will destroy any dream of salvaging a failing business in most cases. It is not unusual for the debtor to be several months behind in rental payments when the petition for reorganization is filed. Also, the lease may provide for termination upon the tenant's insolvency or bankruptcy.

These problems were given serious consideration by Congress when enacting the Bankruptcy Reform Act of 1978.[103] Subject to certain conditions, the debtor in possession or trustee has the right to assume and continue possession under an unexpired lease by curing the default or by providing adequate assurance of cure. Equally as important, a lease may not be terminated solely because of an ipso facto clause which

---

[99] 11 U.S.C. § 1108. Compare B. Rule 11-23, applicable in cases under former Chapter XI, which required the trustee or debtor in possession to obtain a court order to conduct the business.

[100] 11 U.S.C. § 1107(a).

[101] See Chapter 7 *supra* for a discussion of the trustee's powers.

[102] See 11 U.S.C. §§ 1106(a)(1), 704(7). See also B. Rule 11-30 which applied in cases filed under former Chapter XI.

[103] See 11 U.S.C. § 365.

provides for automatic termination upon the insolvency or bankruptcy of the tenant.[104] Normally, the debtor in possession or trustee has until confirmation of the plan to reject or assume the lease. The extraordinary power of the debtor in possession or trustee to reject or assume unexpired leases, despite prior default or a bankruptcy termination clause, is discussed in depth in the chapter on the trustee's powers and the reader should consult that portion of the book.[105]

What are the rights of the parties during the time between the filing of the petition and formal rejection or assumption of the lease which may occur several months later? It should be kept in mind that the automatic stay provision protects the debtor against eviction by normal state process.[106] Therefore, the landlord who wants to evict the defaulting debtor must seek relief from the stay in the bankruptcy court. The court will determine whether the stay will continue until such time as the debtor in possession or trustee formally rejects or assumes the unexpired lease. The standards to be used by the court on this question are identical with the standards used in determining whether relief from the stay is to be granted to a secured party seeking foreclosure.[107] The landlord may be given relief from the stay if not adequately protected against loss, or otherwise "for cause."[108] It can also be argued that relief should be granted when the lease is not needed for the reorganization and the debtor has no equity in the property. It can be expected, however, that courts will be reluctant to give the landlord relief from the automatic stay, except when the landlord is in jeopardy of suffering substantial losses, so that the debtor may have the opportunity to either reject or assume it at a future date. In fact, it is likely that the court will require the debtor in possession or trustee to make the election in a relatively short time period so as to protect the landlord's interests instead of merely granting relief from the stay.[109]

In sum, the debtor-tenant is protected against loss of the premises on a temporary basis by the automatic stay after the petition is filed and on a more permanent basis by the power to reject or assume a lease despite prior default or a bankruptcy termination clause. These protections, however, are subject to rules designed to adequately protect the landlord against financial loss.

---

[104] Compare former B.A. § 70,b). See Queens Blvd. Wine & Liquor Corp. v. Blum, 503 F.2d 202 (2d Cir. 1974).

[105] See Chapter 7 *supra*.

[106] 11 U.S.C. § 362(a)(3).

[107] See ¶ 8.10.

[108] 11 U.S.C. § 362(d).

[109] See ¶ 7.10[6].

[2] Problems With Tenants

Let us assume that a debtor in a chapter 11 case is the lessor of certain real estate. Of course, if the lease is a favorable one from the lessor's standpoint, the debtor in possession or trustee will assume the lease and continue to reap its benefits. In order to assume the lease, however, the debtor must cure any default or provide adequate assurance that cure will occur promptly with respect to the debtor's obligations to provide services as landlord.[110]

If the lease is not favorable for the landlord because the rent is below current market value of the premises, the debtor may prefer to reject it. However, the Bankruptcy Code contains a special provision designed to protect a tenant from eviction in the event that the landlord rejects the lease. Specifically, upon rejection the tenant is given the choice of either treating the lease as terminated by the rejection or remaining in possession of the premises for the balance of the lease term, including renewal or extension of the term enforceable under nonbankruptcy law. If the tenant chooses to remain in possession despite rejection of the lease by the landlord, any damages due to the debtor's failure to provide services or otherwise perform the landlord's obligations under the lease may be offset against the rent.[111] Accordingly, the debtor who is a lessor may discover that problems with an unfavorable tenant may not disappear after the commencement of a reorganization case.

[3] Use, Sale, or Lease of Property in the Ordinary Course of Business

As previously discussed, the debtor in possession may continue the operation of the business after the petition is filed unless a trustee is appointed. The debtor's continued operation will necessitate the use of assets and may also require the lease or sale of property. As long as the use, sale or lease of property is in the ordinary course of business, the debtor in possession or trustee may act without the necessity of obtaining prior approval of the court.[112] Normally, the debtor will transact business without giving notice and without any hearing at all. In brief, the debtor in possession is authorized to manufacture finished products and may buy and sell goods, collect receivables, and enter into contracts in the normal course of business. The debtor in possession may pay cash for needed items and may pay salaries to employees. A

---

[110] See 11 U.S.C. § 365 and ¶ 7.09[3].

[111] See 11 U.S.C. § 365(h) and ¶ 7.09[10].

[112] 11 U.S.C. § 363(c)(1).

debtor operating a chain of retail stores may close several, open new ones, and sign new leases while a manufacturer may acquire new equipment; but all transactions must be similar to those historically carried on by the debtor in the ordinary course of business.

The debtor in possession or trustee may also use, sell or lease property not in the ordinary course of business, but only if court approval is obtained upon notice and a hearing.[113] When the debtor is in doubt as to whether certain transactions are in the ordinary course, it is advisable to treat such borderline conduct as not in the ordinary course and to obtain court approval. In certain instances property may be sold free and clear of liens and security interests.[114]

There are several limitations on the debtor's right to use, sell and lease property after a reorganization petition is filed. First, the court has the power to order the prior approval of all or particular transactions.[115] In essence, if the court is shown cause to keep a very close watch over the debtor's conduct, it may require the debtor to obtain permission for specific activities by limiting its powers to operate. Nonetheless, automatic continuation is the rule, not the exception.

A second limitation relates to adequate protection of the property rights of others. If a party has a property interest in the item, as in the case of a creditor with a security interest in the debtor's assets, the sale of such property by the debtor in possession must not violate any order which gives the secured party relief from the automatic stay against lien enforcement.[116] For example, if the court grants relief to a secured party by conditioning the stay on the debtor's maintaining possession of the collateral, the debtor in possession may not sell it in the ordinary course of business. In addition, the court may comply with the request of any person who has a property interest to give such person adequate protection against loss.[117] For example, when the debtor in possession uses machinery which is the subject of a security interest and the secured party is stayed from foreclosing, the court may order that the

---

[113] 11 U.S.C. § 363(b), derived from former B.A. § 70(f). If the court approves the sale, reversal of such authorization on appeal does not affect the validity of the sale to a good faith purchaser unless the sale was stayed pending the appeal. 11 U.S.C. § 363(m).

[114] 11 U.S.C. § 363(f).

[115] 11 U.S.C. § 363(c)(1).

[116] 11 U.S.C. §§ 361, 363(d). See ¶ 1.09 and ¶ 8.10, for a discussion of adequate protection for secured parties with respect to the stay against lien enforcement in chapter 11 cases.

[117] 11 U.S.C. § 363(e).

debtor provide adequate protection against additional depreciation caused by further use of the machinery. Adequate protection of such interest is further fortified by the Bankruptcy Code's provision granting the secured creditor "superpriority" as an administrative expense to the extent that the protection is otherwise inadequate.[118]

Probably the most important limitation on the debtor's use of property in reorganization cases relates to the use, sale or lease of "cash collateral." Cash collateral includes cash, negotiable instruments, documents of title, securities, deposit accounts, or other cash equivalents in which the debtor's estate and another entity have an interest.[119] An illustration of cash collateral exists when a secured party has a security interest in accounts receivable and the cash proceeds of the accounts receivable. When the accounts are collected and deposited in a bank account, the cash and bank deposit are cash collateral subject to the rights of the secured party. The Bankruptcy Code does not permit the use of cash collateral by the debtor unless the other interested party, i.e., the secured creditor, consents or the court authorizes the use of it after notice and a hearing.[120] The debtor is not free to use cash collateral otherwise. The court may authorize such use only if the secured party is adequately protected against loss.[121]

When the debtor has to use cash collateral in the normal operation of the business and is unable to obtain the secured party's consent, it may be necessary to obtain court approval in a very short time. It takes little imagination to see that a debtor's lifeline may be cut off after the petition for reorganization is filed if an inability exists to use cash collateral on very short notice. This is especially so because businesses in trouble often use accounts receivable as security for loans and, therefore, the only major source of cash flow falls within the category of cash collateral.[122] Congress, too, realized the potential crippling effect of the limitation on the use of cash collateral and therefore provided an ameliorating procedure to give the debtor an early day in court.

The hearing on the use of cash collateral may be preliminary or may be consolidated with the hearing on the question of adequate protection for interested parties. If preliminary only, the court may autho-

---

[118] 11 U.S.C. § 507(b).

[119] 11 U.S.C. § 363(a).

[120] 11 U.S.C. § 363(c)(2).

[121] This requirement applies only if the interested party requests adequate protection. See 11 U.S.C. § 363(e).

[122] According to Section 9-306 of the Uniform Commercial Code, the accounts receivable financier will also have a security interest in the cash proceeds when the accounts are collected.

rize the use, sale or lease of cash collateral if there is a reasonable likelihood that the debtor in possession or trustee will prevail at the final hearing, that is, if it is likely that the secured party will be adequately protected by substituting other collateral, by making periodic payments or otherwise. In such event, the court will permit the use of cash collateral.[123] The statute is clear in requiring that the hearing be "scheduled in accordance with the needs of the debtor" and that "the court shall act promptly" on requests to authorize the use of cash collateral.[124] For example, assume that the debtor in possession has a payroll to meet; it is Friday afternoon and paychecks must be handed out today. If the employees are not paid in the customary manner, not only will pandemonium follow, but there may be no workers available on Monday to operate the business. Under these circumstances, proper notice to the secured creditor or its attorney may be by telephone informing either of an application to be submitted to the court within a few hours for the use of cash collateral to meet the payroll. The court may be satisfied with such notice and may grant authorization after a brief preliminary hearing on the same day whether or not there is an appearance by the secured creditor.[125] Lacking consent of the secured creditor or court authorization to use cash collateral, the debtor in possession is required to segregate and account for all cash collateral within its control.[126]

Because of the headaches which may result from the limitations on the use of cash collateral, the debtor should minimize these problems by adequately planning prior to filing the chapter 11 petition. When the debtor has secured loans from financial institutions, it is prudent to discuss the filing of the reorganization petition with those financial institutions so as to obtain their support for postpetition financing that permits the use of cash collateral. This prepetition arrangement will help to avoid the hazardous consequences of interrupted operations at a most important juncture in the life of the company, namely the transitional period before the debtor becomes a debtor in possession. In this crucial period it is important that regularity and confidence are indicated to suppliers, customers, and employees.

---

[123] The trustee or debtor in possession has the burden of proof on the issue of adequate protection. 11 U.S.C. § 363(e).

[124] 11 U.S.C. § 363(c)(3). See 11 U.S.C. § 102(1) with respect to prompt notice.

[125] See 11 U.S.C. § 102(1) defining "after notice and hearing" and authorizing an act without an actual hearing if notice is given and there is insufficient time for a hearing.

[126] 11 U.S.C. § 363(c)(4).

[4] Banking Facilities

Obviously, business cannot be conducted without banking facilities. As of the date of the commencement of the case, the money in the debtor's bank accounts becomes property of the estate.[127] In theory, the debtor is not entitled to use this money, but the debtor in possession, a newly created legal entity, may use it.[128] As such, old bank accounts are frozen and checks will no longer be honored by banks. New bank accounts will be opened by the debtor in possession immediately after the commencement of the case.

It is common for the debtor in possession to open new accounts at the same banks which serviced the business in prepetition days, as long as the institutions are federally insured depositories. If the institution is not insured by the Federal Deposit Insurance Corporation or by another federal agency, or the deposited sum exceeds the amount of such insurance, the depository will have to post a sufficient bond or securities to protect the funds of the estate.[129] Subject to these rules which are designed to protect the estate, the debtor in possession is free to choose the institution or type of account to open. The use of savings banks and savings and loan associations, as well as commercial banks, is permitted without special court authorization. This degree of leeway is a substantial departure from the former Bankruptcy Act which permitted deposits only in depositories specifically designated by the court.[130]

New accounts that are opened after a reorganization case is commenced require the submission of new signature cards of the officers and new corporate resolutions of the board of directors. The accounts are opened in the individual, partnership or corporate name of the debtor followed by the words "debtor in possession."

Because of restrictions on the use of cash collateral, all cash collateral should be deposited in separate bank accounts so as to keep it segregated from cash which is readily usable by the debtor in possession.[131]

[5] Obtaining Credit and Working Capital

Although the enterprise's assets are protected from creditors by the automatic stay, the business may still be faced with a cash flow problem.

---

[127] 11 U.S.C. § 541(a). See Chapter 4 *supra* for a discussion of property of the estate.

[128] 11 U.S.C. § 363(c)(1).

[129] 11 U.S.C. § 345(b).

[130] See B. Rules 512, 605(b), 10-605, 11-52, which are superseded by 11 U.S.C. § 345(b).

[131] 11 U.S.C. § 363(c)(4).

Accounts receivable must be diligently collected, inventory must be sold and, of course, credit lines must be reestablished.

The debtor in possession or trustee may obtain unsecured credit and incur unsecured debt in the ordinary course of business.[132] Thus, goods may be purchased on credit and unsecured loans may be procured if consistent with the traditional operations of the enterprise. Also, the court, after notice and a hearing, may authorize the procurement of unsecured credit other than in the ordinary course of business.[133]

Why would anybody extend unsecured credit to a debtor in possession? At first glance, this appears to be an ill-advised investment. However, to encourage such extensions of credit, the Bankruptcy Code provides for certain protections. In fact, the debtor in possession can now offer the credit community fairly sound assurances of payment. First, unsecured debts which predated the commencement of the case are frozen by the automatic stay;[134] only current purchases of goods or services need be paid by the estate. Second, while the prepetition indebtedness is frozen, the debtor in possession may use money of the estate to pay the new creditors in the ordinary course of business because these debts are administrative expenses entitled to priority.[135] Such payments do not constitute voidable preferences.[136] Third, in the event that the debtor in possession or trustee cannot solve the firm's troubles and the reorganization case is converted to a liquidation, the postpetition debts qualify as administration claims and will have a priority in distribution.[137] Although suppliers and lenders who extend credit to a debtor in possession or trustee are not assured of certainty of payment, the stay regarding prepetition debts and the administrative expense priority of postpetition debts minimizes the risk which they take. The risk is almost diminished when the debtor in possession has substantial assets which are free of liens and security interests. Moreover, unsecured creditors have a stake in the debtor's survival, for if credit is not extended liquidation may ensue, any hope for recovery on the old debt will be lost, and the creditor may lose a good customer.

Assume that a debtor in possession is unable to obtain unsecured

---

[132] 11 U.S.C. § 364(a).

[133] 11 U.S.C. § 364(b).

[134] 11 U.S.C. § 362(a). See ¶¶ 1.09 and 8.10.

[135] 11 U.S.C. §§ 503(b), 507(a)(1).

[136] See ¶ 7.05 on voidable preferences.

[137] The same priority for administrative expenses applies in liquidation cases.

credit despite these protections. If such credit is needed for the successful rehabilitation of the debtor, the court, after notice and a hearing, may authorize the obtaining of credit by giving the new creditor priority over all other administrative expenses.[138] Accordingly, the creditor will have priority over all other persons who extend credit to the debtor in possession after the commencement of the case. In essence, the new creditor will be receiving a priority within a priority. Also, the court may permit the new creditor to be secured by a lien on property which is not otherwise the subject of any liens, or if the property is already subject to a lien, the court may permit the new creditor to have a junior lien.[139] In extreme cases the court has the power to give the new creditor a lien which is superior or equal to an existing lien on property, but only if necessary to obtain credit and if the prior lienholder is adequately protected.[140] Needless to say, these liens diminish the debtor's ability to obtain credit and, therefore, debtors should make every effort to obtain credit without granting new liens.[141]

The debtor in possession or trustee may take other steps to acquire the working capital needed for a successful reorganization. Subsidiaries or divisions of the corporate debtor which are unprofitable or which serve no useful purpose in the formulation of a reorganization plan may be sold or liquidated.[142] It is common for insolvent subsidiaries to file petitions along with the parent corporation and, with court approval, for the cases to be consolidated or jointly administered. Debtors with huge inventories in retail store operations may sell these assets at public auction with court approval and may dispose of fixtures, equipment and leaseholds in the same manner to provide the enterprise with ready cash which can be used for operating expenses.[143] Also, accounts receivable not already subjected to security interests may be factored or used as collateral for bank loans with court authorization.

---

[138] 11 U.S.C. § 364(c)(1). See, however, Otte v. Manufacturers Hanover Commercial Corp., 596 F.2d 1092 (2d Cir. 1979), in which the court of appeals said that it found nothing in Section 364(c) that advances the case in favor of "cross-collateralization."

[139] 11 U.S.C. §§ 364(c)(2), 364(c)(3).

[140] 11 U.S.C. § 364(d).

[141] Such an effort is required by the Code. See 11 U.S.C. § 364(d).

[142] Court approval is required prior to such sales if not made in the ordinary course of business. 11 U.S.C. § 363(b).

[143] See, for example, *In re* United Merchants & Mfrs., Inc., Dkt. No. 77-B-1513-1888 (S.D.N.Y. 1977), where the inventory, fixtures and leaseholds of a division of the debtor, Robert Hall Clothes, operating 367 retail stores, were sold at auction and a sale consummated of the parent's factoring division.

[6] Internal Problems

An important point which must not be overlooked in reorganization cases concerns employee morale and continued loyalty to the financially troubled debtor. It is not difficult to foresee that the commencement of the chapter 11 case could have a devastating effect on workers at all levels. Why should a person remain loyal and continue to work hard for a business on the brink of destruction? Competitors who are aware of the weak financial condition of the debtor are apt to lure key officials with blandishments of better offers and more security; they may even intimate to major customers that the debtor will wind up liquidating instead of restructuring. If the most valued employees flee the company the chances for successful reorganization will be dim.[144]

For these reasons, the debtor must give serious thought to building up the morale of the organization. In corporate reorganizations, the chief executive must work with the other officers and the board of directors as a team and must minimize internal dissension. Employees on every level should be kept informed so that they understand that chapter 11 means a second opportunity to keep the company alive. Their help must be enlisted in the challenge of saving the business. With the aid of lawyers, accountants and consultants, information releases should be prepared for the press, suppliers, creditors, customers and employees to acquaint them with the reorganization filing and to stress the continuity of the business operation.

No simple solution is available to meet the problem of keeping the staff and customers from severing their affiliations with the debtor. However, a company that has a good working relationship with its staff will generally find that their loyalty and interest will survive reorganization as long as they are confident that the company's ills can be remedied. Likewise, customers who have been pleased with the quality of the debtor's services and products are not apt to leave if they can be convinced of the firm's continuity. Therefore, it will be a drastic mistake for the debtor to be less than diligent in keeping employees and customers informed at all times.

The necessity of maintaining the morale of top executives, however, should be no obstacle in eliminating those who do not fill the

---

[144] See "Company Doctor Sigoloff: 'The Skillful Scalpel' Joins No. 1 Builder," N.Y. Times, Oct. 7, 1979, at 1, § 3, which reported the statement of Sanford S. Sigoloff, formerly an executive of Daylin, Inc. which was reorganized under Chapter XI, with reference to Daylin employees: "The people who work with you to help turn around a troubled company put forth a superhuman effort. . . . All during the trouble they get no rewards, but they endure the stress and strain. They deserve something for that."

qualifications necessary for their specific positions. Creditors' committees often suggest that particular employees be replaced or that unnecessary positions be terminated. No unqualified executive or employee is immune from the severance of employment. The discharge of employees and the termination of positions make it necessary for the debtor to take steps to maintain the morale of the remaining officers and employees. Also, it is a difficult task to replace executives since it is not easy to find a qualified person who will accept a new position with an insolvent company. Such a person may be attracted by the challenge of rebuilding with rewards of salary, bonus, and stock options.[145]

In a succinct and comprehensive comment, Congress indicated the salient features of a successful business in a competitive economy: "The success and even the survival, of a corporation in contemporary markets depends on three elements: First, the ability to attract and hold skilled management; second the ability to obtain credit; and third, the corporation's ability to project to the public an image of vitality. . . ."[146]

¶ 8.12 CREDITORS' COMMITTEES AND EQUITY SECURITY HOLDERS' COMMITTEES

Although in most reorganization cases existing management continues to conduct the debtor's business in the ordinary course after the petition is filed, creditors will want to look over the debtor's shoulder carefully to make sure that their interests are being protected. Of course, it is unwieldy, if not impossible, for every creditor to keep a close eye on the debtor's operations. For this reason, the Bankruptcy Code provides for a mechanism which assures that creditors will be able to oversee the operations and to voice their thoughts throughout the chapter 11 case. This mechanism involves the appointment of committees of creditors and equity security holders.

---

[145] In *In re* J. M. Fields, Inc. Dkt. No. 78-B-1764 (S.D.N.Y. 1978) the court authorized the employment of a new president and chief executive officer for a period of five years at an annual compensation, payment of a sum for his relocation, stock options, deferred benefits, and a cash fund to secure payment of all compensation under the employment agreement. Of course, benefits should be moderated by the size of the debtor and the complexity of the problems.

[146] 124 Cong. Rec. H11101 (daily ed. Sept. 28, 1978). See also *In re* Commonwealth Oil Refining Co., 464 F. Supp. 580, 582 (W.D. Tex. 1979), where the court approved a debtor's agreement with a management concern, empowering it "to seek out and employ management-level personnel under long-term contracts. . . ."

[1] The Appointment of Committees

The court is obligated to appoint a committee of creditors holding unsecured claims "as soon as is practicable" after the order for reorganization relief under chapter 11.[147] This rule represents a substantial departure from Chapter XI of the former Bankruptcy Act which provided for the election of a committee at the creditors' first meeting.[148] The committee will ordinarily consist of those unsecured creditors who hold the seven largest claims of the kinds represented on the committee and who are willing to serve. Alternatively, the court may appoint the members of any informal committee which was organized by unsecured creditors prior to the filing of the reorganization petition as long as the members are fairly chosen and are representative of the different kinds of claims which exist against the debtor.[149] Any party in interest may request at any time that the committee membership or size be changed on the ground that it is not representative of the different kinds of claims.[150] For example, suppliers of goods, institutional lenders, service creditors, nonpriority claims of unions, and other types of creditors may all want to have their own representatives. The court may grant such request after a hearing, on notice to all interested parties. It should be noted, however, that the Code indicates that it is usually appropriate to have seven members on a committee, although there is no fixed ceiling or floor on the number of members.[151]

In addition to the committee of creditors with unsecured claims, the court has the discretion to appoint additional committees of creditors, shareholders, limited partners, or other equity security holders if necessary to assure their adequate representation in the chapter 11 case.[152] As a flexible guideline, the Bankruptcy Code provides that equity security holders' committees shall ordinarily consist of the seven largest holders of equity securities who are willing to serve.[153]

---

[147] 11 U.S.C. § 1102(a)(1).

[148] Former B.A. § 338. See B. Rule 11-27 which is superseded by the Bankruptcy Code.

[149] 11 U.S.C. § 1102(b)(1).

[150] 11 U.S.C. § 1102(c).

[151] Compare B. Rule 11-27(a) which required that the committee in a Chapter XI case consist of not less than three nor more than eleven creditors. Former Chapter X, however, had no ceiling on the number of creditors who could serve on a committee, nor was there any provision for an official election. See former B.A. § 211 and B. Rule 10-211.

[152] 11 U.S.C. § 1102(a)(2).

[153] 11 U.S.C. § 1102(b).

In those jurisdictions which are governed by the U.S. Trustee Pilot Program, the U.S. Trustee makes the appointment of creditors' and equity security holders' committees.[154]

All committee members act in a representative capacity and have fiduciary obligations. Each member of the committee acts for the best interests of its constituents, not in its own private interest.[155] It is for this reason that the court has control over the membership of the committees and may add or remove a member upon the request of any interested party after a hearing on notice.[156] It should be noted also that each member of the creditors' committee must be a creditor. Therefore, the members may be corporate entities or partnerships. In such cases, the creditor usually designates an attorney in fact, such as its credit executive, attorney, or accountant, to carry out its duties as a member.[157]

[2] Functions and Powers of Committees

The creditors' and equity security holders' committees serve very important functions. In general, they gather information about the ongoing operations of the debtor in possession. They provide assistance and supervision for the debtor in possession or a trustee if one is appointed. They actively represent the several classes of creditors or equity security holders by keeping a watchful eye on the debtor and acting quickly if there is a need to be heard. They are also a significant negotiating force when the debtor formulates a plan of reorganization and, if the debtor's plan is rejected, a committee may play a primary role by formulating its own plan. The debtor in possession knows that a successful reorganization requires participation and cooperation from creditors and equity security holders and, therefore, will aim to cooperate with the committees.

Soon after the appointment of a committee, its members will schedule a meeting. If a majority of the members is present, the committee may select and authorize the appointment of attorneys, accountants or other persons to represent it or to perform appropriate services

---

[154] 11 U.S.C. § 151102.

[155] See Mintz v. Joseph Clavin & Co., 4 App. Div. 2d 635 (1st Dep't 1957), *aff'd* 4 N.Y.2d 886 (1958) for a nonbankruptcy case which discusses ethical duties of members of creditors' committees.

[156] 11 U.S.C. § 1102(c).

[157] See Arrow Dairy Co. v. Chase Superior, Inc. 116 F.2d 573 (2d Cir. 1941), where the court held that an attorney representing a creditor could act as a member of the creditors' committee.

for the committee.[158] It is anticipated that attorneys will be chosen to represent committees in most cases and the Code provides for leeway to appoint one or more for each committee. All appointments must be made with court approval and any person employed by a committee may not represent any other entity in connection with the reorganization.[159] This prohibition of joint representation is designed to avoid a serious conflict of interest which results when a lawyer or accountant represents an individual creditor of one class as well as representing the committee of different classes of creditors.

The powers of committees are quite extensive and are set forth in the Bankruptcy Code with particularity.[160] First, a committee has the right to consult with the debtor in possession or trustee concerning the administration of the reorganization case. Second, committees have very broad investigatory powers. The committee may investigate all aspects of the debtor's business operations, including the debtor's acts, conduct, assets, liabilities and financial condition. It may investigate the desirability of continuing the business "and any other matter relevant to the case or to the formulation of a plan." [161] Third, committees play an active role in the actual formulation of a reorganization plan and they make recommendations to creditors and equity security holders concerning proposed plans. Also, the committees may collect and file with the court acceptances and rejections of a plan. If a committee believes that the appointment of a trustee is necessary, it has standing to request that a trustee be so appointed. Moreover, Congress did not intend to limit the powers of committees to those specified above. The Code provides that, in addition to particular powers set forth in the statute, a committee may "perform such other services as are in the interest of those represented." [162]

Not long after a committee is appointed, the debtor in possession or the trustee must meet with the committee to transact "such business as may be necessary and proper." [163] The committee will then meet from time to time either with or without the debtor in possession or trustee as is appropriate under the circumstances of the particular case.

---

[158] 11 U.S.C. § 1103(a).

[159] 11 U.S.C. § 1103(b). See 11 U.S.C. § 101(14) where "entity" is defined to include a person, estate, trust or governmental unit.

[160] These powers are set forth in 11 U.S.C. § 1103(c).

[161] 11 U.S.C. § 1103(c)(2).

[162] 11 U.S.C. § 1103(c)(5).

[163] 11 U.S.C. § 1103(d).

¶ 8.13 TRUSTEES

[1] The Appointment of a Trustee

In consolidating former Chapters X, XI, and XII into the new chapter 11, one of the most difficult issues which Congress had to face was whether the appointment of a trustee should be mandatory in all cases, or whether the debtor should be permitted to remain in possession and control of the business during reorganization.[164]

The legislative history of the Bankruptcy Reform Act of 1978 indicates that Congress was impressed with the track record of many successful cases involving publicly held debt under former Chapter XI where the debtors were left in possession.[165] Congress recognized that most business failures were not caused by dishonest management or fraud, but instead resulted from depressive business cycles or market shifts. Furthermore, by permitting present management to continue in possession, a company in need of immediate reorganization would not be inclined to wait too long before filing a petition because of the fear of losing control by an appointment of a trustee. Congress also recognized that continuity of management increased the likelihood that reorganization would succeed because of the disruption and difficulties which result when a stranger to the business was suddenly put in the driver's seat. Additionally, the appointment of a trustee caused added expense which should be avoided if possible. For these reasons, Congress chose not to make the appointment of a trustee mandatory in reorganization cases.[166]

Nonetheless, cases do arise in which the cause of business failure may be related to incompetent management or fraud by current executives. In such cases, it may be appropriate for a trustee to be appointed and for present management to be supplanted. Accordingly, the Bankruptcy Code provides for enough flexibility to permit courts on a case-by-case basis to appoint trustees when needed.[167] However,

---

[164] In Chapter X cases, the appointment of a trustee was mandatory if liquidated and noncontingent debt was $250,000 or more, and was customary when the debts were lower. Former B.A. § 156; B. Rule 10-202. However, in Chapters XI and XII, the debtor usually remained in possession and the appointment of a receiver or trustee was optional. Former B.A. §§ 332, 342, 432; B. Rules 11-18, 12-17.

[165] See 124 Cong. Rec. H11102 (daily ed. Sept. 28, 1978).

[166] See House Comm. on the Judiciary, Bankruptcy Law Revision, H.R. Rep. No. 95-595, 95th Cong., 1st Sess. 232-234, for a discussion of these considerations.

[167] 11 U.S.C. § 1104.

it is to be remembered that a debtor in possession is the rule and not the exception.

Specifically, the Bankruptcy Code permits the court to appoint a trustee at any time prior to confirmation of a plan, but only on request of a party in interest [168] and after notice and a hearing. After the hearing, the court may appoint a trustee: (1) only "for cause," including but not limited to fraud, dishonesty, incompetence, or gross mismanagement of the affairs of the debtor by current management; or (2) if a trustee's appointment is in the interests of creditors, equity, security holders, and the estate. These standards are quite flexible and give the judge wide discretion in deciding whether it is appropriate to appoint a trustee. The Bankruptcy Code, however, expressly provides that the number of securities holders or the amount of assets or liabilities shall not be considered in determining whether a trustee should be appointed.[169] Congress made it clear that the size of the business and amount of publicly held securities should have no bearing on whether current management ought to be replaced by a trustee.

It must be recalled that one of the reasons for consolidating former Chapters X and XI was to avoid time-consuming and expensive litigation on the question of whether the case should be converted from one rehabilitation chapter to another.[170] In such litigation, courts often focused on the need for the appointment of an independent trustee. Decisions in conversion proceedings, therefore, were based usually on such factors as the public interest, size of the company, fraud, dishonesty, incompetence, or gross mismanagement by current executives.[171] These factors, excluding the assets and liabilities of the debtor and the number of security holders, are similar to the criteria employed under chapter 11 of the Code on the issue of whether a trustee should be appointed.

Therefore, unless the parties in interest and the courts realize that the appointment of a trustee is a procedure to be used sparingly, there is danger that we will again see many time-consuming and expensive trials and appeals concerning trustee appointment. Accordingly, the

---

[168] A U.S. Trustee has standing to request the appointment of a trustee. 11 U.S.C. § 151104.

[169] 11 U.S.C. § 1104(a).

[170] See ¶ 8.02.

[171] See Securities and Exchange Comm'n v. American Trailer Rentals Co., note 22 *supra*, and General Stores Corp. v. Shlensky, 350 U.S. 462 (1956), for a discussion of some of these factors. See also Securities and Exchange Comm'n v. Canandaigua Enterprises Corp., note 24 *supra*, discussing the weakness and strength of Chapters X and XI of the former Act.

recent reform of the bankruptcy laws will not achieve its goal of streamlining reorganization cases and will only constitute semantic infiltration. Indeed, the sentiment of Congress is expressed in this connection as follows: "This [appointment of an examiner instead of a trustee] should adequately represent the needs of public security holders in most cases. . . ." [172]

A caveat should also be presented to the debtor: the risk of litigation for the appointment of a trustee will be minimized if debtors actively consult with committees to help cure the causes which led to insolvency and if they negotiate fairly and openly with regard to a plan. Congress believes that negotiations between the debtor and creditors in connection with the formulation of a plan will lead to rehabilitation in a more profitable fashion than litigation.

Consistent with Congress' preference for allowing a debtor to remain in possession, the Code provides that the court may terminate a trustee's appointment for cause after a hearing on notice.[173] In essence, this provision gives the management a second opportunity to obtain control. This termination must be based on the premise that the cause for the trustee's appointment has been eliminated by the interim therapy or that the results of the trustee's investigations reveal the absence of any wrongdoing or incompetence on the part of management.

Anyone who is appointed to serve as a trustee must be a "disinterested person" [174] and must qualify and meet certain conditions. For a discussion of the qualifications of a trustee, eligibility to serve, compensation, employment of attorneys or other professionals, the U.S. Trustee Pilot Program, and other aspects of the trustee's position, see Chapter 6 of this book.

[2] Duties of the Trustee

In the rare case of a trustee's appointment to replace the debtor in possession, the trustee will take over control and operate the business. In addition to conducting the debtor's business during reorganization, the trustee is obligated to perform certain functions enumerated in the Bankruptcy Code. The trustee must: [175]

(1) Be accountable for all property received;

---

[172] 124 Cong. Rec. H11100 (daily ed. Sept. 28, 1978). See ¶ 8.14 on the appointment of an examiner.

[173] 11 U.S.C. § 1105.

[174] 11 U.S.C. § 1104(c).

[175] These duties are set forth in 11 U.S.C. §§ 1106(a), which is derived

(2) Examine proofs of claims and object to the allowance of any claim that is improper, if a purpose would be served thereby;
(3) Unless the court orders otherwise, furnish information concerning the estate and its administration which is requested by a party in interest;
(4) File with the court and appropriate taxing agencies periodic reports and summaries of the operation of the business, including statements of receipts and disbursements, and such other information as the court requires;
(5) Make a final report and file a final account of the administration of the estate with the court;[176]
(6) If the debtor has not done so, file the list of creditors, schedules of assets and liabilities, and statement of financial affairs;[177]
(7) Unless the court orders otherwise, investigate the acts, conduct, assets, liabilities, and financial condition of the debtor, the operation of the business, the desirability of the continuance of the business, and any other matter relevant to the case or to the formulation of a plan;
(8) As soon as practicable, file a statement as to any investigation and as to any cause of action available to the estate, and transmit a copy to committees, any indenture trustee or any entity as the court may designate;
(9) As soon as practicable, file a reorganization plan, or recommend conversion of the case to one under chapter 7 or chapter 13 of the Code, or recommend dismissal of the case;
(10) File tax returns which the debtor failed to file, or furnish other required information to tax authorities without the trustee subjecting himself to personal liability; and
(11) After confirmation of a plan, file reports which are necessary or ordered by the court.

In the usual case where a trustee is not appointed, the debtor in possession is obligated to perform all these functions except for the investigatory functions described in (7) and (8) above.[178] In such event,

---

from former B.A. §§ 167, 168, and B. Rules 10-208, 10-212(b), 10-213.

[176] If there is a U.S. Trustee in the jurisdiction, a copy of the final account must be filed with the U.S. Trustee as well as with the court. 11 U.S.C. § 15704.

[177] This is a back-up provision as the primary obligation for filing these documents is with the debtor. 11 U.S.C. § 521(1).

[178] 11 U.S.C. § 1107(a).

these investigatory functions will devolve upon the committees unless an examiner is appointed.[179]

¶ 8.14 APPOINTMENT OF AN EXAMINER

There may be situations when the continuance of present management of the debtor is essential to the successful continuation of the business, while there may also be reasonable cause to suspect possible wrongful conduct. In this situation, and in other situations where it will be in the interest of the parties, the court may appoint an examiner instead of appointing a trustee.[180] The appointment of an examiner is a much less restrictive alternative than the appointment of a trustee because a trustee takes control away from the debtor's current management while the appointment of an examiner leaves the debtor in possession with the exclusive right to file a plan within the 120-day period.[181]

The function of an examiner is investigatory, namely to investigate allegations of fraud, dishonesty, incompetence, misconduct, irregularities in the management of the debtor, and other relevant matters.[182] The examiner's duty is to investigate the conduct, assets, liabilities, financial condition, desirability of the continuance of business, as well as other matters relevant to the case or the formulation of a plan. As soon as is practicable, statements must be filed concerning the investigation, including factual findings concerning the affairs of the debtor and any causes of action the debtor may have against present or past employees or others. These statements, or summaries of them, must be given to committees, any indenture trustee, and to anyone else designated by the court. Although the function of an examiner is limited to investigations, the court does have the power to order an examiner to perform any other function usually performed by a trustee that the court orders the debtor in possession not to perform.[183]

In cases in which the debtor's fixed, liquidated, unsecured debts exceed $5 million, the appointment of an examiner appears to be mandatory if a party requests such appointment and if a trustee is not ap-

---

[179] See ¶¶ 8.12, 8.14.

[180] 11 U.S.C. § 1104(b), derived from former B.A. § 168, which gave the examiner broader powers.

[181] See 11 U.S.C. § 1121(b) and ¶ 8.19[1] for a discussion of the debtor's right to file a plan.

[182] See *In re* Nazareth Fair Grounds and Farmer's Market, Inc., 374 F.2d 595 (2d Cir. 1967), where the court of appeals analyzed the services of an examiner.

[183] 11 U.S.C. § 1106(b).

pointed. However, to determine whether there are $5 million in unsecured debts, those for goods, services, or taxes, and debts owed to an insider are not counted.[184] When the debtor has less than $5 million of unsecured debt, the appointment of an examiner may be made when such appointment would be in the best interests of the parties.[185] Basically, examiners will be appointed in situations where there is need for a thorough investigation, but where the facts do not justify depriving the debtor of possession. It is likely that an examiner will be appointed when a hearing on the appointment of a trustee does not produce evidence sufficient to justify the appointment of a trustee. If the examiner's report reveals evidence of wrongdoing, the court may then appoint a trustee to pursue actions against the wrongdoers on behalf of the debtor.[186] It should be noted that an examiner may not be necessary when committees are conducting their own thorough investigation of the debtor. In any event, an examiner may not be appointed unless the court first conducts a hearing on notice to parties in interest.

When the appointment of an examiner is ordered, the court will appoint a disinterested person to serve.[187] In jurisdictions which have the U.S. Trustee Pilot Program, the U.S. Trustee, after consultation with parties in interest, makes the appointment subject to the court's approval.[188]

¶ 8.15 THE RIGHT TO BE HEARD IN REORGANIZATION CASES: THE ROLE OF THE SEC

The number and various types of interests which can be affected by a reorganization prompted Congress to assure that all persons interested in the case are afforded the right to be heard. Accordingly, the Bankruptcy Code provides that any party in interest, including the debtor, the trustee, a committee, a creditor, an equity security holder, or any indenture trustee, has the right to raise, appear and be heard on any issue in a reorganization case.[189] Thus, even if a party in interest

---

[184] 11 U.S.C. § 1104(b)(2).

[185] 11 U.S.C. § 1104(b)(1).

[186] The Code is unclear as to whether an examiner may be authorized to pursue actions on behalf of the debtor. Former B.A. § 216(13) authorized the appointment of an examiner to enforce actions after confirmation of a plan.

[187] 11 U.S.C. § 1104(c).

[188] 11 U.S.C. § 151104(c).

[189] 11 U.S.C. § 1109(b).

is not directly involved in the particular dispute that is being litigated in the bankruptcy court, the party in interest may be heard.

The Code also provides that the SEC has the right to raise, appear and be heard on any issue in a reorganization case.[190] This is a departure from prior reorganization law, however, in that now the SEC's participation is no longer mandatory in any case. Under Chapter X of the former Act, the SEC was required to examine any reorganization plan and file a report when the corporate debtor had scheduled indebtedness exceeding $3 million and discretion rested with the court to submit such plan to the Commission if the indebtedness was under $3 million.[191] These reports, which had to be distributed to creditors and stockholders, were comprehensive and contained among other data the history of the debtor as well as a valuation of assets.[192]

It is not surprising that such SEC participation was time-consuming and complicated and usually caused substantial delay in the confirmation of a plan. Although SEC participation is no longer mandatory, it can be expected that the agency will still play an active role as a watchdog for shareholders and bondholders in cases involving large publicly held corporations. However, the Bankruptcy Code deprives the SEC of the right to initiate an appeal from any judgment or order of the court.[193] It may, nonetheless, file briefs or otherwise participate in an appeal properly initiated by another party.

¶ 8.16 JOINT ADMINISTRATION AND CONSOLIDATION

The Bankruptcy Code does not permit two or more debtors to file a joint petition for relief unless it is filed by a husband and wife.[194] Nonetheless, when there are several related debtors in reorganization cases, such as a general partner and a partnership entity or a parent corporation and its subsidiaries, it will be convenient to have a joint administration of cases.[195] It must be kept in mind that a joint administration does not affect the substantive rights of creditors, interest holders or other parties. The debtors remain separate entities, although there is a joint handling of purely administrative matters to expedite the cases. For example, one set of applications and orders for several

---

[190] 11 U.S.C. § 1109(a).

[191] Former B.A. §§ 172, 173; B. Rule 10-303.

[192] See B. Rule 10-208(c).

[193] 11 U.S.C. § 1109(a).

[194] 11 U.S.C. § 302(a).

[195] See B. Rules 117(b), 11-14. See ¶ 1.08[3] on joint administration of cases.

debtors bearing a joint caption may be authorized instead of utilizing separate orders for each case. Similarly, the court may appoint one trustee or examiner for related cases.

Joint administration of related cases must be distinguished from consolidation, which is a much more drastic step.[196] When cases are consolidated, the debtors are treated as one entity. A leading case on consolidation, *Chemical Bank New York Trust Co. v. Kheel,*[197] illustrates this point. Two corporations, both owned or controlled by one person, were operated as a single unit with little or no attention paid to formalities usually observed in independent corporations. Officers and directors of both corporations were the same, funds were shifted back and forth between them, loans were made back and forth, borrowings made by one corporation were used to pay debts of the other, and other similar activities justified piercing the corporate veils of these related debtors. The corporations' financial condition and intercompany relationships would have made it extremely time-consuming and expensive to conduct an audit because of the practical disregard of corporate lines. The Court of Appeals for the Second Circuit ordered the consolidation of both debtors over the objection of a creditor, holding that:

> The power to consolidate should be used sparingly because of the possibility of unfair treatment of creditors of a corporate debtor who have dealt solely with that debtor without knowledge of its interrelationship with others. Yet in the rare case such as this, where the interrelationships of the group are hopelessly obscured and the time and expense necessary even to attempt to unscramble them so substantial as to threaten the realization of any net assets for all the creditors, equity is not helpless to reach a rough approximation of justice to some rather than deny any to all.
>
> By the order of consolidation, in effect the intercompany claims of the debtor companies are eliminated, the assets of all debtors are treated as common assets and claims of outside creditors against any of the debtors are treated as against the common fund, eliminating a large number of duplicative claims filed against several debtors by creditors uncertain as to which debtor was eventually liable.[198]

Consolidation may also be achieved by providing for it in a reorga-

---

[196] See B. Rule 117(a).

[197] 369 F.2d 845 (2d Cir. 1966).

[198] *Id.* at 847.

nization plan. In *In re Continental Vending Machine Corporation,*[199] for example, the court approved a reorganization plan under former Chapter X which called for treating the properties of parent and subsidiary corporations on the basis of a merger and consolidation for the purpose of dealing with unsecured claims. The plan provided, however, that secured claims be treated as if there were no merger at all. The plan was upheld as being "fair and equitable" [200] to the creditors.

Consolidation is an important tool in the reorganization process, for as the court of appeals indicated, the benefits include elimination of intercompany claims, guaranties,[201] and duplicative claims filed against several debtors when only one liability exists. Moreover, claims of creditors are considered payable out of a common fund thereby making available a single resource for the funding of a plan where some of the debtors may have insufficient funds for that purpose.[202]

Consolidation and joint administration are available in liquidation and reorganization cases. Because of the growth of conglomerates and the increasing number of interconnected corporations, it is likely that in the future more reorganizations will involve consolidations.

¶ 8.17 CONVERSION OR DISMISSAL OF THE CASE

Let us assume that a debtor in a reorganization case decides reorganization is hopeless and liquidation under chapter 7 of the Bankruptcy Code is the only solution. In that event the Code gives the debtor the absolute right to convert a chapter 11 reorganization case to a chapter 7 case. However, this right exists only if the reorganization case

---

[199] 517 F.2d 997 (2d Cir. 1975), *cert. denied* 424 U.S. 913 (1976). See also *In re* Flora Mir Candy Corp., 432 F.2d 1060 (2d Cir. 1970).

[200] See ¶ 8.23[4] for a discussion of "fair and equitable."

[201] See, *In re* Gulfco Inv. Corp., 593 F.2d 921, 928 (10th Cir. 1979):

> "Once the consolidation has been ordered the subject guarantees, which represent multiple claims, are necessarily eliminated. Therefore, an unsecured creditor has only one claim per transaction to be satisfied from the pooled resource. The court was not authorized to eliminate the guarantees . . . absent compelling equitable reasons for doing so. It would depend on a consolidation as well. . . ."

See also Fisher v. Lee Bros. Value World, Inc., 486 F.2d 1037 (9th Cir. 1973); Rhedom Realty Corp. v. Mammoth Mart, Inc., 397 F. Supp. 381 (D. Mass. 1975).

[202] In instances where there are equities existing in favor of certain creditors, however, the consolidation may occur with an opportunity granted to such creditors to establish such equities. See Stone v. Eacho, 127 F.2d 284, 290 (4th Cir. 1942).

was voluntarily commenced, the debtor remained in possession, and the case had not been previously converted to chapter 11 on somebody else's request.[203] In all other situations, the debtor does not have the right to convert the case but may make a request for conversion to liquidation "for cause." [204]

It does not seem likely that debtors, especially corporations, will apply for conversion except in rare cases. Directors and officers of debtor corporations who are about to throw in the towel and give up on saving the business usually disengage themselves from the venture or show signs of pessimism prior to exercising their right to convert to liquidation. This gives creditors and others an opportunity to request the appointment of a trustee to continue the reorganization where such continuance is in the best interests of the parties. Moreover, the debtor and parties in interest have another alternative to chapter 7, namely, the proposing of a plan of reorganization "which may provide for the sale of all or substantially all of the property of the estate, and the distribution of the proceeds of such sale among holders of claims or interests." [205]

Any party in interest may request that a reorganization case be converted to liquidation or that it be dismissed.[206] The court may convert or dismiss, but must first conduct a hearing on notice and find cause for such action. Whether the court dismisses or converts the case depends on what the court deems to be in the best interests of the creditors and the estate. The court is given wide discretion in converting or dismissing cases as evidenced by the fact that the Code enumerates nine illustrations which would constitute sufficient cause for conversion or dismissal. These situations, which are not exhaustive, are as follows: [207]

(1) Continuing loss to or diminution of the estate and the absence of a reasonable likelihood of rehabilitation;

(2) Inability to effectuate a plan;

---

[203] 11 U.S.C. § 1112(a). Once a case is converted by the debtor to a chapter 7 case, the debtor's right to convert the case again is gone. 11 U.S.C. § 706(a).

[204] 11 U.S.C. § 1112(b).

[205] 11 U.S.C. § 1123(b)(4), which overrules the holding in *In re* Pure Penn. Petroleum Co., 188 F.2d 851 (2d Cir. 1951).

[206] 11 U.S.C. § 1112(b).

[207] These illustrations are mentioned in 11 U.S.C. § 1112(b), which is derived in part from former B.A. §§ 236, 376, and B. Rules 10-308, 11-42. For the role of the SEC on this issue, see ¶ 8.15.

(3) Unreasonable delay by the debtor that is prejudicial to creditors;
(4) Failure to propose a plan of reorganization within any time fixed by the court;
(5) Denial of confirmation of every proposed plan and denial of additional time for filing another plan or a modification of a plan;
(6) Revocation of an order of confirmation which was procured by fraud and denial of confirmation of another plan or a modified plan;
(7) Inability to effectuate substantial consummation of a confirmed plan;
(8) Material default by the debtor with respect to a confirmed plan; and
(9) Termination of a plan by reason of the occurrence of a condition specified in the plan.

In weighing these considerations, the court should consider the position of the committees since its determination must be dictated by the best interests of creditors and estate.[208] Also, it should be understood that generally rehabilitation is to be favored over liquidation.

Despite the court's broad powers to dismiss or convert a case for cause, the Bankruptcy Code prohibits the conversion of a reorganization case to a chapter 7 liquidation if the debtor is a farmer or nonprofit organization, unless the debtor requests the conversion.[209] This prohibition is consistent with the protections afforded farmers and nonprofit organizations against involuntary petitions for liquidation.[210]

When the debtor is an individual who has regular income, a chapter 11 reorganization case may be converted to a chapter 13 case if the debtor requests the conversion and if he did not receive a discharge by confirmation of a chapter 11 plan or if the discharge has been revoked.[211]

Of course, the court may not convert a case to another chapter if the debtor would not be otherwise eligible to obtain relief under such chapter.[212]

---

[208] See *In re* International Swimming Pool Corp., 186 F. Supp. 63 (S.D.N.Y. 1960), where the court gave weight to the position of the creditors' committee opposing a motion for indemnity.

[209] 11 U.S.C. § 1112(c).

[210] See ¶ 2.04[2].

[211] 11 U.S.C. § 1112(d).

[212] 11 U.S.C. § 1112(e).

¶ 8.18 CLAIMS AND INTERESTS: SPECIAL PROTECTIONS FOR PARTIALLY SECURED AND NONRECOURSE CREDITORS

In order to participate in the reorganization as a creditor, it is necessary for a claimant to have an allowed claim. Likewise, equity security holders must have allowed interests to participate in the chapter 11 case.[213] A detailed discussion concerning the filing of proofs of claims and interests, the allowance of claims and interests, secured claims, and priorities among claims is contained in Chapter 5 of this book. The rules discussed in that chapter apply in reorganizations as well as in other bankruptcy cases.

The Bankruptcy Code provides that in a reorganization case a proof of claim or interest "is deemed filed" for any claim or interest which appears in the debtor's schedules filed with the court.[214] Accordingly, it is not necessary for creditors and equity security holders to file any documents to preserve their rights as long as their claims and interests are scheduled properly. Unless an objection is made, these scheduled claims and interests will be allowed automatically. In the usual case, most of the creditors' claims and equity security holders' interests will be accurately scheduled. However, this automatic filing provision does not apply to claims or interests which are scheduled as disputed, contingent or unliquidated. Creditors and equity security holders whose claims or interests are not scheduled, or are scheduled as disputed, contingent or unliquidated, should file proofs of claims or interests to protect their rights.[215] In any event, a creditor who desires to rely on the schedules has the responsibility for determining that its claim is accurately listed.

Classification of claims and interests becomes important when a plan is being formulated. The ways in which a class of creditors may be affected in reorganization and the requirements for the confirmation of a plan will be discussed below.[216]

Chapter 11 provides special protections for certain secured creditors and lienors whose claims exceed the value of their collateral. In general, such creditors are treated as having allowed secured claims equal to the value of the collateral and as having allowed unsecured

---

[213] For example, only persons with allowed claims or interests may accept or reject a reorganization plan. 11 U.S.C. § 1126(a).

[214] 11 U.S.C. § 1111(a), derived from B. Rules 10-401, 12-30.

[215] See 11 U.S.C. §§ 501, 502.

[216] See ¶ 8.23.

claims for the balance of the indebtedness, whether or not the creditor has recourse against the debtor under applicable law or by agreement.[217] In essence, the Code bootstraps the nonrecourse lender into the position of a lender with recourse against the debtor so as to give him an allowed claim to the extent that the face amount of the debt exceeds the present value of the collateral. This protection prevents the debtor in possession from keeping the needed collateral as part of the reorganization plan while buying out the nonrecourse creditor at present collateral value and ignoring the face amount of the debt. This protection does not apply, however, if the collateral is sold by the debtor in possession or trustee or is to be sold under the reorganization plan. Furthermore, this treatment of nonrecourse secured creditors also terminates if the class elects to be treated as fully secured creditors under Section 1111(b)(2).[218]

The partially secured creditor, whether on a recourse or nonrecourse basis, is given greater protection if the class of which the claim is a part elects under Section 1111(b)(2) to be treated as having fully secured claims for reorganization purposes. This election, which requires approval by more than half of the class members in number holding at least two-thirds of the claims in amount, may not be made, however, if the actual collateral is of inconsequential value or, in the case of a recourse creditor, the collateral is sold by the debtor in possession or trustee or is to be sold pursuant to the reorganization plan.[219]

The purpose of these protections for partially secured creditors and nonrecourse lenders is to avoid cramming down a plan against such creditors by paying them current value of the collateral at a time when the market with respect to the collateral is depressed. The reorganization plan may have to treat such creditors based on their entire claim and not on just the portion which is covered by the present value of the collateral. These rules are not intended, however, to increase the rights of partially secured or nonrecourse creditors if the reorganization fails and the estate is liquidated.[220]

The effects of these protections for partially secured and nonrecourse creditors are best understood when considered in connection with the requirements for the confirmation of a reorganization plan.[221]

---

[217] 11 U.S.C. § 1111(b)(1)(A).

[218] *Id.*

[219] 11 U.S.C. §§ 1111(b)(1)(B)(i), 1111(b)(1)(B)(ii).

[220] See 124 Cong. Rec. H11103-05 (daily ed. Sept. 28, 1978).

[221] See ¶ 8.23.

¶ 8.19 PROPOSING THE REORGANIZATION PLAN

[1] Who May File The Plan?

As previously discussed, an underlying premise of the Bankruptcy Code is that the debtor should retain control of the business throughout a reorganization case unless there is cause to replace the debtor in possession. Likewise, the Code is designed to give the debtor in possession control over the future of the business by giving the debtor the *exclusive* right to file a reorganization plan during the 120-day period following the filing of a voluntary petition, or, in an involuntary case, following the order for relief.[222] This 120-day period is designed to give the debtor ample time to formulate a plan by negotiating with creditors and other interested parties, and by predicting the future capacity of the enterprise. Thus, the debtor retains a certain amount of control over the reorganization of the business. In the case of a corporate debtor, this provision gives current management a significant role in shaping the company's future. The debtor may file a plan at any time within the 120-day period. In fact, a plan may be filed with the voluntary petition but generally such filing may be of little value unless the debtor has negotiated before the commencement of the case with creditors and the plan has been approved by the creditors' committee.[223]

The debtor loses this exclusive right to file a plan in any of the following three situations: (1) if a trustee is appointed; (2) if the 120-day period expires and the debtor has not filed a plan; or (3) if the debtor does not file a plan which has been accepted, before 180 days after the order for relief under chapter 11, by each class of claims and interests which is impaired under the plan.[224]

Accordingly, the debtor in possession who files a plan within the 120-day period has an additional sixty days to obtain acceptances from creditors and equity security holders. The Code provides, however, that on request of any party in interest and after notice and a hearing, the court may "for cause" reduce or increase the 120-day or 180-day periods.[225] The purpose of this provision is to give the court flexibility to extend the period in unusually large or complex cases or when credi-

---

[222] 11 U.S.C. § 1121(b). See Sugg. Int. B. Rule 3005(a).

[223] See *In re* N.J.B. Prime Investors, 4 Bankr. Dec. 1219 (S.D.N.Y. 1979) where the court stated: "In an unusual departure from the normal, the debtor's petition was accompanied by its plan. . . ."

[224] 11 U.S.C. § 1121(c). See ¶ 8.19[2][b] for a discussion of "impaired" claims and interests. Compare with the phrase "adversely affected" explained in former B.A. § 107.

[225] 11 U.S.C. § 1121(d). See Sugg. Int. B. Rule 3005(c).

tors cause delay. Also, the court may shorten these periods in small cases or when the debtor is found to be delaying the case unnecessarily. The obtaining of acceptances within the time frame of 180 days after the commencement of the case from each class of claims which is impaired puts a strain upon the debtor to obtain the acceptances of not only the unsecured creditors but secured and stockholder interests as well. In all probability time will be extended where the committee of the principal class of creditors has informally approved the plan within the 120 days.

Once the debtor loses the exclusive right to file a plan, any party in interest may file one. In such a case, the debtor, the trustee, a creditor, an equity security holder, a committee, an indenture trustee, or any other party in interest may file a plan.[226]

[2] Provisions Which Must be in the Plan

Chapter 11 of the Bankruptcy Code requires that certain provisions are to be included in every reorganization plan.[227] These mandatory provisions will be discussed separately.

[a] Designation of Classes

A reorganization plan must designate the classes of claims, except for certain priority claims. Also, the plan must designate the classes of interests. All classifications must be based on the nature of the claims or interests and the members of each class must have claims or interests which are substantially similar to the others in that class.[228] Each secured creditor having a distinct interest in the same property, such as first and second mortgages, will ordinarily be placed in a separate class. All unsecured claims of suppliers of inventory and services may be in one class and unsecured institutional lenders may be placed in another, or since all are general creditors, they may be placed in the same class. Subordinated debenture holders often will constitute a separate class, as will stockholders of the same class of common stock. The plan may, however, designate a separate class consisting of every small unsecured

---

[226] 11 U.S.C. § 1121(c). See Sugg. Int. B. Rule 3005(b) requiring the court to fix a time within which a trustee must file a plan or a report of the reasons why a plan cannot be formulated. If a trustee is appointed, other parties in interest may file a plan before the conclusion of the disclosure statement hearing. See Sugg. Int. B. Rules 3005(b), 3006.

[227] 11 U.S.C. § 1123(a).

[228] 11 U.S.C. § 1122(a).

claim that is less than or reduced to an amount approved by the court as reasonable and necessary for administrative convenience.[229]

[b] Specification of Unimpaired Claims and Interests

The plan must specify the classes of claims or interests which are not impaired by the plan.[230] "Impairment" of claims and interests is new terminology in bankruptcy[231] and is important in determining whether a plan may be confirmed without the consent of certain creditors or interest holders. In essence, acceptance of a plan by unimpaired classes is not required for confirmation.[232]

There are three ways in which a class of claims or interests is left unimpaired by the plan.[233] First, the plan may leave unaltered the legal, equitable, and contractual rights of the creditors or interest holders in that class. Second, despite prior defaults, the claims or interests of the class may be reinstated under the plan by the curing of any defaults other than defaults based on mere bankruptcy or insolvency, by reinstating the original maturity dates which existed prior to default and acceleration, by compensating the creditors or interest holders for damages resulting from their reasonable reliance on contractual provisions or applicable law which gives them the right to accelerate payment, and by not otherwise altering the rights of the creditors or interest holders in that class. The third way of leaving a class unimpaired is to provide in the plan that all members of the class receive on the effective date of the plan cash equal to the allowed amount of each claim of its members; that is, a class is not impaired if it is to be paid immediately 100 cents on the dollar.

It should be kept in mind that a class of nonrecourse creditors or partially secured creditors who elect under Section 1111(b)(2) to be treated as fully secured creditors will be impaired unless the members

---

[229] 11 U.S.C. § 1122(b). See "Commonwealth Oil Files Plan Involving Takeover," N.Y. Times, July 24, 1979, at D3, col. 5, discussing a plan under former Chapter XI which provided for a separate class of general unsecured creditors with claims of $5,000 or less which would be paid fully in cash, while others would receive 46.3 percent in cash, 46.3 percent in common stock valued at $7.20 per share, and 7.4 percent in notes.

[230] 11 U.S.C. § 1123(a)(2).

[231] "Impairment" of claims and interests "differs significantly" from the concept of "materially and adversely affected" used in former B.A. § 107. 124 Cong. Rec. H11103 (daily ed. Sept. 28, 1978).

[232] 11 U.S.C. § 1129(a)(8)(B).

[233] These ways are set forth in 11 U.S.C. § 1124.

of the class receive cash equal to the entire amount of their claims.[234] Therefore, a secured creditor who receives cash equal to the value of the collateral, but less than the total allowed claim, is nevertheless impaired. In the case of security holders, each member of the class must receive a cash payment equal to the greater of any fixed liquidation preference or any fixed redemption price provided for in the stock certificate, bond, or other security instrument. Accordingly, a class of common stockholders may not be left unimpaired by providing for a cash payment because such stock does not usually contain fixed liquidation preferences or redemption prices.

[c] Specification of the Treatment of Impaired Classes

The plan must set forth the treatment of all classes of claims or interests which will be impaired by the plan.[235] A plan may impair any class of claims, whether secured or unsecured, and may alter the rights of any stockholders, bondholders, holders of limited partnership rights, and other interest holders.[236]

[d] Equal Treatment for Class Members

Every reorganization plan must provide for the same treatment for each claim or interest of a particular class, except that creditors or interest holders of a class may agree to be treated less favorably.[237] It is not surprising that each secured creditor is often put in a separate class because of the practical necessity to treat each secured creditor differently depending on the type and value of the collateral and amount of debt owed.

[e] Adequate Means for Execution

The plan must provide for adequate means for its execution. How does the debtor expect to fulfill its obligations to creditors and interest holders as impaired by the plan? How will the business be reconstructed to facilitate rehabilitation? The Bankruptcy Code sets forth the following ten illustrations of such adequate means which serve as

---

[234] See ¶ 8.18.
[235] 11 U.S.C. § 1123(a)(3).
[236] 11 U.S.C. § 1123(b)(1).
[237] 11 U.S.C. § 1123(a)(4).

useful guides and suggestions for those who are formulating a reorganization plan: [238]

(1) Debtor's retention of all or part of the property of the estate;
(2) Transfer of all or any part of the estate's property to other entities, whether organized before or to be organized after confirmation of the plan;
(3) Merger or consolidation of the debtor with one or more other entities;
(4) Sale of property, either subject to or free from liens, or the distribution of property among those who have interests in it;
(5) Satisfaction or modification of any mortgage, security interest or other lien;
(6) Cancellation or modification of any indenture or similar instrument;
(7) Curing or waiver of any default;
(8) Extension of a maturity date or change in the interest rate or other term of outstanding securities;
(9) Amendment of the debtor's charter; or
(10) Issuance of securities of the debtor, or of any entity to which the debtor is to transfer property or with which the debtor is to merge or consolidate, in exchange for cash, property, existing securities, or in exchange for claims or interests, or for any other appropriate purpose.

[f] Required Provisions for Corporate Charters Relating to Voting Rights

A reorganization plan must provide for the inclusion in the debtor's corporate charter of a provision which prohibits the issuance of nonvoting equity securities, and which provides for an appropriate distribution of voting power among the classes which have the right to vote. This requirement also applies with respect to corporations with which the debtor will merge or consolidate or to which the debtor will transfer a substantial part of its property. If there are several classes of equity security holders, and one class has a preference over others with respect to dividends, adequate provisions for the election of directors representing the preferred class in the event of default must be contained in the reorganization plan. The rationale behind these requirements is the

---

[238] These illustrations are set forth in 11 U.S.C. § 1123(a)(5) and are derived from former B.A. § 216 relating to Chapter X of the former Act.

protection of all shareholders who have voting privileges and of those who will be receiving securities as part of the reorganization.[239]

[g] Selection of Officers, Directors, or Trustees

The Code requires that reorganization plans contain only provisions that are consistent with the interests of creditors and equity security holders and with public policy with respect to the manner of selection of officers, directors or trustees under the plan and of any successor officers, directors, or trustees.[240]

[3] Optional Provisions That May Be Included in the Plan

The Bankruptcy Code does not attempt to specify every type of provision which may be contained in a reorganization plan. In fact, Congress expressly provided that the plan may contain any "appropriate provision not inconsistent with the applicable provisions" of the Code.[241]

As discussed above, the plan may alter the rights of any class of creditors whether secured or unsecured. It may reduce the amount of each claim and provide for extensions of maturity dates. Secured creditors may be affected by having their collateral replaced by other property or by receiving newly issued shares of stock in substitution for their claims. These are only a few of the many ways in which the plan may affect creditors. Similarly, the interests of stockholders, partners, bondholders and others may be dealt with by substituting other securities for their present interests or by modifying their rights. However, this does not mean that the treatment of creditors and interest holders is limitless. As we will discuss later, restrictions on the impairment of claims and interests result from the requirements for confirmation of the plan.[242] Also, the proponent of a plan must appreciate the importance of obtaining the support of committees and other interested parties which usually requires serious negotiations with committees and the parties who are affected by the plan.

In addition to the impairment of claims and interests, the Code mentions several other optional provisions which may be contained in a plan:

---

[239] 11 U.S.C. § 1123(a)(6). It is questionable whether this provision is applicable to private closely held corporations where the stock ownership is not to be impaired.

[240] 11 U.S.C. § 1123(a)(7).

[241] 11 U.S.C. § 1123(b)(5).

[242] See ¶ 8.23.

[a] Assumption or Rejection of Executory Contracts and Leases

A reorganization plan may provide for the assumption or rejection of any executory contract or unexpired lease of the debtor which was not previously rejected by the debtor in possession or trustee.[243] These provisions may be extremely important to the debtor's rehabilitation, especially when the debtor is saddled with burdensome executory contracts and unfavorable leases. Equally important is the assumption of profitable leases and contracts.[244] The rights, liabilities, and restrictions relating to the assumption or rejection of executory contracts and leases are the same whether the assumption or rejection is made by a trustee in a liquidation case, before confirmation in a chapter 11 case, or as part of a reorganization plan. A discussion of these rights, liabilities and restrictions is contained in Chapter 7 of this book.

[b] Adjustment or Enforcement of Claims and Interests Belonging to the Debtor

The plan may provide for the settlement, adjustment, or enforcement of any claim or interest which belongs to the debtor or to the estate.[245] For example, the debtor may have a substantial cause of action for breach of contract against a former customer or an antitrust claim against a competitor. A vital part of the reorganization may be a provision to approve a favorable settlement of such claims which will provide needed cash to enable the debtor to reverse its financial condition. Alternatively, the plan may provide for the appointment of an agent or representative to enforce or negotiate a settlement of such claims. Similarly, the plan may provide that property interests belonging to the debtor or the estate are to be retained, adjusted, or enforced.

[c] Sale of Property and Distribution of Proceeds

The plan may provide for the sale of all or substantially all of the property of the estate and the distribution of the proceeds to creditors

---

[243] 11 U.S.C. § 1123(b)(2), derived from former B.A. §§ 216(4), 357(2), 461(4). See also 11 U.S.C. § 365.

[244] Generally, the Code does not permit the enforcement of bankruptcy termination clauses which would prevent the assumption of executory contracts and leases. 11 U.S.C. § 365(e). See ¶ 7.10[7]. Compare *In re* Drake Publishers, Inc., 5 Bankr. Dec. 136 (S.D.N.Y. 1978) where a court held under former Chapter XI that authors were entitled to enforce a bankruptcy termination clause against a publisher-debtor upon the debtor's failure to prove that termination would impede rehabilitation.

[245] 11 U.S.C. § 1123(b)(3).

or interest holders. Accordingly, chapter 11 permits "liquidating plans." [246]

[d] Use and Sale of Nonexempt Assets in Cases Concerning an Individual Debtor

Of course, a reorganization plan may provide for the continued use or the sale or lease of property of the debtor or of the estate. However, the Code prohibits use, sale or lease of property which is exempt in cases in which the debtor is an individual, unless the debtor consents or is the proponent of the plan.[247]

¶ 8.20 REQUIREMENTS FOR DISCLOSURE: THE ADEQUATE INFORMATION HEARING

A major concern of Congress in consolidating the rehabilitation chapters of the former Bankruptcy Act into the new chapter 11 was the creation of an appropriate mechanism for providing all parties in interest with adequate information about the debtor and a proposed plan. A premise which underlies the disclosure provisions of chapter 11 is that creditors and security holders must have certain information prior to the acceptance or rejection of a plan in order to make an informed judgment of their own. However, it is also important that the disclosure mechanism has sufficient flexibility to avoid the time and expense of unnecessary reports and hearings. Congress had both of these needs in mind when it fashioned the new disclosure requirements.[248]

An acceptance or rejection of a plan may not be solicited from any interested party after a reorganization case is commenced unless prior to or at the time of the solicitation the party receives a copy of the plan (or a summary of the plan) together with a written disclosure statement.[249] The disclosure statement must contain "adequate information," which is measured by an extremely flexible standard:

> "Adequate information" means information of a kind, and in sufficient detail, as far as is reasonably practicable in light of the nature and history of the debtor and the condition of the debtor's books and records, that would enable a hypothetical reasonable investor typical of holders of claims or interests of the relevant class to make an informed judgment about the plan.[250]

---

[246] 11 U.S.C. § 1123(b)(4).
[247] 11 U.S.C. § 1123(c).
[248] See H.R. Rep. No. 95-595, 95th Cong., 1st Sess. 226 (1977).
[249] 11 U.S.C. § 1125(b).
[250] 11 U.S.C. § 1125(a)(1).

Accordingly, the amount and type of information required depends, in part, on the condition of the debtor's books. That is a recognition that financially troubled businesses often have inadequate and neglected records. Certified audited financial statements or reconstructed books and records may not be required if their cost and inconveniences outweigh the need for that information under the circumstances of the particular case. Also, the Code bases the disclosure standard on the needs of the hypothetical investor who is "reasonable" and "typical" of the relevant class.[251] An insider would obviously not be the typical hypothetical creditor if the class does not consist of insiders. The amount of disclosure required depends on the sophistication of the members of the relevant class and on their ability to obtain information from other sources.

The Suggested Interim Bankruptcy Rules require that a disclosure statement be filed with the plan or thereafter. If the disclosure statement is not filed with the plan, a time limit for such filing must be set by the court.[252] It is conceivable that, in order to comply with the 120-day exclusive period for filing a plan,[253] a debtor may file the plan within the exclusive period and file a disclosure statement shortly thereafter. However, the limitation of sixty additional days required for obtaining acceptances will require expedition in the filing of the statement so that acceptances may be obtained within such time period.[254]

As a protective measure, the written disclosure statement required to be distributed prior to or with the solicitation of acceptances or rejections must be approved by the court after notice and a hearing.[255] The Suggested Interim Bankruptcy Rules provide that the hearing must be held on at least twenty days' notice to the debtor, creditors, equity security holders, and other parties in interest. Objections to the disclosure statement may be filed and served on the debtor, the trustee, if any, all appointed committees, and any other entity designated by the court, at any time prior to approval of the statement or by an earlier date as the court may fix.[256]

The court will apply the "adequate information" standard to the particular circumstances of the case when determining whether a dis-

---

[251] 11 U.S.C. § 1125(a)(1). See also 11 U.S.C. § 1125(a)(2) for a definition of "investor typical of holders of claims or interests of the relevant class."

[252] Sugg. Int. B. Rule 3005(e).

[253] See 11 U.S.C. § 1121(b) and ¶ 8.19[1].

[254] See 11 U.S.C. § 1121(c)(3) and ¶ 8.19[1].

[255] 11 U.S.C. § 1125(b).

[256] Sugg. Int. B. Rule 3006(a).

closure statement should be approved. Although the court in its discretion may dispense with a valuation of the debtor or an appraisal of the debtor's assets,[257] nevertheless, a valuation or appraisal hearing may be essential in order to establish adequate information. For example, if the plan offers unsecured creditors a 25 percent settlement, such creditors will undoubtedly want to know liquidation value of the estate in order to determine that the proposed plan is in their best interests. Similarly, going concern valuation is essential when a plan provides for the issuance of securities or the amendment or elimination of the rights of stockholders. Although the Code provides that it is not necessary for the court to consider the report of an examiner or trustee prior to approving the disclosure statement,[258] the pursuit of substantial causes of action and their evaluation may constitute an important ingredient in any plan and should be part of the disclosure statement.

Although each member of a particular class of creditors or interest holders must receive the same disclosure statement, different statements may be provided to different classes.[259] Some classes may not need the same amount or kind of information as others. Giving shorter statements to certain classes may save printing and distribution costs. In many cases, however, the extra cost of preparing separate statements may be greater than the cost of distributing the most complete statement to all classes. When different disclosure statements are used, each one must be approved in advance by the court.

The flexibility feature of the chapter 11 disclosure provisions may be destroyed if the debtor in possession or other proponent of a plan will be required to comply with nonbankruptcy securities laws. Section 5 of the Securities Act of 1933,[260] Section 14 of the Securities Exchange Act of 1934,[261] and many state securities laws contain strict rules requiring a proxy statement or prospectus whenever public investors are solicited. The cost of developing such a prospectus or proxy statement can be excessive in a complex case. Such expenses and time-consuming procedures can prevent a reorganization from ever succeeding. In recognition of this problem, Congress balanced the need to protect the public investor with the need to protect creditors' rights in bankruptcy cases.[262]

---

[257] 11 U.S.C. § 1125(b).

[258] See 124 Cong. Rec. H11103 (daily ed. Sept. 28, 1978) wherein Rep. Don Edwards, a sponsor of the Bankruptcy Reform Act (H.R. 8200), pointed out that the examiner's investigation "is to proceed on an independent basis from the procedure of the reorganization under chapter 11."

[259] 11 U.S.C. § 1125(c).

[260] 15 U.S.C. § 77e (1970).

[261] 15 U.S.C. § 78n (1970).

[262] See H.R. Rep. No. 95-595, note 248 *supra*, at 227-229.

The result of this balancing process is two-fold: First, the disclosure statement under chapter 11 need not comply with nonbankruptcy securities laws in order to meet the "adequate information" standard.[263] Information similar to that which is ordinarily contained in a proxy statement or prospectus may be required for the reorganization disclosure statement in complex cases. But, the need for such complex and detailed reports will be determined on a case-by-case basis. Second, the public investor is protected to some degree by requiring a court hearing on the approval of all disclosure statements at which the SEC or any similar federal or state government agency or official may appear and be heard, if it so desires.[264]

In cases involving the restructuring of large public corporations, it is likely that the SEC will play an active role at the disclosure statement hearing. The SEC's role is limited, however, in that it does not have the right to initiate an appeal from any order approving a disclosure statement.[265] In essence, if no interested party is motivated to appeal the decision, the SEC or another government body should not be in a position to prolong the reorganization case. As stated in a congressional report on the Bankruptcy Reform Act, "the patient may die on the operating table while the lawyers are diagnosing,"[266] if extensive delays caused by appeals are permitted. Accordingly, the SEC may not take an appeal from the bankruptcy judge's decision but may be heard on an appeal which is initiated by an interested party.

A person who solicits the acceptance or rejection of a reorganization plan or who participates in the offer, issuance, sale or purchase of securities in connection with a plan is protected by a "safe harbor" provision against potential liability which may arise out of the violation of nonbankruptcy securities laws if an approved disclosure statement is used. As long as the person acts in good faith and in compliance with the Bankruptcy Code, such person will not be liable for securities laws violations.[267] This immunity is necessary to protect creditors, com-

---

[263] 11 U.S.C. § 1125(d).

[264] *Id.*

[265] *Id.*

[266] H.R. Rep. No. 95-595, note 248 *supra*, at 229.

[267] 11 U.S.C. § 1125(e). The Bankruptcy Reform Act codifies Ernst & Ernst v. Hochfelder, 425 U.S. 185 (1976), for solicitations in connection with a bankruptcy reorganization based on court-approved disclosure statements. In *Hochfelder*, the Supreme Court held that the civil liability for damages provided under Section 10(b) of the Securities Exchange Act of 1934 and SEC Rule 10b-5 do not extend to good faith, though negligent, omissions or misstatements in connection with the purchase or sale of securities. See H.R. Rep. No. 95-595, note 248 *supra*, at 229-231.

mittees, attorneys, and others involved in a reorganization case who solicit acceptances or rejections by using a court-approved disclosure statement.[268]

When the court approves the disclosure statement, it must fix a time within which creditors and interest holders may accept or reject the plan and may schedule the hearing on confirmation.[269] The Suggested Interim Bankruptcy Rules require that the clerk of the court[270] mail to all creditors and equity security holders: (1) the plan or a summary of the plan approved by the court; (2) the approved disclosure statement; (3) the opinion or a summary of the opinion of the court, if any, approving the disclosure statement; (4) notice of the date fixed, if any, for the confirmation hearing; and (5) such other information as the court may direct. In addition, notice of the deadline for filing acceptances or rejections of the plan and a form of ballot must be mailed to persons entitled to vote on the plan.[271]

¶ 8.21 ACCEPTANCE OF THE PLAN

After a reorganization plan is filed and the disclosure statement is approved, the proponent of the plan solicits acceptances from creditors and interest holders who are impaired by the plan. Those who oppose the plan may solicit rejections. As we will discuss later, a plan may not be confirmed unless each class has accepted it or, in the event of a cram down situation, at least one class has accepted it.[272]

Any holder of a claim or interest which is allowed in the case may accept or reject a plan.[273] If the United States is a creditor or interest

---

[268] See "S.E.C. Acts to Encourage Forecasting of Earnings," N.Y. Times, June 6, 1979, at D6: "[T]he [SEC] agreed to provide companies with a so-called 'safe harbor' against liability if their projections of revenues or earnings have a 'reasonable basis' and were made 'in good faith.' "

[269] Sugg. Int. B. Rule 3006(c).

[270] The court may, however, require a person other than the clerk of the court to bear responsibility for transmitting these notices. See Sugg. Int. B. Rule 3006(e).

[271] Sugg. Int. B. Rule 3006(d). See Sugg. Int. B. Form No. 21 for the form of ballot which is set forth in Appendix B.

[272] See ¶ 8.23.

[273] 11 U.S.C. § 1126(a). See Chapter 5 *supra* on the allowance of claims and interests. The Suggested Interim Bankruptcy Rules provide that the following entities may accept or reject a plan: (1) a creditor whose claim is deemed allowed pursuant to Section 502 of the Bankruptcy Code; (2) a creditor whose claim has been allowed by the court, even if it has been

holder, the Secretary of the Treasury may accept or reject the plan on its behalf.[274] A creditor whose claim has been allowed in part as a secured claim and in part as an unsecured claim may accept or reject a plan in both capacities.[275] If more than one plan is transmitted for a vote, an acceptance or rejection may be filed by each entity entitled to accept or reject for any number of such plans and, if acceptances are filed for more than one plan, the creditor or interest holder may indicate a preference among the plans.[276] The court may permit a creditor or equity security holder to change or withdraw an acceptance or rejection, but only for cause shown and within the time limit set by the court for accepting or rejecting the plan.[277]

Let us assume that a debtor proposed an out-of-court arrangement plan to creditors and obtained acceptances prior to filing a reorganization petition. Later, the debtor files a chapter 11 petition and files the same plan. Will the acceptances obtained prior to commencement of the chapter 11 case be considered as acceptances in the case? The Bankruptcy Code provides that acceptances or rejections obtained prior to the case are effective for chapter 11 purposes, but only if the prepetition solicitation of the acceptances or rejections complies with applicable nonbankruptcy law governing the adequacy of disclosure or, if no such law exists, the information distributed prior to or with the solicitation meets the "adequate information" standard of chapter 11.[278] For this reason, debtors who attempt to work out arrangements with creditors prior to filing a petition for reorganization are advised to take extreme care in meeting bankruptcy and nonbankruptcy disclosure standards.[279]

---

allowed temporarily for the limited purpose of voting on the plan; (3) a creditor who is a security holder of record at the date the order approving the disclosure statement is entered whose claim has not been disallowed; and (4) an equity security holder of record at the date the order approving the disclosure statement is entered whose interest has not been disallowed. Sugg. Int. B. Rule 3007(a). See Sugg. Int. B. Form No. 21, set forth in Appendix B, for the form of a ballot for accepting or rejecting a plan.

[274] 11 U.S.C. § 1126(a).

[275] Sugg. Int. B. Rule 3007(d).

[276] Sugg. Int. B. Rule 3007(c).

[277] Sugg. Int. B. Rule 3007(a).

[278] 11 U.S.C. § 1126(b).

[279] See Sugg. Int. B. Rule 3007(b) which provides, in part, that a prepetition acceptance or rejection may not be effective if the court finds, after a hearing on notice, that the plan was not generally transmitted to creditors and equity security holders or that an unreasonably short time was prescribed for parties to accept or reject the plan.

In order to obtain the acceptance of a class, it is necessary to receive a sufficient number of acceptances based on a required percentage of members. In regard to creditor classes, the plan is deemed accepted by a class if the members who hold at least two-thirds in amount and more than one-half in number of the total allowed claims of the class who vote accept.[280] A plan is deemed accepted by a class of stockholders or other interest holders if it is accepted by the members who hold at least two-thirds in amount of the total allowed interests held by the members of the class who vote.[281] It is important to note that only those members who vote to accept or reject the plan are counted as class members for this purpose. For example, assume that there are 1,000 members of a creditor class with total claims worth $10,000,000. Assume further that 750 members with total allowed claims of $7,500,000 vote to either accept or reject while the remaining 250 members do not vote. For the class to accept the plan, it must be accepted by at least 376 members (more than one-half of those who vote) who hold at least $5,000,000 in allowed claims (two-thirds in amount of the claims held by those who vote). If there is a class of stockholders who collectively hold 1,000 shares of common stock, and the holders of 500 shares vote to either accept or reject, the plan is deemed accepted by the class if the holders of at least 334 shares vote to accept it.

Despite the number of acceptances, however, the court has the power to disqualify any members of a class whose acceptance or rejection is not in good faith, is not solicited or procured in good faith, or is in violation of any provision of the bankruptcy laws. Such disqualification may be made on the request of any party in interest, but only after a hearing on notice.[282] The effect on this designation is to eliminate the objectionable claimant as a member of the relevant class for the purpose of determining whether the class accepts the plan. Also,

---

[280] 11 U.S.C. § 1126(c). Compare with former Chapter X which required acceptance by two-thirds based on the amount of claims filed and allowed in each class regardless of the number of creditors. Former B.A. § 179. See also Section 362(1) of the former Act which required acceptance by a simple majority in number of creditors and amount of filed and allowed claims of each class in Chapter XI cases. Compare B. Rules 10-305(e) and 12-37(d) which provided that the filing of an acceptance or rejection under former Chapter X or XII constituted the filing of a proof of claim or interest for the purpose of computing majorities.

[281] 11 U.S.C. § 1126(d). See former B.A. § 179 which required acceptance by the holders of a simple majority of the stock of each class.

[282] 11 U.S.C. § 1126(e), derived from former B.A. § 203. See also, B. Rule 10-305(d).

the court has the power to designate the exclusion of a claim for voting purposes based on a conflict of interest, such as a person who holds several claims or interests and is a member of several classes.[283]

The Code contains two provisions which make it unnecessary to solicit acceptances or rejections from certain classes. First, if a class is not impaired under a plan, it is deemed to have accepted the plan automatically.[284] Second, if the plan provides for no compensation or payment whatsoever to the members of a particular class, the relevant class is deemed to have rejected the plan regardless of how the members actually vote,[285] in which event the cram down method of confirmation would have to be employed.[286]

¶ 8.22 MODIFICATIONS OF THE PLAN

After the filing of a plan, court approval of the disclosure statement, and solicitation of acceptances, the proponent of the plan may realize that modification will be necessary in order to obtain the required acceptances to permit confirmation. It is not uncommon, therefore, for plans to be modified after they are filed but before confirmation.

The proponent of a plan has the right to modify it at any time prior to confirmation. The old plan as modified becomes the new plan as soon as the proponent files the modification with the court. No hearing or court approval is necessary for the filing of a modification.[287]

After the filing of a modification, the proponent must distribute a court-approved disclosure statement containing adequate information concerning the plan as modified.[288] The type and amount of information which is required to be submitted in the disclosure statement will depend on the particular case. A slight modification may require only minimal information or no information at all if a disclosure statement about the original plan was previously distributed. The court will set a

---

[283] The purpose of this section is to overrule in bankruptcy situations such cases as Aladdin Hotel Co. v. Bloom, 200 F.2d 627 (8th Cir. 1953), a nonbankruptcy case in which the court permitted bondholders, who were also the controlling stockholders, to vote for a plan extending the maturity dates of bonds to the detriment of a minority of bondholders. See H.R. Rep. No. 95-595, 95th Cong., 1st Sess. 411 (1977).

[284] 11 U.S.C. § 1126(f).

[285] 11 U.S.C. § 1126(g).

[286] See 11 U.S.C. § 1129(b) and ¶ 8.23[3].

[287] 11 U.S.C. § 1127(a).

[288] 11 U.S.C. § 1127(c). It is questionable whether such disclosure must be made to parties not affected by the modification who had already accepted the plan. See B. Rules 10-306 and 11-39.

time limit before which any member of a class who voted for the plan prior to the modification may change such vote. Those persons who vote to accept or reject prior to the modification and who do not change their votes within the time limit set by the court will be held to their original votes.[289] This procedure avoids the time and expense of soliciting new votes from every creditor and interest holder.

It should be noted that only a proponent of the plan has the right to file a modification prior to confirmation.[290] Other interested parties who desire to modify the plan must file their own competing plans subject to the rules dealing with the 120-day and 180-day exclusive periods reserved for the debtor to file a plan and to obtain acceptances.[291]

In appropriate situations, it is even possible for a plan to be modified after confirmation. The Bankruptcy Code permits such modification but only if certain requirements are met.[292] First, the plan may not be modified after "substantial consummation." A plan becomes substantially consummated upon the transfer of all or substantially all of the property to be transferred under the plan, the assumption by the debtor or a successor of the business or of the management of substantially all of the property dealt with in the plan, and the commencement of distribution under the plan.[293] When the plan is substantially consummated, the court may not permit modification. Second, the classification of parties and the contents of the plan as modified must conform to the requirements for all plans under chapter 11. Third, only the proponent of the plan or the reorganized debtor has the right to seek a modification after confirmation. Fourth, the modified plan becomes effective only if the court, after notice and a hearing, confirms it in accordance with the voting and other confirmation requirements of chapter 11. Before confirming the plan as modified the court must find that circumstances warrant the modification. Also, the proponent must distribute judicially approved disclosure statements containing adequate information about the modification, and creditors and interest holders must be given an opportunity to change their previous votes before the court confirms the plan as modified.[294]

---

[289] 11 U.S.C. § 1127(d), derived from B. Rule 10-306(b).

[290] 11 U.S.C. § 1127(a).

[291] See 11 U.S.C. § 1121(c) and ¶ 8.19[1].

[292] 11 U.S.C. § 1127(b).

[293] 11 U.S.C. § 1101(2), derived from former B.A. § 229(a) and B. Rule 10-306(c)(2).

[294] 11 U.S.C. §§ 1127(c), 1127(d).

¶ 8.23 CONFIRMATION OF THE PLAN

[1] The Confirmation Hearing

The objective in a reorganization case is the confirmation of the plan. The court may consider the confirmation of a plan only after a hearing on notice.[295] Any party, including a creditor, stockholder, committee, debtor, indenture trustee, or the SEC has the right to object to the confirmation of a plan.[296]

There are two ways that a plan may qualify for confirmation. The first road to confirmation is by obtaining the acceptances of every class which is impaired by the plan. The second way is commonly referred to as the "cram down" method because it permits the court to confirm a plan despite the rejection of an impaired class of creditors or equity security holders. In essence, the plan may be crammed down non-assenting classes as long as there is at least one assenting class. Whether the proponents of a plan seek to obtain confirmation by the acceptance method or by the cram down method, there are several requirements which must be satisfied before the court will confirm a plan.

If more than one plan is proposed which meets the requirements for confirmation, the court is directed by the Code to confirm only one plan after considering the preferences of creditors and equity security holders.[297] This consideration would undoubtedly weigh heavily in favor of the plan which all classes accept rather than a plan which would require a cram down confirmation.

[2] Requirements for Confirmation: The Acceptance Method

The Code sets forth twelve requirements which must be met in

---

[295] 11 U.S.C. § 1128(a). See Sugg. Int. B. Rule 3008(a)(2) dealing with the hearing on confirmation.

[296] 11 U.S.C. §§ 1128(b), 1109. See Sugg. Int. B. Rule 3008(a)(1) on objections to confirmation. See also B. Rule 914 which applies to objections to confirmation.

[297] 11 U.S.C. § 1129(c). Of course, this rule does not prohibit the confirmation of a plan after a prior confirmation is revoked because of fraud. It also does not prevent modification of a plan after confirmation. See 11 U.S.C. § 1127(b). See also *In re* Hartsdale Assocs., 3 Bankr. Dec. 1137 (S.D.N.Y. 1977), where the court measured two competing plans filed under former Chapter XII and accepted the debtor's plan instead of the trustee's plan; *In re* Imperial "400" Nat'l, Inc., 374 F. Supp. 949 (D.N.J. 1974), where the court analyzed four plans proposed under former Chapter X, applying the fair and equitable test.

order for the court to confirm a plan by the acceptance method.[298] Each requirement will be discussed separately.

(1) The plan must comply with all of the applicable provisions of chapter 11. Classification of classes must be proper and the plan must contain those provisions required by the Code.[299]

(2) The proponent of the plan must comply with all of the applicable provisions of chapter 11.[300] Probably the most important requirement relates to the disclosure of information prior to or together with solicitation of acceptances.[301]

(3) The plan must have been proposed in good faith and in accordance with the law. Good faith is not defined in the Code but would appear to be related to the phrase "in accordance with the law." The commission of a bankruptcy crime by the proponent of the plan, such as the concealment of assets or the making of a false oath, may prevent confirmation.[302]

(4) The court may not confirm the plan unless certain protective measures are taken in connection with fees paid or to be paid for expenses relating to the reorganization case. Any payment for services, costs or expenses in connection with the reorganization case which is made or promised by the debtor, the proponent of the plan, or by any person issuing securities or acquiring property under the plan, must have been disclosed to the court. Also, such payments already made must have been reasonable and the payments which are to be fixed after confirmation must be subject to the court's approval on the basis of reasonableness.[303]

(5) The proponent of the plan must have disclosed the identity and affiliations of any person who is proposed to serve as a postconfirmation director, officer or voting trustee of the reorganized debtor, of the debtor's successor, or of an affiliated business participating in a joint plan. The court must be satisfied that the appointment or continued service of such person is consistent with the interests of creditors and equity holders and with public policy. This requirement gives the court the power to make judgments concerning the competence, honesty, and

---

[298] Eleven of the requirements are set forth in 11 U.S.C. § 1129(a), which is derived from former B.A. § 221. The other requirement is contained in 11 U.S.C. § 1129(d), which is derived from former B.A. § 269.

[299] 11 U.S.C. § 1129(a)(1). See 11 U.S.C. § 1123(a).

[300] 11 U.S.C. § 1129(a)(2).

[301] See 11 U.S.C. § 1125.

[302] 11 U.S.C. § 1129(a)(3). See 18 U.S.C. § 152, as amended by Title III Section 314(c) of the Bankruptcy Reform Act.

[303] 11 U.S.C. § 1129(a)(4), derived from former B.A. § 221(4).

experience of those who will be at the helm of the reorganized venture. If the court is not satisfied with the proposed appointments it will in all probability refuse to confirm the plan. Likewise, the proponent is required to disclose the identity of any insider who will be employed or retained by the reorganized debtor and the nature of any compensation paid or to be paid to him.[304]

(6) If there is a regulatory commission which has jurisdiction over the rates of the reorganized debtor, the plan may not be confirmed unless the commission approves any rate change provided for in the plan or, in the alternative, the plan provides that any rate change is expressly conditioned on commission approval.[305]

(7) In enacting the Bankruptcy Code, Congress wanted to be certain that a nonconsenting creditor or equity interest holder was not adversely affected by the reorganization of a debtor which might give such person less than the person would receive if the debtor were liquidated. Accordingly, chapter 11 contains a minimum financial standard, often referred to as the "best interests of creditors" standard, which must be met in order to obtain confirmation.[306] Specifically, the plan may be confirmed only if, with respect to each class of creditors or interest holders, each and every class member has accepted the plan or, in the alternative, each class member will receive or retain under the plan money or property of a value, as of the effective date of the plan, which is not less than the amount which the class member will receive or retain in a liquidation case. Accordingly, every nonassenting creditor and interest holder should receive at least as much cash or property as if a chapter 7 liquidation had taken place.

There are several points to consider about this seventh requirement for confirmation. First, every member of a class must assent to the plan in order to exempt the relevant class from the minimum financial standard.[307] Thus, if ninety-nine percent of the class votes to accept the plan, and one percent either rejects or refrains from voting, the *entire* class must receive at least as much as it would receive in a liquidation case. Second, for the court to determine whether this minimum financial standard is met, it is necessary to determine the value of the assets and

---

[304] 11 U.S.C. § 1129(a)(5). See 11 U.S.C. § 101(25) for a definition of "insider."

[305] 11 U.S.C. § 1129(a)(6).

[306] 11 U.S.C. § 1129(a)(7). This standard derives from Section 366(2) of former Chapter XI. See *In re* Gilchrist Co., 410 F. Supp. 1070, 1075 (E.D. Pa. 1976) for an application of the "best interests of creditors" test under former Chapter XI.

[307] 11 U.S.C. § 1129(a)(7)(A)(i).

to make a hypothetical distribution in liquidation. The court will have to consider priority claims as well as subordination provisions of chapter 11.[308] Third, the *present* value of the distribution to the creditors or interest holders under the plan must be as much as a hypothetical liquidation dividend.[309] Accordingly, if a creditor will receive $10,000 in a liquidation, the reorganization plan may not give the creditor $10,000 to be paid in future installments unless there is a discount of the interest on the installments so that the present value of the deferred cash installments is at least $10,000.[310]

A special rule is contained in chapter 11 with respect to members of secured creditor classes who make a Section 1111(b)(2) election. The reader will recall that a class of secured creditors with collateral worth less than the amount of their claims, thereby being partially secured creditors, may elect to have their entire allowed claims treated as fully secured, even if they have nonrecourse claims.[311] With respect to a class which makes a Section 1111(b)(2) election, each member must receive or retain under the plan money or property of a value, as of the effective date of the plan, which is not less than the value of the collateral which is the subject of the member's security interest.[312] The effect of this rule is that secured creditors who elect to be treated as having fully secured claims under Section 1111(b)(2) are not covered by the "best interests of creditors" standard. For example, if a creditor has a $10,000 claim secured by collateral worth $7,000 in a liquidation case, such creditor will receive $7,000 plus a pro rata share of the estate based on the unsecured deficiency of $3,000. Nonetheless, the chapter 11 plan may provide the creditor with payments having a present value of $7,000 only, thereby depriving the creditor of the pro rata share on the unsecured deficiency. On the other hand, if the secured creditor class did not elect under Section 1111(b)(2), all members will have to receive an amount equal to the value of the collateral plus the pro rata share, if any, based on the deficiency which would be made in a liquidation case.

The rationale for depriving Section 1111(b)(2) creditors of the

---

[308] See 11 U.S.C. §§ 510, 726 and ¶ 5.14, with respect to subordination of claims.

[309] 11 U.S.C. § 1129(a)(7)(A)(ii).

[310] See Klee, "All You Ever Wanted To Know About Cram Down Under the New Bankruptcy Code," 53 Am. Bankr. L.J. 133 (1979), for a series of examples utilizing a discount factor so as to equate deferred cash payments with present values.

[311] See ¶ 8.18.

[312] 11 U.S.C. § 1129(a)(7)(B).

minimum liquidation standard in chapter 11 cases with respect to the unsecured portions of their claims is that they have elected to be treated as if their entire claims are fully secured and, therefore, it is logically consistent to treat them as if they have no deficiency at all. Such creditors choose to have a lien securing the full amount of their allowed claims so that if the value of the collateral increases after the plan is confirmed, the future payments to be made under the plan will be secured. In essence, if the class as a whole assents to the plan and elects to be treated as fully secured under Section 1111(b)(2), a nonassenting member of the class is deprived of the right to receive an amount equal to the liquidation dividend to the extent of a deficiency claim. This will not present a problem, however, because it is unlikely that a secured creditor class will make a Section 1111(b)(2) election and also assent to a plan which gives each member less than will otherwise be received in liquidation. If the plan provides for such unfavorable treatment, the class wili probably reject the plan and will have to be treated more favorably in a cram down situation.[313]

(8) In order to obtain confirmation by the acceptance method, it is necessary for each class of creditors or interest holders which is impaired under the plan to accept it.[314] Again, it is not necessary to have every member of each impaired class vote to accept, as long as the required percentages of acceptances are voted.[315] The acceptance of unimpaired classes is not required because the plan does not affect their rights. If any impaired class fails to accept the plan, either confirmation will be denied or the proponent of the plan will seek confirmation by the cram down method as to this class.

(9) The plan must contain certain provisions which protect priority creditors who have not expressly agreed to a particular treatment. First, administrative expenses, court fees and charges assessed against the estate, and unsecured claims arising in the ordinary course of the debtor's business after the commencement of an involuntary case but before the order for relief or appointment of a trustee, must be paid in full in cash on the effective date of the plan.[316] Such claimants are not required to accept deferred payments or property in lieu of cash, even if they are dissenting members of a class which has accepted the plan. This protection is needed to encourage persons to do business with the

---

[313] A further discussion on the benefits of a Section 1111(b)(2) election is contained in ¶ 8.18.

[314] 11 U.S.C. § 1129(a)(8).

[315] See ¶ 8.21 for a discussion of the percentage requirements for acceptance by a class.

[316] 11 U.S.C. § 1129(a)(9)(A). See 11 U.S.C. §§ 507(a)(1), 507(a)(2).

debtor despite the fact that the debtor is the subject of a reorganization and to assure that court fees and charges are paid.

Second, the allowed unsecured claims for wages, salaries, commissions, contributions to employee benefit plans, and for claims arising out of consumer deposits, to the extent that such claims are entitled to priority in distribution, must be paid in cash. If such claims are held by members of a class which has accepted the plan, the plan may provide for deferred cash payments which, when discounted to determine the present value of such payments, equal the full amount of the allowed priority claims. If the claims are held by members of a class which has not accepted the plan, the priority claims must be paid in full on the effective date of the plan. Property or securities may not be substituted for cash with respect to these claims. Of course, if a member of the priority class agrees to accept lesser payments, this requirement does not apply with respect to that particular creditor.[317]

Third, the government bodies that hold allowed unsecured tax claims entitled to priority must receive deferred cash payments which have a present value on the effective date of the plan equal to the full amount of their respective tax claims. Notwithstanding their priority status, the payments may be deferred, but not for a period of more than six years after the date of the assessment of the relative tax claim.[318]

(10) A plan may not be confirmed unless at least one class of claims has accepted it, but any claims held by insiders are not included for determining the number and amount of acceptances for this purpose. Accordingly, the acceptance of at least one class, excluding the members who are so closely connected with the debtor that their votes may have been cast without objectivity, is required for confirmation.[319] A class which is not impaired is deemed to have accepted the plan and, therefore, satisfies this requirement.[320]

(11) Another requirement for confirmation relates to the likelihood of success of the reorganization. It is intended that only plans which are feasible and likely to succeed shall be confirmed. If the court

---

[317] 11 U.S.C. § 1129(a)(9)(B). See 11 U.S.C. §§ 507(a)(3), 507(a)(4), 507(a)(5).

[318] 11 U.S.C. § 1129(a)(9)(C). See 11 U.S.C. § 507(a)(6). Tax liens are treated the same as secured claims for purposes of confirmation requirements. See 11 U.S.C. § 506(a).

[319] 11 U.S.C. § 1129(a)(10). This provision is designed to codify the holdings in Gardens of Cortez v. John Hancock Mutual Life Ins. Co., 585 F.2d 975 (10th Cir. 1978) and Meyer v. Rowen, 195 F.2d 263 (10th Cir. 1952), and to reject the holding in *In re* Marietta Cobb Apartments Co., 3 Bankr. Dec. 720 (S.D.N.Y. 1970).

[320] See 11 U.S.C. § 1126(f).

finds that confirmation of the plan will probably be followed by either liquidation or the need for further financial reorganization of the debtor or any successor to the debtor, it may not confirm.[321] This requirement does not apply, however, with respect to liquidation and further reorganization which are provided for in the plan itself. Therefore, a liquidating plan may be confirmed in a chapter 11 case.[322]

(12) The final requirement for confirmation relates to the primary purpose of the plan. A plan may not be confirmed if its principal purpose is the avoidance of taxes.[323] Likewise, if the principal purpose of the plan is to avoid the requirements of Section 5 of the Securities Act of 1933 relating to disclosure, the plan may not be confirmed.[324] However, it is important to note that only a governmental unit that is an interested party may object to confirmation on these grounds.

[3] Requirements for Confirmation: The Cram Down Method

In the event that any class of claims or interests which is impaired under the plan fails to accept it by the minimum percentage of votes,[325] the proponent of the plan may request confirmation by an alternative method commonly called the "cram down." The following requirements for confirming a plan by the cram down method are designed to make sure that dissenting classes are treated fairly.

(1) The plan may not be confirmed under the cram down method unless eleven of the twelve requirements discussed above with respect to confirmation by the acceptance method are satisfied. The only requirement which need not be met is the acceptance of all impaired classes, which is listed above as the eighth requirement.[326] Accordingly,

---

[321] 11 U.S.C. § 1129(a)(11), which derives from Section 366(2) of former Chapter XI. See United Properties, Inc. v. Emporium Dep't Stores, Inc., 379 F.2d 55 (8th Cir. 1967), in which confirmation of a plan of arrangement was reversed on appeal because it was not feasible. The appellate court focused on the following facts: (1) the ratio of current assets to current liabilities was less than two to one, (2) the solvency of the debtor was questionable, (3) evidence failed to establish that the debtor could operate at a profit, and (4) the cash flow was inadequate.

[322] See 11 U.S.C. § 1123(b)(4) which expressly allows a plan to provide for the sale of all or substantially all of the property of the estate. See ¶ 8.19[3][c].

[323] 11 U.S.C. § 1129(d). See 11 U.S.C. §§ 346, 1146 for special tax provisions which assist reorganized debtors.

[324] 11 U.S.C. § 1129(d). See 15 U.S.C. § 77(e) and 11 U.S.C. § 1145.

[325] See 11 U.S.C. § 1126 and ¶ 8.21.

[326] 11 U.S.C. § 1129(b)(1).

the plan and its proponent must comply with the provisions of chapter 11, the plan must be proposed in good faith and within the bounds of the law, fees paid in connection with the case must be disclosed and be reasonable, certain disclosures and approval with respect to post-confirmation personnel are required, rates must be approved by governing regulatory commissions, provisions for cash payments to certain priority creditors must be set forth in the plan, and the plan must be likely to succeed in rehabilitating the debtor. Also, the plan may not be confirmed over the objection of a government body if its principal purpose is to avoid taxes or securities laws. Most importantly, at least one class of creditors must accept the plan, excluding insiders for this purpose, so as to prevent the cram down of a plan without at least some acceptance. Additionally, the minimum financial standard commonly referred to as the "best interests of creditors" test is applicable in cram down cases to assure that all dissenting creditors and interest holders, except for secured parties who are in a class that made a Section 1111(b)(2) election, will receive in a reorganization case at least as much money or property as they will receive in liquidation. These requirements are discussed more fully above.

(2) The court may not confirm a plan by the cram down method unless the proponent of the plan so requests.[327] For example, if the proponent seeks confirmation by the acceptance method, but the court finds that one class has failed to accept it, the court may not rewrite the plan to comply with the cram down requirements and confirm; it must deny confirmation and the proponent must make the necessary changes in the plan prior to requesting a cram down confirmation.

(3) The plan may not "discriminate unfairly" with respect to each impaired class of creditors or interest holders that do not accept the plan.[328] The essence of this requirement is that a dissenting class must be treated equally with respect to other classes of equal rank. A dissenting class of unsecured creditors is treated fairly as long as it receives an amount equal to its pro rata share of the total consideration which is to be given to all classes of the same rank, subject to the effects of any subordination agreements between members of the dissenting class and members of another class of equal rank.

This point is too complex to leave without an illustration.[329] Assume that there are three classes of unsecured creditors. Class *A* is

---

[327] *Id.*

[328] *Id.*

[329] This illustration is a variation of one contained in the House of Representatives' report on the bankruptcy reform bill. See H.R. Rep. No. 95-595, 95th Cong., 1st Sess., 416, 417 (1977).

composed of trade creditors, Class *B* is composed of creditors who have agreed to subordinate their claims, and Class *C* is composed of the senior creditors to whom the creditors of Class *B* subordinated their claims. Accordingly, there are trade creditors, junior creditors, and senior creditors, all of whom are unsecured. Suppose further that each class has allowed claims of $100,000 and that the class of trade creditors is the only class that did not accept the proposed plan. If the plan proposes to pay $15,000 to trade creditors, $30,000 to senior creditors, and nothing to junior creditors, the plan will not discriminate unfairly against the trade creditors because they have one-third of the unsecured claims and will receive one-third of the compensation paid to unsecured creditors. Even if the senior creditors of Class *C* receive $25,000 and junior creditors of Class *B* receive $5,000, the trade creditors will not be discriminated against because trade creditors will be receiving $15,000 in either event.

Assume that the plan proposes to pay Class *A* trade creditors $15,000, the Class *B* junior creditors $0, and the Class *C* senior creditors $25,000, and that the senior creditors do not accept the plan. Does the plan discriminate unfairly against the senior creditors? Even though the trade creditors receive less than the senior creditors, the senior creditors are discriminated against because they are entitled to the rights of the subordinated creditors of Class *B* and, accordingly, they must receive two-thirds of the distribution paid to unsecured creditors. Since the plan proposes to pay senior creditors only $25,000 of the total $45,000 distribution to unsecured creditors, the plan may not be confirmed without the acceptance of Class *C* senior creditors.

(4) The final requirement for "cramming down" a plan despite nonacceptance of an impaired class is that the plan will be "fair and equitable" with respect to each dissenting class. The fair and equitable standard is discussed in the following section.

[4] The Fair and Equitable Standard in Cram Down Cases

A plan may not be confirmed over the dissent of an impaired class of creditors or interest holders unless it is "fair and equitable" with respect to the dissenting class.[330] The phrase "fair and equitable" was used in Chapter X of the former Bankruptcy Act and has been construed by the courts as requiring absolute priority among classes ac-

---

[330] 11 U.S.C. § 1129(b)(1).

cording to their rank.[331] Thus, it is not surprising that the fair and equitable standard is often referred to as the "absolute priority rule."[332] In essence, a plan is "fair and equitable" with respect to an impaired class when that class will receive full compensation for its allowed claims before any junior class receives anything. In addition, a plan is not "fair and equitable" if a class which is senior to a dissenting class receives more than 100 percent of the amount of its claim.

It should be kept in mind that the fair and equitable standard applies only with respect to classes that do not accept the plan. Thus, if all classes accept the plan there is no need to consider this standard at all. Also, senior classes that accept the plan have no right to object to confirmation on the ground that junior classes will receive value while the senior class will not be paid in full. Accordingly, this standard will be applied by focusing on the highest ranked dissenting class and on all classes junior to it, as long as no senior class is receiving more than 100 percent of its claims.[333]

The Bankruptcy Code contains guidelines for the application of the fair and equitable standard to secured creditors, unsecured creditors, and interest holders.

[a] Secured Creditors

A plan is fair and equitable with respect to a dissenting class of secured creditors if any one of three alternative conditions is satisfied.

The first alternative way to satisfy this standard is to provide that class members retain their security interests, whether the collateral is kept or is transferred by the debtor, to the extent of their allowed secured claims *and* to give each secured creditor in the class deferred cash payments which aggregate to at least the amount of the allowed secured claim and which have a present value equal to the value of the collateral.[334]

This standard is complicated by the application of Section 1111

---

[331] Former B.A. § 221(2). "Fair and equitable" became "words of art" having a special meaning in reorganization cases. See Case v. Los Angeles Lumber Prods. Co., 308 U.S. 106 (1939) and SEC v. United States Realty & Improvement Co., 310 U.S. 434 (1940).

[332] See Blum & Kaplan, "The Absolute Priority Doctrine in Corporate Reorganizations," 41 U. Chi. L. Rev. 651 (1974).

[333] This represents a departure from the fair and equitable standard in former Chapter X, which required absolute priority for all classes regardless of acceptance.

[334] 11 U.S.C. § 1129(b)(A)(i).

(b)(2) of the Code.[335] The meaning of "allowed secured claim" as used in the previous paragraph will depend on whether the secured class makes a Section 1111(b)(2) election to be treated as fully secured despite the fact that the collateral may be worth less than the amount of the claim. For example, assume that a creditor loaned $15,000,000 to a debtor secured by real estate worth $18,000,000 and the value of the real estate has dropped to $12,000,000 by the date when the debtor filed a chapter 11 petition. If the creditor is alone in a class, makes a Section 1111(b)(2) election, and does not accept the plan, the plan will be fair and equitable with respect to the secured creditor if it provides that the mortgage lien will remain on the land to secure the entire $15,000,000 debt, the face amount of deferred cash payments to be made are at least $15,000,000, and the present value of the present or deferred payments is at least $12,000,000. Because of the Section 1111 (b)(2) election, the entire $15,000,000 claim is deemed secured and must be paid in full eventually despite the $12,000,000 value of the collateral.

It is easy to see that the Bankruptcy Code is designed to prevent the debtor from buying off the partially secured creditor by reducing the claim to the value of the collateral. In order to determine the present value of cash payments, the court must take into account the prevailing interest and discount rates. If the secured creditor does not elect under Section 1111(b)(2), such creditor will not be entitled to the full $15,000,000 in cash payments because the total allowed secured claim will be only $12,000,000 and the creditor would be treated as having an unsecured claim to the extent of $3,000,000.[336] Also, to the extent that the deferred cash payments exceed $12,000,000, such a nonelecting creditor will be unsecured in the event of a future default.[337]

A second alternative for complying with the fair and equitable standard with respect to a class of dissenting secured creditors is for the plan to provide for the realization of the "indubitable equivalent" of their secured claims.[338] Whether or not the secured creditor class makes a Section 1111(b)(2) election, the abandonment of the collateral to the creditors or giving them a lien on similar collateral may satisfy this standard. The electing class may not be deprived of the future appreciation of the collateral which is the purpose of permitting such an election. Present cash payments less than the allowed secured claim will

---

[335] See ¶ 8.18.

[336] See 11 U.S.C. § 506(a).

[337] This illustration is based on a similar one contained in the Congressional Record. See 124 Cong. Rec. H11104 (daily ed. Sept. 28, 1978).

[338] 11 U.S.C. § 1129(b)(2)(A)(iii).

not be the "indubitable equivalent" of the collateral. Again, if the class makes an election under Section 1111(b)(2), the allowed secured claim must equal the full amount of the debt, not just the present value of the collateral. However, unsecured notes or equity securities of the reorganized debtor will not constitute the "indubitable equivalent" of the collateral.[339]

The term "indubitable equivalent" derives from Judge Learned Hand's opinion in *In re Murel Holding Corporation*.[340] That case involved a plan which provided that a mortgagee was compelled to forego all amortization payments for ten years. Since the mortgagee had only a 10 percent margin of value above the loan balance and had to take its chances as to the ultimate value of the property at the end of the ten-year period, as no provision was made for amortization of principal, the mortgagee was not receiving "payment of the most indubitable equivalence" at the time of confirmation. It is conceivable that the court could have held that the "indubitable equivalence" might have been achieved by granting a lien on other property which was self-liquidating or, if it were not needed for the debtor's rehabilitation, by a sale of the property.

The third alternative is to provide in the plan for the sale of the collateral free and clear of liens and for the security interest to attach to the sale proceeds. In addition, the security interest in the proceeds must be treated in accordance with either of the first two alternatives discussed above to meet the fair and equitable standard with respect to the dissenting class of secured creditors.[341]

It is important to emphasize that the Code does not permit the cramming down of a plan on a dissenting secured creditor class by giving the class equity securities in the reorganized debtor. None of the three alternative means of satisfying the fair and equitable rule permits the dissenting secured class to be bought off with newly issued securities which are speculative at best. This is one way that the Code seeks to preserve the sanctity of the security interest by protecting secured creditors in reorganization cases.[342]

---

[339] See the discussion of the "indubitable equivalent" standard in 124 Cong. Rec. H11104 (daily ed. Sept. 28, 1978).

[340] 75 F.2d 941, 942 (2d. Cir. 1935).

[341] 11 U.S.C. § 1129(b)(2)(A)(ii).

[342] Of course, this is not the only way that secured creditors are protected in reorganization cases. See, e.g., 11 U.S.C. § 361 on adequate protection of interests; 11 U.S.C. § 363 on the use, sale or lease of collateral; 11 U.S.C. § 507(b) on super-priority of liens; and 11 U.S.C. § 1111(b)(2) on the election to be treated as fully secured.

[b] Unsecured Claims

There are two ways of satisfying the fair and equitable standard with respect to a dissenting class of unsecured claims. The first way is for the plan to provide for full compensation to the dissenting class.[343] As long as the plan provides that each creditor in the class receives or retains "property" of a present value equal to the allowed amount of the creditor's claim, the plan is fair and equitable as to that class. The term "property" is very broad and, unlike the provision for secured creditors, may include newly issued securities of the reorganized debtor.[344]

When securities are to be issued to a dissenting unsecured class, it becomes necessary to go through a complex valuation process to determine the present worth of the securities. To determine the value of securities, the court must first determine the "going concern" value of the reorganized debtor which involves speculation with respect to future earnings. The court is compelled to make a judgment as to prospective earnings per share of stock and to apply such earnings to arrive at the present value. Liquidation value, original or reproduction costs, book value, and fair market value of the debtor's assets are irrelevant except as these factors relate to earning capacity. As long as there is a reasonable likelihood that the present value of the securities given to the dissenting class equals the amount of the allowed unsecured claims, the plan meets the fair and equitable requirement with respect to that class and may be confirmed without its acceptance.[345]

---

[343] 11 U.S.C. § 1129(b)(2)(B)(i).

[344] 124 Cong. Rec. H11104 (daily ed. Sept. 28, 1978). See Reiter v. Sonotone Corp., 99 S. Ct. 2326, 2330 (1979), an antitrust case in which the court wrote: "The word 'property' has a naturally broad and inclusive meaning. In its dictionary definitions and in common usage 'property' comprehends anything of material value owned or possessed. Money, of course, is a form of property."

[345] See, Consolidated Rock Prods. Co. v. DuBois, 312 U.S. 510, 526 (1941), in which Justice Douglas made the following comment on valuation:

> "Since its application requires a prediction as to what will occur in the future, an estimate, as distinguished from mathematical certitude, is all that can be made. But that estimate must be based on an informed judgment which embraces all facts relevant to future earning capacity and hence to present worth, including, of course, the nature and condition of properties, the past earnings record, and all circumstances which indicate whether or not that record is a reliable criterion of future performance."

See also *In re* Keeshin Freight Lines, Inc., 86 F. Supp. 439 (N.D. Ill. 1949), in which the court estimated the debtor's earnings and applied to it a price-

The second way of satisfying the fair and equitable test with respect to a dissenting class of unsecured creditors is for the plan to give no property or payments to any class which is junior to the dissenting class.[346] Accordingly, if a dissenting unsecured creditor class is to receive property worth only one-half of its allowed claims, the plan may still be fair and equitable if all junior classes, which would include partners or stockholders, are to receive nothing and if no senior class is to receive more than 100 percent of its allowed claims.

[c] Interest Holders

Classes of equity interest holders that are impaired and that do not accept a plan also must receive fair and equitable treatment for the plan to be confirmed. If the debtor is a corporation, such interests include common or preferred stockholders. With respect to a partnership debtor, the interest holders will be limited or general partners.

If members of the interest holder class are entitled to a fixed liquidation preference or redemption price by virtue of their interests, the plan is fair and equitable as to that class if the interest holders receive property, which may consist of newly issued securities, of a present worth equal to the fixed liquidation or redemption price or the present value of their interests, whichever is greater. This requirement applies only when the proposed plan provides for a distribution to other interest holders which are junior to the dissenting class.[347]

Alternatively, the plan may meet the fair and equitable standard with respect to a dissenting equity interest class by providing for no compensation to junior classes.[348] Generally, equity interest holders are on the bottom of the priority ladder. In corporate reorganizations, the common stockholders are at the lowest rung, as are general partners in partnership cases. When the lowest class is also the dissenting class, the fair and equitable test is satisfied as long as no senior class of interest holders or creditors receives more than 100 percent of its allowed claims.

[5] The Effect of Confirmation

Confirmation of a plan marks the beginning of the reorganized debtor's new financial life. New legal relationships are established and

---

earnings multiplier which indicated the rate on which capitalization was based, namely the risk factors involved in the operation of a trucking system.

[346] 11 U.S.C. § 1129(b)(2)(B)(ii).

[347] 11 U.S.C. § 1129 (b)(2)(C)(i).

[348] 11 U.S.C. § 1129(b)(2)(C)(ii).

old ones are modified or terminated. It is at that point in time that the debtor starts a second chance to succeed in business.

Once a plan is confirmed, it becomes binding on the debtor as well as just about everyone who has a financial relationship with the debtor. It is binding on any entity which issues securities or which acquires securities or other property under the plan. In the case of a corporate debtor, all shareholders and owners of other forms of equity interests are bound by the plan. The rights of general partners are fixed by the plan when the debtor is a partnership. Of course, all creditors are bound by the confirmed plan as well, except in rare cases when the debtor will not be entitled to a discharge of certain debts. All of these persons and entities are bound by the plan whether or not they accepted or are impaired by it. Even dissenting classes in cram down cases and dissenting members of accepting classes in all cases are bound.[349] As such, the plan establishes new obligations and new legal relationships.

Confirmation of a plan also ends the life of the bankruptcy estate. By operation of law, all property of the estate is vested in the reorganized debtor, except as otherwise provided in the plan or in the confirmation order.[350] Moreover, the property dealt with by the plan becomes free and clear of all interests and claims of creditors, equity security holders, and general partners of the debtor, subject to the provisions of the plan or confirmation order.[351]

¶ 8.24 DISCHARGE FOR A REORGANIZED DEBTOR

Confirmation of a plan automatically discharges the debtor from any debt that arose prior to the date of confirmation, including those liabilities that arose from the rejection of executory contracts, unexpired leases, and taxes. This discharge is effective as against any creditor, regardless of whether or not a proof of claim has been filed, the claim has been allowed, or the creditor has accepted the plan.[352] Likewise, confirmation of the plan terminates all rights and interests of equity security holders who are dealt with in the plan.[353] Accordingly, the essence of confirmation is that all prior debts and interests are extinguished and replaced by the debts and interests provided for in the plan

[349] 11 U.S.C. § 1141(a). See Sugg. Int. B. Rule 3008(b) and Sugg. Int. B. Form No. 22 (Order Confirming a Plan).

[350] 11 U.S.C. § 1141(b).

[351] 11 U.S.C. § 1141(c).

[352] 11 U.S.C. § 1141(d)(1)(A).

[353] 11 U.S.C. § 1141(d)(1)(B).

or confirmation order. Of course, claims which are unimpaired by the plan remain in full force.

There are two situations when the discharge of debts upon confirmation will not completely release the debtor from preconfirmation obligations. First, if the debtor is an individual, those debts which are nondischargeable in a liquidation case will survive reorganization.[354] As a matter of policy, an individual debtor should not be able to avoid the payment of nondischargeable liabilities, such as alimony and child support, by proceeding under chapter 11. Otherwise, an effective use of the cram down provisions of chapter 11 against creditors with nondischargeable claims would defeat the more important social reasons for having such claims survive bankruptcy.

It is interesting to note that corporate and partnership debtors, which are not entitled to a discharge in liquidation cases at all,[355] will be discharged from all debts in chapter 11 cases. This is so even with respect to those debts which would survive with respect to debtors who are individuals. As discussed in an earlier chapter, many of the nondischargeable debts, such as debts arising from fraud, embezzlement or willful injuries, relate to dishonest or undesirable conduct of the debtor.[356] When the debtor is an individual such debts survive either a liquidation or reorganization. However, it makes sense to discharge such debts in cases of corporate and partnership reorganizations because dishonest management will most likely be replaced and it will be undesirable to penalize new management, as well as shareholders and creditors, for the unscrupulous conduct of former employees. In addition, nondischargeable tax claims also are discharged in corporate reorganizations to avoid uncertainty as to the liabilities of the corporation. Therefore, interested parties in corporate or partnership reorganization cases will have a fixed list of liabilities on which to base their decisions without worrying about nondischargeable debts.[357]

The second exception to the broad discharge rule in reorganization cases applies to a liquidation in a chapter 11 case. If the confirmed plan provides for substantial liquidation, the debtor stops doing business after confirmation, and the debtor will not be entitled to a general

---

[354] 11 U.S.C. § 1141(d)(2). See 11 U.S.C. § 523 and ¶ 3.09 with respect to nondischargeable debts.

[355] See 11 U.S.C. § 727(a)(1) and ¶ 3.03[1].

[356] See ¶ 3.09.

[357] Rep. Don Edwards remarked that "retaining an exception for discharge with respect to nondischargeable taxes would leave an undesirable uncertainty surrounding reorganizations that is unacceptable." 124 Cong. Rec. H11105 (daily ed. Sept. 28, 1978).

discharge in a chapter 7 liquidation case, then confirmation of a chapter 11 plan will not discharge the debtor.[358] Since corporations and partnerships are not entitled to any discharge in chapter 7 cases,[359] it follows that the corporation or partnership which liquidates under the reorganization chapter will not have the benefit of a discharge of debts. This exception is not too important in corporate cases because the life of a corporate debtor usually terminates upon liquidation, but is important in partnership cases since general partners are personally liable for partnership debts.[360]

Despite the discharge of debts upon confirmation, the bankruptcy court may approve a written waiver of discharge executed by the debtor after the commencement of a voluntary reorganization case. In involuntary reorganization cases, the waiver must be executed after the order for relief is approved by the court.[361]

¶ 8.25 EXECUTING THE CONFIRMED PLAN

The debtor is obligated to carry out the plan after confirmation, unless a particular entity was or will be organized for this purpose. The debtor or other executing entity must comply with any court orders relating to the consummation of the plan.[362]

The court has the authority to direct the debtor or any other necessary party to execute or deliver any instrument or to perform any other act necessary for carrying out the plan.[363] For example, the court may order the debtor and any other necessary party to execute a deed to property dealt with by the plan or direct the satisfaction of any lien or the recording of documents to indicate such satisfaction.

It is common for a reorganization plan to contain conditions for participating in a distribution of property or securities. For example,

---

[358] 11 U.S.C. § 1141(d)(3).

[359] See 11 U.S.C. § 727(a)(1) and ¶ 3.03[1].

[360] See *In re* Ira Haupt & Co., 240 F. Supp. 369 (S.D.N.Y. 1965), where the court directed a solvent partner to turn over personal assets to the partnership trustee. See also B. Rule 108(c) requiring the filing of individual schedules for each general partner.

[361] 11 U.S.C. § 1141(d)(4).

[362] 11 U.S.C. § 1142(a). On consummation of the plan, the court will enter a final decree which contains provisions: (1) stating the effect of confirmation and consummation on the creditors and equity security holders of the debtor; (2) discharging the trustee, if any; (3) making such provisions by way of injunction or otherwise as may be equitable; and (4) closing the estate. Sugg. Int. B. Rule 3010(b).

[363] 11 U.S.C. § 1142(b). See Sugg. Int. B. Rule 3010(a).

the plan may require that a stockholder present or surrender securities as a condition for receiving newly issued stock or other property. In such cases, chapter 11 imposes a five-year limitation for meeting these conditions. Any person who fails to meet such conditions within five years from the date on which the confirmation order is entered is forever barred from participating in a distribution under the plan.[364]

¶ 8.26 REVOCATION OF CONFIRMATION PROCURED BY FRAUD

If an order of confirmation was procured by fraud, the bankruptcy judge may revoke the order on request of any interested party. However, the request to revoke must be made within 180 days after the date of entry of the confirmation order. In addition, the court may not revoke unless notice is given to interested parties and a hearing is held on the fraud issue.[365]

Revocation of a confirmation order can be detrimental to persons who acquired rights in good faith reliance on the confirmation of the plan. Therefore, the court is required to make necessary provisions to protect such persons whenever it revokes a confirmation order.[366] Also, any revocation of confirmation must provide for the revocation of the debtor's discharge.[367] After revocation, the court may receive proposals to modify the plan and proceed toward confirmation if to do so will be in the best interest of creditors.[368]

¶ 8.27 EXEMPTION FROM SECURITIES LAWS

The Securities Act of 1933 imposes rigid registration requirements and other restrictions with respect to the issuance or sale of securities.[369] However, the application of these securities laws to the typical chapter 11 case could be detrimental because it would seriously impede the flexibility of the reorganization process. The need to file complex registration statements with regard to the issuance of securities under a plan would be so costly and time-consuming that it could eliminate any chance of a successful reorganization.

---

[364] 11 U.S.C. § 1143.
[365] 11 U.S.C. § 1144.
[366] 11 U.S.C. § 1144(1).
[367] 11 U.S.C. § 1144(2).
[368] See B. Rule 11-42(b).
[369] 15 U.S.C. § 77(e) (1970).

It is not surprising, therefore, that the former Bankruptcy Act afforded special exemptions to debtors in business rehabilitation cases with respect to securities laws.[370] Congress continued and even extended the scope of these limited exemptions from securities laws in the Bankruptcy Code.

Section 1145 of the Bankruptcy Code contains the detailed rules which exempt certain transactions from the scope of federal, state, and local securities laws.[371] In general, the Code exempts from Section 5 of the Securities Act and from similar state laws the issuance of certificates of indebtedness and the issuance of securities under a plan if such securities are issued solely or primarily in exchange for claims against, or equity securities of, the debtor.[372] The exercise of certain conversion privileges in connection with securities issued under the plan is also exempt from the requirements of these securities laws.[373]

Limited exemptions are also provided for the sale of portfolio securities which are owned by the debtor prior to the reorganization case. It is often necessary for the trustee or debtor in possession to sell portfolio securities to raise cash during the reorganization. The exemption relates to the sale of certain securities which were not issued by the debtor or its affiliate.[374]

The Code also provides for limited exemptions in connection with the resale of securities issued under a reorganization plan. The problem arises because the securities laws require a registration statement if securities are taken with a view to distribution. Since many creditors accept a plan which provides for the issuance of new securities to them with a view to reselling the securities immediately, such registration requirements can deter creditors from accepting such a plan. Therefore, the Code grants a limited exemption so that creditors may resell their securities free of registration restrictions.[375] The selling creditors may

---

[370] See former B.A. §§ 264, 393, 518. See also Corotto, "Debtor Relief Proceedings Under the Bankruptcy Act and the Securities Act of 1933: The Registration Requirement and Its Implications," 47 Am. Bankr. L.J. 183 (1973), for a discussion of these exemptions under the former Bankruptcy Act.

[371] For a detailed analysis of these exemptions which goes way beyond the brief discussion in this book, see H.R. Rep. No. 95-595, 95th Cong., 1st Sess. 236-238, 419-421 (1977). Exemptions relating to the Trust Indenture Act of 1939 and other laws are also contained in 11 U.S.C. § 1145. The reader concerned with the details of the securities laws exemptions should consult 11 U.S.C. § 1145.

[372] 11 U.S.C. § 1145(a)(1).

[373] 11 U.S.C. § 1145(a)(2).

[374] 11 U.S.C. § 1145(a)(3).

[375] See 11 U.S.C. § 1145(b).

be required, however, to supply the purchaser with the disclosure statement, as supplemented, in lieu of a prospectus. In this way, the law provides a compromise which protects the public while preserving the flexibility necessary for successful reorganizations.

¶ 8.28 TAXATION OF THE DEBTOR IN A REORGANIZATION CASE

Tax consequences of reorganization may be important in connection with the formulation and successful execution of a plan. The extent to which tax attributes of the debtor, such as net operating losses, may benefit the reorganized debtor may be of particular importance in providing the company with the advantage of offsetting carryforward losses against current income.[376] Tax implications may result from a discharge or reduction of debts, the issuance of stock or other securities in exchange for creditors' claims, and the realization of gain upon the sale of property other than in the regular course of business. The complexity of the tax problems presented in a reorganization case often requires the expertise of an accountant or special tax counsel.

The former Bankruptcy Act contained provisions which dealt the tax treatment of the cancellation or reduction of indebtedness in rehabilitation cases. Specifically, no income was recognized as a result of the cancellation of indebtedness in an insolvency reorganization under Chapter X,[377] arrangement under Chapter XI,[378] or real property arrangement under Chapter XII.[379] The former Act required, however, that the tax basis of the debtor's assets be reduced by a sum equal to the amount that the indebtedness had been decreased, but not below the fair market value of the debtor's property as of the date on which the plan was confirmed.[380]

The Bankruptcy Reform Act repealed the federal tax provisions of the former Act and, in essence, did not replace them.[381] Although the Bankruptcy Code contains three special tax sections, these provisions

---

[376] See Glancy, "Carrying Losses Through Chapter X and Chapter XI Reorganizations," 28 Tax Law. 27 (1974); Plumb, "The Tax Recommendations of the Commission on the Bankruptcy Laws—Reorganizations, Carryovers and the Effects of Debt Reduction," 29 Tax. L. Rev. 227 (1974).

[377] Former B.A. § 268.

[378] Former B.A. § 395.

[379] Former B.A. § 520.

[380] Former B.A. §§ 270, 396, 522.

[381] Title IV Section 401(a) of the Bankruptcy Act repealed the former Bankruptcy Act.

apply to state and local tax and do not affect federal tax consequences.[382] Congress deliberately omitted references to federal taxes in the Bankruptcy Reform Act because a separate bankruptcy tax bill was introduced to deal with such matters. In fact, the proposed Bankruptcy Tax Act, which attempts to strike a balance between federal tax policies and bankruptcy policies, is pending in Congress at the time of this writing.[383] Accordingly, the practitioner should be aware that changes and clarification with respect to tax aspects of reorganization are expected to occur with the probable enactment of legislation in the very near future. Until that time, the reader must refer to the Internal Revenue Code [384] to ascertain what tax benefits, if any, are available to the reorganized debtor.

---

[382] See 11 U.S.C. § 346, 728, 1146.

[383] H.R. 5043 (Bankruptcy Tax Act of 1979), 97th Cong., 1st Sess. See 125 Cong. Rec. H7244 (daily ed. Aug. 2, 1979) for a summary of the provisions of the bill.

[384] 26 U.S.C. §§ 1 et seq.

Chapter 9

DEBT ADJUSTMENTS FOR INDIVIDUALS WITH REGULAR INCOME

¶ 9.01 WHAT IS CHAPTER 13?

The Bankruptcy Code offers several alternative forms of relief for individual debtors experiencing financial difficulty. The most common form of relief, liquidation under chapter 7 of the Code, results in the loss of nonexempt assets and usually a discharge of indebtedness.[1] Individuals in business may seek reorganization under chapter 11 as a

---

[1] See Chapter 1 *supra* on voluntary liquidation cases.

means of rehabilitating and preserving their companies.[2] This chapter focuses on a third alternative for individual debtors provided under chapter 13 of the Code, entitled "Adjustment of Debts of an Individual with Regular Income." [3]

Chapter 13 of the Code is designed to enable individual debtors under court protection and supervision to apply a portion of future earnings to the payment of all or a portion of their debts over an extended period of time. The debtor is protected from creditors by an automatic stay while a plan of repayment is developed and carried out.[4] The policy which underlies chapter 13 is to encourage debtors to pay their debts instead of merely seeking a discharge. For those individuals engaged in business, it is similar in theory to chapter 11 reorganizations in that the purpose is rehabilitation and the preservation and continued use of property instead of the disposition of assets through liquidation.[5]

Chapter 13 of the Code derives from Chapter XIII "Wage Earner Plans" of the former Bankruptcy Act.[6] Added to the former Act by an amendment in 1938, Chapter XIII was intended to give the wage earner a reasonable opportunity to arrange installment payments out of future income so that creditors would receive more money than they otherwise would receive in liquidation, and so that the debtor may avoid the stigma of being adjudicated as a "bankrupt" under the former Act.[7] The justification for pursuing Chapter XIII relief instead of liquidation was one of moral values, namely, it was the right thing to do to pay accrued obligations. This sense of morality was, however, often a difficult course to pursue for many debtors who had to support dependents while overburdened by heavy debts. Moreover, Chapter XIII was inflexible and deficient in several ways: (1) secured parties had the right to veto any plan which affected them; [8] (2) availability was limited to wage earners and not self-employed individuals; [9] (3) plans had to be approved by a vote of the creditors; [10] and (4) it did not prevent creditors from pursuing remedies against codebtors, such as the debtor's spouse or parent who cosigned promissory notes.[11] As a result, Chapter XIII was

[2] See Chapter 8 *supra* on reorganizations.
[3] 11 U.S.C. §§ 1301–1330.
[4] See ¶ 9.06.
[5] See ¶ 8.01.
[6] Former B.A. §§ 601–686.
[7] See Perry v. Commerce Loan Co., 383 U.S. 392 (1966).
[8] Former B.A. §§ 651, 652(1).
[9] Former B.A. §§ 606(3), 603(8).
[10] Former B.A. §§ 651, 652.
[11] See ¶ 9.06.

not used by most individual debtors who sought relief under the former Act.[12]

This chapter focuses on the features of the new chapter 13 and the significant revisions made over the former Chapter XIII. Indeed, the many improvements made by the Code with respect to debt adjustments for individuals will make the new chapter 13 a viable and popular alternative which should be considered seriously by individuals seeking relief from severe financial pressures.

¶ 9.02 ADVANTAGES AND DISADVANTAGES OF SEEKING RELIEF UNDER CHAPTER 13

When should an individual debtor opt for relief under chapter 13 instead of filing a petition for liquidation under chapter 7? The answer to this question depends on many factors, including the debtor's financial situation as well as moral values.

One benefit which a debtor derives from filing a chapter 13 petition is the protection of the debtor's nonexempt assets which would be lost in a liquidation case. Thus, it is important to ascertain the extent to which the debtor's property is nonexempt and the value of these assets. In view of the generosity of the new federal exemptions, many consumer debtors will find that most assets are exempt and, accordingly, will not be lost in liquidation.[13] On the other hand, debtors who place a high value on keeping whatever nonexempt assets they have should consider going the chapter 13 route.

Another factor which should be considered in deciding whether to proceed under chapter 7 or chapter 13 is the likelihood that the debtor's earnings will support the debtor's day-to-day expenses in the future and still leave enough to make periodic payments to pay old debts. However, there seems to be a split of authority as to whether it is necessary for a debtor to offer unsecured creditors any payment under a plan. In *In re Stuart and Sheila Terry,*[14] the court confirmed the plan which offered no payment to unsecured creditors since these creditors would receive no dividend if the debtor were liquidated under chapter 7.

If this case remains as authority, attorneys representing debtors will have to consider whether there exists any reason for filing volun-

---

[12] During the one-year period from July 1, 1976 to June 30, 1977, only 29,422 Chapter XIII petitions were filed while there were a total of 182,210 nonbusiness bankruptcies. See Administrative Office of the U.S. Courts *Tables of Bankruptcy Statistics* (1978).

[13] See ¶ 4.07; 11 U.S.C. § 522.

[14] Collier Bankr. Cas. 2d 525 (W.D. Ark. 1980).

tary petitions under chapter 7 for individual debtors who could avail themselves of the benefits of chapter 13. However, in *In re Iacovini,* the court refused confirmation where the debtors' plans offered nothing to unsecured creditors although the unsecured creditors would receive nothing in liquidation.[15]

The nondischargeability of debts in a liquidation case is another factor to be considered. If there are substantial nondischargeable obligations, such as debts based on larceny, willful and malicious injury to property, or recent income tax liabilities,[16] chapter 13 offers an opportunity to eliminate, reduce, or pay such debts over an extended period of time.[17] In contrast, a liquidation case would not protect the debtor from the enforcement of these nondischargeable obligations. In addition, chapter 13 is available to individuals who may not be eligible for a chapter 7 discharge. For example, a person who received a discharge in a liquidation case within the previous six years may not obtain another discharge in a subsequent chapter 7 case, but may seek relief and receive a discharge under chapter 13.[18]

The stigma attached to a chapter 13 debtor is not as severe as that which attaches to the debtor who files a liquidation case to escape the payment of liabilities. In fact, one of the primary reasons for enacting Chapter XIII of the former Act in 1938 was a desire to avoid "an adjudication of bankruptcy with its attendant stigma."[19] Although the new Code eliminates the labels "bankrupt" and "adjudication" for all debtors, nevertheless a good faith effort to pay past debts under court protection is looked upon more favorably by the community than a total avoidance of liabilities through a discharge. This factor may be important to individuals who are concerned about personal image as well as the ability to obtain credit in the future. Extending credit to someone who, despite past financial misfortunes, has attempted to pay as much as possible from future earnings is much more preferable to creditors than advancing credit to someone who has not even bothered to make the attempt.

Moreover, the debtor's personal sense of morality cannot be ignored in choosing the appropriate insolvency proceeding. The debtor

---

[15] *Id.* at 331 (D. Utah 1980).

[16] See 11 U.S.C. § 523 and ¶ 3.09 for a discussion on exceptions to discharge.

[17] Obligations to pay alimony, maintenance or support, however, are nondischargeable under chapter 13 as well as under chapter 7. 11 U.S.C. §§ 523 (a)(5), 1328(a)(2), 1328(c)(2). See ¶ 9.17.

[18] See 11 U.S.C. § 727(a)(8) and ¶ 9.17.

[19] Note 7 *supra,* at 392, 395.

who feels a moral obligation to pay debts may opt for chapter 13 instead of chapter 7 for that reason.

Financially troubled individuals who own small businesses may have to make a choice between filing a reorganization petition under chapter 11 or a debt adjustment petition under chapter 13.[20] One benefit of proceeding under chapter 13 is that creditor approval of the plan is not required for confirmation.[21] In addition, only the debtor can file a chapter 13 plan.[22] Furthermore, the flexibility and economy of chapter 13 usually make it a more appealing avenue for small business rehabilitation when contrasted with chapter 11 reorganization.

¶ 9.03 STRUCTURE OF CHAPTER 13

The practitioner should realize that chapter 13 does not contain all of the Code provisions applicable in debt adjustment cases. Chapter 1 of the Code contains general provisions, including definitions, which apply in chapter 13 cases.[23] The provisions in chapter 3, which deal with the commencement of the case, trustees, automatic stays, meeting of creditors, examination of the debtor, depositories of money of the estate, and other administrative matters, also are generally applicable.[24] Chapter 5 of the Code applies to chapter 13 cases as well, on such matters as claims, priorities, exemptions, property of the estate, trustee's avoiding powers, and various other issues unless the particular provision indicates otherwise.[25]

The sections contained in chapter 13 apply only to debt adjustments for individuals.

¶ 9.04 WHO MAY FILE A CHAPTER 13 PETITION?

One of the most significant changes made by the new chapter 13 relates to eligibility for relief.[26] Chapter XIII of the former Bankruptcy

---

[20] See ¶ 9.04 on eligibility for filing a chapter 13 petition.

[21] Compare 11 U.S.C. § 1129(a)(10), which requires that at least one class of claims accept a chapter 11 plan, with 11 U.S.C. § 1325, which does not require such acceptance in chapter 13 cases.

[22] 11 U.S.C. § 1321. Compare 11 U.S.C. § 1121 which permits any party in interest to file a reorganization plan after a specified time period. See ¶ 8.19.

[23] 11 U.S.C. §§ 101 et seq.; 11 U.S.C. § 103(a).

[24] 11 U.S.C. §§ 301 et seq.; 11 U.S.C. § 103(a).

[25] 11 U.S.C. §§ 501 et seq.; 11 U.S.C. § 103(a).

[26] See, generally Lee, "Chapter 13 nee Chapter XIII," 53 Am. Bankr. L.J. 303 (1979).

Act was available only to a "wage earner," which means an individual whose principal income is derived from wages, salary or commissions.[27] Self-employed individuals who have small businesses were not permitted to seek relief under Chapter XIII and, as a result, they often resorted to liquidation or an expensive and complex Chapter XI arrangement.

Chapter 13 of the new Code eliminates the distinction between employed workers and sole proprietors. Any individual whose income is sufficiently stable and regular so that payments under a chapter 13 plan can be made, except for stockholders or commodity brokers, qualifies as an "individual with regular income."[28] Thus, self-employed druggists, grocers, and farmers may take advantage of chapter 13 as can the factory worker. Individuals may qualify for chapter 13 relief even if their primary income is from pensions, social security or investments.[29] This expansion of eligibility certainly will make chapter 13 a more popular avenue for financial relief.

The expansion of the scope of chapter 13 made it necessary for Congress to place a monetary limit on eligibility so as to prevent large businesses from using chapter 13 as a means of avoiding chapter 11. It should be noted that a chapter 11 reorganization is designed for the larger business, whether or not it is a sole proprietorship, and that chapter 13 is appropriate for the smaller business. For this reason, the Code provides that chapter 13 is available only to an individual with regular income who owes, on the date of the commencement of the case, noncontingent, liquidated, unsecured debts of less than $100,000 and noncontingent, liquidated, secured debts of less than $350,000.[30] When a joint petition is filed by a husband and wife, the aggregate liabilities of both spouses may not exceed the $100,000 limit for unsecured debts and the $350,000 limit for secured debts.[31]

Let us assume that a husband and wife operate a small business together, say a small grocery store. Whether they are eligible to file a joint petition under chapter 13 may depend on the form of ownership. If the business is a partnership, the business is not eligible for chapter 13 relief. However, if the business is operated as if it is owned by one

---

[27] Former B.A. § 606(8).

[28] 11 U.S.C. § 101(24). See H.R. Rep. No. 95-595, 95th Cong., 1st Sess. 312 (1977). As the House report indicates, the reason for excluding stockbrokers and commodity brokers is so that they may not avoid the customer protection provisions applicable to such debtors under chapter 7. See 11 U.S.C. §§ 741–752, 761–766.

[29] See note 28 *supra*, at 119.

[30] 11 U.S.C. § 109(e).

[31] *Id.* See 11 U.S.C. § 302 which permits joint petitions.

spouse as sole proprietor, that spouse may file a chapter 13 petition alone or together with the other spouse. The facts of the particular case will determine the intended form of ownership. Even in the absence of a formal partnership agreement, an informal or implied partnership arrangement may result in a separate partnership entity which would be ineligible for chapter 13 relief.[32]

¶ 9.05 COMMENCING A CHAPTER 13 CASE

The only way that a chapter 13 case may be commenced is by the filing of a voluntary petition by the individual debtor or, in a joint case, by the husband and wife.[33] For several reasons, the Code does not permit involuntary petitions under chapter 13.[34] As pointed out in a congressional report, the Constitution prohibits involuntary servitude and it has been suggested that a compulsory debt adjustment plan would, in essence, force an individual to work for the benefit of the debtor's creditors. Also, Congress believes that an individual should not be forced into a repayment plan because an unwilling debtor probably would not maintain employment or cooperate in the plan.[35]

Consistent with the policy against involuntary debt adjustments for individuals, the Code provides that a chapter 7 liquidation may not be converted to a chapter 13 case unless the conversion is at the request of the debtor.[36]

Procedures for filing a petition under chapter 13 are substantially the same as those applicable to chapter 7 cases.[37] The rules that govern jurisdiction, abstention, venue, and transfer are the same under chapter 7 and chapter 13. The chapter 13 debtor must submit a list of creditors, schedules, and statement of affairs.[38] Even the $60 filing fee is the same under chapter 7 and chapter 13.[39] Accordingly, the reader interested

---

[32] See note 28 *supra*, at 320.

[33] 11 U.S.C. §§ 301, 302.

[34] 11 U.S.C. § 303(a). See Adam, "Should Chapter XIII Bankruptcy Be Involuntary?," 44 Tex. L. Rev. 533 (1966).

[35] See note 28 *supra*, at 120.

[36] 11 U.S.C. § 706(c).

[37] These procedures are governed by chapter 3 of the Code which is applicable to chapter 13 cases as well as chapter 7 cases. 11 U.S.C. § 103(a).

[38] The chapter 13 statement of affairs should conform to Official Form No. 13-5 as amended by Sugg. Int. B. Rule 13001. A list of exemptions prepared in the manner prescribed by Schedule B-4 of Sugg. Int. B. Form No. 6 must accompany the chapter 13 statement.

[39] 28 U.S.C. § 1930(a)(1), added by B.R.A. § 246(a).

in commencing a chapter 13 case should consult chapter 1 of this book where these procedures and requirements are discussed.

¶ 9.06 AUTOMATIC STAY AND THE PROTECTION OF CODEBTORS

The automatic stay against debt collection and lien enforcement which applies in liquidation and reorganization cases also benefits chapter 13 debtors.[40] The stay temporarily relieves the debtor of financial pressures while affording a breathing spell pending confirmation of a repayment plan. A detailed discussion of the scope of the automatic stay, exceptions to the stay, requirements for the adequate protection of lienholders and property rights, termination and relief from the stay, and enforcement is contained in the first chapter of this book and should be consulted by practitioners involved in chapter 13 cases.

It is common practice for a lender in a consumer loan transaction to require that a friend or relative of the debtor cosign or otherwise guaranty a promissory note with the debtor. In many of these situations the cosigner is not even aware of the legal consequences of acting as a surety. When the debtor is unable to pay the note because of financial reverses, the lender is in a position to use the threat of collection from the cosigner as leverage to extract preferential payments from the debtor. Thus, moral and social pressure placed on the debtor to protect a friend or relative often results in an unfair advantage to a particular lender over others.

Chapter XIII of the former Act was not designed to deal with the pressures relating to the protection of friends and relatives who cosigned with the debtor. Under the former Act, the filing of a petition in a wage earner proceeding did not interfere with the right to enforce the debt against codebtors. In order to protect a codebtor, the wage earner often made arrangements with the lender to reaffirm the debt or to make preferential payments. As stated in a congressional report, "this practice makes Chapter XIII plans [under the former Bankruptcy Act] difficult to consummate, because the debtor has the obligation to the creditor in addition to his obligations under the plan." [41]

In order to cure the problem involving pressure from creditors

---

[40] See 11 U.S.C. §§ 103(a), 362.

[41] Note 28 *supra*, at 122. The only way in which a debtor under former Chapter XIII was able to protect codebtors was to provide for their protection in the plan and to obtain the acceptance of the creditor. See Schraer v. G.A.C. Finance Corp., 408 F.2d 891 (6th Cir. 1969).

based on the liability of friends or relatives who are cosigners on consumer loans, the new chapter 13 contains a special automatic stay provision applicable to codebtors.[42] Specifically, after the commencement of a chapter 13 case a creditor may not act, or commence or continue any civil action, to collect all or any part of a consumer debt from any individual who is liable with the debtor. The stay also applies with respect to persons who put up collateral to secure the debt.

It is important to realize that the automatic stay of collection activities against codebtors is limited to ensure that the lender does not lose any substantive rights with respect to the cosigner's liability. The stay results only in a procedural delay and does not affect the creditor's right to full satisfaction from the debtor and codebtor. In essence, the lender is required to wait for payment under the chapter 13 plan before pursuing remedies against the codebtor. In this way, the codebtor benefits from payments made by the debtor during the chapter 13 case.

Because of its narrow purpose, the automatic stay of action against codebtors has several limitations. First, it only applies to *consumer* debts on which there is an *individual* codebtor.[43] It does not apply to any debts which arose in the ordinary course of the debtor's business. The stay is lifted automatically as soon as the chapter 13 case is closed, dismissed, or converted to a liquidation or reorganization.[44]

The Code contains a special limitation on the scope of the stay of action against codebtors to deal with negotiable instruments. Pursuant to the Uniform Commercial Code, substantive rights of the holder of a negotiable promissory note or check may be affected by the presentment or notice of dishonor of the instrument. For example, the failure to give timely notice of dishonor to the indorser of a negotiable promissory note may result in the maker's discharge.[45] For this reason, the chapter 13 stay expressly permits the holder to present an instrument or give notice of dishonor to a codebtor.[46]

Lenders who are subject to the automatic stay as against codebtors may obtain relief from the stay under certain circumstances. The Code gives the court the power, upon request of a party in interest and after notice and a hearing, to grant relief from the stay in three situations. First, because the stay is aimed at true codebtors, relief may be granted to the extent that the "codebtor" actually received the consideration on

---

[42] 11 U.S.C. § 1301. See note 26 *supra*, at 303, 308–310.

[43] The term "consumer debt" means a debt incurred by an individual primarily for a personal, family, or household purpose. 11 U.S.C. § 101(7).

[44] 11 U.S.C. § 1301(a)(2).

[45] U.C.C. §§ 3-502(1)(a), 3-508(2).

[46] 11 U.S.C. § 1301(b).

which the claim is based. For example, assume that the lender gave a $1,000 loan to the chapter 13 debtor and that both the debtor and a friend signed the promissory note as comakers. Upon discovery that the friend received and spent $500 of the loan proceeds, the court should relieve the lender from the stay as against the friend to the extent of $500. The rationale for this provision is that the cosigner is not a guarantor, but is really a principal debtor, to the extent of the $500 which the cosigner received and used.[47]

The second situation which justifies relief from the automatic stay is when the plan filed by the debtor proposes not to pay the entire claim.[48] For example, if the plan proposes to pay only $700 of the $1,000 claim, the court should permit the creditor to take immediate action against the codebtor to the extent of $300 although the creditor would have to wait to collect $700 in accordance with the payment schedule set forth in the plan. Of course, if the debtor defaults in the payments set forth in the plan, the creditor may request dismissal of the chapter 13 case and, upon dismissal, may collect from the debtor or codebtor the total amount due, including, if the loan contract so provides, postpetition interest, costs, and attorney's fees.[49]

Finally, a creditor may obtain relief from the stay of action against a codebtor if continuation of the stay would result in irreparable harm to the creditor.[50] If there is a real danger that the codebtor's financial condition will deteriorate substantially while the case is pending, the creditor should be able to act without delay. Thus, the stay should be lifted if the codebtor either threatens to leave the locale, files a bankruptcy petition, or is about to terminate employment.[51] Moreover, if there is reasonable cause to believe that the codebtor's property is about to be transferred or is likely to depreciate in value, continuation of the stay may cause irreparable harm to the creditor and appropriate relief should be given.[52]

In light of the automatic stay, it is necessary to protect creditors from the running of the statute of limitations with respect to actions against codebtors. The Code provides that, in the event that the statute of limitations on a claim against a codebtor does not expire prior to the commencement of the chapter 13 case, the period in which the creditor may sue the codebtor does not expire until either the end of the original

---

[47] 11 U.S.C. § 1301(c)(1).
[48] 11 U.S.C. § 1301(c)(2).
[49] See 11 U.S.C. § 1307(c)(5).
[50] 11 U.S.C. § 1301(c)(3).
[51] See H.R. Rep. No. 95-595, 95th Cong., 1st Sess. 426 (1977).
[52] See S. Rep. No. 95-989, 95th Cong., 2d Sess. 139 (1978).

statute of limitations period or thirty days after notice of the termination of the stay, whichever is later.[53]

¶ 9.07 THE TRUSTEE

A trustee serves as the principal administrator in every chapter 13 case. When the volume of cases in a particular judicial district so warrants, the court may appoint one or more standing trustees to serve in most or all of the chapter 13 cases commenced in that district.[54] The reason for encouraging the appointment of standing trustees is to permit those who serve as trustees to acquire expertise through repeated experiences as chapter 13 administrators. If a standing trustee is not appointed, the court will appoint a person to serve as trustee.[55] Creditors do not have the right to elect the trustee.[56]

In the judicial districts which have the U.S. Trustee Pilot Program, the U.S. Trustee may, subject to the Attorney General's approval, appoint one or more standing trustees if the number of cases so warrants.[57] The U.S. Trustee is responsible for supervising the standing trustee in the performance of official duties.[58] If a standing trustee is not appointed, then the U.S. Trustee must serve in chapter 13 cases.[59]

Any person who serves as trustee, including a standing trustee, must satisfy the eligibility requirements and qualify for the position.[60] These requirements, as well as the amount of compensation and employment of attorneys and other professionals, are discussed in Chapter 6 of this book.

The trustee in a chapter 13 case collects a portion of the debtor's income and makes payments to creditors in accordance with the repayment plan.[61] However, it is important to appreciate that the trustee is not merely a disbursing agent.[62] Instead, the trustee has a broad range of responsibilities.

---

[53] 11 U.S.C. § 108(c).

[54] 11 U.S.C. § 1302(d).

[55] 11 U.S.C. § 1302(a).

[56] Compare 11 U.S.C. § 702 which gives creditors the right to elect a trustee in liquidation cases if certain conditions are met.

[57] 28 U.S.C. § 586(b), B.R.A. § 224(a). See ¶ 6.08 for a discussion on the U.S. Trustee Pilot Program.

[58] 28 U.S.C. § 586(a)(3), B.R.A. § 224(a).

[59] 11 U.S.C. § 151302(a).

[60] 11 U.S.C. §§ 321, 322.

[61] See 11 U.S.C. § 1326(b).

[62] See Comment, "The Chapter XIII Trustee: 'Trustee' or Disbursing Agent?," 21 Me. L. Rev. 53 (1969).

The chapter 13 trustee's duties are similar to those of a liquidation trustee in that the chapter 13 trustee has the responsibility for investigating the debtor's financial affairs, accounting for any property received, examining proofs of claims, objecting to the allowance of improper claims, opposing the debtor's discharge when advisable, furnishing information concerning the estate upon the request of interested parties, and making a final report and filing a final account of the administration of the estate.[63] The trustee also may examine the debtor at the meeting of creditors.[64] In addition, the trustee may assume or reject executory contracts and leases, recover preferences and fraudulent conveyances, and assert the other avoiding powers available under the Code.[65]

The chapter 13 trustee is obligated to appear in court and be heard on three important issues. First, the trustee must be heard with respect to the valuation of property subject to a lien.[66] The consumer debtor usually is not knowledgeable with regard to the valuation of assets on the open market. The trustee is called upon to produce evidence of value so as to enable the court to determine the extent of the lienor's secured claim and the amount of the allowable unsecured claim based on the deficiency. Second, the trustee must appear and be heard concerning the confirmation of the plan.[67] The trustee must investigate and present evidence relating to the debtor's ability to make payments pursuant to the plan while having enough income remaining for day-to-day living expenses. It is the trustee's obligation to present proof that the plan either does or does not meet the requirements for confirmation.[68] Third, in the event that a request is made to modify the repayment plan after confirmation, the trustee must appear and be heard concerning justification for amending the plan.[69]

---

[63] See 11 U.S.C. §§ 704, 1302(b)(1). The chapter 13 debtor, however, performs the duty of filing reports of the continued operation of a business. In liquidation cases, the trustee is required to file such reports if the business continues to operate during the pendency of the case. Compare 11 U.S.C. § 704(7) and § 1304(c). See Chapter 6 *supra* for a discussion on these duties.

[64] 11 U.S.C. § 343.

[65] See Chapter 6 *supra* on the trustee's avoiding powers. See also City Nat'l Bank & Trust Co. v. Oliver, 230 F.2d 686 (10th Cir. 1956), in which a Chapter XIII trustee asserted the rights of a lien creditor to avoid an unrecorded chattel mortgage.

[66] 11 U.S.C. § 1302(b)(2)(A).

[67] 11 U.S.C. § 1302(b)(2)(B).

[68] See ¶ 9.14 on the requirements for confirmation.

[69] 11 U.S.C. § 1302(b)(2)(C). See ¶ 9.18 on modification of the plan after confirmation.

In addition to other duties, the chapter 13 trustee performs a counseling function. The Code directs the trustee to advise the debtor other than on legal matters during the chapter 13 case.[70] An experienced standing trustee can give valuable advice on financial matters which may not be within the particular expertise of the debtor's attorney. In this way, the trustee plays an important role by helping the debtor to tailor the plan to the debtor's special needs and circumstances. Once the plan is confirmed, the trustee assists the debtor in performing under it.

As discussed earlier, chapter 13 is available to an individual debtor who is engaged in business as a sole proprietor.[71] In such cases, the trustee has additional duties relating to the continuation of the business. The trustee must investigate the financial condition and the operation of the debtor's business.[72] Among other things, the investigation must deal with the question of whether it is desirable to continue the business. The trustee is responsible for filing "as soon as practicable" a statement of the investigation, including any facts pertaining to fraud, dishonesty, incompetence, mismanagement, or irregularity in the management of the debtor's affairs, or relating to a cause of action available to the estate. A copy or a summary of the statement must be given to the creditor's committee or to any other entity designated by the court.[73]

¶ 9.08 RIGHTS AND POWERS OF THE DEBTOR

An essential feature of a chapter 13 case is that the debtor remains in possession of all assets pending confirmation of the plan. Unless the repayment plan provides otherwise, the debtor also will continue to keep all property for normal use after confirmation without losing it to the trustee or to creditors.[74]

In a liquidation or reorganization case in which a trustee is appointed, the trustee has the right to seek court approval for the use, sale or lease of property outside the ordinary course of business. Such use or disposition of assets beyond the ordinary course of business is not permitted without a hearing on notice.[75] In a chapter 13 case, how-

---

[70] 11 U.S.C. § 1302(b)(3).

[71] See ¶ 9.04. See also 11 U.S.C. § 1304(a) which defines a debtor "engaged in business" as one who is self-employed and who incurs trade credit in the production of income from such employment.

[72] 11 U.S.C. §§ 1302(c), 1106(a)(3).

[73] 11 U.S.C. §§ 1302(c), 1106(a)(4).

[74] 11 U.S.C. § 1306(b).

[75] See 11 U.S.C. § 363(b).

ever, the trustee does not have the authority even to request that property be used, sold or leased outside the ordinary course of business. The exclusive right to seek court approval for such use, sale or lease is given to the debtor.[76] Thus, for example, the chapter 13 debtor may request, upon notice and a hearing, that a car or home be sold, but the trustee has no standing to make the request. This provision is consistent with the policy of maintaining the debtor's control over the property of the estate instead of passing it to the trustee.

When the debtor is engaged in business, the business may continue to operate unless the court orders otherwise.[77] Subject to the same limitations placed on a debtor in possession or trustee in a reorganization case, the chapter 13 debtor has the exclusive right to enter into transactions, including the sale or lease of property of the estate, in the ordinary course of business without notice or a hearing.[78] Moreover, the debtor engaged in business has the same rights as a chapter 11 debtor in possession or trustee with respect to obtaining credit for the business.[79] By giving the debtor this leeway to conduct "business as usual," the commencement of the chapter 13 case should not interfere with the debtor's ability to rehabilitate the debtor's financial situation.

Whether the chapter 13 debtor uses, sells or leases property in the ordinary course of business or, with court approval, outside the normal business activity, Code provisions relating to the adequate protection of lienors or others may not be ignored.[80] Similarly, the use, sale or lease of assets must be consistent with any judicial relief relating to the automatic stay.[81] Limitations on the right to sell property free and clear of property interests which apply in liquidations and reorganizations are also applicable in chapter 13 cases.[82] Finally, the Code provision which invalidates so-called ipso facto clauses, also referred to as bankruptcy clauses, which attempt to terminate or condition the debtor's interest in property based on the debtor's financial condition is applicable in chapter 13 cases as well as in cases under chapter 7 or chapter 11.[83]

---

[76] 11 U.S.C. § 1303.

[77] 11 U.S.C. § 1304(b).

[78] 11 U.S.C. §§ 1304(b), 363(c). See ¶ 8.11[3] for a discussion on the limits relating to the use, sale or lease of property.

[79] 11 U.S.C. §§ 1304(b), 364.

[80] See 11 U.S.C. §§ 361, 363(d), 363(e).

[81] 11 U.S.C. § 363(d).

[82] 11 U.S.C. § 363(f). See ¶ 4.11 for a discussion on the right to sell property free and clear of property interests.

[83] 11 U.S.C. § 363(1). See ¶ 7.10[7].

¶ 9.09 THE FILING AND ALLOWANCE OF CLAIMS

The general provisions of the Code which govern the filing of proofs of claims, allowance of claims, administrative expense claims, secured claims, priorities, codebtor claims, and subordination of claims in liquidation cases also are applicable in chapter 13 cases. These matters are discussed in Chapter 5 of this book.

There are special provisions relating to the filing and allowance of postpetition claims which are applicable in chapter 13 cases only. These provisions permit the filing and allowance of two types of postpetition claims so as to enable certain creditors whose claims arise after the petition is filed to participate in the debt adjustment case along with prepetition creditors. It is important to note, however, that the Code does not compel the filing of these claims, but merely gives the creditor the option of filing. If the postpetition claim is not filed and is not dealt with in the plan, the creditor may have to wait until the close of the case in order to recover payment.[84] It may be beneficial, therefore, for the creditor to participate in the case and receive periodic payments under the plan.

The first type of postpetition claim that may be filed is a claim for taxes that becomes payable to a governmental unit while the case is pending.[85] Although the payment of postpetition tax claims is the responsibility of the debtor, not the estate, taxing authorities may be in the best position to collect these claims by receiving periodic payments under the repayment plan.

The second type of postpetition claim which may be allowed in a chapter 13 case only is a claim based on a consumer debt. It is often necessary for the debtor to obtain credit during the pendency of a chapter 13 case in order to acquire necessary consumer services and goods. In fact, such extension of consumer credit may be essential for the successful performance of the debt adjustment plan. For example, the debtor may have to borrow money for the purpose of repairing the family automobile used to travel to work. On the other hand, there is

---

[84] The automatic stay against acts to obtain possession of property of the estate prevents postpetition creditors from proceeding against the debtor's prepetition assets. 11 U.S.C. § 362(a)(3). Claimants may enforce their postpetition claims not provided for in the plan when the stay terminates. Unless the creditor obtains relief from the stay at an earlier date, it is terminated as soon as the property is vested back in the debtor. 11 U.S.C. § 362(c)(1). This vesting occurs upon confirmation. 11 U.S.C. § 1327(b). Accordingly, the postpetition creditor who does not participate in the case may be stayed from proceeding against assets until a plan is confirmed.

[85] 11 U.S.C. § 1305(a)(1).

a danger that a chapter 13 debtor may incur unnecessary credit which hampers the debtor's ability to perform under the plan. In order to balance these considerations, the Code encourages the extension of credit to a chapter 13 debtor by giving a creditor the option to file a proof of claim based on a consumer debt that arises after the commencement of the case. However, the debt must be for property or services primarily for personal, family or household purposes "necessary for the debtor's performance under the plan" in order to be allowable.[86] Moreover, as another protective measure, the Code mandates the disallowance of the postpetition consumer debt claim if the creditor knew or should have known that prior approval by the trustee of the debtor's incurring the obligation was practicable and was not obtained.[87] Accordingly, the person who extends consumer credit to the chapter 13 debtor after the commencement of the case should first obtain the approval of the trustee so as to preserve the right to file a claim and participate in the chapter 13 plan.

When a proof of claim for a postpetition tax or consumer debt claim is filed, the claim will be either allowed or disallowed in accordance with the same provisions which determine allowability of prepetition claims.[88] For allowability purposes, the postpetition claim is treated as if it had arisen before the date of the filing of the petition. The amount of the claim, however, is to be determined as of the date on which the claim arose.[89]

¶ 9.10 PROPERTY OF THE ESTATE

Section 541 of the Bankruptcy Code, which is discussed in depth in Chapter 4 of this book, determines the property which becomes the estate upon the filing of a bankruptcy petition. All of the property included in the estate pursuant to Section 541 is property of the estate in a chapter 13 case. Similarly, the rules governing exemptions under Section 522 are applicable in chapter 13 cases. Therefore, the practitioner involved in an individual debt adjustment case should consult Chapter 4 of this book.

The nature of a chapter 13 case as an extension of payments over a period of time instead of an immediate liquidation of assets necessitates an expansion of the scope of the estate to include property ac-

---

[86] 11 U.S.C. § 1305(a)(2).
[87] 11 U.S.C. § 1305(c).
[88] 11 U.S.C. §§ 502, 1305(b). See ¶ 5.05 on the allowability of claims.
[89] 11 U.S.C. § 1305(b).

quired during the repayment period. For this reason, the chapter 13 estate includes, in addition to the property specified in Section 541 of the Code, property that the debtor acquires after the commencement of the case but before the case is either closed, dismissed or converted.[90] Moreover, all earnings from services performed by the debtor between the filing of the petition and the close, dismissal or conversion of the case also become property of the estate.[91] The inclusion of such post-petition property and earnings is a significant departure from the scope of the estate in liquidation cases.[92] As a result of this inclusion, the court has jurisdiction over such property and earnings and the automatic stay protects them against collection efforts.[93]

Although the debtor's property becomes the estate, the debtor may retain possession and may continue to use the property.[94] Alternatively, the plan may provide that a part of the estate or specific assets be liquidated to enable the debtor to perform in accordance with the schedule of payments under the plan.[95]

¶ 9.11 CONVERSION OR DISMISSAL

There are special provisions which govern the conversion of a chapter 13 case to a case under a different chapter of the Code. The Code also provides for the dismissal of an individual debt adjustment case in certain situations.

[1] The Debtor's Right to Convert or Dismiss

As discussed earlier, debt adjustments are available to individuals on a voluntary basis only.[96] Unlike liquidations and reorganizations, a chapter 13 case may not be commenced by an involuntary petition. Consistent with the policy of permitting voluntary petitions only, the Code gives the debtor the absolute right to convert a chapter 13 case to a chapter 7 case at any time.[97] The debtor who decides to abandon

---

[90] 11 U.S.C. § 1306(a)(1).

[91] 11 U.S.C. § 1306(a)(2).

[92] See 11 U.S.C. § 541 and ¶ 4.03 with respect to the scope of the estate in a liquidation case.

[93] 11 U.S.C. § 362. See ¶ 1.09 on the scope of the automatic stay.

[94] 11 U.S.C. § 1306(b).

[95] 11 U.S.C. § 1322(b)(8).

[96] See ¶ 9.05.

[97] 11 U.S.C. § 1307(a). See 11 U.S.C. § 348 for the effects of conversion. See also *In re* Hendren, 240 F. Supp. 807 (S.D. Ohio 1965) in which the

the debt adjustment route during the case may switch to liquidation. In fact, any waiver of the debtor's right to so convert the case is unenforceable.[98]

Alternatively, the chapter 13 debtor who changes his or her mind about seeking a debt adjustment may request that the case be dismissed at any time. The right to request dismissal may not be waived. In general, the court has no choice but to grant the debtor's request. However, there is an important exception to the debtor's right to compel dismissal. Let us assume that a petition was filed by or against the debtor under either chapter 7 or chapter 11. Assume further that the case was converted to chapter 13 at the debtor's request. Following the conversion to chapter 13, the debtor may not compel dismissal of the case as a matter of right. Under the Code, the debtor's right to have the case dismissed does not apply if it were converted previously to chapter 13 from chapter 7 or chapter 11.[99] Thus, the debtor who has second thoughts about converting a liquidation or reorganization to a chapter 13 case may insist on another conversion to chapter 7, but may not compel dismissal.

[2] Dismissal or Conversion for Cause

An interested party may request that a chapter 13 case be either dismissed or converted to a liquidation case. The court may not grant such a request, however, unless after notice and a hearing the evidence establishes cause for the dismissal or conversion. Whether the court dismisses or converts the case to chapter 7 depends on what it considers to be in the best interests of creditors and the estate.[100] It is interesting to note, however, that the court may not convert the case without the debtor's consent if the debtor is a farmer.[101] This limitation is consistent with the provision which prohibits involuntary liquidation petitions against farmers.[102]

There are many situations which may justify dismissal or conversion. Although there is no exhaustive list of all such situations, the

---

court held that the debtor may convert a case under former Chapter XIII to a straight bankruptcy case even after the debtor defaulted on the obligations under the plan.

[98] *In re* Hendren, note 97, supra.

[99] 11 U.S.C. § 1307(b).

[100] 11 U.S.C. § 1307(c).

[101] 11 U.S.C. § 1307(e). See § 101(17) and ¶ 2.04[2][a] for the definition of "farmer."

[102] 11 U.S.C. § 303(a).

Bankruptcy Code enumerates seven circumstances which would constitute cause for dismissal or conversion: [103]

(a) Unreasonable delay by the debtor that is prejudicial to creditors;
(b) Nonpayment of any court fees and charges;
(c) Failure to file a plan timely under chapter 13 requirements;
(d) Denial of confirmation of a plan and denial of additional time for filing another plan or a modification of a plan;
(e) Material default by the debtor with respect to a term of a confirmed plan;
(f) Revocation of an order of confirmation and denial of confirmation of a modified plan;
(g) Termination of a confirmed plan by reason of the occurrence of a condition specified in the plan.

[3] Conversion to Chapter 11

The broad eligibility requirements of chapter 13 make it possible for a sole proprietor of a small business to seek an individual debt adjustment instead of a more complex reorganization under chapter 11. It is easy to appreciate that creditors may prefer to have the case proceed under chapter 11 because of greater control. In a chapter 11 case, creditors have the right to vote to accept or reject a plan, except when the cram down approach to confirmation is employed and the absolute priority standard is met.[104] A trustee may be appointed in a reorganization case to oust the debtor from management of the business whereas a chapter 13 debtor stays in control.[105] Chapter 11 requires adequate disclosure statements which are not mandatory in chapter 13 cases.[106] Creditors have the right to file plans in chapter 11 cases after a period of time, but not in chapter 13 cases.[107]

Any interested party who believes that the case should proceed under chapter 11 instead of chapter 13 may request conversion at any time before confirmation of a plan. The court has the discretion to convert a chapter 13 case to a reorganization case after a hearing on notice. Whether the court orders the conversion depends on the need for the

---

[103] 11 U.S.C. § 1307(c).
[104] See 11 U.S.C. § 1129 and ¶ 8.23.
[105] See 11 U.S.C. § 1104 and ¶ 8.13.
[106] See 11 U.S.C. § 1125 and ¶ 8.20.
[107] Compare 11 U.S.C. § 1121 with 11 U.S.C. § 1321.

unique features of chapter 11 under the circumstances.[108] If the debtor is a farmer, however, the case may not be converted to a reorganization case unless it is at the debtor's request.[109]

¶ 9.12 THE PLAN

The heart of a chapter 13 case is the repayment plan. In accordance with the voluntary nature of individual debt adjustments, the debtor is the only one who has the right to file a plan.[110] Unlike reorganization cases, creditors may not propose a plan. The trustee's role in the preparation of the plan is advisory only. The debtor, who is most sensitive to the need to support a family out of future earnings, has the final say with respect to the contents of the plan.[111]

The Bankruptcy Rules provide that the plan must be filed by the debtor either with the petition or within ten days thereafter. This time limitation may be extended for cause shown and on notice to such persons as the court may direct.[112] The court may order the debtor to furnish a sufficient number of copies of the plan to enable the court to include a copy with each notice of the meeting of creditors.[113] If the debtor fails to file a plan within the applicable time period, the court may either dismiss or convert the case to a liquidation case under chapter 7 upon the request of an interested party.[114]

The Bankruptcy Code allows for substantial flexibility with respect to the provisions of a plan. The rationale for such flexibility is that the debtor, in consultation with the debtor's attorney and the trustee, should be able to design a plan which is tailor-made for the particular circumstances of the case.

[1] Provisions That Are Mandatory or Prohibited

In light of the policy of flexibility, the Code mandates only three provisions that must be contained in every chapter 13 plan. First, the plan must provide for the submission of all or a portion of future earnings or other future income to the trustee to the extent that it is neces-

---

[108] 11 U.S.C. § 1307(d).
[109] 11 U.S.C. § 1307(e).
[110] 11 U.S.C. § 1321.
[111] See H.R. Rep. No. 95-595, 95th Cong., 1st Sess. 123 (1977).
[112] B. Rule 13-201(a).
[113] B. Rule 13-201(b).
[114] 11 U.S.C. § 1307(c)(3). See ¶ 9.11[2].

sary for the execution of the plan.[115] The remaining income, although part of the bankruptcy estate,[116] stays within the debtor's control to be used for the support of the debtor and the debtor's family. The portion of future income submitted to the trustee must be placed under the trustee's supervision and control so that the trustee may make payments to creditors in accordance with the terms of the plan. This requirement, however, does not mean that *all* payments to creditors must be made from future income. The plan may provide, if the debtor so desires, that some payments be made from the proceeds of certain assets and other payments to be made from future income. Thus, the plan may provide for partial liquidation of assets to pay creditors.[117] However, at least *some* portion of the debtor's future income must be used to pay creditors in order to meet the first requirement relative to the content of the plan. It is important to note that the Code does not mandate that the debtor deliver the portion of earnings to the trustee. Instead, the plan may provide that the debtor's employer or other source of income make payments directly to the trustee.

The second provision of the plan which is mandatory relates to the payment of priority claims. The plan must provide for full payment of all claims entitled to priority under Section 507 of the Code.[118] These are the same claims which would be entitled to priority in a liquidation case, including administrative expenses, certain wage claims, consumer deposit claims and certain tax claims.[119] The reason for compelling payment in full to these priority creditors is that they should be treated in a chapter 13 case in the same way that they would be treated in a chapter 7 liquidation. Otherwise, they would be penalized by the debtor's choice of pursuing a debt adjustment under chapter 13. The full payment of a priority claim does not have to be made in one lump sum. Instead, the plan may provide for deferred cash payments, the present value of which equals the full amount of the priority claim. Furthermore, this requirement does not apply with respect to a priority creditor who agrees to a different treatment of the claim.[120]

The final type of provision which is required applies only if the

---

[115] 11 U.S.C. § 1322(a)(1). Compare former B.A. § 646(4) which required in Chapter XIII cases submission of future earnings to the supervision and control of the court, not the trustee.

[116] See 11 U.S.C. § 1306(a)(2) and ¶ 9.10.

[117] See 11 U.S.C. § 1322(b)(8) and ¶ 9.12[2]

[118] 11 U.S.C. § 1322(a)(2).

[119] See ¶ 5.13 for a discussion on priority claims.

[120] 11 U.S.C. § 1322(a)(2).

plan classifies claims. If claims are classified, each claim within a particular class must be accorded the same treatment.[121]

In addition to mandating the three provisions mentioned above, the Code clearly prohibits two different provisions. First, the plan may not provide for payments to creditors over a period that is longer than three years, unless the court approves a longer period. The court may not approve a longer period unless cause is shown and the approved period does not exceed five years.[122] Accordingly, the repayment period may not exceed five years in any event and, without court approval based on cause, it may not exceed three years. Second, a claim secured only by a real estate mortgage on the debtor's principal residence may not be modified by any provision of the chapter 13 plan.[123]

[2] Optional Provisions

Subject to the mandatory and prohibited provisions discussed above, there are virtually limitless variations with respect to the contents of a plan. As long as it does not violate any section of chapter 13, the plan may include any "appropriate provision."[124] The Code specifies the following nine optional provisions which may be included in a plan, but it is important to appreciate that the list is not exhaustive:

[a] The Classifications of Claims

The plan may designate classes of unsecured claims in the same way that such claims may be classified in a reorganization case.[125] The members of each class must have claims which are substantially similar to others in the same class. For administrative convenience, a separate class of small claims, such as those under $50, may be placed in a separate class for immediate payment without deferral. The Code provides, however, that the plan may not "discriminate unfairly" against any designated class.[126] The mere fact that classification is permitted, indi-

---

[121] 11 U.S.C. § 1322(a)(3). See ¶ 9.12[2][a].

[122] 11 U.S.C. § 1322(c).

[123] 11 U.S.C. § 1322(b)(2). This provision does not apply to a security interest in a mobile home or other personal property used as a residence. It is important to note that, although the plan may not modify home mortgage payments, the holders of such mortgages are still subject to the automatic stay. See 11 U.S.C. § 362 and ¶ 1.09.

[124] 11 U.S.C. § 1322(b)(10).

[125] 11 U.S.C. § 1322(b)(1). See 11 U.S.C. § 1122 and ¶ 8.19[2][a] for a discussion on the classification of claims in reorganization cases.

[126] 11 U.S.C. § 1322(b)(1). See ¶ 8.23[3] for a discussion of the term "discriminate unfairly" in the context of a reorganization case.

cates that classes may be treated differently. The court has the discretion to forbid different treatment among unsecured creditors when, in the court's view, the difference creates unfair discrimination.

[b] Modifying the Rights of Creditors

The plan may modify the rights of secured or unsecured creditors.[127] With respect to each claim, the plan may be of the extension type, which means that payment is made in full over a period of time, or the composition type, which means that the total payments made to a creditor represent only a portion of the claim.

There are two caveats with respect to any provision which modifies claims. First, as discussed above, a claim secured only by a mortgage on real estate that is the debtor's principal residence may not be modified.[128] Of course, the plan may provide for curing any default on the mortgage, but the original payment requirements may not be altered. Second, the plan will not be confirmed unless holders of claims receive a minimum amount of value. These minimal protections, which depend on whether the claim is secured or unsecured, should be considered when the debtor is formulating the plan. The requirements for confirmation are discussed later in this chapter.[129]

[c] Curing or Waiving Default

The plan may provide that prior default be either cured or that a waiver of default be obtained.[130] This provision may be important with respect to secured creditors who, because of prior default, have the right to accelerate or foreclose. It is important to note, however, that a provision in the plan in connection with the cure or waiver of any default may be subject to the terms of the credit instrument or security agreement.

[d] Concurrent Payments of Secured, Unsecured, and Priority Claims

A plan may not be confirmed unless priority claims are paid in

---

[127] 11 U.S.C. § 1322(b)(2).

[128] See ¶ 9.12[1].

[129] See ¶ 9.14.

[130] 11 U.S.C. § 1322(b)(3). See ¶ 9.12[2][e] with respect to curing default on a long-term obligation.

full,[131] secured creditors receive at least the value of the collateral,[132] and unsecured claims are paid at least their liquidation value.[133] Despite these requirements, however, the Code makes it clear that these different types of claims may be paid concurrently.[134] That is, it is not necessary for priority claims to be paid *before* any other claims are to be paid, as long as the plan provides for the eventual payment of priority claims in full in deferred cash payments. Similarly, unsecured creditors may be paid while secured creditors are being paid.

[e] Curing Default and Maintaining Payment of Long-Term Debts

Long-term debts may present special problems in chapter 13 cases. Assume that the debtor has defaulted by not paying the mortgage on the debtor's home during the two-month period before the commencement of the case. Suppose further that the mortgage loan calls for monthly payments to be made for the next twelve years. May the mortgagee insist on acceleration and foreclosure because of the default? May the debtor deal with future mortgage payments in the plan?

The Code assists the debtor by permitting the plan to provide for the curing of any default "within a reasonable time."[135] Thus, the debtor may avoid loss of the property by proposing the payment of all past due installments as long as the cure is made without undue delay, such as within a month or two after confirmation of the plan. The debtor's right to cure in this manner applies even with respect to a mortgage on a principal residence.[136]

In addition, the plan may provide for the maintenance of normal payments on long-term obligations while the case is pending, even if the last installment is due after the date on which the final payment under the plan is due. For example, the plan may provide that the debtor pay the normal home mortgage payments or automobile loan payments pursuant to the loan instrument during the repayment period of the plan. When all payments have been made under the plan and the case is closed, the debtor may continue to pay these long-term obligations. The effect of this provision is that the debtor may pay in accordance with a contract repayment period which is longer than the period of re-

---

[131] See 11 U.S.C. § 1322(a)(2) and ¶ 9.12[1].
[132] See 11 U.S.C. § 1325(a)(5) and ¶ 9.14[5].
[133] See 11 U.S.C. § 1325(a)(4) and ¶ 9.14[4].
[134] 11 U.S.C. § 1322(b)(4).
[135] 11 U.S.C. § 1322(b)(5).
[136] See ¶ 9.12[2][b].

payment under the plan.[137] Of course, the unpaid installments remaining after the plan is fully executed are not discharged.[138]

[f] Payment of Postpetition Claims

As discussed above, certain claims for tax obligations and consumer debts which arise after the commencement of a chapter 13 case are allowable.[139] Consistent with the policy of allowing such postpetition claims, the Code provides that a plan may call for the payment of all or any part of them.[140]

[g] Assumption or Rejection of Executory Contracts and Unexpired Leases

A trustee in a chapter 13 case has the right to assume or reject executory contracts and unexpired leases at any time before the confirmation of a plan unless the court orders that the trustee decide at an earlier date.[141] The assumption or rejection of executory contracts and unexpired leases is discussed in another part of this book which should be consulted by practitioners involved in chapter 13 cases.[142]

If a particular executory contract or lease was not previously rejected by the trustee, the debt adjustment plan might provide for its assumption or rejection.[143] For example, the plan might reject a contract for a health spa membership, cooking lessons, or an executory contract to purchase unnecessary appliances if the terms of the contract would hamper the debtor's ability to accomplish a successful debt adjustment. The rights, liabilities, and restrictions relating to the assumption or rejection of executory contracts and leases are the same whether it is made by the trustee before confirmation of the plan or as part of the plan itself.

[h] Liquidation of Property

The Code makes it clear that a chapter 13 plan may involve at least partial liquidation of assets to pay claims.[144] The property liqui-

---

[137] Note that the repayment period under the plan may not exceed five years in any event. 11 U.S.C. § 1322(c). See ¶ 9.12[1].

[138] See ¶ 9.17 with respect to discharge.

[139] See ¶ 9.09.

[140] 11 U.S.C. § 1322(b)(6).

[141] See 11 U.S.C. § 365(d)(2).

[142] See ¶ 7.10.

[143] 11 U.S.C. § 1322(b)(7).

[144] 11 U.S.C. § 1322(b)(8).

dated may be part of the bankruptcy estate, including exempt assets, or may be property that belongs to the debtor. Thus, property purchased by the debtor after the petition is filed may be liquidated under the terms of the plan even though such property is not part of the estate. The plan may provide that property be conveyed to creditors directly or, alternatively, that the liquidation proceeds be paid to them.

Since a primary motive for filing a chapter 13 petition instead of pursuing a chapter 7 liquidation is to keep nonexempt assets, it is rare for a chapter 13 plan to provide for liquidation of most or all of the debtor's property. The extent to which a plan provides for liquidation may depend on the sufficiency of future earnings to pay creditors under the plan in addition to supporting the debtor.

[i] Vesting of Property

The plan may provide that property of the estate, including exempt property, vest in the debtor or in any other entity either on confirmation of the plan or at a later date.[145] For example, a plan may provide that the debtor's stocks and bonds vest in a certain creditor upon confirmation in payment of a claim. Unless the plan or the order of confirmation provides otherwise, all property of the estate is vested in the debtor upon confirmation.[146]

¶ 9.13 MODIFICATION OF THE PLAN BEFORE CONFIRMATION

In accordance with the Code's policy of flexibility in the formulation of a plan, chapter 13 gives the debtor the absolute right to modify a previously filed plan at any time before confirmation.[147] No court approval is necessary for the modification to be made. Of course, the plan as modified must conform to the general content requirements for chapter 13 plans. Upon filing a modification, the plan as modified becomes the plan for all purposes.[148]

In certain instances, such as when the proposed plan provides that a secured creditor is to receive less than the value of collateral, the formal acceptance of the plan by the particular creditor may be sought in order to meet the requirements for confirmation.[149] If there has been

---

145 11 U.S.C. § 1322(b)(9).

146 11 U.S.C. § 1327(b). See ¶ 9.15.

147 11 U.S.C. § 1323(a). Compare former B.A. § 653 which required leave of the court to modify a plan prior to confirmation.

148 11 U.S.C. § 1323(b).

149 See ¶ 9.14[5].

an acceptance or rejection by a secured creditor prior to the time when the plan is modified, the acceptance or rejection continues to be effective if the modification does not affect the treatment of the secured creditor under the plan. In such a situation, the secured creditor does not have the right to revoke the acceptance or rejection. However, if the modification does affect the treatment of the secured creditor's claim, the previous acceptance or rejection will not continue to be effective if the creditor revokes or changes it.[150]

¶ 9.14 CONFIRMATION OF THE PLAN

After the debtor files a debt adjustment plan, the court is required to conduct a hearing on notice to all interested parties to consider whether the plan should be confirmed.[151] The Bankruptcy Rules of Procedure require that at least ten days' notice by mail be given to all creditors.[152] Any interested party may appear to object to confirmation. An objection results in a contested matter and the hearing may have to be adjourned to permit discovery and the preparation of evidence.[153]

The trustee is the only party who is required to appear,[154] although the debtor and the debtor's attorney may be present. In preparation for the hearing, the trustee should gather information relating to the value of property secured by nonavoidable liens, the liquidation value of unsecured claims, the likelihood that the debtor will succeed in meeting the proposed payments from future income, and any other issue which may arise with respect to the requirements for confirmation.

The requirements for confirmation of a chapter 13 plan are not as strict nor complex as the requirements for confirmation of a chapter 11 reorganization plan, which is a reason why individual owners of small businesses may prefer proceeding under chapter 13. For example, chapter 13 does not give unsecured creditors the right to vote to accept or reject a plan.[155] Moreover, the absolute priority rule applicable in reorganizations with respect to the cram down method of confirmation does not apply to debt adjustment plans.[156]

---

[150] 11 U.S.C. § 1323(c).

[151] 11 U.S.C. § 1324.

[152] B. Rule 13-203(a).

[153] See B. Rule 914 and ¶ 6.04.

[154] 11 U.S.C. § 1302(b)(2)(B).

[155] Compare former B.A. §§ 651 and 652 which give creditors the right to accept or reject a Chapter XIII plan.

[156] See 11 U.S.C. § 1129(b) and ¶ 8.23[3].

It is interesting to note that chapter 13 of the new Code deletes an important requirement for confirmation under Chapter XIII of the former Act. In addition to removing the need for a creditor vote, the new chapter 13 does not require a finding that the debtor is not guilty of any act which would constitute an objection to discharge.[157] Thus, the debtor who would be deprived of a discharge in a liquidation case may have a plan confirmed under chapter 13 nonetheless.[158]

The Code sets forth six requirements which must be met in order for the court to confirm the plan. Each of these requirements will be discussed separately:

[1] Compliance With the Bankruptcy Code

The plan may not be confirmed unless its complies with the provisions of chapter 13 and with all other applicable provisions of the Bankruptcy Code.[159] For example, if the plan does not contain a required provision for full payment of priority claims, the court may not confirm it.[160] Similarly, the plan may not be confirmed if the debtor does not meet the eligibility requirements for filing a chapter 13 petition.[161]

[2] Payment of Fees and Charges

Confirmation of a plan may not be ordered unless any fee or charge under chapter 123 of Title 28 of the U.S. Code required to be paid before confirmation has been paid.[162] Although the filing fee of $60 may be paid in installments with court approval, in the usual case the fee is paid at the time the petition is filed.[163] In the rare case when the installment method is permitted, the plan will not be confirmed if the debtor is in default on any installment.

In addition, any payments which are required to be paid at or before confirmation according to the terms of the plan must be paid in order for the court to confirm. For example, if the plan proposes to

---

[157] See former B.A. § 656(3).

[158] See 11 U.S.C. § 727 and ¶ 3.03 on objections to discharge in a liquidation case.

[159] 11 U.S.C. § 1325(a)(1), derived from former B.A. § 656(a)(1).

[160] See 11 U.S.C. § 1322(a)(2) and ¶ 9.12[1].

[161] See ¶ 9.04.

[162] 11 U.S.C. § 1325(a)(2).

[163] See 28 U.S.C. § 1930(a)(1), added by B.R.A. § 246(a). See also Sugg. Int. B. Rule 1006(b).

make full payment to a class of unsecured creditors with claims of $25 or less at the time of confirmation, such payment must be made.

[3] Good Faith Proposal

A plan may not be confirmed unless it was proposed by the debtor in good faith and not by any means forbidden by law. Notwithstanding the historical development of this requirement, some courts have interpreted it to mean that a debtor must make a good faith effort to make meaningful payments to unsecured creditors.[164]

[4] Minimum Distribution on Unsecured Claims

Chapter 13 protects holders of allowed unsecured claims by requiring a minimum distribution under the plan. The value, as of the effective date of the plan, of property or cash payments to be distributed under the plan on account of each allowed unsecured claim may not be less than the amount that would be paid to the holder of the claim if the estate were liquidated under chapter 7.[165] This minimum requirement, often referred to as the "best interests of creditors" standard,[166] assures that every unsecured creditor will receive under the plan at least as much as the creditor will be left with after a liquidation.

In order to decide whether the plan meets this requirement, the court must determine the value of nonexempt assets and make a hypothetical distribution in liquidation. Priority status, allowability of claims, validity and value of liens, and other factors that affect the distribution in a chapter 7 liquidation must be taken into consideration.

In addition, the court must determine the value, as of the effective date of the plan, of future payments or property to be distributed to unsecured creditors pursuant to the plan. The effective date of the plan is usually the date when it is confirmed, although the plan may provide for a delay before it is effective. Accordingly, future payments have to be discounted to determine present value. For example, assume that an

---

[164] 11 U.S.C. § 1325(a)(3), derived from former B.A. §§ 651, 656(a)(4). See, e.g., *In re* Iacovini, 5 Bankr. Dec. 1270 (D. Utah 1980).

[165] 11 U.S.C. § 1325(a)(4).

[166] Chapter XIII of the former Bankruptcy Act required that the plan be "for the best interests of the creditors," which means that each creditor receives at least as much as would be recovered in a liquidation case. Former B.A. § 656(a)(2). See ¶ 8.23[2] for a discussion of the "best interests of creditors" standard in the context of a reorganization case.

unsecured creditor will receive $5,000 in liquidation based on a $15,000 allowable claim. The plan may not propose to pay that creditor $5,000 in fifty monthly installments of $100 each because the *present* value of such installments is less than $5,000. In essence, the plan will have to provide for discounting the installments so that present value of the future payments equals $5,000.

It is important to note that the "best interests of creditors" standard applies to all allowed unsecured claims, regardless of whether the plan proposes to deal with such claims. This fact should be taken into consideration by holders of postpetition tax and consumer debt claims, who have the option of filing proofs of claims to be allowed.

[5] Treatment of Secured Claims

It is not mandatory that the plan affect the rights of secured parties. If a secured claim is not dealt with in the plan, the lienor may seek relief from the automatic stay in order to pursue contractual remedies in the event of default.[167] However, if the plan proposes to modify the rights of secured creditors, the plan may not be confirmed unless at least one of three requirements are met with respect to the holder of each allowed secured claim.[168]

One way to satisfy the requirement with respect to an allowed secured claim provided for by the plan is to obtain the acceptance of the secured creditor. If the lienor accepts the plan, the manner in which the creditor is treated under the plan may not be the basis of an objection to confirmation.

Alternatively, the plan may be confirmed if, with respect to the holder of an allowed secured claim who does not accept the plan, it provides that the creditor shall retain the lien, and that the value of payments or property to be distributed to the lienor under the plan is not less than the allowed amount of the secured claim. In determining the value of the property or payments to be distributed under the plan, the *present* value must be determined as of the date when the plan is to become effective, which is usually the date of confirmation. Because the amount of the allowed secured claim is limited to the value of the collateral, the effect of this requirement is that the lienor is entitled to, in terms of present value of payments to be made under the plan, at least the value of the collateral up to the amount of the claim.[169] In

---

[167] See 11 U.S.C. § 362(d) and ¶ 1.09[7].

[168] These requirements are set forth in 11 U.S.C. § 1325(a)(5).

[169] See 11 U.S.C. § 506 and ¶ 5.11[1] on the allowance of secured claims.

lieu of future payments, of course, other property may be conveyed to the secured creditor in order to meet this standard. This alternative is often called a cram down approach to confirmation because it allows for the modification of the secured party's rights without consent.[170]

The third acceptable treatment of allowed secured claims is to provide in the plan that the debtor surrender the collateral to the secured creditor. In this way, the secured party is sure to receive at least the value of the allowed secured claim.

It is important to note that undersecured creditors, i.e., those whose collateral is valued at less than the amount of the debt owed, are treated as having two separate claims.[171] The creditor has an allowable secured claim up to the value of the collateral, and an allowable unsecured claim for the deficiency. In such situations, the plan must give the creditor the liquidation value of the unsecured claim as discussed above, as well as satisfying one of the three requirements with respect to the allowed secured claim. The result of these requirements is that the nonassenting creditor will receive in present value in the chapter 13 case at least as much as will be received in a liquidation case. If these minimum standards are not met, the plan may not be confirmed.

[6] Feasibility of the Plan

The Code prohibits confirmation unless the court makes a determination that the debtor will be able to make all payments under the plan and otherwise to comply with its terms.[172] The trustee's role in this issue is significant. One of the reasons for imposing on the trustee the obligation to investigate the debtor's financial situation, to advise the debtor when formulating a plan, and to appear and be heard at the confirmation hearing is so that the trustee may act as an objective source on the feasibility of the plan under the particular circumstances of the case.[173] Congress made it clear that the debtor's "primary obligation to

---

[170] The availability of the cram down approach is a significant departure from Chapter XIII of the former Act. Under Chapter XIII, every secured party whose claim was "dealt with" by the plan had to accept the plan in order to have the plan confirmed. Former B.A. § 652(1). Compare the cram down requirements in the new chapter 13 with the stricter requirements for a cram down in chapter 11 reorganizations. See 11 U.S.C. § 1129(b)(2)(A) and ¶ 8.23[3].

[171] See 11 U.S.C. § 506 and ¶ 5.11[1].

[172] 11 U.S.C. § 1325(a)(6), derived from former B.A. § 656(a)(2) which required that a Chapter XIII plan be "feasible."

[173] See ¶ 9.07.

support his dependents" must be considered in determining whether the plan is likely to succeed.[174]

¶ 9.15 THE EFFECT OF CONFIRMATION

Confirmation of a plan makes it binding on the debtor and on all creditors. Each creditor is bound by the confirmed plan, whether or not the claim of the creditor is provided for by the plan and whether or not the creditor either has objected to, has accepted, or has rejected the plan.[175]

The Code gives the bankruptcy court broad powers to enforce the confirmed plan. The court may issue any order, process or judgment that is necessary or appropriate to carry out the provisions of the plan.[176] The court may order any entity from whom the debtor receives income, including a trust or a government employer, to pay all or any part of that income to the trustee so that payments under the plan can be made.[177]

Although the confirmed plan becomes effective and binds all creditors, it is important to note that confirmation alone does not result in a discharge of debts. In contrast to the confirmation of a chapter 11 reorganization plan, which results in an immediate discharge of debts and replacement with new obligations spelled out in the plan, the chapter 13 debtor is not discharged until after the plan is fully executed or, in limited situations, when the debtor fails to comply with the plan.[178] As a practical matter, the delay of the discharge until compliance of the plan in most cases does not matter because the binding effect of the plan, the automatic stay, and the court's injunctive powers prevent creditors from enforcing their claims other than as provided for in the plan.

---

[174] H.R. Rep. No. 95-595, 95th Cong., 1st Sess. 124 (1977).

[175] 11 U.S.C. § 1327(a), derived from former B.A. § 657.

[176] See 11 U.S.C. § 105(a). Compare *In re* Jackson, 424 F.2d 1220 (7th Cir. 1970) *cert. denied* 400 U.S. 911 (1970), which held that a bankruptcy court had no authority to grant injunctive relief against the employer of the Chapter XIII debtor.

[177] 11 U.S.C. § 1325(b). See 11 U.S.C. § 101(14) for the definition of "entity." Compare United States v. Krakover, 377 F.2d 104 (10th Cir. 1967), *cert. denied* 389 U.S. 845 (1968), which held that under former Chapter XIII the federal government could not be ordered to pay wages to the trustee.

[178] See 11 U.S.C. § 1328 and ¶ 9.17. Compare 11 U.S.C. § 1141(d) and ¶ 8.24 dealing with discharge in a reorganization case.

A significant effect of confirmation is that it automatically vests all of the property of the estate in the debtor, except as otherwise provided in the plan or the order of confirmation.[179] This result is consistent with the policy of giving the chapter 13 debtor use and enjoyment of assets except for the portion of future income or property to be used to carry out the debt adjustment plan. If the plan provides for the conveyance or liquidation of certain property, then those specific assets do not vest in the debtor and remain as the bankruptcy estate.

When property of the estate vests in the debtor upon confirmation of a plan, it does so free and clear of any claim or interest of any creditor provided for by the plan, except as otherwise indicated in the plan or the order of confirmation.[180] The vesting of property free and clear of liens is significant with respect to the rights of secured creditors. Providing for secured claims in the plan is optional, not mandatory. If a secured claim is not provided for in the plan, the property vests in the debtor subject to the lien and the secured creditor may seek relief from the automatic stay to enforce the contractual right to payment.[181] However, in the event that the plan provides for a secured claim, such as by reducing the amount of each monthly installment, the collateral vests in the debtor upon confirmation free and clear of the security interest unless the plan or confirmation order provides otherwise. For this reason, secured creditors who are asked to accept a plan should insist that the plan provide for the continuation of the lien. If a secured creditor affected by the plan does not accept it and the collateral is not surrendered, the plan *must* provide for the continuation of the lien or else it may not be confirmed.[182] Thus, the plan usually provides that security interests continue in the collateral after confirmation either to induce secured creditors to accept the plan or, in the absence of acceptance, to meet the requirements for confirmation.

¶ 9.16 PAYMENTS PURSUANT TO THE PLAN

The plan must provide for submission to the trustee of so much of the debtor's future income as necessary for compliance with the plan.[183] The trustee receives a portion of the debtor's income which, as part of

---

[179] 11 U.S.C. § 1327(b).

[180] 11 U.S.C. § 1327(c).

[181] See 11 U.S.C. § 362(d) and ¶ 1.09[7] on the right to be relieved from the automatic stay.

[182] 11 U.S.C. § 1325(a)(5)(B). See ¶ 9.14[5].

[183] 11 U.S.C. § 1322(a)(1). See ¶ 9.12[1].

the bankruptcy estate, is within the exclusive jurisdiction and control of the bankruptcy court.[184] If necessary to assure that the trustee will receive the appropriate portion of debtor's income, the court may order any entity from whom the debtor receives income to pay it to the trustee directly.[185] In the usual case, however, the debtor pays a portion of the debtor's income to the trustee without the need to involve the employer.

The trustee acts as the disbursing agent by paying creditors pursuant to the terms of the confirmed plan.[186] The plan or the confirmation order may provide for direct payment by the debtor or a third party to a creditor, thus bypassing the trustee, but such arrangements are rare.

The Code requires that two categories of claims and expenses be paid in full before or simultaneously with payment to any other creditors. First, before any creditor gets paid under the plan, every allowed administrative expense claim and every court fee assessed against the estate must be paid in full.[187] Thus, the $60 filing fee must be paid in full before creditors receive anything under the plan, even if the debtor has permission to pay the fee in installments. This requirement is consistent with the policy of giving these claims and expenses the highest priority in a liquidation case. Second, if a standing trustee is serving in the case, the percentage fee fixed for that trustee must be paid in full before or simultaneously with payment to creditors under the plan.[188]

¶ 9.17 DISCHARGE

There are two ways in which a chapter 13 case may result in a discharge of indebtedness. Regardless of which method is applied, however, the bankruptcy court is required to hold a discharge hearing at which the debtor must appear in person.[189] The purposes and procedures involved with respect to the discharge hearing are discussed in Chapter 3 of this book.[190]

It is interesting to note that the grounds for objecting to a dis-

---

[184] See 11 U.S.C. § 1306(a)(2) and ¶ 9.10 dealing with the debtor's earnings as part of the estate.

[185] 11 U.S.C. § 1325(b).

[186] See 11 U.S.C. § 1326(b).

[187] 11 U.S.C. §§ 1326(a)(1), 151326(1). See 11 U.S.C. § 507(a)(1) and ¶ 5.08 with respect to administrative expenses.

[188] 11 U.S.C. §§ 1326(a)(2), 151326(2). See 11 U.S.C. § 1302(e) and ¶ 6.07[5] dealing with the standing trustee's fee.

[189] 11 U.S.C. § 524(d).

[190] See ¶ 3.07.

charge in liquidation cases do not apply under chapter 13.[191] Thus, individuals who may not receive a discharge under chapter 7, such as persons who failed to keep adequate books and records, should consider seeking chapter 13 relief. Most importantly, a debtor who received a discharge within the previous six years is not barred from obtaining a discharge under chapter 13, although the debtor would not be eligible for a discharge in a chapter 7 liquidation.[192]

Another important aspect of a chapter 13 discharge is that it usually does not prevent a subsequent discharge under chapter 7 within the following six years. If the payments actually made pursuant to the chapter 13 plan total 100 percent of the allowed unsecured claims, i.e., when the plan is of the extension type instead of the composition type, the chapter 13 discharge is not a ground for objection in any subsequent bankruptcy case. Moreover, if the plan was proposed by the debtor in good faith, it was the debtor's best effort, and payment was made of at least 70 percent of the allowed unsecured claims, the chapter 13 discharge is not a bar to another discharge in a liquidation case within the following six years.[193] In the event the proposed plan provides for payment of more than 70 percent, but less than 100 percent, of the allowed unsecured claims, a determination of good faith and best efforts probably will be made by the court upon application of the debtor at the confirmation hearing. For this reason, it may be wise for the chapter 13 debtor to provide in the plan for at least 70 percent payment so that, in the event of future financial difficulty, a chapter 7 discharge would be available.

[1] Discharge Upon Completion of Payments

The most desirable way for the chapter 13 debtor to receive a discharge is to comply fully with the terms of the plan. As soon as practicable after the final payment is made pursuant to the plan, the court is required to grant the debtor a discharge, unless the court approves a written waiver of discharge executed by the debtor after the chapter 13 petition is filed.[194]

The discharge granted after full compliance with the plan is very broad in scope. Debts, whether secured or unsecured, which are provided for by the plan are discharged. The debtor is also released from

---

[191] See 11 U.S.C. § 727 and ¶ 3.03. See also Lee, "Chapter 13 nee Chapter XIII," 53 Am. Bankr. L.J. 303, 323–324 (1979).

[192] See 11 U.S.C. § 727(a)(8).

[193] 11 U.S.C. § 727(a)(9).

[194] 11 U.S.C. § 1328(a).

debts which are disallowed by the court. However, debts which are incurred by the debtor after the commencement of the case and not provided for by the plan are not subject to the discharge.[195]

There are only three types of debts which are excepted from discharge upon full compliance with the plan.[196] As discussed earlier, a long-term debt which, by the terms of the underlying contract, is payable at least in part after the last payment is due under the plan, such as a mortgage loan payable over a period of time exceeding the life of the chapter 13 plan, may be dealt with in the plan.[197] Specifically, the plan may provide for the curing of any default within a reasonable time and the maintenance of payments while the case is pending on such a long-term debt. Obviously, it would be unfair for the debtor to be discharged on this type of obligation because of the mere fact that the plan provided for cure or continuation of payments at the contract rate during the case. Accordingly, such long-term obligations are excepted from discharge.[198]

The second exception to discharge involves a debt to a spouse, former spouse, or child, for alimony, maintenance, or support in connection with a separation agreement, divorce decree or property settlement.[199] This exception does not apply, however, to the extent that the debt was assigned to another entity, such as a state social services department which gave financial support to the debtor's dependents.

Third, a discharge under chapter 13 does not release the debtor from any allowed postpetition consumer debt if prior approval by the trustee of the debtor's incurring the debt was practicable but was not obtained.[200] As discussed earlier, a postpetition consumer debt may be allowed in a chapter 13 case in certain situations.[201] The reader will recall that such a debt must be disallowed if the creditor knew or should have known that prior approval by the trustees of the debtor's incurring the obligation was practicable and was not obtained. That condition on allowability is designed to encourage creditors to seek approval prior to extending consumer credit. Similarly, the Code encourages

---

[195] *Id.*

[196] Compare the exceptions to discharge in liquidation cases under 11 U.S.C. § 523. See ¶ 3.09.

[197] See ¶ 9.12[2][e].

[198] 11 U.S.C. § 1328(a)(1).

[199] 11 U.S.C. § 1328(a)(2). See 11 U.S.C. § 523(a)(5) and ¶ 3.09[5] for a discussion on this exception to discharge.

[200] 11 U.S.C. § 1328(d).

[201] See 11 U.S.C. § 1305(a)(2) and ¶ 9.09 dealing with allowable postpetition consumer debts.

debtors to initiate such approval by excepting the postpetition consumer debt from discharge unless the prior approval of the trustee is obtained.

It is interesting to note that eight categories of obligations which survive a chapter 7 discharge are released in a chapter 13 case upon full compliance with the plan.[202] For example, a debt based on fraud or embezzlement or a tax obligation which is excepted from discharge in a liquidation case will be discharged under chapter 13 by fulfilling the terms of a confirmed plan, whether or not the plan provides for the payment of 100 percent of all claims. For this reason, the debtor who has substantial indebtedness which will not be discharged in a chapter 7 case may well be advised to consider the filing of a chapter 13 petition instead.

[2] Discharge Without Completion of Payments

Let us assume that the debtor fails to complete the payments provided for in the plan. May the debtor receive a discharge nonetheless?

Chapter 13 provides for the so-called "hardship" discharge which may be granted when the debtor has not completed payments under the plan.[203] This type of discharge may be granted at any time after confirmation of the plan. There are several requirements, however, which must be met before the court may grant such a discharge. First, the court must hold a hearing on notice for the purpose of determining whether the discharge should be granted. Second, the court may grant the discharge only if the court finds that the debtor's failure to complete the payments is due to circumstances for which the debtor should not justly be held accountable.[204] For example, the debtor's default under the plan may have been caused by a serious illness which interfered with the debtor's ability to continue employment.

Another requirement for a hardship discharge is that the value, as of the effective date of the plan, of all property and payments actually distributed under the plan on account of each unsecured claim is not less than the amount that would have been paid on such claim if the estate had been liquidated under chapter 7.[205] Thus, the liquidation value standard required for confirmation is also required for a hardship

---

[202] See 11 U.S.C. § 523 and ¶ 3.09.

[203] 11 U.S.C. § 1328(b). See, H.R. Rep. No. 95-595, 95th Cong., 1st Sess. 430 (1977)

[204] 11 U.S.C. § 1328(b)(1).

[205] 11 U.S.C. § 1328(b)(2).

discharge.[206] If any holder of an allowed unsecured claim does not receive at least the liquidation value of the claim, the debtor is not entitled to a hardship discharge.

It is much more preferable for the debtor who is unable to complete payments under the plan to seek a reasonable modification of the plan instead of simply defaulting. For this reason, the Code prohibits the granting of a hardship discharge unless the court is satisfied that modification of the plan is not practicable.[207]

A discharge granted without the completion of payments under the confirmed plan is not as broad as the full compliance discharge discussed above. The hardship discharge applies only with respect to *unsecured* claims provided by the plan or disallowed by the court.[208] In contrast to the full compliance discharge, secured claims are unaffected by the hardship discharge. Moreover, the hardship discharge does not apply to any debts which are nondischargeable in a liquidation case.[209] For example, the chapter 13 debtor may be released from debts based on recent tax claims or embezzlement if the plan is executed in full, but not if a hardship discharge is granted.

A hardship discharge is similar to a full compliance discharge in two respects. First, long-term obligations which are cured and maintained during the pendency of the case, but which outlive the life of the plan, are not affected by any chapter 13 discharge.[210] Second, a hardship discharge is similar to a full compliance discharge in that it does not release the debtor from any allowed postpetition consumer debt if prior approval by the trustee of the debtor's incurring such debt was practicable and was not obtained.[211]

[3] Revocation of Discharge

A chapter 13 discharge may be revoked on request of a party in interest. However, the request for revocation must be made before one year after the discharge is granted, or else any such request is time barred. Moreover, the request for revocation may not be granted unless, after a hearing on notice, the court finds that the discharge was obtained through fraud and that the party seeking the revocation first

---

[206] See 11 U.S.C. § 1325(a)(4) and ¶ 9.14[4].

[207] 11 U.S.C. § 1328(b)(3). See 11 U.S.C. § 1329 and ¶ 9.18 on modification of the plan after confirmation.

[208] 11 U.S.C. § 1328(c).

[209] 11 U.S.C. § 1328(c)(2). See 11 U.S.C. § 523(a) and ¶ 3.09 on exceptions to discharge in liquidation cases.

[210] 11 U.S.C. § 1328(c)(1). See 11 U.S.C. ¶ 1322(b)(5) and ¶ 9.12[2][e].

[211] 11 U.S.C. § 1328(d). See 11 U.S.C. § 1305(a)(2) and ¶ 9.09.

learned of the fraud after the discharge was granted.[212] Consequently, the creditor who has knowledge that a chapter 13 debtor is about to obtain a discharge through fraud must object, if at all, prior to the granting of the discharge.

¶ 9.18 MODIFICATION OF THE PLAN AFTER CONFIRMATION

The debtor's financial situation may deteriorate even further due to unforeseen circumstances after a plan is confirmed. An unexpected medical expense, loss of income, or the birth of an additional dependent may make it impracticable for the debtor to comply with the terms of the plan. In such a case, the debtor may seek a modification of the confirmed plan.

A modification of a confirmed plan may be made in order to either increase or reduce the amount or time of payments on claims of a particular class provided for by the plan.[213] In addition, if a creditor whose claim is provided for in the plan obtains payment from a source other than the debtor or otherwise in a way that is not pursuant to the terms of the plan, the plan may be modified to the extent necessary to take account of such payment.[214] For example, if a codebtor voluntarily pays a claim provided for in the plan, the plan should be modified so that the creditor does not, in total, receive more than 100 percent of the amount of the original claim.

There are several restrictions which limit the debtor's ability to modify a plan after confirmation. The plan as modified must contain the three types of provisions which are required for all chapter 13 plans, including provisions for the submission of future income to the trustee, the full payment of priority claims, and equal treatment of claims within a particular class.[215] The section of chapter 13 which governs optional provisions of the plan are applicable to modified plans as well.[216] Moreover, the requirements for confirmation of a chapter 13 plan apply equally to the modification of a confirmed plan.[217]

If a secured creditor has accepted or rejected the plan prior to confirmation, the acceptance or rejection continues to be effective if the modification after confirmation does not affect the secured creditor's

---

[212] 11 U.S.C. § 1328(e).
[213] 11 U.S.C. §§ 1329(a)(1), 1329(a)(2).
[214] 11 U.S.C. § 1329(a)(3).
[215] 11 U.S.C. § 1329(b)(1). See ¶ 9.12[1].
[216] 11 U.S.C. § 1329(b)(1). See ¶ 9.12[2].
[217] 11 U.S.C. § 1329(b)(1). See ¶ 9.14.

position. Thus, the acceptance or rejection may not be revoked unless the modification deals with the secured claim. If the creditor's treatment is different under the modified plan, the previous acceptance or rejection continues unless revoked.[218]

As discussed earlier, a plan may not provide for payments over a period that is longer than three years, unless the court approves a longer period for cause. In no event may the court approve a period that is longer than five years.[219] A modification after confirmation may not extend this maximum time period. That is, the plan as modified may not provide for payments over a period that is longer than three years after the time when the first payment under the *original* confirmed plan was due. The court, however, may approve a longer period up to five years after the time when the first payment under the original confirmed plan was due, but only if there is cause for such approval.[220]

The plan as modified becomes the plan for all purposes unless, after notice and a hearing, the modification is disapproved by the court.[221] If no person objects to the proposed modification after notice to interested parties, the court may approve it without the need for a hearing.[222] In the event that a hearing is held, the trustee is required to appear and be heard on the appropriateness of the modification.[223]

The debtor who is having difficulty in making the payments under a confirmed plan is not required to seek modification. Clearly, the Code encourages modification when necessary for the same reasons that it encourages rehabilitation and debt adjustment in the first instance. Nonetheless, the debtor who is unable to comply with the terms of the plan may abandon the effort to succeed at debt adjustment by converting the case to a liquidation case under chapter 7 or by seeking a dismissal.[224] If the debtor merely defaults with respect to a material term of the plan, such as by failing to make the required payments to creditors, any party in interest may request that the case either be converted to a chapter 7 liquidation or dismissed.[225] The final alternative for the debtor who is unable to comply with the confirmed plan is to seek a hardship discharge.[226] However, such a discharge is granted only if

---

[218] 11 U.S.C. §§ 1329(b)(1), 1323(c).
[219] See ¶ 9.12[1].
[220] 11 U.S.C. § 1329(c).
[221] 11 U.S.C. § 1329(b)(2).
[222] See 11 U.S.C. § 102(1).
[223] 11 U.S.C. § 1302(b)(2)(C).
[224] See 11 U.S.C. § 1307 and ¶ 9.11.
[225] 11 U.S.C. § 1307(c)(5).
[226] See 11 U.S.C. § 1328(b) and ¶ 9.17[2].

certain requirements are met, including a determination that modification is not practicable.[227]

¶ 9.19 REVOCATION OF A CONFIRMATION ORDER

If an order of confirmation was procured by fraud, the court may revoke the order on request of any party in interest. The court may not revoke a confirmation order, however, unless the request is made within 180 days after the date on which the order was entered. Notice must be given prior to the revocation and, upon the request of any party, a hearing is held to determine whether there was fraud in procuring the order.[228]

Upon revocation of a confirmation order, the court may dispose of the case by dismissing it or, if the best interests of creditors and the estate so dictate, the court may convert the case to a chapter 7 liquidation. Alternatively, the court may fix a time within which the debtor may propose a modification of the plan for confirmation.[229]

---

[227] 11 U.S.C. § 1328(b)(3).

[228] 11 U.S.C. § 1330(a), derived from former B.A. § 671 and B. Rule 13-214(b).

[229] 11 U.S.C. § 1330(b).

Chapter 10

ALTERNATIVE INSOLVENCY PROCEEDINGS

¶ 10.01 AVAILABLE ALTERNATIVES FOR THE INSOLVENT DEBTOR[1]

Credit executives observing their debtors cease operations with the intent of liquidating their assets for the benefit of creditors are often perplexed by the numerous methods of liquidation available.[2] Although the Bankruptcy Code offers a uniform system of liquidation throughout the United States and its territories, alternative insolvency proceedings differ from state to state. Unfortunately, there is a lack of uniformity among states which is not caused by the unique commercial needs of a particular locality, but rather is the product of haphazard growth. Moreover, competing insolvency systems are in existence *within* each state and territory. For example, New York has several statutes which have been either designed or invoked for the liquidation of insolvent estates:

(1) The general assignment for the benefit of creditors under the New York Debtor and Creditor Law[3] and the complementary provisions for the liquidation of claims of secured creditors;[4]
(2) Nonjudicial dissolution of insolvent corporations under Article 10 of the New York Business Corporation Law;[5]
(3) Judicial dissolution of an insolvent corporation under Article 11 of the New York Business Corporation Law;[6] and
(4) Bulk transfer of the assets of an insolvent debtor which is governed by Article 6 of the Uniform Commercial Code.[7]

In addition to these alternatives, the insolvent debtor may attempt to achieve an out-of-court arrangement with creditors. This type of arrangement requires the cooperation of all major creditors in order to

---

[1] Parts of an article by Weintraub, Levin & Sosnoff, "Assignments for the Benefit of Creditors and Competitive Systems for Liquidation of Insolvent Estates," 39 Cornell L.Q. 3 (1953) were used for this chapter with permission of the copyright owner.

[2] See New York Credit Men's Adjustment Bureau, Inc. v. Weiss, 305 N.Y. 1, 110 N.E.2d 397 (1953), where the court discusses the proceedings available to an insolvent.

[3] N.Y. Debt & Cred. Law Art. 2 (McKinney 1945), as amended §§ 4, 12–16, 18, 22, 24 (McKinney Supp. 1978).

[4] N.Y. Debt. & Cred. Law Art. 2A (McKinney 1945), as amended § 30 (McKinney Supp. 1978).

[5] N.Y. Bus. Corp. Law Art. 10 (Nonjudicial Dissolution) §§ 1001–1009 (McKinney 1963), as amended § 1008 (McKinney Supp. 1979).

[6] N.Y. Bus. Corp. Law Art. (McKinney 1963), as amended §§ 1104a, 1111, 1118 (McKinney Supp. 1979).

[7] U.C.C. Art. 6.

be successful. Although such common law composition agreements may be used to achieve liquidation, these arrangements are more common when the debtor seeks to rehabilitate the business without resorting to the need to file a petition for reorganization under chapter 11 of the Bankruptcy Code. The out-of-court arrangement is discussed in greater detail in Chapter 8 of this book.

This conflict between in-court and out-of-court procedures is further accentuated by the Bankruptcy Code which makes available an additional means of liquidation of an insolvent's estate. Since it is axiomatic that an insolvent's estate belongs to the creditors, it follows that any disposition of the debtor's property for the purpose of liquidation and distribution should be in accordance with a design and practice best suited to give creditors the highest return in dollars, as well as to afford a thorough examination and orderly administration.[8]

The general weakness of the out-of-court procedure, however, is its susceptibility to abuse. The fact that there may at times be creditor supervision does not lessen the possibility that the procedure will not protect creditors' interests on every occasion.

It follows, therefore, that without adequate creditor supervision the rights of the creditors can be preserved only in proceedings which safeguard the debtor's assets, not only those assets which are in *custodia legis,* but those which have been transferred somewhere on the eve of insolvency. Preservation of assets is the primary feature of an effective insolvency statute. Equally important is an equitable distribution without preference among general creditors. Interwoven with these principles are simplicity of procedure and economy of operation. What is the extent to which out-of-court and in-court procedures measure up to these standards? An appreciation of these values may aid in understanding the relative merits of each type of insolvency system.

¶ 10.02 THE STATUTORY ASSIGNMENT FOR THE BENEFIT OF CREDITORS

The extensive use of statutory assignments for the benefit of creditors in many states leads to the conclusion that they constitute an important factor in insolvency liquidations. The exploration of the reasons would seem to indicate, first and foremost, their ease of execution. The statutory assignment, like the common law assignment or deed of trust,[9] is a transfer of the insolvent's property to a trustee or assignee for the

---

[8] See ¶ 10.06.

[9] See ¶ 10.03.

purpose of liquidating for the benefit of the insolvent's creditors. The ease of execution of an assignment, usually a simple printed document requiring no initial effort or real expense on the part of the debtor, has been one of the reasons why it has found favor among debtors. Another positive feature of the assignment for the benefit of creditors is that it is an easy way for the debtor to avoid being the subject of a bankruptcy case, as many debtors have the horror of the so-called bankruptcy stigma.[10]

Most statutes have no prohibition against the choice of the debtor's representative as assignee.[11] Although it would be wise in the first instance to execute the assignment to bona fide creditors' associations or representatives, nevertheless the leeway to assign assets to the debtor's attorney has the salutary result of quick immunization of assets as against attaching creditors. Creditors are not remediless in such situations, however, as they can petition for a substitution of the assignee if the facts warrant a finding of misconduct, incompetency or conflict of interest; or creditors may file an involuntary petition for liquidation under chapter 7 of the Bankruptcy Code.[12] Assignments for the benefit of creditors, therefore, serve a useful purpose in preserving assets for the benefit of creditors. Once those assets have been brought under the custody of the assignee or the court, the choice then is with the creditors as to whether bankruptcy or the assignment proceedings will furnish the best results.

The assignment also serves a useful purpose in common law settlements[13] or extensions as an escrow document, i.e., the debtor often agrees with the creditors to pay their obligations over an extended period of time; the assignment document is executed and held in escrow to secure the debtor's promise to make the extended payments. The agreement between the debtor and the creditors provides that in the event the debtor defaults, the creditors may file the assignment and

---

[10] See Harris, "The Bulk Sale As a Vehicle for Effecting Out-of-Court Settlement with Creditors," 55 Com. L.J. 317 (1950): "He is motivated by the desire . . . to escape the stigma of being designated a bankrupt. . . ."

[11] Compare Ark. Stat. Ann. §§ 36-301-308 (1962) which provides for the appointment of a receiver; Cal. [Civ.] Code §§ 3449–3473 (West 1970) as amended (1978) which provides for the assignment by an insolvent in trust to the sheriff who calls a meeting of creditors for the purpose of electing an assignee from their own number.

[12] See 11 U.S.C. § 303(h)(2) and ¶ 2.09[2].

[13] For a discussion of common law assignments, see Weintraub, "Some Practical Aspects of Debtor-Creditor Adjustments for the General Practitioner," a lecture published in two parts: 126 N.Y.L.J. 702, col. 1 (Oct. 2, 1951) and 126 N.Y.L.J. 714, col. 1 (Oct. 3, 1951).

liquidate the assets under it. This assures creditors immediate control over their debtor's estate. The escrow deposit does not bar the debtor from filing a voluntary petition under either chapters 7 or 11 of the Bankruptcy Code.[14]

These uses give assignments a facility and flexibility of operation not possessed by other liquidation proceedings. But, of course, an insolvency statute has other fundamental purposes[15] and the question arises as to what extent the statutory assignment competes with other means of liquidation, such as the Bankruptcy Code, state dissolution proceedings for corporations, and bulk transfers.

¶ 10.03 THE COMMON-LAW ASSIGNMENT OR DEED OF TRUST

The forerunner of the statutory assignment was the common-law assignment for the benefit of creditors or deed of trust. A century or more ago almost all assignments for the benefit of creditors were common law assignments. This was so simply because there were few state statutes regulating assignment proceedings. Debtors were proclaimed to have an "inherent common law right"[16] to make general assignments; or, stated differently, a general assignment "creates an express trust, no legislation is needed to give it validity."[17] Absent fraud, the common-law assignment was invulnerable to attack by objecting creditors.[18]

While most statutes today permit a debtor to do little more than choose an assignee, at common law the debtor had wide discretion in fixing the terms and conditions of the trust. The debtor could execute a partial assignment, prefer one creditor over another, and even demand releases from consenting creditors. Finally, the debtor could endow the assignee with broad discretionary powers in the administration of the trust.[19] The entire proceeding has been appropriately described as:

> [a] private transaction between the debtor and the assignee, with little of the notoriety which its avowed object would seem to acquire, and its effect has not inaptly been characterized as a "bankrupt law made by the debtor for himself."[20]

---

[14] See 11 U.S.C. § 301.

[15] See ¶ 10.01.

[16] Brashear v. West, 32 U.S. (7 Pet.) 608 (1833).

[17] *Glenn On Liquidation*, § 123 at 204 (1935).

[18] *Id.* at 174.

[19] Burrill, *Voluntary Assignments for the Benefit of Creditors*, 23, 24, 171 (6th ed. 1894).

[20] *Id.* at 24.

Creditor control over the "inherent common law right" of debtors to make general assignments seldom came about, and when it did, it was only in a negative fashion upon the discovery of fraud. At such times, an ambitious creditor might sue under statutes outlawing fraudulent conveyances or seek to invoke the equity powers of the courts. Needless to say, such costly and somewhat undefined remedies were rarely pressed.[21]

In the later years of the nineteenth century many aspects of common-law assignments were recognized as abusive: the debtor was too much in command of the parceling out of the assets; there were no anticipatory safeguards against fraud; investigation was not easy; and preferred treatment of friendly creditors was unseemly. Methods were sought which would afford creditors some authority and equal participation in the proceeding, and which would insure the integrity of the assignee. The outcome was the enactment of state statutes regulating assignments for the benefit of creditors.

A few of these statutes, such as those of Maryland[22] and Massachusetts,[23] are very brief. They leave regulation to case law, and as a result assignments continue as private arrangements. Most statutes, however, are comprehensive and specify in detail the steps to be followed in assignment proceedings. Some of the elaborate statutes contain express provisions that they are to be regarded as exclusive,[24] and thereby completely replace common-law assignments. Other statutes, although comprehensive, are silent or ambiguous on the question of exclusiveness.[25]

The problem of what to do with nonconforming assignments is left to the courts. This problem has many phases. It arises when nonconsenting creditors attempt to attack the assignment by levying upon the assets in the assignee's possession. When confronted with such suits, courts render decisions based on the usual considerations: facts, equities, and determinations of legislative intent and policy. Concern with whether the irregularities in the assignments are deliberate or inadvertent is rarely displayed and, with exceptions to be noted below, most of this litigation is treated as involving isolated occurrences. Courts do not

---

[21] *Id.* at 23.

[22] Ann. Code of Md., §§ 15-101 to 15-103 (1975) (Michie Co.).

[23] Mass. Ann. Laws, Ch. 203, §§ 40–42 (Michie/Law. Co-op 1958).

[24] The assignment law of New Jersey provides: "All general assignments for the benefit of creditors shall be made in accordance with the provisions of this chapter." N.J. Stat. Ann. § 2A:19-6 (West 1932).

[25] See, for example, N.Y. Debt. & Cred. Law Art. 2 (McKinney 1945), as amended §§ 4, 12–16, 18, 22–24 (McKinney Supp. 1978).

frequently regard the facts at hand as reflecting a general practice throughout the state.

In suits to upset assignments which do not satisfy statutory requirements, courts have resolved this problem by either declaring them void or, alternatively, by upholding them.

[1] Noncomplying Assignments Declared Void

The court may declare the noncomplying assignment void and permit creditors to continue levying on assets. When an assignor verified his schedule of assets as "just and true" in the face of a statute which required the oath to read "full and complete," the Georgia Supreme Court declared the assignment void and refused a request for permission to amend the affidavit.[26]

The unfeasibility of permitting common-law assignments and statutory assignments to exist side by side in the same state was recognized by a New York court in *Lubinsky v. Hoffman.*[27] In that case, the assignor attempted at the outset to proceed in accordance with New York's Debtor and Creditor Law. However, he failed to acknowledge his assignment as required by Section 3 of that law. When the defect was realized, he tried to amend the instrument of assignment to make it a common law deed of trust. Upon a creditor's suit, the court declared the document void. The decision can be criticized for permitting the attacking creditor to recover in full to the exclusion of other creditors.[28] However, the reasons offered by the court for its refusal to honor the makeshift proceeding are persuasive. Speaking of the New York Debtor and Creditor Law, the court said:

---

[26] Fort v. Martin Tobacco Co., 77 Ga. 111, 1 S.E. 223 (1887). For other cases where the assignments were discarded, see Youghiogheny Ohio Coal Co. v. Anderson, 186 Mich. 349, 152 N.W. 1025 (1915); Haverhill Shoe Novelty Co. v. Leader Shoe Co., 87 N.H. 366, 180 A. 242 (1935); Lubinsky v. Hoffman, 158 Misc. 261, 284 N.Y.S. 549 (Sup. Ct. 1934), *aff'd* 246 App. Div. 803, 285 N.Y.S. 1074 (1st Dep't 1936).

[27] Note 26 *supra.*

[28] Compare Metro Burak, Inc. v. Rosenthal & Rosenthal, Inc., 83 Misc. 2d 637, 372 N.Y.S.2d 781, (Supp. Ct. Richmond County 1975), *aff'd as mdf'd* 51 App. Div. 2d 1003, 380 N.Y.S.2d 758 (2d Dep't 1976), holding that a judgment creditor who has knowledge that an assignment does not strictly comply with the statute may be estopped from asserting priority based on post-assignment levy if the statutory requisites are subsequently met. The court stated that the plaintiff may not take advantage of a mere oversight to claim priority over its fellow creditors who might have continued their own collection procedures had they known what plaintiff was going to do. *Id.* at 761, 380 N.Y.S.2d at 761.

> The only manner in which the property of a debtor may be assigned and distributed for the benefit of creditors is in accordance with the provisions of the debtor and creditor law. Otherwise this law would just be an empty collection of words to be observed according to the whims and fancies of the debtor and his select group of creditors. . . . The debtor and creditor law contains minute specifications of each step in the assignment for the benefit of creditors. The Appellate Division of this department has amplified the statute law by a code of rules, which must be observed in the handling of the debtor's estate.[29]

The rationale of the *Lubinsky* case is incontrovertible. When the state legislature has provided elaborate and comprehensive procedures for conducting general assignments, these procedures should be followed and the assignment should not be left to private arrangement. Any shortcomings in the law can be cured by amendment.

[2] Noncomplying Assignments Upheld

Some courts have held assignments valid despite deviation from the statute. This result is justified generally on the rationale that the assignment, valid at common law, is not invalidated by the statute. An assignment, irregular under the statute, was upheld as valid at common law in *Damaskus v. McCarty-Johnson Heating and Eng'r Co.*[30] The creditor attempted to garnishee property in the hands of the purchaser from the assignee. Striving to avoid the inequalities that would accrue upon the creditor's success, the Colorado court resorted to the oft-heard reasoning that the statute was directory rather than mandatory, and therefore common-law assignments were still legal. Assignees in Colorado, however, are best advised to comply with the statute because, ten years later, the same court ruled that, although common-law assignments were recognized and legal, creditors of the assignor who did not

---

[29] Lubinsky v. Hoffman, note 26 *supra,* at 262, 284 N.Y.S. at 550. The court stated:

> There is nothing effective about a common-law deed of trust unless all of the creditors, including loan and merchandise creditors, join therein. Otherwise, such a common-law deed of trust is void. The Debtor and Creditor law and the rules of the Appellate Division provide for rigid supervision over the estates of insolvent debtors. Parties must not be allowed to deal with insolvents' property at their own smart will. The law has been written into the Debtor and Creditor law and its provisions must be followed and obeyed.

Id. at 263, 284 N.Y.S. at 550, 551.

[30] 88 Colo. 279, 295 P. 490 (1931).

consent to the assignment could levy on the assets in the hands of the assignee just as though such assignment had not been made.[31]

A serious problem is posed in those jurisdictions where, in order to avoid the alleged inconvenience and expense of court supervision that would result from statutory requirements, assignments are consistently and deliberately made outside the assignment statutes. When such dodging of legislative enactments receives court sanction, two equally valid classes of assignments are found to exist side by side in a given jurisdiction: the first is statutory and the other is nonstatutory or common law. This problem exists in California as a result of the leading case of *Brainard v. Fitzgerald.*[32]

Brainard v. Fitzgerald involved an assignment to the secretary of the board of trade of San Francisco "on a printed form used generally by boards of trade." The assignment was for the benefit of creditors generally, but it was conceded by the assignee that it did not comply with the California statute as to its form or recordation. The court ruled that a valid common-law transfer had taken place and held it impervious to an attacking creditor. The court then concluded:

> In the absence of any conflict with or violation of our statutory law, we are not inclined to interfere with the practice developed by local boards of trade of procuring assignments executed in good faith for the benefit of creditors generally.[33]

The result of the decision in the *Brainard* case was to establish for California alternative systems for the execution and administration of general assignments. The first is a free-style, undefined liquidation to be worked out by private arrangement between the debtor and the assignee. Whatever is devised the court will uphold, provided there is no "conflict" with California's statutory law.[34]

---

[31] McKelvy v. Striker, 108 Colo. 320, 116 P.2d 921 (1941). See also International Brown Drilling Corp. v. Ferguson Trucking Co., 347 P.2d 773 (Colo. 1959).

[32] 3 Cal. 2d 157, 44 P.2d 336 (1935). See Shimm, "The Impact of State Law on Bankruptcy," 1971 Duke L.J. 879, 890. See also Comment, 36 Calif. L. Rev. 586, 587 (1948).

[33] *Id.* at 163, 44 P.2d at 339.

[34] See, e.g., The Mechanics Bank of Richmond v. M. H. Rosenberg, 201 Cal. App. 2d 419, 20 Cal. Rptr. 202, 205 (1962) where the court stated that even though the procedure for the statutory assignment for the benefit of creditors was not followed, California law recognized the common law assignment. The court went on to note that while California has two completely independent systems by which an insolvent debtor can assign his property, the common law mode is usually followed because it is less expensive and less complicated than the statutory one.

The second type of general assignment provided for in California is the statutory one. California's comprehensive law[35] provides, among other things, for the filing of assignments, inventories and assignee's bonds; it sets conditions for the examination of assignors; recites methods for the conduct of sales; directs accounting by assignees and fixes their fees. This law also states that certain assignments are void, e.g., assignments which contain preferences or demand releases; and finally, the law provides for priority payment to certain classes of tax[36] and wage claimants.[37] In sum, the California statute is designed to insure the orderly administration of insolvent estates and to shut off the likelihood of any preferential or fraudulent drain of assets.

¶ 10.04 ASSIGNMENTS IN THE VARIOUS STATES AND TERRITORIES

An analysis of the assignment statutes existing in the fifty states, the District of Columbia, Puerto Rico, and the Virgin Islands, shows the existence of such an amorphous group as almost defies classification. The range is from the simplest type, such as exists in Idaho, to the comprehensive type in New York. The Idaho statute is an example of oversimplification in that its sole provision is a mandate that no assignment for the benefit of creditors is valid unless the assignee is a bona fide resident of the state.[38] Such matters as the duties, powers, rights, and remedies of an assignee are ostensibly left to judicial legislation.

At the other extreme of the statutory horizon is the New York law which is the most comprehensive of all assignment statutes.[39] The statute incorporates many sections of the former Bankruptcy Act thereby giving greater rights to the assignee to support the recovery of assets for creditors.[40]

The credit executive checking accounts in fifty-three jurisdictions will want to know whether all or any of these statutes not only provide for an equitable distribution of the assets available for creditors, but

---

[35] Calif. [Civ.] Code §§ 3449–3473 (West 1970).

[36] Cal. [Rev. & Tax.] Code § 6756 (West 1970) as amended (1977).

[37] Cal. [Civ. Proc.] Code § 1204 (West 1972).

[38] Idaho Code § 68-201 (1949).

[39] Note 3, *supra*.

[40] See N.Y. Debt. & Cred. Law § 15 (McKinney 1945) as amended in 1950 (McKinney Supp. 1978). See also Weintraub & Levin, "General Assignment for the Benefit of Creditors: Recent Amendments to the Law," 123 N.Y.L.J. 1786, col. 1, (May 19, 1950) and 123 N.Y.L.J. 1806, col. 1 (May 22, 1950). It will be interesting to see whether this trend is continued under the new Bankruptcy Code.

whether the statutes have at least the minimal provisions for the recovery of preferences and fraudulent conveyances. Finally, creditors will want to know whether participation in the assignment proceeding releases the creditor's claim against the debtor.

A classification of types of state assignment statutes based on the credit executive's viewpoint is possible:

[1] The New York Type [41]

New York offers a comprehensive legal procedure for the liquidation of insolvent estates under court supervision with adequate protection for creditors. Jurisdiction of the proceedings is in the supreme or county court.[42] Provision is made for the form, filing, and acknowledgement of assignments.[43] Although the statute does not clearly indicate that the assignment must include all the debtor's property and must be for the benefit of all creditors, the decisional law is to that effect.[44]

Within twenty days after the assignment, the debtor is required to file a detailed schedule of assets and liabilities.[45] To encourage effective compliance with this requirement, the debtor's attorney is allowed compensation for the services rendered in this connection.[46] This is somewhat similar to the compensation allowable under the Bankruptcy Code to the attorney for the debtor.[47] If the debtor fails to file such schedules, the statute authorizes that the assignee shall prepare and file them instead.

The duties of an assignor are somewhat analogous to those of a debtor in a liquidation case under the Bankruptcy Code. The assignor must comply with all lawful orders of the court, examine the correctness of all claims, deliver to the assignee papers, books, and records, and, if ordered by the court, submit to examination under oath.[48]

---

[41] N.Y. Debt. & Cred. Law Art. 2 (McKinney 1945) as amended § 4, 12–16, 18, 22–24 (McKinney Supp. 1978).

[42] N.Y. Debt. & Cred. Law Art. 2, § 2 (McKinney 1945).

[43] N.Y. Debt. & Cred. Law Art. 2, § 3 (McKinney 1945).

[44] See *In re* General Assignment for Benefit of Creditors of Forty Wall St. Corp., 258 App. Div. 108, 15 N.Y.S.8d 554 (1st Dep't 1939). See also Freeman v. Marine Midland Bank, 419 F. Supp. 440, 447 (E.D.N.Y. 1976).

[45] N.Y. Debt. & Cred. Law § 4 as amended (McKinney Supp. 1978).

[46] N.Y. Debt. & Cred. Law § 4 subd. 6 as amended (McKinney Supp. 1978).

[47] See 11 U.S.C. § 330(a)(1) and ¶ 6.10.

[48] N.Y. Debt. & Cred. Law § 4, as amended (McKinney Supp. 1978). See 11 U.S.C. § 521 on the debtor's duties in a bankruptcy case.

The duties of the assignee likewise run parallel to those of a trustee under the Bankruptcy Code.[49] The assignee must sell the property at public auction unless good cause is shown for a private sale. The statute grants the assignee the authority to advertise for creditors to present claims, and prescribes the form of claim to be used. Before selling any property, the assignee must file a bond in an amount to be fixed by the court, generally in a sum equal to at least the value of the assets. The assignee must collect and reduce the property of the estate to cash, report to the court the disallowance of claims, furnish information regarding the estate to interested parties as requested, keep regular accounts and, finally, close the estate as expeditiously as possible.[50] Failure of the assignee to perform any of these duties is grounds for the judge to remove the assignee on application of a creditor.[51]

It is clear that creditors are afforded a role in the administration of the estate. The statute requires that creditors receive at least ten days' notice of all proposed sales of property, the payment of dividends, the final accounting and the compromise of any controversy.[52] Provision is made for the allowance of claims, including damages for breach of lease, and the principle of setoff is recognized.[53]

The court is given broad power to supervise the proceeding, allow claims, authorize the continuance of the business, and to determine the exemptions of assignors. It may also authorize the assignee to bring an action against persons who have received property in fraud of creditors when such transfers may have been avoided by creditors. Moreover, the court may authorize the institution of a suit to recover a voluntary preference. The court has the additional power to allow the claims of secured creditors in such sums as may be owing above the value of collateral, to permit the assignee to examine parties and witnesses under oath, and to compel their attendance and the production of books.[54]

The court may also require the filing of interim and final reports and, if such reports are acceptable, may discharge the assignee and the assignee's surety. Power is given to the court to approve a composition settlement between the assignor and creditors, to punish contempt re-

---

[49] N.Y. Debt. & Cred. Law § 14, as amended (McKinney Supp. 1978). See 11 U.S.C. § 704 and ¶ 6.07 on duties of a trustee in a bankruptcy case.

[50] N.Y. Debt. & Cred. Law § 14, as amended (McKinney Supp. 1978).

[51] N.Y. Debt. & Cred. Law § 8 (McKinney 1945).

[52] N.Y. Debt. & Cred. Law § 12, as amended (McKinney Supp. 1978).

[53] N.Y. Debt. & Cred. Law § 13, as amended (McKinney Supp. 1978). Compare 11 U.S.C. § 553 on the treatment of the right to set off in bankruptcy cases.

[54] N.Y. Debt. & Cred. Law § 15, as amended (McKinney Supp. 1978).

sulting from any disobedience or any violation of an order, and to restrain by arrest a party or witness from leaving the jurisdiction.[55] Finally, the court is given such power as a surrogate may exercise in reference to an account by an executor or administrator.[56]

One of the most important powers vested in the court is the authority to set aside certain liens.[57] All claims which for want of record or otherwise would not be valid against the claims of creditors of the assignor will not be considered liens against the estate. Thus, unperfected security interests, although valid as against the debtor, are invalid as against the assignee.[58] The concept that the assignee's title is no better than that of the assignor has been abandoned.

Preferences to general creditors are prohibited[59] other than for wages which are limited to a sum not to exceed $1,000 earned by each employee within three months prior to the assignment.[60] Priorities for debts owed to the United States are not contained in the assignment statute but have been made applicable by federal law.[61] The uniform act governing liquidation of secured claims in insolvency proceedings has likewise been made applicable.[62]

New York provides only for a voluntary assignment proceeding commenced at the volition of the debtor alone.[63] New York has no

---

[55] *Id.*

[56] N.Y. Debt. & Cred. Law § 15(17), as amended (McKinney Supp. 1978). This anomalous provision stems historically from the jurisdiction of probate courts over the distribution of insolvent estates. See Williston, "The Effect of the National Bankruptcy Act on State Laws," 22 Harv. L. Rev. 547 (1909).

[57] N.Y. Debt. & Cred. Law § 17 (McKinney 1945).

[58] See U.C.C. § 9-301. See also *In re* General Assignment for the Benefit of Creditors of Nat'l N.Y. Packing & Shipping Co., 82 Misc. 2d 1010, 372 N.Y.S.2d 274 (Sup. Ct. N.Y. County 1975). This is similar to the trustee's avoiding powers under the Bankruptcy Code. See 11 U.S.C. § 544(b) and ¶ 7.01.

[59] N.Y. Debt. & Cred. Law § 23, as amended (McKinney Supp. 1978).

[60] N.Y. Debt. & Cred. Law § 22, as amended (McKinney Supp. 1978). See also §§ 21a, 22(2)(a), which extends the definition of wages to include fringe benefits. Compare 11 U.S.C. § 507(a) with respect to priorities under the Bankruptcy Code.

[61] See 31 U.S.C. § 191.

[62] Article 2A of the N.Y. Debtor & Creditor Law is an adoption of the Uniform Act Fixing Basis of Participation by Secured Creditors in Insolvent Estates, 9 Uniform Laws Annotated, approved by the Commissioners on Uniform State Laws and recommended by them for enactment by the states.

[63] Certain states, however, do provide for the appointment of a receiver by the court upon a creditor's request if the debtor is preferring creditors or

provision whereby preferential or fraudulent transfers by the debtor in contemplation of insolvency shall operate as an assignment of the debtor's property for the benefit of all creditors.[64] Although forced assignments may be extremely useful in those jurisdictions that do not have effective statutes for the recovery of preferential and fraudulent conveyances, they are inconsistent with the voluntary nature of assignment proceedings.

The New York assignment statute is a comprehensive liquidating statute which must be followed to the exclusion of common law assignments. Extensive statutory regulation and close judicial supervision have rendered, for practical purposes, the New York assignment for the benefit of creditors a state bankruptcy proceeding.[65]

[2] The Texas and Virginia Type Statute and the Discharge Question

One of the most perplexing problems relating to assignment statutes is the question of the availability of a discharge to the debtor. The Texas and Virginia statutes are examples of those purporting to grant a debtor a discharge. The Texas statute [66] provides for the discharge of the debtor from the claims of those consenting creditors who have received dividends of at least 33⅓ percent. The Texas creditor may avoid a release by refusing to consent to the assignment. However, a creditor who does not consent to an assignment is not entitled to share in the distribution of the debtor's estate.[67]

The Virginia statute [68] provides that the assignment may contain a provision that consenting creditors are deemed to have discharged the assignor. To what extent are those and similar statutes valid?

The Supreme Court has held that a state assignment statute that grants a discharge to nonconsenting as well as to consenting creditors is void, at least as far as the discharge provision of the statute is con-

---

making fraudulent conveyances in contemplation of insolvency. See, e.g., Ohio Rev. Code Ann. § 1313.56 (1962) Page's Ohio Rev. Code Ann.

[64] Compare Ky. Rev. Stat. § 378.060 (1970) and Pa. Stat. Ann., Tit. 39, §151 (Purdon 1958) which provide that when the debtor makes a preference in contemplation of insolvency, it shall operate to the benefit of all the creditors of the debtor. See Note, 41 Ky. L.J. 450 (1953).

[65] See Shimm, "The Impact of State Law on Bankruptcy," 1971 Duke L.J. 880, 891 (1971).

[66] Tex. Bus. & Com. Code Ann., Tit. 3, § 23.10 (Vernon 1968).

[67] Tex. Bus. & Com. Code Ann., Tit. 3, § 23.30 (Vernon 1968).

[68] Va. Code § 55-159 (1974).

cerned.[69] The discharge of debts is a unique feature of federal bankruptcy legislation which cannot be superseded by state legislation.[70]

The validity of assignment statutes that release only consenting creditors was dealt with in *Johnson v. Star*.[71] The Supreme Court upheld the Texas assignment statute even though participation in the assignment served to release the debtor from the claims of the consenting creditors.[72] Although the Supreme Court has not ruled on the constitutionality of the Virginia assignment statute, it appears that the statute will be upheld because creditors are afforded the opportunity to avoid a release by refraining from participation in the assignment.[73] The creditor who is not satisfied with the assignment has the option of not consenting to it and filing an involuntary petition under the Bankruptcy Code.[74]

[3] The Georgia Type

The Georgia assignment statute[75] allows the assignor, if not a corporation,[76] to prefer one creditor over others.[77] Several states still allow preferences of one sort or another.[78] All such enactments have a basic weakness in not providing for equal distribution. However, the creditor who discovers that the insolvent debtor has preferred one or more creditors may wish to file an involuntary bankruptcy petition under the Bankruptcy Code.[79]

---

[69] Boese v. King, 108 U.S. 379, 2 S. Ct. 765 (1883). See also *In re* Wittstein 166 F. Supp. 122, 124 (D.V.I. 1958); United States v. Rome, 414 F. Supp. 517, 520 (D. Mass. 1976).

[70] The U.S. Constitution gives Congress the power to "establish . . . Uniform Laws on the subject of bankruptcies throughout the United States." U.S. Const., Art. I, § 8, Cl. 4. See *In re* Wisconsin Builders Supply Co., 239 F.2d 649 (7th Cir. 1956).

[71] 287 U.S. 527, 53 S. Ct. 265 (1933).

[72] Note 65 *supra*, at 880, 891.

[73] But see, Note, 36 Va. L. Rev. 813 (1950) where at least one commentator believes that the Virginia assignment statute should be held unconstitutional because of the discharge provision.

[74] See 11 U.S.C. § 303 and Chapter 2 *supra* on involuntary petitions.

[75] Ga. Code Ann. § 28-301-320 (1969).

[76] Ga. Code Ann. § 28-302 (1969).

[77] Ga. Code Ann. § 28-301 (1969).

[78] See, e.g., *id.;* Mont. Rev. Codes Ann. §§ 18-305, 18-309 (1967); N.D. Cent. Code § 13-01-03 (1971). See also Miss. Code Ann. § 85-1-1 (1972); Pollock v. Sykes, 74 Miss. 700, 21 So. 780 (1897); Bradberry v. Adams, 110 Miss. 581, 70 So. 697 (1916).

[79] Although the making of a preference, in and of itself, is not grounds for the filing of an involuntary petition, other grounds may exist. See 11 U.S.C. § 303 and Chapter 2 *supra.*

[4] The Connecticut Type

Under Connecticut law statutory insolvency proceedings have been superseded [80] by the Bankruptcy Code. The state statute is applicable only with regard to debtors who do not qualify for filing a bankruptcy petition or who may not be the subject of an involuntary petition. For example, involuntary insolvency proceedings may be commenced against farmers under Connecticut law [81] because they may not be subjects of involuntary bankruptcy cases.[82] However, the constitutionality of this provision is questionable.[83] The common law-assignment also seems to be void in Connecticut unless all creditors assent thereto.[84]

A number of jurisdictions have no assignment statute at all.[85] In some of these jurisdictions the common-law assignment still exists independent of any statutory regulation.[86] In those jurisdictions where the common-law assignment is held to be void, there is no state method of insolvency liquidation of an individual or partnership. Connecticut, however, does have a statute for the judicial and nonjudicial dissolution of corporations,[87] similar in design to the corporate dissolution statute of New York.[88]

[5] The Idaho Type

The Idaho statute [89] offers no substantial guidance to the assignee as the provisions for executing and administering assignments are sketchy. The Idaho statute provides only that the assignee must be a

---

[80] Conn. Gen. Stat. Ann. § 45-159 (West 1960).

[81] See, e.g., Pitcher v. Standish, 98 A. 93, 90 Conn. 601 (1916).

[82] 11 U.S.C. § 303(a).

[83] See Comment, 1938 Wisc. L. Rev. 302, 312 (1938): "If a state law provides for [involuntary proceedings], it should be held that the law is an insolvency law and that it is inoperative within the field of the Bankruptcy Act."

[84] Conn. Gen. Stat. Ann. § 45-159 (1960), as amended (1979).

[85] Ill. Me., Nev., Ore., Neb., Hawaii, and P.R. have no assignment statutes.

[86] Ill., Me., and Ore. have common law assignments which exist independent of statutory regulation. See J. Walter Thompson Co. v. Whitehead Co., 56 N.E. 1106 (Ill. 1900); Pleasant Hill Cemetery v. Davis, 76 Me. 289 (1884); Hall's Western Auto Supply Co. v. Brock, 400 P.2d 5 (Sup. Ct. Oregon 1965).

[87] Conn. Gen. Stat. Ann. §§ 33-375 et seq. as amended (West 1979).

[88] N.Y. Bus. Corp. Law. Art. 10, 11 (McKinney 1963), as amended §§ 1008, 1104a, 1111, 1118 (McKinney Supp. 1978). See ¶ 10.06.

[89] Idaho Code § 68-201 (1973).

resident of the state; there are no other requirements or provisions in the statute relating to assignments. Several other states have statutes of this nature.[90] The general weakness of these statutes is that they furnish no guide for the assignee, and procedures, rights, and remedies are made to depend upon the uncertainty of decisional law.

¶ 10.05 SHORTCOMINGS OF STATE ASSIGNMENT PROCEEDINGS

Many state assignment statutes were modeled generally after the former Bankruptcy Act. While it is difficult to generalize about these statutes because they differ from state to state, the New York statute, in particular, closely parallels the former Act in many details.[91] For example, the claims of a landlord for damages resulting from the rejection of an unexpired lease on real estate has been limited to a period not to exceed one year, plus an amount equal to the unpaid accrued rent;[92] priority has been granted to wage earners in a sum not exceeding $1,000 for wages earned within three months of the assignment;[93] and fees paid by the assignor to an attorney prior to and in connection with an assignment have been made subject to reexamination and excessive payments are recoverable.[94] It will be interesting to see whether the New York Debtor and Creditor Law is amended to conform with the provisions of the new Bankruptcy Code.

Although the New York statute follows the former Bankruptcy Act closely, it could not compete in many substantial respects with the former Act. The shortcomings of the New York statute, which is the most comprehensive assignment statute, are worthy of discussion.

---

[90] See, e.g., Fla. Stat. Ann. §§ 727.01, 727.04 (West 1969); Ga. Code Ann. §§ 28-303, 28-312, 28-313; Minn. Stat. Ann. § 577.01 (West 1947); Miss. Code Ann. § 85-1-1 (1973); N.D. Cent. Code § 32-26-04 (1976); Va. Code § 55-162 (1974).

[91] See Krause, "Insolvent Debtor Adjustments Under Relevant State Court Statutes As Against Proceedings Under the Bankruptcy Act," 12 Bus. Law 184, 186–189 (1957) for a comparison of New York's assignment law with former Bankruptcy Act.

[92] N.Y. Debt. & Cred. Law § 13, as amended (McKinney Supp. 1978). See former B.A. § 63a(9).

[93] N.Y. Debt. & Cred. Law § 22, as amended (McKinney Supp. 1978). See former B.A. § 64a(2), limiting the wage earner's priority to $600 earned within three months of bankruptcy.

[94] N.Y. Debt. & Cred. Law § 4, as amended (McKinney Supp. 1978). See former B.A. § 60d.

[1] Inability to Deal With Involuntary Preferences

From a liquidation statute with common law vestiges allowing preferential treatment of creditors, the New York statute has grown into one designed for equal distribution of assets to general creditors. The statute originally authorized preferences to general creditors limited to one-third of the estate. The preferences were lawful if contained in the document assigning the debtor's property. The authority for preferential Law Revision Commission whose purpose was to: remove variations between the law as to general assignments and the comparable provisions of the Bankruptcy Act which hinder successful use of the general assignment as an alternative to bankruptcy.[95]

Thereafter, an effective provision was inserted in the statute authorizing the assignee to institute an action to recover a voluntary preference received within four months of the assignment under much the same circumstances as when a trustee may recover a preference under the former Bankruptcy Act.[96] However, although the trustee in bankruptcy may set aside both voluntary and involuntary transfers,[97] the New York provision still leaves an involuntary preference, such as an attachment or judgment lien obtained prior to the assignment, beyond the assignee's avoiding powers.[98]

Statutes of several states provide for the setting aside of such a preferential lien if obtained within a period not exceeding four months prior to the execution of the assignment.[99] Equality of distribution among general creditors necessitates such provisions. The current status of the assignee in New York deprives him of rights which a trustee in bankruptcy enjoys under the Bankruptcy Code to avoid involuntary preferences. Effective administration requires that the assignee have the rights, remedies, and powers similar to those of a bankruptcy trustee. There exists no sound reason to differentiate between voluntary and involuntary preferences.

---

[95] See *Report of the N.Y. Law Revision Commission* 295, 296 (1950), Leg. Doc. 65(1) at 11 and 12 (1950).

[96] N.Y. Debt. & Cred. Law § 15 subd. 6(a), as amended (McKinney Supp. 1978). See former B.A. §§ 60a and 60b. It will be interesting to see whether states such as New York amend their assignment statutes to conform to the new ninety-day preference period contained in the Bankruptcy Code. See 11 U.S.C. § 547.

[97] See 11 U.S.C. § 547 and ¶ 7.05 on preferences.

[98] See *In re* S. Feldman & Co. 237 App. Div. 720, 262 N.Y.S. 681 (1st Dep't 1933); see also note 91 *supra*, at 184, 188.

[99] See, e.g., R.I. Gen. Laws § 10-4-6 (1970) (4 months); Wis. Stat. Ann. § 1218.18(3) (West 1974) (4 months).

The Uniform Commercial Code recognizes the principle that an assignee should have the same powers as a trustee in bankruptcy with respect to unperfected security interests.[100] An unperfected security interest is held to be subordinate to the claim of a lien creditor. The Code defines "lien creditor" as one who has obtained a lien on property by "attachment, levy or the like and includes an assignee for the benefit of creditors . . . and a trustee in bankruptcy . . . or a receiver in equity. . . ."[101]

[2] Lack of Adequate Court Supervision

No insolvency system offers sounder administration than the Bankruptcy Code in providing for the supervision of a liquidation case by the bankruptcy judge and the trustee.[102] They are highly skilled judicial officers whose daily business is bankruptcy and its problems. The day-to-day administration of a bankruptcy case is the responsibility of the trustee, while the bankruptcy judge has broad jurisdiction over virtually all disputes. These judicial officers maintain jurisdiction over a case and its many facets from beginning to end. Their supervision encompasses liquidation of assets as well as problems of allowability of claims.

In state assignment proceedings, courts often do not exercise direct supervision. In the Supreme Court of the State of New York in the counties of New York and Kings, for example, various phases of the proceedings are brought on for hearing at special terms of the court. In these courts several judges pass upon different phases of the proceeding with none having complete supervision of the whole because of the rotation of presiding justices. Moreover, state court judges rarely have the same expertise and experience in liquidation proceedings as federal bankruptcy judges.

[3] Inability to Obtain Discharge

State assignment proceedings do not give the debtor complete relief because of the inability of the states to grant a discharge.[103] While this is an important consideration for the individual, it is an irrelevant shortcoming with respect to the partnership or corporate debtor which is not even entitled to a discharge under the Bankruptcy Code.[104] The in-

---

[100] U.C.C. § 9-301.

[101] *Id.*

[102] See Chapter 6 *supra* for a discussion on the bankruptcy court and trustee.

[103] See ¶ 10.04[2].

[104] See 11 U.S.C. § 727(a)(1) and ¶ 3.03[1].

ability to obtain a discharge of debts is one of the reasons why it is rare for individuals to file an assignment for the benefit of creditors.

[4] Lack of Uniformity—Conflict of Laws

Lack of uniformity among state asssignment statutes may create difficulties in administration. When an assignment is filed in one jurisdiction and property is located in another the problem presented is whether the assignee's title is superior to claims of local creditors. In light of the desirability of having a single law govern the assignment of a debtor's interests rather than as many laws as there are states in which the debtor has property,[105] the general rule is that whether an assignment is effective to transfer the debtor's interests in chattels or intangible rights is determined by the law of the one state which has the most significant relationship to the debtor and the assignment. If the debtor is an individual the state will usually be the state of domicile; if the debtor is a corporation, the state will generally be the state of incorporation.[106] However, this principle does not displace the rights of local creditors to levy upon the assets in their jurisdiction and obtain a lien superior to that of the assignee.[107]

¶ 10.06 WHICH PROCEEDING IS CHEAPER?

There is much speculation as to whether an assignment for the benefit of creditors is cheaper than a federal bankruptcy liquidation. Statistical comparison is difficult because each individual case has its own variables, such as types of assets sold, market conditions, depreciation, and others. Furthermore, it is difficult to measure worthy but often costly and unfruitful efforts to uncover fraudulent and preferential transfers, and to measure the cost of investigating and possibly opposing a debtor's application for a discharge.

In *New York Credit Men's Adjustment Bureau, Inc. v. Weiss,*[108] the argument was made that a sale by an auctioneer was a less expensive administration in the liquidation of assets and would bring greater returns to creditors than a bankruptcy or assignment. Plaintiffs countered that certain values would necessarily be sacrificed: an indepen-

---

[105] *Restatement (Second) of Conflict of Laws*, § 250 Comment *b*, (1971).

[106] *Restatement (Second) of Conflict of Laws*, § 250 (1971).

[107] See Clark v. Williard, 294 U.S. 211, 213 (1935): "Every state has jurisdiction to determine for itself the liability of property within its territorial limits to seizure and sale under the process of its courts."

[108] 305 N.Y. 1, 110 N.E.2d 397 (1953).

dent trustee, an examination of witnesses, and a possible recovery of preferences. Similarly, in a bankruptcy case, even if the costs are somewhat higher, the creditor obtains the advantage of a dignified examination of the debtor and witnesses before a judicial officer and a thorough examination into the debtor's financial history.[109]

From the individual debtor's viewpoint, it must be remembered that the bankruptcy system also provides for a discharge and allows exemptions which may be more significant than those allowed by state exemption laws.[110]

The person interested in commencing an insolvency proceeding, either as the debtor or as a petitioning creditor, should not choose the avenue for relief based on expense alone. In the final analysis, this choice should be founded on a determination of which procedure best satisfies the needs of a particular case.

¶ 10.07 JUDICIAL AND NONJUDICIAL CORPORATE DISSOLUTION PROCEEDINGS

New York, in common with many states, has proceedings for the judicial and nonjudicial dissolution and liquidation of insolvent corporations.[111] A nonjudicial dissolution in New York must be authorized by at least two-thirds of all outstanding stockholders, unless the certificate of incorporation contains a different provision.[112] After dissolution, the corporation ceases to do business but has the power to wind up its affairs, to collect its assets and sell them for cash at public or private sale, and generally to do all other acts appropriate to liquidate its business.[113] A further provision authorizes a distribution of the assets to stockholders entitled to them, but only after paying or adequately providing for the payment of the liabilities of the corporation.[114]

The nonjudicial dissolution statute also provides for corporate action and survival of remedies after dissolution so that the corporation

---

[109] See Gamer, "On Comparing "Friendly Adjustment and Bankruptcy," 16 Cornell L.Q. 35, 66 (1930), where the court stated that "it is submitted that bankruptcy gives much more for its increased costs. . . ." See also note 91 *supra*, at 187-188.

[110] See ¶ 4.07 for a discussion of exemptions.

[111] See N.Y. Bus. Corp. Law Art. 10 (Nonjudicial Dissolution) §§ 1001-1009 and Art. 11 (Judicial Dissolution), as amended § 1008, 1104a, 1111, 1118 (McKinney Supp. 1978).

[112] N.Y. Bus. Corp. Law, Art. 10, §§ 1001, 1002 (McKinney 1963).

[113] N.Y. Bus. Corp. Law, Art. 10, § 1005 (McKinney 1963).

[114] *Id.*

may sue or be sued. Dissolution does not affect any remedy available against the corporation, its directors or officers.[115] Moreover, the statute also provides a time limitation for the filing of claims and the giving of notice to creditors.[116] The court is given the authority,[117] upon a petition by a creditor, director, officer, shareholder, or other, to supervise the adequacy of the notice, to determine the validity or invalidity of any claims presented, to determine the payment or compromise of claims against the corporation, to order the appropriate disposition or destruction of records, to appoint a receiver [118] or to issue an injunction, as well as to grant other miscellaneous relief.

Whereas the nonjudicial dissolution proceeding in New York must be authorized by shareholders, the judicial dissolution proceeding may be initiated by the attorney general who petitions for dissolution,[119] or by a majority of directors who adopt a resolution finding either that the assets of the corporation are not sufficient to discharge liabilities or that a dissolution will be beneficial to the shareholders.[120] A majority of shareholders are given the same right as the directors to adopt a resolution and petition for the dissolution of the corporation.[121] After the judicial dissolution proceeding is commenced by the filing of a petition, the same statutory provisions and procedures which govern nonjudicial proceedings are applicable.[122]

As an alternative means of liquidation, corporate dissolution can compete effectively with the assignment for the benefit of creditors. It is apparent that the dissolution of an insolvent corporation is free from the many restraints which generally prevail in court-controlled liquidation proceedings. In New York, for example, directors are authorized to sell the corporate property at a private or public sale or to continue the business for the purpose of liquidation. Furthermore, directors

---

[115] N.Y. Bus. Corp. Law, Art. 10, § 1006 (McKinney 1963), as amended (McKinney Supp. 1978).

[116] N.Y. Bus. Corp. Law, Art. 10, § 1007 (McKinney 1963).

[117] N.Y. Bus. Corp. Law, Art. 10, § 1008. See also Weintraub & Levin, "Bulk Transfers—A Functional Approach to Article 6 of the Code," in Coogan, Hogan & Vagts, *Secured Transactions Under The UCC* Ch. 22 (1978).

[118] N.Y. Bus. Corp. Law, Art. 10, § 1008(a)(8) (McKinney 1963). See N.Y. Bus. Corp. Law, Art. 12 (McKinney 1963) which provides for the appointment of a receiver by the court in a judicial or nonjudicial dissolution proceeding.

[119] N.Y. Bus. Corp. Law, Art. 11, § 1101 (McKinney 1963).

[120] N.Y. Bus. Corp. Law, Art. 11, § 1102 (McKinney 1963).

[121] N.Y. Bus. Corp. Law, Art. 11, § 1103 (McKinney 1963).

[122] N.Y. Bus. Corp. Law, Art. 11, § 1117 (McKinney 1963).

selling assets are not subject to the Bulk Transfer provisions of Article 6 of the Uniform Commercial Code.[123] In view of these wide powers, corporate dissolution proceedings have a degree of flexibility not present in other liquidation proceedings where the sale of property is subject to court and creditor approval.

Despite this flexibility, certain safeguards are present to protect creditors' interests. Any director who acted in a way adverse to the interests of stockholders and creditors may be held accountable to them for such acts, and causes of action existing against directors for waste and mismanagement continue.[124] For speedy action, the court may compel directors to file accounts[125] and may appoint a receiver to supersede them.[126]

Whether an insolvent corporation belongs in a dissolution proceeding, or whether an assignment for the benefit of creditors will best serve its purpose, is a difficult decision and should be made only after consultation with creditors. In the usual case, creditors also have the option of filing an involuntary petition under the Bankruptcy Code[127] if dissatisfied with the manner in which the debtor is handling the liquidation of the corporation.

From the debtor's point of view, no stigma of an assignment for the benefit of creditors or bankruptcy is attached to the dissolution. For this reason, directors of an insolvent concern look upon this method with general approval. The personal factor of the director assisting in the dissolution also makes for a more efficient liquidation. Furthermore, the elimination of court orders providing for the operation of the business, reports, and authority for procedural steps results in extreme flexibility and minimal expense.

The main disadvantage of dissolution is that the proceeding is only desirable in those cases where there are no complex problems of administration. For example, if the corporation has given preferences voidable under an assignment statute or the Bankruptcy Code, a dissolution proceeding is not feasible for the purpose of their recovery.

---

[123] U.C.C. § 6-103(5) provides that sales made in the course of proceedings for the dissolution of a corporation and of which the creditors of the corporation receive advance notice substantially equivalent to that provided in the Article are excepted from Article 6.

[124] See N.Y. Bus. Corp. Law, Art. 10, §§ 1006, 1007 (McKinney 1963).

[125] See Application of Bittner, 265 App. Div. 490, 39 N.Y.S.2d 658 (1st Dep't 1943).

[126] N.Y. Bus. Corp. Law § 1008(8) and N.Y. Bus. Corp. Law, Art. 12 (1963), as amended (McKinney Supp. 1978).

[127] See 11 U.S.C. § 303 and Chapter 2 *supra*.

¶ 10.08 BULK TRANSFERS

Although not originally intended by the legislature as an insolvency proceeding, a bulk transfer has become, through usage, a means by which an insolvent corporation, partnership, or sole proprietor may sell assets, pay creditors with the proceeds, and liquidate the business. Bulk transfers are governed by Article 6 of the Uniform Commercial Code. Designed to protect the creditors of a business whose assets are being sold in bulk,[128] the Article sets forth specific requirements that must be complied with in order for the sale to be effective against creditors of the transferor.

Section 6-104(1) of the Uniform Commercial Code compels the seller to furnish a signed list of existing creditors.[129] The buyer and seller prepare a schedule of the property transferred[130] and the buyer preserves the list and schedule for six months after the transfer.[131] In addition, an effective transfer requires that the buyer give notice of the transfer to all listed creditors at least ten days before taking possession or paying for the goods.[132] The failure to comply with these provisions will render the transfer ineffective against unlisted and unnotified creditors.[133]

Responsibility for the accuracy and completeness of the list of creditors rests on the seller.[134] Errors and omissions do not render the transfer ineffective unless the buyer has actual knowledge of them.[135] The good faith purchaser of the assets, who purchases goods without actual knowledge of any unlisted creditors and who complies with the provisions of Article 6, becomes immune from liability to such creditors who subsequently learn about the sale.[136]

May the buyer rely on the list of creditors furnished by the seller or does the buyer have the duty to inquire about its accuracy and com-

---

[128] Siegal, "Tabin Corp. v. Climax Boutique—Open Door for Commercial Scoundrels?," 40 Albany L.R., 355 (1976); see also Donnelly & Donnelly, "Commercial Law," 26 Syr. L.R. 233, 251 (1975).

[129] U.C.C. § 6-104(1)(a), (2).

[130] U.C.C. § 6-104(1)(b).

[131] U.C.C. § 6-104(1)(c).

[132] U.C.C. §§ 6-105, 6-107.

[133] See Starman v. John Wolfe, Inc., 490 S.W.2d 377 (1973) where the Missouri Court of Appeals invalidated a bulk transfer and held the transferees liable to a creditor of the transferor for failure to comply with the bulk sale notice provisions.

[134] U.C.C. § 6-104(3).

[135] *Id.*

[136] See Siegal, note 128 *supra.*

pleteness? This question was dealt with in *Adrian Tabin Corporation v. Climax Boutique.*[137] The defendant had purchased a dress business in bulk after obtaining an affidavit from the corporate president stating that no creditors existed and after a lien search revealed no outstanding liens. In fact, a creditor did exist and he sued the buyer to set aside the sale on the ground that the buyer had failed to make a careful inquiry as to the possible existence of creditors and had, therefore, failed to comply with the notice provisions of the Uniform Commercial Code.[138] The New York Court of Appeals interpreted Article 6 literally and held that the Uniform Commercial Code imposes no duty of careful inquiry, and that the transferee in a bulk sale who has no actual knowledge of nonlisted creditors may rely on the affidavit furnished by the transferor.[139] The transfer is not ineffective because of errors or omissions in the list unless the buyer actually knew of such creditors. The suggestion that a business buyer who receives an affidavit stating that there are no creditors is put on notice to inquire because it is highly unlikely that in today's world a going business will have no outstanding debts[140] was rejected.

The bulk sale is an inexpensive and relatively quick method for the debtor having mostly unsecured creditors to wind up and liquidate the business without judicial supervision and without the stigma of bankruptcy.[141] The bulk transfer, however, may not be in the creditors' best interests because, if the provisions of Article 6 are complied with, an unlisted, unsecured creditor may be unable to benefit from the proceeds of the sale or to levy on any assets which are sold. In protecting the rights of the innocent good faith purchaser, the Uniform Commercial Code limits the rights of the unlisted creditors to realize on their claims. Creditors also are disadvantaged when the seller sells the assets at an unreasonable price and/or disappears with the proceeds of the sale. The omitted creditor is not entirely remediless, however, as the creditor may attack the sale as a fraudulent conveyance[142] or may file an involuntary petition in bankruptcy[143] if the applicable requirements for such action exist.

---

[137] 34 N.Y.2d 210, 313 N.E.2d 66, 356 N.Y.S.2d 606 (1974).

[138] 34 N.Y.2d at 212.

[139] *Id.* at 213.

[140] *Id.* at 216.

[141] See Rodden & Carpenter, "Corporate Insolvency—Liquidation or Rehabilitation," 36 Univ. of Colo. L. Rev. 117, 121-124 (1963).

[142] See Uniform Fraudulent Conveyances Act § 7.

[143] See 11 U.S.C. § 303(h) and Chapter 2 *supra.*

¶ 10.09 CONCLUSION

The statutory and nonstatutory methods of liquidation available to the insolvent debtor who does not wish to file a petition in bankruptcy under the federal Bankruptcy Code differ from state to state. Moreover, the alternatives for insolvency under state law vary as to complexity and effectiveness in liquidating the debtor's estate and protecting the creditors' rights. The debtor who is contemplating liquidation must consider the applicable statutes, as well as the relative advantages of available out-of-court and in-court arrangements, in order to ascertain the cheapest, quickest, and most advantageous method. It is impossible to draw general conclusions about the most beneficial insolvency proceeding. The decision depends upon the facts and circumstances of each individual case.

It is usually the debtor who initiates the insolvency proceeding. However, the ultimate choice is with the creditor. A creditor who is dissatisfied with the debtor's choice of state insolvency procedure usually may file an involuntary petition pursuant to the Bankruptcy Code.[144] If the debtor chooses to make an assignment, for example, and appoints a custodian to take charge of the assets, or if the debtor generally fails to pay its debts as they become due, the debtor may be the subject of an involuntary bankruptcy by the creditors' actions.

---

[144] *Id.*

Appendix A: THE BANKRUPTCY CODE

Title I of the Bankruptcy Reform Act of 1978 [Public Law 95-598] contains the Bankruptcy Code. The Code, which applies to all bankruptcy cases commenced on or after October 1, 1979, constitutes Title 11 of the United States Code.

Public Law 95-598
95th Congress

An Act

To establish a uniform Law on the Subject of Bankruptcies.

Be it enacted by the Senate and House of Representatives of the United States of America in Congress assembled,

TITLE I—ENACTMENT OF TITLE 11 OF THE UNITED STATES CODE

SEC. 101. The law relating to bankruptcy is codified and enacted as title 11 of the United States Code, entitled "Bankruptcy", and may be cited as 11 U.S.C. § , as follows:

TITLE 11—BANKRUPTCY

CHAPTER 1—GENERAL PROVISIONS

§ 101. Definitions

In this title—

(1) "accountant" means accountant authorized under applicable law to practice public accounting, and includes professional accounting association, corporation, or partnership, if so authorized;

(2) "affiliate" means—

(A) entity that directly or indirectly owns, controls, or holds with power to vote, 20 percent or more of the outstanding voting securities of the debtor, other than an entity that holds such securities—

(i) in a fiduciary or agency capacity without sole discretionary power to vote such securities; or

(ii) solely to secure a debt, if such entity has not in fact exercised such power to vote;

(B) corporation 20 percent or more of whose outstanding voting securities are directly or indirectly owned, controlled, or held with power to vote, by the debtor, or by an entity that directly or indirectly owns, controls, or holds with power to vote, 20 percent or more of the outstanding voting securities of the debtor, other than an entity that holds such securities—

(i) in a fiduciary or agency capacity without sole discretionary power to vote such securities; or

(ii) solely to secure a debt, if such entity has not in fact exercised such power to vote;

(C) person whose business is operated under a lease or operating agreement by a debtor, or person substantially all of whose property is operated under an operating agreement with the debtor; or

(D) entity that operates the business or all or substantially all of the property of the debtor under a lease or operating agreement;

(3) "attorney" means attorney, professional law association, corporation, or partnership, authorized under applicable law to practice law;

(4) "claim" means—

(A) right to payment, whether or not such right is reduced to judgment, liquidated, unliquidated, fixed, contingent, matured, unmatured, disputed, undisputed, legal, equitable, secured, or unsecured; or

(B) right to an equitable remedy for breach of performance if such breach gives rise to a right to payment, whether or not such right to an equitable remedy is reduced to judgment, fixed, contingent, matured, unmatured, disputed, undisputed, secured, or unsecured;

(5) "commodity broker" means futures commission merchant, foreign futures commission merchant, clearing organization, leverage transaction merchant, or commodity options dealer, as defined in section 761 of this title, with respect to which there is a customer, as defined in section 761(9) of this title;

(6) "community claim" means claim that arose before the commencement of the case concerning the debtor for which property of the kind specified in section 541(a)(2) of this title is liable, whether or not there is any such property at the time of the commencement of the case;

(7) "consumer debt" means debt incurred by an individual primarily for a personal, family, or household purpose;

(8) "corporation"—

(A) includes—

(i) association having a power or privilege that a private corporation, but not an individual or a partnership, possesses;

(ii) partnership association organized under a law that makes only the capital subscribed responsible for the debts of such association;

(iii) joint-stock company;

(iv) unincorporated company or association; or

(v) business trust; but

(B) does not include limited partnership:

(9) "creditor" means—

(A) entity that has a claim against the debtor that arose at the time of or before the order for relief concerning the debtor;

(B) entity that has a claim against the estate of a kind specified in section 502(f), 502(g), 502(h) or 502(i) of this title; or

(C) entity that has a community claim;

(10) "custodian" means—

(A) receiver or trustee of any of the property of the debtor, appointed in a case or proceeding not under this title;

(B) assignee under a general assignment for the benefit of the debtor's creditors; or

(C) trustee, receiver, or agent under applicable law, or under a contract, that is appointed or authorized to take charge of property of the debtor for the purpose of enforcing a lien against such property, or for the purpose of general administration of such property for the benefit of the debtor's creditors;

(11) "debt" means liability on a claim;

(12) "debtor" means person or municipality concerning which a case under this title has been commenced;

(13) "disinterested person" means person that—

(A) is not a creditor, an equity security holder, or an insider;

(B) is not and was not an investment banker for any outstanding security of the debtor;

(C) has not been, within three years before the date of the filing of the petition, an investment banker for a security of the debtor, or an attorney for such an investment banker in connection with the offer, sale, or issuance of a security of the debtor;

(D) is not and was not, within two years before the date of the filing of the petition, a director, officer, or employee of the debtor or of an investment banker specified in subparagraph (B) or (C) of this paragraph; and

(E) does not have an interest materially adverse to the interest of the estate or of any class of creditors or equity security holders, by reason of any direct or indirect relationship to, connection with, or interest in, the debtor or an investment banker specified in subparagraph (B) or (C) of this paragraph, or for any other reason;

(14) "entity" includes person, estate, trust, governmental unit;

(15) "equity security" means—

(A) share in a corporation, whether or not transferable or denominated "stock", or similar security;

(B) interest of a limited partner in a limited partnership; or

(C) warrant or right, other than a right to convert, to purchase, sell, or subscribe to a share, security, or interest of a kind specified in subparagraph (A) or (B) of this paragraph;

(16) "equity security holder" means holder of an equity security of the debtor;

(17) "farmer" means person that received more than 80 percent of such person's gross income during the taxable year of such person immediately preceding the taxable year of such person during which the case under this title concerning such person was commenced from a farming operation owned or operated by such person;

(18) "farming operation" includes farming, tillage of the soil, dairy farming, ranching, production or raising of crops, poultry, or livestock, and production of poultry or livestock products in an unmanufactured state;

(19) "foreign proceeding" means proceeding, whether judicial or administrative and whether or not under bankruptcy law, in a foreign country in which the debtor's domicile, residence, principal place of business, or principal assets were located at the commencement of such proceeding, for the purpose of liquidating an estate, adjusting debts by composition, extension, or discharge, or effecting a reorganization;

(20) "foreign representative" means duly selected trustee, administrator, or other representative of an estate in a foreign proceeding;

(21) "governmental unit" means United States; State; Commonwealth; District; Territory; municipality; foreign state; department, agency, or instrumentality of the United States, a State, a Commonwealth, a District, a Territory, a municipality, or a foreign state; or other foreign or domestic government;

(22) "indenture" means mortgage, deed of trust, or indenture, under which there is outstanding a security, other than a voting-trust certificate, constituting a claim against the debtor, a claim secured by a lien on any of the debtor's property, or an equity security of the debtor;

(23) "indenture trustee" means trustee under an indenture;

(24) "individual with regular income" means individual whose income is sufficiently stable and regular to enable such individual to make payments under a plan under chapter 13 of this title, other than a stock broker or a commodity broker;

(25) "insider" includes—

(A) if the debtor is an individual—

(i) relative of the debtor or of a general partner of the debtor;

(ii) partnership in which the debtor is a general partner;

(iii) general partner of the debtor; or

(iv) corporation of which the debtor is a director, officer, or person in control;

(B) if the debtor is a corporation—

(i) director of the debtor;

(ii) officer of the debtor;

(iii) person in control of the debtor;

(iv) partnership in which the debtor is a general partner;

(v) general partner of the debtor; or

(vi) relative of a general partner, director, officer, or person in control of the debtor;

(C) if the debtor is a partnership—

(i) general partner in the debtor;

(ii) relative of a general partner in, general partner of, or person in control of the debtor;

(iii) partnership in which the debtor is a general partner;

(iv) general partner of the debtor; or

(v) person in control of the debtor;

(D) if the debtor is a municipality, elected official of the debtor or relative of an elected official of the debtor;

(E) affiliate, or insider of an affiliate as if such affiliate were the debtor; and

(F) managing agent of the debtor;

(26) "insolvent" means—

(A) with reference to an entity other than a partnership, financial condition such that the sum of such entity's debts is greater than all of such entity's property, at a fair valuation, exclusive of—

(i) property transferred, concealed, or removed with intent to hinder, delay, or defraud such entity's creditors; and

(ii) property that may be exempted from property of the estate under section 522 of this title; and

(B) with reference to a partnership, financial condition such that the sum of such partnership's debts is greater than the aggregate of, at a fair valuation—

(i) all of such partnership's property, exclusive of property of the kind specified in subparagraph (A)(i) of this paragraph; and

(ii) the sum of the excess of the value of each general partner's separate property, exclusive of property of the kind specified in subparagraph (A)(ii) of this paragraph, over such partner's separate debts;

(27) "judicial lien" means lien obtained by judgment, levy, sequestration, or other legal or equitable process or proceeding;

(28) "lien" means charge against or interest in property to secure payment of a debt or performance of an obligation;

(29) "municipality" means political subdivision or public agency or instrumentality of a State;

(30) "person" includes individual, partnership, and corporation, but does not include governmental unit;

(31) "petition" means petition filed under section 301, 302, 303, or 304 of this title, as the case may be, commencing a case under this title;

(32) "purchaser" means transferee of a voluntary transfer, and includes immediate or mediate transferee of such a transferee;

(33) "railroad" means common carrier by railroad engaged in the transportation of individuals or property or owner of trackage facilities leased by such a common carrier;

(34) "relative" means individual related by affinity or consanguinity within the third degree as determined by the common law, or individual in a step or adoptive relationship within such third degree;

(35) "security"—

(A) includes—

(i) note;

(ii) stock;

(iii) treasury stock;

(iv) bond;

(v) debenture;

(vi) collateral trust certificate;

(vii) pre-organization certificate or subscription;

(viii) transferable share;

(ix) voting-trust certificate;

(x) certificate of deposit;

(xi) certificate of deposit for security;

(xii) investment contract or certificate of interest or

participation in a profit-sharing agreement or in an oil, gas, or mineral royalty or lease, if such contract or interest is the subject of a registration statement filed with the Securities and Exchange Commission under the provisions of the Securities Act of 1933 (15 U.S.C. 77a et seq.), or is exempt under section 3(b) of such Act (15 U.S.C. 77c(b)) from the requirement to file such a statement;

(xiii) interest of a limited partner in a limited partnership;

(xiv) other claim or interest commonly known as "security"; and

(xv) certificate of interest or participation in, temporary or interim certificate for, receipt for, or warrant or right to subscribe to or purchase or sell, a secuity; but

(B) does not include—

(i) currency, check, draft, bill of exchange, or bank letter of credit;

(ii) leverage transaction, as defined in section 761(13) of this title;

(iii) commodity futures contract or forward commodity contract;

(iv) option, warrant, or right to subscribe to or purchase or sell a commodity futures contract;

(v) option to purchase or sell a commodity;

(vi) contract or certificate specified in clause (xii) of subparagraph (A) of this paragraph that is not the subject of such a registration statement filed with the Securities and Exchange Commission and is not exempt under section 3(b) of the Securities Act of 1933 (15 U.S.C. 77c(b)) from the requirement to file such a statement; or

(vii) debt or evidence of indebtedness for goods sold and delivered or services rendered;

(36) "security agreement" means agreement that creates or provides for a security interest;

(37) "security interest" means lien created by an agreement;

(38) "statutory lien" means lien arising solely by force of a statute on specified circumstances or conditions, or lien of distress for rent, whether or not statutory, but does not include security interest or judicial lien, whether or not such interest or lien is provided by or is dependent on a statute and whether or not such interest or lien is made fully effective by statute;

(39) "stockbroker" means person with respect to which there is a customer, as defined in section 741(2) of this title, engaged in the business of effecting transactions in securities—

(A) for the accounts of others; or

(B) with members of the general public, from or for such person's own account; and

(40) "transfer" means every mode, direct or indirect, absolute or conditional, voluntary or involuntary, of disposing of or parting with property or with an interest in property, including retention of title as a security interest.

§ 102. Rules of construction

In this title—

(1) "after notice and a hearing", or a similar phrase—

(A) means after such notice as is appropriate in the particular circumstances, and such opportunity for a hearing as is appropriate in the particular circumstances; but

(B) authorizes an act without an actual hearing if such notice is given properly and if—

(i) such a hearing is not requested timely by a party in interest; or

(ii) there is insufficient time for a hearing to be commenced before such act must be done, and the court authorizes such act;

(2) "claim against the debtor" includes claim against property of the debtor;

(3) "includes" and "including" are not limiting;

(4) "may not" is prohibitive, and not permissive;

(5) "or" is not exclusive;

(6) "order for relief" means entry of an order for relief;

(7) the singular includes the plural; and

(8) a definition, continued in a section of this title that refers to another section of this title, does not, for the purpose of such reference, affect the meaning of a term used in such other section.

§ 103. Applicability of chapters

(a) Except as provided in section 1161 of this title, chapters 1, 3, and 5 of this title apply in a case under chapter 7, 11, or 13 of this title.

(b) Subchapters I and II of chapter 7 of this title apply only in a case under such chapter.

(c) Subchapter III of chapter 7 of this title applies only in a case under such chapter concerning a stockholder.

(d) Subchapter IV of chapter 7 of this title applies only in a case under such chapter concerning a commodity broker except with respect to section 746(c) which applies to margin payments made by any debtor to a commodity broker or forward contract merchant.

(e) Except as provided in section 901 of this title, only chapters 1 and 9 of this title apply in a case under such chapter 9.

(f) Except as provided in section 901 of this title, subchapters I, II, and III of chapter 11 of this title apply only in a case under such chapter.

(g) Subchapter IV of chapter 11 of this title applies only in a case under such chapter concerning a railroad.

(h) Chapter 13 of this title applies only in a case under such chapter.

§ 104. Adjustment of dollar amounts

The Judicial Conference of the United States shall transmit to the Congress and to the President before May 1, 1985, and before May 1 of every sixth year after May 1, 1985, a recommendation for the uniform percentage adjustment of each dollar amount in this title and in section 1930 of title 28.

§ 105. Power of court

(a) The bankruptcy court may issue any order, process, or judgment that is necessary or appropriate to carry out the provisions of this title.

(b) Notwithstanding subsection (a) of this section, a bankruptcy court may not appoint a receiver in a case under this title.

§ 106. Waiver of sovereign immunity

(a) A governmental unit is deemed to have waived sovereign immunity with respect to any claim against such governmental unit that is property of the estate and that arose out of the same transaction or occurrence out of which such governmental unit's claim arose.

(b) There shall be offset against an allowed claim or interest of a governmental unit any claim against such governmental unit that is property of the estate.

(c) Except as provided in subsections (a) and (b) of this section and notwithstanding any assertion of sovereign immunity—

(1) a provision of this title that contains "creditor", "entity", or "governmental unit" applies to governmental units; and

(2) a determination by the court of an issue arising under such a provision binds governmental units.

§ 107. Public access to papers

(a) Except as provided in subsection (b) of this section, a paper filed in a case under this title and the dockets of a bankruptcy court are public records and open to examination by an entity at reasonable times without charge.

(b) On request of a party in interest, the bankruptcy court shall, and on the bankruptcy court's own motion, the bankruptcy court may—

(1) protect an entity with respect to a trade secret or confidential research, development, or commercial information; or

(2) protect a person with respect to scandalous or defamatory matter contained in a paper filed in a case under this title.

§ 108. Extension of time

(a) If applicable law, an order entered in a proceeding, or an agreement fixes a period within which the debtor may commence an action, and such period has not expired before the date of the filing of the petition, the trustee may commence such action only before the later of—

(1) the end of such period, including any suspension of such period occurring on or after the commencement of the case; and

(2) two years after the order for relief.

(b) Except as provided in subsection (a) of this section, if applicable law, an order entered in a proceeding, or an agreement fixes a period within which the debtor or an individual protected under section 1301 of this title may file any pleading, demand, notice, or proof of claim or loss, cure a default, or perform any other similar act, and such period has not expired before the date of the filing of the petition, the trustee may only file, cure, or perform, as the case may be, before the later of—

(1) the end of such period, including any suspension of such period occurring on or after the commencement of the case; and

(2) 60 days after the order for relief.

(c) Except as provided in section 524 of this title, if applicable law, an order entered in a proceeding, or an agreement fixes a period for commencing or continuing a civil action in a court other than a bankruptcy court on a claim against the debtor, or against an individual with respect to which such individual is protected under section 1301 of this title, and such period has not expired before the date of the filing of the petition, then such period does not expire until the later of—

(1) the end of such period, including any suspension of such period occurring on or after the commencement of the case; and

(2) 30 days after notice of the termination or expiration of the stay under section 362, 922, or 1301 of this title, as the case may be, with respect to such claim.

§ 109. Who may be a debtor

(a) Notwithstanding any other provision of this section, only a person that resides in the United States, or has a domicile, a place of business, or property in the United States, or a municipality, may be a debtor under this title.

(b) A person may be a debtor under chapter 7 of this title only if such person is not—

(1) a railroad;

(2) a domestic insurance company, bank, savings bank, cooperative bank, savings and loan association, building and loan association, homestead association, or credit union; or

(3) a foreign insurance company, bank, savings bank, cooperative bank, savings and loan association, building and loan association, homestead association, or credit union, engaged in such business in the United States.

(c) An entity may be a debtor under chapter 9 of this title if and only if such entity—

(1) is a municipality;

(2) is generally authorized to be a debtor under such chapter by State law, or by a governmental officer or organization empowered by State law to authorize such entity to be a debtor under such chapter;

(3) is insolvent or unable to meet such entity's debts as such debts mature;

(4) desires to effect a plan to adjust such debts; and

(5) (A) has obtained the agreement of creditors holding at least a majority in amount of the claims of each class that such entity intends to impair under a plan in a case under such chapter;

(B) has negotiated in good faith with creditors and has failed to obtain the agreement of creditors holding at least a majority in amount of the claims of each class that such entity intends to impair under a plan in a case under such chapter;

(C) is unable to negotiate with creditors because such negotiation is impracticable; or

(D) reasonably believes that a creditor may attempt to obtain a preference.

(d) Only a person that may be a debtor under chapter 7 of this title, except a stockholder or a commodity broker, and a railroad may be a debtor under chapter 11 of this title.

(e) Only an individual with regular income that owes, on the date of the filing of the petition, noncontingent, liquidated, unsecured debts of less than $100.000 and noncontingent, liquidated, secured debts of less than $350,000, or an individual with regular income and such individual's spouse, except a stockbroker or a commodity broker, that owe, on the date of the filing of the petition, noncontingent, liquidated, unsecured debts that aggregate less than $100.000 and noncontingent, liquidated, secured debts of less than $350,000 may be a debtor under chapter 13 of this title.

CHAPTER 3—CASE ADMINISTRATION

SUBCHAPTER I—COMMENCEMENT OF A CASE

§ 301. Voluntary cases

A voluntary case under a chapter of this title is commenced by the filing with the bankruptcy court of a petition under such chapter by an entity that may be a debtor under such chapter. The commencement of a voluntary case under a chapter of this title constitutes an order for relief under such chapter.

§ 302. Joint cases

(a) A joint case under a chapter of this title is commenced by the filing with the bankruptcy court of a single petition under such chapter by an individual that may be a debtor under such chapter and such individual's spouse. The commencement of a joint case under a chapter of this title constitutes an order for relief under such chapter.

(b) After the commencement of a joint case, the court shall determine the extent, if any, to which the debtors' estates shall be consolidated.

§ 303. Involuntary cases

(a) An involuntary case may be commenced only under chapter 7 or 11 of this title, and only against a person, except a farmer or a corporation that is not a moneyed, business, or commercial corporation, that may be a debtor under the chapter under which such case is commenced.

(b) An involuntary case is commenced by the filing with the bankruptcy court of a petition under chapter 7 or 11 of this title—

(1) by three or more entities, each of which is either a holder of a claim against such person that is not contingent as to liability or an indenture trustee representing such a holder, if such claims aggregate at least $5,000 more than the value of any lien on property of the debtor securing such claims held by the holders of such claims;

(2) if there are fewer than 12 such holders, excluding any employee or insider of such person and any transferee of a transfer that is voidable under section 544, 545, 547, 548, 549, or 724(a) of this title, by one or more of such holders that hold in the aggregate at least $5,000 of such claims;

(3) if such person is a partnership—

(A) by fewer than all of the general partners in such partnership; or

(B) if relief has been ordered under this title with respect to all of the general partners in such partnership, by a general partner in such partnership, the trustee of such a general partner, or a holder of a claim against such partnership; or

(4) by a foreign representative of the estate in a foreign proceeding concerning such person.

(c) After the filing of a petition under this section but before the case is dismissed or relief is ordered, a creditor holding an unsecured claim that is not contingent, other than a creditor filing under subsection (b) of this section, may join in the petition with the same effect as if such joining creditor were a petitioning creditor under subsection (b) of this section.

(d) The debtor, or a general partner in a partnership debtor that did not join in the petition, may file an answer to a petition under this section.

(e) After notice and a hearing, and for cause, the court may require the petitioners under this section to file a bond to indemnify the debtor for such amounts as the court may later allow under subsection (i) of this section.

(f) Notwithstanding section 363 of this title, except to the extent that the court orders otherwise, and until an order for relief in the case, any business of the debtor may continue to operate, and the debtor may continue to use, acquire, or dispose of property as if an involuntary case concerning the debtor had not been commenced.

(g) At any time after the commencement of an involuntary case under chapter 7 of this title but before an order for relief in the case, the court, on request of a party in interest, after notice to the debtor and a hearing, and if necessary to preserve the property of the estate or to prevent loss to the estate, may appoint an interim trustee under section 701 of this title to take possession of the property of the estate and to operate any business of the debtor. Before an order for relief, the debtor may regain possession of property in the possession of a trustee ordered appointed under this subsection if the debtor files such bond as the court requires, conditioned on the debtor's accounting for and delivering to the trustee, if there is an order for relief in the case, such property, or the value, as of the date the debtor regains possession, of such property.

(h) If the petition is not timely controverted, the court shall order relief against the debtor in an involuntary case under the chapter under which the petition was filed. Otherwise, after trial, the court shall order relief against the debtor in an involuntary case under the chapter under which the petition was filed, only if—

(1) the debtor is generally not paying such debtor's debts as such debts become due; or

(2) within 120 days before the date of the filing of the petition, a custodian, other than a trustee, receiver, or agent appointed or authorized to take charge of less than substantially all of the property of the debtor for the purpose of enforcing a lien against such property, was appointed or took possession.

(i) If the court dismisses a petition under this section other than on consent of all petitioners and the debtor, and if the debtor does not waive the right to judgment under this subsection, the court may grant judgment—

(1) against the petitioners and in favor of the debtor for—

(A) costs;

(B) a reasonable attorney's fee; or

(C) any damages proximately caused by the taking of possession of the debtor's property by a trustee appointed under subsection (g) of this section or section 1104 of this title; or

(2) against any petitioner that filed the petition in bad faith, for—

(A) any damages proximately caused by such filing; or

(B) punitive damages.

(j) Only after notice to all creditors and a hearing may the court dismiss a petition filed under this section—

(1) on the motion of a petitioner;

(2) on consent of all petitioners and the debtors; or

(3) for want of prosecution.

(k) Notwithstanding subsection (a) of this section, an involuntary case may be commenced against a foreign bank that is not engaged in such business in the United States only under chapter 7 of this title and only if a foreign proceeding concerning such bank is pending.

§ 304. Cases ancillary to foreign proceedings

(a) A case ancillary to a foreign proceeding is commenced by the filing with the bankruptcy court of a petition under this section by a foreign representative.

(b) Subject to the provisions of subsection (c) of this section, if a party in interest does not timely controvert the petition, or after trial, the court may—

(1) enjoin the commencement or continuation of—

(A) any action against—

(i) a debtor with respect to property involved in such foreign proceeding; or

(ii) such property; or

(B) the enforcement of any judgment against the debtor with respect to such property, or any act or the commencement or continuation of any judicial proceeding to create or enforce a lien against the property of such estate;

(2) order turnover of the property of such estate, or the proceeds of such property, to such foreign representative; or

(3) order other appropriate relief.

(c) In determining whether to grant relief under subsection (b) of this section, the court shall be guided by what will best assure an economical and expeditious administration of such estate, consistent with—

(1) just treatment of all holders of claims against or interests in such estate;

(2) protection of claim holders in the United States against prejudice and inconvenience in the processing of claims in such foreign proceeding;

(3) prevention of preferential or fraudulent dispositions of property of such estate;

(4) distribution of proceeds of such estate substantially in accordance with the order prescribed by this title;

(5) comity; and

(6) if appropriate, the provision of an opportunity for a fresh start for the individual that such foreign proceeding concerns.

§ 305. Abstention

(a) The court, after notice and a hearing, may dismiss a case under this title, or may suspend all proceedings in a case under this title, at any time if—

(1) the interests of creditors and the debtor would be better served by such dismissal or suspension; or

(2)(A) there is pending a foreign proceeding: and

(B) the factors specified in section 304(c) of this title warrant such dismissal or suspension.

(b) A foreign representative may seek dismissal or suspension under subsection (a)(2) of this section.

(c) An order under subsection (a) of this section dismissing a case or suspending all proceedings in a case, or a decision not so to dismiss or suspend, is not reviewable by appeal or otherwise.

§ 306. Limited appearance

An appearance in a bankruptcy court by a foreign representative in connection with a petition or request under section 303, 304, or 305 of this title does not submit such foreign representative to the jurisdiction of any court in the United States for any other purpose, but the bankruptcy court may condition any order under section 303, 304, or 305 of this title on compliance by such foreign representative with the orders of such bankruptcy court.

SUBCHAPTER II—OFFICERS

§ 321. Eligibility to serve as trustee

(a) A person may serve as trustee in a case under this title only if such person is—

(1) an individual that is competent to perform the duties of trustee and, in a case under chapter 7 or 13 of this title, resides or has an office in the judicial district within which the case is pending, or in any judicial district adjacent to such district; or

(2) a corporation authorized by such corporation's charter or bylaws to act as trustee, and, in a case under chapter 7 or 13 of this title, having an office in at least one of such districts.

(b) A person that has served as an examiner in a case may not serve as trustee in the case.

§ 322. Qualification of trustee

(a) A person selected under section 701, 702, 703, 1104, 1163, or 1302 of this title to serve as trustee in a case under this title qualifies if before five days after such selection, and before beginning official duties, such person has filed with the court a bond in favor of the United States conditioned on the faithful performance of such official duties.

(b) The court shall determine—

(1) the amount of a bond filed under subsection (a) of this section; and

(2) the sufficiency of the surety on such bond.

(c) A trustee is not liable personally or on such trustee's bond in favor of the United States for any penalty or forfeiture incurred by the debtor.

(d) A proceeding on a trustee's bond may not be commenced after two years after the date on which such trustee was discharged.

§ 323. Role and capacity of trustee

(a) The trustee in a case under this title is the representative of the estate.

(b) The trustee in a case under this title has capacity to sue and be sued.

§ 324. Removal of trustee or examiner

The court, after notice and a hearing, may remove a trustee or an examiner, for cause.

§ 325. Effect of vacancy

A vacancy in the office of trustee during a case does not abate any pending action or proceeding, and the successor trustee shall be substituted as a party in such action or proceeding.

§ 326. Limitation on compensation of trustee

(a) In a case under chapter 7 or 11, the court may allow reasonable compensation under section 330 of this title of the trustee for the trustee's services, payable after the trustee renders such services, not to exceed fifteen percent on the first $1,000 or less, six percent on any amount in excess of $1,000 but not in excess of $3,000, three percent on any amount in excess of $3,000 but not in excess of $20,000, two percent on any amount in excess of $20,000 but not in excess of $50,000, and one percent on any amount in excess of $50,000, upon all moneys disbursed or turned over in the case by the trustee to parties in interest, excluding the debtor, but including holders of secured claims.

(b) In a case under chapter 13 of this title, the court may not allow compensation for services or reimbursement of expenses of a standing trustee appointed under section 1302(d) of this title, but may allow reasonable compensation under section 330 of this title of a trustee appointed under section 1302(a) of this title for the trustee's services, payable after the trustee renders such services, not to exceed five percent upon all payments under the plan.

(c) If more than one person serves as trustee in the case, the aggregate compensation of such persons for such service may not exceed the maximum compensation prescribed for a single trustee by subsection (a) or (b) of this section, as the case may be.

(d) The court may deny allowance of compensation for services and reimbursement of expenses of the trustee if the trustee—

(1) failed to make diligent inquiry into facts that would permit denial of allowance under section 328(c) of this title; or

(2) with knowledge of such facts, employed a professional person under section 327 of this title.

§ 327. Employment of professional persons

(a) Except as otherwise provided in this section, the trustee, with the court's approval, may employ one or more attorneys, accountants, appraisers, auctioneers, or other professional persons, that do not hold or represent an interest adverse to the estate, and that are disinterested persons, to represent or assist the trustee in carrying out the trustee's duties under this title.

(b) If the trustee is authorized to operate the business of the debtor under section 721 or 1108 of this title, and if the debtor has regularly employed attorneys, accountants, or other professional persons on salary, the trustee may retain or replace such professional persons if necessary in the operation of such business.

(c) In a case under chapter 7 or 11 of this title, a person is not disqualified for employment under this section solely because of such person's employment by or representation of a creditor, but may not, while employed by the trustee, represent, in connection with the case, a creditor.

(d) The court may authorize the trustee to act as attorney or accountant for the estate if such authorization is in the best interest of the estate.

(e) The trustee, with the court's approval, may employ, for a specified special purpose, other than to represent the trustee in conducting the case, an attorney that has represented the debtor, if in the best interest of the estate, and if such attorney does not represent or hold any interest adverse to the debtor or to the estate with respect to the matter on which such attorney is to be employed.

(f) The trustee may not employ a person that has served as an examiner in the case.

§ 328. Limitation on compensation of professional persons

(a) The trustee, or a committee appointed under section 1102 of this title, with the court's approval, may employ or authorize the employment of a professional person under section 327 or 1103 of this title, as the case may be, on any reasonable terms and conditions of employment, including on a retainer, on an hourly basis, or on a contingent fee basis. Notwithstanding such terms and conditions, the court may allow compensation different from the compensation provided under such terms and conditions after the conclusion of such employment, if such terms and conditions prove to have been improvident in light of developments unanticipatable at the time of the fixing of such terms and conditions.

(b) If the court has authorized a trustee to serve as an attorney or accountant for the estate under section 327(d) of this title, the court may allow compensation for the trustee's services as such attorney or accountant only to the extent that the trustee performed services as attorney or accountant for the estate and not for performance of any of the trustee's duties that are generally performed by a trustee without the assistance of an attorney or accountant for the estate.

(c) Except as provided in section 327(c), 327(e), or 1107(b) of this title, the court may deny allowance of compensation for services and reimbursement of expenses of a professional person employed under section 327 or 1103 of this title if, at any time during such professional person's employment under section 327 or 1103 of this title, such professional person is not a disinterested person, or represents or holds an interest adverse to the interest of the estate with respect to the matter on which such professional person is employed.

§ 329. Debtor's transactions with attorneys

(a) Any attorney representing a debtor in a case under this title, or in connection with such a case, whether or not such attorney applies for compensation under this title, shall file with the court a statement of the compensation paid or agreed to be paid, if such payment or agreement was made after one year before the date of the filing of the petition, for services rendered or to be rendered in contemplation of and in connection with the case by such attorney, and the source of such compensation.

(b) If such compensation exceeds the reasonable value of any such services, the court may cancel any such agreement, or order the return of any such payment, to the extent excessive, to—

(1) the trustee, if the property transferred—

(A) would have been property of the estate; or

(B) was to be paid by or on behalf of the debtor under a plan under chapter 11 or 13 of this title; or

(2) the entity that made such payment.

§ 330. Compensation of officers

(a) After notice to any parties in interest and to the United States trustee and a hearing, and subject to sections 326, 328, and 329 of this title, the court may award to a trustee, to an examiner, to a professional person employed under section 327 or 1103 of this title, or to the debtor's attorney—

(1) reasonable compensation for actual, necessary services rendered by such trustee, examiner, professional person, or attorney, as the case may be, and by any paraprofessional persons employed by such trustee, professional person, or attorney, as the case may be, based on the time, the nature, the extent, and the value of such services, and the cost of comparable services other than in a case under this title; and

(2) reimbursement for actual, necessary expenses.

(b) There shall be paid from the filing fee in a case under chapter 7 of this title $20 to the trustee serving in such case, after such trustee's services are rendered.

§ 331. Interim compensation

A trustee, an examiner, a debtor's attorney, or any professional person employed under section 327 or 1103 of this title may apply to the court not more than once every 120 days after an order for relief in a case under this title, or more often if the court permits, for such compensation for services rendered before the date of such an application or reimbursement for expenses incurred before such date as is provided under section 330 of this title. After notice and a hearing, the court may allow and disburse to such applicant such compensation or reimbursement.

SUBCHAPTER III—ADMINISTRATION

§ 341. Meetings of creditors and equity security holders

(a) Within a reasonable time after the order for relief in a case under this title, there shall be a meeting of creditors.

(b) The court may order a meeting of any equity security holders.

(c) The court may not preside at, and may not attend, any meeting under this section.

§ 342. Notice

There shall be given such notice as is appropriate of an order for relief in a case under this title.

§ 343. Examination of the debtor

The debtor shall appear and submit to examination under oath at the meeting of creditors under section 341(a) of this title. Creditors, any indenture trustee, or any trustee or examiner in the case may examiner the debtor.

§ 344. Self-incrimination; immunity

Immunity for persons required to submit to examination, to testify, or to provide information in a case under this title may be granted under part V of title 18.

§ 345. Money of estates

(a) A trustee in a case under this title may make such deposit or investment of the money of the estate for which such trustee serves as will yield the maximum reasonable net return on such money, taking into account the safety of such deposit or investment.

(b) Except with respect to a deposit or investment that is insured or guaranteed by the United States or by a department, agency, or instrumentality of the United States or backed by the full faith and credit of the United States, the trustee shall require from an entity with which such money is deposited or invested—

(1) a bond—

(A) in favor of the United States;

(B) secured by the undertaking of a corporate surety approved by the court for the district in which the case is pending; and

(C) conditioned on—

(i) a proper accounting for all money so deposited or invested and for any return on such money;

(ii) prompt repayment of such money and return; and

(iii) faithful performance of duties as a depository; or

(2) the deposit of securities of the kind specified in section 15 of title 6.

§ 346. Special tax provisions

(a) Except to the extent otherwise provided in this section, subsections (b), (c), (d), (e), (g), (h), (i), and (j) of this section apply notwithstanding any State or local law imposing a tax, but subject to the Internal Revenue Code of 1954 (26 U.S.C. 1 et seq.).

(b)(1) In a case under chapter 7 or 11 of this title concerning an individual, any income of the estate may be taxed under a State or local law imposing a tax on or measured by income only to the estate, and may not be taxed to such individual. Except as provided in section 728 of this title, if such individual is a partner in a partnership, any gain or loss resulting from a distribution of property from such partnership, or any distributive share of income, gain, loss, deduction, or credit of such individual that is distributed, or considered distributed, from such partnership, after the commencement of the case is gain, loss, income, deduction, or credit, as the case may be, of the estate.

(2) Except as otherwise provided in this section and in section 728 of this title, any income of the estate in such a case, and any State or local tax on or measured by such income, shall be computed in the same manner as the income and the tax of an estate.

(3) The estate in such a case shall use the same accounting method as the debtor used immediately before the commencement of the case.

(c)(1) The commencement of a case under this title concerning a corporation or a partnership does not effect a change in the status of such corporation or partnership for the purposes of any State or local law imposing a tax on or measured by income. Except as otherwise provided in this section and in section 728 of this title, any income of the estate in such case may be taxed only as though such case had not been commenced.

(2) In such a case, except as provided in section 728 of this title, the trustee shall make any tax return otherwise required by State or local law to be filed by or on behalf of such operation or partnership in the same manner and form as such corporation or partnership, as the case may be, is required to make such return.

(d) In a case under chapter 13 of this title, any income of the estate or the debtor may be taxed under a State or local law imposing a tax on or measured by income only to the debtor, and may not be taxed to the estate.

(e) A claim allowed under section 502(f) or 503 of this title, other than a claim for a tax that is not otherwise deductible or a capital expenditure that is not otherwise deductible, is deductible by the entity to which income of the estate is taxed unless such claim was deducted by another entity, and a deduction for such a claim is deemed to be a deduction attributable to a business.

(f) The trustee shall withhold from any payment of claims for wages, salaries, commissions, dividends, interest, or other payments, or collect, any amount required to be withheld or collected under applicable State or local tax law, and shall pay such withheld or collected amount to the appropriate governmental unit at the time and in the manner required by such tax law, and with the same priority as the claim from which such amount was withheld was paid.

(g)(1) Neither gain nor loss shall be recognized on a transfer—

(A) by operation of law, of property to the estate;

(B) other than a sale, of property from the estate to the debtor; or

(C) in a case under chapter 11 of this title concerning a corporation, of property from the estate to a corporation that is an affiliate participating in a joint plan with the debtor, or that is a successor to the debtor under the plan, except that gain or loss may be recognized to the same extent that such transfer results in the recognition of gain or loss under section 371 of the Internal Revenue Code of 1954 (26 U.S.C. 371).

(2) The transferee of a transfer of a kind specified in this subsection shall take the property transferred with the same character, and with the transferor's basis, as adjusted under subsection (j)(5) of this section, and holding period.

(h) Notwithstanding sections 728(a) and 1146(a) of this title, for the purpose of determining the number of taxable periods during which the debtor or the estate may use a loss carryover or a loss carryback, the taxable period of the debtor during which the case is commenced is deemed not to have been terminated by such commencement.

(i) (1) In a case under chapter 7 or 11 of this title concerning an individual, the estate shall succeed to the debtor's tax attributes, including—

(A) any investment credit carryover;
(B) any recovery exclusion;
(C) any loss carryover;
(D) any foreign tax credit carryover;
(E) any capital loss carryover; and
(F) any claim of right.

(2) After such a case is closed or dismissed, the debtor shall succeed to any tax attribute to which the estate succeeded under paragraph (1) of this subsection but that was not utilized by the estate. The debtor may utilize such tax attributes as though any applicable time limitations on such utilization by the debtor were suspended during the time during which the case was pending.

(3) In such a case, the estate may carry back any loss of the estate to a taxable period of the debtor that ended before the order for relief under such chapter the same as the debtor could have carried back such loss had the debtor incurred such loss and the case under this title had not been commenced, but the debtor may not carry back any loss of the debtor from a taxable period that ends after such order to any taxable period of the debtor that ended before such order until after the case is closed.

(j) (1) Except as otherwise provided in this subsection, income is not realized by the estate, the debtor, or a successor to the debtor by reason of forgiveness or discharge of indebtedness in a case under this title.

(2) For the purposes of any State or local law imposing a tax on or measured by income, a deduction with respect to a liability may not be allowed for any taxable period during or after which such liability is forgiven or discharged under this title. In this paragraph, "a deduction with respect to a liability" includes a capital loss incurred on the disposition of a capital asset with respect to a liability that was incurred in connection with the acquisition of such asset.

(3) Except as provided in paragraph (4) of this subsection, for the purpose of any State or local law imposing a tax on or measured by income, any net operating loss of an individual or corporate debtor, including a net operating loss carryover to such debtor, shall be reduced by the amount of indebtedness forgiven or discharged in a case under this title, except to the extent that such forgiveness or discharge resulted in a disallowance under paragraph (2) of this subsection.

(4) A reduction of a net operating loss or a net operating loss carryover under paragraph (3) of this subsection or of basis under paragraph (5) of this subsection is not required to the extent that the indebtedness of an individual or corporate debtor forgiven or discharged—

(A) consisted of items of a deductible nature that were not deducted by such debtor; or

(B) resulted in an expired net operating loss carryover or other deduction that—

(i) did not offset income for any taxable period; and

(ii) did not contribute to a net operating loss in or a net operating loss carryover to the taxable period during or after which such indebtedness was discharged.

(5) For the purposes of a State or local law imposing a tax on or measured by income, the basis of the debtor's property or of property transferred to an entity required to use the debtor's basis in whole or in part shall be reduced by the lesser of—

(A) (i) the amount by which the indebtedness of the debtor has been forgiven or discharged in a case under this title; minus

(ii) the total amount of adjustments made under paragraphs (2) and (3) of this subsection; and

(B) the amount by which the total basis of the debtor's assets that were property of the estate before such forgiveness or discharge exceeds the debtor's total liabilities that were liabilities both before and after such forgiveness or discharge.

(6) Notwithstanding paragraph (5) of this subsection, basis is not required to be reduced to the extent that the debtor elects to treat as taxable income, of the taxable period in which indebtedness is forgiven or discharged, the amount of indebtedness forgiven or discharged that otherwise would be applied in reduction of basis under paragraph (5) of this subsection.

(7) For the purposes of this subsection, indebtedness with respect to which an equity security, other than an interest of a limited partner in a limited partnership, is issued to the creditor to whom such indebtedness was owned, or that is forgiven as a contribution to capital by an equity security holder other than a limited partner in the debtor, is not forgiven or discharged in a case under this title—

(A) to any extent that such indebtedness did not consist of items of a deductible nature; or

(B) if the issuance of such equity security has the same consequences under a law imposing a tax on or measured by income to such creditor as a payment in cash to such creditor in an amount equal to the fair market value of such equity security, then to the lesser of—

(i) the extent that such issuance has the same such consequences; and

(ii) the extent of such fair market value.

§ 347. Unclaimed property

(a) Ninety days after the final distribution under section 726 or 1326 of this title in a case under chapter 7 or 13 of this title, as the case may be, the trustee shall stop payment on any check remaining unpaid, and any remaining property of the estate shall be paid into the court and disposed of under chapter 129 of title 28.

(b) Any security, money, or other property remaining unclaimed at the expiration of the time allowed in a case under chapter 9 or 11 of this title for the presentation of a security or the performance of any other act as a condition to participation in the distribution under any plan confirmed under section 943(b), 1129, or 1173 of this title, as the case may be, becomes the property of the debtor or of the entity acquiring the assets of the debtor under the plan, as the case may be.

§ 348. Effect of conversion

(a) Conversion of a case from a case under one chapter of this title to a case under another chapter of this title constitutes an order for relief under the chapter to which the case is converted, but, except as provided in subsections (b) and (c) of this section, does not effect a change in the date of the filing of the petition, the commencement of the case, or the order for relief.

(b) Unless the court for cause orders otherwise, in sections 701(a),

727(a)(10), 727(b), 728(a), 728(b), 1102(a), 1110(a)(1), 1121(b), 1121(c), 1141(d)(4), 1146(a), 1146(b), 1301(a), 1305(a), and 1328(a) of this title, "the order for relief under this chapter" in a chapter to which a case has been converted under section 706, 1112, or 1307 of this title means the conversion of such case to such chapter.

(c) Sections 342 and 365(d) of this title apply in a case that has been converted under section 706, 1112, or 1307 of this title, as if the conversion order were the order for relief.

(d) A claim against the estate or the debtor that arises after the order for relief but before conversion in a case that is converted under section 1112 or 1307 of this title, other than a claim specified in section 503(b) of this title, shall be treated for all purposes as if such claim had arisen immediately before the date of the filing of the petition.

(e) Conversion of a case under section 706, 1112, or 1307 of this title terminates the service of any trustee or examiner that is serving in the case before such conversion.

§ 349. Effect of dismissal

(a) Unless the court, for cause, orders otherwise, the dismissal of a case under this title does not bar the discharge, in a later case under this title, of debts that were dischargeable in the case dismissed.

(b) Unless the court, for cause, orders otherwise, a dismissal of a case other than under section 742 of this title—

(1) reinstates—

(A) any proceeding or custodianship superseded under section 543 of this title;

(B) any transfer avoided under section 522, 544, 545, 547, 548, 549, or 724(a) of this title, or preserved under section 510(c)(2), 522(i)(2), or 551 of this title; and

(C) any lien voided under section 506(d) of this title;

(2) vacates any order, judgment, or transfer ordered, under section 522(i)(1), 542, 550, or 553 of this title; and

(3) revests the property of the estate in the entity in which such property was vested immediately before the commencement of the case under this title.

§ 350. Closing and reopening cases

(a) After an estate is fully administered and the court has discharged the trustee, the court shall close the case.

(b) a case may be reopened in the court in which such case was closed to administer assets, to accord relief to the debtor, or for other cause.

SUBCHAPTER IV—ADMINISTRATIVE POWERS

§ 361. Adequate protection

When adequate protection is required under section 362, 363, or 364 of this title of an interest of an entity in property, such adequate protection may be provided by—

(1) requiring the trustee to make periodic cash payments to such entity, to the extent that the stay under section 362 of this title, use, sale, or lease under section 363 of this title, or any grant of a lien under section 364 of this title results in a decrease in the value of such entity's interest in such property;

(2) providing to such entity an additional or replacement lien to the extent that such stay, use, sale, lease, or grant results in a

decrease in the value of such entity's interest in such property; or

(3) granting such other relief, other than entitling such entity to compensation allowable under section 503(b)(1) of this title as an administrative expense, as will result in the realization by such entity of the indubitable equivalent of such entity's interest in such property.

§ 362. Automatic stay

(a) Except as provided in subsection (b) of this section, a petition filed under section 301, 302, or 303 of this title operates as a stay, applicable to all entities, of—

(1) the commencement or continuation, including the issuance or employment of process, of a judicial, administrative, or other proceeding against the debtor that was or could have been commenced before the commencement of the case under this title, or to recover a claim against the debtor that arose before the commencement of the case under this title;

(2) the enforcement, against the debtor or against property of the estate, of a judgment obtained before the commencement of the case under this title;

(3) any act to obtain possession of property of the estate or of property from the estate;

(4) any act to create, perfect, or enforce any lien against property of the estate;

(5) any act to create, perfect, or enforce against property of the debtor any lien to the extent that such lien secures a claim that arose before the commencement of the case under this title;

(6) any act to collect, assess, or recover a claim against the debtor that arose before the commencement of the case under this title;

(7) the setoff of any debt owing to the debtor that arose before the commencement of the case under this title against any claim against the debtor; and

(8) the commencement or continuation of a proceeding before the United States Tax Court concerning the debtor.

(b) The filing of a petition under section 301, 302, or 303 of this title does not operate as a stay—

(1) under subsection (a) of this section, of the commencement or continuation of a criminal action or proceeding against the debtor;

(2) under subsection (a) of this section, of the collection of alimony, maintenance, or support from property that is not property of the estate;

(3) under subsection (a) of this section, of any act to perfect an interest in property to the extent that the trustee's rights and powers are subject to such perfection under section 546(b) of this title;

(4) under subsection (a)(1) of this section, of the commencement or continuation of an action or proceeding by a governmental unit to enforce such governmental unit's police or regulatory power;

(5) under subsection (a)(2) of this section, of the enforcement of a judgment, other than a money judgment, obtained in an action or proceeding by a governmental unit to enforce such governmental unit's police or regulatory power;

(6) under subsection (a)(7) of this section, of the setoff of any mutual debt and claim that are commodity futures contracts,

forward commodity contracts, leverage transactions, options, warrants, rights to purchase or sell commodity futures contracts or securities, or options to purchase or sell commodities or securities;

(7) under subsection (a) of this section, of the commencement of any action by the Secretary of Housing and Urban Development to foreclose a mortgage or deed of trust in any case in which the mortgage or deed of trust held by said Secretary is insured or was formerly insured under the National Housing Act and covers property, or combinations of property, consisting of five or more living units; or

(8) under subsection (a) of this section, of the issuance to the debtor by a governmental unit of a notice of tax deficiency.

(c) Except as provided in subsections (d), (e), and (f) of this section—

(1) the stay of an act against property of the estate under subsection (a) of this section continues until such property is no longer property of the estate; and

(2) the stay of any other act under subsection (a) of this section continues until the earliest of—

(A) the time the case is closed;

(B) the time the case is dismissed; and

(C) if the case is a case under chapter 7 of this title concerning an individual or a case under chapter 9, 11, or 13 of this title, the time a discharge is granted or denied.

(d) On request of a party in interest and after notice and a hearing, the court shall grant relief from the stay provided under subsection (a) of this section, such as by terminating, annulling, modifying, or conditioning such stay—

(1) for cause, including the lack of adequate protection of an interest in property of such party in interest; or

(2) with respect to a stay of an act against property, if—

(A) the debtor does not have an equity in such property; and

(B) such property is not necessary to an effective reorganization.

(e) Thirty days after a request under subsection (d) of this section for relief from the stay of any act against property of the estate under subsection (a) of this section, such stay is terminated with respect to the party in interest making such request, unless the court, after notice and a hearing, orders such stay continued in effect pending, or as a result of, a final hearing and determination under subsection (d) of this section. A hearing under this subsection may be a preliminary hearing, or may be consolidated with the final hearing under subsection (d) of this section. If the hearing under this subsection is a preliminary hearing—

(1) the court shall order such stay so continued if there is a reasonable likelihood that the party opposing relief from such stay will prevail at the final hearing under subsection (d) of this section; and

(2) such final hearing shall be commenced within thirty days after such preliminary hearing.

(f) The court, without a hearing, shall grant such relief from the stay provided under subsection (a) of this section as is necessary to prevent irreparable damage to the interest of an entity in property, if such interest will suffer such damage before there is an opportunity for notice and a hearing under subsection (d) or (e) of this section.

(g) In any hearing under subsection (d) or (e) of this section concerning relief from the stay of any act under subsection (a) of this section—

(1) the party requesting such relief has the burden of proof on the issue of the debtor's equity in property; and

(2) the party opposing such relief has the burden of proof on all other issues.

§ 363. Use, sale, or lease of property

(a) In this section, "cash collateral" means cash, negotiable instruments, documents of title, securities, deposit accounts, or other cash equivalents in which the estate and an entity other than the estate have an interest.

(b) The trustee, after notice and a hearing, may use, sell, or lease, other than in the ordinary course of business, property of the estate.

(c)(1) If the business of the debtor is authorized to be operated under section 721, 1108, or 1304 of this title and unless the court orders otherwise, the trustee may enter into transactions, including the sale or lease of property of the estate, in the ordinary course of business, without notice or a hearing, and may use property of the estate in the ordinary course of business without notice or a hearing.

(2) The trustee may not use, sell, or lease cash collateral under paragraph (1) of this subsection unless—

(A) each entity that has an interest in such cash collateral consents; or

(B) the court, after notice and a hearing, authorizes such use, sale, or lease in accordance with the provisions of this section.

(3) Any hearing under paragraph (2)(B) of this subsection may be a preliminary hearing or may be consolidated with a hearing under subsection (e) of this section, but shall be scheduled in accordance with the needs of the debtor. If the hearing under paragraph (2)(B) of this subsection is a preliminary hearing, the court may authorize such use, sale, or lease only if there is a reasonable likelihood that the trustee will prevail at the final hearing under subsection (e) of this section. The court shall act promptly on any request for authorization under paragraph (2)(B) of this subsection.

(4) Except as provided in paragraph (2) of this subsection, the trustee shall segregate and account for any cash collateral in the trustee's possession, custody, or control.

(d) The trustee may use, sell, or lease property under subsection (b) or (c) of this section only to the extent not inconsistent with any relief granted under section 362(c), 362(d), 362(e), or 362(f) of this title.

(e) Notwithstanding any other provision of this section, at any time, on request of an entity that has an interest in property used, sold, or leased, or proposed to be used, sold, or leased, by the trustee, the court shall prohibit or condition such use, sale, or lease as is necessary to provide adequate protection of such interest. In any hearing under this section, the trustee has the burden of proof on the issue of adequate protection.

(f) The trustee may sell property under subsection (b) or (c) of this section free and clear of any interest in such property of an entity other than the estate, only if—

(1) applicable nonbankruptcy law permits sale of such property free and clear of such interest;

(2) such entity consents;

(3) such interest is a lien and the price at which such property is to be sold is greater than the aggregate value of such interest;

(4) such interest is in bona fide dispute; or

(5) such entity could be compelled, in a legal or equitable proceeding, to accept a money satisfaction of such interest.

(g) Notwithstanding subsection (f) of this section, the trustee may sell property under subsection (b) or (c) of this section free and clear of any vested or contingent right in the nature of dower or curtesy.

(h) Notwithstanding subsection (f) of this section, the trustee may sell both the estate's interest, under subsection (b) or (c) of this section, and the interest of any co-owner in property in which the debtor had, immediately before the commencement of the case, an undivided interest as a tenant in common, joint tenant, or tenant by the entirety, only if—

(1) partition in kind of such property among the estate and such co-owners is impracticable;

(2) sale of the estate's undivided interest in such property would realize significantly less for the estate than sale of such property free of the interests of such co-owners;

(3) the benefit to the estate of a sale of such property free of the interests of co-owners outweighs the detriment, if any, to such co-owners; and

(4) such property is not used in the production, transmission, or distribution, for sale, of electric energy or of natural or synthetic gas for heat, light, or power.

(i) Before the consummation of a sale of property to which subsection (g) or (h) of this section applies, or of property of the estate that was community property of the debtor and the debtor's spouse immediately before the commencement of the case, the debtor's spouse, or a co-owner of such property, as the case may be, may purchase such property at the price at which such sale is to be consummated.

(j) After a sale of property to which subsection (g) or (h) of this section applies, the trustee shall distribute to the debtor's spouse or the co-owners of such property, as the case may be, and to the estate, the proceeds of such sale, less the costs and expenses, not including any compenation of the trustee, of such sale, according to the interests of such spouse or co-owners, and of the estate.

(k) At a sale under subsection (b) of this section of property that is subject to a lien that secures an allowed claim, if the holder of such claim purchases such property, such holder may offset such claim against the purchase price of such property.

(l) The trustee may use, sell, or lease property under subsection (b) or (c) of this section, or a plan under chapter 11 or 13 of this title may provide for the use, sale, or lease of property, notwithstanding any provision in a contract, a lease, or applicable law that is conditioned on the insolvency or financial conditions of the debtor, on the commencement of a case under this title concerning the debtor, or on the appointment of a taking possession by a trustee in a case under this title or a custodian, and that effects, or gives an option to effect, a forfeiture, modification, or termination of the debtor's interests in such property.

(m) The reversal or modification on appeal of an authorization under subsection (b) or (c) of this section of a sale or lease of property does not affect the validity of a sale or lease under such authorization to an entity that purchased or leased such property in good faith, whether or not such entity knew of the pendency of the appeal, unless such authorization and such sale or lease were stayed pending appeal.

(n) The trustee may void a sale under this section if the sale price was controlled by an agreement among potential bidders at such sale, or may recover from a party to such agreement any amount by which the value of the property sold exceeds the price at which such sale was consummated, and may recover any costs, attorneys' fees, or expenses incurred in voiding such sale or recovering such amount. The court may grant judgment in favor of the estate and against any such party that entered into such agreement in willful disregard of this subsection for punitive damages in addition to any recovery under the preceding sentence.

§ 364. Obtaining credit

(a) If the trustee is authorized to operate the business of the debtor under section 721, 1108, or 1304 of this title, unless the court orders otherwise, the trustee may obtain unsecured credit and incur unsecured debt in the ordinary course of business allowable under section 503 (b) (1) of this title as an administrative expense.

(b) The court, after notice and a hearing, may authorize the trustee to obtain unsecured credit or to incur unsecured debt other than under subsection (a) of this section, allowable under section 503(b) (1) of this title as an administrative expense.

(c) If the trustee is unable to obtain unsecured credit allowable under section 503(b) (1) of this title as an administrative expense, the court, after notice and a hearing, may authorize the obtaining of credit or the incurring of debt—

(1) with priority over any or all administrative expenses of the kind specified in section 503(b) or 507(b) of this title;

(2) secured by a lien on property of the estate that is not otherwise subject to a lien; or

(3) secured by a junior lien on property of the estate that is subject to a lien.

(d) (1) The court, after notice and a hearing, may authorize the obtaining of credit or the incurring of debt secured by a senior or equal lien on property of the estate that is subject to a lien only if—

(A) the trustee is unable to obtain such credit otherwise; and

(B) there is adequate protection of the interest of the holder of the lien on the property of the estate on which such senior or equal lien is proposed to be granted.

(2) In any hearing under this subsection, the trustee has the burden of proof on the issue of adequate protection.

(e) The reversal or modification on appeal of an authorization under this section to obtain credit or incur debt, or of a grant under this section of a priority or a lien, does not affect the validity of any debt so incurred, or any priority or lien so granted, to an entity that extended such credit in good faith, whether or not such entity knew of the pendency of the appeal, unless such authorization and the incurring of such debt, or the granting of such priority or lien, were stayed pending appeal.

(f) Except with respect to an entity that is an underwriter as defined in section 1145(b) of this title, section 5 of the Securities Act of 1933 (15 U.S.C. 77e), the Trust Indenture Act of 1939 (15 U.S.C. 77aaa et seq.), and any State or local law requiring registration for offer or sale of a security or registration or licensing of an issuer of, underwriter of, or broker or dealer in, a security does not apply to the offer or sale under this section of a security that is not an equity security.

§ 365. Executory contracts and unexpired leases

(a) Except as provided in sections 765 and 766 of this title and in subsections (b), (c), and (d) of this section, the trustee, subject to the court's approval, may assume or reject any executory contract or unexpired lease of the debtor.

(b) (1) If there has been a default in an executory contract or unexpired lease of the debtor, the trustee may not assume such contract or lease unless, at the time of assumption of such contract or lease, the trustee—

(A) cures, or provides adequate assurance that the trustee will promptly cure, such default;

(B) compensates, or provides adequate assurance that the trustee will promptly compensate, a party other than the debtor to such contract or lease, for any actual pecuniary loss to such party resulting from such default; and

(C) provides adequate assurance of future performance under such contract or lease.

(2) Paragraph (1) of this subsection does not apply to a default that is a breach of a provision relating to—

(A) the insolvency or financial condition of the debtor at any time before the closing of the case;

(B) the commencement of a case under this title; or

(C) the appointment of or taking possession by a trustee in a case under this title or a custodian before such commencement.

(3) For the purposes of paragraph (1) of this section, adequate assurance of future performance of a lease of real property in a shopping center includes adequate assurance—

(A) of the source of rent and other consideration due under such lease;

(B) that any percentage rent due under such lease will not decline substantially;

(C) that assumption or assignment of such lease will not breach substantially any provision, such as a radius, location, use, or exclusivity provision, in any other lease, financing agreement, or master agreement relating to such shopping center; and

(D) that assumption or assignment of such lease will not disrupt substantially any tenant mix or balance in such shopping center.

(4) Notwithstanding any other provision of this section, if there has been a default in an unexpired lease of the debtor, other than a default of a kind specified in paragraph (2) of this subsection, the trustee may not require a lessor to provide services or supplies incidental to such lease before assumption of such lease unless the lessor is compensated under the terms of such lease for any services and supplies provided under such lease before assumption of such lease.

(c) The trustee may not assume or assign an executory contract or unexpired lease of the debtor, whether or not such contract or lease prohibits or restricts assignment of rights or delegation of duties, if—

(1) (A) applicable law excuses a party, other than the debtor, to such contract or lease from accepting performance from or rendering performance to the trustee or an assignee of such contract or lease, whether or not such contract or lease prohibits or restricts assignment of rights or delegation of duties; and

(B) such party does not consent to such assumption or assignment; or

(2) such contract is a contract to make a loan, or extend other debt financing or financial accommodations, to or for the benefit of the debtor, or to issue a security of the debtor.

(d) (1) In a case under chapter 7 of this title, if the trustee does not assume or reject an executory contract or unexpired lease of the debtor within 60 days after the order for relief, or within such additional time as the court, for cause, within such 60-day period, fixes, then such contract or lease is deemed rejected.

(2) In a case under chapter 9, 11, or 13 of this title, the trustee may assume or reject an executory contract or unexpired lease of the debtor at any time before the confirmation of a plan, but the court, on request of any party to such contract or lease, may order the trustee to determine within a specified period of time whether to assume or reject such contract or lease.

(e)(1) Notwithstanding a provision in an executory contract or unexpired lease, or in applicable law, an executory contract or unexpired lease of the debtor may not be terminated or modified, and any right or obligation under such contract or lease may not be terminated or modified, at any time after the commencement of the case solely because of a provision in such contract or lease that is conditioned on—

(A) the insolvency or financial condition of the debtor at any time before the closing of the case;

(B) the commencement of a case under this title; or

(C) the appointment of or taking possession by a trustee in a case under this title or a custodian before such commencement.

(2) Paragraph (1) of this subsection does not apply to an executory contract or unexpired lease of the debtor, whether or not such contract or lease prohibits or restricts assignment of rights or delegation of duties, if—

(A)(i) applicable law excuses a party, other than the debtor, to such contract or lease from accepting performance from or rendering performance to the trustee or to an assignee of such contract or lease, whether or not such contract or lease prohibits or restricts assignment of rights or delegation of duties; and

(ii) such party does not consent to such assumption or assignment; or

(B) such contract is a contract to make a loan, or extend other debt financing or financial accommodations, to or for the benefit of the debtor, or to issue a security of the debtor.

(f)(1) Except as provided in subsection (c) of this section, notwithstanding a provision in an executory contract or unexpired lease of the debtor, or in applicable law, that prohibits, restricts, or conditions the assignment of such contract or lease, the trustee may assign such contract or lease under paragraph (2) of this subsection.

(2) The trustee may assign an executory contract or unexpired lease of the debtor only if—

(A) the trustee assumes such contract or lease in accordance with the provisions of this section; and

(B) adequate assurance of future performance by the assignee of such contract or lease is provided, whether or not there has been a default in such contract or lease.

(3) Notwithstanding a provision in an executory contract or unexpired lease of the debtor, or in applicable law that terminates or modifies, or permits a party other than the debtor to terminate or modify, such contract or lease or a right or obligation under such contract or lease on account of an assignment of such contract or lease, such contract, lease, right, or obligation may not be terminated or modified under such provision because of the assumption or assignment of such contract or lease by the trustee.

(g) Except as provided in subsections (h)(2) and (i)(2) of this section, the rejection of an executory contract or unexpired lease of the debtor constitutes a breach of such contract or lease—

(1) if such contract or lease has not been assumed under this section or under a plan confirmed under chapter 9, 11, or 13 of this title, immediately before the date of the filing of the petition; or

(2) if such contract or lease has been assumed under this section or under a plan confirmed under chapter 9, 11, or 13 of this title—

(A) if before such rejection the case has not been converted under section 1112 or 1307 of this title, at the time of such rejection; or

(B) if before such rejection the case has been converted under section 1112 or 1307 of this title—

(i) immediately before the date of such conversion, if such contract or lease was assumed before such conversion; or

(ii) at the time of such rejection, if such contract or lease was assumed after such conversion.

(h)(1) If the trustee rejects an unexpired lease of real property of the debtor under which the debtor is the lessor, the lessee under such lease may treat the lease as terminated by such rejection, or, in the alternative, may remain in possession for the balance of the term of such lease and any renewal or extension of such term that is enforceable by such lessee under applicable nonbankruptcy law.

(2) If such lessee remains in possession, such lessee may offset against the rent reserved under such lease for the balance of the term after the date of the rejection of such lease, and any such renewal or extension, any damages occurring after such date caused by the nonperformance of any obligation of the debtor after such date, but such lessee does not have any rights against the estate on account of any damages arising after such date from such rejection, other than such offset.

(i)(1) If the trustee rejects an executory contract of the debtor for the sale of real property under which the purchaser is in possession, such purchaser may treat such contract as terminated, or, in the alternative, may remain in possession of such real property.

(2) If such purchaser remains in possession—

(A) such purchaser shall continue to make all payments due under such contract, but may, offset against such payments any damages occurring after the date of the rejection of such contract caused by the nonperformance of any obligation of the debtor after such date, but such purchaser does not have any rights against the estate on account of any damages arising after such date from such rejection, other than such offset; and

(B) the trustee shall deliver title to such purchaser in accordance with the provisions of such contract, but is relieved of all other obligations to perform under such contract.

(j) A purchaser that treats an executory contract as terminated under subsection (i) of this section, or a party whose executory contract to purchase real property from the debtor is rejected and under which such party is not in possession, has a lien on the interest of the debtor in such property for the recovery of any portion of the purchase price that such purchaser or party has paid.

(k) Assignment by the trustee to an entity of a contract or lease assumed under this section relieves the trustee and the estate from any liability for any breach of such contract or lease occurring after such assignment.

§ 366. Utility service

(a) Except as provided in subsection (b) of this section, a utility may not alter, refuse, or discontinue service to, or discriminate against, the trustee or the debtor solely on the basis that a debt owed by the debtor to such utility for service rendered before the order for relief was not paid when due.

(b) Such utility may alter, refuse, or discontinue service if neither the trustee nor the debtor, within 20 days after the date of the order for relief, furnishes adequate assurance of payment, in the form of a deposit or other security, for service after such date. On request of a party in interest and after notice and a hearing, the court may order reasonable modification of the amount of the deposit or other security necessary to provide adequate assurance of payment.

CHAPTER 5—CREDITORS, THE DEBTOR, AND THE ESTATE

SUBCHAPTER I—CREDITORS AND CLAIMS

SUBCHAPTER II—DEBTOR'S DUTIES AND BENEFITS

SUBCHAPTER III—THE ESTATE

SUBCHAPTER I—CREDITORS AND CLAIMS

§ 501. Filing of proofs of claims or interests

(a) A creditor or an indenture trustee may file a proof of claim. An equity security holder may file a proof of interest.

(b) If a creditor does not timely file a proof of such creditor's claim, an entity that is liable to such creditor with the debtor, or that has secured such creditor, may file a proof of such claim.

(c) If a creditor does not timely file a proof of such creditor's claim, the debtor or the trustee may file a proof of such claim.

(d) A claim of a kind specified in section 502(f), 502(g), 502(h) or 502(i) of this title may be filed under subsection (a), (b), or (c) of this section the same as if such claim were a claim against the debtor and had arisen before the date of the filing of the petition.

§ 502. Allowance of claims or interests

(a) A claim or interest, proof of which is filed under section 501 of this title, is deemed allowed, unless a party in interest, including a creditor of a partner in a partnership that is a debtor in a case under chapter 7 of this title, objects.

(b) Except as provided in subsections (f), (g), (h) and (i) of this section, if such objection to a claim is made, the court, after notice and a hearing, shall determine the amount of such claim as of the date of the filing of the petition, and shall allow such claim in such amount, except to the extent that—

(1) such claim is unenforceable against the debtor, and unenforceable against property of the debtor, under any agreement or applicable law for a reason other than because such claim is contingent or unmatured;

(2) such claim is for unmatured interest;

(3) such claim may be offset under section 553 of this title against a debt owing to the debtor;

(4) if such claim is for a tax assessed against property of the estate, such claim exceeds value of the interest of the estate in such property;

(5) if such claim is for services of an insider or attorney of the debtor, such claim exceeds the reasonable value of such services;

(6) the claim is for a debt that is unmatured on the date of the filing of the petition, and that is excepted from discharge under section 523(a)(5) of this title;

(7) if such claim is the claim of a lessor for damages resulting from the termination of a lease of real property, such claim exceeds—

(A) the rent reserved by such lease, without acceleration, for the greater of one year, or 15 percent, not to exceed three years, of the remaining term of such lease, following the earlier of—

(i) the date of the filing of the petition; and

(ii) the date on which such lessor reposessed, or the lessee surrendered, the leased property; plus

(B) any unpaid rent due under such lease, without acceleration, on the earlier of such dates;

(8) if such claim is for damages resulting from the termination of an employment contract, such claim exceeds—

(A) the compensation provided by such contract, without acceleration, for one year following the earlier of—

(i) the date of the filing of the petition; and

(ii) the date on which the employer directed the employee to terminate, or such employee terminated, performance under such contract; plus

(B) the unpaid compensation due under such contract without acceleration, on the earlier of such dates; or

(9) such claim results from a reduction, due to late payment, in the amount of an otherwise applicable credit available to the

debtor in connection with an employment tax on wages, salaries, or commissions earned from the debtor.

(c) There shall be estimated for purpose of allowance under this section—

(1) any contingent or unliquidated claim, fixing or liquidation of which, as the case may be, would unduly delay the closing of the case; or

(2) any right to an equitable remedy for breach of performance if such breach gives rise to a right to payment.

(d) Notwithstanding subsections (a) and (b) of this section, the court shall disallow any claim of any entity from which property is recoverable under section 542, 543, 550, or 553 of this title or that is a transferee of a transfer avoidable under section 522(f), 522(h), 544, 545, 547, 548, 549, or 724(a) of this title, unless such entity or transferee has paid the amount or turned over any such property, for which such entity or transferee is liable under section 522(i), 542, 543, 550, or 553 of this title.

(e)(1) Notwithstanding subsections (a) and (b) of this section and paragraph (2) of this subsection, the court shall disallow any claim for reimbursement or contribution of an entity that is liable with the debtor on, or has secured, the claim of a creditor, to the extent that—

(A) such creditor's claim against the estate is disallowed;

(B) such claim for reimbursement or contribution is contingent as of the time of allowance of such claim for reimbursement or contribution; or

(C) such entity requests subrogation under section 509 of this title to the rights of such creditor.

(2) A claim for reimbursement or contribution of such an entity that becomes fixed after the commencement of the case shall be determined, and shall be allowed under subsection (a), (b), or (c) of this section, or disallowed under subsection (d) of this section, the same as if such claim had become fixed before the date of the filing of the petition.

(f) In an involuntary case, a claim arising in the ordinary course of the debtor's business or financial affairs after the commencement of the case but before the earlier of the appointment of a trustee and the order for relief shall be determined as of the date such claim arises, and shall be allowed under subsection (a), (b), or (c) of this section or disallowed under subsection (d) or (e) of this section, the same as if such claim had arisen before the date of the filing of the petition.

(g) A claim arising from the rejection, under section 365 of this title or under a plan under chapter 9, 11, or 13 of this title, of an executory contract or unexpired lease of the debtor that has not been assumed shall be determined, and shall be allowed under subsection (a), (b), or (c) of this section or disallowed under subsection (d) or (e) of this section, the same as if such claim had arisen before the date of the filing of the petition.

(h) A claim arising from the recovery of property under section 522(i), 550, or 553 of this title shall be determined, and shall be allowed under subsection (a), (b), or (c) of this section, or disallowed under subsection (d) or (e) of this section, the same as if such claim had arisen before the date of the filing of the petition.

(i) A claim that does not arise until after the commencement of the case for a tax entitled to priority under section 507(a)(6) of this title shall be determined, and shall be allowed under subsection (a), (b), or (c) of this section, or disallowed under subsection (d) or (e) of this section, the same as if such claim had arisen before the date of the filing of the petition.

(j) Before a case is closed, a claim that has been allowed may be reconsidered for cause, and reallowed or disallowed according to the equities of the case.

§ 503. Allowance of administrative expenses

(a) An entity may file a request for payment of an administrative expense.

(b) After notice and a hearing, there shall be allowed, administrative expenses, other than claims allowed under section 502(f) of this title, including—

(1)(A) the actual, necessary costs and expenses of preserving the estate, including wages, salaries, or commissions for services rendered after the commencement of the case;

(B) any tax—

(i) incurred by the estate, except a tax of a kind specified in section 507(a)(6) of this title; or

(ii) attributable to an excessive allowance of a tentative carryback adjustment that the estate received, whether the taxable year to which such adjustment relates ended before or after the commencement of the case; and

(C) any fine, penalty, or reduction in credit, relating to a tax of a kind specified in subparagraph (B) of this paragraph;

(2) compensation and reimbursement awarded under section 330 of this title;

(3) the actual, necessary expenses, other than compensation and reimbursement specified in paragraph (4) of this subsection incurred by—

(A) a creditor that files a petition under section 303 of this title;

(B) a creditor that recovers, after the court's approval, for the benefit of the estate any property transferred or concealed by the debtor;

(C) a creditor in connection with the prosecution of a criminal offense relating to the case, or to the business or property of the debtor;

(D) a creditor, an indenture trustee. an equity security holder, or a committee representing creditors or equity security holders other than a committee appointed under section 1102 of this title, in making a substantial contribution in a case under chapter 9 or 11 of this title; or

(E) a custodian superseded under section 543 of this title, and compensation for the services of such custodian;

(4) reasonable compensation for professional services rendered by an attorney or an accountant of an entity whose expense is allowable under paragraph (3) of this subsection, based on the time, the nature, the extent, and the value of such services; and the cost of comparable services other than in a case under this title, and reimbursement for actual, necessary expenses incurred by such attorney or accountant;

(5) reasonable compensation for services rendered by an indenture trustee in making a substantial contribution in a case under chapter 9 or 11 of this title, based on the time, the nature, the extent, and the value of such services, and the cost of comparable services other than in a case under this title; and

(6) the fees and mileage payable under chapter 119 of title 28.

§ 504. Sharing of compensation

(a) Except as provided in subsection (b) of this section, a person receiving compensation or reimbursement under section 503(b)(2) or 503(b)(4) of this title may not share or agree to share—

(1) any such compensation or reimbursement with another person; or

(2) any compensation or reimbursement received by another person under such sections.

(b)(1) A member, partner, or regular associate in a professional association, corporation, or partnership may share compensation or reimbursement received under section 503(b)(2) or 503(b)(4) of this title with another member, partner, or regular associate in such association, corporation, or partnership, and may share in any compensation or reimbursement received under such sections by another member, partner, or regular associate in such association, corporation, or partnership.

(2) An attorney for a creditor that files a petition under section 303 of this title may share compensation and reimbursement received under section 503(b)(4) of this title with any other attorney contributing to the services rendered or expenses incurred by such creditor's attorney.

§ 505. Determination of tax liability

(a)(1) Except as provided in paragraph (2) of this subsection, the court may determine the amount or legality of any tax, any fine or penalty relating to a tax, or any addition to tax, whether or not previously assessed, whether or not paid, and whether or not contested before and adjudicated by a judicial or administrative tribunal of competent jurisdiction.

(2) The court may not so determine—

(A) the amount or legality of a tax, fine, penalty, or addition to tax if such amount or legality was contested before and adjudicated by a judicial or administrative tribunal of competent jurisdiction before the commencement of the case under this title; or

(B) any right of the estate to a tax refund, before the earlier of—

(i) 120 days after the trustee properly requests such refund from the governmental unit from which such refund is claimed; and

(ii) a determination by such governmental unit of such request.

(b) A trustee may request a determination of any unpaid liability of the estate for any tax incurred during the administration of the case by submitting a tax return for such tax and a request for such a determination to the governmental unit charged with responsibility for collection or determination of such tax. Unless such return is fraudulent, or contains a material misrepresentation, the trustee, the debtor, and any successor to the debtor are discharged from any liability for such tax—

(1) upon payment of the tax shown on such return, if—

(A) such governmental unit does not notify the trustee, within 60 days after such request, that such return has been selected for examination; or

(B) such governmental unit does not complete such an examination and notify the trustee of any tax due, within 180 days after such request or within such additional time as the court, for cause, permits;

(2) upon payment of the tax determined by the court, after notice and a hearing, after completion by such governmental unit of such examination; or

(3) upon payment of the tax determined by such governmental unit to be due.

(c) Notwithstanding section 362 of this title, after determination by the court of a tax under this section, the governmental unit charged with responsibility for collection of such tax may assess such tax against the estate, the debtor, or a successor to the debtor, as the case may be, subject to any otherwise applicable law.

§ 506. Determination of secured status

(a) An allowed claim of a creditor secured by a lien on property in which the estate has an interest, or that is subject to setoff under section 553 of this title, is a secured claim to the extent of the value of such creditor's interest in the estate's interest in such property, or to the extent of the amount subject to setoff, as the case may be, and is an unsecured claim to the extent that the value of such creditor's interest or the amount so subject to setoff is less than the amount of such allowed claim. Such value shall be determined in light of the purpose of the valuation and of the proposed disposition or use of such property, and in conjunction with any hearing on such disposition or use or on a plan affecting such creditor's interest.

(b) To the extent that an allowed secured claim is secured by property the value of which, after any recovery under subsection (c) of this section, is greater than the amount of such claim, there shall be allowed to the holder of such claim, interest on such claim, and any reasonable fees, costs, or charges provided under the agreement under which such claim arose.

(c) The trustee may recover from property securing an allowed secured claim the reasonable, necessary costs and expenses of preserving, or disposing of, such property to the extent of any benefit to the holder of such claim.

(d) To the extent that a lien secures a claim against the debtor that is not an allowed secured claim, such lien is void, unless—

(1) a party in interest has not requested that the court determine and allow or disallow such claim under section 502 of this title; or

(2) such claim was disallowed only under section 502(e) of this title.

§ 507. Priorities

(a) The following expenses and claims have priority in the following order:

(1) First, administrative expenses allowed under section 503(b) of this title, and any fees and charges assessed against the estate under chapter 123 of title 28.

(2) Second, unsecured claims allowed under section 502(f) of this title.

(3) Third, allowed unsecured claims for wages, salaries, or commissions, including vacation, severance and sick leave pay—

(A) earned by an individual within 90 days before the date of the filing of the petition or the date of the cessation of the debtor's business, whichever occurs first; but only

(B) to the extent of $2,000 for each such individual.

(4) Fourth, allowed unsecured claims for contributions to employee benefit plans—

(A) arising from services rendered within 180 days before the date of the filing of the petition or the date of the cessation of the debtor's business, whichever occurs first; but only

(B) for each such plan, to the extent of—

(i) the number of employees covered by such plan multiplied by $2,000; less

(ii) the aggregate amount paid to such employees under paragraph (3) of this subsection, plus the aggregate amount paid by the estate on behalf of such employees to any other employee benefit plan.

(5) Fifth, allowed unsecured claims of individuals, to the extent of $900 for each such individual, arising from the deposit, before the commencement of the case, of money in connection with the purchase, lease, or rental of property, or the purchase of services, for the personal, family, or household use of such individuals, that were not delivered or provided.

(6) Sixth, allowed unsecured claims of governmental units, to the extent that such claims are for—

(A) a tax on or measured by income or gross receipts—

(i) for a taxable year ending on or before the date of the filing of the petition for which a return, if required, is last due, including extensions, after three years before the date of the filing of the petition;

(ii) assessed within 240 days, plus any time plus 30 days during which an offer in compromise with respect to such tax that was made within 240 days after such assessment was pending, before the date of the filing of the petition; or

(iii) other than a tax of a kind specified in section 523 (a)(1)(B) or 523(a)(1)(C) of this title, not assessed before, but assessable, under applicable law or by agreement, after, the commencement of the case;

(B) a property tax assessed before the commencement of the case and last payable without penalty after one year before the date of the filing of the petition;

(C) a tax required to be collected or withheld and for which the debtor is liable in whatever capacity;

(D) an employment tax on a wage, salary, or commission of a kind specified in paragraph (3) of this subsection earned from the debtor before the date of the filing of the petition, whether or not actually paid before such date, for which a return is last due, under applicable law or under any extension, after three years before the date of the filing of the petition;

(E) an excise tax on—

(i) a transaction occurring before the date of the filing of the petition for which a return, if required, is last due, under applicable law or under any extension, after three years before the date of the filing of the petition; or

(ii) if a return is not required, a transaction occurring during the three years immediately preceding the date of the filing of the petition;

(F) a customs duty arising out of the importation of merchandise—

(i) entered for consumption within one year before the date of the filing of the petition;

(ii) covered by an entry liquidated or reliquidated within one year before the date of the filing of the petition; or

(iii) entered for consumption within four years before the date of the filing of the petition but unliquidated on such date, if the Secretary of the Treasury certifies that failure to liquidate such entry was due to an investigation pending on such date into assessment of antidumping or countervailing duties or fraud, or if information needed for the proper appraisement or classification of such merchandise was not available to the appropriate customs officer before such date; or

(G) a penalty related to a claim of a kind specified in this paragraph and in compensation for actual pecuniary loss.

(b) If the trustee, under section 362, 363, or 364 of this title, provides adequate protection of the interest of a holder of a claim secured by a lien on property of the debtor and if, notwithstanding such protection, such creditor has a claim allowable under subsection (a)(1) of this section arising from the stay of action against such property under section 362 of this title, from the use, sale, or lease of such property under section 363 of this title, or from the granting of a lien under section 364(d) of this title, then such creditor's claim under such subsection shall have priority over every other claim allowable under such subsection.

(c) For the purpose of subsection (a) of this section, a claim of a governmental unit arising from an erroneous refund or credit of a tax shall be treated the same as a claim for the tax to which such refund or credit relates.

(d) An entity that is subrogated to the rights of a holder of a claim of a kind specified in subsection (a)(3), (a)(4), (a)(5), or (a)(6) of this section is not subrogated to the right of the holder of such claim to priority under such subsection.

§ 508. Effect of distribution other than under this title

(a) If a creditor receives, in a foreign proceeding, payment of, or a transfer of property on account of, a claim that is allowed under this title, such creditor may not receive any payment under this title on account of such claim until each of the other holders of claims on account of which such holders are entitled to share equally with such creditor under this title has received payment under this title equal in value to the consideration received by such creditor in such foreign proceeding.

(b) If a creditor of a partnership debtor receives, from a general partner that is not a debtor in a case under chapter 7 of this title, payment of, or a transfer of property on account of, a claim that is allowed under this title and that is not secured by a lien on property of such partner, such creditor may not receive any payment under this title on account of such claim until each of the other holders of claims on account of which such holders are entitled to share equally with such creditor under this title has received payment under this title equal in value to the consideration received by such creditor from such general partner.

§ 509. Claims of codebtors

(a) Except as provided in subsections (b) and (c) of this section, an entity that is liable with the debtor on, or that has secured, a claim of a creditor, and that pays such claim, is subrogated to the rights of such creditor to the extent of such payment.

(b) Such entity is not subrogated to the rights of such creditor to the extent that—

(1) a claim of such entity for reimbursement or contribution on account of a payment of such creditor's claim is—

(A) allowed under section 502 of this title;

(B) disallowed other than under section 502(e) of this title; or

(C) subordinated under section 510 of this title; or

(2) as between the debtor and such entity, such entity received the consideration for the claim held by such creditor.

(c) The court shall subordinate to the claim of a creditor and for the benefit of such creditor an allowed claim, by way of subrogation under section 509 of this title, or for reimbursement or contribution, of an entity that is liable with the debtor on, or that has secured, such creditor's claim, until such creditor's claim is paid in full, either through payments under this title or otherwise.

§ 510. Subordination

(a) A subordination agreement is enforceable in a case under this title to the same extent that such agreement is enforceable under applicable nonbankruptcy law.

(b) Any claim for recission of a purchase or sale of a security of the debtor or of an affiliate or for damages arising from the purchase or sale of such a security shall be subordinated for purposes of distribution to all claims and interests that are senior or equal to the claim or interest represented by such security.

(c) Notwithstanding subsections (a) and (b) of this section, after notice and a hearing, the court may—

(1) under principles of equitable subordination, subordinate for purposes of distribution all or part of an allowed claim to all or part of another allowed claim or all or part of an allowed interest to all or part of another allowed interest; or

(2) order that any lien securing such a subordinated claim be transferred to the estate.

SUBCHAPTER II—DEBTOR'S DUTIES AND BENEFITS

§ 521. Debtor's duties

The debtor shall—

(1) file a list of creditors, and unless the court orders otherwise, a schedule of assets and liabilities, and a statement of the debtor's financial affairs;

(2) if a trustee is serving in the case, cooperate with the trustee as necessary to enable the trustee to perform the trustee's duties under this title;

(3) if a trustee is serving in the case, surrender to the trustee all property of the estate and any recorded information, including books, documents, records, and papers, relating to property of the estate; and

(4) appear at the hearing required under section 524(d) of this title.

§ 522. Exemptions

(a) In this section—

(1) "dependent" includes spouse, whether or not actually dependent; and

(2) "value" means fair market value as of the date of the filing of the petition.

(b) Notwithstanding section 541 of this title, an individual debtor may exempt from property of the estate either—

(1) property that is specified under subsection (d) of this section, unless the State law that is applicable to the debtor under paragraph (2)(A) of this subsection specifically does not so authorize; or, in the alternative,

(2)(A) any property that is exempt under Federal law, other than subsection (d) of this section, or State or local law that is applicable on the date of the filing of the petition at the place in which the debtor's domicile has been located for the 180 days immediately preceding the date of the filing of the petition, or for a longer portion of such 180-day period than in any other place; and

(B) any interest in property in which the debtor had, immediately before the commencement of the case, an interest as a tenant by the entirety or joint tenant to the extent that such interest as a tenant by the entirety or joint tenant is exempt from process under applicable nonbankruptcy law.

(c) Unless the case is dismissed, property exempted under this section is not liable during or after the case for any debt of the debtor that arose, or that is determined under section 502 of this title as if such claim had arisen before the commencement of the case, except—

(1) a debt of a kind specified in section 523(a)(1) or section 523(a)(5) of this title; or

(2) a lien that is—

(A) not avoided under section 544, 545, 547, 548, 549, or 724(a) of this title;

(B) not voided under section 506(d) of this title; or

(C)(i) a tax lien, notice of which is properly filed; and

(ii) avoided under section 545(2) of this title.

(d) The following property may be exempted under subsection (b)(1) of this section:

(1) The debtor's aggregate interest, not to exceed $7,500 in value, in real property or personal property that the debtor or a dependent of the debtor uses as a residence, in a cooperative that owns property that the debtor or a dependent of the debtor uses as a residence, or in a burial plot for the debtor or a dependent of the debtor.

(2) The debtor's interest, not to exceed $1,200 in value, in one motor vehicle.

(3) The debtor's interest, not to exceed $200 in value in any particular item, in household furnishings, household goods, wearing apparel, appliances, books, animals, crops, or musical instruments, that are held primarily for the personal, family, or household use of the debtor or a dependent of the debtor.

(4) The debtor's aggregate interest, not to exceed $500 in value, in jewelry held primarily for the personal, family, or household use of the debtor or a dependent of the debtor.

(5) The debtor's aggregate interest, not to exceed in value $400 plus any unused amount of the exemption provided under paragraph (1) of this subsection, in any property.

(6) The debtor's aggregate interest, not to exceed $750 in value,

in any implements, professional books, or tools, of the trade of the debtor or the trade of a dependent of the debtor.

(7) Any unmatured life insurance contract owned by the debtor, other than a credit life insurance contract.

(8) The debtor's aggregate interest, not to exceed in value $4,000 less any amount of property of the estate transferred in the manner specified in section 542(d) of this title, in any accrued dividend or interest under, or loan value of, any unmatured life insurance contract owned by the debtor under which the insured is the debtor or an individual of whom the debtor is a dependent.

(9) Professionally prescribed health aids for the debtor or a dependent of the debtor.

(10) The debtor's right to receive—

(A) a social security benefit, unemployment compensation, or a local public assistance benefit;

(B) a veterans' benefit;

(C) a disability, illness, or unemployment benefit;

(D) alimony, support, or separate maintenance, to the extent reasonably necessary for the support of the debtor and any dependent of the debtor;

(E) a payment under a stock bonus, pension, profitsharing, annuity, or similar plan or contract on account of illness, disability, death, age, or length of service, to the extent reasonably necessary for the support of the debtor and any dependent of the debtor, unless—

(i) such plan or contract was established by or under the auspices of an insider that employed the debtor at the time the debtor's rights under such plan or contract arose;

(ii) such payment is on account of age or length of service; and

(iii) such plan or contract does not qualify under section 401(a), 403(a), 403(b), 408, or 409 of the Internal Revenue Code of 1954 (26 U.S.C. 401(a), 403(a), 403(b), 408, or 409).

(11) The debtor's right to receive, or property that is traceable to—

(A) an award under a crime victim's reparation law;

(B) a payment on account of the wrongful death of an individual of whom the debtor was a dependent, to the extent reasonably necessary for the support of the debtor and any dependent of the debtor;

(C) a payment under a life insurance contract that insured the life of an individual of whom the debtor was a dependent on the date of such individual's death, to the extent reasonably necessary for the support of the debtor and any dependent of the debtor;

(D) a payment, not to exceed $7,500, on account of personal bodily injury, not including pain and suffering or compensation for actual pecuniary loss, of the debtor or an individual of whom the debtor is a dependent; or

(E) a payment in compensation of loss of future earnings of the debtor or an individual of whom the debtor is or was a dependent, to the extent reasonably necessary for the support of the debtor and any dependent of the debtor.

(e) A waiver of exemptions executed in favor of a creditor that holds an unsecured claim against the debtor is unenforceable in a case under this title with respect to such claim against property that the debtor may exempt under subsection (b) of this section. A waiver by the debtor of a power under subsection (f) or (h) of this section to avoid a transfer, under subsection (g) or (i) of this section to exempt property, or under subsection (i) of this section to recover property or to preserve a transfer, is unenforceable in a case under this title.

(f) Notwithstanding any waiver of exemptions, the debtor may avoid the fixing of a lien on an interest of the debtor in property to the extent that such lien impairs an exemption to which the debtor would have been entitled under subsection (b) of this section, if such lien is—

(1) a judicial lien; or

(2) a nonpossessory, nonpurchase-money security interest in any—

(A) household furnishings, household goods, wearing apparel, appliances, books, animals, crops, musical instruments, or jewelry that are held primarily for the personal, family, or household use of the debtor or a dependent of the debtor;

(B) implements, professional books, or tools, of the trade of the debtor or the trade of a dependent of the debtor; or

(C) professionally prescribed health aids for the debtor or a dependent of the debtor.

(g) Notwithstanding sections 550 and 551 of this title, the debtor may exempt under subsection (b) of this section property that the trustee recovers under section 510(c)(2), 542, 543, 550, 551, or 553 of this title, to the extent that the debtor could have exempted such property under subsection (b) of this section if such property had not been transferred, if—

(1)(A) such transfer was not a voluntary transfer of such property by the debtor; and

(B) the debtor did not conceal such property; or

(2) the debtor could have avoided such transfer under subsection (f)(2) of this section.

(h) The debtor may avoid a transfer of property of the debtor or recover a setoff to the extent that the debtor could have exempted such property under subsection (g)(1) of this section if the trustee had avoided such transfer, if—

(1) such transfer is avoidable by the trustee under section 544, 545, 547, 548, 549, or 724(a) of this title or recoverable by the trustee under section 553 of this tittle; and

(2) the trustee does not attempt to avoid such transfer.

(i)(1) If the debtor avoids a transfer or recovers a setoff under subsection (f) or (h) of this section, the debtor may recover in the manner prescribed by, and subject to the limitations of, section 550 of this title, the same as if the trustee had avoided such transfer, and may exempt any property so recovered under subsection (b) of this section.

(2) Notwithstanding section 551 of this title, a transfer avoided under section 544, 545, 547, 548, 549, or 724(a) of this title, under subsection (f) or (h) of this section, or property recovered under section 553 of this title, may be preserved for the benefit of the debtor to the extent that the debtor may exempt such property under subsection (g) of his section or paragraph (1) of this subsection.

(j) Notwithstanding subsections (g) and (i) of this section, the debtor may exempt a particular kind of property under subsections (g) and (i) of this section only to the extent that the debtor has exempted less property in value of such kind than that to which the debtor is entitled under subsection (b) of this section.

(k) Property that the debtor exempts under this section is not liable for payment of any administrative expense except—

(1) the aliquot share of the costs and expenses of avoiding a transfer of property that the debtor exempts under subsection (g) of this section, or of recovery of such property, that is attributable to the value of the portion of such property exempted in relation to the value of the property recovered; and

(2) any costs and expenses of avoiding a transfer under subsection (f) or (h) of this section, or of recovery of property under subsection (i)(1) of this section, that the debtor has not paid.

(l) The debtor shall file a list of property that the debtor claims as exempt under subsection (b) of this section. If the debtor does not file such a list, a dependent of the debtor may file such a list, or may claim property as exempt from property of the estate on behalf of the debtor. Unless a party in interest objects, the property claimed as exempt on such list is exempt.

(m) This section shall apply separately with respect to each debtor in a joint case.

§ 523. Exceptions to discharge

(a) A discharge under section 727, 1141, or 1328(b) of this title does not discharge an individual debtor from any debt—

(1) for a tax or a customs duty—

(A) of the kind and for the periods specified in section 507(a)(2) or 507(a)(6) of this title, whether or not a claim for such tax was filed or allowed;

(B) with respect to which a return, if required—

(i) was not filed; or

(ii) was filed after the date on which such return was last due, under applicable law or under any extension, and after two years before the date of the filing of the petition; or

(C) with respect to which the debtor made a fraudulent return or willfully attempted in any manner to evade or defeat such tax;

(2) for obtaining money, property, services, or an extension, renewal, or refinance of credit, by—

(A) false pretenses, a false representation, or actual fraud, other than a statement respecting the debtor's or an insider's financial condition; or

(B) use of a statement in writing—

(i) that is materially false;

(ii) respecting the debtor's or an insider's financial condition;

(iii) on which the creditor to whom the debtor is liable for obtaining such money, property, services, or credit reasonably relied; and

(iv) that the debtor caused to be made or published with intent to deceive;

(3) neither listed nor scheduled under section 521(1) of this title, with the name, if known to the debtor, of the creditor to whom such debt is owed, in time to permit—

(A) if such debt is not of a kind specified in paragraph (2), (4), or (6) of this subsection, timely filing of a proof of claim, unless such creditor had notice or actual knowledge of the case in time for such timely filing; or

(B) if such debt is of a kind specified in paragraph (2), (4), or (6) of this subsection, timely filing of a proof of claim and timely request for a determination of dischargeability of such debt under one of such paragraphs, unless such creditor had notice or actual knowledge of the case in time for such timely filing and request;

(4) for fraud or defalcation while acting in a fiduciary capacity, embezzlement, or larceny;

(5) to a spouse, former spouse, or child of the debtor, for alimony to, maintenance for, or support of such spouse or child, in connection with a separation agreement, divorce decree, or property settlement agreement, but not to the extent that—

(A) such debt is assigned to another entity, voluntarily, by operation of law, or otherwise; or

(B) such debt includes a liability designated as alimony, maintenance, or support, unless such liability is actually in the nature of alimony, maintenance, or support;

(6) for willful and malicious injury by the debtor to another entity or to the property of another entity;

(7) to the extent such debt is for a fine, penalty, or forfeiture payable to and for the benefit of a governmental unit, and is not compensation for actual pecuniary loss, other than a tax penalty—

(A) relating to a tax of a kind not specified in paragraph (1) of this subsection; or

(B) imposed with respect to a transaction or event that occurred before three years before the date of the filing of the petition;

(8) to a governmental unit, or a nonprofit institution of higher education, for an educational loan, unless—

(A) such loan first became due before five years before the date of the filing of the petition; or

(B) excepting such debt from discharge under this paragraph will impose an undue hardship on the debtor and the debtor's dependents; or

(9) that was or could have been listed or scheduled by the debtor in a prior case concerning the debtor under this title or under the Bankruptcy Act in which the debtor waived discharge, or was denied a discharge under section 727(a) (2), (3), (4), (5), (6), or (7) of this title, or under section 14c (1), (2), (3), (4), (6), or (7) of such Act.

(b) Notwithstanding subsection (a) of this section, a debt that was excepted from discharge under subsection (a)(1), (a)(3), or (a)(8) of this section, under section 17a(1), 17a(3), or 17a(5) of the Bankruptcy Act, under section 439A of the Higher Education Act of 1965 (20 U.S.C. 1087-3), or under section 733(g) of the Public Health Services Act (42 U.S.C. 294f) in a prior case concerning the debtor under this title, or under the Bankruptcy Act, is dischargeable in a case under this title unless, by the terms of subsection (a) of this section, such debt is not dischargeable in the case under this title.

(c) Except as provided in subsection (a)(3)(B) of this section, the debtor shall be discharged from a debt specified in paragraph (2), (4), or (6) of subsection (a) of this section, unless, on request of the creditor to whom such debt is owed, and after notice and a hearing, the court determines such debt to be excepted from discharge under paragraph (2), (4), or (6), as the case may be, of subsection (a) of this section.

(d) If a creditor requests a determination of dischargeability of a consumer debt under subsection (a)(2) of this section, and such debt is discharged, the court shall grant judgment against such creditor and in favor of the debtor for the costs of, and a reasonable attorney's fee for, the proceeding to determine dischargeability, unless such granting of judgment would be clearly inequitable.

§ 524. Effect of discharge

(a) A discharge in a case under this title—

(1) voids any judgment at any time obtained, to the extent that such judgment is a determination of the personal liability of the debtor with respect to any debt discharged under section 727, 944, 1141, or 1328 of this title. whether or not discharge of such debt is waived;

(2) operates as an injunction against the commencement or continuation of an action, the employment of process, or any act, to collect, recover or offset any such debt as a personal liability of the debtor, or from property of the debtor, whether or not discharge of such debt is waived; and

(3) operates as an injunction against the commencement or continuation of an action, the employment of process, or any act, to collect or recover from, or offset against, property of the debtor of the kind specified in section 541(a)(2) of this title that is acquired after the commencement of the case, on account of any allowable community claim, except a community claim that is excepted from discharge under section 523 or 1328(c)(1) of this title, or that would be so excepted, determined in accordance with the provisions of sections 523(c) and 523(d) of this title, in a case concerning the debtor's spouse commenced on the date of the filing of the petition in the case concerning the debtor, whether or not discharge of the debt based on such community claim is waived.

(b) Subsection (a)(3) of this section does not apply if—

(1)(A) the debtor's spouse is a debtor in a case under this title, or a bankrupt or a debtor in a case under the Bankruptcy Act, commenced within six years of the date of the filing of the petition in the case concerning the debtor; and

(B) the court does not grant the debtor's spouse a discharge in such case concerning the debtor's spouse; or

(2)(A) the court would not grant the debtor's spouse a discharge in a case under chapter 7 of this title concerning such spouse commenced on the date of the filing of the petition in the case concerning the debtor; and

(B) a determination that the court would not so grant such discharge is made by the bankruptcy court within the time and in the manner provided for a determination under section 727 of this title of whether a debtor is granted a discharge.

(c) An agreement between a holder of a claim and the debtor, the consideration for which, in whole or in part, is based on a debt that is dischargeable in a case under this title is enforceable only to any extent enforceable under applicable nonbankruptcy law, whether or not discharge of such debt is waived, only if—

(1) such agreement was made before the granting of the discharge under section 727, 1141, or 1328 of this title;

(2) the debtor has not rescinded such agreement within 30 days after such agreement becomes enforceable;

(3) the provisions of subsection (d) of this section have been complied with; and

(4) in a case concerning an individual, to the extent that such debt is a consumer debt that is not secured by real property of the debtor, the court approves such agreement as—

(A)(i) not imposing an undue hardship on the debtor or a dependent of the debtor; and

(ii) in the best interest of the debtor; or

(B)(i) entered into in good faith; and

(ii) in settlement of litigation under section 523 of this title, or providing for redemption under section 722 of this title.

(d) In a case concerning an individual, when the court has determined whether to grant or not to grant a discharge under section 727, 1141, or 1328 of this title, the court shall hold a hearing at which the debtor shall appear in person. At such hearing, the court shall inform the debtor that a discharge has been granted or the reason why a discharge has not been granted. If a discharge has been granted and if the debtor desires to make an agreement of the kind specified in subsection (c) of this section, then at such hearing the court shall—

(1) inform the debtor—

(A) that such an agreement is not required under this title, under nonbankruptcy law, or under any agreement not made in accordance with the provisions of subsection (c) of this section; and

(B) of the legal effect and consequences of—

(i) an agreement of the kind specified in subsection (c) of this section; and

(ii) a default under such an agreement;

(2) determine whether the agreement that the debtor desires to make complies with the requirements of subsection (c)(4) of this subsection, if the consideration for such agreement is based in whole or in part on a consumer debt that is not secured by real property of the debtor.

(e) Except as provided in subsection (a)(3) of this section, discharge of a debt of the debtor does not affect the liability of any other entity on, or the property of any other entity for, such debt.

§ 525. Protection against discriminatory treatment

Except as provided in Perishable Agricultural Commodities Act, 1930 (7 U.S.C. 499a–499s), the Packers and Stockyards Act, 1921 (7 U.S.C. 181–229), and section 1 of the Act entitled "An Act making appropriations for the Department of Agriculture for the fiscal year ending June 30, 1944, and for other purposes," approved July 12, 1943 (57 Stat. 422; 7 U.S.C. 204), a governmental unit may not deny, revoke, suspend, or refuse to renew a license, permit, charter, franchise, or other similar grant to, condition such a grant to, discriminate with respect to such a grant against, deny employment to, terminate the employment of, or discriminate with respect to employment against, a person that is or has been a debtor under this title or a bankrupt or a debtor under the Bankruptcy Act, or another person with whom such bankrupt or debtor has been associated, solely because such bankrupt or debtor is or has been a debtor under this title or a bankrupt or debtor under the Bankruptcy Act, has been insolvent before the commencement of the case under this title, or during the case but before the debtor is granted or denied a discharge, or has not paid a debt that is dischargeable in the case under this title or that was discharged under the Bankruptcy Act.

SUBCHAPTER III—THE ESTATE

§ 541. Property of the estate

(a) The commencement of a case under under section 301, 302, or 303 of this title creates an estate. Such estate is comprised of all the following property, wherever located:

(1) Except as provided in subsections (b) and (c)(2) of this section, all legal or equitable interests of the debtor in property as of the commencement of the case.

(2) All interests of the debtor and the debtor's spouse in community property as of the commencement of the case that is—

(A) under the sole, equal, or joint management and control of the debtor; or

(B) liable for an allowable claim against the debtor, or for both an allowable claim against the debtor and an allowable claim against the debtor's spouse, to the extent that such interest is so liable.

(3) Any interest in property that the trustee recovers under section 543, 550, 553, or 723 of this title.

(4) Any interest in property preserved for the benefit of or ordered transferred to the estate under section 510(c) or 551 of this title.

(5) An interest in property that would have been property of the estate if such interest had been an interest of the debtor on the date of the filing of the petition, and that the debtor acquires or becomes entitled to acquire within 180 days after such date—

(A) by bequest, devise, or inheritance;

(B) as a result of a property settlement agreement with the debtor's spouse, or of an interlocutory or final divorce decree; or

(C) as a beneficiary of a life insurance policy or of a death benefit plan.

(6) Proceeds, product, offspring, rents, and profits of or from property of the estate, except such as are earnings from services performed by an individual debtor after the commencement of the case.

(7) Any interest in property that the estate acquires after the commencement of the case.

(b) Property of the estate does not include any power that the debtor may only exercise solely for the benefit of an entity other than the debtor.

(c)(1) Except as provided in paragraph (2) of this subsection, an interest of the debtor in property becomes property of the estate under subsection (a)(1), (a)(2), or (a)(5) of this section notwithstanding any provision—

(A) that restricts or conditions transfer of such interest by the debtor; or

(B) that is conditioned on the insolvency or financial condition of the debtor, on the commencement of a case under this title, or on the appointment of or the taking possession by a trustee in a case under this title or a custodian, and that effects or gives an option to effect a forfeiture, modification, or termination of the debtor's interest in property.

(2) A restriction on the transfer of a beneficial interest of the debtor in a trust that is enforceable under applicable nonbankruptcy law is enforceable in a case under this title.

(d) Property in which the debtor holds, as of the commencement of the case, only legal title and not an equitable interest, such as a mortgage secured by real property, or an interest in such a mortgage, sold by the debtor but as to which the debtor retains legal title to service or supervise the servicing of such mortgage or interest, becomes property of the estate under subsection (a) of this section only to the extent of the debtor's legal title to such property, but not to the extent of any equitable interest in such property that the debtor does not hold.

(e) The estate shall have the benefit of any defense available to the debtor as against an entity other than the estate, including statutes of limitation, statutes of frauds, usury, and other personal defenses. A waiver of any such defense by the debtor after the commencement of the case does not bind the estate.

§ 542. Turnover of property to the estate

(a) Except as provided in subsection (c) or (d) of this section, an entity, other than a custodian, in possession, custody, or control, during the case, of property that the trustee may use, sell, or lease under section 363 of this title, or that the debtor may exempt under section 522 of this title, shall deliver to the trustee, and account for, such property or the value of such property, unless such property is of inconsequential value or benefit to the estate.

(b) Except as provided in subsection (c) or (d) of this section, an entity that owes a debt that is property of the estate and that is matured, payable on demand, or payable on order, shall pay such debt to, or on the order of, the trustee, except to the extent that such debt may be offset under section 553 of this title against a claim against the debtor.

(c) Except as provided in section 362(a)(7) of this title, an entity that has neither actual notice nor actual knowledge of the commencement of the case concerning the debtor may transfer property of the estate, or pay a debt owing to the debtor, in good faith and other than in the manner specified in subsection (d) of this section, to an entity other than the trustee, with the same effect as to the entity making such transfer or payment as if the case under this title concerning the debtor had not been commenced.

(d) A life insurance company may transfer property of the estate or property of the debtor to such company in good faith, with the same effect with respect to such company as if the case under this title concerning the debtor had not been commenced, if such transfer is to pay a premium or to carry out a nonforfeiture insurance option, and is required to be made automatically, under a life insurance contract with such company that was entered into before the date of the filing of the petition and that is property of the estate.

(e) Subject to any applicable privilege, after notice and a hearing, the court may order an attorney, accountant, or other person that holds recorded information, including books, documents, records, and papers, relating to the debtor's property or financial affairs, to disclose such recorded information to the trustee.

§ 543. Turnover of property by a custodian

(a) A custodian with knowledge of the commencement of a case under this title concerning the debtor may not make any disbursement from, or take any action in the administration of, property of the debtor, proceeds of such property, or property of the estate, in the possession, custody, or control of such custodian, except such action as is necessary to preserve such property.

(b) A custodian shall—

(1) deliver to the trustee any property of the debtor transferred to such custodian, or proceeds of such property, that is in such custodian's possession, custody, or control on the date that such custodian acquires knowledge of the commencement of the case; and

(2) file an accounting of any property of the debtor, or proceeds of such property, that, at any time, came into the possession, custody, or control of such custodian.

(c) The court, after notice and a hearing, shall—

(1) protect all entities to which a custodian has become obligated with respect to such property;

(2) provide for the payment of reasonable compensation for services rendered and costs and expenses incurred by such custodian; and

(3) surcharge such custodian, other than an assignee for the benefit of the debtor's creditors that was appointed or took possession more than 120 days before the date of the filing of the petition, for any improper or excessive disbursement, other than a disbursement that has been made in accordance with applicable law or approved, after notice and a hearing, by a court of competent jurisdiction before the commencement of the case under this title.

(d) The bankruptcy court may, after notice and a hearing, excuse compliance with subsection (a), (b), or (c) of this section, if the interests of creditors, and, if the debtor is not insolvent, of equity security holders, would be better served by permitting a custodian to continue in possession, custody, or control of such property.

§ 544. Trustee as lien creditor and as successor to certain creditors and purchasers

(a) The trustee shall have, as of the commencement of the case, and without regard to any knowledge of the trustee or of any creditor, the rights and powers of, or may avoid any transfer of property of the debtor or any obligation incurred by the debtor that is voidable by—

(1) a creditor that extends credit to the debtor at the time of the commencement of the case, and that obtains, at such time and with respect to such credit, a judicial lien on all property on which a creditor on a simple contract could have obtained a judicial lien, whether or not such a creditor exists;

(2) a creditor that extends credit to the debtor at the time of the commencement of the case, and obtains, at such time and with respect to such credit, an execution against the debtor that is returned unsatisfied at such time, whether or not such a creditor exists; and

(3) a bona fide purchaser of real property from the debtor, against whom applicable law permits such transfer to be perfected, that obtains the status of a bona fide purchaser at the time of the commencement of the case, whether or not such a purchaser exists.

(b) The trustee may avoid any transfer of an interest of the debtor in property or any obligation incurred by the debtor that is voidable under applicable law by a creditor holding an unsecured claim that is allowable under section 502 of this title or that is not allowable only under section 502(e) of this title.

§ 545. Statutory liens

The trustee may avoid the fixing of a statutory lien on property of the debtor to the extent that such lien—

(1) first becomes effective against the debtor—

(A) when a case under this title concerning the debtor is is commenced;

(B) when an insolvency proceeding other than under this title concerning the debtor is commenced;

(C) when a custodian is apponted or takes possession;

(D) when the debtor becomes insolvent;

(E) when the debtor's financial condition fails to meet a specified standard; or

(F) at the time of an execution against property of the debtor levied at the instance of an entity other than the holder of such statutory lien;

(2) is not perfected or enforceable on the date of the filing of the petition against a bona fide purchaser that purchases such property on the date of the filing of the petition, whether or not such a purchaser exists;

(3) is for rent; or

(4) is a lien of distress for rent.

§ 546. Limitations on avoiding powers

(a) An action or proceeding under section 544, 545, 547, 548, or 553 of this title may not be commenced after the earlier of—

(1) two years after the appointment of a trustee under section 702, 1104, 1163, or 1302 of this title; and

(2) the time the case is closed or dismissed.

(b) The rights and powers of the trustee under section 544, 545, or 549 of this title are subject to any generally applicable law that permits perfection of an interest in property to be effective against an entity that acquires rights in such property before the date of such perfection. If such law requires seizure of such property or commencement of an action to accomplish such perfection, and such property has not been seized or such action has not been commenced before the date of the filing of the petition, such interest in such property shall be perfected by notice within the time fixed by such law for such seizure or commencement.

(c) The rights and powers of the trustee under sections 544(a), 545, 547, and 549 of this title are subject to any statutory right or common-law right of a seller, in the ordinary course of such seller's business, of goods to the debtor to reclaim such goods if the debtor has received such goods while insolvent, but—

(1) such a seller may not reclaim any such goods unless such seller demands in writing reclamation of such goods before ten days after receipt of such goods by the debtor; and

(2) the court may deny reclamation to a seller with such a right of reclamation that has made such a demand only if court—

(A) grants the claim of such a seller priority as an administrative expense; or

(B) secures such claim by a lien.

§ 547. Preferences

(a) In this section—

(1) "inventory" means personal property leased or furnished, held for sale or lease, or to be furnished under a contract for

service, raw materials, work in process, or materials used or consumed in a business, including farm products such as crops or livestock, held for sale or lease;

(2) "new value" means money or money's worth in goods, services, or new credit, or release by a transferee of property previously transferred to such transferee in a transaction that is neither void nor voidable by the debtor or the trustee under any applicable law, but does not include an obligation substituted for an existing obligation;

(3) "receivable" means right to payment, whether or not such right has been earned by performance; and

(4) a debt for a tax is incurred on the day when such tax is last payable, including any extension, without penalty.

(b) Except as provided in subsection (c) of this section, the trustee may avoid any transfer of property of the debtor—

(1) to or for the benefit of a creditor;

(2) for or on account of an antecedent debt owed by the debtor before such transfer was made;

(3) made while the debtor was insolvent;

(4) made—

(A) on or within 90 days before the date of the filing of the petition; or

(B) between 90 days and one year before the date of the filing of the petition, if such creditor, at the time of such transfer—

(i) was an insider; and

(ii) had reasonable cause to believe the debtor was insolvent at the time of such transfer; and

(5) that enables such creditor to receive more than such creditor would receive if—

(A) the case were a case under chapter 7 of this title;

(B) the transfer had not been made; and

(C) such creditor received payment of such debt to the extent provided by the provisions of this title.

(c) The trustee may not avoid under this section a transfer—

(1) to the extent that such transfer was—

(A) intended by the debtor and the creditor to or for whose benefit such transfer was made to be a contemporaneous exchange for new value given to the debtor; and

(B) in fact a substantially contemporaneous exchange;

(2) to the extent that such transfer was—

(A) in payment of a debt incurred in the ordinary course of business or financial affairs of the debtor and the transferee;

(B) made not later than 45 days after such debt was incurred;

(C) made in the ordinary course of business or financial affairs of the debtor and the transferee; and

(D) made according to ordinary business terms;

(3) of a security interest in property acquired by the debtor—

(A) to the extent such security interest secures new value that was—

(i) given at or after the signing of a security agreement that contains a description of such property as collateral;

(ii) given by or on behalf of the secured party under such agreement;

(iii) given to enable the debtor to acquire such property; and

(iv) in fact used by the debtor to acquire such property; and

(B) that is perfected before 10 days after such security interest attaches;

(4) to or for the benefit of a creditor, to the extent that, after such transfer, such creditor gave new value to or for the benefit of the debtor—

(A) not secured by an otherwise unavoidable security interest; and

(B) on account of which new value the debtor did not make an otherwise unavoidable transfer to or for the benefit of such creditor;

(5) of a perfected security interest in inventory or a receivable or the proceeds of either, except to the extent that the aggregate of all such transfers to the transferee caused a reduction, as of the date of the filing of the petition and to the prejudice of other creditors holding unsecured claims, of any amount by which the debt secured by such security interest exceeded the value of all security interest for such debt on the later of—

(A)(i) with respect to a transfer to which subsection (b)(4)(A) of this section applies, 90 days before the date of the filing of the petition; or

(ii) with respect to a transfer to which subsection (b)(4)(B) of this section applies, one year before the date of the filing of the petition; and

(B) the date on which new value was first given under the security agreement creating such security interest; or

(6) that is the fixing of a statutory lien that is not avoidable under section 545 of this title.

(d) A trustee may avoid a transfer of property of the debtor transferred to secure reimbursement of a surety that furnished a bond or other obligation to dissolve a judicial lien that would have been avoidable by the trustee under subsection (b) of this section. The liability of such surety under such bond or obligation shall be discharged to the extent of the value of such property recovered by the trustee or the amount paid to the trustee.

(e)(1) For the purposes of this section—

(A) a transfer of real property other than fixtures, but including the interest of a seller or purchaser under a contract for the sale of real property, is perfected when a bona fide purchaser of such property from the debtor against whom applicable law permits such transfer to be perfected cannot acquire an interest that is superior to the interest of the transferee; and

(B) a transfer of a fixture or property other than real property is perfected when a creditor on a simple contract cannot acquire a judicial lien that is superior to the interest of the transferee.

(2) For the purposes of this section, except as provided in paragraph (3) of this subsection, a transfer is made—

(A) at the time such transfer takes effect between the transferor and the transferee, if such transfer is perfected at, or within 10 days after, such time;

(B) at the time such transfer is perfected, if such transfer is perfected after such 10 days; or

(C) immediately before the date of the filing of the petition, if such transfer is not perfected at the later of—

(i) the commencement of the case; and

(ii) 10 days after such transfer takes effect between the transferor and the transferee.

(3) For the purposes of this section, a transfer is not made until the debtor has acquired rights in the property transferred.

(f) For the purposes of this section, the debtor is presumed to have been insolvent on and during the 90 days immediately preceding the date of the filing of the petition.

§ 548. Fraudulent transfers and obligations

(a) The trustee may avoid any transfer of an interest of the debtor in property, or any obligation incurred by the debtor, that was made or incurred on or within one year before the date of the filing of the petition, if the debtor—

(1) made such transfer or incurred such obligation with actual intent to hinder, delay, or defraud any entity to which the debtor was or became, on or after the date that such transfer occurred or such obligation was incurred, indebted; or

(2)(A) received less than a reasonably equivalent value in exchange for such transfer or obligation; and

(B)(i) was insolvent on the date that such transfer was made or such obligation was incurred, or became insolvent as a result of such transfer or obligation;

(ii) was engaged in business, or was about to engage in business or a transaction, for which any property remaining with the debtor was an unreasonably small capital; or

(iii) intended to incur, or believed that the debtor would incur, debts that would be beyond the debtor's ability to pay as such debts matured.

(b) The trustee of a partnership debtor may avoid any transfer of an interest of the debtor in property, or any obligation incurred by the debtor, that was made or incurred on or within one year before the date of the filing of the petition, to a general partner in the debtor, if the debtor was insolvent on the date such transfer was made or such obligation was incurred, or became insolvent as a result of such transfer or obligation.

(c) Except to the extent that a transfer or obligation voidable under this section is voidable under section 544, 545, or 547 of this title, a transferee or obligee of such a transfer or obligation that takes for value and in good faith has a lien on any interest transferred, may retain any lien transferred, or may enforce any obligation incurred, as the case may be, to the extent that such transferee or obligee gave value to the debtor in exchange for such transfer or obligation.

(d)(1) For the purposes of this section, a transfer is made when such transfer becomes so far perfected that a bona fide purchaser from the debtor against whom such transfer could have been perfected cannot acquire an interest in the property transferred that is superior to the interest in such property of the transferee, but if such transfer is not so perfected before the commencement of the case, such transfer occurs immediately before the date of the filing of the petition.

(2) In this section—

(A) "value" means property, or satisfaction or securing of a present or antecedent debt of the debtor, but does not include an unperformed promise to furnish support to the debtor or to a relative of the debtor; and

(B) a commodity broker or forward contract merchant that receives a margin payment, as defined in section 761(15) of this title, takes for value.

§ 549. Postpetition transactions

(a) Except as provided in subsection (b) and (c) of this section, the trustee may avoid a transfer of property of the estate—

(1) that occurs after the commencement of the case; and

(2)(A) that is authorized under section 303(f) or 542(c) of this title; or

(B) that is not authorized under this title or by the court.

(b) In an involuntary case, a transfer that occurs after the commencement of such case but before the order for relief is valid against the trustee to the extent of any value, including services, but not including satisfaction or securing of a debt that arose before the commencement of the case, given after the commencement of the case in exchange for such transfer, notwithstanding any notice or knowledge of the case that the transferee has.

(c) The trustee may not avoid under subsection (a) of this section a transfer, to a good faith purchaser without knowledge of the commencement of the case and for present fair equivalent value or to a purchaser at a judicial sale, of real property located other than in the county in which the case is commenced, unless a copy of the petition was filed in the office where conveyances of real property in such county are recorded before such transfer was so far perfected that a bona fide purchaser of such property against whom applicable law permits such transfer to be perfected cannot acquire an interest that is superior to the interest of such good faith or judicial sale purchaser. A good faith purchaser, without knowledge of the commencement of the case and for less than present fair equivalent value, of real property located other than in the county in which the case is commenced, under a transfer that the trustee may avoid under this section, has a lien on the property transferred to the extent of any present value given, unless a copy of the petition was so filed before such transfer was so perfected.

(d) An action or proceeding under this section may not be commenced after the earlier of—

(1) two years after the date of the transfer sought to be avoided; and

(2) the time the case is closed or dismissed.

§ 550. Liability of transferee of avoided transfer

(a) Except as otherwise provided in this section, to the extent that a transfer is avoided under section 544, 545, 547, 548, 549, or 724(a) of this title, the trustee may recover, for the benefit of the estate, the property transferred, or, if the court so orders, the value of such property, from—

(1) the initial transferee of such transfer or the entity for whose benefit such transfer was made; or

(2) any immediate or mediate transferee of such initial transferee.

(b) The trustee may not recover under section (a)(2) of this section from—

(1) a transferee that takes for value, including satisfaction or securing of a present or antecedent debt, in good faith, and without knowledge of the voidability of the transfer avoided; or

(2) any immediate or mediate good faith transferee of such transferee.

(c) The trustee is entitled to only a single satisfaction under subsection (a) of this section.

(d) (1) A good faith transferee from whom the trustee may recover under subsection (a) of this section has a lien on the property recovered to secure the lesser of—

(A) the cost, to such transferee, of any improvement made after the transfer, less the amount of any profit realized by such transferee from such property; and

(B) any increase in value as a result of such improvement, of the property transferred.

(2) In this subsection, "improvement" includes—

(A) physical additions or changes to the property transferred;

(B) repairs to such property;

(C) payment of any tax on such property;

(D) payment of any debt secured by a lien on such property;

(E) discharge of any lien against such property that is superior or equal to the rights of the trustee; and

(F) preservation of such property.

(e) An action or proceeding under this section may not be commenced after the earlier of—

(1) one year after the avoidance of the transfer on account of which recovery under this section is sought; and

(2) the time the case is closed or dismissed.

§ 551. Automatic preservation of avoided transfer

Any transfer avoided under section 522, 544, 545, 547, 548, 549, or 724(a) of this title, or any lien void under section 506(d) of this title, is preserved for the benefit of the estate but only with respect to property of the estate.

§ 552. Postpetition effect of security interest

(a) Except as provided in subsection (b) of this section, property acquired by the estate or by the debtor after the commencement of the case is not subject to any lien resulting from any security agreement entered into by the debtor before the commencement of the case.

(b) Except as provided in sections 363, 506(c), 544, 545, 547, and 548 of this title, if the debtor and a secured party enter into a security agreement before the commencement of the case and if the security interest created by such security agreement extends to property of the debtor acquired before the commencement of the case and to proceeds, product, offspring, rents, or profits of such property, then such security interest extends to such proceeds, product, offspring, rents, or profits acquired by the estate after the commencement of the case to the extent provided by such security agreement and by applicable nonbankruptcy law, except to the extent that the court, after notice and a hearing and based on the equities of the case, orders otherwise.

§ 553. Setoff

(a) Except as otherwise provided in this section and in sections 362 and 363 of this title, this title does not affect any right of a creditor to offset a mutual debt owing by such creditor to the debtor that arose before the commencement of the case under this title against a claim of such creditor against the debtor that arose before the commencement of the case, except to the extent that—

(1) the claim of such creditor against the debtor is disallowed other than under section 502(b)(3) of this title;

(2) such claim was transferred, by an entity other than the debtor, to such creditor—

(A) after the commencement of the case; or

(B) (i) after 90 days before the date of the filing of the petition; and

(ii) while the debtor was insolvent; or

(3) the debt owed to the debtor by such creditor was incurred by such creditor—

(A) after 90 days before the date of the filing of the petition;

(B) while the debtor was insolvent; and

(C) for the purpose of obtaining a right of setoff against the debtor.

(b) (1) Except with respect to a setoff of a kind described in section 362(b)(6) or 365(h)(1) of this title, if a creditor offsets a mutual debt owing to the debtor against a claim against the debtor on or within 90 days before the date of the filing of the petition, then the trustee may recover from such creditor the amount so offset to the extent that any insufficiency on the date of such setoff is less than the insufficiency on the later of—

(A) 90 days before the date of the filing of the petition; and

(B) the first date during the 90 days immediately preceding the date of the filing of the petition on which there is an insufficiency.

(2) In this subsection, "insufficiency" means amount, if any, by which a claim against the debtor exceeds a mutual debt owing to the debtor by the holder of such claim.

(c) For the purposes of this section, the debtor is presumed to have been insolvent on and during the 90 days immediately preceding the date of the filing of the petition.

§ 554. Abandonment of property of the estate

(a) After notice and a hearing, the trustee may abandon any property of the estate that is burdensome to the estate or that is of inconsequential value to the estate.

(b) On request of a party in interest and after notice and a hearing, the court may order the trustee to abandon any property of the estate that is burdensome to the estate or that is of inconsequential value to the estate.

(c) Unless the court orders otherwise, any property that is scheduled under section 521(1) of this title and that is not administered before a case is closed under section 350 of this title is deemed abandoned.

(d) Unless the court orders otherwise, property of the estate that is not abandoned under section (a) or (b) of this section and that is not administered in the case remains property of the estate.

CHAPTER 7—LIQUIDATION

SUBCHAPTER I—OFFICERS AND ADMINISTRATION

Sec.

SUBCHAPTER II—COLLECTION, LIQUIDATION, AND DISTRIBUTION OF THE ESTATE

SUBCHAPTER III—STOCKBROKER LIQUIDATION

SUBCHAPTER IV—COMMODITY BROKER LIQUIDATION

SUBCHAPTER I—OFFICERS AND ADMINISTRATION

§ 701. Interim trustee

(a) Promptly after the order for relief under this chapter, the court shall appoint one disinterested person that is a member of the panel of private trustees established under section 604(f) of title 28 or that was serving as trustee in the case immediately before the order for relief under this chapter to serve as interim trustee in the case.

(b) The service of an interim trustee under this section terminates when a trustee elected or designated under section 702 of this title to serve as trustee in the case qualifies under section 322 of this title.

(c) An interim trustee serving under this section is a trustee in a case under this title.

§ 702. Election of trustee

(a) A creditor may vote for a candidate for trustee only if such creditor—

(1) holds an allowable, undisputed, fixed, liquidated, unsecured claim of a kind entitled to distribution under section 726(a)(2), 726(a)(3), or 726(a)(4) of this title;

(2) does not have an interest materially adverse, other than an equity interest that is not substantial in relation to such creditor's interest as a creditor, to the interest of creditors entitled to such distribution; and

(3) is not an insider.

(b) At the meeting of creditors under section 341 of this title, creditors may elect one person to serve as trustee in the case if election of a trustee is requested by creditors that may vote under subsection (a) of this section, and that hold at least 20 percent in amount of the claims specified in subsection (a)(1) of this section that are held by creditors that may vote under subsection (a) of this section.

(c) A candidate for trustee is elected trustee if—

(1) creditors holding at least 20 percent in amount of the claims specified in subsection (a)(1) of this section that are held by creditors that may vote under subsection (a) of this section vote; and

(2) such candidate receives the votes of creditors holding a majority in amount of claims specified in subsection (a)(1) of this section that are held by creditors that vote for trustee.

(d) If a trustee is not elected under subsection (c) of this section, then the interim trustee shall serve as trustee in the case.

§ 703. Successor trustee

(a) If a trustee dies or resigns during a case, fails to qualify under section 322 of this title, or is removed under section 324 of this title, creditors may elect, in the manner specified in section 702 of this title, a person to fill the vacancy in the office of trustee.

(b) Pending election of a trustee under subsection (a) of this section, if necessary to preserve or prevent loss to the estate, the court may appoint an interim trustee in the manner specified in section 701(a) of this title. Sections 701(b) and 701(c) of this title apply to such interim trustee.

(c) If creditors do not elect a successor trustee under subsection (a) of this section, or if a trustee is needed in a case reopened under section 350 of this title, then the court shall appoint one disinterested person that is a member of the panel of private trustees established under section 604(f) of title 28 to serve as trustee in the case.

§ 704. Duties of trustee

The trustee shall—

(1) collect and reduce to money the property of the estate for which such trustee serves, and close up such estate as expeditiously as is compatible with the best interests of parties in interest;

(2) be accountable for all property received;

(3) investigate the financial affairs of the debtor;

(4) if a purpose would be served, examine proofs of claims and object to the allowance of any claim that is improper;

(5) if advisable, oppose the discharge of the debtor;

(6) unless the court orders otherwise, furnish such information concerning the estate and the estate's administration as is requested by a party in interest;

(7) if the business of the debtor is authorized to be operated, file with the court and with any governmental unit charged with responsibility for collection or determination of any tax arising out of such operation, periodic reports and summaries of the operation of such business, including a statement of receipts and disbursements, and such other information as the court requires; and

(8) make a final report and file a final account of the administration of the estate with the court.

§ 705. Creditors' committee

(a) At the meeting under section 341(a) of this title, creditors that may vote for a trustee under section 702(a) of this title may elect a committee of not fewer than three, and not more than eleven, creditors, each of whom holds an allowable unsecured claim of a kind entitled to distribution under section 726(a)(2) of this title.

(b) A committee elected under subsection (a) of this section may consult with the trustee in connection with the administration of the estate, make recommendations to the trustee respecting the performance of the trustee's duties, and submit to the court any question affecting the administration of the estate.

§ 706. Conversion

(a) The debtor may convert a case under this chapter to a case under chapter 11 or 13 of this title at any time, if the case has not been converted under section 1112 or 1307 of this title. Any waiver of the right to convert a case under this subsection is unenforceable.

(b) On request of a party in interest and after notice and a hearing, the court may convert a case under this chapter to a case under chapter 11 of this title at any time.

(c) The court may not convert a case under this chapter to a case under chapter 13 of this title unless the debtor requests such conversion.

(d) Notwithstanding any other provision of this section, a case may not be converted to a case under another chapter of this title unless the debtor may be a debtor under such chapter.

§ 707. Dismissal

The court may dismiss a case under this chapter only after notice and a hearing and only for cause, including—

(1) unreasonable delay by the debtor that is prejudicial to creditors; and

(2) nonpayment of any fees and charges required under chapter 123 of title 28.

SUBCHAPTER II—COLLECTION, LIQUIDATION, AND DISTRIBUTION OF THE ESTATE

§ 721. Authorization to operate business

The court may authorize the trustee to operate the business of the debtor for a limited period, if such operation is in the best interest of the estate and consistent with the orderly liquidation of the estate.

§ 722. Redemption

An individual debtor may, whether or not the debtor has waived the right to redeem under this section, redeem tangible personal property intended primarily for personal, family, or household use, from a lien securing a dischargeable consumer debt, if such property is exempted under section 522 of this title or has been abandoned under section 554 of this title, by paying the holder of such lien the amount of the allowed secured claim of such holder that is secured by such lien.

§ 723. Rights of partnership trustee against general partners

(a) If there is a deficiency of property of the estate to pay in full all claims allowed in a case under this title concerning a partnership, then each general partner in such partnership is liable to the trustee for the full amount of such deficiency.

(b) To the extent practicable, the trustee shall first seek recovery of such deficiency from any general partner in such partnership that is not a debtor in a case under this title. Pending determination of such deficiency, the court may order any such partner to provide the estate with indemnity for, or assurance of payment of, any deficiency recoverable from such partner, or not to dispose of property.

(c) Notwithstanding section 728(c) of this title, the trustee has a claim against the estate of each general partner in such partnership that is a debtor in a case under this title for the full amount of all claims of creditors allowed in the case concerning such partnership. Notwithstanding section 502 of this title, there shall not be allowed in such case a claim against such partner on which both such partner and such partnership are liable, except to any extent that such claim is secured only by property of such partner and not be property of such partnership. The claim of the trustee under this subsection is entitled to distribution in such case under section 726(a) of this title the same as any other claim of the kind specified in such section.

(d) If the aggregate that the trustee recovers from the estates of general partners under subsection (c) of this section is greater than any deficiency not recovered under subsection (b) of this section, the court, after notice and a hearing, shall determine an equitable distribution of the surplus so recovered, and the trustee shall distribute such surplus to the estates of the general partners in such partnership according to such determination.

§ 724. Treatment of certain liens

(a) The trustee may avoid a lien that secures a claim of a kind specified in section 726(a)(4) of this title.

(b) Property in which the estate has an interest and that is subject to a lien that is not avoidable under this title and that secures an allowed claim for taxes, or proceeds of such property, shall be distributed—

(1) first, to any holder of an allowed claim secured by a lien on such property that is not avoidable under this title and that is senior to such tax lien;

(2) second, to claims specified in sections 507(a)(1), 507(a)(2), 507(a)(3), 507(a)(4), and 507(a)(5) of this title, to the extent of the amount of such allowed tax claim that is secured by such tax lien;

(3) third, to the holder of such tax lien, to any extent that such holder's allowed claim that is secured by such tax lien exceeds any amount distributed under paragraph (2) of this subsection;

(4) fourth, to any holder of an allowed claim secured by a lien on such property that is not avoidable under this title and that is junior to such tax lien;

(5) fifth, to the holder of such tax lien, to the extent that such holder's allowed claim secured by such tax lien is not paid under paragraph (3) of this subsection; and

(6) sixth, to the estate.

(c) If more than one creditor is entitled to distribution under a particular paragraph of subsection (b) of this section, distribution to such creditors under such paragraph shall be in the same order as distribution to such creditors would have been other than under this section.

(d) A statutory lien whose priority is determined in the same manner as the priority of a tax lien under section 6323 of the Internal Revenue Code of 1954 (26 U.S.C. 6323) shall be treated under subsection (b) of this section the same as a tax lien.

§ 725. Disposition of certain property

After the commencement of a case under this chapter, but before final distribution under section 726 of this title, the trustee, after notice and a hearing, shall dispose of any property in which an entity other than the estate has an interest, such as a lien, and that has not been disposed of under another section of this title.

§ 726. Distribution of property of the estate

(a) Except as provided in section 510 of this title, property of the estate shall be distributed—

(1) first, in payment of claims of the kind specified in, and in the order specified in, section 507 of this title;

(2) second, in payment of any allowed unsecured claim, other than a claim of a kind specified in paragraph (1), (3), or (4) of this subsection, proof of which is—

(A) timely filed under section 501(a) of this title;

(B) timely filed under section 501(b) or 501(c) of this title; or

(C) tardily filed under section 501(a) of this title, if—

(i) the creditor that holds such claim did not have notice or actual knowledge of the case in time for timely filing of a proof of such claim under section 501(a) of this title; and

(ii) proof of such claim is filed in time to permit payment of such claim;

(3) third, in payment of any allowed unsecured claim proof of which is tardily filed under section 501(a) of this title, other than a claim of the kind specified in paragraph (2)(C) of this subsection;

(4) fourth, in payment of any allowed claim, whether secured or unsecured, for any fine, penalty, or forfeiture, or for multiple, exemplary, or punitive damages, arising before the earlier of the order for relief or the appointment of a trustee, to the extent that such fine, penalty, forfeiture, or damages are not compensation for actual pecuniary loss suffered by the holder of such claim;

(5) fifth, in payment of interest at the legal rate from the date of the filing of the petition, on any claim paid under paragraph (1), (2), (3), or (4) of this subsection; and

(6) sixth, to the debtor.

(b) Payment on claims of a kind specified in paragraph (1), (2), (3), (4), (5), or (6) of section 507(a) of this title, or in paragraph (2), (3), (4), or (5) of subsection (a) of this section, shall be made pro rata among claims of the kind specified in a particular paragraph, except that in a case that has been converted to this chapter under section 1112 or 1307 of this title, administrative expenses incurred under this chapter after such conversion have priority over administrative expenses incurred under any other chapter of this title or under this chapter before such conversion and over any expenses of a custodian superseded under section 543 of this title.

(c) Notwithstanding subsections (a) and (b) of this section, if there is property of the kind specified in section 541(a)(2) of this title, or proceeds of such property, in the estate, such property or proceeds shall be segregated from other property of the estate, and such property or proceeds and other property of the estate shall be distributed as follows:

(1) Administrative expenses shall be paid either from property of the kind specified in section 541(a)(2) of this title, or from other property of the estate, as the interest of justice requires.

(2) Claims other than for administrative expenses shall be paid

in the order specified in subsection (a) of this section, and, with respect to claims of a kind specified in a particular paragraph of section 507 of this title or subsection (a) of this section, in the following order and manner:

(A) First, community claims against the debtor or the debtor's spouse shall be paid from property of the kind specified in section 541(a)(2) of this title, except to the extent that such property is solely liable for debts of the debtor.

(B) Second, to the extent that community claims against the debtor are not paid under subparagraph (A) of this paragraph, such community claims shall be paid from property of the kind specified in section 541(a)(2) of this title that is solely liable for debts of the debtor.

(C) Third, to the extent that all claims against the debtor including community claims against the debtor are not paid under subparagraph (A) or (B) of this paragraph such claims shall be paid from property of the estate other than property of the kind specified in section 541(a)(2) of this title.

(D) Fourth, to the extent that community claims against the debtor or the debtor's spouse are not paid under subparagraph (A), (B), or (C) of this paragraph, such claims shall be paid from all remaining property of the estate.

§ 727. Discharge

(a) The court shall grant the debtor a discharge, unless—

(1) the debtor is not an individual;

(2) the debtor, with intent to hinder, delay, or defraud a creditor or an officer of the estate charged with custody of property under this title, has transferred, removed, destroyed, mutilated, or concealed, or has permitted to be transferred, removed, destroyed, mutilated, or concealed—

(A) property of the debtor, within one year before the date of the filing of the petition; or

(B) property of the estate, after the date of the filing of the petition;

(3) the debtor has concealed, destroyed, mutilated, falsified, or failed to keep or preserve any recorded information, including books, documents, records, and papers, from which the debtor's financial condition or business transactions might be ascertained, unless such act or failure to act was justified under all of the circumstances of the case;

(4) the debtor knowingly and fraudulently, in or in connection with the case—

(A) made a false oath or account;

(B) presented or used a false claim;

(C) gave, offered, received, or attempted to obtain money, property, or advantage, or a promise of money, property, or advantage, for acting or forbearing to act; or

(D) withheld from an officer of the estate entitled to possession under this title, any recorded information, including books, documents, records, and papers, relating to the debtor's property or financial affairs;

(5) the debtor has failed to explain satisfactorily, before determination of denial of discharge under this paragraph, any loss of assets or deficiency of assets to meet the debtor's liabilities;

(6) the debtor has refused, in the case—

(A) to obey any lawful order of the court, other than an order to respond to a material question or to testify;

(B) on the ground of privilege against self-incrimination, to respond to a material question approved by the court or to testify, after the debtor has been granted immunity with respect to the matter concerning which such privilege was invoked; or

(C) on a ground other than the property invoked privilege against self-incrimination, to respond to a material question approved by the court or to testify;

(7) the debtor has committed any act specified in paragraph (2), (3), (4), (5), or (6) of this subsection, on or within one year before the date of the filing of the petition, or during the case, in connection with another case concerning an insider;

(8) the debtor has been granted a discharge under this section, under section 1141 of this title, or under section 14, 371 or 476 of the Bankruptcy Act, in a case commenced within six years before the date of the filing of the petition;

(9) the debtor has been granted a discharge under section 1328 of this title, or under section 660 or 661 of the Bankruptcy Act, in a case commenced within six years before the date of the filing of the petition, unless payments under the plan in such case totaled at least—

(A) 100 percent of the allowed unsecured claims in such case; or

(B) (i) 70 percent of such claims; and

(ii) the plan was proposed by the debtor in good faith, and was the debtor's best effort; or

(10) the court approves a written waiver of discharge executed by the debtor after the order for relief under this chapter.

(b) Except as provided in section 523 of this title, a discharge under subsection (a) of this section discharges the debtor from all debts that arose before the date of the order for relief under this chapter, and any liability on a claim that is determined under section 502 of this title as if such claim had arisen before the commencement of the case, whether or not a proof of claim based on any such debt or liability is filed under section 501 of this title, and whether or not a claim based on any such debt or liability is allowed under section 502 of this title.

(c)(1) The trustee or a creditor may object to discharge under subsection (a) of this section.

(2) On request of a party in interest, the court may order the trustee to examine the acts and conduct of the debtor to determine whether a ground exists for denial of discharge.

(d) On request of the trustee or a creditor, and after notice and a hearing, the court shall revoke a discharge granted under subsection (a) of this section if—

(1) such discharge was obtained through the fraud of the debtor, and the requesting party did not know of such fraud until after the granting of such discharge;

(2) the debtor acquired property that is property of the estate, or became entitled to acquire property that would be property of the estate, and knowingly and fraudulently failed to report the acquisition of, or entitlement to, such property, or to deliver or surrender such property to the trustee; or

(3) the debtor committed an act specified in subsection (a)(6) of this section.

(e) The trustee or a creditor may request a revocation of a discharge—

(1) under subsection (d)(1) of this section, within one year after such discharge was granted; or

(2) under subsection (d)(2) or (d)(3) of this section, before the later of—

(A) one year after the granting of such discharge; and

(B) the date the case is closed.

§ 728. Special tax provisions

(a) For the purposes of any State or local law imposing a tax on or measured by income, the taxable period of a debtor that is an individual shall terminate on the date of the order for relief under this chapter, unless the case was converted under section 1112 of this title.

(b) Notwithstanding any State or local law imposing a tax on or measured by income, the trustee shall make tax returns of income for the estate of an individual debtor in a case under this chapter or for a debtor that is a corporation in a case under this chapter only if such estate or corporation has net taxable income for the entire period after the order for relief under this chapter during which the case is pending. If such entity has such income, or if the debtor is a partnership, then the trustee shall make and file a return of income for each taxable period during which the case was pending after the order for relief under this chapter.

(c) If there are pending a case under this chapter concerning a partnership and a case under this chapter concerning a partner in such partnership, a governmental unit's claim for any unpaid liability of such partner for a State or local tax on or measured by income, to the extent that such liability arose from the inclusion in such partner's taxable income, of earnings of such partnership that were not withdrawn by such partner, is a claim only against such partnership.

(d) Notwithstanding section 541 of this title, if there are pending a case under this chapter concerning a partnership and a case under this chapter concerning a partner in such partnership, then any State or local tax refund or reduction of tax of such partner that would have otherwise been property of the estate of such partner under section 541 of this title—

(1) is property of the estate of such partnership to the extent that such tax refund or reduction of tax is fairly apportionable to losses sustained by such partnership and not reimbursed by such partner; and

(2) is property of the estate of such partner otherwise.

SUBCHAPTER III—STOCKBROKER LIQUIDATION

§ 741. Definitions for this subchapter

In this subchapter—

(1) "Commission" means Securities and Exchange Commission;

(2) "customer" includes—

(A) entity with whom the debtor deals as principal or agent and that holds a claim against the debtor on account of a security received, acquired, or held by the debtor in the ordinary course of business as a stockbroker from or for the securities account or accounts of such entity—

(i) for safekeeping;

(ii) with a view to sale;

(iii) to cover a consummated sale;
(iv) pursuant to a purchase;
(v) as collateral under a security agreement; or
(vi) for the purpose of effecting registration of transfer; and

(B) entity that holds a claim against the debtor arising out of—

(i) a sale or conversion of a security received, acquired, or held as specified in subparagraph (A) of this paragraph; or

(ii) a deposit of cash, a security, or other property with the debtor for the purpose of purchasing or selling a security;

(3) "customer name security" means security—

(A) held for the account of a customer on the date of the filing of the petition by or on behalf of the debtor;

(B) registered in such customer's name on such date or in the process of being so registered under instructions from the debtor; and

(C) not in a form transferable by delivery on such date;

(4) "customer property" means cash, security, or other property, and proceeds of such cash, security, or property, at any time received, acquired, or held by or for the account of the debtor, from or for the securities account of a customer—

(A) including—

(i) property that was unlawfully converted and that is property of the estate;

(ii) a security held as property of the debtor to the extent such security is necessary to meet a net equity claim based on a security of the same class and series of an issuer;

(iii) resources provided through the use or realization of a customer's debit cash balance or a debit item includible in the Formula for Determination of Reserve Requirement for Brokers and Dealers as promulgated by the Commission under the Securities Exchange Act of 1934 (15 U.S.C. 78a et seq.); and

(iv) other property of the debtor that any applicable law, rule, or regulation requires to be set aside or held for the benefit of a customer, unless including such property as customer property would not significantly increase customer property; but

(B) not including—

(i) a customer name security delivered to or reclaimed by a customer under section 751 of this title; or

(ii) property to the extent that a customer does not have a claim against the debtor based on such property;

(5) "net equity" means, with respect to the aggregate of all of a customer's accounts that such customer holds in the same capacity—

(A) (i) aggregate dollar balance that would remain in such accounts after the liquidation, by sale or purchase, at the time of the filing of the petition of all securities positions in all such accounts, except customer name securities of such customer; minus

(ii) any claim of the debtor against such customer that

would have been owing immediately after such liquidation; plus

(B) any payment by such customer to the trustee, within 60 days after notice under section 342 of this title, of any business related claim of the debtor against such customer;

(6) "SIPC" means Security Investor Protection Corporation.

§ 742. Effect of section 362 of this title in this subchapter

Notwithstanding section 362 of this title, SIPC may file an application for a protective decree under the Securities Investor Protection Act of 1970 (15 U.S.C. 78aaa et seq.). The filing of such application stays all proceedings in the case under this chapter unless and until such application is dismissed. If SIPC completes the liquidation of the debtor, then the court shall dismiss the case.

§ 743. Notice

The clerk shall give the notice required by section 342(a) of this title to SIPC and to the Commission.

§ 744. Executory contracts

Notwithstanding section 365(d)(1) of this title, the trustee shall assume or reject, under section 365 of this title, any executory contract of the debtor for the purchase or sale of a security in the ordinary course of the debtor's business, within a reasonable time after the date of the order for relief, not to exceed 30 days. If the trustee does not assume such a contract within such time, such contract is rejected.

§ 745. Treatment of accounts

(a) Accounts held by a particular customer in separate capacities shall be treated as accounts of separate customers.

(b) If a stockbroker or a bank holds a customer net equity claim against the debtor that arose out of a transaction for a customer of such stockbroker or bank, each such customer of such stockbroker or bank shall be treated as a separate customer of the debtor.

(c) A trustee's account specified as such on the debtor's books, and supported by a trust deed filed with, and qualified as such by, the Internal Revenue Service, and under the Internal Revenue Code of 1954 (26 U.S.C. 1 et seq.), shall be treated as a separate customer account for each beneficiary under such trustee account.

§ 746. Extent of customer claim

(a) If, after the date of the filing of the petition, an entity effects, with respect to cash or a security, a transaction with the debtor, in a manner that would have made such entity a customer with respect to such cash or security had such transaction occurred before such date, and such transaction was effected by such entity in good faith and before the qualification under section 322 of this title of a trustee, such entity shall be deemed a customer, and the date of such transaction shall be deemed to be the date of the filing of the petition for the purpose of determining such entity's net equity with respect to such cash or security.

(b) An entity does not have a claim as a customer to the extent that such entity has a claim for cash or a security that, by contract, agreement, understanding, or operation of law, is—

(1) part of the capital of the debtor; or

(2) is subordinated to the claims of any or all creditors.

§ 747. Subordination of certain customer claims

Except as provided in section 510 of this title, unless all other customer net equity claims have been paid in full, the trustee may not pay in full or pay in part, directly or indirectly, any net equity claim of a customer that was, on the date such claim arose—

(1) an insider;

(2) a beneficial owner of at least five percent of any class of equity securities of the debtor, other than—

(A) nonconvertible stock having fixed preferential dividend and liquidation rights; or

(B) interests of limited partners in a limited partnership;

(3) a limited partner with a participation of at least five percent in the net assets or net profits of the debtor; or

(4) an entity that, directly or indirectly, through agreement or otherwise, exercised or had the power to exercise control over the management or policies of the debtor.

§ 748. Reduction of securities to money

As soon as practicable after the date of the order for relief, the trustee shall reduce to money, consistent with good market practice, all securities held as property of the estate, except for customer name securities delivered or reclaimed under section 751 of this title.

§ 749. Voidable transfers

Any transfer of property that, except for such transfer, would have been customer property, may be avoided by the trustee, and shall be treated as customer property, if and to the extent that the trustee avoids such transfer under section 544, 545, 547, 548, 549, or 724(a) of this title. For the purpose of such sections, the property so transferred shall be deemed to have been property of the debtor and, if such transfer was made to a customer or for a customer's benefit, such customer shall be deemed, for the purposes of this section, to have been a creditor.

§ 750. Distribution of securities

The trustee may not distribute a security except under section 751 of this title.

§ 751. Customer name securities

The trustee shall deliver any customer name security to or on behalf of the customer entitled to such security, unless such customer has a negative net equity. With the approval of the trustee, a customer may reclaim a customer name security after payment to the trustee, within such period as the trustee allows, of any claim of the debtor against such customer to the extent that such customer will not have a negative net equity after such payment.

§ 752. Customer property

(a) The trustee shall distribute customer property ratably to customers on the basis and to the extent of such customers allowed net equity claims and in priority to all other claims, except claims specified in section 507(a)(1) of this title that are attributable to the administration of customer property.

(b)(1) The trustee shall distribute customer property in excess of that distributed under subsection (a) of this section in accordance with section 726 of this title.

(2) Except as provided in section 510 of this title, if a customer is not paid the full amount of such customer's allowed net equity claim from customer property, the unpaid portion of such claim is a claim entitled to distribution under section 726(a) of this title.

(c) Subject to section 741(4)(B) of this title, any cash or security remaining after the liquidation of a security interest created under a security agreement made by the debtor shall be apportioned between the general estate and customer property in the proportion that the general property of the debtor and the cash or securities of customers were subject to such security interest.

SUBCHAPTER IV—COMMODITY BROKER LIQUIDATION

§ 761. Definitions for this subchapter

In this subchapter—

(1) "Act" means Commodity Exchange Act (7 U.S.C. 1 et seq.);

(2) "clearing organization" means organization that clears commodity contracts on, or subject to the rules of, a contract market or board of trade;

(3) "Commission" means Commodity Futures Trading Commission;

(4) "commodity contract" means—

(A) if the debtor is a futures commission merchant, contract for the purchase or sale of a commodity for future delivery on, or subject to the rules of, a contract market or board of trade;

(B) if the debtor is a foreign futures commission merchant, foreign future;

(C) if the debtor is a leverage transaction merchant, leverage transaction;

(D) if the debtor is a clearing organization, contract for the purchase or sale of a commodity for future delivery on, or subject to the rules of, a contract market or board of trade that is cleared by the debtor; or

(E) if the debtor is a commodity options dealer, commodity option;

(5) "commodity option" means agreement or transaction subject to regulation under section 4c(b) of the Act (7 U.S.C. 6c(b));

(6) "commodity options dealer" means person that extends credit to, or that accepts cash, a security, or other property from, a customer of such person for the purchase or sale of an interest in a commodity option;

(7) "contract market" means board of trade designated as a contract market by the Commission under the Act;

(8) "contract of sale", "commodity", "future delivery", "board of trade", and "futures commission merchant" have the meanings assigned to those terms in the Act;

(9) "customer" means—

(A) if the debtor is a futures commission merchant—

(i) entity for or with whom the debtor deals and that holds a claim against the debtor on account of a commodity contract made, received, acquired, or held by or through the debtor in the ordinary course of the debtor's business as a futures commission merchant from or for the commodity futures account of such entity; or

(ii) entity that holds a claim against the debtor arising out of—

(I) the making, liquidation, or change in the value of a commodity contract of a kind specified in clause (i) of this subparagraph;

(II) a deposit or payment of cash, a security, or other property with the debtor for the purpose of making or margining such a commodity contract; or

(III) the making or taking of delivery on such a commodity contract;

(B) if the debtor is a foreign futures commission merchant—

(i) entity for or with whom the debtor deals and that holds a claim against the debtor on account of a commodity contract made, received, acquired, or held by or through the debtor in the ordinary course of the debtor's business as a foreign futures commission merchant from or for the foreign futures account of such entity; or

(ii) entity that holds a claim against the debtor arising out of—

(I) the making, liquidation, or change in value of a commodity contract of a kind specified in clause (i) of this subparagraph;

(II) a deposit or payment of cash, a security, or other property with the debtor for the purpose of making or margining such a commodity contract; or

(III) the making or taking of delivery on such a commodity contract;

(C) if the debtor is a leverage transaction merchant—

(i) entity for or with whom the debtor deals and that holds a claim against the debtor on account of a commodity contract engaged in by or with the debtor in the ordinary course of the debtor's business as a leverage transaction merchant from or for the leverage account of such entity;

(ii) entity that hold a claim against the debtor arising out of—

(I) the making, liquidation, or change in value of a commodity contract of a kind specified in clause (i) of this subparagraph;

(II) a deposit or payment of cash, a security, or other property with the debtor for the purpose of entering into or margining such a commodity contract; or

(III) the making or taking of delivery on such a commodity contract;

(D) if the debtor is a clearing organization, clearing member of the debtor with whom the debtor deals and that holds a claim against the debtor on account of cash, a security, or other property received by the debtor to margin, guarantee, or secure a commodity contract in such clearing member's proprietary account or customers' account; or

(E) if the debtor is a commodity options dealer—

(i) entity for or with whom the debtor deals and that holds a claim on account of a commodity contract made, received, acquired, or held by or through the debtor in the ordinary course of the debtor's business as a commodity options dealer from or for the commodity options account of such entity; or

(ii) entity that holds a claim against the debtor arising out of—

(I) the making of, liquidation of, exercise of, or a change in value of, a commodity contract of a kind specified in clause (i) of this subparagraph; or

(II) a deposit or payment of cash, a security, or other property with the debtor for the purpose of making, exercising, or margining such a commodity contract;

(10) "customer property" means cash, a security, or other property, or proceeds of such cash, security, or property, at any time received, acquired, or held by or for the account of the debtor, from or for the account of a customer—

(A) including—

(i) property received, acquired, or held to margin, guarantee, secure, purchase, or sell a commodity contract;

(ii) profits or contractual or other rights accruing to a customer as a result of a commodity contract;

(iii) an open commodity contract;

(iv) specifically identifiable customer property;

(v) warehouse receipt or other document held by the debtor evidencing ownership of or title to property to be delivered to fulfill a commodity contract from or for the account of a customer;

(vi) cash, a security, or other property received by the debtor as payment for a commodity to be delivered to fulfill a commodity contract from or for the account of a customer;

(vii) a security held as property of the debtor to the extent such security is necessary to meet a net equity claim based on a security of the same class and series of an issuer;

(viii) property that was unlawfully converted and that is property of the estate; and

(ix) other property of the debtor that any applicable law, rule, or regulation requires to be set aside or held for the benefit of a customer, unless including such property as customer property would not significantly increase customer property; but

(B) not including property to the extent that a customer does not have a claim against the debtor based on such property;

(11) "foreign future" means contract for the purchase or sale of a commodity for future delivery on, or subject to the rules of, a board of trade outside the United States;

(12) "foreign futures commission merchant" means entity engaged in soliciting or accepting orders for the purchase or sale of a foreign future or that, in connection with such a solicitation or acceptance, accepts cash, a security, or other property or extends credit, to margin, guarantee, or secure any trade or contract that results from such a solicitation or acceptance;

(13) "leverage transaction" means agreement that is subject to regulation under section 217 of the Commodity Futures Trading Commission Act of 1974 (7 U.S.C. 15a), and that is commonly known to the commodities trade as a margin account, margin contract, leverage account, or leverage contract;

(14) "leverage transaction merchant" means person that is engaged in the business of engaging in leverage transactions;

(15) "margin payment" means payment or deposit of cash, a security, or other property, that is commonly known to the commodities trade as original margin, initial margin, maintenance margin, or variation margin, including a daily variation settlement payment;

(16) "member property" means customer property at any time received, acquired, or held by or for the account of a debtor that is a clearing organization, from or for the proprietary account of a customer that is a clearing member of the debtor; and

(17) "net equity" means, subject to such rules and regulations as the Commission promulgates under the Act, with respect to the aggregate of all of a customer's accounts that such customer holds in the same capacity—

(A) balance remaining in such customer's accounts immediately after—

(i) all commodity contracts of such customer have been transferred, liquidated, or become identified for delivery; and

(ii) all obligations of such customer to the debtor have been offset; plus

(B) the value, as of the date of return under section 766 of this title, of any specifically identifiable customer property actually returned to such customer before the date specified in subparagraph (A) of this paragraph; plus

(C) the value, as of the date of transfer, of—

(i) any commodity contract to which such customer is entitled that is transferred to another person under section 766 of this title; and

(ii) any cash, security, or other property of such customer transferred to such other person under section 766 of this title to margin or secure such transferred commodity contract.

§ 762. Notice to the Commission and right to be heard

(a) The clerk shall give the notice required by section 342 of this title to the Commission.

(b) The Commission may raise and may appear and be heard on any issue in a case under this chapter.

§ 763. Treatment of accounts

(a) Accounts held by a particular customer in separate capacities shall be deemed to be accounts of separate customers.

(b) A member of a clearing organization shall be deemed to hold such member's proprietary account in a separate capacity from such member's customers' account.

(c) The net equity in a customer's account may not be offset against the net equity in the account of any other customer.

§ 764. Voidable transfers

(a) Except as otherwise provided in this section, any transfer of property that, except for such transfer, would have been customer property, may be avoided by the trustee, and shall be treated as customer property, if and to the extent that the trustee avoids such transfer under section 544, 545, 547, 548, 549, or 724(a) of this title. For the purpose of such sections, the property so transferred is deemed to have been property of the debtor, and, if such transfer was made to a customer or for a customer's benefit, such customer is deemed, for the purposes of this section, to have been a creditor.

(b) Notwithstanding sections 544, 545, 547, 548, 549, and 724(a) of this title, the trustee may not avoid a transfer made before five days after the date of the filing of the petition, if such transfer is approved by the Commission by rule or order, either before or after such transfer, and if such transfer is—

(1) a transfer of a commodity contract entered into or carried by or through the debtor on behalf of a customer, and of any cash, securities, or other property margining or securing such commodity contract; or

(2) the liquidation of a commodity contract entered into or carried by or through the debtor on behalf of a customer.

(c) Notwithstanding sections 544, 545, 547, 548, and 724(a) of this title, the trustee may not avoid a transfer that is a margin payment to or deposit with a commodity broker or forward contract merchant or is a settlement payment made by a clearing organization and that occurs before the commencement of the case, except under section 548(a)(1) of this title.

§ 765. Customer instructions

(a) The notice under section 342 of this title to customers shall instruct each customer—

(1) to file a proof of such customer's claim promptly, and to specify in such claim any specifically identifiable security, property, or commodity contract; and

(2) to instruct the trustee of such customer's desired disposition, including transfer under section 766 of this title or liquidation, of any commodity contract specifically identified to such customer.

(b) The trustee shall comply, to the extent practicable, with any instruction received from a customer regarding such customer's desired disposition of any commodity contract specifically identified to such customer. If the trustee has transferred, under section 766 of this title, such a commitment, the trustee shall transmit any such instruction to the commodity broker to whom such commodity contract was so transferred.

§ 766. Treatment of customer property

(a) The trustee shall answer all margin calls with respect to a specifically identifiable commodity contract of a customer until such time as the trustee returns or transfers such commodity contract, but the trustee may not make a margin payment that has the effect of a distribution of more than that to which such customer is entitled under subsection (h) or (i) of this section.

(b) The trustee shall prevent any open commodity contract that is being actively traded as of the date of the filing of the petition from remaining open after the last day of trading in such commodity contract, or into the first day on which notice of intent to deliver on such commodity contract may be tendered, whichever occurs first. With respect to any commodity contract that has remained open after the last day of trading in such commodity contract or with respect to which delivery must be made or accepted under the rules of contract market on which such commodity contract was made, the trustee may operate the business of the debtor for the purpose of—

(1) accepting or making tender of notice of intent to deliver the physical commodity underlying such commodity contract;

(2) facilitating delivery of such commodity; or

(3) disposing of such commodity if a party to such commodity contract defaults.

(c) The trustee shall return promptly to a customer any specifically identifiable security, property, or commodity contract to which such customer is entitled, or shall transfer, on such customer's behalf, such security, property, or commodity contract to a commodity broker that is not a debtor under this title, subject to such rules or regulations as the Commission may prescribe, to the extent that the value of such security, property, or commodity contract does not exceed the amount to which such customer would be entitled under subsection (h) or (i) of this section if such security, property, or commodity contract were not returned or transferred under this subsection.

(d) If the value of a specifically identifiable security, property, or commodity contract exceeds such amount, then the customer to whom such security, property, or commodity contract is specifically identified may deposit cash with the trustee equal to the difference between the value of such security, property, or commodity contract and such amount, and the trustee shall—

(1) return promptly such security, property, or commodity contract to such customer; or

(2) transfer, on such customer's behalf, such security, property, or commodity contract to a commodity broker that is not a debtor under this title, subject to such rules or regulations as the Commission may prescribe.

(e) Subject to subsection (b) of this section, the trustee shall liquidate any commodity contract that—

(1) is identified to a particular customer and with respect to which such customer has not timely instructed the trustee as to the desired disposition of such commodity contract;

(2) cannot be transferred under subsection (c) of this section; or

(3) cannot be identified to a particular customer.

(f) As soon as practicable after the commencement of the case, the trustee shall reduce to money, consistent with good market practice, all securities and other property, other than commodity contracts, held as property of the estate, except for specifically identifiable securities or property distributable under subsection (h) or (i) of this section.

(g) The trustee may not distribute a security or other property except under subsection (h) or (i) of this section.

(h) Except as provided in subsection (b) of this section, the trustee shall distribute customer property ratably to customers on the basis and to the extent of such customers' allowed net equity claims, and in priority to all other claims, except claims of a kind specified in section 507(a)(1) of this title that are attributable to the administration of customer property. Such distribution shall be in the form of—

(1) cash;

(2) the return or transfer, under subsection (c) or (d) of this section, of specifically identifiable customer securities, property, or commodity contracts; or

(3) payment of margin calls under subsection (a) of this section.

(i) If the debtor is a clearing organization, the trustee shall distribute—

(1) customer property, other than member property, ratably to customers on the basis and to the extent of such customers' allowed net equity claims based on such customers' accounts other than proprietary accounts, and in priority to all other claims, except claims of a kind specified in section 507(a)(1) of this title that are attributable to the administration of such customer property; and

(2) member property ratably to customers on the basis and to the extent of such customers' allowed net equity claims based on such customers' proprietary accounts, and in priority to all other claims, except claims of a kind specified in section 507(a)(1) of this title that are attributable to the administration of member property or customer property.

(j)(1) The trustee shall distribute customer property in excess of that distributed under subsection (h) or (i) of this section in accordance with section 726 of this title.

(2) Except as provided in section 510 of this title, if a customer is not paid the full amount of such customer's allowed net equity claim from customer property, the unpaid portion of such claim is a claim entitled to distribution under section 726(a) of this title.

CHAPTER 9—ADJUSTMENT OF DEBTS OF A MUNICIPALITY

SUBCHAPTER I—GENERAL PROVISIONS

§ 901. Applicability of other sections of this title

(a) Sections 301, 344, 347(b), 349, 350(b), 361, 362, 364(c), 364(d), 364(e), 364(f), 365, 366, 501, 502, 503, 504, 506, 507(a)(1), 509, 510, 524(a)(1), 524(a)(2), 544, 545, 546, 547, 548, 549(a), 549(c), 549(d), 550, 551, 552, 553, 1102, 1103, 1109, 1111(b) 1122, 1123(a)(1), 1123(a)(2), 1123(a)(3), 1123(a)(4), 1123(a)(5), 1123(b), 1124, 1125, 1126(a), 1126(b), 1126(c), 1126(e), 1126(f), 1126(g), 1127(d), 1128, 1129(a)(2), 1129(a)(3), 1129(a)(8), 1129(a)(10), 1129(b)(1), 1129(b)(2)(A), 1129(b)(2)(B), 1142(b), 1143, 1144, and 1145 of this title apply in a case under this chapter.

(b) A term used in a section of this title made applicable in a case under this chapter by subsection (a) of this section or section 103(e) of this title has the meaning defined for such term for the purpose of such applicable section, unless such term is otherwise defined in section 902 of this title.

(c) A section made applicable in a case under this chapter by subsection (a) of this section that is operative if the business of the debtor is authorized to be operated is operative in a case under this chapter.

§ 902. Definitions for this chapter

In this chapter—

(1) "property of the estate", when used in a section that is made applicable in a case under this chapter by section 103(e) or 901 of this title, means property of the debtor;

(2) "special tax payer" means record owner or holder of title, legal or equitable, to real property against which has been levied a special assessment or special tax the proceeds of which are the sole source of payment of an obligation issued by the debtor to defray the cost of an improvement relating to such real property;

(3) "special tax payer affected by the plan" means special tax payer with respect to whose real property the plan proposes to increase the proportion of special assessments or special taxes referred to in paragraph (2) of this section assessed against such real property; and

(4) "trustee", when used in a section that is made applicable in a case under this chapter by section 103(e) or 901 of this title, means debtor, except as provided in section 926 of this title.

§ 903. Reservation of State power to control municipalities

This chapter does not limit or impair the power of a State to control, by legislation or otherwise, a municipality of or in such State in the exercise of the political or governmental powers of such municipality, including expenditures for such exercise, but—

(1) a State law prescribing a method of composition of indebtedness of such municipality may not bind any creditor that does not consent to such composition; and

(2) a judgment entered under such a law may not bind a creditor to that does not consent to such composition.

§ 904. Limitation on jurisdiction and powers of court

Notwithstanding any power of the court, unless the debtor consents or the plan so provides, the court may not, by any stay, order, or decree, in the case or otherwise, interfere with—

(1) any of the political or governmental powers of the debtor;

(2) any of the property or revenues of the debtor; or

(3) the debtor's use or enjoyment of any income-producing property.

SUBCHAPER II—ADMINISTRATION

§ 921. Petition and proceedings relating to petition

(a) Notwithstanding sections 109(c) and 301 of this title, a case under this chapter concerning an unincorporated tax or special assessment district that does not have such district's own officials is commenced by the filing under section 301 of this title of a petition under this chapter by such district's governing authority or the board or body having authority to levy taxes or assessments to meet the obligations of such district.

(b) The chief judge of the court of appeals for the circuit embracing the district in which the case is commenced shall designate the bankruptcy judge to conduct the case.

(c) After an objection to the petition, the court, after notice and a hearing, may dismiss the petition, if the debtor did not file the petition in good faith, or if the petition does not meet the requirements of this title.

(e) If the petition is not dismissed under subsection (d) of this section, the court shall order relief under this chapter.

(f) The court may not, on account of an appeal from an order for relief, delay any proceeding under this chapter in the case in which the appeal is being taken; nor shall any court order a stay of such proceeding pending such appeal. The reversal on appeal of a finding of jurisdiction does not affect the validity of any debt incurred that is authorized by the court under section 364(c) or 364(d) of this title.

§ 922. Automatic stay of enforcement of claims against the debtor

(a) A petition filed under this chapter operates as a stay, in addition to the stay provided by section 362 of this title, applicable to all entities, of—

(1) the commencement or continuation, including the issuance or employment of process, of judicial, administrative, or other proceeding against an officer or inhabitant of the debtor that seeks to enforce a claim against the debtor; and

(2) the enforcement of a lien on or arising out of taxes or assessments owed to the debtor.

(b) Subsections (c), (d), (e), (f), and (g) of section 362 of this title apply to a stay under subsection (a) of this section the same as such subsections apply to a stay under section 362(a) of this title.

§ 923. Notice

There shall be given notice of the commencement of a case under this chapter, notice of an order for relief under this chapter, and notice of the dismissal of a case under this chapter. Such notice shall also be published at least once a week for three successive weeks in at least one newspaper of general circulation published within the district in which the case is commenced, and in such other newspaper having a general circulation among bond dealers and bondholders as the court designates.

§ 924. List of creditors

The debtor shall file a list of creditors.

§ 925. Effect of list of claims

A proof of claim is deemed filed under section 501 of this title for any claim that appears in the list filed under section 924 of this title, except a claim that is listed as disputed, contingent, or unliquidated.

§ 926. Avoiding powers

If the debtor refuses to pursue a cause of action under section 544, 545, 547, 548, 549(a), or 550 of this title, then on request of a creditor, the court may appoint a trustee to pursue such cause of action.

§ 927. Dismissal

(a) After notice and a hearing, the court may dismiss a case under this chapter for cause, including—

(1) want of prosecution;

(2) unreasonable delay by the debtor that is prejudicial to creditors;

(3) failure to propose a plan within the time fixed under section 941 of this title;

(4) if a plan is not accepted within any time fixed by the court;

(5) denial of confirmation of a plan under section 943(b) of this title and denial of additional time for filing another plan or a modification of a plan; or

(6) if the court has retained jurisdiction after confirmation of a plan—

(A) material default by the debtor with respect to a term of such plan; or

(B) termination of such plan by reason of the occurrence of a condition specified in such plan.

(b) The court shall dismiss a case under this chapter if confirmation is refused.

SUBCHAPTER III—THE PLAN

§ 941. Filing of plan

The debtor shall file a plan for the adjustment of the debtor's debts. If such a plan is not filed with the petition, the debtor shall file such a plan at such later time as the court fixes.

§ 942. Modification of plan

The debtor may modify the plan at any time before confirmation, but may not modify the plan so that the plan as modified fails to meet the requirements of this chapter. After the debtor files a modification, the plan as modified becomes the plan.

§ 943. Confirmation

(a) A special tax payer may object to confirmation of a plan.

(b) The court shall confirm the plan if—

(1) the plan complies with the provisions of this title made applicable by sections 103(e) and 901 of this title;

(2) the plan complies with the provisions of this chapter;

(3) all amounts to be paid by the debtor or by any person for services or expenses in the case or incident to the plan have been fully disclosed and are reasonable;

(4) the debtor is not prohibited by law from taking any action necessary to be taken to carry out the plan;

(5) the plan provides that each holder of a claim of the kind specified in section 507(a)(1) of this title will receive, on account of such claim, property of a value, as of the effective date of the plan, equal to the allowed amount of such claim, except to the extent that the holder of a particular claim of such kind has waived such payment on such claim; and

(6) the plan is in the best interests of creditors and is feasible.

§ 944. Effect of confirmation

(a) The provisions of a confirmed plan bind the debtor and any creditor, whether or not—

(1) a proof of such creditor's claim is filed or deemed filed under section 501 of this title;

(2) such claim is allowed under section 502 of this title; or

(3) such creditor has accepted the plan.

(b) Except as provided in subsection (c) of this section, the debtor is discharged from all debts as of the time when—

(1) the plan is confirmed;

(2) the debtor deposits any consideration to be distributed under the plan with a disbursing agent appointed by the court; and

(3) the court has determined—

(A) that any security so deposited will constitute, after distribution, a valid legal obligation of the debtor; and

(B) that any provision made to pay or secure payment of such obligation is valid.

(c) The debtor is not discharged under subsection (b) of this section from any debt—

(1) excepted from discharge by the plan or order confirming the plan; or

(2) owed to an entity that, before confirmation of the plan, had neither notice nor actual knowledge of the case.

§ 945. Continuing jurisdiction and closing of the case

(a) The court may retain jurisdiction over the case for such period of time as is necessary for the successful execution of the plan.

(b) Except as provided in subsection (a) of this section, the court shall close the case when administration of the case has been completed.

§ 946. Effect of exchange of securities before the date of the filing of the petition

The exchange of a new security under the plan for a claim covered by the plan, whether such exchange occurred before or after the date of the filing of the petition, does not limit or impair the effectiveness of the plan or of any provision of this chapter. The amount and number specified in section 1126(c) of this title include the amount and number of claims formerly held by a creditor that has participated in any such exchange.

CHAPTER 11—REORGANIZATION

SUBCHAPTER I—OFFICERS AND ADMINISTRATION

Sec.

SUBCHAPTER II—THE PLAN

SUBCHAPTER III—POSTCONFIRMATION MATTERS

SUBCHAPTER IV—RAILROAD REORGANIZATION

SUBCHAPTER I—OFFICERS AND ADMINISTRATION

§ 1101. Definitions for this chapter

In this chapter—

(1) "debtor in possession" means debtor except when a person that has qualified under section 322 of this title is serving as trustee in the case;

(2) "substantial consummation" means—

(A) transfer of all or substantially all of the property proposed by the plan to be transferred;

(B) assumption by the debtor or by the successor to the debtor under the plan of the business or of the management of all or substantially all of the property dealt with by the plan; and

(C) commencement of distribution under the plan.

§ 1102. Creditors' and equity security holders' committees

(a)(1) As soon as practicable after the order for relief under this chapter, the court shall appoint a committee of creditors holding unsecured claims.

(2) On request of a party in interest, the court may order the appointment of additional committees of creditors or of equity security holders if necessary to assure adequate representation of creditors or of equity security holders. The court shall appoint any such committee.

(b)(1) A committee of creditors appointed under subsection (a) of this section shall ordinarily consist of the persons, willing to serve, that hold the seven largest claims against the debtor of the kinds represented on such committee, or of the members of a committee organized by creditors before the order for relief under this chapter, if such committee was fairly chosen and is representative of the different kinds of claims to be represented.

(2) A committee of equity security holders appointed under subsection (a)(2) of this section shall ordinarily consist of the persons, willing to serve, that hold the seven largest amounts of equity securities of the debtor of the kinds represented on such committee.

(c) On request of a party in interest and after notice and a hearing, the court may change the membership or the size of a committee appointed under subsection (a) of this section if the membership of such committee is not representative of the different kinds of claims or interests to be represented.

§ 1103. Powers and duties of committees

(a) At a scheduled meeting of a committee appointed under section 1102 of this title, at which a majority of the members of such committee are present, and with the court's approval, such committee may select and authorize the employment by such committee of one or more attorneys, accountants, or other agents, to represent or perform services for such committee.

(b) A person employed to represent a committee appointed under section 1102 of this title may not, while employed by such committee, represent any other entity in connection with the case.

(c) A committee appointed under section 1102 of this title may—

(1) consult with the trustee or debtor in possession concerning the administration of the case;

(2) investigate the acts, conduct, assets, liabilities, and financial condition of the debtor, the operation of the debtor's business and the desirability of the continuance of such business, and any other matter relevant to the case or to the formulation of a plan;

(3) participate in the formulation of a plan, advise those represented by such committee of such committee's recommendations as to any plan formulated, and collect and file with the court acceptances of a plan;

(4) request the appointment of a trustee or examiner under section 1104 of this title, if a trustee or examiner, as the case may be, has not previously been appointed under this chapter in the case; and

(5) perform such other services as are in the interest of those represented.

(d) As soon as practicable after the appointment of a committee under section 1102 of this title, the trustee shall meet with such committee to transact such business as may be necessary and proper.

§ 1104. Appointment of trustee or examiner

(a) At any time after the commencement of the case but before confirmation of a plan, on request of a party in interest, and after notice and a hearing, the court shall order the appointment of a trustee—

(1) for cause, including fraud, dishonesty, incompetence, or gross mismanagement of the affairs of the debtor by current management, either before or after the commencement of the case, or similar cause, but not including the number of holders of securities of the debtor or the amount of assets or liabilities of the debtor; or

(2) if such appointment is in the interests of creditors, any equity security holders, and other interests of the estate, without regard to the number of holders of securities of the debtor or the amount of assets or liabilities of the debtor.

(b) If the court does not order the appointment of a trustee under this section, then at any time before the confirmation of a plan, on request of a party in interest, and after notice and a hearing, the court shall order the appointment of an examiner to conduct such an investigation of the debtor as is appropriate, including an investigation of any allegations of fraud, dishonesty, incompetence, misconduct, mismanagement, or irregularity in the management of the affairs of the debtor of or by current or former management of the debtor, if—

(1) such appointment is in the interests of creditors, any equity security holders, and other interests of the estate; or

(2) the debtor's fixed, liquidated, unsecured debts, other than debts for goods, services, or taxes, or owing to an insider, exceed $5,000,000.

(c) If the court orders the appointment of a trustee or an examiner, if a trustee or an examiner dies or resigns during the case or is removed under section 324 of this title, or if a trustee fails to qualify under section 322 of this title, then the court shall appoint one disinterested person to serve as trustee or examiner, as the case may be, in the case.

§ 1105. Termination of trustee's appointment

At any time before confirmation of a plan, on request of a party in interest, and after notice and a hearing, the court may terminate the trustee's appointment and restore the debtor to possession and management of the property of the estate, and operation of the debtor's business.

§ 1106. Duties of trustee and examiner

(a) A trustee shall—

(1) perform the duties of a trustee specified in sections 704(2), 704(4), 704(6), 704(7), and 704(8) of this title;

(2) if the debtor has not done so, file the list, schedule, and statement required under section 521(1) of this title;

(3) except to the extent that the court orders otherwise, investigate the acts, conduct, assets, liabilities, and financial condition of the debtor, the operation of the debtor's business and the desirability of the continuance of such business, and any other matter relevant to the case or to the formulation of a plan;

(4) as soon as practicable—

(A) file a statement of any investigation conducted under paragraph (3) of this subsection, including any fact ascertained pertaining to fraud, dishonesty, incompetence, misconduct, mismanagement, or irregularity in the management of the affairs of the debtor, or to a cause of action available to the estate; and

(B) transmit a copy or a summary of any such statement to any creditors' committee or equity security holders' committee, to any indenture trustee, and to such other entity as the court designates;

(5) as soon as practicable, file a plan under section 1121 of this title, file a report of why the trustee will not file a plan, or recommend conversion of the case to a case under chapter 7 or 13 of this title or dismissal of the case;

(6) for any year for which the debtor has not filed a tax return required by law, furnish, without personal liability, such information as may be required by the governmental unit with which such tax return was to be filed, in light of the condition of the debtor's books and records and the availability of such information; and

(7) after confirmation of a plan, file such reports as are necessary or as the court orders.

(b) An examiner appointed under section 1104(c) of this title shall perform the duties specified in paragraphs (3) and (4) of subsection (a) of this section, and any other duties of the trustee that the court orders the debtor in possession not to perform.

§ 1107. Rights, powers, and duties of debtor in possession

(a) Subject to any limitations on a trustee under this chapter, and to such limitations or conditions as the court prescribes, a debtor in possession shall have all the rights, other than the right to compensation under section 330 of this title, and powers, and shall perform all the functions and duties, except the duties specified in sections 1106(a)(2), (3), and (4) of this title, of a trustee serving in a case under this chapter.

(b) Notwithstanding section 327(a) of this title, a person is not disqualified for employment under section 327 of this title by a debtor in possession solely because of such person's employment by or representation of the debtor before the commencement of the case.

§ 1108. Authorization to operate business

Unless the court orders otherwise, the trustee may operate the debtor's business.

§ 1109. Right to be heard

(a) The Securities and Exchange Commission may raise and may appear and be heard on any issue in a case under this chapter, but the Securities and Exchange Commission may not appeal from any judgment, order, or decree entered in the case.

(b) A party in interest, including the debtor, the trustee, a creditors' committee, an equity security holders' committee, a creditor, an equity security holder, or any indenture trustee, may raise and may appear and be heard on any issue in a case under this chapter.

§ 1110. Aircraft equipment and vessels

(a) The right of a secured party with a purchase-money equipment security interest in, or of a lessor or conditional vendor of, whether as trustee or otherwise, aircraft, aircraft engines, propellers, appliances, or spare parts, as defined in section 101 of the Federal Aviation Act of 1958 (49 U.S.C. 1301), or vessels of the United States, as defined in subsection B(4) of the Ship Mortgage Act, 1920 (46 U.S.C. 911(4)), that are subject to a purchase-money equipment security interest granted by, leased to, or conditionally sold to, a debtor that is an air carrier operating under a certificate of convenience and necessity issued by the Civil Aeronautics Board, or a water carrier that holds a certificate of public convenience and necessity or permit issued by the Interstate Commerce Commission, as the case may be, to take possession of such equipment in compliance with the provisions of a purchase-money equipment security agreement, lease, or conditional sale contract, as the case may be, is not affected by section 362 or 363 of this title or by any power of the court to enjoin such taking of possession, unless—

(1) before 60 days after the date of the order for relief under this chapter, the trustee, subject to the court's approval, agrees to perform all obligations of the debtor that become due on or after such date under such security agreement, lease, or conditional sale contract, as the case may be; and

(2) any default, other than a default of a kind specified in section 365(b)(2) of this title, under such security agreement, lease, or conditional sale contract, as the case may be—

(A) that occurred before such date is cured before the expiration of such 60-day period; and

(B) that occurs after such date is cured before the later of—

(i) 30 days after the date of such default; and

(ii) the expiration of such 60-day period.

(b) The trustee and the secured party, lessor, or conditional vendor, as the case may be, whose right to take possession is protected under subsection (a) of this section may agree, subject to the court's approval, to extend the 60-day period specified in subsection (a)(1) of this section.

§ 1111. Claims and interests

(a) A proof of claim or interest is deemed filed under section 501 of this title for any claim or interest that appears in the schedules filed under section 521(1) or 1106(a)(2) of this title, except a claim or interest that is scheduled as disputed, contingent, or unliquidated.

(b)(1)(A) A claim secured by a lien on property of the estate shall be allowed or disallowed under section 502 of this title the same as if the holder of such claim had recourse against the debtor on account of such claim, whether or not such holder has such recourse, unless—

(i) the class of which such claim is a part elects, by at least two-thirds in amount and more than half in number of allowed claims of such class, application of paragraph (2) of this subsection; or

(ii) such holder does not have such recourse and such property is sold under section 363 of this title or is to be sold under the plan.

(B) A class of claims may not elect application of paragraph (2) of this subsection if—

(i) the interest on account of such claims of the holders of such claims in such property is of inconsequential value; or

(ii) the holder of a claim of such class has recourse against the debtor on account of such claim and such property is sold under section 363 of this title or is to be sold under the plan.

(2) If such an election is made, then notwithstanding section 506(a) of this title, such claim is a secured claim to the extent that such claim is allowed.

§ 1112. Conversion or dismissal

(a) The debtor may convert a case under this chapter to a case under chapter 7 of this title unless—

(1) the debtor is not a debtor in possession;

(2) the case is an involuntary case originally commenced under this chapter; or

(3) the case was converted to a case under this chapter on other than the debtor's request.

(b) Except as provided in subsection (c) of this section, on request of a party in interest, and after notice and a hearing, the court may convert a case under this chapter to a case under chapter 7 of this title or may dismiss a case under this chapter, whichever is in the best interest of creditors and the estate, for cause, including—

(1) continuing loss to or diminution of the estate and absence of a reasonable likelihood of rehabilitation;

(2) inability to effectuate a plan;

(3) unreasonable delay by the debtor that is prejudicial to creditors;

(4) failure to propose a plan under section 1121 of this title within any time fixed by the court;

(5) denial of confirmation of every proposed plan and denial of additional time for filing another plan or a modification of a plan;

(6) revocation of an order of confirmation under section 1144 of this title, and denial of confirmation of another plan or a modified plan under section 1129 of this title;

(7) inability to effectuate substantial consummation of a confirmed plan;

(8) material default by the debtor with respect to a confirmed plan; and

(9) termination of a plan by reason of the occurrence of a condition specified in the plan.

(c) The court may not convert a case under this chapter to a case under chapter 7 of this title if the debtor is a farmer or a corporation that is not a moneyed, business, or commercial corporation, unless the debtor requests such conversion.

(d) The court may convert a case under this chapter to a case under chapter 13 of this title only if—

(1) the debtor requests such conversion; and

(2) the debtor has not been discharged under section 1141(d) of this title.

(e) Notwithstanding any other provision of this section, a case may not be converted to a case under another chapter of this title unless the debtor may be a debtor under such chapter.

SUBCHAPTER II—THE PLAN

§ 1121. Who may file a plan

(a) The debtor may file a plan with a petition commencing a voluntary case, or at any time in a voluntary case or an involuntary case.

(b) Except as otherwise provided in this section, only the debtor may file a plan until after 120 days after the date of the order for relief under this chapter.

(c) Any party in interest, including the debtor, the trustee, a creditors' committee, an equity security holders' committee, a creditor, an equity security holder, or any indenture trustee, may file a plan if and only if—

(1) a trustee has been appointed under this chapter;

(2) the debtor has not filed a plan before 120 days after the date of the order for relief under this chapter; or

(3) the debtor has not filed a plan that has been accepted, before 180 days after the date of the order for relief under this chapter, by each class the claims or interests of which are impaired under the plan.

(d) On request of a party in interest and after notice and a hearing, the court may for cause reduce or increase the 120-day period or the 180-day period referred to in this section.

§ 1122. Classification of claims or interests

(a) Except as provided in subsection (b) of this section, a plan may place a claim or an interest in a particular class only if such claim or interest is substantially similar to the other claims or interests of such class.

(b) A plan may designate a separate class of claims consisting only of every unsecured claim that is less than or reduced to an amount that the court approves as reasonable and necessary for administrative convenience.

§ 1123. Contents of plan

(a) A plan shall—

(1) designate, subject to section 1122 of this title, classes of claims other than claims of a kind specified in section 507(a)(1), 507(a)(2), or 507(a)(6) of this title and classes of interests;

(2) specify any class of claims or interests that is not impaired under the plan;

(3) shall specify the treatment of any class of claims or interests that is impaired under the plan;

(4) provide the same treatment for each claim or interest of a particular class, unless the holder of a particular claim or interest agrees to a less favorable treatment of such particular claim or interest;

(5) provide adequate means for the plan's execution, such as—

(A) retention by the debtor of all or any part of the property of the estate;

(B) transfer of all or any part of the property of the estate to one or more entities, whether organized before or after the confirmation of such plan;

(C) merger or consolidation of the debtor with one or more persons;

(D) sale of all or any part of the property of the estate, either subject to or free of any lien, or the distribution of all or any part of the property of the estate among those having an interest in such property of the estate;

(E) satisfaction or modification of any lien;

(F) cancellation or modification of any indenture or similar instrument;

(G) curing or waiving any default;

(H) extension of a maturity date or a change in an interest rate or other term of outstanding securities;

(I) amendment of the debtor's charter; or

(J) issuance of securities of the debtor, or of any entity referred to in subparagraph (B) or (C) of this paragraph, for cash, for property, for existing securities, or in exchange for claims or interests, or for any other appropriate purpose;

(6) provide for the inclusion in the charter of the debtor, if the debtor is a corporation, or of any corporation referred to in paragraph (5)(B) or (5)(C) of this subsection, of a provision prohibiting the issuance of nonvoting equity securities, and providing, as to the several classes of securities possessing voting power, an appropriate distribution of such power among such classes, including, in the case of any class of equity securities having a preference over another class of equity securities with respect to dividends, adequate provisions for the election of directors representing such preferred class in the event of default in the payment of such dividends; and

(7) contain only provisions that are consistent with the interests of creditors and equity security holders and with public policy with respect to the manner of selection of any officer, director, or trustee under the plan and any successor to such officer, director, or trustee.

(b) Subject to subsection (a) of this section, a plan may—

(1) impair or leave unimpaired any class of claims, secured or unsecured, or of interests;

(2) subject to section 365 of this title, provide for the assumption or rejection of any executory contract or unexpired lease of the debtor not previously rejected under section 365 of this title;

(3) provide for—

(A) the settlement or adjustment of any claim or interest belonging to the debtor or to the estate; or

(B) the retention and enforcement by the debtor, by the trustee, or by a representative of the estate appointed for such purpose, of any such claim or interest;

(4) provide for the sale of all or substantially all of the property of the estate, and the distribution of the proceeds of such sale among holders of claims or interests; and

(5) include any other appropriate provision not inconsistent with the applicable provisions of this title.

(c) In a case concerning an individual, a plan proposed by an entity other than the debtor may not provide for the use, sale, or lease of property exempted under section 522 of this title, unless the debtor consents to such use, sale, or lease.

§ 1124. Impairment of claims or interests

Except as provided in section 1123(a)(4) of this title, a class of claims or interests is impaired under a plan unless, with respect to each claim or interest of such class, the plan—

(1) leaves unaltered the legal, equitable, and contractual rights to which such claim or interest entitles the holder of such claim or interest;

(2) notwithstanding any contractual provision or applicable law that entitles the holder of such claim or interest to demand or receive accelerated payment of such claim or interest after the occurrence of a default—

(A) cures any such default, other than a default of a kind specified in section 365(b)(2) of this title, that occurred before or after the commencement of the case under this title;

(B) reinstates the maturity of such claim or interest as such maturity existed before such default;

(C) compensates the holder of such claim or interest for any damages incurred as a result of any reasonable reliance by such holder on such contractual provision or such applicable law; and

(D) does not otherwise alter the legal, equitable, or contractual rights to which such claim or interest entitles the holder of such claim or interest; or

(3) provides that, on the effective date of the plan, the holder of such claim or interest receives, on account of such claim or interest, cash equal to—

(A) with respect to a claim, the allowed amount of such claim; or

(B) with respect to an interest, if applicable, the greater of—

(i) any fixed liquidation preference to which the terms of any security representing such interest entitle the holder of such interest; and

(ii) any fixed price at which the debtor, under the terms of such security, may redeem such security from such holder.

§ 1125. Postpetition disclosure and solicitation

(a) In this section—

(1) "adequate information" means information of a kind, and in sufficient detail, as far as is reasonably practicable in light of the nature and history of the debtor and the condition of the debtor's books and records, that would enable a hypothetical reasonable investor typical of holders of claims or interests of the relevant class to make an informed judgment about the plan; and

(2) "investor typical of holders of claims or interests of the relevant class" means investor having—

(A) a claim or interest of the relevant class;

(B) such a relationship with debtor as the holders of other claims or interests of such class generally have; and

(C) such ability to obtain such information from sources other than the disclosure required by this section as holders claims or interests in such class generally have.

(b) An acceptance or rejection of a plan may not be solicited after the commencement of the case under this title from a holder of a claim or interest with respect to such claim or interest, unless, at the time of or before such solicitation, there is transmitted to such holder the plan or a summary of the plan, and a written disclosure statement approved, after notice and a hearing, by the court as containing adequate information. The court may approve a disclosure statement without a valuation of the debtor or an appraisal of the debtor's assets.

(c) The same disclosure statement shall be transmitted to each holder of a claim or interest of a particular class, but there may be transmitted different disclosure statements, differing in amount, detail, or kind of information, as between classes.

(d) Whether a disclosure statement contains adequate information is not governed by any otherwise applicable nonbankruptcy law, rule, or regulation, but an agency or official whose duty is to administer or enforce such a law, rule, or regulation may be heard on the issue of whether a disclosure statement contains adequate information. Such an agency or official may not appeal from an order approving a disclosure statement.

(e) A person that solicits, in good faith and in compliance with the applicable provisions of this title, or that participates, in good faith and in compliance with the applicable provisions of this title, in the offer, issuance, sale, or purchase of a security, offered or sold under the plan, of the debtor, of an affiliate participating in a joint plan with the debtor, or of a newly organized successor to the debtor under the plan, is not liable, on account of such solicitation or participation, for violation of any applicable law, rule, or regulation governing the offer, issuance, sale, or purchase of securities.

§ 1126. Acceptance of plan

(a) The holder of a claim or interest allowed under section 502 of this title may accept or reject a plan. If the United States is a creditor or equity security holder, the Secretary of the Treasury may accept or reject the plan on behalf of the United States.

(b) For the purposes of subsections (c) and (d) of this section, a holder of a claim or interest that has accepted or rejected the plan before the commencement of the case under this title is deemed to have accepted or rejected such plan, as the case may be, if—

(1) the solicitation of such acceptance or rejection was in compliance with any applicable nonbankruptcy law, rule, or regulation governing the adequacy of disclosure in connection with such solicitation; or

(2) if there is not any such law, rule, or regulation, such acceptance or rejection was solicited after disclosure to such holder of adequate information, as defined in section 1125(a)(1) of this title.

(c) A class of claims has accepted a plan if such plan has been accepted by creditors, other than any entity designated under subsection (e) of this section, that hold at least two-thirds in amount and more than one-half in number of the allowed claims of such class held by creditors, other than any entity designated under subsection (e) of this section, that have accepted or rejected such plan.

(d) A class of interests has accepted a plan if such plan has been accepted by holders of such interests other than any entity designated under subsection (e) of this section, that hold at least two-thirds in amount of the allowed interests of such class held by holders of such interests, other than any entity designated under subsection (e) of this section, that have accepted or rejected such plan.

(e) On request of a party in interest, and after notice and a hearing the court may designate any entity whose acceptance or rejection of such plan was not in good faith, or was not solicited or procured in good faith or in accordance with the provisions of this title.

(f) Notwithstanding any other provision of this section, a class that is not impaired under a plan is deemed to have accepted the plan, and solicititation of acceptances with respect to such class from the holders of claims or interest of such class is not required.

(g) Notwithstanding any other provision of this section, a class is deemed not to have accepted a plan if such plan provides that the claims or interests of such class do not entitle the holders of such claims or interests to any payment or compensation under the plan on account of such claims or interests.

§ 1127. Modification of plan

(a) The proponent of a plan may modify such plan at any time before confirmation, but may not modify such plan so that such plan as modified fails to meet the requirements of sections 1122 and 1123 of this title. After the proponent files a modification with the court, the plan as modified becomes the plan.

(b) The proponent of a plan or the reorganized debtor may modify such plan at any time after confirmation of such plan and before substantial consummation of such plan, but may not modify such plan so that such plan as modified fails to meet the requirements of sections 1122 and 1123 of this title. Such plan as modified under this subsection becomes the plan only if the court, after notice and a hearing, confirms such plan, as modified, under section 1129 of this title, and circumstances warrant such modification.

(c) The proponent of a modification shall comply with section 1125 of this title with respect to the plan as modified.

(d) Any holder of a claim or interest that has accepted or rejected a plan is deemed to have accepted or rejected, as the case may be, such plan as modified, unless, within the time fixed by the court, such holder changes such holder's previous acceptance or rejection.

§ 1128. Confirmation hearing

(a) After notice, the court shall hold a hearing on confirmation of a plan.

(b) A party in interest may object to confirmation of a plan.

§ 1129. Confirmation of plan

(a) The court shall confirm a plan only if all of the following requirements are met:

(1) The plan complies with the applicable provisions of this chapter.

(2) The proponent of the plan complies with the applicable provisions of this chapter.

(3) The plan has been proposed in good faith and not by any means forbidden by law.

(4) (A) Any payment made or promised by the proponent, by the debtor, or by a person issuing securities or acquiring property

under the plan, for services or for costs and expenses in, or in connection with, the case, or in connection with the plan and incident to the case, has been disclosed to the court; and

(B) (i) any such payment made before confirmation of the plan is reasonable; or

(ii) if such payment is to be fixed after confirmation of the plan, such payment is subject to the approval of the court as reasonable.

(5) (A) (i) The proponent of the plan has disclosed the identity and affiliations of any individual proposed to serve, after confirmation of the plan, as a director, officer, or voting trustee of the debtor, an affiliate of the debtor participating in a joint plan with the debtor, or a successor to the debtor under the plan; and

(ii) the appointment to, or continuance in, such office of such individual, is consistent with the interests of creditors and equity security holders and with public policy.

(B) The proponent of the plan has disclosed the identity of any insider that will be employed or retained by the reorganized debtor, and the nature of any compensation for such insider.

(6) Any regulatory commission with jurisdiction, after confirmation of the plan, over the rates of the debtor has approved any rate change provided for in the plan, or such rate change is expressly conditioned on such approval.

(7) With respect to each class—

(A) each holder of a claim or interest of such class—

(i) has accepted the plan; or

(ii) will receive or retain under the plan on account of such claim or interest property of a value, as of the effective date of the plan, that is not less than the amount that such holder would so receive or retain if the debtor were liquidated under chapter 7 of this title on such date; or

(B) if section 1111(b)(2) of this title applies to the claims of such class, each holder of a claim of such class will receive or retain under the plan on account of such claim property of a value, as of the effective date of the plan, that is not less than the value of such creditor's interest in the estate's interest in the property that secures such claims.

(8) With respect to each class—

(A) such class has accepted the plan; or

(B) such class is not impaired under the plan.

(9) Except to the extent that the holder of a particular claim has agreed to a different treatment of such claim, the plan provides that—

(A) with respect to a claim of a kind specified in section 507(a)(1) or 507(a)(2) of this title, on the effective date of the plan, the holder of such claim will receive on account of such claim cash equal to the allowed amount of such claim;

(B) with respect to a class of claims of a kind specified in section 507(a)(3), 507(a)(4), or 507(a)(5) of this title, each holder of a claim of such class will receive—

(i) if such class has accepted the plan, deferred cash payments of a value, as of the effective date of the plan, equal to the allowed amount of such claim; or

(ii) if such class has not accepted the plan, cash on the effective date of the plan equal to the allowed amount of such claim; and

(C) with respect to a claim of a kind specified in section 507(a)(6) of this title, the holder of such claim will receive on account of such claim deferred cash payments, over a period not exceeding six years after the date of assessment of such claim, of a value, as of the effective date of the plan, equal to the allowed amount of such claim.

(10) At least one class of claims has accepted the plan, determined without including any acceptance of the plan by any insider holding a claim of such class.

(11) Confirmation of the plan is not likely to be followed by the liquidation, or the need for further financial reorganization, of the debtor or any successor to the debtor under the plan, unless such liquidation or reorganization is proposed in the plan.

(b)(1) Notwithstanding section 510(a) of this title, if all of the applicable requirements of subsection (a) of this section other than paragraph (8) are met with respect to a plan, the court, on request of the proponent of the plan, shall confirm the plan notwithstanding the requirements of such paragraph if the plan does not discriminate unfairly, and is fair and equitable, with respect to each class of claims or interests that is impaired under, and has not accepted, the plan.

(2) For the purpose of this subsection, the condition that a plan be fair and equitable with respect to a class includes the following requirements:

(A) With respect to a class of secured claims, the plan provides—

(i)(I) that the holders of such claims retain the lien securing such claims, whether the property subject to such lien is retained by the debtor or transferred to another entity, to the extent of the allowed amount of such claims; and

(II) that each holder of a claim of such class receive on account of such claim deferred cash payments totaling at least the allowed amount of such claim, of a value, as of the effective date of the plan, of at least the value of such holder's interest in the estate's interest in such property;

(ii) for the sale, subject to section 363(k) of this title, of any property that is subject to the lien securing such claims, free and clear of such lien, with such lien to attach to the proceeds of such sale, and the treatment of such lien on proceeds under clause (i) or (iii) of this subparagraph; or

(iii) for the realization by such holders of the indubitable equivalent of such claims.

(B) With respect to a class of unsecured claims—

(i) the plan provides that each holder of a claim of such class receive or retain on account of such claim property of a value, as of the effective date of the plan, equal to the allowed amount of such claim; or

(ii) the holder of any claim or interest that is junior to the claims of such class will not receive or retain on account of such junior claim or interest any property.

(C) With respect to a class of interests—

(i) the plan provides that each holder of an interest of such class receive or retain on account of such claim property of a value, as of the effective date of the plan, equal to the greatest of the allowed amount of any fixed liquidation preference to which such holder is entitled, any fixed redemption price to which such holder is entitled, and the value of such interest; or

(ii) the holder of any interest that is junior to the interests of such class will not receive or retain under the plan on account of such junior interest any property.

(c) Notwithstanding subsections (a) and (b) of this section and except as provided in section 1127(b) of this title, the court may confirm only one plan, unless the order of confirmation in the case has been revoked under section 1144 of this title. If the requirements of subsections (a) and (b) of this section are met with respect to more than one plan, the court shall consider the preferences of creditors and equity security holders in determining which plan to confirm.

(d) Notwithstanding any other provision of this section, on request of a party in interest that is a governmental unit, the court may not confirm a plan if the principal purpose of the plan is the avoidance of taxes or the avoidance of section 5 of the Securities Act of 1933 (15 U.S.C. 77e).

SUBCHAPTER III—POSTCONFIRMATION MATTERS

§ 1141. Effect of confirmation

(a) Except as provided in subsections (d)(2) and (d)(3) of this section, the provisions of a confirmed plan bind the debtor, any entity issuing securities under the plan, any entity acquiring property under the plan, and any creditor or equity security holder of, or general partner in, the debtor, whether or not the claim or interest of such creditor, equity security holder, or general partner is impaired under the plan and whether or not such creditor, equity security holder, or general partner has accepted the plan.

(b) Except as otherwise provided in the plan or the order confirming the plan, the confirmation of a plan vests all of the property of the estate in the debtor.

(c) After confirmation of a plan, the property dealt with by the plan is free and clear of all claims and interests of creditors, of equity security holders, and of general partners in the debtor, except as otherwise provided in the plan or in the order confirming the plan.

(d)(1) Except as otherwise provided in this subsection, in the plan, or in the order confirming the plan, the confirmation of a plan—

(A) discharges the debtor from any debt that arose before the date of such confirmation, and any debt of a kind specified in section 502(g), 502(h), or 502(i) of this title, whether or not—

(i) a proof of the claim based on such debt is filed or deemed filed under section 501 of this title;

(ii) such claim is allowed under section 502 of this title; or

(iii) the holder of such claim has accepted the plan; and

(B) terminates all rights and interests of equity security holders and general partners provided for by the plan.

(2) The confirmation of a plan does not discharge an individual debtor from any debt excepted from discharge under section 523 of this title.

(3) The confirmation of a plan does not discharge a debtor if—

(A) the plan provides for the liquidation of all or substantially all of the property of the estate;

(B) the debtor does not engage in business after consummation of the plan; and

(C) the debtor would be denied a discharge under section 727(a) of this title if the case were a case under chapter 7 of this title.

(4) The court may approve a written waiver of discharge executed by the debtor after the order for relief under this chapter.

§ 1142. Execution of plan

(a) Notwithstanding any otherwise applicable nonbankruptcy law, rule, or regulation relating to financial condition, the debtor and any entity organized or to be organized for the purpose of carrying out the plan shall carry out the plan, and shall comply with any orders of the court.

(b) The court may direct the debtor and any other necessary party to execute or deliver or to join in the execution or delivery of any instrument required to effect a transfer of property dealt with by confirmed plan, and to perform any other act, including the satisfaction of any lien, that is necessary for the consummation of the plan.

§ 1143. Distribution

If a plan requires presentment or surrender of a security or the performance of any other act as a condition to participation in distribution under the plan, such action shall be taken not later than five years after the date of the entry of the order of confirmation. Any entity that has not within such time presented or surrendered such entity's security or taken any such other action that the plan requires may not participate in distribution under the plan.

§ 1144. Revocation of an order of confirmation

On request of a party in interest at any time before 180 days after the date of the entry of the order of confirmation, and after notice and a hearing, the court may revoke such order if such order was procured by fraud. An order under this section revoking an order of confirmation shall—

(1) contain such provisions as are necessary to protect any entity acquiring rights in good faith reliance on the order of confirmation; and

(2) revoke the discharge of the debtor.

§ 1145. Exemption from securities laws

(a) Except with respect to an entity that is an underwriter as defined in subsection (b) of this section, section 5 of the Securities Act of 1933 (15 U.S.C. 77e) and any State or local law requiring registration for offer or sale of a security or registration or licensing of an issuer of, underwriter of, or broker or dealer in, a security does not apply to—

(1) the offer or sale under a plan of a security of the debtor, of an affiliate participating in a joint plan with the debtor, or of a successor to the debtor under the plan—

(A) in exchange for a claim against, an interest in, or a claim for an administrative expense in the case concerning, the debtor or such affiliate; or

(B) principally in such exchange and partly for cash or property;

(2) the offer of a security through any warrant, option, right to subscribe, or conversion privilege that was sold in the manner specified in paragraph (1) of this subsection, or the sale of a security upon the exercise of such a warrant, option, right, or privilege;

(3) the offer or sale, other than under a plan, of a security of an issuer other than the debtor or an affiliate, if—

(A) such security was owned by the debtor on the date of the filing of the petition;

(B) the issuer of such security is—

(i) required to file reports under section 13 of the Securities Exchange Act of 1934 (15 U.S.C. 78m); and

(ii) in compliance with all applicable requirements for the continuance of trading in such security on the date of such offer or sale; and

(C) such offer or sale is of securities that do not exceed—

(i) during the two-year period immediately following the date of the filing of the petition, four percent of the securities of such class outstanding on such date; and

(ii) during any 180-day period following such two-year period, one percent of the securities outstanding at the beginning of such 180-day period; or

(4) a transaction by a stockholder in a security that is executed after a transaction of a kind specified in paragraph (1) or (2) of this subsection in such security and before the expiration of 40 days after the first date on which such security was bona fide offered to the public by the issuer or by or through an underwriter, if such stockbroker provides, at the time of or before such transaction by such stockholder, a disclosure statement approved under section 1125 of this title, and, if the court orders, information supplementing such disclosure statement.

(b)(1) Except as provided in paragraph (2) of this subsection, an entity is an underwriter under section 2(11) of the Securities Act of 1933 (15 U.S.C. 77b(11)), if such entity—

(A) purchases a claim against, interest in, or claim for an administrative expense in the case concerning, the debtor, if such purchase is with a view to distribution of any security received or to be received in exchange for such a claim or interest;

(B) offers to sell securities offered or sold under the plan for the holders of such securities;

(C) offers to buy securities offered or sold under the plan for the holders of such securities, if such offer to buy is—

(i) with a view to distribution of such securities; and

(ii) under an agreement made in connection with the plan, with the consummation of the plan, or with the offer or sale of securities under the plan; or

(D) is an issuer, as used in such section 2(11), with respect to such securities.

(2) An entity is not an underwriter under section 2(11) of the Securities Act of 1933 or under paragraph (1) of this subsection with respect to an agreement that provides only for—

(A)(i) the matching combination of fractional interests in securities offered or sold under the plan into whole interests; or

(ii) the purchase or sale of such fractional interests among entities receiving such fractional interests under the plan; or

(B) the purchase or sale for such entities of such fractional or whole interests as are necessary to adjust for any remaining fractional interests after such matching.

(3) An entity other than an entity of the kind specified in paragraph (1) of this subsection is not an underwriter under section 2(11) of the Securities Act of 1933 with respect to any securities offered or sold to such entity in the manner specified in subsection (a)(1) of this section.

(c) An offer or sale of securities of the kind and in the manner specified under subsection (a)(1) of this section is deemed to be a public offering.

(d) The Trust Indenture Act of 1939 (15 U.S.C. 77aaa et seq.) does not apply to a commercial note issued under the plan that matures not later than one year after the effective date of the plan.

§ 1146. Special tax provisions

(a) For the purposes of any State or local law imposing a tax on or measured by income, the taxable period of a debtor that is an individual shall terminate on the date of the order for relief under this chapter, unless the case was converted under section 706 of this title.

(b) The trustee shall make a State or local tax return of income for the estate of an individual debtor in a case under this chapter for each taxable period after the order for relief under this chapter during which the case is pending.

(c) The issuance, transfer, or exchange of a security, or the making or delivery of an instrument of transfer under a plan confirmed under section 1129 of this title, may not be taxed under any State or local law imposing a stamp tax or similar tax.

(d) The court may authorize the proponent of a plan to request a determination, limited to questions of law, by a State or local governmental unit charged with responsibility for collection or determination of a tax on or measured by income, of the tax effects, under section 346 of this title and under the law imposing such tax, of the plan. In the event of an actual controversy, the court may declare such effects after the earlier of—

(1) the date on which such governmental unit responds to the request under this subsection; and

(2) 270 days after such request.

SUBCHAPTER IV—RAILROAD REORGANIZATION

§ 1161. Inapplicability of other sections

Sections 341, 343, 1102(a)(1), 1104, 1105, 1107, 1129(a)(7), and 1129(c) of this title do not apply in a case concerning a railroad.

§ 1162. Definition

In this subchapter, "Commission" means Interstate Commerce Commission.

§ 1163. Appointment of trustee

As soon as practicable after the order for relief, the Secretary of Transportation shall submit a list of five disinterested persons that are qualified and willing to serve as trustee in the case. The court shall appoint one of such persons to serve as trustee in the case.

§ 1164. Right to be heard

The Commission, the Department of Transportation, and any State or local commission having regulatory jurisdiction over the debtor may raise and may appear and be heard on any issue in a case under this chapter, but may not appeal from any judgment, order, or decree entered in the case.

§ 1165. Protection of the public interest

In applying sections 1166, 1167, 1169, 1170, 1171, 1172, 1173, and 1174 of this title, the court and the trustee shall consider the public interest in addition to the interests of the debtor, creditors, and equity security holders.

§ 1166. Effect of Interstate Commerce Act and of Federal, State, or local regulations

Except with respect to abandonment under section 1170 of this title, or merger, modification of the financial structure of the debtor, or issuance or sale of securities under a plan, the trustee and the debtor are subject to the provisions of the Interstate Commerce Act (49 U.S.C. 1 et seq.) that are applicable to railroads, and the trustee is subject to orders of any Federal, State, or local regulatory body to the same extent as the debtor would be if a petition commencing the case under this chapter had not been filed, but—

(1) any such order that would require the expenditure, or the incurring of an obligation for the expenditure, of money from the estate is not effective unless approved by the court; and

(2) the provisions of this chapter are subject to section 601(b) of the Regional Rail Reorganization Act of 1973 (45 U.S.C. 791(b)).

§ 1167. Collective bargaining agreements

Notwithstanding section 365 of this title, neither the court nor the trustee may change the wages or working conditions of employees of the debtor established by a collective bargaining agreement that is subject to the Railway Labor Act (45 U.S.C. 151 et seq.) except in accordance with section 6 of such Act (45 U.S.C. 156).

§ 1168. Rolling stock equipment

(a) The right of a secured party with a purchase-money equipment security interest in, or of a lessor or conditional vendor of, whether as trustee or otherwise, rolling stock equipment or accessories used on such equipment, including superstructures and racks, that are subject to a purchase-money equipment security interest granted by, leased to, or conditionally sold to, the debtor to take possession of such equipment in compliance with the provisions of a purchase-money equipment security agreement, lease, or conditional sale contract, as the case may be, is not affected by section 362 or 363 of this title or by any power of the court to enjoin such taking of possession, unless—

(1) before 60 days after the date of the commencement of a case under this chapter, the trustee, subject to the court's approval, agrees to perform all obligations of the debtor under such security agreement, lease, or conditional sale contract, as the case may be; and

(2) any default, other than a default of a kind specified in section 365(b)(2) of this title, under such security agreement, lease, or conditional sale contract, as the case may be—

(A) that occurred before such date and is an event of default therewith is cured before the expiration of such 60-day period; and

(B) that occurs or becomes an event of default after such date is cured before the later of—

(i) 30 days after the date of such default or event of default; and

(ii) the expiration of such 60-day period.

(b) The trustee and the secured party, lessor, or conditional vendor, as the case may be, whose right to take possession is protected under subsection (a) of this section, may agree, subject to the court's approval to extend the 60-day period specified in subsection (a)(1) of this section.

§ 1169. Effect of rejection of lease of railroad line

(a) Except as provided in subsection (b) of this section, if a lease of a line of railroad under which the debtor is the lessee is rejected under section 365 of this title, and if the trustee, within such time as the court fixes, and with the court's approval, elects not to operate the leased line, the lessor under such lease, after such approval, shall operate the line.

(b) If operation of such line by such lessor is impracticable or contrary to the public interest, the court, on request of such lessor, and after notice and a hearing, shall order the trustee to continue operation of such line for the account of such lessor until abandonment is ordered under section 1170 of this title, or until such operation is otherwise lawfully terminated, whichever occurs first.

(c) During any such operation, such lessor is deemed a carrier subject to the provisions of the Interstate Commerce Act (49 U.S.C. 1 et seq.) that are applicable to railroads.

§ 1170. Abandonment of railroad line

(a) The court, after notice and a hearing, may authorize the abandonment of a railroad line if such abandonment is—

(1) (A) in the best interest of the estate; or

(B) essential to the formulation of a plan; and

(2) consistent with the public interest.

(b) If, except for the pendency of the case under this chapter, such abandonment would require approval by the Commission under a law of the United States, the trustee shall initiate an appropriate application for such abandonment with the Commission. The court may fix a time within which the Commission shall report to the court on such application.

(c) After the court receives the report of the Commission, or the expiration of the time fixed under subsection (b) of this section, whichever occurs first, the court may authorize such abandonment after notice to the Commission, the Secretary of Transportation, the trustee, any party in interest that has requested notice, any affected shipper or community, and any other entity prescribed by the court, and a hearing.

(d) (1) Enforcement of an order authorizing such abandonment shall be stayed until the time for taking an appeal has expired, or, if an appeal is timely taken, until such order has become final.

(2) If an order authorizing the abandonment of a railroad line is appealed, the court, on request of a party in interest, may authorize termination of service on a line or a portion of a line pending the determination of such appeal, after notice to the Commission, the Secretary of Transportation, the trustee, any party in interest that has requested notice, any affected shipper or community, and any other entity prescribed by the court, and a hearing. An appellant may not obtain a stay of the enforcement of an order authorizing such termination by the giving of a supersedeas bond or otherwise, during the pendency of such appeal.

§ 1171. Priority claims

(a) There shall be paid as an administrative expense any claim of an individual or of the personal representative of a deceased individual against the debtor or the estate, for personal injury to or death of such individual arising out of the operation of the debtor or the estate, whether such claim arose before or after the commencement of the case.

(b) Any unsecured claim against the debtor that would have been entitled to priority if a receiver in equity of the property of the debtor had been appointed by a Federal court on the date of the order for relief under this title shall be entitled to such priority in the case under this chapter.

§ 1172. Contents of plan

(a) In addition to the provisions required or permitted under section 1123 of this title, a plan—

(1) shall specify the extent to and the means by which the debtor's rail service is proposed to be continued, and the extent to which any of the debtor's rail service is proposed to be terminated; and

(2) may include a provision for—

(A) the transfer of any or all of the operating railroad lines of the debtor to another operating railroad; or

(B) abandonment of any railroad line in accordance with section 1170 of this title.

(b) If, except for the pendency of the case under this chapter, transfer of, or operation of or over, any of the debtor's rail lines by an entity other than the debtor or a successor to the debtor under the plan would require approval by the Commission under a law of the United States, then a plan may not propose such a transfer or such operation unless the proponent of the plan initiates an appropriate application for such a transfer or such operation with the Commission and, within such time as the court may fix, not exceeding 180 days, the Commission, with or without a hearing, as the Commission may determine, and with or without modification or condition, approves such application, or does not act on such application. Any action or order of the Commission approving, modifying, conditioning, or disapproving such application is subject to review by the court only under sections 706(2)(A), 706(2)(B), 706(2)(C), and 706(2)(D) of title 5.

§ 1173. Confirmation of plan

(a) The court shall confirm a plan if—

(1) the applicable requirements of section 1129 of this title have been met;

(2) each creditor or equity security holder will receive or retain under the plan property of a value, as of the effective date of the plan, that is not less than the value of property that each such creditor or equity security holder would so receive or retain if all of the operating railroad lines of the debtor were sold, and the proceeds of such sale, and the other property of the estate, were distributed under chapter 7 of this title on such date;

(3) in light of the debtor's past earnings and the probable prospective earnings of the reorganized debtor, there will be adequate coverage by such prospective earnings of any fixed charges, such as interest on debt, amortization of funded debt, and rent for leased railroads, provided for by the plan; and

(4) the plan is compatible with the public interest.

(b) If the requirements of subsection (a) of this section are met with respect to more than one plan, the court shall confirm the plan that is most likely to maintain adequate rail service in the public interest.

§ 1174. Liquidation

On request of a party in interest and after notice and a hearing, the court may, or, if a plan has not been confirmed under section 1173 of this title before five years after the date of the order for relief, the court shall, order the trustee to cease the debtor's operation and to collect and reduce to money all of the property of the estate in the same manner as if the case were a case under chapter 7 of this title.

CHAPTER 13—ADJUSTMENT OF DEBTS OF AN INDIVIDUAL WITH REGULAR INCOME

SUBCHAPTER I—OFFICERS, ADMINISTRATION, AND THE ESTATE

Sec.

SUBCHAPTER II—THE PLAN

SUBCHAPTER I—OFFICERS, ADMINISTRATION, AND THE ESTATE

§ 1301. Stay of action against codebtor

(a) Except as provided in subsections (b) and (c) of this section, after the order for relief under this chapter, a creditor may not act, or commence or continue any civil action, to collect all or any part of a consumer debt of the debtor from any individual that is liable on such debt with the debtor, or that secured such debt, unless—

(1) such individual became liable on or secured such debt in the ordinary course of such individual's business; or

(2) the case is closed, dismissed, or converted to a case under chapter 7 or 11 of this title.

(b) A creditor may present a negotiable instrument, and may give notice of dishonor of such an instrument.

(c) On request of a party in interest and after notice and a hearing, the court shall grant relief from the stay provided by subsection (a) of this section with respect to a creditor, to the extent that—

(1) as between the debtor and the individual protected under subsection (a) of this section, such individual received the consideration for the claim held by such creditor;

(2) the plan filed by the debtor proposes not to pay such claim; or

(3) such creditor's interest would be irreparably harmed by such stay.

§ 1302. Trustee

(a) If the court has appointed an individual under subsection (d) of this section to serve as standing trustee in cases under this chapter and if such individual qualifies under section 322 of this title, then such individual shall serve as trustee in the case. Otherwise, the court shall appoint a person to serve as trustee in the case.

(b) The trustee shall—

(1) perform the duties specified in sections 704(2), 704(3), 704(4), 704(5), 704(6), and 704(8) of this title;

(2) appear and be heard at any hearing that concerns—

(A) the value of property subject to a lien;

(B) confirmation of a plan; or

(C) modification of the plan after confirmation; and

(3) advise, other than on legal matters, and assist the debtor in performance under the plan.

(c) If the debtor is engaged in business, then in addition to the duties specified in subsection (b) of this section, the trustee shall perform the duties specified in sections 1106(a)(3) and 1106(a)(4) of this title.

(d) If the number of cases under this chapter commenced in a particular judicial district so warrant, the court may appoint one or more individuals to serve as standing trustee for such district in cases under this chapter.

(e)(1) A court that has appointed an individual under subsection (d) of this section to serve as standing trustee in cases under this chapter shall fix—

(A) a maximum annual compensation for such individual, not to exceed the lowest annual rate of basic pay in effect for grade GS–16 of the General Schedule prescribed under section 5332 of title 5; and

(B) a percentage fee, not to exceed ten percent, based on such maximum annual compensation and the actual, necessary expenses incurred by such individual as standing trustee.

(2) Such individual shall collect such percentage fee from all payments under plans in the cases under this chapter for which such individual serves as standing trustee. Such individual shall pay annually to the Treasury—

(A) any amount by which the actual compensation of such individual exceeds five percent upon all payments under plans in cases under this chapter for which such individual serves as standing trustee; and

(B) any amount by which the percentage fee fixed under paragraph (1)(B) of this subsection for all such cases exceeds—

(i) such individual's actual compensation for such cases, as adjusted under subparagraph (A) of this paragraph; plus

(ii) the actual, necessary expenses incurred by such individual as standing trustee in such cases.

§ 1303. Rights and powers of debtor

Subject to any limitations on a trustee under this chapter, the debtor shall have, exclusive of the trustee, the rights and powers of a trustee under sections 363(b), 363(d), 363(e), 363(f), and 363(l), of this title.

§ 1304. Debtor engaged in business

(a) A debtor that is self-employed and incurs trade credit in the production of income from such employment is engaged in business.

(b) Unless the court orders otherwise, a debtor engaged in business may operate the business of the debtor, and, subject to any limitations on a trustee under sections 363(c) and 364 of this title and to such limitations or conditions as the court prescribes, shall have, exclusive of the trustee, the rights and powers of the trustee under such sections.

(c) A debtor engaged in business shall perform the duties of the trustee specified in section 704(7) of this title.

§ 1305. Filing and allowance of postpetition claims

(a) A proof of claim may be filed by any entity that holds a claim against the debtor—

(1) for taxes that become payable to a governmental unit while the case is pending; or

(2) that is a consumer debt, that arises after the date of the order for relief under this chapter, and that is for property or services necessary for the debtor's performance under the plan.

(b) Except as provided in subsection (c) of this section, a claim filed under subsection (a) of this section shall be allowed or disallowed under section 502 of this title, but shall be determined as of the date such claim arises, and shall be allowed under section 502(a), 502(b), or 502(c) of this title, or disallowed under section 502(d) or 502(e) of this title, the same as if such claim had arisen before the date of the filing of the petition.

(c) A claim filed under subsection (a)(2) of this section shall be disallowed if the holder of such claim knew or should have known that prior approval by the trustee of the debtor's incurring the obligation was practicable and was not obtained.

§ 1306. Property of the estate

(a) Property of the estate includes, in addition to the property specified in section 541 of this title—

(1) all property of the kind specified in such section that the debtor acquires after the commencement of the case but before the case is closed, dismissed, or converted to a case under chapter 7 or 11 of this title, whichever occurs first; and

(2) earnings from services performed by the debtor after the commencement of the case but before the case is closed, dismissed, or converted to a case under chapter 7 or 11 of this title, whichever occurs first.

(b) Except as provided in a confirmed plan or order confirming a plan, the debtor shall remain in possession of all property of the estate.

§ 1307. Conversion or dismissal

(a) The debtor may convert a case under this chapter to a case under chapter 7 of this title at any time. Any waiver of the right to convert under this subsection is unenforceable.

(b) On request of the debtor at any time if the case has not been converted under section 706 or 1112 of this title, the court shall dismiss a case under this chapter. Any waiver of the right to dismiss under this subsection is unenforceable.

(c) Except as provided in subsection (e) of this section, on request of a party in interest and after notice and a hearing, the court may convert a case under this chapter to a case under chapter 7 of this title, or may dismiss a case under this chapter, whichever is in the best interests of creditors and the estate, for cause, including—

(1) unreasonable delay by the debtor that is prejudicial to creditors;

(2) nonpayment of any fees and charges required under chapter 123 of title 28;

(3) failure to file a plan timely under section 1321 of this title;

(4) denial of confirmation of a plan under section 1325 of this title and denial of additional time for filing another plan or a modification of a plan;

(5) material default by the debtor with respect to a term of a confirmed plan;

(6) revocation of the order of confirmation under section 1330 of this title, and denial of confirmation of a modified plan under section 1329 of this title; and

(7) termination of a confirmed plan by reason of the occurrence of a condition specified in the plan.

(d) Except as provided in subsection (e) of this section, at any time before the confirmation of a plan under section 1325 of this title, on request of a party in interest and after notice and a hearing, the court may convert a case under this chapter to a case under chapter 11 of this title.

(e) The court may not convert a case under this chapter to a case under chapter 7 or 11 of this title if the debtor is a farmer, unless the debtor requests such conversion.

(f) Notwithstanding any other provision of this section, a case may not be converted to a case under another chapter of this title unless the debtor may be a debtor under such chapter.

SUBCHAPTER II—THE PLAN

§ 1321. Filing of plan

The debtor shall file a plan.

§ 1322. Contents of plan

(a) The plan shall—

(1) provide for the submission of all or such portion of future earnings or other future income of the debtor to the supervision and control of the trustee as is necessary for the execution of the plan;

(2) provide for the full payment, in deferred cash payments of all claims entitled to priority under section 507 of this title, unless the holder of a particular claim agrees to a different treatment of such claim; and

(3) if the plan classifies claims, provide the same treatment for each claim within a particular class.

(b) Subject to subsections (a) and (c) of this section, the plan may—

(1) designate a class or classes of unsecured claims, as provided in section 1122 of this title, but may not discriminate unfairly against any class so designated;

(2) modify the rights of holders of secured claims, other than a claim secured only by a security interest in real property that is the debtor's principal residence, or of holders of unsecured claims;

(3) provide for the curing or waiving of any default;

(4) provide for payments on any unsecured claim to be made concurrently with payments on any secured claim or any unsecured claim;

(5) notwithstanding paragraph (2) of this subsection, provide for the curing of any default within a reasonable time and maintenance of payments while the case is pending on any unsecured claim or secured claim on which the last payment is due after the date on which the final payment under the plan is due;

(6) provide for the payment of all or any part of any claim allowed under section 1305 of this title;

(7) provide for the assumption or rejection of any executory contract or unexpired lease of the debtor not previously rejected under section 365 of this title;

(8) provide for the payment of all or any part of a claim against the debtor from property of the estate or property of the debtor;

(9) provide for the vesting of property of the estate, on confirmation of the plan or at a later time, in the debtor or in any other entity; and

(10) include any other appropriate provision not inconsistent with this title.

(c) The plan may not provide for payments over a period that is longer than three years, unless the court, for cause, approves a longer period, but the court may not approve a period that is longer than five years.

§ 1323. Modification of plan before confirmation

(a) The debtor may modify the plan at any time before confirmation, but may not modify the plan so that the plan as modified fails to meet the requirements of section 1322 of this title.

(b) After the debtor files a modification under this section, the plan as modified becomes the plan.

(c) Any holder of a secured claim that has accepted or rejected the plan is deemed to have accepted or rejected, as the case may be, the plan as modified, unless the modification provides for a change in the rights of such holder from what such rights were under the plan before modification, and such holder changes such holder's previous acceptance or rejection.

§ 1324. Confirmation hearing

After notice, the court shall hold a hearing on the confirmation of the plan. A party in interest may object to the confirmation of the plan.

§ 1325. Confirmation of plan

(a) The court shall confirm a plan if—

(1) the plan complies with the provisions of this chapter and with other applicable provisions of this title;

(2) any fee, charge, or amount required under chapter 123 of title 28, or by the plan, to be paid before confirmation, has been paid;

(3) the plan has been proposed in good faith and not by any means forbidden by law;

(4) the value, as of the effective date of the plan, of property to be distributed under the plan on account of each allowed unsecured claim is not less than the amount that would be paid on such claim if the estate of the debtor were liquidated under chapter 7 of this title on such date;

(5) with respect to each allowed secured claim provided for by the plan—

(A) the holder of such claim has accepted the plan;

(B)(i) the plan provides that the holder of such claim retain the lien securing such claim; and

(ii) the value, as of the effective date of the plan, of property to be distributed under the plan on account of such claim is not less than the allowed amount of such claim; or

(C) the debtor surrenders the property securing such claim to such holder; and

(6) the debtor will be able to make all payments under the plan and to comply with the plan.

(b) After confirmation of a plan, the court may order any entity from whom the debtor receives income to pay all or any part of such income to the trustee.

§ 1326. Payments

(a) Before or at the time of each payment to creditors under the plan, there shall be paid—

(1) any unpaid claim of the kind specified in section 507(a)(1) of this title; and

(2) if a standing trustee appointed under section 1302(d) is serving in the case, the percentage fee fixed for such standing trustee under section 1302(e) of this title.

(b) Except as otherwise provided in the plan or in the order confirming the plan, the trustee shall make payments to creditors under the plan.

§ 1327. Effect of confirmation

(a) The provisions of a confirmed plan bind the debtor and each creditor, whether or not the claim of such creditor is provided for by the plan, and whether or not such creditor has objected to, has accepted, or has rejected the plan.

(b) Except as otherwise provided in the plan or the order confirming the plan, the confirmation of a plan vests all of the property of the estate in the debtor.

(c) Except as otherwise provided in the plan or in the order confirming the plan, the property vesting in the debtor under subsection (b) of this section is free and clear of any claim or interest of any creditor provided for by the plan.

§ 1328. Discharge

(a) As soon as practicable after completion by the debtor of all payments under the plan, unless the court approves a written waiver of discharge executed by the debtor after the order for relief under this chapter, the court shall grant the debtor a discharge of all debts provided for by the plan or disallowed under section 502 of this title, except any debt—

(1) provided for under section 1322(b)(5) of this title; or

(2) of the kind specified in section 523(a)(5) of this title.

(b) At any time after the confirmation of the plan and after notice and a hearing, the court may grant a discharge to a debtor that has not completed payments under the plan only if—

(1) the debtor's failure to complete such payments is due to circumstances for which the debtor should not justly be held accountable;

(2) the value, as of the effective date of the plan, of property actually distributed under the plan on account of each allowed unsecured claim is not less than the amount that would have been paid on such claim if the estate of the debtor had been liquidated under chapter 7 of this title on such date; and

(3) modification of the plan under section 1329 of this title is not practicable.

(c) A discharge granted under subsection (b) of this section discharges the debtor from all unsecured debts provided for by the plan or disallowed under section 502 of this title, except any debt—

(1) provided for under section 1322(b)(5) of this title; or

(2) of a kind specified in section 523(a) of this title.

(d) Notwithstanding any other provision of this section, a discharge granted under this section does not discharge the debtor from any debt based on an allowed claim filed under section 1305(a)(2) of this title if prior approval by the trustee of the debtor's incurring such debt was practicable and was not obtained.

(e) On request of a party in interest before one year after a discharge under this section is granted, and after notice and a hearing, the court may revoke such discharge only if—

(1) such discharge was obtained through fraud; and

(2) knowledge of such fraud came to the requesting party after such discharge was granted.

§ 1329. Modification of plan after confirmation

(a) At any time after confirmation but before the completion of payments under a plan, the plan may be modified to—

(1) increase or reduce the amount of payments on claims of a particular class provided for by the plan;

(2) extend or reduce the time for such payments; or

(3) alter the amount of the distribution to a creditor whose claim is provided for by the plan, to the extent necessary to take account of any payment of such claim other than under the plan.

(b)(1) Sections 1322(a), 1322(b), and 1323(c) of this title and the requirements of section 1325(a) of this title apply to any modification under subsection (a) of this section.

(2) The plan as modified becomes the plan unless, after notice and a hearing, such modification is disapproved.

(c) A plan modified under this section may not provide for payments over a period that expires after three years after the time that the first payment under the original confirmed plan was due, unless the court, for cause, approves a longer period, but the court may not approve a period that expires after five years after such time.

§ 1330. Revocation of an order of confirmation

(a) On request of a party in interest at any time within 180 days after the date of the entry of an order of confirmation under section 1325 of this title, and after notice and a hearing, the court may revoke such order if such order was procured by fraud.

(b) If the court revokes an order of confirmation under subsection (a) of this section, the court shall dispose of the case under section 1307 of this title, unless, within the time fixed by the court, the debtor proposes and the court confirms a modification of the plan under section 1329 of this title.

CHAPTER 15—UNITED STATES TRUSTEES

Sec.

SUBCHAPTER VII—LIQUIDATION

SUBCHAPTER XI—REORGANIZATION

SUBCHAPTER XIII—ADJUSTMENT OF DEBTS OF AN INDIVIDUAL WITH REGULAR INCOME

§ 1501. Applicability of chapter

This chapter applies only in cases under this title pending in the following districts:

(1) District of Maine, District of New Hampshire, District of Massachusetts, and District of Rhode Island.

(2) Southern District of New York.

(3) District of Delaware and District of New Jersey.

(4) Eastern District of Virginia and District of District of Columbia.

(5) Northern District of Alabama.

(6) Northern District of Texas.

(7) Northern District of Illinois.

(8) District of Minnesota, District of North Dakota, and District of South Dakota.

(9) Central District of California.

(10) District of Colorado and District of Kansas.

SUBCHAPTER I—GENERAL PROVISIONS

§ 15101. Definitions

In this title—

(1) "entity" includes United States trustee; and

(2) "governmental unit" does not include United States trustee while serving as a trustee in a case under this title.

§ 15102. Rule of construction

In this title, a reference to a section that is made inapplicable under section 15103(f) of this chapter refers to the section of this chapter that replaces such inapplicable section.

§ 15103. Applicability of subchapters and sections

(a) Subchapters I and III of this chapter apply in a case under chapter 7, 11, or 13 of this title, except that section 15343 of this title does not apply in a case concerning a railroad.

(b) Subchapter VII of this chapter applies only in a case under chapter 7 of this title.

(c) Subchapter XI of this chapter applies only in a case under chapter 11 of this title that does not concern a railroad.

(d) Section 151163 of this title applies only in a case concerning a railroad.

(e) Subchapter XIII of this chapter applies only in a case under chapter 13 of this title.

(f) Sections 303(g), 322(b), 324, 326(b), 343, 345(b), 701(a), 703(b), 703(c), 704(8), 727(c), 727(d), 727(e), 1102(a), 1104, 1105, 1163, 1302(a), 1302(d), 1302(e), and 1326(a) of this title do not apply in a case under this title.

SUBCHAPTER III—CASE ADMINISTRATION

§ 15303. Involuntary cases

At any time after the commencement of an involuntary case under chapter 7 of this title but before an order for relief in the case, the court, on request of a party in interest, after notice to the debtor and a hearing, and if necessary to preserve the property of the estate or to prevent loss to the estate, may order the United States trustee to appoint an interim trustee under section 15701 of this title to take possession of the property of the estate and to operate any business of the debtor. Before an order for relief, the debtor may regain possession of property in the possession of a trustee ordered appointed under this subsection if the debtor files such bond as the court requires, conditioned on the debtor's accounting for and delivering to the trustee if there is an order for relief in the case, such property, or the value, as of the date the debtor regains possession, of such property.

§ 15321. Eligibility to serve as trustee

The United States trustee for the judicial district in which the case is pending is eligible to serve as trustee in the case.

§ 15322. Qualification of trustee

(a) A United States trustee qualifies whenever such trustee serves in a case under this title.

(b) The United States trustee shall determine—

(1) the amount of a bond filed under section 322(a)(2); and

(2) the sufficiency of the surety on such bond.

§ 15324. Removal of trustee or examiner

The court, after notice and a hearing, may remove a trustee other than the United States trustee, or an examiner, for cause.

§ 15326. Limitation on compensation of trustee

In a case under chapter 13 of this title, the court may not allow compensation for services or reimbursement of expenses of the United States trustee or of a standing trustee appointed under section 586(b) of title 28, but may allow reasonable compensation under section 330 of this title of a trustee appointed under section 1302(a) of this title for the trustee's services, payable after the trustee renders such services, not to exceed five percent upon all payments under the plan.

§ 15330. Compensation of officers

In a case in which the United States trustee serves as trustee, the compensation of the trustee under section 330 of this title shall be paid to the clerk of the bankruptcy court, and by the clerk, into the Treasury.

§ 15343. Examination of the debtor

The debtor shall appear and submit to examination under oath at the meeting of creditors under section 341(a) of this title. Creditors, any indenture trustee, any trustee or examiner in the case, or the United States trustee may examine the debtor.

§ 15345. Money of estates

(a) Except with respect to a deposit or investment that is insured or guaranteed by the United States or by a department, agency, or instrumentality of the United States or backed by the full faith and credit of the United States, the trustee shall require from an entity with which such money is deposited or invested—

(1) a bond—

(A) in favor of the United States;

(B) secured by the undertaking of a corporate surety approved by the United States trustee for the district in which the case is pending; and

(C) conditioned on—

(i) a proper accounting for all money so deposited or invested and for any return on such money;

(ii) prompt repayment of such money and return; and

(iii) faithful performance of duties as a depository; or

(2) the deposit of securities of the kind specified in section 15 of title 6.

(b) The United States trustee may aggregate money of estates for which such United States trustee serves as trustee for deposit or investment under this section, in order to increase the return on such money, taking into account the safety of such deposit or investment. The United States trustee shall maintain complete records identifying separately the money of each estate included in such an aggregation. Any return on any such deposit or investment shall be paid by the United States trustee into the Treasury.

SUBCHAPTER VII—LIQUIDATION

§ 15701. Interim trustee

(a) Promptly after the order for relief under chapter 7 of this title, the United States trustee shall appoint one disinterested person that is a member of the panel of private trustee established under section 586(a)(1) of title 28 or that was serving as trustee in the case immediately before the order for relief under this chapter to serve as interim trustee in the case.

(b) If none of such persons is willing to serve as interim trustee in the case, then the United States trustee shall serve as interim trustee in the case.

§ 15703. Successor trustee

(a) Pending election of a trustee under section 703(a) of this title, if necessary to preserve or prevent loss to the estate, the United States trustee may appoint an interim trustee in the manner specified in section 15701(a) of this title. Section 701(b) and 701(c) of this title apply to such interim trustee.

(b) If creditors do not elect a successor trustee under section 703(a) of this title, or if a trustee is needed in a case reopened under section 350 of this title, then the United States truste shall serve, or shall appoint one disinterested person that is a member of the panel of private trustees established under section 586(a)(1) of title 28 to serve, as trustee in the case.

§ 15704. Duties of trustee

The trustee shall make a final report and file a final account of the administration of the estate with the court and with the United States trustee.

§ 15727. Discharge

(a)(1) The trustee, a creditor, or the United States trustee may object to discharge under section 727(a) of this title.

(2) On request of a party in interest, the court may order the United States trustee to examine the acts and conduct of the debtor to determine whether a ground exists for denial of discharge.

(b) On request of the trustee, a creditor, or the United States trustee, and after notice and a hearing, the court shall revoke a discharge granted under section 727(a) of this title if—

(1) such discharge was obtained through the fraud of the debtor, and the requesting party did not know of such fraud until after the granting of such discharge;

(2) the debtor acquired property that is property of the estate, or became entitled to acquire property that would be property of the estate, and knowingly and fraudulently failed to report the acquisition of, or entitlement to, such property, or to deliver or surrender such property to the trustee; or

(3) the debtor committed an act specified in section 727(a)(6) of this title.

(c) The trustee, a creditor, or the United States trustee may request a revocation of a discharge—

(1) under section 727(d)(1) of this title within one year after such discharge was granted; or

(2) under section 727(d)(2) or 727(d)(3) of this title before the later of—

(A) one year after the granting of such discharge; and

(B) the date the case is closed.

SUBCHAPTER XI—REORGANIZATION

§ 151102. Creditors' and equity security holders' committees

(a) As soon as practicable after the order for relief under chapter 11 of this title, the United States trustee shall appoint a committee of creditors holding unsecured claims.

(b) On request of a party in interest of the court may order the appointment of additional committees of creditors or of equity security holders if necessary to assure adequate representation of creditors or of equity security holders. The United States trustee shall appoint any such committee.

§ 151104. Appointment of trustee or examiner

(a) At any time after the commencement of the case but before confirmation of a plan, on request of a party in interest or the United States trustee, and after notice and a hearing, the court shall order the appointment of a trustee—

(1) for cause, including fraud, dishonesty, incompetence, or gross mismanagement of the affairs of the debtor by current management, either before or after the commencement of the case, or similar cause, but not including the number of holders of securities of the debtor or the amount of assets or liabilities of the debtor; or

(2) if such appointment is in the interests of creditors, any equity security holders, and other interests of the estate, without regard to the number of holders of securities of the debtor or the amount of assets or liabilities of the debtor.

(b) If the court does not order the appointment of a trustee under this section, then at any time before the confirmation of a plan, on request of a party in interest or the United States trustee, and after notice and a hearing, the court shall order the appointment of an examiner to conduct such an investigation of the debtor as is appropriate, including an investigation of any allegations of fraud, dishonesty, incompetence, misconduct, mismanagement, or irregularity in the management of the affairs of the debtor of or by current or former management of the debtor, if—

(1) such appointment is in the best interest of creditors, any equity security holders, and other interests of the estate; or

(2) the debtor's fixed, liquidated, unsecured debts, other than debts for goods, services, or taxes, or owing to an insider, exceed $5,000,000.

(c) If the court orders the appointment of a trustee or an examiner, if a trustee or an examiner dies or resigns during the case or is removed under section 324 of this title, or if a trustee fails to qualify under section 322 of this title, then the United States trustee, after consultation with parties in interest, shall appoint, subject to the court's approval, one disinterested person other than the United States trustee to serve as trustee or examiner, as the case may be, in the case.

§ 151105. Termination of trustee's appointment

At any time before confirmation of a plan, on request of a party in interest or the United States trustee, and after notice and a hearing, the court may terminate the trustee's appointment and restore the debtor to possession and management of the property of the estate, and operation of the debtor's business.

§ 151!63. Appointment of trustee

As soon as practicable after the order for relief the Secretary of Transportation shall submit a list of five disinterested persons that are qualified and willing to serve as trustee in the case. The United States trustee shall appoint one of such persons to serve as trustee in the case.

SUBCHAPTER XIII—ADJUSTMENT OF DEBTS OF AN INDIVIDUAL WITH REGULAR INCOME

§ 151302. Trustee

(a) If the United States trustee has appointed an individual under section 586(b) of title 28 to serve as standing trustee in cases under chapter 13 of this title and if such individual qualifies under section 322 of this title, then such individual shall serve as trustee in the case. The United States trustee shall serve as trustee in the case otherwise.

(b) The trustee shall—

(1) perform the duties specified in sections 704(2), 704(3), 704(4), 704(5), 704(6), and 704(8) of this title;

(2) appear and be heard at any hearing that concerns—

(A) the value of property subject to a lien;

(B) confirmation of a plan; or

(C) modification of the plan after confirmation; and

(3) advise, other than on legal matters, and assist the debtor in performance under the plan.

§ 151326. Payments

Before or at the time of each payment to creditors under the plan, there shall be paid—

(1) any unpaid claim of the kind specified in section 507(a)(1) of this title; and

(2) if a standing trustee appointed under section 586(b) of title 28 is serving in the case, the percentage fee fixed for such standing trustee under section 586(e)(1)(B) of title 28.

TITLE II—AMENDMENTS TO TITLE 28 OF THE UNITED STATES CODE AND TO THE FEDERAL RULES OF EVIDENCE

SEC. 201. (a) Title 28 of the United States Code is amended by inserting immediately after chapter 5 the following:

"CHAPTER 6—BANKRUPTCY COURTS

"Sec.
"151. Creation and composition of bankruptcy courts.
"152. Appointment of bankruptcy judges.
"153. Tenure and residence of bankruptcy judges.
"154. Salaries of bankruptcy judges.
"155. Chief judge; precedence of bankruptcy judges.
"156. Division of business among bankruptcy judges.
"157. Times of holding court.
"158. Accommodations at places for holding court.
"159. Vacant judgeship as affecting proceedings.
"160. Appellate panels.

"§ 151. Creation and composition of bankruptcy courts

"(a) There shall be in each judicial district, as an adjunct to the district court for such district, a bankruptcy court which shall be a court of record known as the United States Bankruptcy Court for the district.

"(b) Each bankruptcy court shall consist of the bankruptcy judge or judges for the district in regular active service. Justices or judges designated and assigned shall be competent to sit as judges of the bankruptcy court.

"(c) Except as otherwise provided by law, or rule or order of court, the judicial power of a bankruptcy court with respect to any action, suit or proceeding may be exercised by a single bankruptcy judge, who may preside alone and hold a regular or special session of court at the same time other sessions are held by other bankruptcy judges.

"§ 152. Appointment of bankruptcy judges

"The President shall appoint, by and with the advice and consent of the Senate, bankruptcy judges for the several judicial districts. In each instance, the President shall give due consideration to the recommended nominee or nominees of the Judicial Council of the Circuit within which an appointment is to be made.

"§ 153. Tenure and residence of bankruptcy judges

"(a) Each bankruptcy judge shall hold office for a term of 14 years. but may continue to perform the duties of his office until his successor takes office, unless such office has been eliminated.

"(b) Removal of a bankruptcy judge during the term for which he is appointed shall be only for incompetency, misconduct, neglect of duty, or physical or mental disability. Removal shall be by the judicial council of the circuit or circuits in which the bankruptcy judge serves, but removal may not occur unless a majority of all the judges of such circuit council or councils concur in the order of removal. Before any order of removal may be entered, a full specification of the charges shall be furnished to the bankruptcy judge, and he shall be accorded an opportunity to be heard on the charges. Any cause for removal of any bankruptcy judge coming to the knowledge of the Director of the Administrative Office of the United States Courts shall be reported by him to the chief judge of the circuit or circuits in which he serves, and a copy of the report shall at the same time be transmitted to the circuit council or councils and to the bankruptcy judge.

"(c) Each bankruptcy judge shall reside in the district or one of the districts for which he is appointed, or within 20 miles of his official station.

"(d) If the public interest and the nature of the business of a bankruptcy court require that a bankruptcy judge should maintain his abode at or near a particular part of the district the judicial council of the circuit may so declare and may make an appropriate order. If the bankruptcy judges of such a district are unable to agree as to which of them shall maintain his abode at or near the place or within the area specified in such an order the judicial council of the circuit may decide which of them shall do so.

"§ 154. Salaries of bankruptcy judges

"Each judge of a bankruptcy court shall receive a salary at an annual rate of $50,000, subject to adjustment under section 225 of the Federal Salary Act of 1967 (2 U.S.C. 351–361), and section 461 of this title.

"§ 155. Chief judge; precedence of bankruptcy judges

"(a) In each district having more than one judge the bankruptcy judge in regular active service who is senior in commission and under seventy years of age shall be the chief judge of the bankruptcy court. If all the bankruptcy judges in regular active service are 70 years of age or older the youngest shall act as chief judge until a judge has been appointed and qualified who is under 70 years of age, but a judge may not act as chief judge until he has served as a bankruptcy judge for one year.

"(b) The chief judge shall have precedence and preside at any session which he attends.

"Other bankruptcy judges shall have precedence and preside according to the seniority of their commissions. Judges whose commissions bear the same date shall have precedence according to seniority in age.

"(c) A judge whose commission extends over more than one district shall be junior to all bankruptcy judges except in the district in which he resided at the time he entered upon the duties of his office.

"(d) If the chief judge desires to be relieved of his duties as chief judge while retaining his active status as a bankruptcy judge, he may so certify to the chief judge of the court of appeals for the circuit in which the bankruptcy judge serves, and thereafter the bankruptcy judge in active service next in precedence and willing to serve shall be designated by the chief judge of the court of appeals as the chief judge of the bankruptcy court.

"(e) If a chief judge is temporarily unable to perform his duties as such, they shall be performed by the bankruptcy judge in active service, present in the district and able and qualified to act, who is next in precedence.

"(f) Service as a referee in bankruptcy or as a bankruptcy judge under the Bankruptcy Act shall be taken into account in the determination of seniority of commission under this section.

"§ 156. Division of business among bankruptcy judges

"The business of a bankruptcy court having more than one judge shall be divided among the judges as provided by the rules and orders of the court.

"The chief judge of the bankruptcy court shall be responsible for the observance of such rules and orders, and shall divide the business and assign the cases so far as such rules and orders do not otherwise prescribe.

"If the bankruptcy judges in any district are unable to agree upon the adoption of rules or orders for that purpose the judicial council of the circuit shall make the necessary orders.

"§ 157. Times of holding court

"(a) The bankruptcy court at each designated location shall be deemed to be in continuous session on all business days throughout the year.

"(b) Each bankruptcy court may establish by local rule or order schedules of court sessions at designated places of holding court other than the headquarters office of the court. Such schedules may be pretermitted by order of the court.

"(c) Bankruptcy court may be held at any place within the territory served, in any case, on order of the bankruptcy court, for the convenience of the parties, on such notice as the bankruptcy court orders.

"§ 158. Accommodations at places for holding court

"Court shall be held only at places where Federal quarters and accommodations are available, or suitable quarters and accommodations are furnished without cost to the United States. The foregoing restrictions shall not, however, preclude the Administrator of General Services, at the request of the Director of the Administrative Office of the United States Courts, from providing such court quarters and accommodations as the Administrator determines can appropriately be made available at places where court is authorized by law to be held, but only if such court quarters and accommodations have been approved as necessary by the judicial council of the appropriate circuit.

"§ 159. Vacant judgeship as affecting proceedings

"When the office of a bankruptcy judge becomes vacant, all pending process, pleadings and proceedings shall, when necessary, be continued by the clerk until a judge is appointed or designated to hold such court.

"§ 160. Appellate panels

"(a) If the circuit council of a circuit orders application of this section to a district within such circuit, the chief judge of each circuit shall designate panels of three bankruptcy judges to hear appeals from judgments, orders, and decrees of the bankruptcy court of the United States for such district. Except as provided in section 293(e) of this title, a panel shall be composed only of bankruptcy judges for districts located in the circuit in which the appeal arises. The chief judge shall designate a sufficient number of such panels so that appeals may be heard and disposed of expeditiously.

"(b) A panel designated under subsection (a) of this section may not hear an appeal from a judgment, order, or decree entered by a member of the panel.

"(c) When hearing an appeal, a panel designated under subsection (a) of this section shall sit at a place convenient to the parties to the appeal.".

(b) The table of chapters of part I of title 28 of the United States Code is amended by inserting immediately after the item relating to chapter 5 of such title the following:

"6. Bankruptcy courts .... 151".

SEC. 202. Section 291(c) of title 28 of the United States Code is amended by inserting "or bankruptcy" immediately after "to hold a district".

SEC. 203. Section 292(b) of title 28 of the United States Code is amended by inserting "or a bankruptcy court" immediately after "to hold a district court".

SEC. 204. Section 292(d) of title 28 of the United States Code is amended—

(1) by striking out "either";

(2) by inserting "bankruptcy court," immediately after "in a"; and

(3) by inserting a comma immediately after "district court".

SEC. 205. Section 293 of title 28 of the United States Code is amended by adding at the end thereof the following:

"(e)(1) The Chief Justice of the United States may designate and assign temporarily a bankruptcy judge of one circuit for service in a bankruptcy court in another circuit upon presentation of a certificate of necessity by the chief judge or circuit justice of the circuit wherein the need arises.

"(2) The chief judge of a circuit may, in the public interest, designate and assign temporarily a bankruptcy judge of the circuit to hold a bankruptcy court in any district within the circuit.".

SEC. 206. Section 294 of title 28 of the United States Code is amended—

(1) in subsection (c), by deleting "or district" and inserting "district or bankruptcy judge"; and

(2) in subsection (d), by striking out "or district judge" and inserting in lieu thereof ", district judge or bankruptcy judge".

SEC. 207. Section 295 of title 28 of the United States Code is amended by striking out "or district" and inserting in lieu thereof "district, or bankruptcy".

SEC. 208. Section 331 of title 28 of the United States Code is amended—

(1) by striking out "and a district judge from each judicial circuit" in the first sentence of the first paragraph thereof and inserting "a district judge from each judicial circuit, and two bankruptcy judges" in lieu thereof;

(2) by inserting "circuit and district" in the second paragraph—

(A) immediately after "amended section the";

(B) immediately after "for one year, the"; and

(C) immediately after "two years and the";

(3) by inserting immediately after the second paragraph the following: "The bankruptcy judges to be summoned shall be chosen at large by all the bankruptcy judges. Each bankruptcy judge chosen shall serve as a member of the conference for three successive years, except that in the year following the effective date of this sentence the bankruptcy judges shall choose one bankruptcy judge to serve for two years.";

(4) by inserting "or a bankruptcy judge chosen by the bankruptcy judges" immediately after "judges of the circuit" in the first sentence in the third paragraph; and

(5) by inserting "or any other bankruptcy judge" immediately before the period in the first sentence in the third paragraph.

SEC. 209. Section 332(d) of title 28 of the United States Code is amended by inserting "and bankruptcy judges" immediately after "The district judges".

SEC. 210. Section 333 of title 28 of the United States Code is amended by striking out "and district" and inserting in lieu thereof ", district, and bankruptcy".

SEC. 211. Section 376(a)(2)(A) of title 28 of the United States Code is amended by inserting ", or (iii) in the case of a bankruptcy judge, after retirement under section 337 of this title" immediately before the semicolon.

SEC. 213. Section 451 of title 28 of the United States Code is amended—

(1) by inserting a comma and "and bankruptcy courts, the judges of which are entitled to hold office for a term of 14 years" immediately before the period at the end of the paragraph beginning with "The term 'court of the United States' "; and

(2) by inserting a comma and "and judge of the bankruptcy courts, the judges of which are entitled to hold office for a term of 14 years" immediately before the period at the end of the paragraph beginning with "The term 'judge of the United States' ".

SEC. 214. (a) Sections 455(a) and 455(e) of title 28 of the United States Code are each amended by striking out "magistrate, or referee in bankruptcy" each place it appears and inserting in lieu thereof "or magistrate".

(b) The heading for section 455 of title 28 of the United States Code is amended by striking out **"magistrate, or referee in bankruptcy"** and inserting in lieu thereof, **"or magistrate"**.

(c) The item relating to section 455 in the table of sections of chapter 21 of title 28 of the United States Code is amended by striking out "magistrate, or referee in bankruptcy" and inserting in lieu thereof "or magistrate".

SEC. 215. Section 456 of title 28 of the United States Code is amended—

(1) by striking out "and the United States District Court for the District of Columbia," and inserting in lieu thereof "the United States District Court for the District of Columbia, and the United States Bankruptcy Court for the District of Columbia,";

(2) by striking out "and district" and inserting in lieu thereof ", district and bankruptcy"; and

(3) by striking out "and each district judge" and inserting in lieu thereof ", each district judge; and each bankruptcy judge".

SEC. 216. Section 457 of title 28 of the United States Code is amended by inserting "of bankruptcy courts," immediately after "The record".

SEC. 217. (a) The heading for section 460 of title 28 of the United States Code is amended by striking out **"Alaska,"**.

(b) The item relating to section 460 in the table of sections of chapter 21 of title 28 of the United States Code is amended by striking out "Alaska,".

SEC. 218. Section 506 of title 28 of the United States Code is amended by striking out "nine" and inserting in lieu thereof "ten".

SEC. 219. (a) Section 526(a)(1) of title 28 of the United States Code is amended by striking out "and marshals" and inserting in lieu thereof ", marshals, and trustees".

(b) The heading for section 526 of title 28 of the United States Code is amended by striking out "**and marshals**" and inserting in lieu thereof "**, marshals, and trustee**".

(c) The item relating to section 526 in the table of sections of chapter 31 of title 28 of the United States Code is amended by striking out "**and marshals**" and inserting in lieu thereof "**, marshals, and trustees**".

SEC. 220. Section 526(a)(2) of title 28 of the United States Code is amended—

(1) by striking out "referees,";

(2) by striking out "and receivers in bankruptcy" and inserting in lieu thereof "in cases under title 11"; and

(3) by striking out "commissioners" and inserting "magistrates" in lieu thereof.

SEC. 221. Section 569(a) of title 28 of the United States Code is amended by striking out "of the district court" and inserting in lieu thereof "of the bankruptcy, of the district court,".

SEC. 222. Section 571(a) of title 28 of the United States Code is amended—

(1) by striking out "and of the marshals" and inserting in lieu thereof "of the marshals"; and

(2) by inserting ", and of the United States trustees, their assistants, staff and other employees" immediately after "clerical assistance".

SEC. 223. Section 571(b) of title 28 of the United States Code is amended by striking out "and district" and inserting in lieu thereof ", district, and bankruptcy".

SEC. 224. (a) Title 28 of the United States Code is amended by inserting immediately after chapter 37 the following:

"CHAPTER 39—UNITED STATES TRUSTEES

"Sec.

"§ 581. United States trustees

"(a) The Attorney General shall appoint one United States trustee for each of the following districts or groups of districts:

"(1) District of Maine, District of New Hampshire, District of Massachusetts, and District of Rhode Island.

"(2) Southern District of New York.

"(3) District of Delaware and District of New Jersey.

"(4) Eastern District of Virginia and District of District of Columbia.

"(5) Northern District of Alabama.

"(6) Northern District of Texas.

"(7) Northern District of Illinois.

"(8) District of Minnesota, District of North Dakota, District of South Dakota.

"(9) Central District of California.

"(10) District of Colorado and District of Kansas.

"(b) Each United States trustee shall be appointed for a term of seven years. On the expiration of his term, a United States trustee shall continue to perform the duties of his Office until his successor is appointed and qualifies.

"(c) Each United States trustee is subject to removal for cause by the Attorney General.

"§ 582. Assistant United States trustees

"(a) The Attorney General may appoint one or more assistant United States trustees in any district when the public interest so requires.

"(b) Each assistant United States trustee is subject to removal for cause by the Attorney General.

"§ 583. Oath of office

"Each United States trustee and assistant United States trustee, before taking office, shall take an oath to execute faithfully his duties.

"§ 584. Official stations

"The Attorney General may determine the official stations of the United States trustees and assistant United States trustees within the districts for which they were appointed.

"§ 585. Vacancies

"The Attorney General may appoint an acting United States trustee for a district in which the office of United States trustee is vacant, or may designate a United States trustee for another judicial district to serve as trustee for the district in which such vacancy exists. The individual so appointed or designated may serve until the earlier of 90 days after such appointment or designation, as the case may be, or the date on which the vacancy is filled by appointment under section 581 of this title.

"§ 586. Duties; supervision by Attorney General

"(a) Each United States trustee, within his district, shall—

"(1) establish, maintain, and supervise a panel of private trustees that are eligible and available to serve as trustees in cases under chapter 7 of title 11;

"(2) serve as and perform the duties of a trustee in a case under title 11 when required under title 11 to serve as trustee in such a case;

"(3) supervise the administration of cases and trustees in cases under chapter 7, 11, or 13 of title 11;

"(4) deposit or invest under section 345 of title 11 money received as trustee in cases under title 11;

"(5) perform the duties prescribed for the United States trustee under title 11; and

"(6) make such reports as the Attorney General directs.

"(b) If the number of cases under chapter 13 of title 11 commenced in a particular judicial district so warrant, the United States trustee for such district may, subject to the approval of the Attorney General, appoint one or more individuals to serve as standing trustee, or designate one or more assistant United States trustee, in cases under such chapter. The United States trustee for such district shall supervise any such individual appointed as standing trustee in the performance of the duties of standing trustee.

"(c) Each United States trustee shall be under the general supervision of the Attorney General, who shall provide general coordination and assistance to the United States trustees.

"(d) The Attorney General shall prescribe by rule qualifications for membership on the panels established by United States trustees under subsection (a)(1) of this section, and qualifications for appointment under subsection (b) of this section to serve as standing trustee in cases under chapter 13 of title 11. The Attorney General may not require that an individual be an attorney in order to qualify for appointment under subsection (b) of this section to serve as standing trustee in cases under chapter 13 of title 11.

"(e)(1) The Attorney General, after consultation with a United States trustee that has appointed an individual under subsection (b) of this section to serve as standing trustee in cases under chapter 13 of title 11, shall fix—

"(A) a maximum annual compensation for such individual, not to exceed the lowest annual rate of basic pay in effect for grade GS–16 of the General Schedule prescribed under section 5332 of title 5; and

"(B) a percentage fee, not to exceed ten percent, based on such maximum annual compensation and the actual, necessary expenses incurred by such individual as standing trustee.

"(2) Such individual shall collect such percentage fee from all payments under plans in the cases under chapter 13 of title 11 for which such individual serves as standing trustee. Such individual shall pay to the United States trustee, and the United States trustee shall pay to the Treasury—

"(A) any amount by which the actual compensation of such individual exceeds five percent upon all payments under plans in cases under chapter 13 of title 11 for which such individual serves as standing trustee; and

"(B) any amount by which the percentage for all such cases exceeds—

"(i) such individual actual compensation for such cases, as adjusted under subparagraph (A) of this paragraph; plus

"(ii) the actual, necessary expenses incurred by such individual as standing trustee in such cases.

"§ 587. Salaries

"The Attorney General shall fix the annual salaries of United States trustees and assistant United States trustees at rates of compensation not to exceed the lowest annual rate of basic pay in effect for grade GS–16 of the General Schedule prescribed under section 5332 of title 5.

"§ 588. Expenses

"Necessary office expenses of the United States trustee shall be allowed when authorized by the Attorney General.

"§ 589. Staff and other employees

"The United States trustee may employ staff and other employees on approval of the Attorney General.".

(b) The table of chapters of part II of title 28 of the United States Code is amended by inserting at the end thereof the following:

"39. United States Trustees .... 581".

SEC. 225. (a) Section 604(a) of title 28 of the United States Code is amended—

(1) by redesignating paragraph (13) as paragraph (14); and

(2) by inserting immediately after paragraph (12) the following:

"(13) Lay before Congress, annually, statistical tables that will accurately reflect the business transacted by the several bankruptcy courts, and all other pertinent data relating to such courts;".

(b) Section 604 of title 28 of the United States Code, is amended by adding at the end thereof the following:

"(f) For each bankruptcy court, the Director shall name qualified persons to membership on the panel of trustees. The number and qualifications of persons named to membership on the panel of trustees shall be determined by rules and regulations to be adopted by the Director. An individual named to membership on the panel of trustees shall have a residency or office in the State served by the court or in any adjacent State. A corporation named to membership on the panel of trustees shall be authorized by its charter or by law to act as trustee and shall have an office in the State served by the court. The Director on his own initiative may at any time remove for cause a person named to a panel of trustees or remove a trustee appointed from the panel.".

SEC. 226. Section 610 of title 28 of the United States Code is amended by striking out "and district courts" and inserting in lieu thereof ", district courts, and bankruptcy courts".

SEC. 227. Section 620(b)(3) of title 28 of the United States Code is amended—

(1) by striking out "referees,"; and

(2) by striking out "commissioners" and inserting "magistrates" in lieu thereof.

SEC. 228. Section 621(a)(2) of title 28 of the United States Code is amended by striking out "and three active judges of the district courts of the United States" and inserting in lieu thereof ", three active judges of the district courts of the United States, one active judge of the bankruptcy courts of the United States".

SEC. 229. Section 621(b) of title 28 of the United States Code is amended by striking out everything after "years" down through "That a" and inserting in lieu thereof ". A".

SEC. 230. Chapter 42 of title 28 of the United States Code is amended—

(1) by striking out section 629; and

(2) by striking out the item relating to section 629 in the table of sections.

SEC. 231. Section 631(c) of title 28 of the United States Code is amended—

(1) by striking out "of the conference, a part-time referee in bankruptcy or" and inserting in lieu thereof "of the conference,"; and

(2) by striking out "magistrate and part-time referee in bankruptcy," and inserting in lieu thereof "magistrate and".

SEC. 232. Section 634(a) of title 28 of the United States Code is amended by striking out "for full-time and part-time United States magistrates not to exceed the rates now or hereafter provided for full-time and part-time referees in bankruptcy, respectively, referred to in section 40a of the Bankruptcy Act (11 U.S.C. 68(a)), as amended,", and inserting in lieu thereof "not to exceed $48,500 per annum, subject to adjustment in accordance with section 225 of the Federal Salary Act of 1967 and section 461 of this title,".

SEC. 233. (a) Title 28 of the United States Code is amended by inserting immediately after chapter 49 the following:

"CHAPTER 50—BANKRUPTCY COURTS

"§ 771. Clerks

"(a) Based on need each bankruptcy court may appoint a clerk who shall be subject to removal only by the court.

"(b) The clerk may appoint, with the approval of the court, necessary deputies, clerical assistants, and employees in such number as may be approved by the Director of the Administrative Office of the United States Courts. Such deputies, clerical assistants, and employees shall be subject to removal only by the clerk with the approval of the court. If there is no clerk, the Bankruptcy Judge shall perform the duties of this subsection.

"(c) The clerk of each bankruptcy court shall reside in the district for which he is appointed. The bankruptcy court may designate places within the district for the offices of the clerk and his deputies, and their official stations.

"(d) A clerk of a bankruptcy court or his deputy or assistant shall not receive any compensation or emoluments through any office or position to which he is appointed by the court, other than that received as such clerk, deputy or assistant, whether from the United States or from private litigants.

"(e) The clerk of each bankruptcy court shall pay into the Treasury all fees, costs and other moneys collected by him, except uncollected fees not required by Act of Congress to be prepaid.

"He shall make returns thereof to the Director of the Administrative Office of the United States Courts under regulations prescribed by him.

"§ 772. Other employees

"Bankruptcy judges may appoint necessary other employees, including law clerks and secretaries, subject to any limitation on the aggregate salaries of such employees which may be imposed by law.

"§ 773. Records of proceedings; reporters

"(a) The bankruptcy court shall require a record to be made, whenever practicable, of all proceedings in cases had in open court. The Judicial Conference shall prescribe that the record be taken by electronic sound recording means, by a court reporter appointed or employed by such bankruptcy court to take a verbatim record by shorthand or mechanical means, or by an employee of such court designated by such court to take such a verbatim record.

"(b) On the request of a party to a proceeding that has been recorded who has agreed to pay the fee for a transcript, or a judge of the bankruptcy court, a transcript of the original record of the requested parts of such proceeding shall be made and delivered promptly to such party or judge. Any such transcript that is certified shall be deemed prima facie a correct statement of the testimony taken and proceedings had. No transcript of the proceedings of the bankruptcy court shall be considered as official except those made from certified records.

"(c) Fees for transcripts furnished in proceedings to persons permitted to appeal in forma pauperis shall be paid by the United States out of money appropriated for that purpose if the trial judge or a circuit judge certifies that the appeal is not frivolous (but presents a substantial question).

"§ 774. Power to appoint

"Whenever a majority of the bankruptcy judges of any bankruptcy court cannot agree upon the appointment of any officer of such court, the chief judge shall make such appointment.

"§ 775. Salaries of employees

"The salary of an individual appointed or employed under section 771(a), 772, or 773(a) of this title shall be the same as the salary of an individual appointed or employed under section 751(a), 752, or 753(a) of this title, as the case may be. The salaries of individuals appointed under section 771(b) of this title shall be comparable to the salaries of individuals appointed under section 751(b) of this title.".

(b) The table of chapters of part III of title 28 of the United States Code is amended by inserting immediately after the item relating to chapter 49 the following:

"50. Bankruptcy Courts .... 771".

SEC. 234. Section 957(a) of title 28 of the United States Code is amended by inserting "or bankruptcy court" immediately after "district court".

SEC. 235. Section 959(b) of title 28 of the United States Code is amended by striking out "A" and inserting in lieu thereof "Except as provided in section 1166 of title 11, a".

SEC. 236. (a) Chapter 83 of title 28 of the United States Code is amended by inserting immediately after section 1292 the following:

"§ 1293. Bankruptcy appeals

"(a) The courts of appeals shall have jurisdiction of appeals from all final decisions of panels designated under section 160(a) of this title.

"(b) Notwithstanding section 1482 of this title, a court of appeals shall have jurisdiction of an appeal from a final judgment, order, or decree of an appellate panel created under section 160 or a District court of the United States or from a final judgment, order, or decree of a bankruptcy court of the United States if the parties to such appeal agree to a direct appeal to the court of appeals.".

(b) The table of sections of chapter 83 of title 28 of the United States Code is amended by inserting immediately after the item relating to section 1292 the following:

"1293. Bankruptcy appeals.".

SEC. 237. Section 1294 of title 28 of the United States Code is amended—

(1) by striking out "district and territorial" and inserting in lieu thereof "district, bankruptcy, and territorial";

(2) by striking out the period at the end thereof and inserting a semicolon; and

(3) by adding at the end thereof the following:

"(5) From a panel designated under section 160(a) of this title to the court of appeals for the circuit in which the panel was so designated;

"(6) From a bankruptcy court of the United States to the court of appeals for the circuit embracing the district in which the bankruptcy court is located.".

SEC. 238. (a) Section 1334 of title 28 of the United States Code is amended to read as follows:

"§ 1334. Bankruptcy appeals

"(a) The district courts for districts for which panels have not been ordered appointed under section 160 of this title shall have jurisdiction of appeals from all final judgments, orders, and decrees of bankruptcy courts.

"(b) The district courts for such districts shall have jurisdiction of appeals from interlocutory orders and decrees of bankruptcy courts, but only by leave of the district court to which the appeal is taken.

"(c) A district court may not refer an appeal under that section to a magistrate or to a special master.".

(b) The table of sections of chapter 85 of title 28 of the United States Code is amended by striking out the item relating to section 1334 and inserting in lieu thereof the following:

"1334. Bankruptcy appeals.".

SEC. 239. Section 1360(a) of title 28 of the United States Code is amended by striking out "within the Territory" and inserting in lieu thereof "within the State".

SEC. 240. (a) Chapter 87 of title 28 of the United States Code is amended by adding at the end thereof the following:

"§ 1408. Bankruptcy appeals

"An appeal under section 1334 of this title from a judgment, order, or decree of a bankruptcy court may be brought only in the judicial district in which such bankruptcy court is located.".

(b) The table of sections of chapter 87 of title 28 of the United States Code is amended by adding at the end thereof the following:

"1408. Bankruptcy appeals.".

SEC. 241. (a) Title 28 of the United States Code is amended by inserting immediately after chapter 89 the following:

"CHAPTER 90—DISTRICT COURTS AND BANKRUPTCY COURTS

"Sec.
"1471. Jurisdiction.
"1472. Venue of cases under title 11.
"1473. Venue of proceedings arising under or related to cases under title 11.
"1474. Venue of cases ancillary to foreign proceedings.
"1475. Change of venue.
"1476. Creation or alteration of district or division.
"1477. Cure or waiver of defects.
"1478. Removal to the bankruptcy courts.
"1479. Provisional remedies; security.
"1480. Jury trials.
"1481. Powers of bankruptcy court.
"1482. Appeals.

"§ 1471. Jurisdiction

"(a) Except as provided in susbection (b) of this section, the district courts shall have original and exclusive jurisdiction of all cases under title 11.

"(b) Notwithstanding any Act of Congress that confers exclusive jurisdiction on a court or courts other than the district courts, the district courts shall have original but not exclusive jurisdiction of all civil proceedings arising under title 11 or arising in or related to cases under title 11.

"(c) The bankruptcy court for the district in which a case under title 11 is commenced shall exercise all of the jurisdiction conferred by this section on the district courts.

"(d) Subsection (b) or (c) of this section does not prevent a district court or a bankruptcy court, in the interest of justice, from abstaining from hearing a particular proceeding arising under title 11 or arising in or related to a case under title 11. Such abstention, or a decision not to abstain, is not reviewable by appeal or otherwise.

"(e) The bankruptcy court in which a case under title 11 is commenced shall have exclusive jurisdiction of all of the property, wherever located, of the debtor, as of the commencement of such case.

§ 1472. Venue of cases under title 11

"Except as provided in section 1474 of this title, a case under title 11 may be commenced in the bankruptcy court for a district—

"(1) in which the domicile, residence, principal place of business, in the United States, or principal assets, in the United States, of the person or entity that is the subject of such case have been located for the 180 days immediately preceding such commencement, or for a longer portion of such 180-day period than the domicile, residence, principal place of business, in the United States, or principle assets, in the United States, of such person were located in any other district; or

"(2) in which there is pending a case under title 11 concerning such person's affiliate, general partner, or partnership.

"§ 1473. Venue of proceedings arising under or related to cases under title 11

"(a) Except as provided in subsections (b) and (d) of this section, a proceeding arising in or related to a case under title 11 may be commenced in the bankruptcy court in which such case is pending.

"(b) Except as provided in subsection (d) of this section, a trustee in a case under title 11 may commence a proceeding arising in or related to such case to recover a money judgment of or property worth less than $1,000 or a consumer debt of less than $5,000 only in the bankruptcy court for the district in which a defendant resides.

"(c) Except as provided in section (b) of this section, a trustee in a case under title 11 may commence a proceeding arising in or related to such case as statutory successor to the debtor or creditors under section 541 or 544(b) of title 11 in the bankruptcy court for the district where the State or Federal court sits in which, under applicable nonbankruptcy venue provisions, the debtor or creditors, as the case may be, may have commenced an action on which such proceeding is based if the case under title 11 had not been commenced.

"(d) A trustee may commence a proceeding arising under title 11 or arising in or related to a case under title 11 based on a claim arising after the commencement of such case from the operation of the business of the debtor only in the bankruptcy court for the district where a State or Federal court sits in which, under applicable nonbankruptcy venue provisions, an action on such claim may have been brought.

"(e) A proceeding arising in or related to a case under title 11, based on a claim arising after the commencement of such case from the operation of the business of the debtor, may be commenced against the representative of the estate in such case in the bankruptcy court for the district where the State or Federal court sits in which the party commencing such proceeding may, under applicable nonbankruptcy venue provisions, have brought an action on such claim, or in the bankruptcy court in which such case in pending.

"§ 1474. Venue of cases ancillary to foreign proceedings

"(a) A case under section 304 of title 11 to enjoin the commencement or continuation of an action or proceeding in a State or Federal court, or the enforcement of a judgment, may be commenced only in the bankruptcy court for the district where the State or Federal court sits in which is pending the action or proceeding against which the injunction is sought.

"(b) A case under section 304 of title 11 to enjoin the enforcement of a lien against property, or to require turnover of property of an estate, may be commenced only in the bankruptcy court for the district in which such property is found.

"(c) A case under section 304 of title 11, other than a case specified in subsection (a) or (b) of this section, may be commenced only in the bankruptcy court for the district in which is located the principal assets in the United States, of the estate that is the subject of such case.

"§ 1475. Change of venue

"A bankruptcy court may transfer a case under title 11 or a proceeding arising under or related to such a case to a bankruptcy court for another district, in the interest of justice and for the convenience of the parties.

"§ 1476. Creation or alteration of district or division

"Cases or proceedings pending at the time of the creation of a new district or division or transfer of a county or territory from one division or district to another may be tried in the district or division as it existed at the institution of the case or proceeding, or in the district or division so created or to which the county or territory is so transferred as the parties shall agree or the court direct.

"§ 1477. Cure or waiver of defects

"(a) The bankruptcy court of a district in which is filed a case or proceeding laying venue in the wrong division or district may, in the interest of justice and for the convenience of the parties, retain such case or proceeding, or may transfer, under section 1475 of this title, such case or proceeding to any other district or division.

"(b) Nothing in this chapter shall impair the jurisdiction of a bankruptcy court of any matter involving a party who does not interpose timely and sufficient objection to the venue.

"§ 1478. Removal to the bankruptcy courts

"(a) A party may remove any claim or cause of action in a civil action, other than a proceeding before the United States Tax Court or a civil action by a Government unit to enforce such governmental unit's police or regulatory power, to the bankruptcy court for the district where such civil action is pending, if the bankruptcy courts have jurisdiction over such claim or cause of action.

"(b) The court to which such claim or cause of action is removed may remand such claim or cause of action on any equitable ground. An order under this subsection remanding a claim or cause of action, or a decision not so remanding, is not reviewable by appeal or otherwise.

"§ 1479. Provisional remedies; security

"(a) Whenever any action is removed to a bankruptcy court under section 1478 of this title, any attachment or sequestration of the goods or estate of the defendant in such action shall hold the goods or estate to answer the final judgment or decree in the same manner as they would have been held to answer final judgment or decree had it been rendered by the court from which the action was removed, unless the attachment or sequestration is invalidated under applicable law.

"(b) Any bond, undertaking, or security given by either party in an action prior to removal under section 1478 of this title shall remain valid and effectual notwithstanding such removal, unless such bond, undertaking, or other security is invalidated under applicable law.

"(c) All injunctions, orders, or other proceedings in an action prior to removal of such action under section 1478 of this title shall remain in full force and effect until dissolved or modified by the bankruptcy court.

"§ 1480. Jury trials

"(a) Except as provided in subsection (b) of this section, this chapter and title 11 do not affect any right to trial by jury, in a case under title 11 or in a proceeding arising under title 11 or arising in or related to a case under title 11, that is provided by any statute in effect on September 30, 1979.

"(b) The bankruptcy court may order the issues arising under section 303 of title 11 to be tried without a jury.

"§ 1481. Powers of bankruptcy court

"A bankruptcy court shall have the powers of a court of equity, law, and admiralty, but may not enjoin another court or punish a criminal contempt not committed in the presence of the judge of the court or warranting a punishment of imprisonment.

"§ 1482. Appeals

"(a) Panels designated under section 160(a) of this title shall have jurisdiction of appeals from all final judgments, orders, and decrees of bankruptcy courts.

"(b) Panels designated under section 160(a) of this title shall have jurisdiction of appeals from interlocutory judgments, orders, and decrees of bankruptcy courts, but only by leave of the panel to which the appeal is taken.".

(b) The table of chapters of part IV of title 28 of the United States Code is amended by inserting immediately after the item relating to chapter 89 the following:

"90. District Courts and Bankruptcy Courts............................ 1471".

SEC. 242. Section 1656 of title 28 of the United States Code is amended by inserting "or in a bankruptcy court" immediately after "a district court".

SEC. 243. Section 1869(f) of title 28 of the United States Code is amended by inserting "chapter 6 of title 28, United States Code," immediately after "chapter 5 of title 28, United States Code,".

SEC. 244. Section 1914(a) of title 28 of the United States Code is amended by striking out "$15" and inserting "$60" in lieu thereof.

SEC. 245. Section 1923(b) of title 28 of the United States Code is amended by inserting "and United States trustees" immediately after "United States attorneys".

SEC. 246. (a) Chapter 123 of title 28 of the United States Code is amended by inserting immediately after section 1929 the following:

"§ 1930. Bankruptcy courts

"(a) Notwithstanding section 1915 of this title, the parties commencing a case under title 11 shall pay to the clerk of the bankruptcy court the following filing fees:

"(1) For a case commenced under chapter 7 or 13 of title 11, $60.

"(2) For a case commenced under chapter 9 of title 11, $300.

"(3) For a case commenced under chapter 11 of title 11 that does not concern a railroad, as defined in section 101 of title 11, $200.

"(4) For a case commenced under chapter 11 of title 11 concerning a railroad, as so defined, $500.

An individual commencing a voluntary case or a joint case under title 11 may pay such fee in installments.

"(b) The Judicial Conference of the United States may prescribe additional fees in cases under title 11 of the same kind as the Judicial Conference prescribes under section 1914(b) of this title.

"(c) Upon the filing of any separate or joint notice of appeal or application for appeal or upon the receipt of any order allowing, or notice of the allowance of, an appeal or a writ of certiorari $5 shall be paid to the clerk of the bankruptcy court, by the appellant or petitioner.

"(d) Whenever any case or proceeding is dismissed in any bankruptcy court for want of jurisdiction, such court may order the payment of just costs.

"(e) The clerk of the bankruptcy court may collect only the fees prescribed under this section.".

(b) The table of sections of chapter 123 of title 28 of the United States Code is amended by adding at the end thereof the following:

"1930. Bankruptcy courts.".

SEC. 247. Section 2075 of title 28 of the United States Code is amended by—

(1) striking out "under the Bankruptcy Act" and inserting in lieu thereof "in cases under title 11"; and

(2) by striking out the last sentence thereof.

SEC. 248. Section 2107 of title 28 of the United States Code is amended—

(1) by inserting "or the bankruptcy court" immediately after "district court"; and

(2) by striking out the final paragraph.

SEC. 249. Section 2201 of title 28 of the United States Code is amended by inserting "or a proceeding under section 505 or 1146 of title 11" immediately after "the Internal Revenue Code of 1954".

SEC. 250. (a) Chapter 153 of title 28 of the United States Code is amended by adding at the end thereof the following:

"§ 2256. Habeas corpus from bankruptcy courts

"A bankruptcy court may issue a writ of habeas corpus—

"(1) when appropriate to bring a person before the court—

"(A) for examination;

"(B) to testify; or

"(C) to perform a duty imposed on such person under this title; or

"(2) ordering the release of a debtor in a case under title 11 in custody under the judgment of a Federal or State court if—

"(A) such debtor was arrested or imprisoned on process in any civil action;

"(B) such process was issued for the collection of a debt—

"(i) dischargeable under title 11; or

"(ii) that is or will be provided for in a plan under chapter 11 or 13 of title 11; and

"(C) before the issuance of such writ, notice and a hearing have been afforded the adverse party of such debtor in custody to contest the issuance of such writ.".

(b) The table of sections for chapter 153 of title 28 of the United States Code is amended by adding at the end thereof the following:

"2256. Habeas corpus from bankruptcy courts.".

SEC. 251. (a) Rule 1101(a) of the Federal Rules of Evidence is amended by striking out ", referees in bankruptcy,".

(b) Rule 1101(b) of the Federal Rules of Evidence is amended by striking out "the Bankruptcy Act" and inserting in lieu thereof "title 11, United States Code".

SEC. 252. Rule 1101(a) of the Federal Rules of Evidence is amended by inserting "the United States bankruptcy courts," immediately after "the United States district courts,".

Appendix B:

FORMS

Form No. *Page*

Most of the forms contained in this Appendix are the Suggested Interim Bankruptcy Forms drafted by the Advisory Committee on Bankruptcy Rules of the Judicial Conference of the United States. The Suggested Forms are designed to meet the requirements of the Bankruptcy Code and to provide guidance until the promulgation of new Official Forms. The use of these Suggested Forms is mandatory in jurisdictions which have adopted them by local court rule.

Several of the forms contained in the Appendix are based on the Official Forms in Bankruptcy prescribed by the Supreme Court of the United States for use under the former Bankruptcy Act. These forms, which are amended by the authors to conform to the requirements of the new Bankruptcy Code, are applicable until new Official Forms are promulgated.

The practitioner should consult local court rules to determine whether there are additional or different required forms.

Form No. 1

VOLUNTARY CASE: DEBTOR'S PETITION

NOTE: This form is Suggested Interim Bankruptcy Form No. 1. It may be used to commence a voluntary case under chapter 7, 11, or 13 of the Bankruptcy Code.

The title of the case, in the caption of the form, should include other names used by the debtor, such as trade names, married names and maiden names. This will help enable creditors to identify properly the debtor when notices and orders are transmitted to the creditors.

The unsworn declaration at the end of the petition conforms with Public Law 94-550 (90 Stat. 2534, 28 U.S.C. § 1746 (1976)), which permits the declaration to be made in the form indicated with the same force and effect as a sworn statement.

UNITED STATES BANKRUPTCY COURT
FOR THE .... DISTRICT
OF ....

In re ...., Debtor [*include here all names used by debtor within last six years*]	Case No. ....

VOLUNTARY CASE: DEBTOR'S PETITION

1. Petitioner's post-office address is ....

2. Petitioner has resided [*or* has had his domicile *or* has had his principal place of business *or* has had his principal assets] within this district for the preceding 180 days [*or* for a longer portion of the preceding 180 days than in any other district].

3. Petitioner is qualified to file this petition and is entitled to the benefits of title 11, United States Code as a voluntary debtor.

[*If appropriate*] 4. A copy of petitioner's proposed plan, dated ...., ..., is attached [*or* Petitioner intends to file a plan pursuant to chapter 11 [*or* chapter 13] of title 11, United States Code].

WHEREFORE, petitioner prays for relief in accordance with chapter 7 [*or* chapter 11 *or* chapter 13] of title 11, United States Code.

Signed: ....,
Attorney for Petitioner

Address: ....,
....

[*Petitioner signs if not represented by attorney*]

. . . .,
Petitioner

I, ..., the petitioner named in the foregoing petition, certify under penalty of perjury that the foregoing is true and correct.

Executed on . . . .

Signature: . . . .
Petitioner

Form No. 2

VOLUNTARY CASE: DEBTORS' JOINT PETITION

NOTE: This form is Suggested Interim Bankruptcy Form No. 2. This form may be used by a debtor and spouse to commence, voluntarily, a case under chapter 7, Liquidation, chapter 11, Reorganization, or chapter 13, Adjustment of Debts of an Individual with Regular Income.

See the Note to Form No. 1 for discussion of the unsworn declaration at the end of the form.

UNITED STATES BANKRUPTCY COURT
FOR THE .... DISTRICT
OF ....

In re

..........................,
Debtors [*include here all names used by debtors within last six years*] } Case No. ....

VOLUNTARY CASE: DEBTORS' JOINT PETITION

1. Petitioners' post-office address is ....

2. Petitioners have resided [*or* have had their domicile *or* have had their principal place of business *or* have had their principal assets] within this district for the preceding 180 days [*or* for a longer portion of the preceding 180 days than in any other district].

3. Petitioners are qualified to file this petition and are entitled to the benefits of title 11, United States Code as voluntary debtors.

[*If appropriate*] 4. A copy of petitioners' proposed plan, dated ...., ..., is attached [*or* Petitioners intend to file a plan pursuant to chapter 11 [*or* chapter 13] of title 11, United States Code].

WHEREFORE, petitioners pray for relief in accordance with chapter 7 [*or* chapter 11 *or* chapter 13] of title 11, United States Code.

Signed: ....,
Attorney for Petitioners

Address: ....,
....

[*Petitioners sign if not represented by attorney*]

........................,
........................,
Petitioners

We, ..., and ...., the petitioners named in the foregoing petition, certify under penalty of perjury that the foregoing is true and correct.

Executed on ....

Signature: ....

Signature: ....
Petitioners

Form No. 3

APPLICATION TO PAY FILING FEES IN INSTALLMENTS

NOTE: This form is Suggested Interim Bankruptcy Form No. 3.

[*Caption, other than designation, as in Form No. 1*]

APPLICATION TO PAY FILING FEES IN INSTALLMENTS

1. Applicant is filing herewith a petition commencing a voluntary [*or* joint] case under title 11, United States Code.

2. He is unable to pay the filing fees except in installments.

3. He proposes to pay such fees to the clerk of the bankruptcy court upon the following terms:

....

....

....

4. He has paid no money and transferred no property to his attorney for services in connection with this case or any pending case under title 11, United States Code, and he will make no payment or transfer to his attorney for such services until the filing fees are paid in full.

WHEREFORE applicant prays that he be permitted to pay the filing fees in installments.

Dated: .... Signed: ....

Applicant

Address: ....

....

Form No. 4

ORDER FOR PAYMENT OF FILING FEES IN INSTALLMENTS

NOTE: This form is Suggested Interim Bankruptcy Form No. 4.

[*Caption, other than designation, as in Form No. 1*]

ORDER FOR PAYMENT OF FILING FEES IN INSTALLMENTS

The application of the debtor for permission to pay the filing fees in this case in installments having been heard;

It is ordered that the debtor pay the filing fees still owing, namely, $. . . . ., as follows: . . . .

It is further ordered that all payments be made at the office of the clerk of the United States Bankruptcy Court located at . . . ., and that until the filing fees are paid in full, the debtor shall pay no money and shall transfer no property to his attorney, and his attorney shall accept no money or property from the debtor for services in connection with this case.

Dated: . . . .

BY THE COURT

. . . . ,
Bankruptcy Judge

Form No. 5

UNSWORN DECLARATION UNDER PENALTY OF PERJURY ON BEHALF OF A CORPORATION OR PARTNERSHIP

NOTE: This form is Suggested Interim Bankruptcy Form No. 5. 28 U.S.C. § 1746 permits an unsworn declaration to be used in lieu of a verification. See Note to Form No. 1.

I, ... , [the president *or other officer or* an authorized agent of the corporation] [*or* a member *or* an authorized agent of the partnership] named as petitioner in the foregoing petition, certify under penalty of perjury that the foregoing is true and correct, and that the filing of this petition on behalf of the [corporation] [*or* partnership] has been authorized.

Executed on . . . .

Signature: . . . .

Form No. 6

SCHEDULES OF ASSETS AND LIABILITIES

NOTE: This form is Suggested Interim Bankruptcy Form No. 6.

The unsworn declarations at the end of the form are in conformity with 28 U.S.C. § 1746. See Note to Form No. 1.

[*Caption, other than designation, as in Form No. 1*]

SCHEDULE A.—STATEMENT OF ALL LIABILITIES OF DEBTOR

Schedules A-1, A-2, and A-3 must include all the claims against the debtor or his property as of the date of the filing of the petition by or against him.

SCHEDULE A-1.—CREDITORS HAVING PRIORITY

(1) Nature of claim	(2) Name of creditor and complete mailing address including zip code [if unknown, so state]	(3) Specify when claim was incurred and the consideration therefor; when claim is contingent, unliquidated, disputed, or subject to setoff, evidenced by a judgment, negotiable instrument, or other writing, or incurred as partner or joint contractor, so indicate; specify name of any partner or joint contractor on any debt	(4) Indicate if claim is contingent, unliquidated or disputed	(5) Amount of claim

a. Wages, salary, and commissions, including vacation, severance and sick leave pay owing to workmen, servants, clerks, or traveling or city salesmen on salary or commission basis, whole or part time, whether or not selling exclusively for the debtor, not exceeding $2,000 to each, earned within ninety days before filing of petition or cessation of business, if earlier (specify date) $..........

b. Contributions to employee benefit plan for services rendered within 180 days before filing of petition or cessation of business, if earlier (specify date)

c. Deposits by individuals, not exceeding $900 for each for purchase, lease, or rental of property or services for personal, family, or household use that were not delivered or provided

d. Taxes owing [itemize by type of tax and taxing authority]

(1) To the United States
(2) To any state
(3) To any other taxing authority

Total $..........

SCHEDULE A-2.—CREDITORS HOLDING SECURITY

(1) Name of creditor and complete mailing address including zip code [if unknown, so state]	(2) Description of security and date when obtained by creditor	(3) Specify when claim was incurred and the consideration therefor; when claim is contingent, unliquidated, disputed, or subject to setoff, evidenced by a judgment, negotiable instrument, or other writing, or incurred as partner or joint contractor, so indicate; specify name of any partner or joint contractor on any debt	(4) Indicate if claim is contingent, unliquidated or disputed	(5) Market value	(6) Amount of claim without deduction of value of security
				$..........	$..........

Total $..........

SCHEDULE A-3. CREDITORS HAVING UNSECURED CLAIMS WITHOUT PRIORITY

Name of creditor [including last known holder of any negotiable instrument] complete mailing address including zip code [if unknown, so state]	Specify when claim was incurred and the consideration therefor; when claim is contingent, unliquidated, disputed, subject to setoff, evidenced by a judgment, negotiable instrument, or other writing, or incurred as partner or joint contractor, so indicate; specify name of any partner or joint contractor on any debt	Amount of claim
		$..........

Total $..........

SCHEDULE B—STATEMENT OF ALL PROPERTY OF DEBTOR

Schedules B-1, B-2, B-3, and B-4 must include all property of the debtor as of the date of the filing of the petition by or against him.

SCHEDULE B-1.—REAL PROPERTY

Description and location of all real property in which debtor has an interest [including equitable and future interests, interests in estates by the entirety, community property, life estates, leaseholds, and rights and powers exercisable for his own benefit]	Nature of interest [specify all deeds and written instruments relating thereto]	Market value of debtor's interest without deduction for secured claims listed in Schedule A-2 or exemptions claimed in Schedule B-4
		$..........

Total $..........

SCHEDULE B-2.—PERSONAL PROPERTY

Type of property	Description and location	Market value of debtor's interest without deduction for secured claims listed in Schedule A-2 or exemption claimed in Schedule B-4

a. Cash on hand $..........

b. Deposits of money with banking institutions, savings and loan associations, credit unions, public utility companies, landlords, and others

c. Household goods, supplies and furnishings

d. Books, pictures, and other art objects; stamp, coin, and other collections

e. Wearing apparel, jewelry, firearms, sports equipment, and other personal possessions

f. Automobiles, trucks, trailers, and other vehicles

g. Boats, motors, and their accessories

h. Livestock, poultry, and other animals

i. Farming supplies and implements

j. Office equipment, furnishings, and supplies

k. Machinery, fixtures, equipment, and supplies [other than those listed in Items j and l] used in business

l. Inventory

m. Tangible personal property of any other description

n. Patents, copyrights, franchises, and other general intangibles [specify all documents and writings relating thereto]

o. Government and corporate bonds and other negotiable and nonnegotiable instruments

p. Other liquidated debts owing debtor

q. Contingent and unliquidated claims of every nature, including counterclaims of the debtor [give estimated value of each]

r. Interests in insurance policies [itemize surrender or refund values of each]

s. Annuities

t. Stock and interests in incorporated and unincorporated companies [itemize separately]

u. Interests in partnerships

v. Equitable and future interests, life estates, and rights or powers exercisable for the benefit of the debtor (other than those listed in schedule B-1) [specify all written instruments relating thereto]

Total $..........

SCHEDULE B-3.—PROPERTY NOT OTHERWISE SCHEDULED

Type of property	Description and location	Market value of debtor's interest without deduction for secured claims listed in Schedule A-2 or exemption claimed in Schedule B-4
a. Property transferred under assignment for benefit of creditors, within 120 days prior to filing of petition [specify date of assignment, name and address of assignee, amount realized therefrom by the assignee, and disposition of proceeds so far as known to debtor]		$..........
b. Property of any kind not otherwise scheduled		
	Total	$..........

Debtor selects the following property as exempt pursuant to 11 U.S.C. § 522(d) [*or* the laws of the State of ....]

SCHEDULE B-4.—PROPERTY CLAIMED AS EXEMPT

Type of property	Location, description, and, so far as relevant to the claim of exemption, present use of property	Specify statute creating the exemption	Value claimed exempt
			$..........
		Total	$..........

SUMMARY OF DEBTS AND PROPERTY [FROM THE STATEMENTS OF THE DEBTOR IN SCHEDULES A AND B]

Schedule		Total
	Debts	
A-1/a,b	Wages, etc. having priority	
A-1(c)	Deposits of money	
A-1/d(1)	Taxes owing United States	
A-1/d(2)	Taxes owing states	
A-1/d(3)	Taxes owing other taxing authorities	
A-2	Secured claims	
A-3	Unsecured claims without priority	
	Schedule A total	$..........
	Property	
B-1	Real property [total value]	
B-2/a	Cash on hand	
B-2/b	Deposits	
B-2/c	Household goods	
B-2/d	Books, pictures, and collections	
B-2/e	Wearing apparel and personal possessions	
B-2/f	Automobiles and other vehicles	
B-2/g	Boats, motors, and accessories	
B-2/h	Livestock and other animals	
B-2/i	Farming supplies and implements	
B-2/j	Office equipment and supplies	
B-2/k	Machinery, equipment, and supplies used in business	
B-2/l	Inventory	
B-2/m	Other tangible personal property	
B-2/n	Patents and other general intangibles	
B-2/o	Bonds and other instruments	
B-2/p	Other liquidated debts	

B-2/q	Contingent and unliquidated claims
B-2/r	Interests in insurance policies
B-2/s	Annuities
B-2/t	Interests in corporations and unincorporated companies
B-2/u	Interests in partnerships
B-2/v	Equitable and future interests, rights, and powers in personalty
B-3/a	Property assigned for benefit of creditors
B-3/b	Property not otherwise scheduled

Schedule B total $..........

UNSWORN DECLARATION UNDER PENALTY OF PERJURY OF INDIVIDUAL TO SCHEDULES A AND B

I, ..., certify under penalty of perjury that I have read the foregoing schedules, consisting of .... sheets, and that they are true and correct to the best of my knowledge, information, and belief.

Executed on ....

Signature: ....

UNSWORN DECLARATION UNDER PENALTY OF PERJURY ON BEHALF OF CORPORATION OR PARTNERSHIP TO SCHEDULES A AND B

I, ..., [the president *or other officer* or an authorized agent of the corporation] [*or* a member *or* an authorized agent of the partnership] named as debtor in this case, certify under penalty of perjury that I have read the foregoing schedules, consisting of .... sheets, and that they are true and correct to the best of my knowledge, information, and belief.

Executed on ....

Signature: ....

Form No. 7

STATEMENT OF FINANCIAL AFFAIRS FOR DEBTOR NOT ENGAGED IN BUSINESS

NOTE: This form is Suggested Interim Bankruptcy Form No. 7.

See Note to Form No. 1 for discussion of unsworn statement at the end of this form.

[*Caption, other than designation, as in Form No. 1*]

STATEMENT OF FINANCIAL AFFAIRS FOR DEBTOR NOT ENGAGED IN BUSINESS

Each question should be answered or the failure to answer explained. If the answer is "none," this should be stated. If additional space is needed for the answer to any question, a separate sheet, properly identified and made a part hereof, should be used and attached.

The term, "original petition," as used in the following questions, shall mean the petition filed under Rule 1002, 1003, or 1004.

1. *Name and residence.*

a. What is your full name and social security number?

b. Have you used, or been known by, any other names within the six years immmediately preceding the filing of the original petition herein? (If so, give particulars.)

c. Where do you now reside?

d. Where else have you resided during the six years immediately preceding the filing of the original petition herein?

2. *Occupation and income.*

a. What is your occupation?

b. Where are you now employed? (Give the name and address of your employer, or the address at which you carry on your trade or profession, and the length of time you have been so employed or engaged.)

c. Have you been in a partnership with anyone, or engaged in any business during the six years immediately preceding the filing of the original petition herein? (If so, give particulars, including names, dates, and places.)

d. What amount of income have you received from your trade or profession during each of the two calendar years immediately preceding the filing of the original petition herein?

e. What amount of income have you received from other sources during each of these two years? (Give particulars, including each source, and the amount received therefrom.)

3. *Tax returns and refunds.*

a. Where did you file your federal and state income tax returns for the two years immediately preceding the filing of the original petition herein?

b. What tax refunds (income and other) have you received during the year immediately preceding the filing of the original petition herein?

c. To what tax refunds (income or other), if any, are you, or may you be, entitled? (Give particulars, including information as to any refund payable jointly to you and your spouse or any other person.)

4. *Bank accounts and safe deposit boxes.*

a. What bank accounts have you maintained, alone or together with any other person, and in your own or any other name within the two years immediately preceding the filing of the original petition herein? (Give the name and address of each bank, the name in which the deposit is maintained, and the name and address of every other person authorized to make withdrawals from such account.)

b. What safe deposit box or boxes or other depository or depositories have you kept or used for your securities, cash, or other valuables within the two years immediately preceding the filing of the original petition herein? (Give the name and address of the bank or other depository, the name in which each box or other depository was kept, the name and address of every other person who had the right of access thereto, a brief description of the contents thereof, and, if the box has been surrendered, state when surrendered, or, if transferred, when transferred, and the name and address of the transferee.)

5. *Books and records.*

a. Have you kept books of account or records relating to your affairs within the two years immediately preceding the filing of the original petition herein?

b. In whose possession are these books or records? (Give names and addresses.)

c. If any of these books or records are not available, explain.

d. Have any books of account or records relating to your affairs been destroyed, lost, or otherwise disposed of within the two years immediately preceding the filing of the original petition herein? (If so, give particulars, including date of destruction, loss, or disposition, and reason therefor.)

6. *Property held for another person.* What property do you hold for any other person? (Give name and address of each person, and describe the property, or value thereof, and all writings relating thereto.)

7. *Prior bankruptcy.* What cases under the Bankruptcy Act or title 11, United States Code have previously been brought by or against you? (State the location of the bankruptcy court, the nature and number of each case, the date when it was filed, and whether a discharge was granted or refused, the case was dismissed, or a composition, arrangement, or plan was confirmed.)

8. *Receiverships, general assignments, and other modes of liquidation.*

a. Was any of your property, at the time of the filing of the original petition herein, in the hands of a receiver, trustee, or other liquidating agent? (If so, give a brief description of the property, the name and address of the receiver, trustee, or other agent, and, if the agent was appointed in a court proceeding, the name and location of the court, the title and number of the case, and the nature thereof.)

b. Have you made any assignment of your property for the benefit of your creditors, or any general settlement with your creditors, within one year immediately preceding the filing of the original petition herein? (If so, give dates, the name and address of the assignee, and a brief statement of the terms of assignment or settlement.)

9. *Property in hands of third person.* Is any other person holding anything of value in which you have an interest? (Give name and address, location and description of the property, and circumstances of the holding.)

10. *Suits, executions, and attachments.*

a. Were you a party to any suit pending at the time of the filing of the original petition herein? (If so, give the name and location of the court and the title and nature of the proceeding.)

b. Were you a party to any suit terminated within the year immediately preceding the filing of the original petition herein? (If so, give the name and location of the court, the title and nature of the proceeding, and the result.)

c. Has any of your property been attached, garnished, or seized under any legal or equitable process within the year immediately preceding the filing of the original petition herein? (If so, describe the property seized or person garnished, and at whose suit.)

11. *Loans repaid.* What repayments on loans in whole or in part have you made during the year immediately preceding the filing of the original petition herein? (Give the name and address of the lender, the amount of the loan and when received, the amounts and dates of payments and, if the lender is a relative or insider, the relationship.)

12. *Transfers of property.*

a. Have you made any gifts, other than ordinary and usual presents to family members and charitable donations, during the year immediately preceding the filing of the original petition herein? (If so, give names and addresses of donees and dates, description, and value of gifts.)

b. Have you made any other transfer, absolute or for the purpose of security, or any other disposition, of real or tangible personal property during the year immediately preceding the filing of the original petition herein? (Give a description of the property, the date of the transfer or disposition, to whom transferred or how disposed of, and, if the transferee is a relative or insider, the relationship, the consideration, if any, received therefor, and the disposition of such consideration.)

13. *Repossessions and returns.* Has any property been returned to, or repossessed by, the seller or by a secured party during the year immediately preceding the filing of the original petition herein? (If so, give particulars including the name and address of the party getting the property and its description and value.)

14. *Losses.*

a. Have you suffered any losses from fire, theft, or gambling during the year immediately preceding or since the filing of the original petition herein? (If so, give particulars, including dates, names, and places, and the amounts of money or value and general description of property lost.)

b. Was the loss covered in whole or part by insurance? (If so, give particulars.)

15. *Payments or transfers to attorneys.*

a. Have you consulted an attorney during the year immediately preceding or since the filing of the original petition herein? (Give dates, name and address.)

b. Have you during the year immediately preceding or since the filing of the original petition herein paid any money or transferred any property to the attorney or to any other person on his behalf? (If so, give particulars, including amount paid or value of property transferred and date of payment or transfer.)

c. Have you, either during the year immediately preceding or since the filing of the original petition herein, agreed to pay any money or transfer any property to an attorney at law, or to any other person on his behalf? (If so, give particulars, including amount and terms of obligation.)

I, ..., certify under penalty of perjury that I have read the answers contained in the foregoing statement of financial affairs and that they are true and correct to the best of my knowledge, information, and belief.

Executed ....

.........................,
Debtor

Form No. 8

STATEMENT OF FINANCIAL AFFAIRS FOR DEBTOR ENGAGED IN BUSINESS

NOTE: This form is Suggested Interim Bankruptcy Form No. 8.

[*Caption, other than designation, as in Form No. 1*]

STATEMENT OF FINANCIAL AFFAIRS FOR DEBTOR ENGAGED IN BUSINESS

Each question should be answered or the failure to answer explained. If the answer is "none," this should be stated. If additional space is needed for the answer to any question, a separate sheet properly identified and made a part hereof, should be used and attached.

If the debtor is a partnership or a corporation, the questions shall be deemed to be addressed to, and shall be answered on behalf of, the partnership or corporation; and the statement shall be certified by a member of the partnership or by a duly authorized officer of the corporation.

The term, "original petition," as used in the following questions, shall mean the petition filed under Rule 1002, 1003, or 1004.

1. *Nature, location, and name of business.*

a. Under what name and where do you carry on your business?

b. In what business are you engaged? (If business operations have been terminated, give the date of such termination.)

c. When did you commence such business?

d. Where else, and under what other names, have you carried on business within the six years immediately preceding the filing of the original petition herein? (Give street addresses, the names of any partners, joint adventurers, or other associates, the nature of the business, and the periods for which it was carried on.)

e. What is your employer identification number? Your social security number?

2. *Books and records.*

a. By whom, or under whose supervision, have your books of account and records been kept during the two years immediately preceding the filing of the original petition herein? (Give names, addresses, and periods of time.)

b. By whom have your books of account and records been audited during the two years immediately preceding the filing of the original petition herein? (Give names, addresses, and dates of audits.)

c. In whose possession are your books of account and records? (Give names and addresses.)

d. If any of these books or records are not available, explain.

e. Have any books of account or records relating to your affairs been destroyed, lost, or otherwise disposed of within the two years immediately preceding the filing of the original petition herein? (If so, give particulars, including date of destruction, loss, or disposition, and reason therefor.)

3. *Financial statements.* Have you issued any written financial statements within the two years immediately preceding the filing of the original petition herein? (Give dates, and the names and addresses of the persons to whom issued, including mercantile and trade agencies.)

4. *Inventories.*

a. When was the last inventory of your property taken?

b. By whom, or under whose supervision, was this inventory taken?

c. What was the amount, in dollars, of the inventory? (State whether the inventory was taken at cost, market, or otherwise.)

d. When was the next prior inventory of your property taken?

e. By whom, or under whose supervision, was this inventory taken?

f. What was the amount, in dollars, of the inventory? (State whether the inventory was taken at cost, market, or otherwise.)

g. In whose possession are the records of the two inventories above referred to? (Give names and addresses.)

5. *Income other than from operation of business.* What amount of income, other than from operation of your business, have you received during each of the two years immediately preceding the filing of the original petition herein? (Give particulars, including each source, and the amount received therefrom.)

6. *Tax returns and refunds.*

a. In whose possession are copies of your federal and state income tax returns for the three years immediately preceding the filing of the original petition herein?

b. What tax refunds (income or other) have you received during the two years immediately preceding the filing of the original petition herein?

c. To what tax refunds (income or other), if any, are you, or may you be, entitled? (Give particulars, including information as to any refund payable jointly to you and your spouse or any other person.)

7. *Bank accounts and safe deposit boxes.*

a. What bank accounts have you maintained, alone or together with any other person, and in your own or any other name, within the two years immediately preceding the filing of the original petition herein? (Give the name and address of each bank, the name in which the deposit was maintained, and the name and address of every person authorized to make withdrawals from such account.)

b. What safe deposit box or boxes or other depository or depositories have you kept or used for your securities, cash, or other valuables within the two years immediately preceding the filing of the original petition herein? (Give the name and address of the bank or other depository, the name in which each box or other depository was kept, the name and address of every person who had the right of access thereto, a description of the contents thereof, and, if the box has been surrendered, state when surrendered or, if transferred, when transferred and the name and address of the transferee.)

8. *Property held for another person.* What property do you hold for any other person? (Give name and address of each person, and describe the property, the amount or value thereof and all writings relating thereto.)

9. *Prior bankruptcy proceedings.* What cases under the Bankruptcy Act or title 11, United States Code have previously been brought by or against you? (State the location of the bankruptcy court, the nature and number of the case, and whether a discharge was granted or refused, the case was dismissed, or a composition, arrangement, or plan was confirmed.)

10. *Receiverships, general assignments, and other modes of liquidation.*

a. Was any of your property, at the time of the filing of the original petition herein, in the hands of a receiver, trustee, or other liquidating agent? (If so, give a brief description of the property and the name and address of the receiver, trustee, or other agent, and, if the agent was appointed in a court proceeding, the name and location of the court, the title and number of the case, and the nature thereof.)

b. Have you made any assignment of your property for the benefit of your creditors, or any general settlement with your creditors, within the two years immediately preceding the filing of the original petition herein? (If so, give dates, the name and address of the assignee, and a brief statement of the terms of assignment or settlement.)

11. *Property in hands of third person.* Is any other person holding anything of value in which you have an interest? (Give name and address, location and description of the property, and circumstances of the holding.)

12. *Suits, executions, and attachments.*

a. Were you a party to any suit pending at the time of the filing of the original petition herein? (If so, give the name and location of the court and the title and nature of the proceeding.)

b. Were you a party to any suit terminated within the year immediately preceding the filing of the original petition herein? (If so, give the name and location of the court, the title and nature of the proceeding, and the result.)

c. Has any of your property been attached, garnished, or seized under any legal or equitable process within the year immediately preceding the filing of the original petition herein? (If so, describe the property seized or person garnished, and at whose suit.)

13. *Payments on loans and installment purchases.* What repayments on loans in whole or in part, and what payments on installment purchases of goods and services, have you made during the year immediately preceding the filing of the original petition herein? (Give the names and addresses of the persons receiving payment, the amounts of the loans and of the purchase price of the goods and services, the dates of the original transactions, the amounts and dates of payments, and, if any of the payees are your relatives or insiders, the relationship; if the debtor is a partnership and any of the payees is or was a partner or a relative of a partner, state the relationship; if the debtor is a corporation and any of the payees is or was an officer, director, or stockholder, or a relative of an officer, director, or stockholder, state the relationship.)

14. *Transfers of property.*

a. Have you made any gifts, other than ordinary and usual presents to family members and charitable donations during the year immediately preceding the filing of the original petition herein? (If so, give names and addresses of donees and dates, description, and value of gifts.)

b. Have you made any other transfer, absolute or for the purpose of security, or any other disposition which was not in the ordinary course of business during the year immediately preceding the filing of the original petition herein? (Give a description of the property, the date of the transfer or disposition, to whom transferred or how disposed of, and state whether the transferee is a relative, partner, shareholder, officer, director, or insider, the consideration, if any, received for the property, and the disposition of such consideration.)

15. *Accounts and other receivables.* Have you assigned, either absolutely or as security, any of your accounts or other receivables during the year immediately preceding the filing of the original petition herein? (If so, give names and addresses of assignees.)

16. *Repossessions and returns.* Has any property been returned to, or repossessed by, the seller or by a secured party during the year immediately preceding the filing of the original petition herein? (If so, give particulars, including the name and address of the party getting the property and its description and value.)

17. *Business leases.* If you are a tenant of business property, what is the name and address of your landlord, the amount of your rental, the date to which rent had been paid at the time of the filing of the original petition herein, and the amount of security held by the landlord?

18. *Losses.*

a. Have you suffered any losses from fire, theft, or gambling during the year immediately preceding the filing of the original petition herein? (If so, give particulars, including dates, names, and places, and the amounts of money or value and general description of property lost.)

b. Was the loss covered in whole or part by insurance? (If so, give particulars.)

19. *Withdrawals.*

a. If you are an individual proprietor of your business, what personal withdrawals of any kind have you made from the business during the year immediately preceding the filing of the original petition herein?

b. If the debtor is a partnership or corporation, what withdrawals, in any form (including compensation, bonuses or loans), have been made or received by any member of the partnership, or by any officer, director, insider, managing executive, or shareholder of the corporation, during the year immediately preceding the filing of the original petition herein? (Give the name and designation or relationship to the debtor of each person, the dates and amounts of withdrawals, and the nature or purpose thereof.)

20. *Payments or transfers to attorneys.*

a. Have you consulted an attorney during the year immediately preceding or since the filing of the original petition herein? (Give date, name, and address.)

b. Have you during the year immediately preceding or since the filing of the original petition herein paid any money or transferred any property to the attorney, or to any other person on his behalf? (If so, give particulars, including amount paid or value of property transferred and date of payment or transfer.)

c. Have you, either during the year immediately preceding or since the filing of the original petition herein, agreed to pay any money or transfer any property to an attorney at law, or to any other person on his behalf? (If so, give particulars, including amount and terms of obligation.)

(If the debtor is a partnership or corporation, the following additional questions should be answered.)

21. *Members of partnership; officers, directors, managers, and principal stockholders of corporation.*

a. What is the name and address of each member of the partnership, or the name, title, and address of each officer, director, insider, and managing executive, and of each stockholder holding 20 per cent or more of the issued and outstanding stock, of the corporation?

b. During the year immediately preceding the filing of the original petition herein, has any member withdrawn from the partnership, or any officer, director, insider, or managing executive of the corporation terminated his relationship, or any stockholder holding 20 per cent or more of the issued stock disposed of more than 50 per cent of his holdings? (If so, give name and address and reason for withdrawal, termination, or disposition, if known.)

c. Has any person acquired or disposed of 20 per cent or more of the stock of the corporation during the year immediately preceding the filing of the petition? (If so, give name and address and particulars.)

I, ..., certify under penalty of perjury that I have read the answers contained in the foregoing statement of affairs and that they are true and correct to the best of my knowledge, information, and belief.

Executed on ....

Signature: ....

[*Person certifying for partnership or corporation should indicate position or relationship to debtor.*]

Form No. 9

CHAPTER 13 STATEMENT

NOTE: This form is based on Official Form No. 13-5 which is applicable in cases under chapter 13 of the Code. However, changes contained in chapter 13 make it necessary for additional information to be furnished.

Suggested Interim Bankruptcy Rule 13001 (a) requires that the Chapter 13 Statement be accompanied by a statement, prepared in the manner prescribed by Schedule B-4 of the Schedules of Assets and Liabilities (see Form No. 6), of the exemption law which would be selected and the property which would be claimed as exempt if the debtor's estate were liquidated under chapter 7 of the Code. The reason for this requirement is that confirmation of a plan may not be obtained unless distributions are equal to or greater than distributions which would be made in a liquidation case. See 11 U.S.C. § 1325(a)(4).

When the debtor is engaged in business, the debtor is required to file a Statement of Financial Affairs, prepared in the manner prescribed by Form No. 8, together with the Chapter 13 Statement. See Suggested Interim Bankruptcy Rule 13001(b).

[*Caption, other than description, as in Form No. 1*]

CHAPTER 13 STATEMENT

Each question should be answered or the failure to answer explained. If the answer is "none," this should be stated. If additional space is needed for the answer to any question, a separate sheet, properly identified and made a part hereof, should be used and attached.

The term "original petition," as used in the following questions, shall mean the original petition filed by or against you which originated the pending bankruptcy case.

This form must be completed in full whether a single or a joint petition is filed. When information is requested for "each" or "either spouse filing a petition" it should be supplied for both when a joint petition is filed.

1. *Name and residence.*
   a. Give full name:
      Husband: ....
      Wife: ....
   b. Where does each spouse filing a petition now reside?
      (1) Mailing address:
          Husband: ....
          Wife: ....
      (2) City or town:
          Husband: ....
          Wife: ....

(3) Telephone number:
Husband: . . . .
Wife: . . . .

c. What does each spouse filing a petition consider his or her residence, if different from that listed in b, above?
Husband: . . . .
Wife: . . . .

2. *Occupation and income.*

a. Give present occupation of each spouse filing a petition. (If more than one, list all for each spouse filing a petition.)
Husband: . . . .
. . . .
Wife: . . . .
. . . .

b. What is the name, address, and telephone number of present employer or (employers) of each spouse filing a petition? (Include also any identifying badge or card number with employer.)
Husband: . . . .
. . . .
Wife: . . . .
. . . .

c. How long has each spouse filing a petition been employed by present employer?
Husband: . . . .
. . . .
Wife: . . . .
. . . .

d. If either spouse filing a petition has not been employed by present employer for a period of one year, state the name of prior employer(s) and nature of employment during that period.
Husband: . . . .
. . . .
. . . .
Wife: . . . .
. . . .
. . . .

e. Has either spouse filing a petition operated a business, in partnership or otherwise, during the past three years? (If so, give the particulars, including names, dates, and places.)
Husband: . . . .
. . . .
Wife: . . . .
. . . .

f. Answer the following questions for each spouse whether single or joint petition is filed unless spouses are separated and a single petition is filed:

(1) Is your current pay period:

	Husband	*Wife*
(a) Weekly	. . . .	. . . .

(b) Semi-monthly ....
(c) Monthly ....
(d) Other (specify) ....

(2) What are your gross wages, salary or commissions per pay period?

	Husband	*Wife*
	$..........	$..........

(3) What are your payroll deductions per pay period for:

	Husband	*Wife*
(a) Payroll taxes (including social security)	$..........	$..........
(b) Insurance	....	....
(c) Credit union	....	....
(d) Union dues	....	....
(e) Other (specify)	....	....

(4) What is your take-home pay per pay period?

	Husband	*Wife*
	$..........	$..........

(5) Is your employment subject to seasonal or other change?

	Husband	*Wife*
	....	....

(6) What was the amount of your gross income for the last calendar year?

	Husband	*Wife*
	$..........	$..........

(7) Has either of you made any wage assignments or allotments? (If so, indicate which spouse's wages assigned or allotted, the name and address of the person to whom assigned or allotted, and the amount owing, if any, to such person. If allotment or assignment is to a creditor, his claim should also be listed in Item 11a.)

....
....
....

3. *Dependents.* (To be answered for each spouse whether single or joint petition is filed unless spouses are separated and a single petition is filed.)

a. Does either of you pay [*or* receive] alimony, maintenance, or support? ...... If so, how much per month? $..........
For whose support? (Give name, age, and relationship to you.)
Husband: ....
....
....
Wife: ....
....
....

b. List all other dependents, other than present spouse, not listed in a, above. (Give name, age, and relationship to you.)
Husband: ....
....
....

Wife: ....
....
....

4. *Budget.*
   a. Give estimated average future monthly income for each spouse whether single or joint petition is filed unless spouses are separated and a single petition is filed.
      (1) Husband's monthly take-home pay $..........
      (2) Wife's monthly take-home pay ....
      (3) Other monthly income (specify) ....
      Total $..........
   b. Give estimated average future monthly expenses of family (not including debts to be paid under plan), consisting of:
      (1) Rent or home mortgage payment (include lot rental for trailer) $..........
      (2) Utilities (electricity ...., heat ...., water ...., Telephone ....) ....
      (3) Food ....
      (4) Clothing ....
      (5) Laundry and cleaning ....
      (6) Newspapers, periodicals, and books (including school books) ....
      (7) Medical and drug expenses ....
      (8) Insurance (not deducted from wages)
         (a) Auto ....
         (b) Other ....
      (9) Transportation (not including auto payments to be paid under plan) ....
      (10) Recreation ....
      (11) Club and union dues (not deducted from wages) ....
      (12) Taxes (not deducted from wages) ....
      (13) Alimony, maintenance, or support payments ....
      (14) Other payments for support of dependents not living at home ....
      (15) Other (specify)
         ....
         ....
         ....
      Total $..........
   c. Excess of estimated future monthly income (last line of Item 4a, above) over estimated future expenses (last line of Item 4b, above) $..........
   d. Total amount to be paid each month under plan $..........

5. *Payment of attorney.*
   a. How much have you agreed to pay or what

property have you agreed to transfer to your attorney in connection with this case? $..........

b. How much have you paid or what have you transferred to him? $..........

6. *Tax refunds.* (To be answered for each spouse whether single or joint petition is filed unless spouses are separated and a single petition is filed.)

To what tax refunds (income or other), if any, is either of you, or may either of you be, entitled? (Give particulars, including information as to any refunds payable jointly to you or any other person. All such refunds should also be listed in Item 13b.)

....

....

7. *Bank accounts and safe deposit boxes.* (To be answered for each spouse whether single or joint petition is filed unless spouses are separated and a single petition is filed.)

a. Does either of you currently have any bank or savings and loan accounts, checking or savings? (If so, give name and address of bank, nature of account, current balance, and name and address of every other person authorized to make withdrawals from the account. Such accounts should also be listed in Items 13b.)

....

....

b. Does either of you currently keep any safe deposit boxes or other depositories? (If so, give name and address of bank or other depository, name and address of every other person who has a right of access thereto, and a brief description of the contents thereof, which should also be listed in Item 13b.)

....

....

8. *Prior Bankruptcy.*

What proceedings under the Bankruptcy Act have previously been brought by or against either spouse filing a petition? (State the location of the bankruptcy court, the nature and number of each proceeding, the date when it was filed, and whether a discharge was granted or refused, the proceeding was dismissed, or a composition, arrangement, or plan was confirmed.)

....

....

9. *Foreclosures, executions, and attachments.* (To be answered for each spouse whether single or joint petition is filed unless spouses are separated and a single petition is filed.)

a. Is any of the property of either of you, including real estate, involved in a foreclosure proceeding, in or out of court? (If so, identify the property and the person foreclosing.)

....

....

b. Has any property or income of either of you been attached, garnished, or seized under any legal or equitable process within the four months immediately preceding the filing of the original petition herein? If so, describe the property seized, or person garnished, and at whose suit.)

. . . .

. . . .

10. *Repossessions and returns.* (To be answered for each spouse whether single or joint petition is filed unless spouses are separated and a single petition is filed.)

Has any property of either of you been returned to, repossessed, or seized by the seller or by any other party, including a landlord, during the four months immediately preceding the filing of the original petition herein? (If so, give particulars, including the name and address of the party getting the property and its description and value.)

. . . .

. . . .

. . . .

. . . .

11. *Debts.* (To be answered for each spouse whether single or joint petition is filed.)

a. *Secured Debts.* List all debts which are or may be secured by real or personal property. (Indicate in sixth column, if debt payable in installments, the amount of each installment, the installment period (monthly, weekly, or other) and number of installments in arrears, if any. Indicate in last column whether husband or wife solely liable, or whether you are jointly liable.)

Creditor's name and complete mailing address including zip code [if unknown, so state]	Consideration or basis for debt	Amount claimed by creditor	If disputed, amount admitted by debtor	Description of collateral [include year and make of automobile]	Installment amount, period, and number of installments in arrears	Husband or wife solely liable, or jointly liable
....	....	....	....	....	....	....
....	....	....	....	....	....	....
....	....	....	....	....	....	....
....	....	....	....	....	....	....
....	....	....	....	....	....	....
....	....	....	....	....	....	....
....	....	....	....	....	....	....

b. *Unsecured Debts.* List all other debts, liquidated and unliquidated, including taxes, attorneys' fees and tort claims.

Creditor's complete mailing address including zip code [if unknown, so state]	Consideration or basis for debt	Amount claimed by creditor	If disputed, amount admitted by debtor	Husband or wife solely liable, or jointly liable
....	....	....	....	....
....	....	....	....	....
....	....	....	....	....
....	....	....	....	....
....	....	....	....	....
....	....	....	....	....
....	....	....	....	....

12. *Codebtors.* (To be answered for each spouse whether single or joint petition is filed.)

a. Are any other persons liable, as cosigners or in any other manner, on any of the debts of either of you or are either of you so liable on the debts of others? (If so, give particulars, indicating which spouse liable and including names of creditors, nature of debt, names and addresses of codebtors, and their relationship, if any, to you.)

....

....

....

b. If so, have such codebtors made any payments on such debts? (Give name of each codebtor and amount paid by him.)

....

....

....

c. Have either of you made any payments on such debts? (If so, specify total amount paid to each creditor, whether paid by husband or wife, and name of codebtor.)

....

....

....

13. *Property*. (To be answered for each spouse whether single or joint petition is filed.)

a. *Real Property*. List all real property owned by either of you at date of filing of original petition herein. (Indicate in last column whether owned solely by husband or wife, or jointly.)

Description and location of property	Name of any co-owner other than spouse	Present market value (without deduction for mortgage or other security interest)	Amount of mortgage or other security interest on this property	Name of mortgagee or other secured creditor	Value claimed exempt, if any	Owned solely by husband or wife or jointly
....	....	....	....	....	....	....
....	....	....	....	....	....	....
....	....	....	....	....	....	....
....	....	....	....	....	....	....
....	....	....	....	....	....	....
....	....	....	....	....	....	....
....	....	....	....	....	....	....

b. *Personal Property*. List all other property, owned by either of you at date of filing of original petition herein.

Description	Location of property if not at debtor's residence	Name of any co-owner other than spouse	Present market value (without deduction for mortgage or other security interest)	Amount of mortgage or other security interest on this property	Name of mortgagee or other secured creditor	Value claimed exempt, if any	Owned solely by husband, or wife, or jointly
Autos [give year and make]							
....	....	....	$............	$............	$............	....	....
....	....	....	....	....	....	....	....
Household goods							
....	....	....	....	....	....	....	....
....	....	....	....	....	....	....	....
Personal effects							
....	....	....	....	....	....	....	....
....	....	....	....	....	....	....	....
Other (specify)							
....	....	....	....	....	....	....	....
....	....	....	....	....	....	....	....

[*To be signed and verified by both spouses when joint petition is filed.*]

STATE OF .... }
COUNTY OF .... } ss:

I, ..., do hereby swear that I have read the answers contained in the foregoing statement, consisting of ...... sheets, and that they are true and complete to the best of my knowledge, information, and belief.

....
Husband

Subscribed and sworn to before me
on ....

..........................,
....
[*Official character*]

I, ..., do hereby swear that I have read the answers contained in the foregoing statement, consisting of ...... sheets, and that they are true and complete to the best of my knowledge, information, and belief.

....
Wife

Subscribed and sworn to before me
on ....

..........................,
....
[*Official character*]
Attorney for Debtor(s):

..........................,
Name
....
Address

Form No. 10

INVOLUNTARY CASE: CREDITORS' PETITION

NOTE: This form is Suggested Interim Bankruptcy Form No. 9.
28 U.S.C. § 1746 permits the unsworn declaration in lieu of a verification. See Note to Form No. 1.

[*Caption, other than designation, as in Form No. 1*]

INVOLUNTARY CASE: CREDITORS' PETITION

1. Petitioners, ..., of * ...., and ...., of * ...., and ...., of * ...., are creditors of ...., of * ...., holding claims against him, not contingent as to liability, amounting in the aggregate, in excess of the value of any lien held by them on the debtor's property securing such claims, to $5000 or over. The nature and amount of petitioners' claims are as follows:
....
....
....

2. The debtor has had his principal place of business [*or* his domicile *or* his principal assets *or* has resided] within this district for the 180 days preceding the filing of this petition [*or* for a longer portion of the 180 days preceding the filing of this petition than in any other district].

3. The debtor is a person against whom an order for relief may be entered under title 11, United States Code.

4. [The debtor is generally not paying his debts as they become due as indicated by the following ....
....]
or [within 120 days preceding the filing of this petition, a custodian was appointed for *or* has taken possession of substantially all of the property of the debtor, as follows:
....
....]

WHEREFORE petitioners pray that an order of relief be entered against .... under chapter 7 [*or* 11] of title 11, United States Code.

Signed: ....,
....
Attorney for Petitioners

Address: ....
....

[*Petitioners sign if not represented by attorney*]

---

* State post-office address

. . . . ,
. . . . ,
. . . . ,
Petitioners

I, ... , one of the petitioners named in the foregoing petition, certify under penalty of perjury that the foregoing is true and correct according to the best of my knowledge, information, and belief.

Executed on . . . .

Signature: . . . . ,
Petitioner

Form No. 11

SUMMONS TO DEBTOR

NOTE: This form is Suggested Interim Bankruptcy Form No. 10.

[*Caption, other than designation, as in Form No. 1*]

SUMMONS

To the above-named debtor:

A petition under title 11, United States Code having been filed on ...., in this court of bankruptcy, praying for an order for relief under 11 U.S.C. chapter 7 [*or* 11],

You are hereby summoned and required to file with this court and to serve upon the petitioners' attorney, whose address is ...., a motion or an answer * to the petition which is herewith served upon you, on or before .... If you fail to do so, the order for relief will be entered.

....
Clerk of Bankruptcy Court

By: ....
Deputy Clerk

[SEAL OF THE UNITED STATES BANKRUPTCY COURT]

Date of issuance: ....

---

* If you make a motion, as you may in accordance with Bankruptcy Rule 112, that rule governs the time within which your answer must be served.

Form No. 12

ORDER FOR RELIEF

NOTE: This form is Suggested Interim Bankruptcy Form No. 11. It is appropriate for use when relief is ordered on an involuntary petition filed with respect to chapter 7 (Liquidation) or chapter 11 (Reorganization).

[*Caption, other than designation, as in Form No. 1*]

ORDER FOR RELIEF

On consideration of the petition filed on .... against the above-named debtor, an order for relief under chapter 7 [*or* 11] of title 11 of the United States Code is GRANTED.

Dated: ....

BY THE COURT

.........................,
Bankruptcy Judge

Form No. 13

APPOINTMENT OF COMMITTEE OF UNSECURED CREDITORS IN A CHAPTER 9 MUNICIPALITY OR CHAPTER 11 REORGANIZATION CASE

NOTE: This form is Suggested Interim Bankruptcy Form No. 12.

[*Caption, other than designation, as in Form No. 1*]

APPOINTMENT OF COMMITTEE OF UNSECURED CREDITORS IN A CHAPTER 9 MUNICIPALITY OR 11 REORGANIZATION CASE

The following creditors of the above-named debtor holding the seven largest unsecured claims [*or* who are members of a committee organized by creditors before the order for relief under chapter 9 (*or* 11) of the Bankruptcy Code which was fairly chosen and is representative of the different kinds of claims to be represented] and who are willing to serve are appointed to the committee of unsecured creditors:

1. .... of * ....
....

2. .... of * ....
....

3. .... of * ....
....

4. .... of * ....
....

5. .... of * ....
....

6. .... of * ....
....

7. .... of * ....
....

Dated: ....

BY THE COURT

....
Bankruptcy Judge

---

* State post-office address

Form No. 14

ORDER FOR MEETING OF CREDITORS AND RELATED ORDERS, COMBINED WITH NOTICE THEREOF AND OF AUTOMATIC STAY

NOTE: This form is Suggested Interim Bankruptcy Form No. 13. It can be used for cases filed under chapter 7, 11, or 13.

[*Caption, other than designation, as in Form No. 1*]

ORDER FOR MEETING OF CREDITORS AND FIXING TIMES FOR FILING OBJECTIONS TO DISCHARGE AND FOR FILING COMPLAINTS TO DETERMINE DISCHARGEABILITY OF CERTAIN DEBTS, COMBINED WITH NOTICE THEREOF AND OF AUTOMATIC STAY

To the debtor, his creditors, and other parties in interest:

An order for relief under 11 U.S.C. chapter 7 [*or,* 11, *or* 13] having been entered on a petition filed by [*or* against] .... of * ...., on .... it is ordered, and notice is hereby given, that:

1. A meeting of creditors pursuant to 11 U.S.C. § 341(a) shall be held at .... on .... at .... o'clock . . m.
2. The debtor shall appear in person [*or, if the debtor is a partnership,* by a general partner, *or, if the debtor is a corporation,* by its president *or other executive officer*] at that time and place for the purpose of being examined.
3. [*If the debtor is an individual*] .... is fixed as the last day for the filing of objections to the discharge of the debtor.
4. [*If the debtor is an individual*] .... is fixed as the last day for the filing of a complaint to determine the dischargeability of any debt pursuant to 11 U.S.C. § 523(c).

You are further notified that:

The meeting may be continued or adjourned from time to time by notice at the meeting, without further written notice to creditors.

At the meeting the creditors may file their claims, [elect a trustee as permitted by law, designate a person to supervise the meeting, elect a committee of creditors,] examine the debtor, and transact such other business as may properly come before the meeting.

As a result of the filing of the petition, certain acts and proceedings against the debtor and his property are stayed as provided in 11 U.S.C. § 362(a).

[*If the debtor is an individual*] If no objection to the discharge of the debtor is filed on or before the last day fixed therefor as stated in subparagraph 3 above, the debtor will be granted his discharge. If no complaint to determine the dischargeability of a debt under clause (2), (4), or (6) of 11

---

* State post-office address

U.S.C. § 523(a) is filed within the time fixed therefor as stated in subparagraph 4 above, the debt may be discharged.

[*For a chapter 7 or 13 case*] In order to have his claim allowed so that he may share in any distribution from the estate, a creditor must file a claim, whether or not he is included in the list of creditors filed by the debtor. Claims which are not filed within six months after the above date set for the meeting of creditors will not be allowed, except as otherwise provided by law. A claim may be filed in the office of the undersigned bankruptcy judge on an official form prescribed for a proof of claim.

[*If a no-asset or nominal asset case, the following paragraph may be used in lieu of the preceding paragraph.*] It appears from the schedules of the debtor that there are no assets from which any dividend can be paid to creditors. It is unnecessary for any creditor to file his claim at this time in order to share in any distribution from the estate. If it subsequently appears that there are assets from which a dividend may be paid, creditors will be so notified and given an opportunity to file their claims.

Unless the court extends the time, any objection to the debtor's claim of exempt property (Schedule B-4) must be filed within fifteen days after the above date set for the meeting of creditors.

[*For a chapter 11 case*] The debtor [*or* trustee] has filed or will file a list of creditors and equity security holders pursuant to Rule 1007. Any creditor holding a listed claim which is not listed as disputed, contingent, or unliquidated as to amount, may, but need not, file a proof of claim in this case. Creditors whose claims are not listed or whose claims are listed as disputed, contingent, or unliquidated as to amount and who desire to participate in the case or share in any distribution must file their proofs of claim on or before ...., which date is hereby fixed as the last day for filing a proof of claim [*or, if appropriate,* on or before a date to be later fixed of which you will be notified]. Any creditor who desires to rely on the list has the responsibility for determining that he is accurately listed.

[*If appropriate*] .... of * .... has been appointed [interim] trustee of the estate of the above-named debtor.

Dated: ....

BY THE COURT

........................,
Bankruptcy Judge

* State post-office address

Form No. 15

PROOF OF CLAIM

NOTE: This form is based on Official Form No. 15.

[*Caption, other than designation, as in Form No. 1*]

PROOF OF CLAIM

1. [*If claimant is an individual claiming for himself*] The undersigned, who is the claimant herein, resides at * . . . .

[*If claimant is a partnership claiming through a member*] The undersigned, who resides at * . . . . , is a member of . . . . , a partnership, composed of the undersigned and . . . . , of * . . . . , and doing business at * . . . . , and is authorized to make this proof of claim in behalf of the partnership.

[*If claimant is a corporation claiming through an authorized officer*] The undersigned, who resides at * . . . . , is the . . . . of . . . . , a corporation organized under the laws of . . . . and doing business at * . . . . , and is authorized to make this proof of claim on behalf of the corporation.

[*If claim is made by agent*] The undersigned, who resides at * . . . . , is the agent of . . . . , of . . . . , and is authorized to make this proof of claim on behalf of the claimant.

2. The debtor was, at the time of the filing of the petition initiating this case, and still is indebted [*or* liable] to this claimant, in the sum of $. . . . . . .

3. The consideration for this debt [*or* ground of liability] is as follows: . . . .

4. [*If the claim is founded on writing*] The writing on which this claim is founded (or a duplicate thereof) is attached hereto [*or* cannot be attached for the reason set forth in the statement attached hereto].

5. [*If appropriate*] This claim is founded on an open account, which became [*or* will become] due on . . . . , as shown by the itemized statement attached hereto. Unless it is attached hereto or its absence is explained in an attached statement, no note or other negotiable instrument has been received for the account or any part of it.

6. No judgment has been rendered on the claim except . . . .

7. The amount of all payments on this claim has been credited and deducted for the purpose of making this proof of claim.

8. This claim is not subject to any setoff or counterclaim except . . . .

9. No security interest is held for this claim except . . . .

[*If security interest in property of the debtor is claimed*] The undersigned

---

* State post-office address

claims the security interest under the writing referred to in paragraph 4 hereof [*or* under a separate writing which (or a duplicate of which) is attached hereto, *or* under a separate writing which cannot be attached hereto for the reason set forth in the statement attached hereto]. Evidence of perfection of such security interest is also attached hereto.

10. This claim is a general unsecured claim, except to the extent that the security interest, if any, described in paragraph 9 is sufficient to satisfy the claim. [*If priority is claimed, state the amount and basis thereof.*] . . . .
. . . .
. . . .

Dated: . . . .

Signed: . . . .

Penalty for Presenting Fraudulent Claim. Fine of not more than $5,000 or imprisonment for not more than 5 years or both—Title 18, U.S.C., § 152.

Form No. 16

PROOF OF CLAIM FOR WAGES, SALARY, OR COMMISSIONS

NOTE: This form is Suggested Interim Bankruptcy Form No. 14.
See 11 U.S.C. § 507(a)(3) which gives priority to such claims.

[*Caption, other than designation, as in Form No. 1*]

PROOF OF CLAIM FOR WAGES, SALARY, OR COMMISSIONS

1. The debtor owes the claimant computed as follows: $..........

(a) wages, salary, or commissions for services performed from .... to ...., at the following rate or rates of compensation .... $..........

[*if appropriate*]

(b) allowances and benefits, such as vacation and severance and sick leave pay [specify] .... $..........

Total amount claimed $..........

2. The claimant demands priority to the extent permitted by 11 U.S.C. §§ 507(a)(3) and 507(a)(4).

3. The claimant has received no payment, no security, and no check or other evidence of this debt except as follows: ....

Dated: ....

Signed: ....
Claimant

Social Security Number: ....
Address: ....,
....

Penalty for Presenting Fraudulent Claim. Fine of not more than $5,000 or imprisonment for not more than five years or both—Title 18, U.S.C., § 152.

Form No. 17

PROOF OF MULTIPLE CLAIMS FOR WAGES, SALARY, OR COMMISSIONS

NOTE: This form is Suggested Interim Bankruptcy Form No. 15.

[*Caption, other than designation, as in Form No. 1*]

PROOF OF MULTIPLE CLAIMS FOR WAGES,
SALARY, OR COMMISSIONS

1. The undersigned, whose address is * . . . ., is the agent of the claimants listed in the statement appended to this proof of claim and is authorized to make this proof of claim on their behalf.

2. The debtor owes the claimants $. . . . ., computed as indicated in the appended statement.

3. The claimaint demands priority to the extent permitted by 11 U.S.C. §§ 507(a)(3), 507(a)(4).

4. The claimants have received no payment, no security, and no check or other evidence of this debt except as follows: . . . .
. . . .

Dated: . . . .

Signed: . . . .

Penalty for Presenting Fraudulent Claim. Fine of not more than $5,000 or imprisonment for not more than five years or both—Title 18, U.S.C., § 152.

STATEMENT OF WAGE CLAIMS

Name, Address, & Social Security Numbers	Dates services rendered, rates of pay, & fringe benefits	Contributions to employee benefit plans	Amounts Claimed

* State post-office address

Form No. 18

GENERAL POWER OF ATTORNEY

NOTE: This form is based on Official Form No. 13.

[*Caption, other than designation, as in Form No. 1*]

GENERAL POWER OF ATTORNEY

To .... of * ...., and .... of * ....:

The undersigned claimant hereby authorizes you, or any one of you, as attorney in fact for the undersigned and with full power of substitution, to vote on any question that may be lawfully submitted to creditors of the debtor in the above-entitled case; [*if appropriate*] to vote for a trustee of the estate of the debtor and for a committee of creditors; to receive dividends; and in general to perform any act not constituting the practice of law for the undersigned in all matters arising in this case.

Dated: ....

Signed: ....
[*If appropriate*] By ....
as ....
Address: ....,
....

[*If executed by an individual*] Acknowledged before me on ....
[*If executed on behalf of a partnership*] Acknowledged before me on ...., by ...., who says that he is a member of the partnership named above and is authorized to execute this power of attorney in its behalf.
[*If executed on behalf of a corporation*] Acknowledged before me on ...., by ...., who says that he is .... of the corporation named above and is authorized to execute this power of attorney in its behalf.

.........................,
....
Official character

---

* State post-office address

Form No. 19

SPECIAL POWER OF ATTORNEY

NOTE: This form is based on Official Form No. 14.

[*Caption, other than designation, as in Form No. 1*]

SPECIAL POWER OF ATTORNEY

To .... of * ...., and .... of * ....:

The undersigned claimant hereby authorizes you, or any one of you, as attorney in fact for the undersigned [*if desired:* and with full power of substitution,] to attend the first meeting of creditors of the debtor or any adjournment thereof, and to vote in my behalf on any question that may be lawfully submitted to creditors at such meeting or adjourned meeting, and for a trustee or trustees of the estate of the debtor.

Dated: ....

Signed: ....
[*If appropriate*] *By* ....
as ....
Address: ....
........................,
....

[*If executed by an individual*] Acknowledged before me on ....

[*If executed on behalf of a partnership*] Acknowledged before me on ...., by ...., who says that he is a member of the partnership named above and is authorized to execute this power of attorney in its behalf.

[*If executed on behalf of a corporation*] Acknowledged before me on ...., by .... who says that he is .... of the corporation named above and is authorized to execute this power of attorney in its behalf.

........................,
....
[*Official character*]

* State post-office address

Form No. 20

ORDER APPOINTING TRUSTEE AND FIXING THE AMOUNT OF HIS BOND

NOTE: This form is Suggested Interim Bankruptcy Form No. 16. It is for use only in a chapter 7 case. Pursuant to 11 U.S.C. § 701, the court is to appoint an interim trustee promptly after the order for relief.

[*Caption, other than designation, as in Form No. 1*]

ORDER APPOINTING TRUSTEE AND FIXING THE AMOUNT OF HIS BOND

(1) ...., of * ...., is hereby appointed trustee of the estate of the above-named debtor.

(2) The amount of the bond of the trustee is fixed at $...........

Dated: ....

BY THE COURT

.........................,
Bankruptcy Judge

* State post-office address

Form No. 21

ORDER APPROVING ELECTION OF TRUSTEE AND FIXING THE AMOUNT OF HIS BOND

NOTE: This form is Suggested Interim Bankruptcy Form No. 17.

Creditors may elect a trustee pursuant to 11 U.S.C. § 702. If none is elected the interim trustee becomes the trustee.

[*Caption, other than designation, as in Form No. 1*]

ORDER APPROVING ELECTION OF TRUSTEE AND
FIXING THE AMOUNT OF HIS BOND

(1) ...., of * ...., is hereby approved as the elected [*or* is hereby appointed] trustee of the estate of the above-named debtor.

(2) The amount of the bond of the trustee is fixed at $..........

Dated: ....

BY THE COURT

.........................,
Bankruptcy Judge

---

* State post-office address

Form No. 22

NOTICE TO TRUSTEE OF HIS SELECTION AND OF TIME FIXED FOR FILING A COMPLAINT OBJECTING TO DISCHARGE OF DEBTOR

NOTE: This form is Suggested Interim Bankruptcy Form No. 18.

[*Caption, other than designation, as in Form No. 1*]

NOTICE TO TRUSTEE OF HIS SELECTION AND OF TIME FIXED FOR FILING A COMPLAINT OBJECTING TO DISCHARGE OF DEBTOR

To . . . ., of * . . . .:

You are hereby notified of your election [*or* appointment] as trustee of the estate of the above-named debtor. The amount of your bond has been fixed at $. . . . . You are required to notify Hon. . . . ., Bankruptcy Judge, at . . . ., in writing and within five days after receipt of this notice of your acceptance or rejection of the office. If you accept, your bond must be filed with the court on or before . . . .

You are further notified that . . . . has been fixed as the last day for the filing by you or any other party in interest of a complaint objecting to the discharge of the debtor.

Dated: . . . .

. . . .
Clerk of the
Bankruptcy Court

* State post-office address

Form No. 23

DISCHARGE OF DEBTOR

NOTE: This form is Suggested Interim Bankruptcy Form No. 19.

[*Caption, other than designation, as in Form No. 1*]

DISCHARGE OF DEBTOR

It appearing that the person named above has filed a petition commencing a case under title 11, United States Code on ...., and an order for relief was entered under chapter 7 and that no complaint objecting to the discharge of the debtor was filed within the time fixed by the court [*or* that a complaint objecting to discharge of the debtor was filed and, after due notice and hearing, was not sustained]; it is ordered that

1. The above-named debtor is released from all dischargeable debts.
2. Any judgment heretofore or hereafter obtained in any court other than this court is null and void as a determination of the personal liability of the debtor with respect to any of the following:

   (a) debts dischargeable under 11 U.S.C. § 523;
   (b) unless heretofore determined by order of this court to be nondischargeable, debts alleged to be excepted from discharge under clauses (2), (4) and (6) of 11 U.S.C. § 523(a);
   (c) debts determined by this court to be discharged under 11 U.S.C. § 523(d).

3. All creditors whose debts are discharged by this order and all creditors whose judgments are declared null and void by paragraph 2 above are enjoined from instituting or continuing any action or employing any process to collect such debts as personal liabilities of the above-named bankrupt.

Dated: ....

BY THE COURT

....
Bankruptcy Judge

Form No. 24

ORDER APPROVING DISCLOSURE STATEMENT AND FIXING TIME FOR FILING ACCEPTANCES OR REJECTIONS OF PLAN, COMBINED WITH NOTICE THEREOF

NOTE: This form is Suggested Interim Bankruptcy Form No. 20.

[*Caption, other than designation, as in Form No. 1*]

ORDER APPROVING DISCLOSURE STATEMENT AND FIXING TIME FOR FILING ACCEPTANCES OR REJECTIONS OF PLAN, COMBINED WITH NOTICE THEREOF

A disclosure statement under chapter 11 of the Bankruptcy Code having been filed by ...., on .... [*if appropriate,* and by ...., on ....], referring to a plan under chapter 11 of the Code filed by ...., on .... [*if appropriate,* and by ...., on .... respectively] [*if appropriate,* as modified by a modification filed on ....]; and

It having been determined after hearing on notice that the disclosure statement [*or* statements] contain[s] adequate information;

It is ordered, and notice is hereby given, that:

A. The disclosure statement filed by .... dated ....
[*if appropriate,* and by ...., dated] is [are] approved.

B. .... is fixed as the last day for filing written acceptances or rejections of the plan [*or* plans] referred to above.

C. Within .... days after the entry of this order, the plan [*or* plans] [*or* a summary *or* summaries thereof approved by the court], and a summary approved by the court of its opinion, if any, dated ...., approving the disclosure statement [*or* statements] shall be transmitted by mail to creditors, equity security holders and other parties in interest as provided in Rule 3006(d).

D. If acceptances are filed for more than one plan, preferences among the plans so accepted may be indicated.

[*If appropriate*] E. .... is fixed for the hearing on confirmation of the plan [*or* plans].

Dated: ....

BY THE COURT

....
Bankruptcy Judge

[*If the court directs that a copy of the opinion should be transmitted in lieu of or in addition to the summary thereof, the appropriate change should be made in paragraph C of this order.*]

Form No. 25

BALLOT FOR ACCEPTING OR REJECTING PLAN

NOTE: This form is Suggested Interim Bankruptcy Form No. 21.

[*Caption, other than designation, as in Form No. 1*]

BALLOT FOR ACCEPTING OR REJECTING PLAN

The plan referred to in this ballot can be confirmed by the court and thereby made binding on you if it is accepted by the holders of two-thirds in amount and more than one-half in number of claims in each class and the holders of two-thirds in amount of equity security interests in each class voting on the plan. In the event the requisite acceptances are not obtained, the court may nevertheless confirm the plan if the court finds that the plan accords fair and equitable treatment to the class rejecting it. To have your vote count you must complete and return this ballot.

[*If equity security holder*] The undersigned, the holder of [*state number*] .... shares of [*describe type*] .... stock of the above-named debtor, represented by Certificate(s) No. ...., registered in the name of ....

[*If bondholder, debenture holder, or other debt security holder*] The undersigned, the holder of [*state unpaid principal amount*] $............ of [*describe security*] .... of the above-named debtor, with a stated maturity date of .... [*if applicable* registered in the name of ....] [*if applicable* bearing serial number(s) ....],

[*If holder of general claim*] The undersigned, a creditor of the above-named debtor in the unpaid principal amount of $............,

[Check One Box]

☐ Accepts
☐ Rejects

the plan for the reorganization of the above-named debtor.

Dated: ....

Print or type name: ....
Signed: ....
[*If appropriate*] By: ....
as: ....
Address: ....
....

Return this ballot on or before ....

to:
Name: ....
Address: ....
....

This form may be modified as necessary to include descriptions of as many plans as may have been transmitted on which a vote will be taken. The form should be tailored, in that event, so that creditors and equity security holders may express preferences among the plans they wish to accept. The following may be an additional paragraph for such use:

[*If more than one plan is accepted, the following may but need not be completed.*] The undersigned prefers the plans accepted herein in the following order: [*Describe plans*]

1. ....
2. ....

Form No. 26

ORDER CONFIRMING PLAN

NOTE: This form is Suggested Interim Bankruptcy Form No. 22.

[*Caption, other than designation, as in Form No. 1*]

ORDER CONFIRMING PLAN

The plan under chapter 11 of the Bankruptcy Code filed by ...., on .... [*if appropriate,* as modified by a modification filed on ....,] and the plan or a summary thereof having been transmitted to creditors and equity security holders; and

It having been determined after hearing on notice:

1. That the plan has been accepted in writing by the creditors and equity security holders whose acceptance is required by law; and
2. That the provisions of chapter 11 of the Code have been complied with; that the plan has been proposed in good faith and not by any means forbidden by law; and
3. Each holder of a claim or interest has accepted the plan [*or* will receive or retain under the plan property of a value, as of the effective date of the plan, that is not less than the amount that such holder would receive or retain if the debtor were liquidated under chapter 7 of the Code on such date] [*or,* the plan does not discriminate unfairly, and is fair and equitable, with respect to each class of claims or interests that is impaired under, and has not accepted the plan]; and
4. All payments made or promised by the debtor or by a person issuing securities or acquiring property under the plan or by any other person for services or for costs and expenses, or in connection with, the plan and incident to the case, have been fully disclosed to the court and are reasonable or, if to be fixed after confirmation of the plan, will be subject to the approval of the court; and
5. The identity, qualifications, and affiliations of the persons who are to be directors or officers, or voting trustees, if any, of the debtor [and an affiliate of the debtor participating in a joint plan with the debtor] [*or* a successor to the debtor under the plan], after confirmation of the plan, have been fully disclosed, and the appointment of such persons to such offices, or their continuance therein, is equitable, and consistent with the interests of the creditors and equity security holders and with public policy; and
6. The identity of any insiders that will be employed or retained by the debtor and his compensation have been fully disclosed; and

[*If applicable*] 7. Any regulatory commission with jurisdiction, after confirmation of the plan, over the rates of the debtor has approved any rate change provided for in the plan [*or* any rate change is expressly conditioned on approval of any regulatory agency having jurisdiction over the rates of the debtor; and]

[*If appropriate*] 8. Confirmation of the plan is not likely to be followed by the liquidation, or the need for further financial reorganization, of the debtor or any successor to the debtor under the plan;]:

It is ordered that:

The plan filed by ...., on ...., a copy of which plan is attached hereto, is confirmed.

Dated: ....

BY THE COURT

....
Bankruptcy Judge

Form No. 27

NOTICE OF FILING FINAL ACCOUNT

NOTE: This form is Suggested Interim Bankruptcy Form No. 23.

[*Caption, other than designation, as in Form No. 1*]

NOTICE OF FILING OF FINAL ACCOUNT(S) OF TRUSTEE, OF HEARING ON APPLICATIONS FOR COMPENSATION (AND OF HEARING ON ABANDONMENT OF PROPERTY BY THE TRUSTEE)

To the creditors:

The final report(s) and account(s) of the trustee in this case having been filed,

Notice is hereby given, that there will be a hearing held at . . . ., ..., on . . . ., at . . . . . . o'clock . . m., for the purpose [*as appropriate*] of examining and passing on the report(s) and account(s), acting on applications for compensation, and transacting such other business as may properly come before the court. Attendance by creditors is welcomed but not required.

The following applications for compensation have been filed:

Applicants	Commission of Fees	Expenses
. . . . Interim Trustee	$.	$. . . . .
. . . . Trustee	. . . .	. . . .
. . . . Attorney for debtor	. . . .	. . . .
. . . . Attorney for interim trustee	. . . .	. . . .
. . . . Attorney for trustee	. . . .	. . . .
. . . . Attorney for petitioning creditors	. . . .	. . . .
. . . .	. . . .	. . . .

Creditors may be heard before the applications are determined.

The account of the trustee shows total receipts of $. . . . ., and total disbursements of $. . . . . The balance on hand is $. . . . .

In addition to expenses of administration as may be allowed by the court, liens and priority claims totalling $. . . . ., must be paid in advance of any dividend to general creditors.

Claims of general creditors totalling $. . . . . have been allowed.

[*If appropriate*] The trustee's application to abandon the following property will be heard and acted on:

. . . .

. . . .

The debtor has [not] been discharged.

Dated: . . . .

BY THE COURT

. . . . ,
Bankruptcy Judge

TABLE OF BANKRUPTCY CODE SECTIONS

(Title 11, U.S. Code)

[*References are to paragraphs (¶).*]

[*References are to paragraphs (¶).*]

[*References are to paragraphs (¶).*]

[*References are to paragraphs (¶).*]

[References are to paragraphs (¶).]

[*References are to paragraphs (¶).*]

[References are to paragraphs (¶).]

[*References are to paragraphs (¶).*]

[*References are to paragraphs (¶).*]

TABLE OF TITLE 28 SECTIONS, U.S. CODE

[*References are to paragraphs (¶).*]

TABLE OF FORMER BANKRUPTCY ACT SECTIONS

(Former Title 11, U.S. Code)

[*References are to paragraphs (¶).*]

[*References are to paragraphs* (¶).]

[*References are to paragraphs (¶).*]

TABLE OF RULES OF BANKRUPTCY PROCEDURE

[References are to paragraphs (¶).]

[*References are to paragraphs (¶).*]

[*References are to paragraphs (¶).*]

TABLE OF SUGGESTED INTERIM BANKRUPTCY RULES

[*References are to paragraphs (¶).*]

TABLE OF CASES

[*References are to paragraphs (¶).*]

[*References are to paragraphs (¶).*]

C

D

[*References are to paragraphs (¶).*]

E

F

G

[*References are to paragraphs (¶).*]

H

I

[*References are to paragraphs* (¶).]

J

K

L

[*References are to paragraphs (¶).*]

[*References are to paragraphs (¶).*]

[*References are to paragraphs* (¶).]

S

T

[References are to paragraphs (¶).]

[*References are to paragraphs (¶).*]

Y

Z

INDEX

[References are to paragraphs (¶).]

[*References are to paragraphs (¶).*]

[*References are to paragraphs (¶).*]

[*References are to paragraphs (¶).*]

B

[*References are to paragraphs (¶).*]

[*References are to paragraphs (¶).*]

[*References are to paragraphs (¶).*]

[*References are to paragraphs (¶).*]

[*References are to paragraphs (¶).*]

[*References are to paragraphs (¶).*]

[*References are to paragraphs (¶).*]

[*References are to paragraphs* (¶).]

[*References are to paragraphs (¶).*]

[*References are to paragraphs (¶).*]

[*References are to paragraphs (¶).*]

[*References are to paragraphs (¶).*]

F

[*References are to paragraphs (¶).*]

[*References are to paragraphs (¶).*]

G

[*References are to paragraphs (¶).*]

[*References are to paragraphs (¶).*]

[*References are to paragraphs (¶).*]

[*References are to paragraphs (¶).*]

[*References are to paragraphs (¶).*]

[*References are to paragraphs (¶).*]

[*References are to paragraphs (¶).*]

[*References are to paragraphs (¶).*]

[*References are to paragraphs (¶).*]

[*References are to paragraphs (¶).*]

[*References are to paragraphs (¶).*]

[*References are to paragraphs (¶).*]

S

[*References are to paragraphs (¶).*]

[*References are to paragraphs* (¶).]

[*References are to paragraphs (¶).*]

[*References are to paragraphs (¶).*]

[*References are to paragraphs (¶).*]

[*References are to paragraphs (¶).*]

W

[*References are to paragraphs (¶).*]